Image of Health

Elizabeth Barrington
Judy Stamm

CHAPTER 7 Nutrition
MyPlate Supplement

Elizabeth Barrington currently serves as a professor in the Department of Physical Education & Health at San Diego Mesa College where she has taught Health and Lifestyles and Physical Education classes since 1988. Elizabeth holds a M.P.H. with an emphasis in Health Promotion & Behavioral Medicine from San Diego State University, an A.A. in Psychology from Miramar College, and a B.A. in Behavioral Science from National University.

Judy Stamm has been a professor of health education since 1976. She has a Ph.D. in Higher Education from UCLA, a M.S. in Physical Education from California State Polytechnic University, and a B.A. in Political Science from San Diego State University. She currently serves as part-time Assistant Athletic Director and Online Health Education faculty at San Diego City College.

Hayden-McNeil Publishing
14903 Pilot Drive
Plymouth, MI 48170
Phone 734-455-7900 ■ Fax 734-455-3901
www.hmpublishing.com

Barrington-Stamm 3743-1 F11

ISBN 978-073803743-1

9 780738 037431

90000

SECOND PRINTING

Image of Health

Elizabeth Barrington, MPH
San Diego Mesa College

Judy Stamm, PhD
San Diego City College

HAYDEN **HM** MᶜNEIL

Table of Contents

Acknowledgements

Many people have helped us as we worked to complete this textbook. Any errors are ours, but we must share credit for positive aspects with many thanks to the following people:

Marc Barrington

Manny Bautista

Ellie Bewley

Tracy Brennan

Dottie Cordell

Clare Elkins

Cheryl Flanders

Bushra Jonna

Kathy McGinnis

Katie Winters

Andrea Milburn

Pam Rogers

Carlotta Seeley

Amy Shefferd

Jan Stamm

Lorri Sulpizio

Lee Ann Taylor

Sarah Wilkins

Lisa Williams

And much gratitude to the extraordinary publishing team at Hayden-McNeil.

Unit One

Accepting Responsibility for
Personal Health

Chapter 1
Language of Health

Chapter 2
Health Care Choices

Chapter 3
Stress and Mental Health

UNIT ONE

UNIT ONE

Image of Health

Language of Health

THE LANGUAGE OF HEALTH

- Dimensions of Wellness
- Dynamic Wellness: A Lifetime Goal
- Approaches to Health and Wellness
- Health in Perspective

WELLNESS INFLUENCES

- National Health Goals and Trends
- Personal and Cultural Influences
- Diversity and Health

EXPLORING BEHAVIOR CHANGE

- Health Belief Model
- Transtheoretical/Stages of Change Model
- Considering Behavior Change

MANAGING YOUR HEALTH

- Becoming an Informed Consumer
- Health in the College Years

RESPONSIBILITY AND ACCOUNTABILITY

- Taking Responsibility for Your Health
- Focusing on Accountability

Student Learning Outcomes

LEARNING OUTCOME	APPLYING IT TO YOUR LIFE
List and describe the dimensions of wellness and resources for obtaining them.	Develop your wellness goals and list the behaviors and strategies you will use to achieve them.
Describe changes in life expectancy over the last 100 years, and explain why the Healthy People Initiative can influence quantity and quality of years of life.	Investigate the factors that influence your health and identify steps you can take to maximize your health potential.
Describe how diversity factors can affect health.	Identify diversity factors that affect your health and list strategies you can use to overcome them.
List the stages of behavior change.	Identify a behavior you would like to change, begin, or eliminate in your life and create a behavior change plan to help you succeed with this.
List methods you would use to evaluate research or a health article or claim.	Consider your current health and what you have tried to maintain or improve it. Critique these actions based on your knowledge of health research.

Assess Your Knowledge

1. What is the average life expectancy for a person living in the United States today?
   a. About 95 years
   b. About 84 years
   c. About 77 years
   d. About 63 years

2. What major health changes have improved life expectancy since the 1900s?
   a. Chronic diseases have been eliminated.
   b. Vaccinations, sanitation and advances in knowledge have increased longevity.
   c. Antibiotics have reduced death rates.
   d. Incidence of cancer has been reduced.

3. How do infectious diseases differ from chronic diseases?
   a. Infectious diseases are transmitted from person to person, while chronic diseases are of long duration.
   b. Infectious diseases involve lifestyle behaviors, and chronic diseases involve a pathogen.
   c. Infectious diseases kill; chronic diseases do not kill.
   d. Infectious diseases do not kill; chronic diseases do kill.

4. The dimensions of wellness include:
   a. Physical health, nutritional health, and mental health.
   b. Physical, social, emotional health, intellectual health, spiritual health, and environmental health.
   c. Absence of disease, physical wellness, social, emotional health, intellectual health, spiritual health, and environmental health.
   d. Absence of disease, social, emotional health, intellectual health, spiritual health, and financial health.

5. What are the main goals of the Healthy People 2010 initiative?
   a. Increase life expectancy and improve nutrition for all.
   b. Increase life expectancy for minorities and extend health care to all persons.
   c. Increase quality and years of healthy life and eliminate health disparities.
   d. Improve education and access to health information for all persons.

Answers:

1. c; 2. b; 3. a; 4. b; 5. b.

The Language of Health

Imagine yourself sitting in the waiting room of the campus health center. You are there because of a nagging cough that will not go away. You spent about an hour on the Internet earlier in the day, checking out what the problem might be—anything from a lingering cold to lung cancer—and you have a list of questions to ask the doctor.

What does this scenario say about you and your **health**? First, you are taking responsibility for your health, recognizing when you need to see a health care professional and taking action. Second, you prepared for this visit. By doing online research, you have a general idea of what the doctor might be looking for and discussing with you today. You are taking a proactive approach to your health. Third, you are committed to following the doctor's direction, and are showing you are accountable.

This text presents the dual theme of taking **responsibility** for your health and being accountable for it.

Taking responsibility for your health involves a proactive approach. It encompasses everything from making exercise a part of your daily life to becoming an informed health consumer. **Accountability**, being answerable, is closely related to responsibility. But to whom are you accountable? To yourself? To your closest relatives and friends? To society? The answer, of course, is all of these—and more. As an individual, you owe it to yourself to stay healthy, to make the most of your life, and to maximize life expectancy and the quality of your life. As a parent, a sibling, a student, an employee, a friend, and a neighbor, you have the responsibility to participate in your family life, your social network, the workplace, your community, and the world.

Key Terms

Health: Soundness of body and mind; freedom from disease or ailment: *to have one's health; to lose one's health.*

Responsibility: A sense of ownership of actions and choices.

Accountability: The willingness to be answerable for consequences of actions and choices.

This chapter introduces you to health and **wellness** and the many factors that influence them. It illustrates how physical, emotional, intellectual, spiritual, social, and environmental factors are intertwined and need to be in balance for you to achieve dynamic wellness. The chapter also takes a look at our national health goals and the world in which we live—a society composed of individuals of different cultures, races, and socioeconomic levels. Another central theme is behavior change, a tool for improving every aspect of your health. The chapter ends with a discussion of managing your health, which includes learning to become an informed consumer. With the information and tools in this chapter, you can consider this very important question: Are you ready to make a personal commitment to health?

Key Term

Wellness: An approach to health care that emphasizes preventing illness and prolonging vital life.

The terms *health* and *wellness* are often used interchangeably. However, they are somewhat different. Health refers to the condition of an individual at any given time. It reflects soundness of body and mind and freedom from disease or abnormality. So if you have just had a physical examination and been given a "clean bill of health" by your doctor, you could consider yourself in good health. In contrast, wellness refers to a lifestyle approach that emphasizes preventing illness and prolonging a vital life. So if you have a plan for healthy living that you follow, including regular physical activity, a nutritious diet, adequate sleep, and a good balance between work and play, you can say that you are taking a wellness approach to your life.

More than sixty years ago, the World Health Organization defined *health* as a state of complete mental, physical, and social well-being, not merely the absence of disease or **infirmity**.[1] This simple definition encompasses so much, but it fails to address the dynamic nature of health. Your health is in a constant state of flux. Although you may pay attention to your health only when you experience negative symptoms, some aspects of your well-being are constantly changing throughout each day.

Vital health depends on your ability to efficiently respond to daily challenges, including physical, mental, emotional, and even financial challenges. Vital health is our ability to restore and sustain a state of balance, and to live to our maximum potential.

Key Term

Infirmity: Physical or mental weakness.

Dimensions of Wellness

Personal wellness is influenced by many decisions that you make every day. In this section you will learn about the six dynamic interrelated dimensions of wellness.

Physical Wellness

Physical wellness involves feeling well, being able to do ordinary tasks, having good nutrition, having regular sleep patterns, being able to exercise, and being able to manage your life. It is based on responsible decision-making, such as practicing safer sex, avoiding the use or abuse of harmful substances, paying attention to safety issues, and

making sure that you have routine physical examinations and vaccinations. If your physical health is impaired, all other aspects of your life will be affected.

Emotional Wellness

Emotional wellness is the ability to participate in the world around you. It is reflected in your attitudes, sense of self, confidence level, and relationships. It is how you express yourself as you enjoy, appreciate, and react to events and individuals in your life. You laugh, you cry, you get angry, you are somber, and you are calm. Your emotional health is a mirror of the other dimensions of wellness. When a change occurs in another dimension, your emotional wellness may shift out of balance or return into balance.

Intellectual Wellness

Intellectual wellness involves the thinking dimension, allowing you to analyze, reason, compute, and comprehend. It means that you can learn and change behaviors. Intellectual wellness also lets you express your creative side in activities such as writing, music, and art. The intellectual dimension facilitates your success as a student. By pursuing a college degree, you are improving your intellectual health. Learning new skills and new information throughout life will improve the quality of your life.

Spiritual Wellness

Spirituality is the most individual and subjective of the dimensions of wellness. For one person, it may involve participating in an organized religion. For another, it may mean finding meaning in life by exploring the beauty of nature, doing volunteer work, creating art, or working for a cause. One of the common elements in spirituality is a search for meaning and purpose in life: What is important to you? What contributions can you make? Another is a core belief system that underlies your decisions, your actions, and your relationships with others. A sense of spirituality often results in a "concept of oneness," which is an identity or harmony with those things that bring meaning to life.

Critical Thinking Question: If you are a spiritual person, what benefits do you think you get from your spirituality? If you do not consider yourself a spiritual person, how might your life improve if you were to embrace some type of spirituality?

Social Wellness

Most people have three levels in their social network. The primary network includes parents, siblings, partner, spouse, or anyone you live with or see on a daily basis. The secondary social network is made up of extended family members, and friends, classmates, co-workers, and employers. The third level includes everyone else in your life, such as distant family members, friends, and acquaintances with whom you do not have regular contact. The ease or difficulty of day-to-day functioning depends on social networks, especially your primary network. Ideally, they are the support people in your life who encourage and support your endeavors and help keep you calm and balanced. Or, in some cases, they may be the cause of your stress.

Environmental Wellness

Environmental wellness is often taken for granted, assuming that there will always be clean water to drink and clean air to breathe and that sewage and trash disposal will be handled. The quality of the air and water, the level of noise, exposure to chemicals, and the density of the population affect your environmental wellness. The safety of your neighborhood, the availability of recreational areas, and the condition of the food supply are all matters that affect environmental wellness. In addition, these conditions have an impact on other areas of your wellness.

Interconnection of Dimensions of Wellness

If you are unwell in any dimension of your health, other dimensions may also be affected. For example, if you are not physically well, you may experience depression, which would negatively affect your mental health. This, in turn, would affect your emotional and maybe even your intellectual wellness. If you lack self-confidence and have low self-esteem, your ability to interact with others, both socially and emotionally, will also suffer. Some researchers consider other areas, such as occupational wellness and financial wellness. If you are engaged in a job or career that you enjoy and find rewarding, that affects your wellness in a positive way. Similarly, if your financial situation is stable and you are able to live comfortably within your means, you are enjoying financial wellness.

All the dimensions of health need to be in balance and at the highest possible level to achieve an optimum level of wellness. Figure 1-1 illustrates how each dimension interacts with others and can affect overall well-being.

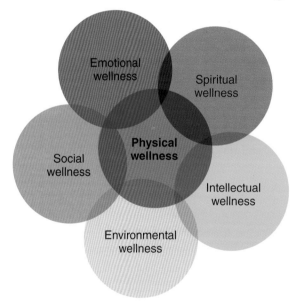

FIGURE 1-1. Dimensions of wellness.

Challenge Question: List and describe each of the dimensions of wellness.

Dynamic Wellness: A Lifetime Goal

Being healthy reflects soundness of body and mind and freedom from disease or abnormality. In an optimal world, each person would have this all the time, but health is dynamic. However, wellness can be pursued even as you face illness or abnormality. By exercising and eating recommended foods, a diabetic can strive to achieve blood sugar control. Someone dealing with mild depression can pursue physical and spiritual wellness, which may help improve his or her mental state. Reading this chapter is helping your intellectual wellness. These are just beginning steps; there is more that you can do.

Self-Care

Self-care involves taking responsibility for your own health. It includes choosing behaviors that promote wellness and staying informed about health care issues so that you will be prepared to make good decisions for your health.

The choices you make about self-care will either enhance or undermine your personal health. If you are a young adult just starting college, the decisions you make and the behaviors you engage in will affect your level of wellness, both today and in the future. Positive self-care includes wearing a seat belt and selecting nutritious foods. Negative self-care is driving after drinking alcohol, not managing stress, and not getting adequate rest. Appropriate self-care is a choice, just as inappropriate self-care is a choice.

An important part of self-care is knowing when to seek medical treatment or ask for help. "Image of Health in Depth: When To Seek Medical Treatment" lists some of the common reasons for seeking medical treatment. Most college campuses offer a variety of programs and services, including medical care, mental health counseling, nutrition, and physical activity classes. Responsible self-care involves seeking out those programs and services that aid in health promotion that will help you meet your needs.

Image of Health in Depth

When to Seek Medical Treatment
Generally, you should seek the advice of a medical practitioner when any of the following conditions exist:

1. Uncontrolled bleeding.

2. Persistent symptoms such as a high fever that does not abate, coughing that lasts longer than about 14 days, sores that do not heal, and hoarseness that lasts longer than about three weeks.

3. Severe pain, major injuries and other emergencies.

4. Unusual symptoms such as unexplained lumps, changes in a mole, difficulty swallowing, vision changes, unexplained weight loss, changes in bowel or bladder habits.

5. Reoccurring symptoms such as headaches, stomachaches, and backaches.

As you evaluate symptoms, consider how urgent they may be. Sometimes, a single symptom might warrant an appointment with a doctor, whereas a combination of symptoms might warrant a trip to an urgent care center. Severe symptoms such as chest pain, uncontrollable vomiting and diarrhea, poisoning, drug overdose, stupor, or loss of consciousness would indicate the need to seek emergency treatment immediately.

Holistic Health

Holistic health is a nontraditional approach that focuses on integration of the many dimensions of health. Practitioners of holistic health emphasize the importance of mind-body health and believe that optimal wellness can be achieved by finding a balance, called **homeostasis**, between mind and body. Holistic health care is characterized by a prevention-oriented approach rather than the cure-oriented protocol exemplified by Western medicine. It focuses on self-care and preventive behaviors rather than medication and therapy. Proponents believe that it is possible to reduce the risk of many diseases by living a holistic lifestyle.

Key Terms

Holistic: Emphasizing the importance of the whole and the interdependence of its parts.

Homeostasis: A state of balance—the ability of the body to physiologically regulate its inner environment in response to fluctuations in the outside environment.

Personal Health

Personal health is defined as the interaction of all aspects of health that are unique to each individual. It is not static but constantly changing—day to day and even hour to hour. Taking responsibility for your personal health means that you understand yourself and your health needs. If you know what makes you happy or sad, energized or fatigued, feeling optimally well or unwell, you can be more accountable for your personal health by making more appropriate choices. Making your personal health a top priority does not mean that you care for yourself more than others. It means that you take responsibility for your personal health first so that you can be fully engaged in your life.

Community Health

Community health refers to the environment, resources, safety, neighborhood, and livability of our homes and community. The neighborhood or community is an important component of American life, and it has a profound influence on health. If children grow up in communities where there is gang activity, where the streets are unsafe, where schools are inadequate, where public services are lacking, and where the closest store is a liquor store, that environment will affect their view of the world, their behavior, and ultimately their health. The community environment affects our ability to interact socially and emotionally with others, and may play a role in whether we have high or low self-esteem.

Approaches to Health and Wellness

Dr. Halbert Dunn, First Director of the National Office for Health Statistics, introduced the idea of a high level of wellness as a definition for health.[2] Dunn considered wellness a way of functioning that is integrated, dynamic, and oriented toward maximizing one's potential, given one's circumstances. His definition also suggests that each individual is accountable for his or her own health.

Managing your health involves a combination of approaches. If you recognize that something is wrong with you physically, you may seek medical intervention. To practice disease prevention, you would combine personal responsibility through your behaviors, such as hand washing, with medical prevention, such as obtaining appropriate vaccinations and having regular screenings. To practice health promotion, you would combine these efforts with an ongoing quest for health and wellness knowledge and recognition of your accountability for your health. If you practice wellness, first and foremost you choose to assume responsibility for the quality of your life. You begin with a conscious decision to shape a healthy lifestyle. Wellness is a mindset, a predisposition to adopt a series of key principles in your life that lead to high levels of well-being and life satisfaction.

Health Promotion

Health promotion requires both individual and public responsibility. It is up to you to engage in health promotion by taking care of your own health. In addition, society and government have a responsibility for health promotion through public education. This might include public service announcements on TV and radio promoting healthy behaviors, billboards and advertisements that advise of the risks of unhealthy behaviors, and even requiring comprehensive health education classes in schools and universities.

Disease Prevention

A responsible approach to disease prevention requires that you take certain precautions on an everyday basis:

- Wash your hands frequently, especially before eating and after using the toilet.

- Practice abstinence or safer sex to avoid sexually transmitted diseases and unplanned pregnancies.

- Practice safe food preparation and storage at home.

- Keep immunizations up to date for yourself and your children.

- Try not to expose others if you have the flu or a bad cold, and try to avoid contact with those that are so infected.

- Get recommended screenings at appropriate intervals to ensure early detection of potential disease.

- Choose to eat a nutritious diet and to exercise regularly.

- Practice stress and anger management.

- Drink responsibly if you choose to drink alcohol.

Self-Treatment

Despite practicing your own health promotion and disease prevention, it is inevitable that some health issues will occur. Depending on symptomology, the cheapest method to start is self-treatment. It involves knowing your body and understanding its signals. Common forms of self-treatment are:

- Self-treatment for the symptoms of colds, cuts, and minor pains.

- Learning first aid, and to help others, cardiopulmonary resuscitation (CPR).

- Use of home pregnancy testing kits, Human immunodeficiency virus (HIV) test kits, blood glucose testing kits, and others as necessary.

- Learning how to relax, to step back and take time out when necessary.

- Knowing when to seek professional care.

Medical Intervention

If you suspect that you have an **infectious disease**, such as influenza or genital warts, you may seek medical intervention from your campus health care provider, a health care clinic, or a physician. If you are diagnosed with a **chronic disease**, such as breast or testicular cancer, the medical intervention may involve specialized treatment such as surgery, radiation therapy, or chemotherapy, or all three. If you were injured in an automobile crash, you would seek emergency care. It is important to recognize when medical intervention is required and when self-care is appropriate.

Health in Perspective

During the past century, the causes of death in the United States have changed and our longevity has increased. Many of the health threats that were widespread 100 years ago, such as pneumonia and typhoid, are under control or eliminated today. Through measures such as vaccination, improved sanitation, and advances in knowledge, people can expect to live longer.

Changes in Life Expectancy

In the early 1900s, most individuals gave little thought to physical fitness or mental health. They were more concerned about having enough food to eat and warding off diseases. They hoped that their children would live past age five as that would improve their chance of living to "old age."[3] Unfortunately, at that time many children did not survive until their fifth birthday, and parents could expect to lose about half of their children. Infectious diseases and poor sanitation were the killers of the day. In 1900, life expectancy averaged about 47 years for whites and about 33 years for blacks, reflecting the high rate of mortality among infants and young children.[4]

Table 1-1. Life Expectancy at Time of Birth

IF YOU WERE BORN IN:	YOUR PROJECTED LIFE EXPECTANCY WOULD BE:	
	Whites	**Blacks**
1900	47.6 years	33 years
1950	69.1 years	60.8 years
2000	77.6 years	71.9 years
2003	77.6 years	72.3 years
2005	77.9 years	72.8 years

(Source: National Vital Statistics Reports, 2006.)

In the United States today, we have improved sanitation and routine vaccination against childhood diseases. Largely because of these efforts and the discovery of antibiotics, life expectancy has almost doubled since 1900. Table 1-1 shows the 2006 National Vital Statistics Report for life expectancy across time at birth. Although we are living longer, we are still not living long, *healthful* lives. Some data suggests that on average, our last 10 years of life are impaired by chronic disease. For instance, researcher Dr. Michael Molla determined that in 2002, the total life expectancy for whites was predicted to be 77.7 years. However, they would have only 67.5 years of a healthy life and ten years of impaired health.[5] Figure 1-2 illustrates how ill health adversely affects the quality of life in later years.

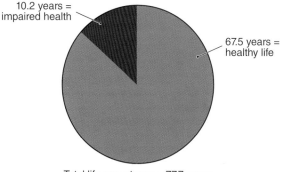

10.2 years = impaired health

67.5 years = healthy life

Total life expectancy = 77.7 years

FIGURE 1-2. Years of healthy life as a proportion of life expectancy in the U.S. population.

Source: National Center for Health Statistics, 2008 Deaths: Preliminary Data for 2006. National Vital Statistics Reports 56(16); National Center for Health Statistics. Healthy People 2010. Midcourse Review. Hyattsville, Md.: Public Health Service.

Challenge Question: What are the major issues that have resulted in longer life expectancy since 1900?

Death and Disability

Of all Americans who die each year, seven of every ten ultimately die of chronic disease, amounting to more than 1.7 million people, and affecting the quality of life for over 90 million.[6] Chronic illnesses and disability from such diseases result in extended pain and suffering and drastically reduce the quality of life for many Americans.

These conditions cause major limitations in activity for more than one of every ten Americans, or 25 million people.[7] It is important to consider that by improving our health-related behaviors today, we could postpone or prevent the onset of chronic diseases and improve our quality of life.

Although the United States has great wealth and freedom, the number of healthy Americans lags behind those in other developed nations. For example, the United States recently became the nation with the highest rate of obesity in the world. Table 1-2 compares the United States rate of obesity with other countries.

Table 1-2.

RANK	COUNTRY	PERCENTAGE OF POPULATION WITH A BODY MASS INDEX GREATER THAN 30kg/SQ. METERS
1	United States	30.6%
2	Mexico	24.2%
3	United Kingdom	23%
4	Slovakia	22.4%
5	Greece	21.9%
6	Australia	21.7%
7	New Zealand	20.9%
8	Hungary	18.8%
9	Luxembourg	18.4%
10	Czech Republic	14.8%
11	Canada	14.3%
12	Spain	13.1%
13	Ireland	13%
14	Germany	12.9%
15	Portugal	12.8%

(Source: NationMaster.com Health Statistics > Obesity (most recent) by country. Downloaded from http://www.nationmaster.com/graph/hea_obe-health-obesity; July 20, 2010.)

We continue to have high smoking rates, resulting in the deaths of about 440,000 Americans a year.[8,9] The Centers for Disease Control and Prevention (CDCP) estimated that in 2001, there were approximately 75,766 deaths due to alcohol, and that this cost about 30 **years of potential life lost** for each death. In addition, our reliance on the automobile results in high levels of pollution and a sedentary lifestyle, both of which adversely affect our health. Altogether, Americans are not achieving a high enough level of health and wellness. In fact, behaviors are causing earlier onset of chronic diseases and potentially earlier deaths. Changes in behavior such as better nutritional choices, exercising, not smoking and moderate or no drinking would reduce these risks.

Key Term

Years of potential life lost: Estimate of the average number of years a person would have lived had they not died prematurely.

Table 1-3. Leading Causes of Death in the United States, 2007

1.	Diseases of the heart
2.	Malignant neoplasms (cancers)
3.	Cerebrovascular diseases (stroke)
4.	Chronic lower respiratory diseases
5.	Accidents (unintentional injuries)
6.	Alzheimer's disease
7.	Diabetes mellitus
8.	Influenza and pneumonia
9.	Nephritis, nephrotic syndrome, and nephrosis (kidney disease)
10.	Septicemia
11.	Intentional self-harm (suicide)
12.	Chronic liver disease and cirrhosis
13.	Essential hypertension and hypertensive renal disease (hypertension)
14.	Parkinson's disease
15.	Assault (homicide)

(Source: U.S. Department of Health and Human Services. Centers for Disease Control and Prevention. National Center for Health Statistics. National Vital Statistics System. Deaths: Final Data for 2007. Jiaquan Xu, Kenneth Kochanek, Sherry Murphy, Betzaida Tejada-Vera.)

Lifestyle behaviors that may impair health or even lead to an earlier death are those behaviors that are chosen and for which we are accountable. For instance, drinking and driving increases your risk of a car accident. Not participating in any form of exercise may increase your risk for several diseases. According to an article published in the *Journal of the American Medical Association*, the leading *lifestyle* causes of death in 2000 were tobacco use, poor diet and physical inactivity, and alcohol consumption.[7] Today, lifestyle behaviors are responsible for at least 37% of all deaths in the United States.

Critical Thinking Question: Why would an educated person maintain lifestyle behaviors that they know might lead to chronic illness and an earlier death?

Table 1-4. Actual Lifestyle Causes of Death in the United States in 1990 and 2000*

ACTUAL CAUSE	NO. (%) IN 1990	NO. (%) IN 2000
Tobacco	400,000 (19)	435,000 (18.1)
Poor Diet and Physical Inactivity	300,000 (14)	400,000 (16.6)
Alcohol Consumption	100,000 (5)	85,000 (3.5)
Microbial Agents	90,000 (4)	75,000 (3.1)
Toxic Agents	60,000 (3)	55,000 (2.3)
Motor Vehicles	25,000 (1)	43,000 (1.8)
Firearms	35,000 (2)	29,000 (1.2)
Sexual Behavior	30,000 (1)	20,000 (0.8)
Illicit Drug Use	20,000 (<1)	17,000 (0.7)

*Mokdad, A.H., et al, 2004. Actual Causes of Death in the United States, 2000. *JAMA* 2004; 291:1238–1245.[7]

The actual causes of death shown in Table 1-4 underscore these findings. Tobacco use is a primary cause for heart disease and cancer. Poor nutrition and physical inactivity can lead to heart disease, cancer, and diabetes. Alcohol consumption is often associated with accidents involving motor vehicles and motorized equipment. In fact, seven of the leading causes of death in the United States are associated with lifestyle risk factors that can be modified. This is quite different from the causes of death in the early 1900s, which were infectious diseases and poor sanitation. In the early 1900s, most people engaged in manual labor, which amounted to daily physical activity.

Eating habits were influenced by seasonal availability and restricted by certain limited food sources, such as meat. Today, diets have shifted from one based on vegetables and minimally processed food, to one based on animal products and highly processed foods.[9] Today's sedentary lifestyle, together with poor dietary habits, substantially increase the risk for coronary artery disease, hypertension, stroke, diabetes, obesity, osteoporosis, and certain cancers and account for about 400,000 deaths in the United States each year. If physical activity patterns and eating habits were more like those of that earlier generation, we might be living longer and healthier lives today.[10]

Wellness Influences

Personal wellness may be influenced by not only an individual's behavior, but by governmental direction, cultural influences, and diversity influences.

National Health Goals and Trends

Personal health behavior change was the focus of most of the earliest health promotion initiatives planned in the United States. It was assumed that people would change their behavior if provided with knowledge from a reliable source.[11] So, if a large public health campaign advised us to exercise, we would then begin to exercise. Unfortunately, this did not prove to be true. A broad campaign produced only minor change in the population. A shift in emphasis occurred with the publication of the first *Healthy People* report in 1980. This report combined broad community health goals with targets for individual behavior change and established national health objectives. In addition, it served as the basis for the development of state and community plans. Each report assesses various aspects of public health and establishes goals for specific targets to be achieved within certain time frames.

Healthy People Initiative

Healthy People 2010 is the Federal health promotion agenda for the United States.[12] Built on the best scientific knowledge available, it offers a simple but powerful idea: to provide health objectives in a format that enables diverse groups to combine their efforts and work as a team.

One of the main goals of the initiative is to help individuals both increase life expectancy and quality of life. A healthy population is our most valuable resource, whereas a sick population diminishes our economy and drains our creativity. Another goal is the elimination, not just the reduction, of health disparities for all minority groups. Under these main goals are hundreds of other target goals to encourage a more active lifestyle, improve nutrition, reduce abuse of various substances, and reduce the incidence of chronic and infectious diseases. Several federal agencies work with the Healthy People Consortium and the Coalition for Healthier Cities and Communities toward achieving these goals, supporting organizations that hold health fairs, screenings, and promote healthy choices.

Image of Health in Depth

Healthy People 2010 Main Goals

Goal 1: Increase Quality and Years of Healthy Life
The first goal of *Healthy People 2010* is to help individuals of all ages increase life expectancy *and* improve quality of life.

Goal 2: Eliminate Health Disparities
The second goal of *Healthy People 2010* is to eliminate health disparities among segments of the population, including differences that occur by gender, race or ethnicity, education or income, disability, geographic location, or sexual orientation.

Critical Thinking Question: In what ways could your college campus work to achieve the two major *Healthy People 2010* health goals?

The Trend Toward Wellness

Today the top three causes of death in the United States—cardiovascular diseases, cancers, and stroke—involve lifestyle factors: the result of choices we make on a daily basis. These include choices such as smoking, not exercising, eating non-nutritionally dense foods, and poor stress management. Of course, some people *do* choose to behave in a responsible manner. The fact that these lifestyle choices are under our direct control makes wellness an achievable goal, and illustrates our own responsibility and consequential accountability.

The trend toward wellness is exemplified by the fitness craze that began in the 1980s. Even your local grocery store may be promoting wellness by encouraging the consumption of more produce. This might be seen with graphics of fruits and vegetables on grocery bags or the promotion of the "Five-A-Day" program, designed to encourage individuals to consume at least five servings of fruit and vegetables each day. However, the most important component in the trend toward wellness is the individual. Many of the choices you make each day move you either toward better health, or away from it. If you are a sedentary person, you may look at people who jog by your house, and think: "I wish I could do that." If you are overweight, you may wonder how thinner people manage to stay thin. Yet the choice to make a behavior change is up to you. If you make a commitment to adopt healthier behaviors today, you are making a commitment to the ultimate goal of wellness—one step at a time, one change at a time, and one better decision at a time.

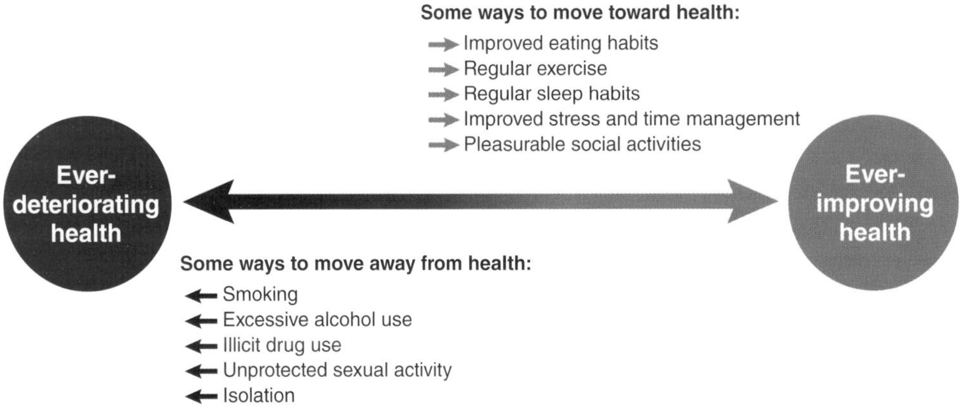

Some ways to move toward health:
➡ Improved eating habits
➡ Regular exercise
➡ Regular sleep habits
➡ Improved stress and time management
➡ Pleasurable social activities

Ever-deteriorating health ⬅━━━━━━━━━➡ Ever-improving health

Some ways to move away from health:
⬅ Smoking
⬅ Excessive alcohol use
⬅ Illicit drug use
⬅ Unprotected sexual activity
⬅ Isolation

FIGURE 1-3. The wellness continuum.

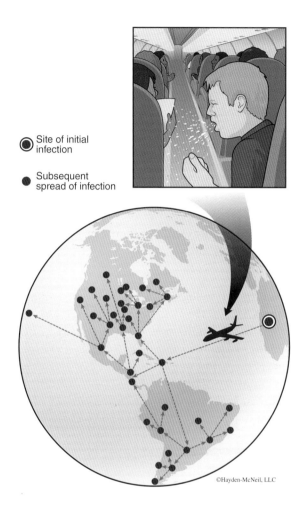

● Site of initial infection

● Subsequent spread of infection

©Hayden-McNeil, LLC

FIGURE 1-4. Exponential spread of disease.

Globalization of Health Issues

With the advent of international travel, health issues no longer remain "local" issues. This was exemplified in the winter of 2002, when the deadly **SARS** virus emerged in southern China. It quickly spread across the Far East, and was then transported via airline passengers to Singapore and Canada. As deaths from SARS occurred, travelers adopted surgical masks and some individuals refused to leave their communities. Ongoing travel by infected but non-symptomatic people moved the virus, while those who chose to curtail their usual business activities slowed economic movement. Each of these had a potential worldwide impact. Figure 1-4 represents how one individual could spread an infectious disease from just one person to an exponential number.

> **Key Term**
>
> **Severe acute respiratory syndrome (SARS)**: A respiratory disease in humans caused by the SARS corona virus (SARS-CoV) and resulting in a death rate of almost 10%.

In April 2009, the first cases of H1N1 flu virus were identified in the U.S. Although most people who become infected recover without hospitalization, the virus can have a deadly potential in people with impaired immune systems and in the elderly. On June 11, 2009, the WHO declared that H1N1 was now **pandemic**, meaning it had spread worldwide.

> **Key Term**
>
> **Pandemic**: An infection that spreads globally to almost every continent.

Personal and Cultural Influences

The earliest influence on your health came from your parents, who were responsible for everything from your nutritional requirements to your emotional needs during childhood. Today, there are many influences on your health, including family history, behavior patterns, social/peer group, the environment, and media and society.

Family History

Your family or genetic background has some influence on your health. For example, if you have a family history of heart disease or breast cancer, you may have an increased risk for these diseases. Similarly, certain diseases, such as **sickle cell disease** or **Tay-Sachs disease**, have a known genetic link. Sickle cell disease is a condition caused by a genetic mutation that affects the oxygen-carrying capacity of red blood cells. Affecting mainly individuals of African descent, this lifelong disease causes fatigue, anemia, pain, organ damage, and other serious symptoms. Tay-Sachs disease, which primarily affects individuals of Eastern European Jewish ancestry, is a fatal genetic disorder that destroys the nervous system in children.[13]

If you know your family history and recognize that you have an increased risk for a certain disease, you can be proactive and incorporate behaviors into your life to lessen the risk. However, with a genetic condition, you will only be able to manage the disease, not avoid it. The Human Genome Project, discussed in the accompanying Image of Health in Depth, addresses how research might help people with specific genetic conditions.

Key Terms

Sickle cell disease: Disease in which sickle-shaped red blood cells block the flow of oxygen-rich blood.

Tay–Sachs disease: Fatal genetic disorder that destroys the nervous system in children. It primarily affects people of Eastern European Jewish ancestry.

Image of Health in Depth

The Human Genome Project

The U.S. Human **Genome** Project (HGP) was a 13-year effort coordinated by the U.S. Department of Energy and the National Institutes of Health. The project goals were to:

- Identify all the approximately 20,000 to 25,000 **genes** in human DNA

- Determine the sequences of the 3 billion chemical base pairs that make up human DNA

- Store this information in databases

- Improve tools for data analysis

- Transfer related technologies to the private sector

- Address the ethical, legal, and social issues (ELSI) that may arise from the project

Although the project was officially at an end when these goals were reached, its work is ongoing. The knowledge gained from the HGP has opened up new areas of research that will continue for years. Gene therapy, for example, is a technique for correcting defective genes responsible for the development of disease. The most common approach to this therapy is to insert a normal gene into a nonspecific location with the genome to replace a nonfunctional gene. Another area for development is pharmacogenetics, which is the study of how an individual's genetic inheritance affects the body's response to drugs. This type of study has the potential for producing more powerful and safer drugs, developing better vaccines, and decreasing the overall cost of health care, among other things.

(Source: National Human Genome Research Institute. U.S. Department of Energy, Office of Science, Office of Biological and Environmental Research, Human Genome Program. August, 2006.)

Key Terms

Genome: The entire DNA (deoxyribonucleic acid) in an organism, including its genes. DNA is made up of four similar chemicals called bases and are abbreviated A, T, C and G. These bases are repeated millions or billions of times throughout a genome. The human genome has 3 billion pairs of bases. The order of the bases is extremely important and dictates whether an organism is human or another species.

Gene: The basic physical and functional units of heredity that carry information for developing the proteins that determine the characteristics of specific organisms. When genes are altered so that the proteins cannot carry out their normal functions, genetic disorders can result.

Behavior Patterns

Patterns of behavior, your lifestyle choices, greatly influence personal health, either positively or negatively. You make choices that improve your health, and you may make choices that work against your health and wellness. Look again at Figure 1-3 illustrating behaviors that move you toward or away from health. What positive behaviors do you choose to maintain and what negative behaviors are keeping you from more optimal health?

Social and Peer Group

Like adolescence, the college years are considered a time of great peer pressure. You probably realize that you are influenced by your friends in many ways, such as choices in music, fashion, study habits, and even in your sleep patterns. Yet there are also more subtle forms of influence that are important to consider. When you and your friends get together, are you more likely to meet in a bar or at a gym? Does your social group prefer fast food or healthy low-fat food? Do your friends use recreational drugs? Do they engage in heavy drinking and irresponsible driving? The answers to these questions will tell you something about your own health behaviors. Perhaps answering these questions will make you think about making different choices. If you are committed to making a behavior change, you may need to make adjustments in your social group. For example, if you are trying to stop smoking, you may need to avoid spending time with friends who smoke. Otherwise, you will be *setting* yourself up for potential failure.

Environmental Influences

Many environmental influences affect your health, including climate, temperature, weather patterns, air quality, noise, population density, and traffic. Your personal environment, such as your neighborhood, also has an influence on your health. If you live in a neighborhood that offers opportunities for exercise, such as bike paths and recreational facilities, you are more likely to be physically active. If your area has many fast-food restaurants, you may find yourself patronizing them rather than cooking at home or seeking out restaurants that have more healthful food choices.

Media and Society

Health information is all around us--on the Internet, in the news, in magazines, in advertisements, and on television and radio. However, not all of it is reliable because some information is inaccurate or not reported fully. Part of your responsibility as an informed consumer is to determine whether information is reliable or not. Chapter 2 shows how you can evaluate information you find.

Taking a critical thinking approach to health information is important in dealing with this information wisely. Critical thinking is the mental process of actively and skillfully analyzing concepts, evaluating and synthesizing information and applying this information to reach an answer or conclusion.

Critical Thinking Question: Consider health advertisements that you have recently seen and identify the underlying messages that may not be true.

Diversity and Health

Health may be affected by sex, gender, sexual orientation, race, culture, socioeconomic status and education, and disabilities. These components may act individually or collectively to affect health.

Sex and Gender

Sex refers to the set of biological and physiological characteristics that define an individual as male or female. For reasons of anatomy, certain diseases affect only one sex. Prostate cancer, for example, occurs in males only. Similarly, cervical cancer affects only females. **Gender** refers to the roles, behaviors, and characteristics that society associates with males and females. These differences also affect health and wellness. For example, risk-taking behavior is more common in men than women, and is perhaps endorsed by society as appropriate. The more risks one takes, the higher the likelihood of accidents and even death. The female role is more often seen as the role of a nurturer and as such, females may be more likely to be part of a supportive social network. In times of stress, this network can help reduce the trauma of stress for women.

Women have a longer life expectancy than men, known as "the female advantage," and white women have the longest life expectancy of all. How much of this "advantage" has to do with gender itself, and how much of it can be explained by differences in behavior? Women tend to form ongoing friendships, which can help to support their mental and physical well being. Compared to men, women are more likely to undergo regular health screenings, to seek professional medical help when they are sick, and to be more concerned about weight control.[14] All of these factors contribute to longevity and disease prevention in women.

Key Terms

Sex: The biological and physical characteristics that define an individual as either female or male.

Gender: Roles, behaviors and characteristics that society associates with males and females.

Sexual Orientation

Sexual orientation, defined as one's natural preference in sexual partners leads to a predilection for homosexuality, heterosexuality or bisexuality. America's gay and lesbian population comprises a diverse community with disparate health concerns. Major health issues for gay men are human immune-deficiency virus and acquired immune deficiency syndrome (HIV/AIDS) and other sexually transmitted diseases, substance abuse, depression, and suicide.[15,16,17,18,19]

 Gay male adolescents are two to three times more likely than their heterosexual peers to attempt suicide.[20,21,22] Some evidence suggests lesbians have higher rates of smoking, overweight, alcohol abuse, and stress than heterosexual women.[23,24,25] In addition, the homophobic issues that surround personal, family, and social acceptance of sexual orientation can place significant burden on an individual's mental health and personal safety.

Ethnicity and Culture

Ethnicity and culture also influence causes of death. Table 1-5 illustrates some of these differences.

Challenge Question: How do causes of death differ for black males and white males throughout their lives?

Critical Thinking Question: Why do health differences exist among different ethnicities?

As you consider the leading causes of death for these groups, it is important to note that HIV, accidents, unintentional injuries and homicide, heart disease, and cancer are all influenced by behavior. It is not an exaggeration to say that behaviors and lifestyle choices are harming health—and even killing us.

Critical Thinking Question: What behaviors practiced by college students might increase the risk of an early death?

Table 1-5. Causes of Death by Ethnic Group

AGE	BLACK MALES	WHITE MALES	NATIVE AMERICAN OR ALASKAN MALES	PACIFIC ISLANDER MALES	BLACK FEMALES	WHITE FEMALES	NATIVE AMERICAN OR ALASKAN FEMALES	PACIFIC ISLANDER FEMALES
<15 years	Unintentional Injuries	Unintentional Injuries	Unintentional Injuries	Unintentional Injuries	Unintentional Injuries	Unintentional Injuries	Unintentional Injuries	Unintentional Injuries
15–34 years	Homicide	Unintentional Injuries	Unintentional Injuries	Unintentional Injuries	15–24 Unintentional Injuries 24–34 HIV	Unintentional Injuries	Unintentional Injuries	15–24 Unintentional Injuries 24–34 Cancer
35–44	Heart Disease	Unintentional Injuries	Unintentional Injuries	Cancer	Cancer	Cancer	Unintentional Injuries	Cancer
45–54	Heart Disease	Heart Disease	Heart Disease	Cancer	Cancer	Cancer	Cancer	Cancer
55–64	Cancer	Cancer	Cancer	Cancer	Cancer	Cancer	Cancer	Cancer
65+	Heart Disease	Heart Disease	Heart Disease	Heart Disease	Heart Disease	65–74 Cancer 74+ Heart Disease	Heart Disease	Heart Disease

Data shown by race include persons of Hispanic origin, because race and Hispanic origin are reported separately on death certificate.
(Source: National Center for Health Statistics, 2004.)

Socioeconomic Status and Education

The connection between socioeconomic status, education, and health issues is complex. Although overall mortality rates fell sharply during the twentieth century throughout the developed world, the mortality rates in lower socioeconomic and educational status groups are still higher than those of groups with higher corresponding levels.[26] The reasons for mortality are complex within any **cohort**, but researchers have identified that people of lower education and lower socioeconomic status tend to smoke more, have higher levels of obesity, and either lack access to medical care, or the available medical care is of poor quality.[27]

Key Term

Cohort: A group of persons sharing a particular statistical or demographic characteristic.

Achieving the two main public health goals, to increase quality and years of life for all and to eliminate health disparities, must involve improving the socioeconomic status and education for certain groups.

Disability Issues

According to the U.S. Census Bureau's 2002 Survey of Income and Program Participation (SIPP), an estimated 51.2 million people in the United States, or about 18.1% of people who are not in institutions or the military, have a disability.[28] These disabilities range from those who are permanently disabled and unable to care for themselves in any way, to those that are temporarily disabled and who may or may not need assistance.

Although disabled people may be healthy, their health may be affected by the severity of the disability, access to health care, and the level of support provided by family, friends, and the community. Many people with a disability have several health challenges, making their daily care and their health care rise to a level of special care. They may need to see a specialist for their main disability, and they may also need transport to doctor visits and related home care.

Exploring Behavior Change

If behavior change were easy, all attempts at change such as weight loss, smoking cessation, or exercise regimens would succeed. But as you review your history, you may find countless examples where you have failed. Why is health behavior so difficult to change?

With many personal behavior changes, you can see the consequences quickly. If you put in extra study time for a test, you will probably earn a higher grade than usual. With health behaviors, both the positive *and* negative consequences can be far removed from the behavior. For example, if you begin an exercise program, you may not see the benefits for many weeks. But if you maintain that exercise program, you are establishing the foundation for a healthier and potentially longer life. By contrast, if you maintain a diet high in fat, animal products, and processed food, the quality of your life and your longevity will be impaired by increasing the risk for obesity and chronic diseases.

Research related to human behavior, including how it can be changed and how behavior change can be maintained, is ongoing. In this section, two of the leading theories of behavior change are examined. Understanding these theories may help you understand why you have or have not been able to successfully change, and maintain a behavior change.

Health Belief Model

The Health Belief Model of behavior was developed in the 1950's by social psychologists Godfrey Hochbaum, Irwin Rosenstock, and Stephen Kegels.[29] Their main conclusions were that human behavior is based on four factors:

- Perceived susceptibility: The individual's belief about his/her chances of getting the condition.

- Perceived severity: The person's opinion of how serious the condition and its consequences might be.

- Perceived benefits: The person's belief that the action taken will reduce the risk or seriousness of the impact.

- Perceived barriers: The person's opinion of the costs, both tangible and psychological, of the target action.

Two other components were added later:

- Cues to action: Factors that produce readiness for change.

- Self-efficacy: Confidence in one's ability to take action and succeed.

If you find out that a close relative of yours has been diagnosed with terminal lung cancer and you are a smoker, you may realize that you are a likely candidate for lung cancer (perceived susceptibility). Considering your relative's situation, you may focus on the possibility of failing health and death (perceived severity). At the same time, you realize that you will gain some immediate and long-term benefits when you stop smoking (perceived benefits), such as easier breathing and the potential for a longer life. You may also realize that you are going to face some challenges in trying to quit smoking (perceived barriers), including knowing it is an addiction and the influence of smoking friends. All of these thoughts may result in a decision to stop smoking (cues to action), but to succeed you need to believe in your ability to be successful (self-efficacy).

Transtheoretical/Stages of Change Model

Prochaska and DiClemente developed the Transtheoretical Model (TTM) as a result of their research into how behavior is learned, maintained, or eliminated.[30] The model lists six stages of change: pre-contemplation, contemplation, preparation, action, maintenance, and termination. Although the stages are listed as sequential steps here, throughout the process of change a person may move backward or forward between stages.

Precontemplation Stage

In the precontemplation stage, you may not be aware that you have a behavior that needs to be changed. If someone has pointed out that there are risks associated with a behavior, such as being overweight, you may deny that these risks are real or serious enough to warrant change. You may have already tried and failed to change the target behavior, and view the situation as hopeless. The motivation to change is not present at this stage. In this stage, people often have an **external locus of control** and blame others, or situations for their own behavior.

Contemplation Stage

In the contemplation stage, you are thinking about making a health behavior change. You may be considering the pros and cons of such a commitment. If losing weight is the issue, you may be thinking about how good it will feel to be slimmer, but you may also be worried about depriving yourself of your favorite foods. Another possibility at this stage is that you have made the decision to change and are thinking about starting within the next six months.

Key Term

External locus of control: Perception that events in your life occur by chance or because of actions outside your control.

Preparation Stage

In the preparation stage, you are thinking seriously about changing and are making plans for the change. If weight loss is your goal, you will probably be considering different food plans, support groups, and approaches to exercise. This is the time to identify people who can help and support you in your new behavior. It is also a time to anticipate any obstacles you may face and plan strategies to overcome them. At this point, you are about one month from starting to change.

Action Stage

In the action stage, you are actively involved in changing a health behavior. You are trying to avoid situations that could tempt you to fall back into your old behavior. You are using positive self-talk to remind yourself that what you are doing is worth the effort and you are staying focused on what you expect to gain.

Throughout the process of change, episodes of relapse are likely to occur. A relapse is commonly associated with an unexpected situation, a lack of planning, or even lack of time. When a relapse does occur, it's important to address it immediately so that the relapse does not cause you to give up. Look back over your past successes and consider the methods you used to stay on target. If changing health behavior were easy, we would not have so many obese people, sedentary people, smokers, or drug users.

Maintenance Stage

At the maintenance stage, you have been successful with your new behavior for over six months. You have experienced some minor setbacks, but you have managed to get back on track. You are still using the strategies that helped you get to this point, and are using positive self-talk to remind yourself about your success in overcoming obstacles. You realize that you still have challenges ahead, but you have plans for this. You are in charge of your health.

Termination Stage

When you reach the termination stage, your new health behavior is firmly entrenched and you are not tempted to go back to your old behavior. Think about the behaviors you have successfully changed in your life. You may have

to think very hard because if you are at the termination stage, you may have forgotten that they ever occurred. But knowing you have achieved success previously will help build your self-efficacy so that you achieve success with your next behavior change.

Considering Behavior Change

If behavior change is to be successful, the decision to make the change should be your decision. You must believe that there are greater rewards to changing than maintaining the behavior. In order to help assure success, consider your self-efficacy related to your goal. Positive self-talk can help increase self-efficacy.

Critical Thinking Question: Of all your behaviors, which has the greatest negative impact on your health? Are you ready to change this behavior?

Joaquin's Story:
A Smoker's Wake-Up Call

During his first year of college, Joaquin experienced some breathing problems and underwent a chest X-ray. The results of the X-ray were unclear, but they suggested the possibility of cancer. Although he had been a smoker since age 13, Joaquin was shocked by this news. After a week of waiting while his doctor consulted with a specialist, Joaquin found out that the suspicious area was not cancer. Although Joaquin was relieved, he promised himself that he would quit smoking.

Joaquin talked to his doctor about various approaches to quitting. He also called his friend, Karen, who stopped smoking a year earlier. They talked about potential obstacles—what to do about socializing with friends who

smoke, how to break the habit of having a cigarette after meals, and how to watch TV without smoking. Karen suggested that Joaquin tell his smoking friends that he wouldn't be able to socialize with them for the first few months while he was trying to quit. Instead of having a cigarette after meals, they decided that Joaquin could plan to start another routine, like brushing his teeth immediately after dinner and going for a walk. To avoid smoking while watching TV, Joaquin thought he'd try going to the library most evenings. That way he'd still see some of his friends, get a lot of work done, and be distracted from smoking.

Joaquin enlisted the help of his family and closest friends, explaining that he would need their help to reach his goal. Everyone agreed to help, so Joaquin felt ready to start.

Joaquin signed a behavior change contract with Karen as his witness. His start date was set for 1 month from that day. Joaquin was excited but also worried about whether or not he would succeed. He felt good about the reward system he had planned. For every week that he managed to avoid smoking, he would do something special—buy himself a new CD, take a day trip, or have a friend over for dinner.

The first week was especially hard, but he tapped into all his resources. He called Karen often. He went to his first support group meeting and talked to someone who was also struggling. He started walking and going to the library in the evenings, and developed a new routine that did not include smoking.

But by the third week Joaquin had bumped into a smoking friend and found himself taking

a cigarette without any hesitation. That night he called Karen and told her what happened. Karen was understanding and supportive. She told Joaquin that she had had similar lapses but that she just started over again. Over the next several months, Joaquin had occasional setbacks but he always got back on track. Gradually, things got easier. He wasn't always thinking about smoking. He actually enjoyed his walking sessions and had begun running. And his time at the library had improved his grades. He was feeling positive and energetic and was breathing more easily.

By the end of one year, Joaquin was a nonsmoker. Sometimes he was tempted to smoke, but felt confident that he had the problem under his control. He was proud of his accomplishment and was enjoying the rewards of his new lifestyle. ■

Social psychologist Julian Rotter identified certain traits in people that predicted how they would interpret life's outcomes and how well they might succeed in life.[31] People with an **internal locus of control** believe that they control their own destiny, whereas those with an external locus of control believe that their fate is largely determined by chance or by other people. People with an internal locus of control have been shown to perform better in school, have better relationships and careers, and are more satisfied with most areas of their life. Individuals with an external locus of control may think that their poor college grades are the fault of the instructor or a badly written test, rather than their own study habits. They are less likely to accept responsibility for relationship problems or career failures. People in this group do not welcome challenges and will abandon trying to change behavior when they confront difficulty or obstacles. These individuals are generally not very happy or satisfied with their lives.

> **Key Term**
>
> **Internal locus of control**: Perception that you control and are responsible for events in your life.

Most people are not purely internally or externally motivated. Motivation often depends on the situation. As you attempt a behavior change, it is important for you to have an internal locus of control about the behavior. You need to believe that you have the skills to make the change, that you can overcome the barriers you will face, and that you will be successful. At the end of the chapter, there is an exercise to determine your level of readiness for change.

Developing a Plan for Behavior Change

Once a pattern of behavior has become established, it takes hard work to break the pattern. Begin by developing a realistic plan or contract that will work for you. Creating a plan is worth the effort because it provides a focus and a guide to follow throughout the process of change, which may take several weeks or months.

Motivation Maximizer

Motivation: The Key to Behavior Change

Did you ever experience a "moment of truth"? Maybe it was a glance in the mirror, an offhand remark by a friend, a visit to the doctor, or news of a relative's illness or death. Whatever happened, you said to yourself: "I need to make this change, and I'm going to do it."

At a time like this your motivation level is very high. You feel strong, decisive, determined, and self-confident. But as time passes, your motivation is likely to waver. Obstacles get in the way, laziness takes over, or more immediate things call for your attention. To keep your motivation level high, use the following strategies:

- *Evaluate your goal.* Is your goal realistic? If your goal is to lose 10 pounds in two weeks, you will probably fail. But if your goal is more realistic—to lose 10 pounds in two months—you will have a much better chance of success.

- *Use positive self-talk.* Give yourself credit for what you are doing. Every time you do something "right," such as going for a walk instead of smoking a cigarette after a meal, tell yourself what a great thing that is. And when you get off the track, dismiss all negative thoughts ("I'll never succeed. I'm just not strong enough…"). Replace them with positive ones ("I had one cigarette. That was a mistake, but it's not the end of the world. I'm going to try harder next time.")

- *Create a support group.* Share your commitment with your friends, family, and co-workers. People who truly care about you will want to help you succeed, so let them be a resource for you. If your friends know you are trying to lose weight, they may plan on having low-calorie snacks at the next party.

- *Give yourself rewards.* Rewards are effective because they reinforce the new behavior you are practicing. Go to see a movie, buy yourself a new CD, have a massage, or go out for coffee with a friend to celebrate each little success. Don't wait until you've reached your big goal. It's the little rewards that will keep you going.

- *Keep your eyes on the prize.* Remind yourself that this change is something you are doing for yourself. Even though it involves hard work and is difficult, you are giving yourself a gift, and you will be the one to enjoy the benefits.

- *Take it one day at a time.* Focus on your target behavior on a daily basis. The days will turn into weeks and months before you know it!

An important preliminary step for behavior change is setting a goal that is specific and within a realistic timeframe. A sedentary person might decide to begin or increase daily walking. To make the goal specific, the plan might be a 30-minute walk three times a week, and the timeframe might be Monday, Wednesday, and Friday during lunch hour. This goal is now specific and realistic.

Many people find it helpful to use a behavior change contract to formalize their plan. The contract explains goals (both short-term and long-term), describes strategies for action, and puts the plan in a timeframe. Behavior change contracts are effective because they represent a strong commitment to change.

Confronting Barriers to Change

As you consider behavior change, think about factors that worked against your efforts at change in the past. Were there certain people who hindered you rather than helped you? Did some situations make things difficult for you? Considering these barriers *in advance* allows you to plan to avoid them or overcome them. Having a strategy will make it much easier to deal with these challenges.

Common Behavior Change Obstacles

Behavior change usually fails for three reasons. The first is a lack of adequate planning. To help ensure success, clearly identify your target behavior, and then establish a specific, goal-oriented plan toward achieving it.

The second reason for behavior change failure is an inability to anticipate and plan for obstacles to success. By anticipating events that might cause failure, you will have a plan ready to overcome them. Without a plan for overcoming such obstacles, you are not in control.

The third reason for behavior change failure is lack of reinforcement. With health behavior changes, it might take months to see the end result. Still, positive changes may be happening in your body. It is up to you to practice positive self-talk and remind yourself of the benefits to come and the negative consequences that you are working to prevent. Setting up a system of incremental rewards is another effective way of reinforcing the new behavior.

Challenge Question: What are the key ways you can help promote success when planning a behavior change?

Steps to Successful Behavior Change

If you are trying to change an existing behavior: Each time the behavior occurs, write down what you were thinking, what your mood was, who you were with, and what you were doing. In this way, you will begin to identify the cues that trigger this unwanted behavior. At the end of the two weeks, review what you have written to see if patterns exist. By identifying and assessing the situations, people, or emotions that may make change more difficult, you can develop ways to counteract these forces. You will need to either avoid some situations or people or be more aware of the influences these "triggers" have so that you can plan to overcome them.

If you are trying to start a new behavior: Make a list of the factors that prevent you from practicing this behavior. The list might include lack of time, laziness, or even friends or family members who are negative influences. "Image of Health in Depth: Overcoming Obstacles" shows how you might organize this list.

Image of Health in Depth

Overcoming Obstacles

OBSTACLES I CAN CONTROL	WHAT I WILL DO	OBSTACLES I CANNOT CONTROL	WHAT I WILL DO
Laziness	Sign up for an exercise class	Friends do not exercise	Try to develop new friendships in the exercise class
Lack of time	Maintain a routine and include the new behavior in it	School and work take up most of my time	Manage my free time better so I prioritize this new behavior
Lack of interest	Develop a list of the good things this behavior will result in	Neighborhood is unsafe for walking at night	Plan to walk at school or work or in the morning when it is light

By identifying barriers to the target behavior and developing potential solutions to them, you increase your chances of success.

BEHAVIOR CHANGE CONTRACT

My Goal: _____ (write down your specific goal).

Ensure that it can be measured in some way. For instance, if you are trying to improve your eating habits, consider statements like "At the end of this behavior change, I will be eating seven servings of fruits and vegetables each day, consuming meat only twice each week, and eating only whole grains. I will limit fast food to no more than once every month." If you are trying to start an exercise regimen, consider "At the end of this behavior change, I will be able to run three miles without stopping."

I will begin this plan on: _____.

My behavior change steps are: In this section, create a series of small steps that lead toward your overall goal. Start small so you ensure success. Gradually build, but remember, if you fail in one step, you go back to the previous step. For the running example, the steps might include:

Week 1: I will get up at 6:30 am, Monday, Wednesday, and Friday and walk around the block four times. I will time myself each day and at the end of the week, I will have reduced how long it takes me from my first day.

Week 2: I will get up at 6:30 am, Monday, Wednesday, and Friday and alternate running and walking around the block four times. I will time how long it takes me, and when possible, will reduce the time spent walking.

Week 3: I will get up at 6:30 am five days a week and will run around the block twice, walk once, and run around the block twice more.

Week 4: I will measure a route that is one mile long. During week 4, I will run for as long as I can, then walk for one minute, and then continue running and walking until I complete the mile. I will do this five days a week.

Week 5: I will run the entire mile five times this week.

Week 6: I will increase the distance by a quarter of a mile and run it three times this week. On one weekend day, I will attempt to run one and one-half miles.

Week 7: I will continue to increase my distance as my stamina and strength allow and maintain my five-day-a-week regimen, with one day being my longest run.

Week 8: By the end of this week, I will run two miles without stopping, on most days of the week.

The reasons I am making this change are: _____

_____

Anticipated benefits of change: _____ (list the benefits you anticipate).

_____

Anticipated consequences if I do not change: _____ (list the negative impact of maintaining this behavior).

_____

Obstacles I may encounter and how I will overcome them:

OBSTACLE	MY PLAN TO OVERCOME THIS

My support resources include: List names of friends, support meetings, classes and other resources you can use here. Set a goal for how frequently you will access these resources (daily, weekly, in person, by phone, etc.).

My reward system will be:

At end of successful week 1	Purchase new DVD (insert rewards that matter to you.)
At end of successful week 2	
At end of successful week 3	
At end of successful week 4	

In the unlikely event I decide to abolish this plan, I agree to _____

In this area, insert some consequence that matters to you. Good ideas include giving one of your supporters a sum of money that would be donated to a cause you do not want to support. Or, you might agree to do a large task for someone else that would be time consuming and unpleasant for you.

I commit to making this change because it matters to me. I know I have the knowledge, ability, and determination to succeed.

Your signature: _____   Date: _____

Witnessed by: _____   Date: _____

Consider the benefits of the behavior change. Make a list of the benefits you anticipate from this new behavior. Some of these benefits may be immediate (e.g., saving money by not buying cigarettes) and some may be in the future (e.g., lessening your risk of chronic diseases).

Create an action plan. For many people, an effective tool to use is the behavior change contract. Many believe that there is a higher chance of success if the SMART objectives are used. This mnemonic is helpful to establish objectives and determine their usefulness for the individual.

SMART objectives include:

S   Is your objective *specific*? What is the observable action or behavior you are expecting? Is it linked to a rate, a number, or a frequency?

M   Is your objective *measurable*? With some behavior change, this might be easy to achieve. You plan to walk rapidly for thirty minutes three times each week. But how would you measure your success with dietary changes? This would involve more specificity.

A   Is your objective *achievable*? Although success may seem likely, this does not make it easy or simple. Your objective must be such that it motivates you, not causes you to feel incompetent or incapable.

R   Is your objective *relevant*? When you achieve success, will it really matter to you? This indicates its relevance.

T   What is the *time* plan for all of this? When will you start? Is a finish date necessary or the end objective clearly defined so you know when it is achieved?

One of the benefits of using a behavior change contract is that a specific plan is established. By establishing your goal, your strategies and a timeframe, you are making your plans very clear. Since this is a document that someone else will witness and you will sign, it becomes a formal promise that you are committed to change. For many people, it carries more weight than a verbal promise.

Managing Your Health

Health is dynamic process. It can change at any time, moving in a positive or negative direction. It is important to keep in mind that you have a strong measure of control over how to manage your health. However, to make good decisions, it is essential to become an informed health consumer.

Becoming an Informed Consumer

Your responsibility is to learn how to sift through information and find out what is reliable and what is not. In that way, you can use information to make health decisions that are appropriate for you.

Understanding Health Research

Qualified scientists consider research published in a peer-reviewed journal the most valid and reliable, because it must go through a rigorous review process.

Newspapers and magazines commonly present medical or health information that may be less reliable than that found in scientific journals. Since this information is routinely condensed, only partial facts or misrepresented information may be presented. Although this distortion may not be intentional, the final information may be faulty.

Health information posted on the Internet may come from highly reliable sources, such as government agencies and well-respected hospitals and colleges. However, individuals or groups without the necessary credentials or knowledge to support the material may also present it.

Table 1-6 lists factors that should be considered when you are evaluating health studies.

Table 1-6. Factors to Consider when Evaluating Research Studies

FACTOR	EXPLANATION
Subjects in the study	Generally, the larger the number of subjects and the more accurately they represent the population, the more reliable the results will be.
Type of study	Epidemiological studies use observation and interviews to trace relationships between cause and effect. They may suggest the need for more research in an area, but they are not reliable sources for making behavior change. Their results need to be validated with more trials.
	Clinical or interventional studies use trials where two or more groups are compared. They are strictly controlled scientific studies where either a drug, medical device, or other intervention is being tested. Clinical studies generally involve experimental groups who receive the drug, device, or other intervention, and control groups who differ only in that they do not receive this. In drug testing, the second group receives a placebo, which is just a sugar pill. The study is more reliable if members for each group are randomly selected and distributed into the groups. To control for subject bias, none of the participants know if they are in the experimental or control group. Researcher bias can be eliminated by making it a double blind study where even they do not know who is receiving the active intervention or the placebo. Multi-center studies involve conducting the research at multiple sites. This improves the results by ensuring a more diverse and bigger population.
	Meta-analysis work combines the results of a large group of similar studies to see if the results remain constant. These are more reliable than individual studies.
Who are the researchers, and who funded the research?	Researchers should not have any bias in the work that they do. Specifically, they should not expect to receive financial gain from their results. Research funding should also come from an unbiased source. This latter objective can become difficult. Pharmaceutical companies establish drug trials to test their own new drugs. Researchers and study participants may be paid to be part of the study. The government tries to prevent any bias by having independent monitors who assess drug trials.
Where was the study published?	Studies that are published in reputable scientific journals are more likely to be reliable and contain **valid research** because of the peer-review process involved. Studies that you might read about in magazines may not have undergone rigorous control and peer review.
Is it the first study of its kind?	Studies that have been replicated and continue to show the same results are more reliable than first-time studies. First-time studies provide interesting information that other scientists will try to replicate, but they should not be the basis for behavior change.
Size of study	Studies that involve large numbers of people tend to produce more **reliable data** than smaller studies. Smaller studies are usually done to test for safety, and if this is proved, larger populations are then studied.

Key Terms

Reliable data: data can be considered broadly reliable if the same results (or ones that are broadly similar) can be gained by a different researcher asking the same questions to the same (or statistically similar) groups / individuals.

Valid research: Research that produces results correctly inferred or deduced from a premise. It presents a valid conclusion.

Challenge Question: What methods would you use to evaluate a study published in a magazine that you read?

Evaluating Health Information

As a college student, you may not have access to health research studies. You may get your health information from newspapers, magazines, television, radio, or the Internet. Each of these sources can provide accurate information, but it may be unintentionally distorted or misrepresented. Studies have shown that consumers consider television to be more accurate than newspaper reports, but as the use of the Internet continues to expand, many consumers now use it as their source for health information.[32] The U.S. National Library of Medicine and National Institutes of Health have created a Web site to help evaluate health Web sites. (http://www.nlm.nih.gov/medlineplus/healthywebsurfing.html)

At this site, the following steps are suggested:

- Consider the source
- Focus on quality
- Consult a health professional
- Be cyber-skeptic
- Look for evidence
- Check for currency
- Beware of bias
- Protect your privacy

Miracles are not sold. Unscrupulous marketers prey on consumers' fears, and make billions of dollars on unproven products and services that might also be risky. If you are unsure about something, contact a professional organization, your physician, or the Better Business Bureau in your community.

Health in the College Years

The college years present many new opportunities and new challenges. It may be the first time that you are living away from your parents. You might need to combine both work and school, leaving little time for anything else. Yet with all these new stresses and responsibilities, it is also an important time to focus on health management.

Access to Health Care

In some cases, college students are able to remain on their parents' insurance plans until they reach a certain age. Some colleges have either the option of paying a health fee for health care services or the fee is mandatory. Services might include an on-campus physician or nurse and discounted prescriptions. Some colleges offer preventive health care, and some may offer psychological health care. For most college students, the campus health center may be the best option. Another option for uninsured college students is to take advantage of community health clinics, which usually charge income-based fees and sometimes offer free services.

Individual Concerns

Due to a generally younger age, most students have a relatively high standard of health. However, some individuals may need to manage a chronic disease, such as diabetes, or a disability, such as multiple sclerosis. If you are in generally good health, this is a good time to focus on strengthening the healthy habits that you already have and targeting areas for improvement. With strong health habits in your younger years, you will be setting the stage for better health for a lifetime.

Health Goals

You are in the process of learning more about your health. You know how to evaluate health information and how to access health care. You have learned how to assess your behavior and how to change it. You are becoming a responsible and accountable party to your own health. Now is the time to establish basic groundwork for a healthy lifestyle. As a responsible individual, you know you can affect your health outcome by choosing appropriate health enhancing habits and behaviors.

A Lifetime Approach to Wellness

During the college years, you might not consider what your life will be like when you are aged 50 and older. Although your interests are likely to change by then, your desire to live as full a life as possible will not.

Many of the choices you make today will determine what you will be able to do when older. Now is the time to improve or work on all positive health behaviors. It is a good time to ensure you practice disease prevention by checking the status of immunizations and practicing self-examinations. It is also the time to take a preventive approach to your health. Good health requires a lifetime of commitment. Improving your health behaviors today and maintaining them through time will help build a foundation for a lifetime of good health.

▼

Responsibility and Accountability

In this first chapter, emphasis is on the responsibility and accountability each person holds for health and wellness. To succeed we must make informed choices, make changes based on knowledge, and establish control by affecting our life outcome.

Taking Responsibility for Your Health

Every day you make choices that affect your level of health and wellness. Whether they are made consciously or not, these choices can have a positive or negative impact on your health. If you drank too much alcohol last night, today you are ill because of it. If you exercised before coming to class today, your energy levels will be higher. While studying this book's approach to health, you will be challenged to view your choices in terms of responsibility. As in other areas, responsibility refers to a sense of ownership of actions and choices. Responsibility includes keeping yourself informed about health matters, making good health choices, and taking a proactive approach to your health. In general, it means taking your health seriously, recognizing that your health is under your control and that you can make changes to improve your health.

Focusing on Accountability

Closely related to responsibility is the idea of accountability, which is the state of being answerable for actions and choices. Underlying accountability is a willingness to accept responsibility for your health. But to whom are you accountable? First and foremost, to yourself. To live a full and rewarding life, you owe it to yourself to make choices that support good health. If you take care of your health, you will increase your chances of being able to be a good relative, friend, and member of society.

Responsibility and accountability are choices you make. They are under your control and you can make changes if they do not provide the outcome you want.

Summary

Language of Health

- Health refers to the condition of a person at a given moment in time. Wellness refers to an approach that prevents illness and promotes a long, vital life. Approaches to health and wellness impact outcome and can include self-care, holistic health, personal health, and community health.

- The WHO defined health as a state of complete mental, physical, and social well-being and not merely the absence of disease or infirmity.

- Responsibility for health means making good health choices and taking a proactive approach to your health. Accountability for your health shows a willingness to accept responsibility for decisions that affect your health.

- The dimensions of wellness include physical, emotional, intellectual, spiritual, social, environmental, and other factors.

- Health promotion refers to efforts by you, and by various organizations and agencies that promote well-being.

- In the 1900s, infectious diseases and poor sanitary conditions caused most deaths. Today, more people die from chronic diseases.

- Life expectancy has increased from about 47 years in 1900 to about 77 years today, but for most people, the last years of their life are impaired due to chronic disease. Most chronic diseases are determined by self-selected behaviors such as smoking, poor nutrition habits, and sedentary behavior.

Wellness Influences

- The first National Health goals were announced in 1980. The most recent goals are for the year 2010 and include eliminating health disparities across groups, and increasing the quality and years of healthy life for all.

- Behavior is the biggest contributor to your health and wellness profile. Each of us has the responsibility and must become accountable for our own health.

- Gender and sexual orientation may increase the risk for certain diseases and behaviors. Ethnicity and culture can have both a positive and negative impact on health.

- Lower socioeconomic and education groups face higher mortality rates than others.

- Over 50 million people have a disability. Without community support, the health of disabled individuals can be compromised.

Exploring Behavior Change

- The Health Belief Model examines the influence perceived susceptibility, severity of disease has on behavior change and how barriers and benefits of change may influence whether someone is motivated to change.

- The Transtheoretical Model of Behavior Change lists six stages: pre-contemplation, contemplation, planning, action, maintenance, and termination.

Managing Your Health

- To effectively manage your health, it is necessary to understand how to interpret health information. Quality research is published in peer-reviewed journals and when repeated, shows the same results.

- A variety of resources are available for the insured and uninsured.

- Setting health goals requires a lifetime commitment. Improving behaviors today, and maintaining those changes, will help assure you of a lower risk of disease and may promote longevity.

Reassessing Your Knowledge

1. What are the three leading causes of death in the USA today? What behaviors affect these causes?

2. How do death rates and causes differ across age, gender and ethnic groups? Why are certain groups prone to certain causes of death and how can this be changed?

3. Why do you think people continue to behave in unhealthy ways when they know this behavior will lead to disease and/or death?

4. What could your college do to promote behavior that is more healthful?

5. Describe why people with an internal locus of control might be more successful with behavior change than those with an external locus of control.

To answer these questions, you might choose to work in groups with your colleagues. Check your answers against the written material in the text, and reread those sections where you made errors.

Health Assessment Toolbox

http://www.realage.com/
This site provides a fill in the blank format to determine the status of your health. Once the survey is completed, you are told your current "age" health, which might be younger or older than you are!

http://americanheart.org/
Click on the getting healthy icon and then choose from a variety of information that will help you maintain your heart health.

http://www.healthstatus.com/
This site offers a variety of tests ranging from body mass index to blood alcohol estimator and daily calorie expenditure.

http://markhenri.com/health/stress.html
This site provides access to the Holmes and Rahe Social Readjustment scale, which evaluates the amount of stress in your life and uses the result to project future illness.

Vocabulary Challenge
Match the term in the left-hand column with its correct definition in the right-hand column.

TERM		DEFINITION
Infirmity		A. An identity or harmony with those things that bring meaning to our lives
Self-efficacy		B. State or rate of sickness
Concept of oneness		C. Spread through contact with an infected individual
Morbidity		D. Data with which results can be replicated
Mortality		E. Feeble or weak in body or health
Infectious disease		F. Loss of life; death rate
Chronic disease		G. Confidence in one's ability to take action and succeed
Reliable data		H. Research that produces a valid conclusion
Valid research		I. Disease that lasts over a long period of time
Dementia		J. Loss of cognitive awareness

Answers
E; G; A; B; F; C; I; D; H; J.

Exploring the Internet

Department of Health and Human Services
Healthy People 2010: National Health Promotion and Disease Prevention Objectives for the Year 2010
http://www.healthypeople.gov

Centers for Disease Control and Prevention
Information on health and safety topics, and statistics for morbidity and death in the USA.
http://www.cdc.gov

Tufts University Health and Nutrition Newsletter
A guide to living longer and healthier.
http://healthletter.tufts.edu

UC Berkeley Wellness Letter
The newsletter of nutrition, fitness and self-care.
http://www.berkeleywellness.com

Understanding Those Medical Research Articles
Pointers to help you wade through scientific journals.
http://www.craighospital.org/SCI/METS/articles.asp

Behavior Change Links
A list of sites on the Web to help you successfully change your behaviors.
http://www.social-marketing.com/BCLinks.html

Evaluating Resources on the Internet
How do you know if the sites you are looking at are reliable and valid? The National Institutes of Health has a web site to help you evaluate what you see on the web.
http://nccam.nih.gov/health/webresources/

Agency for Health Care Research and Quality
This is the Nation's leading Federal agency for research on health care quality, costs, outcomes, and patient safety.
http://www.ahcpr.gov

Selected References

1. "Constitution of the World Health Organization," *Chronicles of the World Health Organization*, Geneva, Switzerland. 1:29–43. 1948.

2. Dunn, H.L. *High Level Wellness*, Beatty Press, Arlington, VA. 1961.

3. Cutler, D.M., and Meara, E. *Changes in the Age Distribution of Mortality over the 20th Century*, Harvard University Press. September, 2001.

4. National Vital Statistics Report. Volume 58, No. 21. U.S. Life Tables, 2006. Elizabeth Arias, Division of Vital Statistics.

5. Molla, et al. "Summary Measures of Population Health, Methods for Calculating Healthy Life Expectancy" *Healthy People 2010 #21*, August 2001, Statistical Notes.

6. Centers for Disease Control and Prevention, National Center for Chronic Disease Prevention and Health Promotion (NCCDPHP) 4770 Buford Hwy, NE. MS K-40, Atlanta, GA 30341-3717. Downloaded May, 2007.

7. Mokdad, A.H, Marks, J.S., Stroup, D.F., and Gerberding, J.L. "Actual Causes of Death in the United States, 2000." *JAMA*, 291: 1238–1245. 2004.

8. Nelson, D.E., Kirkendall, R.S., and Lawton, R.L., et al.: Surveillance for smoking-attributable mortality and years of potential life lost, by state—United States, 1990. *Morbidity and Mortality Weekly Report: CDC Surveillance Summary*, 43(1): 1–8. 1994.

9. Bente, L., and Gerrier, S. Selected Food Highlights of the 20th Century: U.S. Food Supply Series. *Family Economics and Nutrition Review*, 14: 43–52. 2002.

10. Centers for Disease Control. *Morbidity and Mortality Weekly Report*, 53(37): 866–870. September 24, 2004.

11. Bennett, P., and Murphy, S. *Psychology of Health Promotion*. Buckingham, UK: Open University Press. 1997.

12. *Healthy People 2010 and Steps to a Healthier U.S.* U.S. Department of Health and Human Services Office of Disease Prevention and Health Promotion; 1101 Wootton Parkway, Suite LL100 Rockville, MD 20852.

13. National Institute of Neurological Disorders and Stroke. NINDS Tay-Sachs Disease Information Page. National Institutes of Health. Downloaded July 20, 2010 from www.ninds.nih.gov/disorders/taysachs/taysachs.htim.

14. Utilization of Ambulatory Medical Care by Women: United States, 1997–98. Series Report 13, No. 149. 51 pp. (PHS) 2001-1720. National Center for Health Statistics, July, 2001.

15. Fifield, L., Latham, J., and Phillips, C. Alcoholism in the Gay Community: The Price of Alienation, isolation, and Oppression. A Project of the Gay Community Services Center, 1977.

16. Lohrenz, L., Connelly, J., Coyne, L., and Sare, K. Alcohol Problems in Several Midwestern Homosexual Communities. *Journal of Studies on Alcohol and Drugs,* 39: 1959–1963. 1978.

17. Stall, R, and Wiley, J. A comparison of alcohol and drug use patterns of homosexual and heterosexual men: the San Francisco men's health study. *Drug Alcohol Dependence* 22:63–73, 1988.

18. Skinner, W.F.. The prevalence and demographic predictors of illicit and licit drug use among lesbians and gay men. *American Journal of Public Health,* 84: 1307–1310. 1994.

19. Skinner, W.F., and Otis, M.D. Drug and Alcohol Use among Lesbian and Gay People in a Southern U.S.: Sample. *Journal of Homosexuality,* 30: 59–91. 1996.

20. Bagley, C., and Tremblay, P. Elevated Rates of Suicidal Behavior in Gay, Lesbian and Bisexual Youth. *Crisis,* 21(3): 111–17. PubMed, 2000.

21. Kulkin, H.S., Chauvin, E.A., and Percle, G.A. Suicide among Gay and Lesbian Adolescents and Young Adults: a Review of the Literature. *Journal of Homosexuality,* 40(1): 1–29. PubMed Abstract, 2000.

22. Leslie, M.B., Stein, J.A., and Rothermam-Borus, M.J. Sex-Specific Predictors of Suicidality among Runaway Youth. *Child and Adolescent Psychology,* 31(1): 27–40. PubMed Abstract, 2002.

23. American Lung Association Report Highlights Higher Smoking Rates in Lesbian, Gay, Bisexual and Transgender (LGBT) Community Statement by Jane Warner, President and CEO, American Lung Association in California Sacramento, CA. June 29, 2010.

24. Aaron, D.J., Markovic, N., Danielson, M.E., Honnold, J., Janosky, E., and Schmidt, N.J. Behavioral risk factors for disease and preventive health practices among lesbians. *American Journal of Public Health,* 91(6): 972–975. June, 2001.

25. Bernhard, L.A., and Applegate, J.M. Comparison of Stress and Stress Management Strategies between Lesbian and Heterosexual Women. *Health Care for Women International,* 20(4): 335–347. July–August, 1999.

26. Steenland, K, Henley, J., Calle, E., and Thun, M. Individual and Area-Level Socioeconomic Status Variables as Predictors of Mortality in a Cohort of 179,383 Persons. *American Journal of Epidemiology,* 159: 1047–1056. 2004.

27. Shahar, I.S., Vardi, H., Shahar, A., and Fraser, D. Diets and Eating Habits in High and Low Socioeconomic Groups. *Nutrition,* 21(5): 559–566. 2003.

28. "Disability and Health" National Health Interview Survey, Department of Health and Human Services, Centers for Disease Control and Prevention, 1992. See http://www.cdc.gov/ncbdd/dh/disability prevalence.htm

29. Hochbaum, G., Rosenstock, I., and Kegals, S. "Health Belief Model." *U.S. Public Health Service,* 1952.

30. Prochaska, J.O., and DiClemente, C. "Transtheoretical therapy toward a more integrative model of change," *Psychotherapy: Theory, Research and Practice,* 19(3): 276–287. 1982.

31. Rotter, J.B. "Generalized Expectancies for Internal versus External Control of Reinforcement," *Psychological Monographs,* 80. (Whole No. 609). 1966.

32. Eastin, M. Credibility Assessments of Online Health Information: The Effects of Source Expertise and Knowledge of Content. Retrieved February 22, 2007, from http://jcmc.indiana.edu/vol 6/issue 4/estin.html

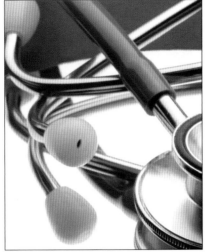

Image of Health

Health Care Choices

YOU AND YOUR WELL-BEING

- Treatment Options
- When to Seek Professional Medical Help
- Types of Treatment

CONVENTIONAL HEALTH PROFESSIONALS

- Choosing a Physician
- The Primary Care Physician
- Other Health Care Team Members
- Secondary Care Physicians
  - Endocrinologists
  - Oncologists
  - Radiologists
  - Ophthalmologists and Other Eye Specialists
- Dentists and Other Dental Professionals

CONVENTIONAL TREATMENTS

- Prescription Drugs
- Drug Labels
  - Patient Counseling Information
  - Brand Name versus Generic Prescription Drugs
  - Questions to Ask About Prescription Drugs

- Over-the-Counter Drugs
  - Safety Issues
- Malpractice
- Pros and Cons of Conventional Medicine

COMPLEMENTARY AND ALTERNATIVE MEDICAL PRACTICES

- Traditional Chinese Medicine
  - Homeopathy
  - Naturopathy
  - Acupuncture
- Mind-Body Practices
  - Hypnosis
  - Meditation
- Herbs and Botanical Remedies
  - Potential Risks with Herbs and Botanical Remedies
  - Potential Benefits from Herbs and Botanical Remedies
- Pros and Cons of Complementary and Alternative Practices
- Evaluating Herbs and Botanical Remedies
- Evaluating CAM Therapies

THE COST OF HEALTH CARE

- Health Insurance Plans
  - Fee for Service
  - Health Maintenance Organizations
  - Preferred Provider Organizations
  - Point of Service Plans
- Government Insurance Plans
  - Medicare
  - Medicaid
  - National Health Insurance

HEALTH ADVERTISING

- Evaluating Health Advertising
- Steps to Take

RESPONSIBILITY AND ACCOUNTABILITY

- Taking Responsibility for Your Health
- Focusing on Accountability

Student Learning Outcomes

LEARNING OUTCOME	APPLYING IT TO YOUR LIFE
State measures you can use to assess your health.	At your age, which are the best assessment methods, and what treatment options are available for you?
Identify criteria you would use to assess a prescription drug, an over-the-counter drug (OTC), or an herbal/botanical remedy.	How do the prescriptions, OTC drugs, and herbal or botanical remedies that are available to you meet the criteria you have established for yourself.
State options that you have for complementary and alternative medical practices.	What questions would you ask a practitioner of one of these methods to determine whether or not you would use it?
List the different kinds of insurance plans that are available today.	Identify what insurance plan is best suited for you.
Identify steps you would take in evaluating health advertising	Look at any product within your home that makes a health claim and identify any concerns you have with the claim.

Assess Your Knowledge

1. Health risk assessments are:
   a. Examinations conducted in a doctor's office.
   b. Examinations conducted in a hospital setting.
   c. Tests to determine your knowledge of health.
   d. Questions that might predict your risk of a particular health issue.

2. Western medicine is also called:
   a. Empirical medicine.
   b. Allopathic medicine.
   c. Pharmaceutical medicine.
   d. Drug-based medicine.

3. An optometrist is:
   a. A physician who specializes in the care of eyes.
   b. A surgeon who conducts eye surgery only.
   c. A trained and licensed person who can prescribe and fit glasses.
   d. A person trained to make eyeglasses.

4. Laws of Conscience refer to:
   a. A series of rights that a professional can follow relative to medical care.
   b. A series of rights that a consumer can follow relative to medical care.
   c. A series of laws concerning the risks and benefits of a prescribed medication.
   d. A series of alternative treatments that must be made available to a patient.

5. Traditional Chinese Medicine has less risk since it is based on natural products and herbs.
   a. True.
   b. False.

Answers:

1. d; 2. b; 3. c; 4. a; 5. b.

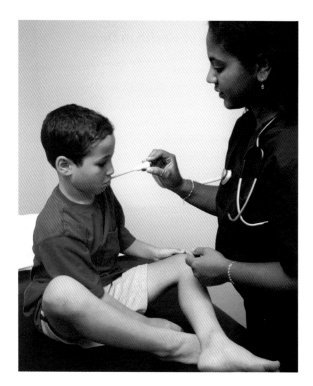

Today, when you awoke, it is likely that you noticed your health only if you felt unwell or tired. This is a typical way of managing personal health: it is taken for granted, until it is taken away. From Chapter 1, you learned that many health issues are caused by our own behavior, while some are inherited; others are the result of infection and others from as yet unknown causes. To know how to manage each requires that you become informed and then make appropriate choices.

This chapter will provide you with information to help you choose between self-care, conventional Western medicine, or **allopathic medicine** and **complimentary** and **alternative medicine**.

Key Terms

Allopathic medicine: Traditional Western medicine that treats disease using conventional evidence-based medical therapies.

Complementary medicine: A type of medical practice that may be performed along with traditional Western medicine practices, such as music therapy while undergoing surgery.

Alternative medicine: A non-western form of medical practice, such as the use of botanicals to treat disease.

In this chapter, you will learn to make informed choices about over-the-counter drugs, prescription drugs, and herbal and botanical remedies. You will also learn how to select between different insurance options and how to evaluate health advertising.

You and Your Well-Being

When you awoke this morning, you subconsciously conducted a self-assessment of your well-being. Were you ready to wake up? Was your sleep restorative or disruptive? Were you ready to face another day? As a result of this self-assessment, you evaluated your current state of health.

Treatment Options

If you determine that you need treatment for any health issue, there are a variety of options including self-care, professional conventional care, over the counter (OTCs) remedies, prescription drugs, and a variety of alternative and complementary medical practices. Depending on the symptoms experienced, most people start treatment with self-care. This may include improved stress management, sleeping habits, nutrition, and perhaps more exercise. Or it may involve the use of self-medication with OTCs or herbal and botanical remedies.

When to Seek Professional Medical Care

Generally, you should seek professional medical care if your symptoms are:

Unusual: Unusual symptoms include finding an unexplained lump or swelling, having blood in your urine or stool, unexplained and ongoing fatigue and weakness, unexplained weight gain or loss, particularly rapid onset, or changes in vision.

Severe: If pain is severe and not alleviated by use of an over-the-counter **analgesic**, or if you are injured, or have uncontrolled bleeding.

Persistent: If symptoms do not go away, medical care may be necessary. A fever that continues more than a few days, a cold that lasts longer than ten days, or a sore that does not heal are examples of persistent symptoms that might warrant medical attention.

Recurrent: If symptoms are recurring, medical care may be indicated. Frequent headaches, stomachaches, or recurring urinary tract infections all may indicate that you need to see a doctor.

> **Key Term**
>
> **Analgesic**: Agent used to suppress pain. This may be an OTC drug such as aspirin or a prescription drug such as Vicodin.

In 2009, eighty-three percent of adults had contact with a health care professional. Women are more likely to visit a physician than men, and as people age, they see a physician more frequently. Almost ninety-two percent of children saw a health care professional and more than 904 million physician office visits were made.[1] Table 2-1 shows the number of visits made by selected patient characteristics to patient care facilities in 2008.

Table 2-2 shows the type of practitioner people see most often. Most visits were made to general and family practitioners, followed by internal medicine practitioners and then pediatricians. Cost of care increases as you move from seeing a general practitioner to a specialized practitioner. The most frequent medical diagnosis for office visits included essential hypertension (high blood pressure,) acute upper respiratory infections, arthropathies (joint diseases,) spinal disorders, malignant neoplasms, and diabetes.

Types of Treatment

When you decide that you need to see a physician, what level of care is appropriate? As a general rule, symptoms that are appropriate for primary care, as opposed to urgent care or an emergency room visit, are symptoms that will not worsen over the next 24 hours. The least expensive form of conventional medical care is with a **primary care physician** (PCP). For college students, this may be available on campus.

> **Key Term**
>
> **Primary Care Physician (PCP)**: A physician who provides the first contact for a person with an undiagnosed health concern as well as continuing care for a variety of medical conditions. PCPs generally do not have a medical specialty or perform surgery.

Image of Health in Depth

Self-Care Assessments

There are several things that can be done routinely at home to help protect your health and to assess any risks that you might face. Breast self-exams and testicular self-exams, when done properly and regularly, will help with the early detection of breast or testicular cancer. Home pregnancy testing kits might determine if a missed period is due to pregnancy. Diabetics can test blood sugars, and those with hypertension can assess their blood pressure. At your last visit to the dentist, you may have learned that proper oral care could help reduce the risk of cardiovascular disease. Routine self-examinations and over-the-counter home tests available today may help to protect health and reduce health care costs.

You can also use Health Risk Assessment (HRA) forms that are available at many medical organization Internet sites such as American Heart Association, American Cancer Society, and American Diabetes Association. These assessments ask a series of questions to help predict your risk for a specific disease. An example of a general health risk assessment, is provided within this chapter.

Some cities offer urgent care facilities that provides walk-in care for symptoms that must be addressed immediately and cannot wait for an opening in a doctor's schedule. Urgent care is more expensive than care provided by a primary care physician, but cheaper than emergency room care. A situation that warrants urgent care is a condition that could be expected to seriously worsen if not treated within 24 hours. This includes flu, strep throat, or other infections; a high fever that has lasted for several days; foreign material in the eye; sprain or pain following a fall; or a cut, sore, or burn that does not heal.

Emergency room visits are expensive but necessary to treat the sudden onset of a severe medical condition with symptoms that may include severe pain. An emergency is a case that without immediate medical attention, you could reasonably expect serious jeopardy to health, serious impairment to bodily function, serious dysfunction of any body organ or part, or possibly death.

Challenge Question: When should you choose emergency care over urgent care, and urgent care over a visit to your physician?

Table 2-1. Selected Patient and Ambulatory Care Visits to Selected Providers, 2008

SELECTED PATIENT AND PROVIDER CHARACTERISTICS	TOTAL	PHYSICIAN OFFICES	HOSPITAL OUTPATIENT DEPTS.	HOSPITAL EMERGENCY DEPARTMENTS
All ages	1,189.6	995.0	109.9	123.8
<15 years of age	192.7	147.2	22.3	23.2
15–24 years of age	105.3	73.9	11.6	19.8
25–44 years of age	256.0	194.6	26.2	35.2
45–64 years of age	341.6	284.1	31.1	26.3
65–74 years of age	144.9	127.1	10.3	7.5
75 and older	149.2	129.0	8.4	11.8
Male	482.5	383.3	42.5	56.7
Female	707.1	527.7	67.4	67.0
White	970.9	802.4	79.2	89.4
Black	158.4	104.0	25.4	29.0
Asian	43.9	38.4	2.9	2.6
Native Hawaiian or Other Pacific Islander	5.6*	4.5*	0.3	0.8*
American Indian or Alaskan Native	4.4	3.0	0.4*	1.0*
More than one race reported	6.4	3.6	1.7*	1.1*

*Figures do not meet standards of reliability or precision

(Table 2-1. Selected patient and provider characteristics for ambulatory care visits to physician offices and hospital outpatient and emergency departments: United States, 2008. Extracted from: Hsiao, C.J., Cherry, D.K., Beatty, P.C., Rechtsteiner, E.A.. National Ambulatory Medical Care Survey: 2007 summary.National health statistics reports; no 27. Hyattsville, MD: National Center for Health Statistics. 2010.)

Table 2-2. Number of Visits to Different Medical Practitioners in 2007

PHYSICIAN CHARACTERISTICS	# OF VISITS IN THOUSANDS IN 2007	# OF VISITS PER 1,000 PERSONS PER YEAR
General and family practice	227,817	76.9
Internal medicine	143,722	48.5
Pediatrics	130,832	189.2
Obstetrics and gynecology	74,296	60.7
Ophthalmology	58,994	19.9
Orthopedic surgery	51,258	17.3
Dermatology	44,874	15.1
Psychiatry	32,660	11.0
Cardiovascular diseases	32,431	10.9
Otolaryngology	20,204	6.8
General surgery	19,636	6.6
Urology	18,914	6.4
Neurology	17,559	5.9
Oncology	15,581	5.3
All other specialties	10,554	35.6

(Extracted from: Hsiao, C.J., Cherry, DK, Beatty, P.C., Rechtsteiner, E.A.. National Ambulatory Medical Care Survey: 2007 summary. National health statistics reports; no 27. Hyattsville, MD: National Center for Health Statistics. 2010.)

GENERAL HEALTH RISK ASSESSMENT

1. How would you describe your health?
   a. Excellent
   b. Very good
   c. Average
   d. Less than average

2. Do you exercise at least three hours each week?
   a. Always
   b. Sometimes
   c. Rarely
   d. Never

3. How often do you use sunscreen?
   a. Every day
   b. Most days
   c. Rarely
   d. Never

4. How often do you wear a seat belt when driving or being driven?
   a. Always
   b. Sometimes
   c. Rarely
   d. Never

5. How often do you eat red meat, pork, cheese, fried foods, and fast foods?
   a. Daily
   b. Sometimes
   c. Rarely
   d. Never

6. How often do you eat at least four servings of vegetables in a day?

   a. Daily
   b. Sometimes
   c. Rarely
   d. Never

7. How often do you eat at least two servings of fruit in a day?
   a. Daily
   b. Sometimes
   c. Rarely
   d. Never

8. How often do you drink more than one alcoholic beverage per day if you are a woman, or more than two alcoholic beverages per day if you are a man?
   a. Never
   b. Rarely
   c. Sometimes
   d. Daily

9. In the past year, have you experienced one or more major stressful events, such as losing a job, relocating, or ending a relationship?
   a. No
   b. Yes, just one
   c. Yes, more than one

10. During the last year, has stress impacted your health, sleeping habits, or eating habits?
    a. Never
    b. Yes, it has impacted me on occasion
    c. Yes, it has impacted me frequently

11. Do you smoke cigarettes, cigars, or a pipe, or use chewing tobacco?
    a. Never
    b. Once in a great while
    c. Yes, most days
    d. Yes, every day

12. Do you abuse any prescription or OTC medications or use any illicit drugs?
    a. Never
    b. Never use illicit drugs, but do occasionally use pharmaceuticals above the recommended dose
    c. Yes, on some days
    d. Yes, every day

Scoring:
If you chose mostly As, you are doing a great job with your health. Keep it up!

If you chose mostly Bs, you are on the right track. Look at those areas where you can make improvements.

If you chose mostly Cs or Ds, you need to consider making some changes to avoid negative health consequences.

This Health Risk Assessment is just a guide. It is not intended to diagnose or treat any condition. Please see a licensed health care professional for help with any conditions that concern you.

Conventional Health Professionals

In 2008, healthcare provided 14.3 million jobs for wage and salary workers.[2] From the local pharmacist to a specialized surgeon, choices in health care professionals are abundant. Conventional Western medicine is based on scientific belief as opposed to faith, or common sense. The use of **pharmaceuticals** and advances in medical technology has helped to extend life. Western medicine, and those who practice it, believes a medical diagnosis is based on:

Empirical Evidence: evidence that is objective, can be observed, repeated under controlled conditions and observed by others.

Rational Evidence: logical rules are followed based on known facts.

Testable Evidence: evidence that can be verified with repeat testing and lead to predictions if the same conditions occur again.

Parsimonious Evidence: the evidence explains events with the fewest number of assumptions.

General Evidence: the evidence has reaching explanatory power.

Rigorously Evaluated Evidence: the evidence is constantly being re-evaluated and produces the same results.

Tentative Evidence: scientists are willing to consider that their explanations may be faulty and are open to alternative explanations.

> **Key Term**
>
> **Pharmaceuticals**: Prescription drugs and over-the-counter drugs

Challenge Question: What is empirical evidence?

Choosing a Physician

Medical treatment for people with health insurance typically begins with a PCP who can make the decision to refer a patient to a specialist if necessary. Uninsured individuals will find it less costly to visit a PCP or a clinic that specializes in care for the under- or uninsured.

The Primary Care Physician

Primary care physicians do not specialize in a particular area of medicine, and may include family practitioners, internal medicine practitioners, and pediatricians. Some insurance companies now permit women to see an obstetric-gynecologist as a PCP for routine pelvic exams. The PCP conducts annual examinations and routine screenings, treats minor injuries and illnesses, and provides necessary follow-up care. Primary care is usually conducted in the doctor's office. Within the practice, the physician may have nurses and medical assistants working, and some busy practices may also employ **nurse practitioners** or **physician's assistants (PAs)**. This relatively new level of care may soon surpass primary care physicians as the first avenue of care, and some PAs are now training as specialists in certain areas.[3]

> **Key Term**
>
> **Nurse practitioner/physician's assistant (PA)**: A registered nurse who has received special training and can perform many of the duties of a physician.

Image of Health in Depth

Choosing a Primary Care Physician

Before the abundance of health insurance plans and choices that exist today, patients chose primary care physicians most often based on referrals and proximity to their homes. Today, insurance plans may limit choice to only those providers within the plan, and services outside the plan may incur higher cost for the patient. But even within the plan, how do you best select your primary care physician? With or without insurance, there are some steps that will help you select your primary care physician. Three types of medical practice are considered primary care:

1. **Family practice**. A family practitioner is a physician who specializes in general family care.

2. **Internal medicine**. An internist is a physician who diagnoses and medically treats diseases in adults without performing surgery. Internists may have a subspecialty that focuses on a specific part of the body, such as the heart or lungs; a specific disease, like diabetes or arthritis; or a particular age group, such as adolescents or the elderly.

3. **Pediatrics**. Pediatricians care for and treat children from birth through teens. They commonly have subspecialties, such as pediatric cardiology, gastroenterology, prenatal medicine, or surgery.

Choosing a physician becomes easier if you follow some simple steps:

- If you have recently moved, ask your current doctor for a referral.

- Determine your preferences for a doctor such as gender, age, hospital associations and location and seek out a practitioner that meets them. Reputable hospitals usually offer a referral service but it cannot vouch for the physician's quality of care.

- Local medical societies often offer directories of membership, but like hospitals, they cannot vouch for quality. However, if you have a chronic disease like diabetes or arthritis, you may find that there are member chapters that you can visit. At meetings you can discuss the experiences that other patients have had with different physicians.

- If you belong to a managed care plan, check the background training and services of doctors associated with your plan.

Other Health Care Team Members

Health care team members include allied health care providers such as nurses, nursing aids, physical therapists, social workers, registered dieticians, and midwives. Your PCP may determine that you need to see a specialist for a particular ailment or as a regular part of treatment. This secondary care involves specialized treatment not provided by a primary care physician and is more expensive than primary care. A referral may be based either on symptoms or an existing condition.

> **Key Term**
>
> **Secondary care**: Care provided to a patient who has been referred to the specialist by a primary care physician.

Secondary Care Physicians

Under an insurance plan, this higher-level care usually requires a referral. Secondary care physicians do not usually have first contact with a patient, and their practices are limited to their specialties.

Endocrinologists

Endocrinology is the science of glandular disorders. For most endocrinologists, the larger part of their practice will be **diabetes** care, but these specialists also work with patients who have thyroid diseases, metabolic and hormonal disorders, and cancers of the endocrine glands.

Oncologists

Oncology is the study of cancer: how it begins, how it spreads, and how it can be treated. Oncologists treat patients with cancer and may refer patients for surgery and radiation treatments.

Radiologists

Radiologists are physicians with advanced training in X-rays and other imaging techniques. This specialized training allows them to diagnose and treat diseases identified by radiologic techniques.

Ophthalmologists and Other Eye Specialists

Ophthalmology is the branch of medicine that deals with diseases and surgery of the visual pathways, including the eye and brain. Since ophthalmologists perform surgery, they are classified as surgeons. Although **optometrists** are sometimes confused with ophthalmologists, optometrists are not physicians, but trained and licensed individuals who evaluate visual problems, and write prescriptions for eyeglasses. **Opticians** are technicians under optometry, and receive on the job training or may undergo an apprenticeship of up to two years. Opticians examine written prescriptions to determine the specifications of lenses. They recommend eyeglass frames, lenses, and lens coatings after considering the prescription and the patient's occupation, habits, and facial features.

Key Terms

Endocrinology: The branch of medicine dealing with the endocrine glands and their secretions.

Diabetes: A metabolic disorder in which the body ceases to either use or make insulin efficiently.

Oncology: The branch of medicine dealing with tumors, including cancerous tumors.

Radiologists: Physicians who are specially trained to interpret medical X-rays.

Ophthalmologists: Licensed physicians specialized in the medical care and surgery of the eyes.

Optometrist: A trained and licensed individual who can prescribe and fit eyeglasses.

Optician: A technician who makes and fits eyeglasses based on prescriptions.

Table 2-3 lists other secondary care specialists.

Table 2-3. Other Medical Specialties

ALLERGISTS	Physicians licensed to diagnose and treat allergies.
ANESTHESIOLOGISTS	Physicians specifically trained to administer sedating drugs or drugs that induce unconsciousness prior to surgery.
CARDIOLOGISTS	Physicians who diagnose and treat diseases of the heart and blood vessels.
DERMATOLOGISTS	Physicians who diagnose and treat diseases of the skin.
GASTROENTEROLOGISTS	Physicians who diagnose and treat disorders of the stomach and intestinal tract.
HEMATOLOGISTS	Physicians who diagnose and treat blood related diseases and disorders.
OBSTETRICIAN-GYNECOLOGISTS	Physicians who are specialized in the care, diagnosis, and treatment of the female reproductive tract, including pregnancy management.
ORTHOPEDISTS	Physicians who specialize in the care of bones and joints.
NEPHROLOGISTS	Physicians who specialize in the care of the kidneys.
RHEUMATOLOGISTS	Physicians who specialize in the care of joints and soft tissues.
PEDIATRICIANS	Physicians specialized in the care, diagnosis, and treatment of childhood diseases (usually up to age 18).
PULMONARY SPECIALISTS	Physicians who diagnose and treat respiratory system disorders.
RHEUMATOLOGISTS	Physicians who specialize in the treatment of rheumatism.

Dentists and Other Dental Professionals

Dentists specialize in the care of teeth, and can write prescriptions, and perform oral surgery and screenings for oral cancer. Even though 60 percent of the population visits a dentist annually, only about 15 percent of patients receive an oral cancer screening.[4] There are several dental specialties, such as orthodontists, who specialize in straightening teeth; endodontic dentists, who specialize in diseases of the root or tissue of the tooth; and periodontists, who specialize in gum disease. Allied dental health workers include hygienists who are trained to clean teeth, and may take X-rays, make molds for crowns, and may remove sutures.

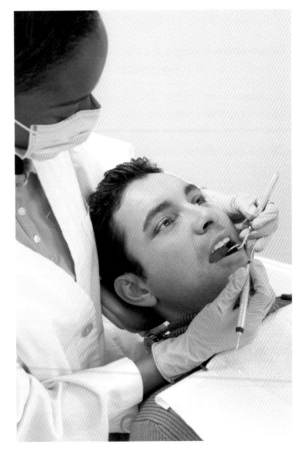

Challenge Questions: Differentiate between an ophthalmologist, an optometrist, and an optician.

Conventional Treatments

Western medical practitioners rely on the scientific method in their practice and treatments. When using drugs and therapies, they are more likely to use those that have been proven effective and safe by the Center for Drug Evaluation and Research (CDER), a subsection of the Food and Drug Administration (FDA).

Prescription Drugs

Prescription drugs are medications monitored by the FDA and which have undergone testing to prove that they will produce a desired and expected result. Like all other drugs, prescription drugs are not without risk, and some can be abused while others may be addicting. About 1.7 billion prescriptions are written annually in medical offices, costing about $203.6 billion each year.[5]

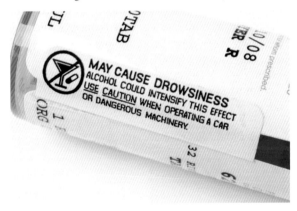

Image of Health in Depth

The Cost of American Pharmaceuticals

For many Americans, the cost of prescription drugs is so high that they either cannot afford it, or they do not take drugs as prescribed—perhaps so the medication will last longer. What causes drugs to be so expensive? Pharmaceutical companies explain that the cost is to cover research and development of new drugs. In 2002, the estimated cost to bring a new drug to market was $802 million.[6] With a potential market share of over two billion dollars, spending eight hundred million does not seem so much. But other factors are involved.

Drug companies spend large sums of money on the concept and development of a new drug, then apply for FDA approval to test the drug. Clinical trials are the next stage of the process. These trials usually occur in three phases:

First phase: Healthy individuals receive the drug to determine dosage levels, absorption and excretion rates and to evaluate side effects. Quite often, these first phase trials occur outside of the USA to save money and to avoid the time delay of getting clinical trial approval.

Second phase: Patients with the targeted disease or condition receive the treatment. Hundreds of patients may be involved at this stage of testing when researchers evaluate the safety and **efficacy** of the drug. Patients and researchers are all paid.

Third phase: Trials involve multi-center trials and the number of patients can range into thousands. At this stage of testing, researchers are establishing firm evidence on the drug's safety and efficacy. Data are collected and analyzed and the results are sent to the FDA for approval and permission to market the drug. The pharmaceutical company pays all participants.

On average, it takes about six years from the start of clinical trials to submission for market release with the FDA. If the drug is not approved, the costs incurred up to that point are lost. If approved, the company has the remaining portion of twenty years to exclusively market the drug. After twenty years, the patent expires and the formula becomes **generic**. Sometimes pharmaceutical companies will *pay* manufacturers of generic drugs to not make a generic version of their drug after its patent has expired or they may marginally change the drug to prevent or inhibit its entry into the generic market.

Although major pharmaceutical companies conduct research and may spend up to 60 percent of their budget researching drugs, the bulk of biotechnology research is done at government institutions and financed by government sponsored research grants.[7]

In January 2011, the Obama administration announced plans to develop the National Center for Advancing Translational Sciences. This center will seek ways to leverage science to bring new ideas and materials to the attention of the pharmaceutical industry by demonstrating their values.[8]

Key Terms

Efficacy: The therapeutic effect of a given intervention.

Generic: A non-branded product.

Challenge Question: At what point in time does a brand name drug become generic?

Critical Thinking Question: The U.S. is the only country that does not have price controls on prescription drugs. In what ways might we benefit and/or suffer if we had government-controlled pricing on all prescription drugs?

The Institutes of Medicine states that according to one estimate, 80 percent of all U.S. adults use a prescription drug, an OTC drug or a dietary supplement every week, and nearly one third of adults will take five or more medications weekly. These drugs can extend lives, manage disease, treat symptoms and alleviate depression. Commonly prescribed drugs include analgesics, **non-steroidal anti-inflammatory agents** (NSAIDs), and **antiemetic** and **antipyretic** agents. NSAIDs are the most prescribed drugs in the USA, although there are also over-the-counter NSAIDs available. These drugs are used to treat arthritis, sports injuries, and post-surgery swelling and pain. In 2005, the FDA required that all NSAIDs, both prescription and non-prescription, include information showing that the drugs might increase cardiovascular disease and gastrointestinal bleeding.[9]

Although events such as this are unusual, they do occur. In an attempt to minimize risk issues, the FDA introduced new drug labels and inserts for drugs.

Key Terms

Anti-inflammatory drugs: Drugs that reduce inflammation.

Antiemetic drugs: Drugs that prevent nausea and vomiting.

Anti-pyretic drugs: Drugs that prevent or reduce fever by lowering body temperature.

Drug Labels

In 2006, the FDA unveiled a major revision to the format for prescription drug information, commonly called the package insert. This insert provides healthcare professionals clear and concise prescribing information to help manage the risks of medication use and reduce medical errors. Research shows that prioritizing the warning information on prescriptions could help reduce the more than 300,000 adverse medication-related emergencies that occur in hospitals each year.[10]

Patient Counseling Information

The drug insert is designed to help doctors advise patients about important uses and limitations of the medication. It also serves as a guide for discussions about the potential risks involved in a specific treatment and steps for managing those risks.

Today, every prescription medication is accompanied by dosage instructions, including what to do if you miss a dose, and potential side effects. In addition, dispensing pharmacists are required to offer counseling on drug prescriptions.

The elderly make up about 12 percent of the U.S. population, yet they use up to 33 percent of all prescription drugs.[11] Drug inserts, together with counseling, may help the elderly reduce risks from prescription drug use. The new label laws may also help protect those consumers who purchase drugs through online pharmaceutical companies.

Brand Name versus Generic Prescription Drugs

All generic drugs must be reviewed and approved by the FDA. These drugs are copies of brand name drugs and must be used with the same dosage and type of administration. Generic drugs always contain the same active ingredient and in some instances are made by the same manufacturer as the brand name drugs. They are packaged differently and they may have a different shape or form (e.g., a tablet versus a capsule), since trade laws do not allow generic drugs to look like their brand name counterparts. The differences between brand name and generic drugs may be in color, flavor, or the inactive and inert ingredients.

Generic drugs are usually much less expensive, since the brand name drugs include the cost of research, advertising and promotion, which inflate the price. Not all drugs have a generic equivalent.

Questions to Ask About Prescription Drugs

The FDA revised a list of questions for consumers to ask about prescription drugs in July 2001.[12] Asking these questions may help improve safety in using the drug and help improve the efficacy of the drug.

Before taking a prescription drug, you should know:

- What is the medicine's name, and what is it supposed to do?

- How and when is it taken, and for how long?

- While taking this medicine, should you avoid:

  - Certain foods or dietary supplements?

  - Caffeine, alcohol, or other beverages?

- Other medicines, either prescription or OTC?

- Certain activities, such as driving or smoking?

- Will this new medicine work safely with prescription and OTC medicines you may already be taking?

- Are there side effects, and what should you do if they occur?

- Will the medicine affect sleep or activity level?

- What should you do if you miss a dose?

More information for making your drugs work safely and effectively can be found at: **http://www.fda.gov/fdac/reprints/medtips.html.**

Over-the-Counter Drugs

As with prescription drugs, the CDER oversees all OTC drugs ensuring they are properly labeled and that their benefits outweigh their risks.

Safety Issues

Over-the-counter drugs generally have these characteristics:

- Their benefits outweigh their risks.

- The potential for misuse and abuse is low.

- Consumers can use them for self-diagnosed conditions.

- They can be adequately labeled.

- Health practitioners are not needed for the safe and effective use of the product.

When consumers use an OTC drug, they are self-diagnosing, self-prescribing and self-administering a drug. If an error is made at any one of these steps, then potential problems can result. Consumers may make an error in diagnosis, may take the wrong medication, and may take a medication that treats more symptoms than they are experiencing, or may take too much or too little of the drug to generate **therapeutic value**. Some OTC medications can lead to overuse as in the case of nasal sprays. Overuse of nasal sprays can increase the swelling in the nasal linings increasing congestion which leads to more frequent use and potentially higher dosing that can last for months or even years.

Key Term

Therapeutic value: The value of a procedure or product relative to its ability to treat or cure a disease or condition.

Occasionally some prescription drugs will be released into the OTC marketplace if their strength is reduced by reformulation, or if the prescribing instructions reduce the dosage. More than fifty-six such prescription drugs are now available OTC and as many twenty-five or more are added each year.

All OTC products must have a label that reflects Food and Drug Administration (FDA) requirements. The label must include the type and quantity of active ingredients, alcohol content, side effects, warnings against inappropriate use and instructions for proper use. Brand name OTC drugs are now frequently available as generic drugs. Your local pharmacist may carry both a brand name aspirin and exactly the same product carrying the store's logo, which is the generic version. As with prescription generic drugs, OTC generics do not differ from their brand name counterparts relative to active ingredients and dosing. "Image of Health In Depth Generic vs. Brand Name OTC Drugs" details this.

Image of Health in Depth

Generic versus Brand Name OTC Drugs

Over-the-counter brand name drugs and their generic counterparts are chemically the same, although they may have different branding names, colors, shapes and fillers. Generic drugs must have **bioequivalence** with brand name drugs relative to active ingredient, dosage amount, and the way it is taken. Bioequivalence is the condition in which different formulations of the same drug or chemical are equally absorbed. Generic drugs cannot be more than 20 percent different from the **bioavailability** of the brand name drug. Bioavailability is the amount of time the drug takes to be used by the body. Generic drugs have the same amount of active ingredient, but the amount of time it takes your body to absorb the drug may be slightly different.

Key Terms

Bioequivalence: The condition in which different formulations of the same drug or chemical are equally absorbed by the body.

Bioavailability: The extent to which a medication or nutrient can be used by the body.

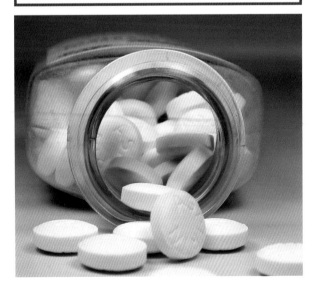

Laws of Conscience

Although physicians and pharmacists are professionally obligated to provide all patients with non-discriminating access to medical services and pharmaceuticals, not all of them may follow this obligation. Some physicians may refuse to perform abortions, and some pharmacists may refuse to provide emergency contraception on the grounds that it violates their conscience. Today, many states have some aspect of laws of conscience, and under such laws professionals can:

- Refuse patients' rights to stop the use of painful or futile treatments.

- Refuse to vaccinate a child for chicken pox.

- Refuse to provide, fill, or transfer any prescription for birth control pills, or emergency contraception (even in the case of a rape victim).

- Refuse to discuss end of life options or follow health directives with terminally ill patients.

- Refuse to advise infertile couples of new reproductive technologies.

It is important to know if your views differ from those of your physician or pharmacist so you can access care that supports your own values and beliefs.

Informed Consent

An informed consent is a written communication between a physician and a patient that results in the patient authorizing or agreeing to specific medical treatments.

The physician is required to disclose and discuss with the patient:

- The patient's diagnosis, if known.

- The nature and purpose of a proposed treatment or procedure.

- The risks and benefits of a proposed treatment or procedure.

- Alternative treatments (regardless of their cost or the extent to which the treatment options are covered by health insurance).

- The risks and benefits of the alternative treatment or procedure.

- The risks and benefits of not receiving or undergoing a treatment or procedure.

As a result, the patient is provided an opportunity to ask questions, elicit a better understanding of the treatment or procedure such that he or she can make an informed decision to either accept or refuse the course of treatment.

Malpractice

Malpractice implies that a medical professional has failed to follow generally accepted professional standards, and that the breach of duty has resulted in injury. In medical cases this means that a health care provider has caused a patient injury. If proven in a court of law, the patient may be entitled to damages and the health care provider may lose the right to practice.

All physicians, hospitals, and clinics carry medical malpractice insurance. This insurance is extremely expensive, and its cost is passed on to the consumer. Each year, 1 in 7 physicians are sued and medical liability suits are filed against 50 percent of neurosurgeons.[13, 14]

Key Term

Malpractice: Failure of a medical professional to render proper services through reprehensible ignorance or negligence or through criminal intent, especially when injury or loss follows.

Pros and Cons of Conventional Medicine

Conventional medicine continues to improve, offering more cures, better pain and disease management and earlier diagnosis. Ongoing research by medical practitioners provides patients with potentially more knowledge, better choice availability and faster resolutions.

Conventional medicine can be very expensive, and there are no guarantees that treatment will be successful. Modern medicine is highly technical, and for the over 50 million Americans who do not have health insurance, it may be unavailable.[15] Even for those with health insurance, co-payments continue to increase, and some of the medicines and treatments prescribed for them may not be covered by their insurance plans. In March 2010, Congress passed the Affordable Health Care Act. The act proposed better health security by holding health insurance companies accountable, lowering health care costs, guaranteeing more choices, expanding health care to most uninsured individuals.

Complementary and Alternative Medicine

Complementary and alternative medicine (CAM) includes those practices not considered part of conventional Western medicine. Complementary medicine is sometimes practiced along with Western medicine, whereas alternative medicine is usually practiced independently of western therapies. CAM therapies are continually evolving, and as those therapies are proven to be effective and considered safe, they may become part of Western medical practice.

The FDA does not control alternative medicines and ingredients are not verified, nor are CAM procedures always standard among practitioners. Despite this, the National Institutes of Health now has a section devoted to CAM studies and some results are encouraging. Table 2-4 lists and briefly describes several of the alternative medicine practices.

Traditional Chinese Medicine

Traditional Chinese medicine (TCM) is a range of medical practices used in China that developed over several thousand years, including herbal medicine, acupuncture, and massage. TCM does not usually operate within a structured paradigm, but some practitioners make efforts to bring practices into a more standard medical framework.

Practitioners believe that the human body operates like a small universe, with all parts interconnected. If one element is not working properly, other elements will be affected. In this holistic approach to medicine the practitioner will treat an "imbalance" in the system rather than an infectious agent. Because there is no standard for treating an imbalance, patients presenting with the same symptoms might receive different therapies. The goal of TCM is to restore the balance of **qi**, which is believed to be the basis of health and vitality in Eastern medicine.

Table 2-4. Alternative Medical Practices

PRACTICE	EXPECTED EFFECTS
Dietary regimens, including fasting, liquid diets, macrobiotics diets, and raw produce diets.	Purported to treat or cure cancers and other diseases, although no proof exists.
Herbal remedies	Herbal remedies are not required to submit evidence of safety or proof that they work in any way. Expected effects that are promoted range from memory improvement to cold prevention. Care should be taken when using these products because they can produce serious adverse effects.
Osteopathic medicine touch therapy	Western trained physicians may also practice osteopathic manipulation therapy. Osteopathic medical students spend approximately 200 hours of training in the art of osteopathic manipulative medicine. This system of hands-on techniques helps alleviate pain, restore motion, support the body's natural functions, and influence the body's structure to help it function more efficiently.
	Touch therapy practitioners claim it works to reduce pain and enhance the body's restorative processes. The therapist's hands never touch the patient, but rather direct a process of energy exchange, where the practitioner gently manipulates the body's energy field flow. In 1998, Journal of the American Medical Association published research showing practitioners were unable to substantiate touch therapy's most fundamental claim and that this represents unrefuted evidence that touch therapy claims are groundless and further professional use is unjustified.[16]
Chiropractic medicine	Chiropractic therapy focuses on diagnosing, treating, and preventing medical disorders of the musculoskeletal system. The chiropractic's premise is that spinal joint misalignment can interfere with the nervous system and result in diminished health and some insurance companies now cover chiropractic care. There is evidence that spinal manipulation is effective for the treatment of acute low back pain, tension headaches, and some musculoskeletal issues, but not all studies support this conclusion. There are no objective controlled trials with definitive conclusions for or against chiropractic claims concerning other health benefits.[17]
Massage therapy and bodywork	Massage and bodywork provides stress and anxiety relief. Massage is one of the oldest healing arts dating back 3,000 years. Any activity that involves applying pressure or vibration to soft body tissues, including muscles, tendons, ligaments, joints and connective tissue, may be called bodywork.
Energy Therapies	Practitioners of energy therapies believe that illness is caused by a disruption or disturbance of energy in the biofield. Asian practitioners have long postulated that the flow and balance of life energies is necessary for maintaining health.
Qigong	Qigong is the practice of different breathing patterns with various physical postures and motions of the body. Practitioners use it as a health maintenance tool and also as a therapeutic tool.
Reiqi	Reiqi is a form of spiritual or faith based healing. Practitioners' use a "laying on of the hands" together with air movement that they claim will channel qi energy from disembodied spirits.

The safety of TCM depends on the therapy being used. Occasionally, herbal products may cause an allergic reaction, poisoning, or even death. Some Chinese remedies include arsenic, based on the presumption that to treat a poison, one must use a poison. Other safety issues include the lack of regulation and standards for ingredients, and potential lax standards of cleanliness when herbs are mixed. As a responsible consumer, you must evaluate whether any herbal or botanical remedy you buy contains the ingredients it purports to contain, and whether those ingredients are in a form that can be absorbed and used by your body. The FDA regulates ingredients, dosage, and efficacy with over-the-counter and prescription drugs, but there is no oversight on any herbal or botanical remedy.

Key Term

Qi: A term used in Chinese culture that is said to be part of every living thing, seen as a life force or spiritual energy.

Acupuncture

Acupuncture aims to restore and maintain health through the stimulation of specific points in the body with the use of needles. According to TCM, the body is a delicate balance of two opposing forces, yin and yang. Yin represents the cold, slow, or passive principle while yang represents the hot, excited, or active principle. These two forces must work in concert with one another to achieve a balanced state. Imbalance results in blocking the flow of vital energy (qi) along pathways known as meridians. The FDA regulates acupuncture needles for one-time use only by licensed practitioners, and the needles must be sterile and non-toxic. Some evidence shows that acupuncture does provide pain relief and can improve function.[18,19,20]

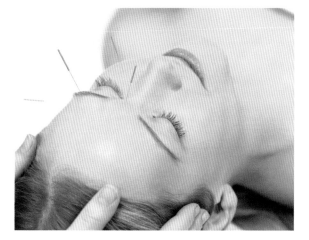

Homeopathy

The principles of homoeopathy are based on the doctrine of vitalism, where it is believed that life forces cannot be explained by physical or chemical forces but rather are self-determined. Homeopathy also includes the concept that similars cure similars, meaning that if a known substance or event has caused you to become ill, then the same substance or event can cause you to become well. Homeopathic practitioners believe human life is based on an energetic vital force, which harmonizes all natural processes and manifests as vitality. When this vital force is mistuned by energy depleting factors symptoms appear that are associated with disease.

Homeopathic remedies are tested on healthy volunteers in clinical trials called provings. During a proving, healthy, human volunteers take a highly diluted remedy until they experience symptoms that are similar to those exhibited by a patient.[21] Practitioners believe this provides an exact illustration of the symptoms that will cure an ill patient. When a homoeopath studies an ill patient, he is searching for a remedy that produced similar symptoms during a proving, and has been clinically confirmed, based on homeopathic methods, to remove those symptoms. In this way, the practitioner matches the symptoms of the patient with the symptoms of the similar remedy. So far, collective research has failed to support these claims.[22]

Key Term

Homeopathy: The method of treating disease by drugs, given in minute doses that would produce, in a healthy person, symptoms similar to those of the disease

---

Naturopathy

Naturopathy (also called naturopathic medicine) is a practice intended to improve health and treat disease by assisting the body's innate ability to recover from illness and injury. A number of different practices may be used, including acupuncture, manual therapy, dietary therapy, and herbalism. Although this school of medical philosophy began in the U.S., it is now practiced around the world. Naturopathic practitioners do not use invasive surgery or synthetic drugs, instead using herbs and foods. Occasionally, these practitioners will refer their patients out to other medical specialties.

> **Key Term**
>
> **Naturopathy**: A system or method of treating disease that employs no surgery or synthetic drugs, but uses diets, herbs, vitamins, and massage to assist the natural healing processes.

Critical Thinking Question: Describe the differences between homeopathy and naturopathy.

Mind-Body Practices

Mind-body practices are those practices that integrate the mind with the body. Substantial evidence shows that mind-body practices enhance quality of life, reduce psychological stress, and improve mental health outcomes.[23]

Hypnosis

Hypnosis, or hypnotherapy, is an altered state of consciousness typically achieved with the assistance of a hypnotherapist. Although its medical uses are not clearly understood, hypnosis appears to help with conditions ranging from pain to asthma.

Under hypnosis, patients' attention is more focused; they are more responsive to suggestions, more open and less critical or disbelieving. The hypnotherapist works to help patients gain control over behavior, emotions, and physical well-being.

The National Institutes of Health has approved hypnotherapy for the treatment of chronic pain, and some preliminary studies suggest it may be used to:

- Inhibit smoking, bed-wetting, and overeating.

- Reduce fear, stress, and anxiety.

- Treat and ease the symptoms of asthma.

- Lower blood pressure.

- Control pain during dental and surgical procedures.

- Control pain during childbirth and hasten delivery.

- Reduce the intensity of headaches and migraines.

- Control nausea and vomiting associated with chemotherapy.

Most states do not regulate hypnotherapists, and not all patients achieve the same benefits with its use. Patients should use the same care in their selection process as they would for any other practitioner.

Meditation

Meditation is thought practice that results in relaxation and stress reduction. Practitioners believe that with practice peace, serenity, calming, and eventually the ability to open oneself to new insights is achieved. During meditation, people clear their minds of all thoughts such that they achieve a sense of separation. During this time, images may occur that cause happiness, energy, sleepiness, and even tears.

Key Terms

Hypnosis: An altered state of consciousness typically achieved with the assistance of a hypnotherapist.

Meditation: Thought practice that results in relaxation and stress reduction.

Herbal and Botanical Remedies

Herbs and botanicals are parts of plants thought to have medicinal or therapeutic properties. Herbs are a subset of botanicals. Although consumers frequently consider something that is "natural" to be safer than something that has been "chemically" created, herbal and botanical remedies, as with prescription and OTC drugs, cannot be presumed to be without risk. Herbal and botanical remedies are not regulated by any agency. There is no authority that oversees whether the active ingredients have bioavailability, and the ingredients are not evaluated to guarantee quality or therapeutic value. The only requirement for companies manufacturing these products is that labels carry a statement showing the FDA has not evaluated claims.

Potential Risks with Herbs and Botanicals

In North America, there have been documented cases of clinical poisoning from herbal remedies that involved mercury or lead. Additionally, it is possible to find unlabelled pharmaceuticals co-mingling with herbal remedies. The FDA issued warnings in 2003 and 2004 against some herbal sexual enhancement products that contained unreported but significant levels of prescription drugs such as Cialis and Viagra. Individuals with cardiovascular disease could experience serious side effects from an herb that included these pharmaceuticals.

Potential Benefits from Herbs and Botanicals

There are herbal remedies that may relieve some symptoms and may have minimum risk associated with them. In some European countries, St. John's Wart may be prescribed for simple depression and small studies have provided evidence for its effectiveness. However, two large studies showed that the herb was no more effective than a placebo.[24] Echinacea is the best-selling herb in the U.S. and it is believed to stimulate the immune system, although no reliable studies have proven this. Gingko biloba is another popular herb, but lacks scientific evidence to support its use for memory enhancement.[25]

Consumers should use the same caution with herbal remedies and supplements as they would with any other product. Responsible individuals will talk with their doctors about the pros and cons of any supplement they might choose to take. Herbal remedies are not regulated and so testing them for efficacy is difficult. When a product is not regulated, no authority oversees its manufacture to ensure it contains what it claims to contain and in the quantities listed. As a result, a bottle of ginseng, listing tablets that contain 1,000 milligrams, may or may not contain that amount. Without regulation, the product may not even be in a form that can be absorbed by the human body. Manufacturers cannot claim that their products produce certain results only that they "may" produce results. Labels must also indicate that claims have not been tested. Herbal manufacturers have resisted oversight by the FDA possibly because methods used to test their products would be inappropriate or perhaps because it would ultimately increase their costs. Until oversight with appropriate methods is developed, herbal products should be used with caution.

Challenge Question: What are some of the positives and negatives for herbal remedies?

Pros and Cons of Alternative and Complementary Therapies

Since there are few set standards for CAM procedures, determining appropriate tests is challenging. The efficacy of CAM therapies can be difficult to prove using the scientific method since the scientific method is based on being able to observe, measure and empirically test new information or knowledge. When using the scientific method to test a procedure, any practitioner must be able to replicate that exact procedure and produce the same result. For instance, if one nurse takes a patient's blood pressure, a test performed on the same patient moments later by a second nurse should show the same blood pressure readings. Since the existence of ying, yang, and qi cannot be observed or measured, it is difficult to quantify results. Practitioners base efficacy of their therapies on the perceived outcome experienced by the patient that may be a result of the therapy, or it may be a placebo effect, or it may have occurred without intervention.

Conventional medicine practitioners are highly trained and licensed, whereas licensing and training is not required in all states for CAM practitioners.

However, some CAM therapies have been shown to achieve specific, positive results. Massage therapy may not improve blood flow, but it can reduce stress, and chiropractic medicine has been shown to reduce back pain in patients. Chiropractors are not trained radiographers, so their use of X-rays may not be a wise investment for the consumer. Acupuncture has been shown to reduce post-surgery pain and with the additional requirement of single-use, sterile, non-toxic needles, risks with acupuncture have been reduced. Patients should still verify that the acupuncturist has completed training and is licensed to practice.

If you choose to use any CAM therapy, ensure that the therapist has undergone training and obtained a license if this is available in your state. Your physician may be able to offer you guidance in selecting a CAM therapist. When you visit the practitioner, ask pertinent questions such as:

1. What will my treatment entail?

2. How many treatments are necessary?

3. What can I expect as a result of treatment?

4. What risks are involved in this treatment?

5. How can I be sure that any herbal treatments contain what they purport to contain in the quantity listed, and in a form that can be digested by my body?

6. Is there any known risk for these herbal products?

7. Are there any products that I should not use when taking these herbal products?

8. Is there any evidence that these treatments and the herbal products actually work?

9. What happens if I experience no benefit from this therapy?

Table 2-5 shows the percentage of people using different forms of complimentary and alternative therapies in the United States.

Table 2-5. Uses of Complementary and Alternative Therapies in the United States

THERAPY	PERCENT WHO EVER USED THERAPY
Prayer	55.3
Natural products (non-vitamin, non-mineral)	25.0
Chiropractic care	19.9
Deep breathing exercises	14.6
Meditation	10.2
Massage	9.3
Yoga	7.5
Diet-based therapies	6.8
Progressive relaxation	4.2
Acupuncture	4.0
Megavitamin therapy	3.9
Homeopathic treatment	3.6
Guided imagery	3.0
T'ai chi	2.5
Hypnosis	1.8
Energy healing therapy/Reiki	1.1
Biofeedback	1.0
Any therapy	74.6

(Source: Barnes, P.M., et al. 2004. Complementary and alternative medicine use among adults: United States, 2002. *Seminars In Integrative Medicine*, 2(2): 54–71. June, 2004.)

Integrative Medicine

With the increasing popularity of CAM therapies, some Western practitioners are now integrating CAM with conventional medicine. The best example of this is Andrew Weil, M.D., who followed his Harvard training as a physician with research into herbs and other CAM therapies. He has authored many books and has an extensive integrated medical practice.

The Cost of Health Care

The U.S. is the only Western, industrialized country that does not provide health insurance for all citizens though it is the leading country for health research and pharmaceutical production. Insurance, when used and managed properly can be cost saving to both the insurance provider and the insured. The insurance carrier may provide preventative medical services such as vaccinations, annual exams, and recommended screenings, while the insured individual reduces cost by practicing health-enhancing behaviors and using a PCP as a first choice as opposed to urgent care or the emergency room. With any insurance, costs are shared among all members of the plan and those in need utilize services when necessary. In effect, the healthy pay for the sick, just as good drivers offset the cost of poor drivers with car insurance. However, if the population is not adopting healthier habits and preventative behaviors, health insurance becomes exceptionally costly.

Image of Health in Depth

National Health Care Spending
In 2008, health care spending in the United States surpassed $2.3 trillion[26], and is projected to reach $3 trillion in 2011. Health care spending is now projected to reach $4.2 trillion by 2016.[27]

Health care spending accounted for 10.7 percent of the gross domestic product (GDP) in Switzerland, 10.5 percent in Germany, 10.4 percent in Canada, and 11.2 percent in France, according to the Organization for Economic Cooperation and Development.[28] Each of these countries has a national health care plan. In the USA, health care spending was 17.6 percent of the GDP in 2009.[29]

Health care spending in the U.S. is 4.3 times the amount spent on national defense.[30]

Although over 50 million Americans are uninsured, the United States spends more on health care than other industrialized nations who provide health insurance to all their citizens.

Health Insurance Plans
Choosing a health insurance plan is like making any other major expensive purchase. It requires knowledge, research, and evaluation. Each type of insurance has a list of pros and cons and there is no single "best" plan. Rather, insurance should be chosen based on needs, marital status and on whether you have or plan to have children. For example, if you are married but have no children, it might be better to purchase two individual plans rather than the expense of a family plan. For college students, the best option is usually to remain on their parents' plan for as long as possible and then move to the medical services that may be provided on campus. Many campuses now have a health services office where you might be able to

see a physician or nurse, and discounted prescriptions are often available. Some colleges also offer group and individual psychological counseling. A health fee included in registration fees usually covers the cost of these services and there may be the option of extending this service to include hospitalization. As a responsible student, you should utilize these services to receive appropriate vaccinations, screenings, and routine examinations.

Fee-for-Service Plans (Traditional Health Insurance)
Fee-for-service plans generally offer a choice of any doctor, any hospital and the ability to switch doctors at will. Fee-for-service requires a monthly premium and an annual deductable. The annual deductible must be met before the insurance will begin to pay expenses. For example, a plan might require that the insured pay the first $1,000 in expenses and then twenty percent of all doctor bills, while the insurance company pays the remaining eighty percent. With fee-for-service, the insured must keep track of all medical expenses and submit claims.

To control costs, **fee-for-service insurance plans** set maximum amounts that will be covered in any one year, and they may limit the amount paid on particular services. For instance, the plan may determine the reasonable and customary fee for setting a broken arm to be $175, and this is the amount used to determine their eighty percent portion. If your doctor charges you $225, you are responsible for the difference between $175 and $225 ($50) and twenty percent of the $175 ($35). With other plans insurance companies negotiates fees for services with doctors and hospitals. With fee-for-service plans, this is the responsibility of the patient. Your doctor may agree to negotiate a price or agree to provide services at the insurance company's set fee. Fee-for-service plans often limit types of care that are covered, and preventive health care such as immunizations and well-child care may not be covered.

Health Maintenance Organizations

Health maintenance organizations (HMOs) are prepaid health plans where members pay a monthly premium for comprehensive care for members and their families. This includes physician appointments, hospital stays, emergencies, surgery, lab tests, X-rays and therapy. The HMO has contracted with specific doctors, hospitals, and pharmacies to provide care at established costs. The insured may pay a co-payment for each office visit, hospital stay, or emergency room treatment. These costs are generally adjusted according to the service being received where a small co-payment may be required to see a doctor, a higher co-payment for urgent care, and higher again for emergency room treatment. HMOs cover preventive health care, and because preventive health care can help control costs for the insurance company, HMOs encourage members to take advantage of this. Additionally, having higher co-payments for some comprehensive services may encourage patients to seek out a primary care physician (PCP) whenever possible.

Under an HMO, you select your doctor from a list of participating doctors and you cannot select a doctor from outside the plan. Hospital and pharmacy choice is also limited to control costs.

Preferred Provider Organizations

Preferred provider organizations (PPOs) are a combination of fee-for-service and HMO plans. As with an HMO, there are a limited number of pharmacies, hospitals and doctors to choose from. Most of your medical bills are covered when you choose an approved provider but there is a larger co-payment with this plan than with an HMO. An advantage of the PPO is that you can select a physician outside of the plan though using an outside provider increases co-payment, and may reduce your coverage.

Point of Service Plans

Point of Service plans are similar to HMOs and PPOs. Policyholders choose a primary care physician from an approved list. The physician may refer the patient to doctors not included in the plan's network, but costs will not be covered completely. Medical claim forms for all visits that occur within network are handled for the patient. When patients go outside the network, they become responsible for submitting full documentation for reimbursement including bills, prescriptions and receipts. These plans are generally more expensive than HMOs and PPOs. They work well for people who travel frequently outside of their health care network area.

Shannon's Story

During her college years, Shannon did not have health insurance, since she was young and healthy, but she was not concerned.

Although sexually active, Shannon did not see a doctor for a regular physical examination. She considered it but knew it would be expensive. Of course, she could have gone to the health clinic on the campus, but that was time consuming. She used the reasoning that she was never sick, so she didn't need a doctor.

A few years passed and Shannon was planning to start a family. However, she was having difficulty getting pregnant. Now insured, she made an appointment with her physician who told her that her fallopian tubes were blocked possibly due to pelvic inflammatory disease (PID). She learned that PID might have been caused by chlamydia, the leading cause of PID or gonorrhea, the second leading cause of PID, both of which are typically asymptomatic in women. Shannon learned that are diseases are

prevalent in sexually active men and women, and both are easily treated and cured with antibiotics. Her doctor explained that had she been having a regular examination, screening for sexually transmitted infections might have been advised.

Looking back, Shannon realized that if she had been responsible, taken the time to seek medical care regularly, she might have avoided this situation. Instead, she was now forced to become accountable for her past choices. For Shannon, the price was surgery to

unblock the fallopian tubes. For other less fortunate women, the tubes may become permanently blocked if these sexually transmitted diseases are left untreated. ■

Government Insurance Options

Through social security taxes, all employed individuals pay into the **Medicare** plan run by the Federal government. States and the federal government jointly fund **Medicaid**.

Medicare

Medicare is the health insurance program for Americans aged 65 and older and for certain disabled Americans. To qualify for Medicare, you must also be eligible to receive Social Security or Railroad Retirement benefits.

There are two parts to Medicare: Part A is free and covers hospital insurance. As with fee-for-service, HMOs, and PPOs, Medicare will restrict the cost paid for services. The second part of Medicare is supplementary insurance, known as Part B, and if elected, requires a premium. This supplementary insurance provides payments for doctors and related services. Selecting the right Medicare plan can be time consuming and difficult.

The best source of information is the handbook "Medicare and You" a free booklet that explains how Medicare works and what benefits are provided (www.medicare.gov/spotlights.asp).

Medicaid

Medicaid provides health coverage for some low-income people who cannot afford to buy insurance or have inadequate medical insurance. Individual states operate this plan, and each state decides who is eligible and the scope of health coverage that is offered.

Critical Thinking Question: Based on your reading, how would you evaluate your health insurance plan if you have one, and if you do not, what sort of plan is best suited for you?

> **Key Terms**
>
> **Fee-for-service insurance**: A health insurance plan in which the consumer pays a monthly premium, and after spending a pre-determined amount on medical care each year, then pays a percentage of expenses incurred while the plan pays the remainder.
>
> **Health maintenance organizations**: Health insurance plans where the consumer pays a monthly premium, selects medical treatment from a list of physicians, and pays only a co-payment at each visit.
>
> **Preferred provider organizations**: A combination of a fee-for-service plan and an HMO.
>
> **Point of service**: Similar to HMOs and PPOs, but work better for people who travel frequently outside of their health care network.
>
> **Medicare**: Government health insurance for those over 65 years of age.
>
> **Medicaid**: Government health insurance for the indigent and disabled.

National Health Insurance

Over 50 million people, representing 16.7 percent of the population, including more than 7 million children under age 18, had no health insurance in 2009 compared to 15.4 percent in 2008. As the number of uninsured people increases, the costs of health care increases since the uninsured often use emergency care services for health needs. If they are unable to pay the bill, this cost is eventually absorbed in higher medical care costs and higher insurance premiums. Although the government has medicare and medicaid,, this still leaves an uninsured gap in the population. Since a healthy population is one of the country's most important assets, alternate forms of insurance may need to be examined for this population.

In March 2010 congress passed into law the Affordable Health Care Act. The new law bans lifetime limits, restricts the use of annual limits on health insurance, and bans dropping coverage when a patient needs it the most. Discriminating against children with pre-existing conditions is prohibited and recommended services such as mammograms, immunizations, and pre-natal care are covered.

Which Plan Is Right for You?

For each group, choose the statement 1 or 2 that best describes how you feel:

1. Having complete freedom to choose doctors and hospitals is the most important thing to me in a health plan, even if it costs more.

2. Holding down my costs is the most important thing to me, even if it means limiting some of my choices.

1. I travel frequently or have children that live away from me, and we may need to see doctors in other parts of the country.

2. I do not travel frequently, and almost all care for my family is needed in our local area.

1. I don't mind a health insurance plan that includes filling out forms or keeping receipts, then sending them in for payment.

2. I prefer not to fill out forms or keep receipts; I want my care covered without a lot of paperwork.

1. In addition to my premiums, I am willing to pay for routine and preventive care, such as office visits, checkups, and shots. I also like knowing that I can get an appointment for these services when I need one.

2. I want a health plan that includes routine and preventive care. I don't mind if I have to wait for these services to be scheduled for an available appointment with my doctor.

1. If I need to see a specialist, I will likely ask my doctor for a recommendation, but I want to decide whom to go to and when. I don't want to have to see my primary care doctor before I can see a specialist.

2. I don't mind if I need a referral from my primary care doctor before I can see a specialist. If my doctor doesn't think I need special services, that is fine with me.

> If your answers are mostly 1s: You want to make your own health care choices, even if it costs you more and takes more paperwork. Fee-for-service may be the best plan for you.
>
> If your answers are mostly 2s: You are willing to give up some choices to hold down your medical costs, and you also want help in managing your care. Consider a health maintenance organization.
>
> If your answers are some 1s and some 2s: You might want to look for a plan such as a preferred provider organization, which combines some of the features of fee-for-service and health maintenance organization coverage.

(Source: AHCPR, 1992.)

This new Act does not put the government in charge of health insurance. Rather, it strengthens existing employer-based health insurance while improving market fairness for consumers by implementing landmark consumer protections. Although portions of the new law are already in place, remaining components will be put into practice by 2014 if the Act is unchallenged.

Critical Thinking Question: How will the Health Care Reform Act change your health insurance options?

Image of Health in Depth

Unequal Treatment: Disparities in Health Care
In 1999, Congress requested that the Institute of Medicine conduct a study to assess disparities in health care among U.S. racial and ethnic minorities and non-minorities.[31] The report showed extensive inequities, even when members of the minority groups had the same income, insurance coverage and medical conditions as whites, including the following:

Racial and ethnic minorities are less likely to receive routine medical procedures, and experience a lower quality of health services.

Minorities are less likely to be given appropriate cardiac medications, to undergo bypass surgery, or to receive kidney dialysis or transplants.

Minorities are more likely to undergo lower limb amputations for diabetes and other conditions.

Disparities are found across different settings, including public and private hospitals and clinics, and teaching and non-teaching hospitals.

Disparities in care are associated with high mortality among minorities.[32]

Critical Thinking Question: What do you think might cause the disparity that exists in health care across ethnic groups?

Health and Advertising

The Federal Trade Commission (FTC) is the government agency that enforces laws and regulations pertaining to advertising. The three main laws are:

1. Advertising must be truthful and non-deceptive.

2. Advertisers must have evidence to back up their claims.

3. Advertisements cannot be unfair.

Even with these laws, advertisers find ways to manipulate words or research to support advertisements. Consumers may take the view that there is nothing to lose by trying a product. But with health-related products, there may be risk. If products do not provide the results that were promoted, consumers lose money. But more importantly, health fraud, or quackery, has an emotional cost. Trying untested products may interfere with effective prescribed medications.

The long-standing advice "if it sounds too good to be true, it probably isn't true" is never more appropriately used than with health advertising. To avoid being misled by unethical marketers, consider the following when looking at promotions:

1. **Does the product promise quick results or cures?**

   This is an example of being "too good to be true." Many dieting products make promises about quick, easy weight loss but the only successful, guaranteed way to lose weight is with calorie reductions and long, slow endurance activity.

2. **Does the product promote that the medical industry does not want you to know about this because they will lose money?**

   If a health product works, marketers will want it promoted by the medical industry to increase their personal profit. Manufacturers would want medical authorities to endorse their product and prove its effectiveness with scientific research.

3. **Does the product diminish the value of scientific health research?**

   Some marketers prey on the concept that scientific research should always be questioned. They may cite remedies used in previous times that worked, but were never tested or promote products by suggesting they have been used for generations in another country. From Chapter 1, you know that health research should be carefully evaluated, and that studies that have both validity and reliability are a solid endorsement.

4. **Does the product state hundreds or thousands or even millions of people have used it successfully?**

   The idea that so many people have used something might persuade us that the product is safe and reliable. Of course, the company does not support its statements with any proof that can be validated.

5. **Does the product offer a money back guarantee, except for shipping and handling?**

   This common ploy is used extensively in television advertising. The idea that you can try the product "free" and without any risk can sound very attractive. Read the small print carefully. Sometimes these products are worth less than what you pay for shipping and handling. The fee charged has a built-in profit margin. And many people forget to submit forms for rebates and refunds. The company knows that many people will buy the product planning to return it if they are dissatisfied, but often fail to do so.

6. **Does the product promote that it can be used to treat or cure a variety of different ailments?**

   No product or medicine can cure a variety of conditions or diseases. If a treatment or cure is available, your physician will know about it and will tell you.

7. **Does the product suggest that "natural" or "herbal" is better than products that are chemically produced?**

   Guidelines for establishing that a product is "natural" change from state to state. The term is ambiguous and hard to define. Promoting something as "herbal" suggests that something natural must be better. There are no scientific results to support the claim that natural or herbal is superior to other manufactured products and in some instances, the product may cause harm.

8. **Does the product suggest that it has been used successfully elsewhere but kept secret in the U.S., and only now has become available?**

   The world keeps getting smaller and people travel more. If there is some new treatment or new drug in another country, it will be known about in this country.

9. **Does the product use testimonials or case histories to support its claims?**

   Consumers like testimonials because we may identify with the person promoting the product. For example, in an advertisement to promote a weight loss product the model may appear overweight or even obese in the before picture, and after using the product now has a perfect body. The model may say that he tried every diet, every exercise and nothing worked, and you may relate to that. Invariably, these promotions will state the advertised results are not typical. It may even be that the model made other major changes that might have caused the weight loss.

Steps to Take

Health advertising is ubiquitous and as long as it remains profitable, it will continue. Before buying any advertised, promoted commercial product to improve or change your health, think about what you can do without the product to generate the change you want. This is probably a better choice, but it might take effort and the results may not be seen for a length of time. If you are still considering an advertised product, ask for a written explanation of how the product works, including copies of any research that support the claims. Do not believe testimonials or products that might be endorsed by someone purporting to be a doctor.

The American Cancer Society and the Arthritis Foundation keep track of unproven and ineffective treatment methods. If you have a specific condition, check information on their Web site, or seek the advice of a physician.

Responsibility and Accountability

This chapter focused on health care choices available to you when you become sick. Responsibly choosing the best health insurance plan for yourself, as well as arming yourself with knowledge so you can evaluate both traditional and alternate health care remedies effectively, will work to improve your health.

Taking Responsibility for Your Health

Responsibility in the area of health care choices and applications will not only help you manage your health, but will also help manage health care resources. Ensuring that you select the appropriate, lowest price level of care for your needs benefits you and keeps health care costs lower. Responsibly performing self-exams, practicing preventive measures, and being aware of risks that you might face all help create a better outcome.

Focusing on Accountability

Being accountable for your health and your health care means that you evaluate therapies so you can ask the right questions and make better choices. When prescribed a medication, taking that medication according to the directions and completing it according to the prescription shows accountability. You are also accountable by practicing self-care to maintain your health, and by seeking professional care early if your symptoms do not improve. Combining responsibility with accountability will help keep health care costs in better control, and may help improve the availability of health care to those who are under-insured and uninsured.

Summary

You and Your Well-Being

- Professional help is needed when a patient experiences unusual, severe, persistent, or recurrent symptoms.

- Treatment options include self-care, primary care, urgent care, and emergency room care.

- Health self-assessment might involve evaluating any symptoms you experience, assessing your risk with an HRA or seeking a health screening from a professional. As a result, you might opt for self-treatment, or seek the care of a physician. Self-treatments can be beneficial but are not without risk, and may delay you from seeing a professional.

Conventional Health Care Professionals

- Conventional Western medicine is based in scientific belief and medical diagnoses are based on empirical, rational, testable, parsimonious, general, rigorously evaluated, and tentative evidence.

- A variety of health care professionals are available, ranging from a primary care provider, to secondary care doctors who specialize, to dentists and allied health care workers. Selecting the right professional is key to achieving the desired outcome.

Conventional Treatments

- Prescription drugs are controlled by the FDA and have been shown to produce the desired results. Occasionally, prescription drugs are released into the OTC market.

- More than 3,000 OTC drugs are available. Some treat individual symptoms while others treat multiple symptoms. OTC drugs are regulated by the FDA and must meet certain criteria.

Complementary and Alternative Medical Practices

- Herbal and botanical treatments are also available over the counter. These are not monitored by any federal agency, and may or may not contain the ingredients listed or perform the expected outcome.

- CAM practitioners are becoming more available. As some CAM therapies are proven to work, they may be integrated into conventional medicine, and covered by health insurance. CAM includes traditional Chinese medicine, mind-body practices, and herbs and botanical remedies.

The Cost of Health Care

- A variety of insurance plans are available to help cover health care cost. Options include fee-for-service plans, health maintenance organizations, preferred provider organizations, and point of service plans.

- Medicare and Medicaid are government health insurance plans. Medicare is for those over 65 or disabled, while Medicaid, offered by individual states, is for low-income citizens who cannot afford or have inadequate medical insurance.

- Over 50 million people do not have health insurance, including more than 7 million children.

- The Affordable Health Care Act may improve insurance options and provide affordable insurance.

Health and Advertising

- Since consumers want good health and may want quick, easy ways to achieve it, health product advertising becomes a profitable arena for manufacturers.

- Before purchasing any products, or treatments, the information provided should be carefully evaluated.

Reassessing Your Knowledge

1. List symptoms that would warrant a visit to a physician.

2. Differentiate between primary and secondary care and name some types of practices that would meet each type of care.

3. Explain the issues with use of any drug. How are drugs monitored, and what controls are in place to ensure their efficacy? Consider OTC, herbal, and prescription drugs when answering this question.

4. Describe the different kinds of health insurance plans that are available, and list the pros and cons of each.

5. Describe four common methods of promoting a health product.

To answer these questions, you might choose to work in groups with your colleagues. Check your answers against the written material in the test, and reread those sections where you made errors.

Health Assessment Toolbox

Health Risk Assessments
This site offers a variety of health assessments.
http://www.healthstatus.com/assessments.html

American Heart Association Learn and Live Quiz
By taking a simple quiz, you will be forwarded to information that will help you live a longer and healthier life.
http://www.americanheart.org/presenter.jhtml?identifier=3019149

American Heart Association Delicious Decisions
Browse a variety of recipes to help you make heat healthy eating a lifetime habit.
http://www.deliciousdecisions.org/

Your Disease Risk
Siteman Cancer Center at the Washington School of Medicine has created an assessment to determine your risk in developing any of five different diseases.
http://www.yourdiseaserisk.wustl.edu/

Ten-Year Cardiovascular Disease Risk Calculator
This site will assess your risk of having a heart attack in the next ten years.
http://hp2010.nhlbihin.net/atpiii/calculator.asp?usertype=pub

Partnership for Healthy Weight Management
This site provides a tool to determine your body mass index that can then be compared to risk factors associated with it.
http://www2.niddk.nih.gov/

Melanoma Risk Assessment Tool
The American Cancer Society has put together a short assessment to determine your risk for melanoma.
http://www.cancer.gov

Sexually Transmitted Diseases (STDs) Risk Assessment
Created by the University of Iowa, this site will assess your risk and provide you with information about the major STDs.
http://www.uihealthcare.com/depts/med/obgyn/pat-edu/stds/stdrisk.html

Assessing your Risk for Drug and Alcohol Addiction
This site, provided by the Department of Labor offers information on risk for addiction and signs of addiction.
http://www.dol.gov/asp/programs/drugs/working-partners/sab/addiction.asp#q11

Health Management Tools
This comprehensive site offers assessment for issues ranging from depression to stress.
http://www.dol.gov/asp/programs/drugs/working-partners/sab/addiction.asp#q11

Discovery Health
Provided by the Discovery Channel, at this site you will find a nutrition assessment along with a variety of personality assessments.
http://health.discovery.com/tools/assessments.html

Vocabulary Challenge
Match the term in the left-hand column with its correct definition in the right-hand column.

TERM		DEFINITION
Synergistic effect	A.	Product that relieves pain
Primary care	B.	Diverse medical and health care systems not part of conventional medicine
Allopathic medicine	C.	Treatment and rehabilitation efforts provided in hospital setting
Optometrist	D.	Person who is licensed to make and fit eyeglasses
Additive effects	E.	Person who is trained to examine eyes and prescribe eyeglasses
Tertiary care	F.	Disease management in doctor's office or hospital setting
Analgesic	G.	One drug potentiates the effect of the second drug
Complementary and alternative medicine	H.	Preventative care, routine screenings, and treatment of routine illnesses
Optician	I.	Combined drug effects are not exaggerated
Secondary care	J.	Medical practice based on scientifically validated methods

G, H, J, E, I, C, A, B, D, F.
Answers

Exploring the Internet

Evaluating Health Insurance Plans

Your guide to objective information about the various plans that are offered.

http://www.consumerreports.org/health/insurance/health-insurance/how-to-pick-health-insurance/compare-health-plans.htm

The American Association of Health Plans

Additional resources to consult when evaluating quality of health care plans.

http://Home.gwi.net/global/evaluating_health_plans.htm

American Medical Association

Journals, research, medical ethics and membership information.

http://www.ama-assn.org/

American Cancer Society

Prevention techniques and warning signals.

http://www.cancer.org/docroot/home/index.asp

American Institute for Cancer Research

Fosters research on diet and cancer prevention and educates the public about the results.

http://www.aicr.org/site/PageServer

National Center for Complimentary and Alternative Medicine, National Institutes of Health

Offers information about complimentary and alternative medicine from the National Institutes of Health.

http://nccam.nih.gov/

National Center for Complimentary and Alternative Medicine

Offers information about current NIH funded clinical trials.

http://nccam.nih.gov/

Evaluating Health Web Sites

Information on evaluating Internet pages that promote health products and services.

http://nnlm.gov/outreach/consumer/evalsite.html

Medline Plus: Guide to Healthy Web Surfing

What you should look for when evaluating the quality of health information on websites.

http://www.nlm.nih.gov/medlineplus/healthywebsurfing.html

Primary, Secondary and Tertiary Prevention Definitions and practice.

http://www.fhea.com/CertificatgionCols/level_prevention.htm

Racial and Ethnic Health Disparities: On the Road from Research to Practice

http://heb.sagepub.com

Selected References

1. Summary Health Statistics for U.S. Adults: National Health Interview Survey, 2009, Table 37; Summary Health Statistics for U.S. Children. National Health Interview Survey, 2009, Table 37; National Ambulatory Medical Care Survey: 2007. Summary Tables 1, 9, and 13.

2. U.S. Department of Labor. Bureau of Labor Statistics. *Career Guide to Industries*, 2010–2011 Edition.

3. Hooker, R.S., and Berlin, L.E. Trends in the Supply of Physician Assistants and Nurse Practitioners in the United States. *Health Affairs,* 21(5): 178–181. 2002.

4. Applebaum, E., Ruhlen, T.N., Kronenberg, F., Hayes, C., and Peters, E.S. Oral Cancer Knowledge, Attitudes and Practices: A Survey of Dentists and Primary Care Physicians in Massachusetts. *Journal of the American Dental Association,* 140: 461–467. 2009.

5. Catlin A., Cowan C., Hartman M., and Heffler S. The National Health Expenditure Accounts Team. National Health Spending in 2006: A Year of Change for Prescription Drugs. *Health Affairs,* 27(1): 14–29. 2008. Doi 10.1377/hlthaff.27.1.14

6. DiMasi J.A., Hansen R.W., and Grabowski H.G. The Price of Innovation: New Estimates of Drug Development Costs. *Journal of Health Economics*, 22(2): 151–85. May, 2003.

7. Gagnon M.A., and Lexchin, J. The Cost of Pushing Pills: A New Estimate of Pharmaceutical Promotion Expenditures in the United States. *PLoS Medicine* 5(1). 2008. el.doi:10.1371/journal.pmed.0050001

8. Collins, F.S., Briggs, J., Fauci, A., et al. Separating Fact and Fiction: News About the Proposed National Center for Advancing Translational Sciences. Feedback. National Institutes of Health. Downloaded January 28, 2011, from http://feedback.nih.gov/index.php/category/ncats/

9. U.S.F.D.A. Weekly News, April 7, 2005. Downloaded March 17, 2010, from http://www.fda.gov/Drugs/DrugSafety/PostmarketDrugSafetyInformationforPatientsandProviders/ucm103420.htm

10. Requirements on the Content and Format of Labeling for Human Prescription Drug and Biological Products, January 24, 2006. Effective June 30, 2006. USFDA, Center for Drug Evaluation and Research. Rules and Regulations. *Federal Register*, 71(15): 3922–3997. January 24, 2006.

11. Benshoff, J., Harrawood, L., and Koch, D. Substance Abuse and the Elderly: Unique Issues and Concerns. *Journal of Rehabilitation*, 69(2): 43–48. 2003.

12. Food and Drug Administration. Center for Drug Evaluation and Research. What questions should I ask my health care provider before taking a new medication? Downloaded January 28, 2011, from http://www.fda.gov/Drugs/default.htm

13. Kereiakes, D.J., and Willerson, J.T., Health Care on Trial. America's Medical Malpractice Crisis. *Circulation*, 109: 2939–2941. 2004.

14. Anderson, R.E. Defending the Practice of Medicine. *Archives of Internal Medicine*, 164: 1173–1178. 2004.

15. United States Census 2010. Downloaded February 8, 2011, from http://2010.census.gov/2010census/

16. Rosa, L., Rosa, E., Sarner, L., and Barrett, S. A Close Look at Therapeutic Touch. *Journal of the American Medical Association*, 279(13): 1005–1010. 1998. doi: 10.1001/jama.279.13.1005

17. Balon, J. A Comparison of Active and Simulated Chiropractic Manipulation as Adjunctive Treatment for Childhood Asthma. *New England Journal of Medicine,* 339: 1013–1020. 1998.

18. Balon, J. A Comparison of Active and Simulated Chiropractic Manipulation as Adjunctive Treatment for Childhood Asthma. *New England Journal of Medicine,* 339: 1013–1020. 1998.

19. Berman, B.M., Lao, L., Langenberg, P., et al. Effectiveness of Acupuncture as Adjunctive Therapy in Osteoarthritis of the Knee: A Randomized, Controlled Trial. *Annals of Internal Medicine*, 141(12): 901–910. 2004.

20. Ernst, E. Acupuncture—A Critical Analysis. *Journal of Internal Medicine*, 259(2): 125–137. 2006.

21. Ernst, E. A Systematic Review of Systematic Reviews of Homeopathy. *British Journal of Clinical Pharmacology,* 54(6): 577–582. 2002. doi:10.1046/j.1365-2125.2002.01699.x, PMID 12492603

22. Shang, A., Huwiler-Müntener, K., Nartey, L., Jüni, P., Dörig, S., Sterne, J.A., Pewsner, D., and Egger, M. Are the Clinical Effects of Homoeopathy Placebo Effects? Comparative Study of Placebo-Controlled Trials of Homoeopathy and Allopathy. *Lancet* 366(9487): 726–732. 2005. doi:10.1016/S0140-6736 (05) 67177-2, PMID 16125589

23. National Institutes of Health, National Center for Complimentary and Alternative Medicine. Blue Ribbon Intramural Research Strategic Planning Panel. June 5, 2009, pp.4.

24. Hypericum Depression Trial Study Group. Effect of Hypericum Perforatum (St. John's Wort) in Major Depressive Disorder: a Randomized, Controlled Trial. *JAMA*, 287: 1807–1814. 2002.

25. DeKosky, S.T., Williamson, J.D., Fitzpatrick, A.L., et al. Gingko Biloba for Prevention of Dementia A Randomized Controlled Trial. *JAMA*, 300(19): 2253–2262. 2008.

26. Centers for Medicare and Medicaid Services, Office of the Actuary, National Health Statistics Group, National Health Care Expenditures Data, January 2010.

27. Poisal, J.A., et al., Health Spending Projections Through 2016: Modest Changes Obscure Part D's Impact, *Health Affairs*, W242–253. February 21, 2007.

28. Organisation for Economic Co-operation and Development. Total Expenditure on Health as Percentage of Gross Domestic Product. November 25, 2010. Downloaded January 31, 2011, from http://www.oecd-ilibrary.org/social-issues-migration-health/health-key-tables-from-oecd_20758480

29. Centers for Medicare and Medicaid Services, Office of the Actuary, National Health Statistics Group, National Health Care Expenditures Data, January 2010.

30. California Health Care Foundation. Health Care Costs 101-2005. March 2, 2005. http://www.chcf.org/

31. Nelson, A. Unequal Treatment: Confronting Racial and Ethnic Disparities in Healthcare. *Journal of the National Medical Association*, 94(8): 666–668. August, 2002.

32. Bach, P.B., Pham, H.H., Schrag, D., Ramsey, T.C., and Hargraves, J.L. Primary Care Physicians Who Treat Blacks and Whites. *New England Journal of Medicine*, 351(6): 575–584. August 5, 2004.

33. Bach, P.B., Pham, H.H., Schrag, D., Ramsey, T.C., and Hargraves, J.L. Primary Care Physicians Who Treat Blacks and Whites. *New England Journal of Medicine,* 351(6): 575–584. August 5, 2004.

Image of Health

Stress and Mental Health

DEFINING STRESS

- General Adaptation Syndrome
- Stress and Disease
  - Cardiovascular Disease
  - Cancer
- Personality and Stress

MANAGING STRESS

- Evaluate Your Stress
- Finding Your Own Stress Level
- Stress Scales
- Proven Stress Management Techniques
- Unresolved Stress
- Negative Coping Methods
  - Alcohol and Stress
  - Marijuana and Stress

DEFINING MENTAL HEALTH

- Psychosocial Health
- The Transition to Adulthood
- Maslow's Hierarchy of Needs

INFLUENCES ON MENTAL HEALTH

- Social Support
- Self Esteem
- Spirituality
- Self-Directed versus Other-Directed
- Happiness
- Decision-Making

MENTAL DISORDERS

- Depression and Mania
  - Major Depression
  - Bipolar Disorder
  - Minor Depression
- Suicide
- Anxiety Disorders, Obsessions, and Compulsions
  - Panic Disorder
  - Agoraphobia
  - Post-Traumatic Stress Syndrome
  - Obsessions and Compulsions
  - Schizophrenia and Other Psychoses

TREATMENT APPROACHES FOR MENTAL HEALTH

- Counseling and Psychotherapy
- Finding the Right Therapist
- Medical Treatment
- Self-Help Options

RESPONSIBILITY AND ACCOUNTABILITY

- Taking Responsibility for Your Mental Health
- Focusing on Accountability

Student Learning Outcomes

LEARNING OUTCOME	APPLYING IT TO YOUR LIFE
Use the General Adaptation Syndrome to describe the body's physical reaction to different types of stressors.	Identify the effects of stress on your body and well-being.
Identify stress management techniques.	Develop a strategy to keep stressors from disrupting your life.
Define the psychosocial components of mental health.	Develop a profile of your mental health using the psychosocial components.
List factors that influence mental health.	Identify circumstances that will foster good personal mental health.
List and define the major mental health disorders.	Recognize any symptoms of mental health disorders you and those around you may have.
Describe treatment options for mental health issues.	Seek appropriate treatment methods for yourself as necessary and for those in your primary social group.

Assess Your Knowledge

1. Psychosocial health includes the four dimensions of wellness:
   a. Emotional, exuberant, homeostatic, resolved
   b. Emotional, intellectual, social, spiritual
   c. Intellectual, homeostatic, resourceful, spiritual
   d. Intellectual, self-actualized, dependent, spiritual

2. Risk factors for suicide include:
   a. Excess energy, hallucinations, depression
   b. Subliminal suggestion, anomie, mania
   c. Family violence, substance abuse, depression
   d. Reactive impulse, spontaneity, mania

3. According to Maslow's hierarchy of needs:
   a. All needs must be met in order to be stress free.
   b. Basic needs must be met before higher level needs can be realized.
   c. Self-actualized people have no basic needs.
   d. All needs can be satisfied by financial wealth.

4. The three parts of General Adaptation Syndrome (GAS) are:
   a. Alarm, confusion, despair
   b. Resistance, resolution, relaxation
   c. Alarm, resistance, exhaustion
   d. Resistance, homeostasis, resolution

5. A stress trigger is:
   a. Something that initiates the stress response.
   b. A constant repetitive stress.
   c. A stress reliever.
   d. An enormous amount of stress.

Answers:

1. b, 2. c, 3. b, 4. c, 5. a

Life in modern America is full of expectations, opportunities, successes, and defeats. Although much about American life is positive, the fast pace and constant bombardment with various stimuli can cause stress, which can affect mental health. Striving to maintain or catch up, striving to acquire more, to be more, striving even to be viewed the way you want to be viewed can all add to the stress load.

As individuals seek more and more, some basic things that bring pleasure to life are sometimes not recognized. The pressure to be more productive, to constantly multitask, and to do everything at an above-average level can be unrealistic. A generation ago, attending college full time was considered a full-time job. Today, many students attend college full time, in addition to working part-time or even full-time jobs; some students are parents, with family responsibilities; and all students attempt to balance a social life with other obligations and still maintain passing grades. With only twenty-four hours in each day, there is simply not enough time to do everything that they want or need to do.

As you read this, you may be thinking, "This sounds like my life." Now think about how stressed you are, and what it might take to feel that your life is in balance. As a result of reading this chapter, you may be able to set better priorities, reduce unnecessary obligations, make time for yourself, and learn to manage stress more effectively and protect your mental health.

Defining Stress

In the 1930s, Hans Selye, a Viennese physician and endocrinologist, was the first to analyze human stress, and spent a lifetime analyzing its effects. He wrote the first paper on human stress syndrome in 1936. According to Selye, "Stress is the nonspecific response of the body to any demand, whether it is caused by, or results in, pleasant or unpleasant conditions."[1] A **stressor** can be physical, emotional, or mental. It can be a person in your life, such as a parent, child, boss, spouse, or partner. Physical stress can appear when your body gets worn down and tired, or it may occur when recovering from a surgery. Emotional stress causes feelings such as grief about a loved one who is ill, concern about a personal health issue, worry about relationship issues, or anxiety about your finances. There is also mental stress, such as test anxiety, making difficult decisions, and concern about anticipated events.

Because life will occasionally be stressful for everyone, your goal should not be to erase all stress. In fact, a little stress is good for you—it makes you perform better and accomplish more. There are two types of stress, and both affect the body in a similar way. **Eustress** is caused by positive events in your life, such as graduation, marriage, promotion, athletic competition, or any positive accomplishment. **Distress** is caused by negative events in life, such as failing a test, being denied a job promotion, the breakup of a relationship, or illness.

Key Terms

Stressor: An activity, experience, event, person, or thing that initiates the stress response.

Eustress: from the Greek *eu* = good, as in euphoria.

Distress: from the Latin *dis* = bad, as in dissonance, disagreement.

FIGURE 3-1. A wedding can produce eustress.

During both eustress and distress, the body undergoes the same nonspecific responses to various positive or negative stimuli. However, according to Selye, eustress causes much less damage to the body than distress, indicating that positive stress encourages the body to adapt to change.[2]

Two people exposed to an identical stressor can have completely different reactions—the difference is how each *perceives* the stressor. For example, children are often fearful of many things with which they have no experience. They may be afraid of other people, dogs, loud noises, fast movement, or anything else they are not accustomed to. As children grow, develop, and have more experiences, they often become less afraid, and eventually perhaps not afraid at all. In other words, a young child may perceive many things as dangerous or frightening; however, as the child gets older, he will realize that most of these things are completely safe.

The same phenomenon occurs with stress, which helps explain different reactions to the same stressor. One individual may have learned that the potential stressor is not dangerous or frightening and remains calm, or has learned to adapt to a familiar stressful situation. The individual who has been negatively affected by the same stressor is initially alarmed, and though the stress is familiar or nonthreatening, finds it difficult to relax and adapt. Ideally, you will learn from experience that what you once perceived as stressful does not affect you in a negative way. When this occurs, you have successfully adapted to a personal stressor.

General Adaptation Syndrome

General Adaptation Syndrome (GAS) illustrates how the human body adapts to stress. All human activities have a certain degree of stress associated with them. According to Selye, the body's ability to successfully adapt depends on the severity of the stressor, as well as a genetic predisposition for stress adaptation.[3] The incidences of **high blood pressure**, **cardiovascular disease**, and cancer are more frequent for people who have difficulty coping with stress; so your ability to adapt to personal stress will lessen the possibility of various stress-related diseases. For people who have difficulty adapting to change, stress appears to negatively affect the immune system, making them much more susceptible to chronic diseases.[4]

> **Key Terms**
>
> **High blood pressure**: A serious condition in which either systolic or diastolic blood pressure remains above normal, possibly leading to coronary heart disease, heart failure, stroke, or kidney disease.
>
> **Cardiovascular disease**: The term used to describe various forms of disease related to the heart and blood vessels.

The general adaptation syndrome consists of three stages—alarm, resistance, and exhaustion—and involves two major systems of the body, the autonomic nervous system and the endocrine system. The autonomic nervous system, consisting of the parasympathetic and sympathetic systems, is responsible for controlling involuntary body functions such as heart rate, respiration, and digestion. The sympathetic nervous system allows the body to function under stress and initiates the **fight-or-flight response**, while the parasympathetic nervous system is in constant opposition to the sympathetic system, attempting to bring the body to **homeostasis**. The endocrine system regulates hormones that are released from various glands in the body. During the stress response, the adrenal glands produce adrenaline, which helps the body cope with both physical and mental stress by raising blood pressure and heart rate. The autonomic nervous system and endocrine system are both activated during the stress response.

> **Key Terms**
>
> **Fight-or-flight response**: The body's response to extreme stress, during which the endocrine system releases stress hormones such as cortisol and adrenaline, and the autonomic nervous system elevates heart rate, blood pressure, and respiration.
>
> **Homeostasis**: Maintaining equilibrium between interdependent elements, especially those maintained by physiological processes.

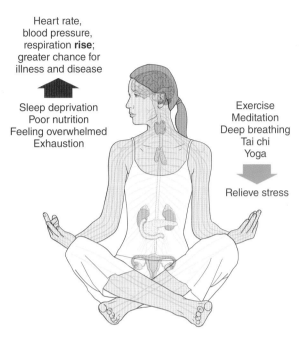

Heart rate, blood pressure, respiration **rise**; greater chance for illness and disease

Sleep deprivation
Poor nutrition
Feeling overwhelmed
Exhaustion

Exercise
Meditation
Deep breathing
Tai chi
Yoga

Relieve stress

During the alarm stage, also known as the fight-or-flight response, the body reacts to a stressor by elevating heart rate, respiration, and blood pressure, and depressing the digestive and immune systems. The resistance stage allows the body to adapt in order to reduce the effects of the continued stressor, and in the exhaustion stage, the body is too fatigued by the continual stress and cannot continue to adapt. Over time, continual unrelieved stress may cause the immune system to be compromised, resulting in illness or disease. However, in most cases the exhaustion stage is not reached, because the body is able to resist the stressor and learns to adapt. The process of the body adapting to stress in order to maintain equilibrium is called homeostasis.

▶**Challenge Question**: Describe the physiologic changes that occur in the body in response to stress.

Unrelieved stress that causes the body to reach exhaustion is a risk factor for both cardiovascular disease and cancer. It is also possible to have a short-term experience with GAS: during exercise, it is common to experience all three stages. However, in most instances exhaustion is reversible or short-lived. For example, if you decide to go for a run in the morning, your muscles and cardiovascular system will experience immediate stress, but your body will adapt to allow more efficiency in your running. Even if you run too fast or too far and reach exhaustion, when you rest you will soon recover and be back to normal. In this example, you moved through the three stages of GAS, but adapted and recovered with no ill effects.

For college students, personal behavior can impact the stress response. When a student is sleep deprived, poorly nourished, overwhelmed by college life, and behind in classes, he can easily reach the exhaustion and illness stage of GAS. For a student with a serious eating disorder such as anorexia, the stress and severity of this illness can lead to the exhaustion stage and possibly death. Stress can be physical, mental, or emotional. It can be your body's reaction to an infection, illness, surgery, an injury, death, or divorce. In most instances, your body experiences alarm, but is quickly able to resist and adapt to the stress.

Many occurrences of everyday life can be stressful for some people. Although some stress can help you perform better and accomplish more, there is a balance that must be reached, and everyone adapts to life stressors differently. Ideally, you will recognize the stressors in your life and learn to adapt so that you manage your stress effectively. The following is a list of common stressors that almost everyone will experience in their lives. Note how many of these common stressors are currently affecting you.

- *Change* causes stress. Any change in your life that takes you out of your comfort zone can be a stressor. Examples: A new semester of classes, new job, new relationship, new marriage, or new baby.

- *Conflict* causes stress. Disagreements with your family, partner, spouse, employer, and coworkers are stressors. Conflict also occurs when making difficult decisions.

- *Overload* causes stress. When your life has too many commitments and responsibilities, it can be difficult or impossible to keep up. When this happens, you are experiencing overload, and possibly **burnout**.

- *Financial worry* causes stress. If you never seem to have enough money, can't pay your bills, or are overextended on your credit cards, you could be experiencing a very real stress.

- *Environmental factors* cause stress. Common environmental stressors include noise, crowding, traffic, and weather. Although you may not be able to control most of these factors, they are still stressors.

> **Key Term**
>
> **Burnout**: Psychological exhaustion and diminished efficiency resulting from overwork or prolonged exposure to stress.

Stress and Disease

It is generally accepted that too much unrelieved stress has a negative effect on overall health. **Psychoneuroimmunology** is the branch of medicine that studies the negative effects of stress that may lead to cardiovascular disease, cancer, diabetes, and many other chronic diseases. Unrelieved stress particularly affects the immune system, causing more susceptibility to chronic illness such as ulcers, heart attacks, gastrointestinal disorders, and cancer.[4]

> **Key Term**
>
> **Psychoneuroimmunology**: A branch of medicine concerned with how emotions affect the immune system.

Cardiovascular Disease

Although there is not a definite link between stress and cardiovascular disease, when combined with other risk factors such as smoking, high cholesterol, and high blood pressure, unalleviated stress seems to exacerbate those factors. It is also thought that hormones the body releases during the stress response, particularly adrenaline and cortisol, subject the body to persistent, long-term effects that may contribute to cardiovascular disease.[5,6] Stress causes some people to overeat and become obese, thereby directly resulting in high blood pressure. In general, those who are less able to manage personal stress may have more risk factors for cardiovascular disease than those who manage stress well.

Cancer

The link between chronic stress and cancer focuses on the affect the endocrine system has on the immune system. Under stress, the endocrine system becomes more active in releasing stress hormones, especially cortisol, that may compromise the immune system. When stress is constant, immune system responses may be altered, making the body more susceptible to disease, including cancer, as well as autoimmune diseases such as lupus and chronic fatigue syndrome.[7,8]

Personality and Stress

Evidence indicates that personality type may be a predictor of stress level and ability to manage personal stress. Two individuals may react differently to an identical stressor: A workaholic who strives for perfection, who may be impatient, highly competitive, hostile, aggressive, and unable to relax, is a type A personality. Type A individuals may be very successful, but are at increased risk for stress-related illnesses. A type B personality is more patient, friendly, calm, and able to relax. Type B individuals can also be successful, but tend to experience far fewer stress-related illnesses.

Further evidence shows that rather than personality type, a propensity toward anger is a more reliable predictor of **coronary heart disease** (CHD). If you are easy to anger and/or react to stressful events by expressing anger, the risk for cardiovascular diseases increases.[9]

> ▶**Challenge Question**: Describe some of the negative consequences that may occur as the result of unrelieved stress.

> **Key Term**
>
> **Coronary heart disease**: Failure of coronary circulation to supply adequate circulation to the cardiac muscle and surrounding tissue.

Managing Stress

Life is constantly changing, so a careful self-assessment of current stressors and their effects may lead to an effective stress management plan, starting with a simple evaluation of your current stress level as you consider the dynamic changes in your life.

Evaluate Your Stress

Take a minute now to do a simple personal stress evaluation. On a piece of paper, make a list of your negative stressors. This is not something you need to think much about, and should only take a couple of minutes. List anything that comes to mind that you find stressful in your life right now. Remember that a person, a situation, or a circumstance can produce stress; it can be your boss, your partner or spouse, your job, or lack of money. If you are feeling some stress, you should be able to list the cause and may have around six to ten items on your list.

Examine your list and decide which of these stressors you have control over—those you can realistically do something about—and make a check mark next to those. But what about the stressors you have less control over? First, evaluate them to determine how much control you really have. What if one of your stressors is a person; for example, your boss? In this case, you may not be able to take immediate action because you need your job. However, you can work toward accepting this as a stress, and learn to adopt some helpful stress management techniques.

If the stressful person is a partner or spouse, you have some serious introspection ahead. Changes can be made to relieve some of your stress, but this cannot be accomplished alone. You must involve your partner or spouse, though it may not be a good idea to announce that you have discovered they are the source of your stress! You may want to review some of the information on relationships in Chapter 4, but remember that there are unlimited possibilities toward resolving stressful difficulties in any relationship. It does, however, require that you establish a mutual desire toward finding a resolution, and a willingness to honestly communicate and work toward a solution.

For stressors that you may control, make a plan to eliminate or lessen the impact they have on your life. You really do have control, and you must take responsibility for your own stress management. Remember that a component of good mental health is learning how to identify and relieve your personal stressors. This is behavior that can be learned, and with practice you can get better at it. It is a measure of adult maturity.

Critical Thinking Question: What changes can you make in your life to reduce personal stress?

We all have stress triggers, and your goal is to identify those that affect you. For some, a stressor may occur when driving a car. People are often in a hurry, and someone driving slowly may be annoying, especially if you are late and they are impeding your progress. If you are often annoyed while driving, this is a stressor or stress trigger for you. Some people are impatient and dislike waiting in line for anything. If you find yourself getting angry in this situation, you know this is a stressor for you.

You must be accountable for managing your stress—it cannot be the responsibility of someone else. If you are late to your first class because you got up late, don't put the blame on traffic, your inability to find parking, or your roommate. If you had gotten up earlier, you would have been on time and relieved some of your stress. This is an important feature of stress management, but some adults never learn to be personally accountable. They spend a lifetime blaming their stress on other people and life circumstances, which means they will never be able to gain control of their own stress.

Once you have identified some stressors, you may begin to adjust your life to minimize their impact. You have control, but it does take some discipline. Most college students could greatly reduce stress by improving personal time management. Many people have difficulty accurately gauging how long it takes to perform the tasks required in their daily lives. Even if you carefully plan your daily events, there is always something that will interfere with your plans. You end up running out of time, either late for events or unable to get everything done—both are significant stressors. If you are as busy as the typical college student, you may have difficulty catching up once you get behind. This in turn adds more stress.

Image of Health

Reducing Test Stress for Students

One of the most stressful events for a college student is taking a test. Testing can produce a level of stress and anxiety that may affect the ability to concentrate, leading to poor performance. The following guidelines may help reduce text anxiety:

1. Prepare often and early. It is better to study each day for several days before a test, rather than waiting until the last minute. This improves memory retention.

2. Cramming the night before a test is not a productive way to retain information. It causes you to be less alert and unable to recall information.

3. Read the text in small segments and self-test to recall what you have read. Recall is more difficult when reading a large passage. Try it in smaller segments, and your retention should improve.

4. Take practice tests that are available either in the textbook or online. Like anything else, you can improve your test-taking skills with practice.

5. Manage your time carefully when taking a test. Don't spend too much time on any one question—if you are having trouble, move to the next question. If you have time later, you can go back.

6. Carefully read each question completely even if you think you know the answer. This keeps you from misreading a question and selecting a wrong answer.

7. Be careful about changing answers. Your first impression is usually correct.

8. Test taking is a skill. You can improve simply with the experience of taking more tests.

A common stressful progression occurs when a student enrolls in too many courses and is then unable keep up with all of the work required. The student may try to balance the overload of classes by doing the minimal amount of work in each, or may ignore some classes completely in order to prepare for a test or project in another class. This behavior is a prescription for extreme stress and poor performance in classes. Under these conditions, it would be better to drop a class, catch up in the rest of the classes, and ultimately perform much better in the remaining classes.

Notice that the stressful situation described above is caused entirely by the student. However, a student living this stressful nightmare may find plenty of people and events to blame for this dilemma. When faced with a situation that seems extremely stressful, it may be time to mentally step back and try to make an unbiased analysis of the problem. You will then be better able to identify some possible solutions. Individuals who manage their stress well are able to do this, and it is a behavior that can be learned. When you find yourself in a cycle of extreme stress, it is time to take charge of the situation and make some changes. Even if change does not completely alleviate your stress, you are taking a proactive approach, which is better than allowing a continuing cycle of stress to disrupt your life.

As you begin to take charge of your personal stress management, you will get better at it. As you learned in Chapter 1, the first step toward behavior change occurs when an individual commits to making that change. Learning how to manage your stress is one of the most important contributions you can make toward living an optimally healthy life.

Finding Your Own Stress Level

The times that are most stressful in our lives are when there is the most change. This is one of the reasons college students experience so much stress. The decisions you make from ages 18 to 25 can have a profound effect on the rest of your life, including graduating from college or choosing a career, marriage, children, work, and family. The decisions you make regarding your health can also either reduce or accelerate your stress. If you choose to drink excessively, use drugs, smoke, deprive yourself of sleep, and eat poorly, you will have much more distress in your life and more difficulty managing your stress. These are all choices you are responsible for—you are the primary caretaker for your own stress, and you are the only one who is accountable for personal stress management.

Image of Health in Depth

Stress Scales

There are several stress scale instruments available to evaluate personal levels of stress. One of the most widely used is a ten-question Perceived Stress Scale developed by Dr. Sheldon Cohen.[10] Although this is not a diagnostic instrument, it is the most widely used instrument to evaluate the perception of stress.

Perceived Stress Scale

The questions in this scale ask you about your feelings and thoughts *during the last month*. In each case, you will be asked to indicate by circling *how often* you felt or thought a certain way.

0 = Never   1 = Almost Never   2 = Sometimes   3 = Fairly Often   4 = Very Often

1. In the last month, how often have you been upset because of something that happened unexpectedly?
    0   1   2   3   4

2. In the last month, how often have you felt that you were unable to control the important things in your life?
    0   1   2   3   4

3. In the last month, how often have you felt nervous and "stressed"?
    0   1   2   3   4

4. In the last month, how often have you felt confident about your ability to handle your personal problems?
    0   1   2   3   4

5. In the last month, how often have you felt that things were going your way?
    0   1   2   3   4

6. In the last month, how often have you found that you could not cope with all the things that you had to do?
    0   1   2   3   4

7. In the last month, how often have you been able to control irritations in your life?
    0   1   2   3   4

8. In the last month, how often have you felt that you were on top of things?
    0   1   2   3   4

9. In the last month, how often have you been angered because of things that were outside of your control?
    0   1   2   3   4

10. In the last month, how often have you felt difficulties were piling up so high that you could not overcome them?
    0   1   2   3   4

Scoring: Add up your total value and compare it with the average that has been shown for your age or ethnic group. The higher your score, the higher is your stress level. Supporting research has shown that higher scores predict a lack of ability to do some things successfully, like quit smoking, manage blood sugar levels in diabetics, and account for a higher frequency of colds. Higher scores also indicate a likelihood of depression accompanying stressful events.

Men	Average 12.1
Women	Average 13.7
Age 18–29	Average 14.2
Age 30–44	Average 13.0
Age 45–54	Average 12.6
Age 55–64	Average 11.9
Age 65+	Average 12.0

Race Averages	
White	12.8
Black	14.7
Hispanic	14.0
Other	14.1

(Source: Cohen, S., Kamarck, T., and Mermelstein, R. A global measure of perceived stress. *Journal of Health and Social Behavior*, 24: 385–396, 1983.)

Proven Stress Management Techniques

Developing a stress management plan is really about creating personal guidelines to bring order to your life. Certain influences in our daily lives bring either a measure of peace and joy or of stress and despair. A goal of this chapter is to encourage you to identify those factors that fall into the peace and joy category, and reduce those in the stress and despair category.

Consider your typical morning. Do you get up early, exercise, and have time to read the paper or time for spiritual reflection? Do you eat breakfast and allow plenty of time for the tasks you must accomplish before you go to school or work? Are you happy when you get to school or work, or is every morning an unsettling experience? Do you get up late, never exercise or eat breakfast, and seem to be constantly running behind and stressed out about it? Are you in trouble at school or work because you are often late? Are you cranky at work because it seems as if your employer is criticizing you? Are you tired all of the time? Do you hate mornings because they are so stressful? In this case, more peace and joy can happen if you were to just get up earlier!

Managing stress is about making choices, being accountable, and taking responsibility for your personal time management. Try to have a general daily living plan, especially a schedule for eating and sleeping. Although it does not need to be exact, regular eating and sleeping patterns reduce stress.

Motivation Maximizer

Make a Stress-Free Living Space

If you are feeling overwhelmed, unable to imagine how to control the stressors in your life, start with something simple. A strategy that may provide an immediate improvement to your stress level is to make a stress-free living space. Try the following four guidelines for a more stress-free you!

1. Even if you think you are comfortable with clutter, straighten up your room, apartment, or house. Putting your living space in order ensures that you can find the things you need, and creates a more peaceful, less chaotic environment.

2. Have a place for everything, especially keys, your wallet, and any items you use daily. Have a place for everything, and put everything in its place!

3. Keep track of supplies, food, or other items you need to replace before you run out.

4. Create your personal sanctuary that no one else will disturb. This can simply be the corner of a room, but it is yours, and yours alone. Ask others to respect this area.

Remember that as a young adult, it is your responsibility to control your personal living space. Don't underestimate the importance this part of your environment has on your level of stress and personal well-being.

There is no single stress management technique that works for everyone. Those who are good at personal stress management may choose an assortment of techniques that they can adjust according to the stressor. Applying the following techniques may help you manage your personal stress:

- Simplify your life. Learn to say yes to things you want in your life and no to those things you don't want in your life.

- Stop doing so many things by learning personal limitations.

- Exercise daily, even if it means walking just ten minutes per day. In a week you have walked for seventy minutes and relieved some stress.

- Practice deep breathing. See "Image of Health in Depth: Breathing" for a simple breathing exercise that can help you relax.

- Make a realistic time management plan. Use a daily planner, or make a list of the things to accomplish each day. Make sure to plan some personal time for fun and relaxation.

- Manage your finances responsibly. Create a budget and stick to it. If you have trouble managing your finances, a financial advisor or peer counselor may be able to help you develop a plan.

- Resolve any difficulties with a partner or spouse. See Chapter 4 for more information on relationships and communication.

- Explore your spiritual side. Practice meditation, explore an organized religion, visit a park or other natural setting. Be grateful for the fundamentally important and positive things in your life.

- Make time for yourself and for people you enjoy. Social time with friends and family is a wonderful stress reliever.

Image of Health in Depth

Breathing

Some of the best-known models for relaxation and stress relief involve a focus on breathing. Yoga, meditation, tai chi, and massage encourage a focus on breathing. The objective is to clear the mind and increase the flow of oxygen into the body. Taking long, slow, deep breaths creates a calming effect, causing relaxation. For a simple breathing relaxation exercise, do the following:

- Find a quiet place where you won't be interrupted.

- Sit in a comfortable chair, hands in lap, feet flat on floor.

- Close your eyes.

- Concentrate on taking a long inhalation. Count to eight slowly as you breathe in.

- Count to eight slowly as you breathe out.

- Complete at least four inhalations and exhalations using this eight count. Focus on slowly counting and breathing deeply in and out.

- As you continue with deep breathing, focus on your feet, lower back, neck, or any personal stress area.

- Refocus on just breathing for a complete sixteen count.

- If your mind starts to wander, bring your attention back to your breath.

As you practice deep breathing and are able to relax, it may be possible to slow your breathing to as few as four complete breaths (inhalations and exhalations) per minute. Deep breathing is a proven relaxation technique that can help calm you during stressful, busy times.

Unresolved Stress

Sometimes, identifying the real cause of personal stress is difficult. You may exhibit signs and symptoms of stress and seek stress relief in various ways, even though a specific stressor has not been identified. This may be because the stressor cannot be resolved, such as in cases of extreme loss. Loss of a spouse through death or divorce; a home destroyed by fire, tornado or hurricane; a financial crisis because of unemployment; you or a loved one diagnosed with a terminal illness—in these examples, the individual identifies the source of the stress, but may not be able to identify how to resolve such an enormous, life-changing stressor.

No matter how successful you are at stress management, there will be times in your life when you experience either a succession of stressful events, or one major stress event, such as the death of a spouse, partner, or close family member. Stress management is not about eliminating the pain of loss; it is about learning positive coping skills to get you through difficult times. It is not unusual for even the best stress managers to have a difficult time dealing with a major stressful life event. This can lead to the exhaustion phase of general adaptation syndrome, possibly compromising personal immunity to the point where illness is inevitable.

Negative Coping Methods

There are a number of negative coping methods that may seem attractive to individuals having difficulty dealing with the stress in their lives. These are behavior choices that may seem like a positive solution at the time, but can ultimately lead to progressively more stress.

Alcohol and Stress

Although there are many other options for dealing with stress, some people drink alcohol, believing it effectively helps to calm them. For many people, having a glass of wine at the end of a difficult, stressful day is an ideal way to relax. Since alcohol is a central nervous system depressant, it causes the body to slow down, making an individual feel more relaxed.

As a college student, you will have many opportunities to drink alcohol. However, your choice of alcohol as a stress management tool may not be the choice most compatible with being a good student. In addition, many young adults struggle with depression, and alcohol is certainly not the best antidote for depression. Alcohol consumption also takes time away from your busy life. While you are partying and recovering from alcohol use, other students are studying and making more productive use of their time.

Marijuana and Stress

Some people argue that marijuana is an effective stress reliever. Tetrahydrocannabinol (THC), the primary active ingredient in marijuana, causes some people to feel relaxed; however, it makes others hyperactive. The problem with using marijuana for stress relief, aside from it being an illegal drug, is that it affects cognition—analytical ability and especially memory become impaired.[11] Marijuana use is therefore not the most productive stress management solution for college students, for whom success is largely determined by intellectual development and comprehensive memory retention. Additionally, progressive use of both alcohol and marijuana may lead to dependency, requiring more time using these drugs to get the desired effect.

On most college campuses today, students may have easy access to alcohol, marijuana, and other drugs, and it is a personal choice whether to use alcohol or other drugs. Your ability to make a decision compatible with your lifestyle and your goals depends on your willingness to take responsibility for your life, and accept accountability for personal behaviors. Take the time to consider what is really most important for you and your future goals.

Defining Mental Health

We all must learn to manage day-to-day stress, but some people may struggle with deeper issues that go beyond external stressors. Some individuals may have trouble coping with life changes or events, struggling to maintain good mental health.

As you look around your college classroom or spend time with your friends, consider: one in four of you will experience at least one episode of depression or anxiety during your lifetime.[12] Is there anything you can do to help yourself avoid this experience? Fortunately there is, if you are willing to accept responsibility for personal mental health and accountability for personal behavior.

Mental health is the foundation for how we conduct our daily lives. It is how we feel, how we think, and how we cope with both positive and negative events in our lives. Our personal mental health is the result of many factors, including our genetics, the environment we live in, and the choices we make regarding our well-being. Through the decisions we make, we have control over many aspects of personal mental health. Although you cannot guarantee that you are mentally healthy, you can choose to create a personal environment that fosters good mental health. This is the ability to create a positive living environment that makes you happy, productive, capable of intimacy, and at peace with your place in the world.

Psychosocial Health

Psychosocial health refers to the dimensions of wellness that affect mental health, including emotional, intellectual, social, and spiritual wellness. These dimensions are varied, personal, and unique to each individual. Differences in ethnicity, cultural diversity, gender, and life experiences generate a unique mental health blueprint for each person.

Key Term

Psychosocial health: The interrelation of social factors and individual thought and behavior, including the emotional, intellectual, social, and spiritual wellness components.

▶**Critical Thinking Question**: Describe how you can find balance in your personal life that will allow you to function at an optimum level.

Psychosocial health, like physical health, is not static. You do not feel the same every day—there are ups and downs, depending on variables relating to your current experiences.

Because life is unpredictable and dynamic, personal mental health depends on your ability to adapt and cope with changing situations and circumstances. For most people, this requires the ability to make minor adjustments so that the important elements of your life remain stable. The good and challenging aspects of marriage or a relationship, the loss of a job, a promotion, or a new baby are typical changes that require personal adjustments to ensure good mental health. Sometimes, changes in your life may be more challenging and require greater coping skills, such as the breakup of a marriage or relationship, or the illness or death of a loved one.

Under any of these circumstances, mental health is challenged. People have varying responses to crisis events, reacting and coping differently. Ideally, you will find a balance in your personal life that will allow you to grow, adapt, and function at an optimal level. Finding balance

can be facilitated by learning how to create a positive living environment, how to set emotional boundaries for yourself and others, and how to find what makes you happy and productive.

▶**Challenge Question**: List and describe the four psychosocial components of mental health.

The Transition to Adulthood

Making the transition from adolescence to adulthood has profound implications for personal mental health. When making the transition from high school to college or work, many people find that they are making independent decisions about their lives for the first time. Depending on their level of maturity, they may embrace this challenge and grow emotionally, or they may falter and have difficulty coping.

For some, the new freedom that comes with adult responsibilities is tantalizing. You choose to do what you want, simply because you can. Adolescents may show responsible development and accountability, but may not always make the best decisions. Because they place a high value on peer acceptance, they may be easily influenced by their friends. This new freedom can be a prescription for anxiety and depression, two categories of mental illness that affect a large percentage of adolescents and young adults.

Although some adolescents may feel their parents are interfering with their lives, the maturation process occurs more smoothly with parental involvement. In fact, it is a time when good parenting and other mentally healthy role models are essential.

Support during adolescence comes primarily from parents, but can be enhanced by any authority figure, especially one whom the adolescent respects. Ideally, the mature adult helps bring mental and emotional stability to the adolescent's evolving mental health. These individuals become touchstones of support while allowing the adolescent freedom to grow, develop, and move toward becoming an autonomous young adult. All adults evolve through this process, and no adult experiences this evolution in the same way or at the same pace.

Two Diverse College Experiences

The following describes two experiences of coping with change and evolving maturity.

Josh's Story

Josh was very excited to start a new chapter in life. He enjoyed high school and was ready to move on to college. As a result of his success in soccer, he received an athletic scholarship to a small university hundreds of miles from his home. Although Josh had not done well academically in high school, the recruiter told him that he would receive counseling and tutoring to help him stay on track academically and remain eligible for the soccer team.

The first semester was great fun for Josh. After going through rush week, he joined a fraternity and soon discovered the opportunities to drink and party every night. Josh loved to party and enjoyed the attention from the girls who were attracted to him. College life was better than he expected, particularly because his parents weren't telling him what to do. Josh believed his parents had never understood him, and was happy to be independent and away from them.

At the end of the first semester, the coach reprimanded Josh for his poor grades. He was told he must improve his grades and become a more responsible student if he wanted to stay on the soccer team. The coach asked how frequently Josh had seen his counselor and used the tutoring services. He told his coach that his schedule and their open appointments did not match up; this could not be seen as his fault! Later, Josh complained to his friends that his coach was so old, he just could not relate to college life. Josh decided he would at least try to attend classes regularly. The 8 a.m. class was a problem—he either slept in, or was still suffering from too much alcohol from the night before. Josh considered that if his friends would stop throwing these all-night parties, academic life might get easier.

Before long, Josh was on academic probation and was not allowed to play soccer. He was doing poorly in his classes and was becoming increasingly depressed. The only time he really felt any relief was when he was drinking, so he started drinking earlier in the day.

Josh was depressed, drinking more frequently, and finding that college was not much fun anymore. He discovered he really didn't have any friends unless he was drinking, and considered dropping out of college to return home. This depressed him even more, because he knew he would be seen as a failure by his parents, family, and friends. He could not understand how his life could take such a devastating turn in such a short time. ■

Andy's Story

Andy was very excited to attend college. His high school experience was positive, but he was ready to move away from his hometown. He was a good high school basketball player, and was recruited to play on the college basketball team. Before fall classes began, he received and read the recommended reading list from his college, realizing it helped prepare him for his first semester classes. He applied for and received college financial aid and got a part-time job working in a coffee house on campus. He joined a fraternity because it was more economical housing, but he was alarmed at how frequently his fraternity brothers drank and stayed up late. Because of the goals he had set for himself and the promises he had made to his parents, he decided not to participate in the heavy drinking. He made friends with many interesting women in his classes and at the coffee house where he worked, and joined a study group with some members of his basketball team.

He also spent some time deciding on his immediate goals for college. He narrowed down the choice of a possible major and minor and enrolled in classes in each discipline. He made an appointment with a college counselor and developed an education plan to help him stay on track for graduation. Because he was very busy with a full load a classes, his part-time job, and playing on the basketball team, he organized his week into realistic time frames.

Andy enjoyed the discipline his time management practices required, and he was careful to allow some time for relaxation and fun. Although busy, he did well in his classes, met many new friends, and managed to save a little money for semester break. He looked forward to visiting his family and friends in his hometown over the holidays, but after a few days found himself longing to return to college to resume his new life. Andy was thrilled by all that he was learning and accomplishing in college, and felt empowered because he was on the right track, and really felt in control of his life. ■

▶**Critical Thinking Question**: Why is Josh having so much difficulty? What can he do about it?

▶**Critical Thinking Question**: What are the keys to Andy's success? What can you apply to your life from this example?

Although Josh and Andy have similar backgrounds, Josh exhibits the characteristics of adolescence, while Andy exhibits the characteristics of adulthood. Josh is eager and open to opportunities for fun, and there is little adult influence to encourage him to act responsibly. He is on his own, accountable for his own behavior. Like many adolescents, Josh chooses to focus on immediate gratification, not on the consequences of his actions. Even when his life starts to fall apart, when he is on academic probation, dropped from the soccer team, and drinking heavily, he still does not accept accountability for his personal behavior. He places the blame on other people and situations, never on himself. These are all characteristics of immature behavior. At this point in his life, Josh needs more direction and nurturing—he is unable to be successful on his own. Andy is successful primarily because he set goals, managed his time well, and made better choices. His success in these endeavors built self-esteem and self-confidence; he is empowered because his personal plan is working successfully.

Since young people mature from adolescence to adulthood at different rates, not everyone can be expected to be successful in college or in the workforce right after high school. However, there are skills and behaviors that can be learned to enhance student success, including:

- *Setting both short- and long-term goals.* Long-term goals may include graduating with a college degree or completing a certificate for employment. Short-term goals include completing a class with a passing grade or better.

- *Establishing personal priorities.* Setting priorities according to your personal interests.

- *Learning how to manage time.* Making sure there is enough time in each day for all of your responsibilities, while still leaving some time just for you.

- *Establishing regular sleep patterns.* Most people need 7–8 hours of sleep each night. It is important to go to sleep around the same time each day.

- *Making time for you.* It is important to have a little time each day to listen to music, exercise, read, or anything else you enjoy.

- *Finding time to exercise.* Exercise is good for stress management and weight control, and provides your body and brain with more oxygen.

- *Learning to regulate and improve diet.* Regular patterns of eating a healthy diet make you feel better, have more energy, and help regulate your weight.

- *Making time for fun with friends and family.* It is important to have fun. Surround yourself with people who make you laugh and with whom you enjoy spending time.

Maslow's Hierarchy of Needs

Good mental health depends on an environment in which a foundation of basic needs is met in order to achieve higher-level, more complex human growth needs.

In 1954, Abraham Maslow developed a theory to explain human motivation. This theory, called a hierarchy of human needs, is illustrated by a pyramid consisting of four deficiency needs and one growth need. The needs are physiological, safety, belongingness and love, and esteem. Maslow described deficiency needs in terms of potency: the more powerful needs are at the base of the pyramid; The less powerful needs are those higher-level needs that are distinctively human, and only humans are capable of achieving higher-level needs.

With deficiency needs, the individual feels anxious if these needs are not met, but feels nothing if the needs are met. As a growth need, **self-actualization** is based on the premise that deficiency needs must be met before a higher level or growth can be realized. Self-actualization includes morality, creativity, spontaneity, the ability to problem-solve, lack of prejudice, acceptance of facts, and becoming all you can be. In 1970, two lower-level growth needs were added: aesthetic needs, and a need to know and understand. According to Maslow, the fulfillment of growth needs provide further motivation, allowing individuals to achieve their full potential. An additional higher-level growth need was added: **transcendence**, a state in which individuals not only realize their highest potential, but also the full potential of human beings at large.[12]

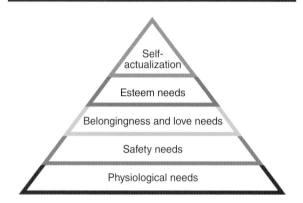
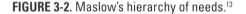

FIGURE 3-2. Maslow's hierarchy of needs.[13]

Maslow's basic premise is that as individuals satisfy deficiency needs and progress up the pyramid, they move into of the growth need of self-actualization and self-transcendence. Reaching self-actualization means finding self-fulfillment and reaching their highest potential. Self-transcendence means moving beyond the ego, helping others find self-fulfillment and realize their potential.[14]

Influences on Mental Health

Personal **self-esteem**, outlook on life, and **self-worth** all contribute to your personal level of mental health, your happiness, the way you view the world, and the way you live. In general, personal outlook is formed by all the life events you have experienced up to this point. Some of these events are of your own choosing, but many reflect the unpredictable nature of life. These life events are both positive and negative, are different for everyone, and have made you the person you are today. Acknowledging your personal life history is of fundamental importance in assessing your personal mental health. The responsibility of changing your life in ways that will enhance your mental health is almost entirely yours.

Social Support

Your primary level of social support includes those with whom you live and spend time with on a daily basis. This is your inner circle, and should consist of one or more people you can depend on and trust completely. Your secondary level of social support is made up of friends and extended family members with whom you may have frequent contact but do not live. These individuals can have an important influence on your mental health, because they may be more positive substitutes for your primary social support. It is not unusual, especially in dysfunctional families, to place a great deal of reliance on a secondary support group because those individuals are dependable and caring. In a dysfunctional family, the characteristics of dependability, caring, and compassion are usually absent, making your secondary support system even more important.

A major influence on personal mental health is your family. Is your family loving, nurturing, encouraging, and generally very supportive of you? Or, is your family dysfunctional, uninvolved, distant, and generally not supportive? Perhaps your family is not a presence in your life, due to death, divorce, or estrangement. Maybe your relationship with your family is a combination of some of these factors. It is important to recognize the pluses and minuses in your family, identifying factors you consider necessary when you have your own family. Since your family is your primary circle of social support, it is important to identify family characteristics for which you are grateful, and those you would like to improve. Responsibility for personal mental wellness involves recognizing the impact your family has on your mental health.

Self-Esteem

Learning how to build self-esteem is important in developing adult-level maturity. Self-esteem is the result of life events that have influenced your confidence in your value as an individual reflecting feelings of self-worth. It is essential to feel good about yourself and to recognize your self-worth. By the time you reach college, you have had many experiences that have contributed to your current level of self-esteem. Influences on self-esteem come from parents or other authority figures, and can be positive or negative. Building self-esteem depends on intrinsic values that develop differently for everyone, such as, self-acceptance, self-responsibility, assertiveness, integrity, and living purposefully with awareness. One of the best ways to improve self-esteem is to learn how to set goals.

▶**Critical Thinking Question**: Identify some experiences in your life that have influenced your self-esteem, both positively and negatively.

Goal setting involves creating a realistic plan you can put into action in order to accomplish a goal, and is important to help you know where you are going, to identify how to get there, and to know when you have arrived. Start with goals you know you can accomplish. When you have made a commitment to accomplish a goal, you must do what is necessary to be successful.

Accomplishing a goal is a taste of success, or a "win," and it is quite empowering. This is not just an exercise in goal setting, although it is instructive in teaching you how to set realistic goals. It is really a way of building self-esteem or self-confidence, and is behavior that can be learned. As you set and accomplish goals, you become more skilled at setting goals and gain a realistic sense of what you can and cannot accomplish successfully. Those who learn to do this have more self-confidence, are able to set realistic goals, and tend to be very successful in their endeavors.

Unfortunately, some students seem to set themselves up for failure by either setting unrealistic goals or not setting any goals at all. These students enroll in too many classes without much thought about the work required to be successful. They have poor time-management skills, seldom completing things on time. They have not identified specific goals, so they have no plan to stay on track and believe they can catch up after falling behind in all of their classes. They are initially very surprised, then angry when they do poorly in the majority of their classes. It is easy to blame this on the instructor, the textbook, poorly designed tests, irritating classmates—anything but their own behavior. They may quickly fall below minimum academic standards for the college and be placed on academic probation. They may now feel a sense of failure, have lost confidence in their abilities, and wonder if college is really for them. Throughout this experience, there is little sense of responsibility and accountability for personal actions.

This type of behavior is personally destructive and can become a pattern that overlaps in all areas of life, building negative self-esteem. It can best be addressed by setting goals and improving time management skills. The importance of setting goals, even if they seem minimal, should not be underestimated. It is the process that is important, as it teaches you how to have a more orderly life, note your accomplishments, and identify your successes.

If you are a student using this textbook in a college-level introductory health course, you have already established a few short-term goals: learning about health, satisfying a college requirement, and completing the course. It is important to recognize short-term goals, in order to feel a sense of accomplishment when you complete them, thereby improving self-esteem. Typical long-term goals for a college student are graduation or the completion of a certificate for training and employment in your chosen career. You should recognize either as a major accomplishment, which should bring an element of joy to your life and empower you with self-confidence and positive self-esteem.

When you begin to have a more ordered life, your mental health will improve. You will be more organized and be able to accomplish more. By setting goals, you will have a better life plan, because you have learned how to chart the direction your life is taking. Think of short-term goals as guideposts on a path toward greater achievement and success.

Motivation Maximizer

Taking Charge of Your Life

If you have decided to take responsibility for your health and be accountable for the decisions you make, you are ready to make you the number-one person in your life. This does not mean you don't care about others; it means you have decided to be the best you can be. Giving 100 percent to every goal means you must set priorities and determine the people and resources available to help you reach your goals. Visualize being the best you can be in:

- Your classes

- Your family

- Your relationships

- Your work

Giving 100 percent to what is important to you enriches your life, as well as the lives of those around you. It makes you a more giving person, enables you to keep your life in balance, and most important, it makes you successful. You really can accomplish more and reach your goals, building self-confidence and self-esteem and making you feel like a winner.[15] When this happens, you know you really have taken charge of your life.

Spirituality

The spiritual dimension of psychosocial health is personal and unique to each individual. For those who embrace this dimension, spirituality can have a very positive influence on mental health. It is a tool that can bring stability, rejuvenation, stress relief, and comfort. Personal expression of spirituality can be found in many contexts. It can be organized religion, meditation, yoga, tai chi, a walk in nature, a good run, or a combination of any of these, and more. Spirituality is both a personal belief system and personal behavior that makes us feel well.

Because it is restorative, spirituality is especially effective for psychosocial wellness. For individuals who embrace a spiritual component of wellness, personal spiritual expression has a grounding effect. It is a dependable antidote for the stress of daily life, bringing a feeling of calmness or peace. It is a human dimension of wellness that can be developed by anyone; it is part of self-care and requires that you take responsibility for your own personal spiritual wellness and psychological health.

Self-Directed versus Other-Directed

One component that affects decision-making during early adulthood is whether an individual is more **self-directed** or **other-directed**. As children, we are directed by our parents and other adults in positions of authority. As children grow, develop emotionally, and become more self-sufficient, they begin the transition toward becoming more self-directed. Adolescence is often a time of great conflict between parents and teenagers, arising over who is making decisions for whom. This is a natural process that allows teenagers to learn how to make important decisions for themselves. Becoming self-directed requires self-responsibility and accountability, and is a growth process that occurs at a different pace for everyone.

Ideally, by early adulthood this transition is mostly in place, and the individual is self-directed, able to make responsible decisions, and not afraid of being accountable for those decisions. However, there are some adults who are never completely self-directed. These individuals have difficulty making decisions, and in being accountable for the decisions they do make. Adults who are other-directed generally have lower self-esteem, lack confidence in their abilities, and often have difficulty in relationships, conflict with their families, and unsatisfying experiences in the workplace.

If you recognize that you are not completely self-directed and think it is important to change, you must examine your relationship with those who are making decisions for you. It may be a parent, spouse or partner, or friend. Becoming self-directed is a gradual process that occurs by first noticing the level of decision-making being made for you, then making an effort to assume responsibility for your own decision-making.

Key Terms

Self-directed: Able to make decisions for oneself, autonomous.

Other-directed: Depend on others to make decisions for you.

Happiness

Choosing to be happy is part of being self-directed, and is the responsibility of each individual. Although it is a common misconception that personal happiness is somehow the responsibility of others in our lives, much personal happiness is of our own choosing. Laughter and humor are known to defuse stress and contribute to feelings of wellbeing and improved mental health. In *Anatomy of an Illness as Perceived by the Patient*, his seminal work on the relationship between laughter and healing, Norman Cousins describes the importance of laughter.[16] Another key to happiness is gratitude: it is important to recognize and be grateful for what is important and positive in your life. It is also important to convey these feelings of gratitude to your family and others for whom you are grateful. Ideally, this is a reciprocal arrangement, but reciprocity should not be a requirement.

We all have different resources and experiences to build a personal happiness template. Our parents and home life, our current life situation, and even our family tree influence us. If you come from a family of generally happy people, you have learned the value of happiness and are more likely to strive toward achieving happiness for yourself. If your family was grumpy and depressed, you may have learned this behavior and therefore may be more likely to be unhappy.

Decision-Making

We all know someone who always seems to make the right decisions under almost any circumstances. How did that person get so good at this? It takes practice, planning, and courage to listen to yourself, to trust your gut feelings

and learn from mistakes. And it can be learned. As you begin to trust yourself and start making good decisions, you become empowered, increasing feelings of self-worth. Even when, after making a poor decision, you learn to avoid making the same mistake again, you are gaining confidence in your decision-making abilities.

Gut feeling is sometimes called intuition, an innate sense of knowing what is right. You will not always be correct, but you can learn to trust your intuitive sense and may find that you are very often more right than wrong. All humans have the ability to develop personal intuition, and all of us can expand this dimension in our lives. Taking control raises self-esteem and makes you a more confident, self-directed person.

Mental Disorders

Some of the volatility in life is self-induced. This is especially true for young people of high school and college age. Adolescents and young adults that lack fully developed adult maturity may not have good coping skills, and may not easily adapt to changing situations. The inability to set realistic goals, along with poor time management skills, nutrition, and sleep habits, are detrimental to good mental health. If drugs and alcohol are part of a lifestyle, the prospects for good mental health diminish considerably, possibly even causing poor mental health in those who would otherwise be mentally healthy.

By the time you reach college, you have probably been exposed to a few individuals who exhibit symptoms of poor mental health—you may even consider yourself to be one of them. You have also probably noticed that there can be a stigma attached to such an individual. If someone you know is in an accident and breaks his arm, you can relate to the pain and discomfort this person is feeling. But if someone you know must be hospitalized because he suffers from depression and has attempted suicide, it may be more difficult to imagine yourself in his place, unless you have experienced this yourself.

For the mentally healthy, the thought of struggling with mental illness may be troubling, and not viewed the same as a physical illness. This is the primary reason that a stigma against mental illness exists: mental health is viewed differently from physical health. To experience physical illness or injury is a condition from which most of us will recover. You probably even know what to expect.

If you break an arm, you wear a cast, the arm heals, and you are back to normal. Mental illness is maybe more frightening. You don't know what to expect, and treatment and recovery depend on many variables. You fear that perhaps you may not recover, or may not recover completely, or that mental illness will change you in an unpredictable and undesirable way. Most people are also reluctant to disclose details of personal mental illness to friends and family, because they expect a negative reaction. Although there is much you can do to influence the state of your own mental health, in some cases poor mental health persists.

▶**Challenge Question**: Explain why some people view mental illness differently from physical illness.

There are many different types of mental disorders, and some are misunderstood. The following section describes the most common types of disorders: depression, mania, anxiety disorders, and psychoses. Although it is not a mental illness, there is also a discussion on suicide, since individuals who are experiencing a mental illness are more prone to suicide.

Depression and Mania

In the United States, more than twenty-six million people experience depressive illness each year.[17] Most of these individuals will go undiagnosed and untreated. Although individuals who are depressed may be aware of their depression, many do not seek treatment because they do not think they can be helped. The National Institutes for Mental Health (NIMH) describes **depressive disorder** as an illness that involves the body, mood, and thoughts. It affects the way a person eats and sleeps, the way he feels about himself, and the way he thinks about things. A depressive disorder is not the same as a passing blue mood, nor is it a sign of personal weakness, or a condition that can be willed or wished away. People with a depressive illness cannot merely "pull themselves together" and get better. Without treatment, symptoms can last for weeks, months, or years. Appropriate treatment, however, can help most people who suffer from depression.[18]

The NIMH recognizes three types of depression: **major depression**, **minor depression** (or **dysthymia**), and **bipolar disorder**.

Key Terms

Depressive disorder: A group of symptoms that reflects a sad or irritable mood beyond normal sadness or grief, characterized by increasingly severe symptoms of a longer duration.

Major depression: Severe, disabling depression that keeps a person from functioning.

Minor depression (dysthymia): Minor depression that does not seriously disable the person, but keeps him from functioning at an optimal level.

Bipolar disorder: Formerly called manic depression, characterized by severe mood swings from high (manic) to low (depression), with episodes of normal moods in between.

Major Depression

Though a major, disabling depressive illness may occur only once in a lifetime, it is far more likely to be a recurring issue. Although major depression may be found in families over several generations, it may also occur in people who have no family history of depression. The risk of a genetic predisposition for depression is only 3 percent; other brain chemistry and environmental factors are usually the cause.[19]

There are many symptoms of depression and mania, and not everyone who suffers from depression experiences all symptoms. The severity of symptoms can vary over time with each individual. Symptoms of depression may include:

- Persistent sad, anxious, or "empty" mood.

- Feelings of hopelessness, pessimism.

- Feelings of guilt, worthlessness, helplessness.

- Loss of interest or pleasure in activities that were once enjoyed, including sex.

- Decreased energy, fatigue, being "slowed down."

- Difficulty concentrating, remembering, making decisions.

- Insomnia, early morning awakening, or oversleeping.

- Loss of appetite and weight loss, or overeating and weight gain.

- Thoughts of death or suicide; suicide attempts.

- Restlessness, irritability.

- Persistent physical symptoms that do not respond to treatment, such as headaches, digestive disorders, and chronic pain.

Bipolar Disorder

Bipolar disorder (also known as manic-depressive disorder) is not as common as other depressive illnesses. This disorder involves extreme mood changes from severe highs (mania) to severe lows (depression). The manic state may include delusions of grandeur, such as when the individual has elevated expectations of future accomplishments that are impossible to achieve. It may also include episodes of unacceptable behavior toward others in a public situation. Symptoms of mania may include the following:

- Abnormal or excessive elation.

- Unusual irritability.

- Decreased need for sleep.

- Grandiose ideas.

- Increased talking.

- Racing thoughts.

- Increased sexual desire.

- Markedly increased energy.

- Poor judgment.

- Inappropriate social behavior.

Minor Depression

The most common mental illness among college students is minor depression. Symptoms of mild depression are not disabling, but those with minor depression do not function adequately or feel well. Unfortunately, it is possible for minor depression to progress to major depression when there is a consistent increase in the frequency, duration, and intensity of depressive episodes.

Minor depression is generally linked to a feeling of loss, thoughts that life is spiraling out of control, and a feeling of powerlessness or impending doom. People who are depressed usually have no energy, may sleep more or be unable to sleep, and are not interested in things that previously gave them pleasure. The depressed person feels unable to control the direction of his life, and does not know what to do about it. These are feelings that make a person susceptible to binge behavior involving food, alcohol, or drugs, all of which are poor coping mechanisms the depressed person uses to cause temporarily relief.

For some people, depression may be triggered by a loss. Typical causes include:

- Death of a spouse, partner, or close family member.

- Breakup of a relationship.

- Loss of a job.

- Failure to get a promotion or failure to perform well academically.

- Loss of a family pet.

- Moving, leaving friends, a familiar house and neighborhood.

Depression can be caused by a series of traumatic events, and exacerbated by low self-esteem and the inability to cope with major life changes. An inability to adapt to change can be a cause of depression, and can be problematic at any age. For the young adult, however, the magnitude of change is greater than at any other time during life, except perhaps for changes that occur at the end of life.

Consider the life changes that can occur during the ages of 18–30. The quantity and quality of education and choice of career are decisions that are typically made during this time. Those who are better educated are generally healthier, or at least more knowledgeable about personal health. They also earn more money during their lifetimes, and will therefore have better access to health care. Young adults will also make decisions about whether to get married and have children. Having children will greatly impact your life for 18–20 years or longer, and may cause the delay of some of your personal goals. A career decision may require relocation, possibly to a new part of the country, or an unfamiliar part of the world.

Or perhaps your life will change unpredictably because of a choice you made without really considering the consequences of that choice. The following three examples are all possible real-life scenarios that can affect young adults.

1. You choose to have unprotected sex, and discover that you are pregnant or responsible for fathering a child.

2. You choose to temporarily quit college because you need to work to make a car or rent payment.

3. You choose to drop out of college and work to help your family, who are experiencing a financial crisis.

In each of these examples, a choice must be made that will change the direction of your life. If you have established goals and are committed to them, you will need to make adjustments, but you can still accomplish your goals. If you have not established personal goals and have not really considered what you will do with your future, these life-changing events will cause you to move in unplanned directions and may lead you to feel that your life is spinning out of control.

▶**Challenge Question:** Describe some of the causes of mild depression.

Image of Health in Depth

Don't Become a Victim

It is important to recognize that you have the ability to adapt to changes in your life, especially changes that result from the decisions you make. The ability to adapt to change is a sign of good mental health, whereas difficulty adapting to changes in your life can lead to depression and anxiety. This may create the feeling that you are a victim of circumstance and powerless to control your life. If you are not taking responsibility for your decisions and are not accountable for your actions, it is easy to fall into the role of being a victim.

- Victims are not accountable, blaming the misfortune in their lives on someone else or on their life circumstances.

- Victims do not accept responsibility for their unfortunate life situations, even if caused by decisions they made.

- Victims have low self-esteem and little self-confidence in their ability to rectify their life situations.

- Victims prefer to be other-directed because they do not trust their ability to make decisions for themselves.

- Victims are likely candidates for depression and anxiety because they see no way of improving their life situation.

▶**Critical Thinking Question:** How does a person who is living the life of a victim break out of this destructive cycle?

An individual may progress from a cyclical pattern of ups and downs in depression to a fairly constant state of depression—a sign that the individual may be moving toward a major depression. Indications that depression is becoming more severe include answering "all of the time" or "most of the time" to two or more of the following:

- So sad that nothing can cheer you up

- Nervous

- Hopeless

- Worthless

- Restless

- Everything is an effort

At this point, it becomes difficult for the individual to cope with life, and medical or psychiatric intervention and possibly hospitalization may be required. The depressed individual may also verbalize thoughts of suicide.

Suicide

USA National Suicide Hotlines
Call toll free, 24 hours a day, seven days a week.
(800) 448-3000
TTY (800) 448-7833
http://suicidehotlines.com/national.html

Although suicide is not a mental disorder, this important topic deserves attention because individuals who are experiencing a mental disorder are more prone to suicide. For the extremely depressed person, suicide may seem like the only viable option. A suicidal person sees his life as spiraling out of control and completely hopeless. Suicide is also a possibility for people with other mental disorders that are not depressive in nature.

It is important to seriously acknowledge talk of suicide. When a depressed individual begins to talk about suicide, it means he has probably been thinking about it for some time. Signs that a suicide attempt is imminent include giving away treasured possessions, surreptitiously saying goodbye to family and friends, and isolation from everyday life. Even at this critical stage of depression, help is available and treatment can be successful. Often, these signs are not recognized or taken seriously until after a suicide or a suicide attempt.

Just as most mental health disorders can be treated, suicide is considered a preventable public health problem. It is estimated that for every suicide death, there are eight to twenty-five suicide attempts. Suicide is the third leading cause of death among 15–24-year-olds, and four times as many males as females die from suicide in this age group. Ninety percent of people who kill themselves have a mental disorder, a substance abuse problem, or both. The majority suffer from depression, and the drugs of choice are alcohol and cocaine.[20]

Risk factors for suicide include:

- Diagnosed or undiagnosed depression.

- Alcohol, cocaine, or other drug abuse.

- Family history of depression and substance abuse.

- Family violence including emotional, physical, and sexual abuse.

- Firearms in the home.

- Family history of incarceration.

- Exposure to or awareness of suicidal behavior.

In 2005, more than 32,000 suicides occurred in the U.S. for all age groups. This is the equivalent of 88 suicides per day, or one suicide every 16 minutes. Firearms are the most commonly used method of suicide among males, and poisoning is the most common method among females.[21]

Image of Health in Depth

Incidence of Suicide by Age and Gender
2005, United States
Suicide Injury Deaths and Rates per 100,000
All Races, Both Sexes, Ages 15 to 24

SEX	NUMBER OF DEATHS	POPULATION	CRUDE RATE	AGE-ADJUSTED RATE**
Males	3,498	21,661,634	16.15	15.97
Females	714	20,454,361	3.49	3.47
Total	4,212	42,115,995	10.00	–

(Source: CDC, National Center for Injury Prevention and Control, 2005.)

It is important to note that although traumatic life events, when combined with depression and drug use, may lead to suicidal thoughts or even attempts, millions of Americans with several risk factors will never attempt suicide. Suicide is not considered a typical response, even to extreme stress. However, many people do not seek treatment for depression because they don't think they can be helped, and may not even recognize that they are depressed. Because ninety percent of suicides have a history of depression, it is very important to seek treatment for depression for yourself or a family member. Correct diagnosis and treatment for depression has the potential to save many lives.

There are many medical and therapeutic options to treat depression. Brain chemical changes, especially a lack of serotonin, is evident in people who are depressed. A low level of serotonin has also been discovered in the brains of suicide victims post mortem.[22] Many depressed people are helped through individual or group psychotherapy, where reasons for the depression can be explored and potentially alleviated. Electroconvulsive Therapy (ECT) has also been used to successfully treat depression, and when successful, works faster than drug treatment options. There is always a preventative option for suicide.

▶**Challenge Question**: Describe some of the risk factors for suicide.

Anxiety Disorders; Obsessions and Compulsions

In any given year, approximately 40 million Americans will have an **anxiety disorder**. These disorders often occur in conjunction with depression or substance abuse. The average age for the first episode is 21.5 years, and most individuals experience more than one type of anxiety disorder—a term that is sometimes applied to extreme stress or some of the specific disorders described in the next section.

> **Key Term**
>
> **Anxiety disorder**: A psychoneurotic disorder, sometimes called free-floating anxiety, characterized by anxiety unattached to any obvious source and often accompanied by physiological manifestations of fear.

Panic Disorder

Panic disorder, characterized by panic attacks, occurs when a person becomes fearful about something that is not dangerous. There may be anxiety about an event or situation that has not yet happened, or the panic attack happens during a stressful event or experience.

Agoraphobia

Agoraphobia commonly occurs in people who suffer from panic attacks. The individual is afraid of being in a place or situation from which they cannot escape, or in which they cannot get help in the event of a panic attack. Approximately 2 million American adults suffer from this disorder.[23] Because of this fear, many sufferers avoid situations that require them to be alone outside their home. They refuse to travel by car, bus, or plane, and dislike crowded places.

> **Key Terms**
>
> **Panic disorder**: An anxiety disorder characterized by severe recurring episodes of fear and terror.
>
> **Agoraphobia**: A fear of being in places where help may not be available, including fear of being outside, in crowds, or on bridges.

Post-Traumatic Stress Syndrome

Post-traumatic stress syndrome (PTSS) is caused by a specific real-life trauma that may compromise mental health. Some people are victims of child abuse, assault, rape, military combat, or serious accident or illness.

The post traumatic time period for recovery varies for each individual, possibly taking years, depending on the debilitating effects of the trauma. In the early stages of recovery, trauma victims may have difficulty sleeping. Even while awake they may be unable rid themselves of images of the trauma, and in some cases, images and thoughts of the trauma become an obsession. Intellectually, a trauma victim knows that replaying the trauma in thoughts and dreams is impeding the healing process, but feels powerless to eliminate the images from his mind. For most people, elapsed time is a great healer. Support of family and friends, counseling, and a return to a normal routine of life may eventually cause the destructive thoughts, images, and dreams to lessen and resolve completely. Occasionally, even years after recovery and with a return to good mental health, something may trigger a flashback to the trauma, which can cause a temporary relapse. In some cases, the individual may experience the same symptoms that occurred right after the initial trauma, but the recovery period is generally much shorter.

Victims of assault or rape often suffer from PTSS. A woman who is raped does not want to have thoughts and dreams about the rape. Unfortunately, though, as a result of this trauma, it is not uncommon for her to develop compulsive, frequent thoughts in which she replays the rape in excruciating detail. The trauma of rape has a residual effect on everyone who is emotionally close to the rape victim, such as her partner, spouse, or parents. Recovery takes time, and is facilitated by a mutual support system and counseling.

Many military veterans returning from war suffer from PTSS. Coming home from a war zone and trying to resume a normal life is a difficult adjustment for everyone, including the family and friends of the returning veteran. Mental health is compromised, and some individuals have a difficult time making the transition from a combat lifestyle to a residential community and family life. Factors that may facilitate a post-war immersion into American society include a strong family or social support system, as well as contact with other veterans who are also having difficulty adjusting to a non-military life.

> **Key Term**
>
> **Post-traumatic stress syndrome**: Persistent mental and emotional stress occurring as a result of injury or severe psychological shock.

Obsessions and Compulsions

Some individuals who suffer from post-traumatic stress syndrome (PTSS) are obsessed with recurring thoughts and dreams of the trauma they experienced. In this case, an **obsession** is an unwanted thought, replaying in an endless loop and negatively affecting mental health. Although often associated with PTSS, some individuals have obsessive thoughts unrelated to a trauma. For example, stalkers have obsessive thoughts about individuals who may not even know them. People also describe obsessions with food, gambling, a person, a workplace, shopping, sex, and exercise. In most cases, individuals recognize their obsessions, but seem unable to stop the obsessive thoughts. When these thoughts interfere with daily life, it can be detrimental to mental health.

A **compulsion** is an unwanted act that is difficult or impossible for an individual to control. Compulsions often work in tandem with obsessions. For a stalker who has obsessive thoughts about a person, the next step may be to physically stalk the person. The stalker is now acting on both an obsession and a compulsion. For movie stars and other famous people, being physically stalked by a fan that is obsessed with them is not an uncommon experience.

A compulsion can also present itself through a repetitive pattern. This could be a task that must be completed in a specific order and in tedious detail, such as dressing in the morning, when everything must be put on in a certain order and manner. Another example is excessive hand washing, in which the individual feels compelled to wash his hands after touching anything. This may involve hand washing for hours each day, becoming so time-consuming that it is disabling. A compulsion can also involve counting, tapping, or teeth clicking. The compulsive individual will tap or click a pattern that must be completed. This pattern can be long or extensive, and is certainly a distraction from normal functioning. Treatment involves convincing the compulsive individual to break the pattern through therapeutic intervention. When it is difficult for the person to function in daily life, both obsessions and compulsions are severe.

> **Key Terms**
>
> **Obsession**: An idea or feeling that completely occupies the mind.
>
> **Compulsion**: An irresistible urge to behave in a certain way, especially against one's conscious wishes.

When obsessions and compulsions become a regular pattern of thoughts and behaviors that are senseless and distressing, the group of symptoms is called obsessive-compulsive disorder (OCD). People with OCD have a difficult time overcoming these symptoms, and because they try to keep repetitive thoughts and behaviors secret, they often do not seek treatment. Symptoms typically begin during teenage years or young adulthood.

Image of Health in Depth

As Good as It Gets

In the movie *As Good as it Gets*, Jack Nicholson plays the part of an obsessive-compulsive character named Melvin. He lives his life as a semi-recluse and has a series of patterns for most of his daily living. He will not step on any cracks in the sidewalk while walking to his favorite restaurant. He visits this restaurant every day, sitting in the same seat each time. He brings his own utensils and insists on the same waitress. He has an extensive routine for locking the many locks on his apartment door. He is alarmed by germs and will not shake hands with anyone. He is a classic obsessive-compulsive personality.

Schizophrenia and Other Psychoses

A **psychosis** is a serious mental disorder that is indicated by disorganized thoughts resulting in faulty beliefs. One of the more severe psychoses is **schizophrenia**, which affects only 1% of the population. The onset of symptoms often occurs in adolescence or early adulthood, and includes hearing voices that others do not hear, or seeing things that others do not see. Some schizophrenics hear voices that instruct them to do various and possibly destructive things. Schizophrenics are not in touch with reality; they cannot think logically, may have difficulty with personal care, and cannot live a normal life. Although there is no known cause for schizophrenia, it seems to be a combination of both genetic and environmental factors. The risk for schizophrenia increases to 10% if a primary family member is afflicted with the illness.

Other psychoses include paranoia, obsessive-compulsive disorders, or delusional behavior. A psychosis can be due to drug and alcohol use, or may be genetic or environmental.

Key Terms

Schizophrenia: A breakdown in the relation between thought, emotion, and behavior, leading to withdrawal from reality into fantasy and delusion.

Psychosis: A severe mental disorder in which thought and emotions are so impaired that contact is lost with external reality.

Image of Health in Depth

Neurotic vs. Psychotic Behavior

The terms neurotic and psychotic are often used interchangeably, but they actually mean different things. It is possible for an individual to exhibit many of the characteristic symptoms found in psychotic individuals but not actually be psychotic. A psychotic is an individual who has lost touch with reality and may behave in bizarre and unpredictable ways. A neurotic person is overanxious, oversensitive, or obsessive, but is still in touch with reality. A neurotic person may suffer from depression, paranoia, panic disorder, or obsessive-compulsive disorder; he has difficulty adapting to changes, to his life situation, and has deficient coping skills. This may cause significant emotional distress, but is not as severe as psychotic behavior.

Treatment Approaches for Mental Health

Although you cannot completely change mental health by changing your behaviors, you can increase behaviors that are known to improve mental health and decrease those that are known to be detrimental, such as abusing alcohol and other drugs. Good mental health is determined by many variables, but may depend on personal choices made by each individual.

Image of Health in Depth

Mock Therapy Session

It is your responsibility to be personally accountable for your own mental health, and there are many self-help alternatives. One possibility is to do a self-analysis by preparing for a mock therapy session. Imagine that you have made an appointment to talk to a counselor or therapist about your struggle with anxiety and depression. Assume that this is a first session and you are meeting this counselor or therapist for the first time. Consider how you will introduce yourself and how you will explain the source and degree of your mental discomfort.

Identifying what you believe are the sources of your mental discomfort and how you are trying to cope is not only useful for helping yourself, but also essential information for a therapist. As you consider the source of your discomfort, try to identify how you might be able to change, control, or eliminate it.

Image of Health in Depth

Gender and Seeking Help

In general, women seek treatment for mental health and medical issues more often than men. Men tend to wait to see if a mental or other medical problem will resolve itself. Seeking medical assistance, especially for mental health, is a sign of weakness for some men. These men may be taught from childhood that they are the stronger gender, and recognizing and accepting that they have a mental health or even a physical medical problem is very difficult. Data shows that fewer men than women seek treatment for anxiety or depressive disorders, but more men than women seek treatment for substance abuse disorders. This suggests that men are more likely to use drugs and alcohol to cope with mental health difficulties. **http://www. hcp.med.harvard.edu/ncs/ftpdir/table_ncsr_LT-prevgenderxage.pdf**

Counseling and Psychotherapy

When mental health becomes compromised, an individual may benefit from counseling or psychotherapy. The severity of the stress or mental dysfunction will dictate the type of therapist required. Counseling provides help with personal or psychological issues by someone who is trained to offer psychological support. On a college campus, this may be a peer counselor who has been trained to offer support to fellow students, or it may be a professional counselor who specializes in mental health issues for college students. Counseling may involve more than one session, or the issue may be resolved or referred after one session. Psychotherapy consists of regularly scheduled therapy sessions with a trained psychotherapist to resolve mental health issues unique to each individual. A student may seek the help of a psychotherapist either from counselor referral, or because the student himself recognizes symptoms of poor mental health and seeks treatment.

One advantage of being a student on a college campus is the number of mental health resources that are usually available, either on campus or by referral. Peer or group counseling can be beneficial for both stress relief and help for depression. Away from home for the first time, many freshmen may struggle with homesickness and depression. Talking to a trained peer counselor who has likely experienced the same freshman loneliness and depression can be very helpful. Campus support groups offer an opportunity to meet regularly with individuals struggling with similar problems—there are often support groups for Alcoholics Anonymous (AA), and for individuals who struggle with depression, shyness, anxiety disorders, or eating disorders.

Psychotherapy has many benefits, especially if the therapist and patient are compatible and able to form a bond of trust. Just as it is important to have a confident, trusting relationship with your primary medical doctor, it is important to find a therapist with whom you feel comfortable and whom you trust to help you.

Finding the Right Therapist

When looking for a therapist, it may be helpful to ask friends or family members for a referral, or to do some research on the Internet. At your first appointment, you should pay attention to your intuition as to whether this is the right person for you. You should feel comfortable and confident that the therapist can help you; if you do not, this may not be the right therapist for you. You should also recognize that successful therapy often takes a long time, sometimes years. The best therapist for you is not necessarily the most expensive or the most experienced. You should discuss insurance and ability to pay on your initial visit. You should also recognize that therapy is not an extravagance, and that money spent on your mental health may be money well spent. Your goal is to feel better and to learn to help yourself become mentally and emotionally strong. Sometimes, becoming mentally and emotionally strong is just a matter of taking the time for the healing process to work, but often, therapy can facilitate the healing and recovery process.

Medical Treatment

There are an enormous number of treatment options for all types of psychological illnesses. The role of the medical practitioner is to determine the extent of psychological illness, make a diagnosis, and recommend a treatment protocol. It is the responsibility of the patient, or those who are responsible for the patient, to explore all possible avenues of treatment. A decision about treatment should be made after all options have been explored and the patient feels comfortable with the treatment protocol. Just as treatment for a physical illness is facilitated by the acceptance and support of the patient, successful treatment for a psychological illness depends on patient confidence and support of the treatment.

During your initial visit with a medical professional, it is necessary to establish a patient history. If you are seeking treatment for the first time, you will need to describe your symptoms, how long you have been experiencing these symptoms, and how much your life has been disrupted by the feelings you are having. Your medical professional may recommend several self-help options as a first level of treatment, or perhaps a series of counseling sessions.

If an individual is suffering from a severe mental illness such as major depression or schizophrenia, the medical professional should be a psychiatrist, a medical doctor who can prescribe drugs as part of a treatment protocol and is qualified to treat severe mental illnesses. With the exception of two states, a psychologist cannot prescribe drugs.[24] Although treatment with drugs may turn out to be the best treatment protocol, there may be other non-drug options that should be explored first. It is the responsibility of the patient or those responsible for the patient to recognize that what may be the most expedient treatment may not be the most appropriate treatment.

Self-Help Options

Just as it is important to have a personal plan to stay physically healthy, it is also important to have a personal plan to stay mentally healthy. We all have different psychological needs, and different tolerances for situations and stressors in our daily lives. Almost everyone can recognize when something is physically harmful, but it is also important to recognize when something is mentally harmful.

Managing intermittent bouts of mild depression or anxiety can sometimes be accomplished with some simple self-help options.

- Talk to a friend about troubling issues in your life.

- Commit to a behavior change. Quit smoking, quit drinking, or lose weight.

- Check the campus health center or the Internet for support groups, or see if your campus offers group or individual therapy.

- Make time for yourself.

- Resume or start an activity that you really enjoy or that interests you.

- Keep a journal.

- Write down your dreams.

- Read a good book.

- Take a class just for fun.

- Practice yoga or tai chi.

- Play music or sing.

The human body is amazingly resilient and can withstand an enormous amount of physical and mental stress, sometimes for years. However, there is a breaking point for everyone, and it is important to take action before this point is reached. If you do not experience an improvement in your wellbeing from practicing the above techniques, seek the help of a counselor or medical professional.

Responsibility and Accountability

Accepting that good personal mental health is largely determined by self-responsibility is an important component of being accountable for decisions and behaviors that affect your life.

Taking Responsibility for Your Mental Health

Gender, age, individual differences, and diverse life experiences make behavior choices and self-responsibility unique for everyone.

At this point in your life, you should be aware of personal conditions, choices, and behaviors that cause you additional stress, anxiety, or depression. You have control over many of these things in the choices that you make, including sleep, nutritional choices, exercise, drugs, alcohol, smoking, and financial responsibility. The company you keep also influences much of your behavior. It is difficult to stop drinking and smoking if all of your friends drink and smoke!

Focusing on Accountability

The person you are today is a result of every experience that has occurred in your life so far. For young adults, it is life experience that has the most profound effect on mental health. Some young adults have benefited from a childhood and adolescence that was nurturing and provided every opportunity for success. Some young adults are still trying to recover from a traumatic childhood and adolescence, and struggle with depression and low self-esteem. Young adulthood is the time of your life when you are finally in charge of you. It is a time when previous life experiences seem to matter less, and personal choices for your current and future life matter more. When you begin to make decisions that will affect personal mental and emotional health, you have an opportunity to facilitate your best personal mental health environment.

Summary

Defining Stress

- The General Adaptation Syndrome (GAS) is an illustration of the human body adapting to stress.

- Eustress is good stress while distress is negative stress.

- Two people exposed to the same stressor may *perceive* the stressor differently.

- Homeostasis is a balanced state.

- Unrelieved stress may cause the body to reach exhaustion.

- Burnout results from prolonged exposure to stress.

- Psychoneuroimmunology is the study of the effects of stress on the incidence of chronic disease.

Managing Stress

- Putting your life in order is about making choices, being accountable, and taking responsibility for your personal time management.

- A careful and accurate self-assessment of current stressors and the effect they have on you makes a personal stress management plan more practical.

- Unrelieved stress is linked to a higher incidence of ulcers, heart attacks, gastrointestinal disorders, and cancer.

Defining Mental Health

- Maslow's basic premise is that as individuals satisfy basic needs, they move into the realm of self-actualization and self-transcendence.

- For the college freshman or post high school young person, the progression from adolescence to adulthood has profound consequences for personal mental health.

- Psychosocial health includes emotional, intellectual, social, and spiritual wellness.

Influences on Mental Health

- A self-directed individual is able to make responsible decisions and is not afraid of being accountable for those decisions.

- Building self-esteem requires goal setting, making a realistic plan to accomplish the goal, and putting a plan into action.

- Choosing to be happy is part of being self-directed.

Mental Disorders

- One in four adults over the age of eighteen suffers from a diagnosable mental disorder in any given year.

- In the United States, almost ten percent of the population or more than 20 million people experience depressive illness each year.

- The most common mental illness among college students is depression.

- Suicide is the third leading cause of death among 15–24 year olds.

- The average age for a first episode of an anxiety disorder is 21.5 years and most individuals experience more than one type of anxiety disorder.

- Posttraumatic stress syndrome is caused by a traumatic event and can negatively affect mental health.

- An obsession is an unwanted thought.

- A compulsion is an unwanted act that is difficult or impossible for an individual to control.

- Only about one percent of the population is affected by schizophrenia. There is no known cause, but there is a genetic link with a higher incidence in people whose parent or sibling has the disease.

Treatment Approaches for Mental Health

- It is your responsibility to be personally accountable for your own mental health, and there are many self-help alternatives.

- A decision about medical treatment for mental health should be made after all options have been explored and the patient feels comfortable with the treatment protocol.

- Spirituality can have a very positive influence on psychological health.

- The psychologically healthy adult is emotionally mature and autonomous, responsible and accountable for personal decisions, able to adapt to change, capable of intimacy, and has normal fluctuations in mood.

Reassessing Your Knowledge

1. How can you evaluate the stressors in your life?

2. Name three things that can help you have a more stress-free life.

3. Describe the dimensions of psychosocial wellness.

4. Why do you think depression is the most common mental illness among college students?

5. What are some of the risk factors for suicide?

To answer these questions, you might choose to work in groups with your colleagues. Check your answers against the written material in the text, and reread those sections where you made errors.

Health Assessment Toolbox

American Association of Suicidology
If you are in crisis or need immediate help.
http://www.suicidology.org/web/guest/home

How Stressed Are You?
Interactive stress quiz.
http://www.teachhealth.com/

Internet Mental Health
Mental health information and diagnostic criteria.
http://www.mentalhealth.com/

Mind Body Medicine
Massachusetts General Hospital
http://www.massgeneral.org/bhi/basics/

National Sleep Foundation
Sleep is vital to our health and well-being.
http://www.sleepfoundation.org/

SAMHSA
Substance Abuse and Mental Health Services Administration
http://store.samhsa.gov/home

Vocabulary Challenge

Match the term in the left-hand column with its correct definition in the right-hand column.

TERM		DEFINITION
Mania	A.	A brain disorder causing a person to be out of touch with reality
Psychoneuroimmunology	B.	Negative stress
Compulsion	C.	Positive stress
Emotional Wellness	D.	A stimulus that initiates the stress response
Obsession	E.	An unwanted act
Eustress	F.	An unwanted thought
Stressor	G.	Extreme elevated mood change
Distress	H.	Illness that involves the body, mood, and thoughts
Schizophrenia	I.	How you express yourself based on how you feel and react to events in your life
Depression	J.	How emotions affect the immune system

Answers
G; J; E; I; F; C; D; B; A; H.

Applying What You Have Learned

1. How could you help a family member through a difficult stressful experience?

2. What steps would you take to help someone improve his time management skills?

3. What things could you do to make your personal life more stress free?

4. What suggestions could you give to someone who is struggling with low self-esteem?

5. How can you help someone who has many symptoms of depression?

6. Why do you think it is important to consider a spiritual dimension in your life?

Exploring the Internet

National Institute of Mental Health
http://www.nimh.nih.gov/

Mayo Clinic Health Information
http://www.mayoclinic.com/

The National Foundation for Depressive Illness
http://www.depression.org

The National Institute of Mental Health
http://www.nimh.nih.gov

Selected References

1. Selye, H.A. Syndrome Produced by Diverse Nocuous Agents. *Nature,* 138: 32. 1936.

2. Selye, H. *The Stress of Life.* McGraw-Hill, New York. 1956 (Revised edition, 1976).

3. Ibid.

4. Ader, R., Felton, D., and Cohen, N. *Psychoneuroimmunology,* Academic Press Inc., 2007.

5. Irwin, M., and Vedhara, K. *Human Psychoneuroimmunology,* Oxford University Press, 2005.

6. Gump, B.B., and Matthews, K.A. "Special intervention reduces CVD mortality for adherent participants in the Multiple Risk Factor Intervention Trial, *Annals of Behavioral Medicine,* 2003.

7. Kiecolt-Glaser, J.K., and Glaser, R. PsychoneuroImmunology and Cancer: Fact of Fiction? *European Journal of Cancer,* 35. 1999.

8. Herbert, T.B. and Cohen, S. Stress and Immunity in Humans: a Meta-Analytic View. *Psychosomatic Medicine,* 1993.

9. Williams J.E., Paton C.C., Siegler I.C., Eigenbrodt, M.L., Nieto, F.J., and Tyroler, H.A. Anger Proneness Predicts Coronary Heart Disease Risk: Prospective Analysis from the Atherosclerosis Risk in Communities (ARIC) Study. *Circulation,* 101(17): 2034–2039. May 2, 2000.

10. Cohen, S., Kamarck, T., and Mermelstein, R. A Global Measure of Perceived Stress. *Journal of Health and Social Behavior,* 24: 385–396. 1983.

11. Jacobsen, L.K., Mencl, W.E., and Westerfield, M. Impact of Cannabis Use on Brain Function in Adolescents. *Ann. N.Y. Acad. Sci.* 1021: 384–390. 2004.

12. Kessler, R.C., Chiu, W.T., Demler, O., and Walters, E.E. Prevalence, Severity, and Comorbidity of Twelve-Month DSM-IV Disorders in the National Comorbidity Survey Replication (NCS-R). *Archives of General Psychiatry,* 62(6): 617–27. June, 2005.

13. Maslow, A. *Motivation and Personality,* 2nd Edition, New York: Harper and Row. 1970.

14. Huitt, W. Maslow's Hierarchy of Needs. *Educational Psychology Interactive.* Valdosta, GA: Valdosta State University. 2007. Retrieved July 25, 2010 from http://www.edpsycinteractive.org/topics/regsys/maslow.html

15. Huitt, W. Self-concept and self-esteem. *Educational Psychology Interactive.* Valdosta, GA: Valdosta State University. 2009. Retrieved July 25, 2010, from http://www.edpsycinteractive.org/topics/regsys/self.html

16. Cousins, N. *Anatomy Of An Illness As Perceived By The Patient Norman Cousin.* January 1979. Publisher WW Norton and Co. Inc., 1979.

17. The Numbers Count: Mental Disorders in America. National Institute of Mental Health. Downloaded July 25, 2010, from http://www.nimh.nih.gov/health/publications/the-numbers-count-mental-disorders-in-america/index.shtml

18. Elkin, I., Shea, T., and Watkins, J.T., National Institute of Mental Health Treatment of Depression Collaborative Research Program. General Effectiveness of Treatments. *Archives of General Psychiatry*, 45. November, 1989.

19. Tsuang, M.T., Bar, J.L., Stone, W. S., and Faraone, S.V. Gene-Environment Interactions in Mental Disorders. *World Psychiatry*. June, 2004.

20. Minino, A.M., Arias, E., Kochanek, K.D., Murphy, S.L., and Smith, B.L. Deaths: Final Data for 2000. National Vital Statistics Reports. *National Center for Health Statistics*, 50(15). 2002.

21. Incidence of Suicide by Age and Gender, Centers for Disease Control and Prevention, National Center for Injury Prevention and Control, CDC, 2005.

22. Heeringen, C., Audenaert, K., Van Laere, K., et al. Prefrontal 5-HT2an Receptor Binding Index, Hopelessness and Personality Characteristics in Attempted Suicide. *Journal of Affective Disorders*, 74(2): 149–158. April, 2003.

23. Kessler, R.C., Chiu, W.T., Demler, O., and Walters, E.E. Prevalence and Comorbitidy of Twelve-Month SDM-IV Disorders in the National Comorbidity Survey Replication (NCSR). *Archives of General Psychiatry*, 62(6): 617–627. June, 2005.

24. LeVine, E.S. Experiences From the Frontline: Prescribing in New Mexico. *American Psychological Association*, Psychological Services. February, 2007.

Unit Two

Relationships, Sexuality, and Family Planning

Chapter 4
Communication and Relationships

Chapter 5
Sexual Health and Reproduction

Chapter 6
Family Planning

UNIT TWO

Image of Health

Communication and Relationships

Student Learning Outcomes

LEARNING OUTCOME	APPLYING IT TO YOUR LIFE
Describe some keys to effective communication.	Identify the level of effectiveness you think you have when communicating with others.
Describe the effects self-concept and self-esteem have on relationships.	Assess your own level of self-esteem and your perception about the effect it has on your relationships with others.
List the components of the Triangular Theory of Love.	Identify these components in a personal relationship you have with someone you care about.
Identify some factors present in a committed relationship.	List the factors that are most important to you in a committed relationship.
Identify some factors that should be considered before choosing to have a family.	Describe the most important factors for you when considering whether to start a family.
Describe some of the issues that may cause a relationship to fail.	Identify some issues that may cause relationship failure for you.

Assess Your Knowledge

1. The types of messages involved in the communication process include:
   a. Verbal, nonverbal, and meta.
   b. Verbal, intrinsic, and cathartic.
   c. Verbal, nonverbal, and subliminal.
   d. Verbal, intrinsic, and deceptive.

2. Gender identity is:
   a. The same as sexual orientation.
   b. The gender to which you most closely identify.
   c. The same as androgynous identity.
   d. Determined at adolescence.

3. Intimate relationships:
   a. Are the same as sexual relationships.
   b. Can be between family members, friends, or with a romantic partner.
   c. Are not necessary in a committed relationship.
   d. Are only possible if you are married.

4. A committed relationship is dependent on:
   a. Marriage.
   b. Respect, shared values, and equality.
   c. Dual employment.
   d. Sex.

5. Divorce:
   a. Occurs in 50% of marriages.
   b. Is almost always the best option when there are difficulties in a marriage.
   c. Can usually be avoided by seeing a marriage counselor.
   d. Rarely happens after 20 years of marriage.

Answers:

1. a; 2. b; 3. b; 4. b; 5. a.

The Communication Process

A variety of styles make up the communication process, including verbal, nonverbal, and meta messages. Verbal messages are most obvious, occurring when two or more people are in conversation. Nonverbal messages are communicated primarily by body language and facial expressions, and often occur simultaneously with verbal messages. A meta message has an underlying meaning or an implicit message, and may be used in advertising to encourage product interest at an almost subliminal level.

Communication Goals

In **communication**, your primary goal should be to convey your thoughts and ideas clearly and accurately, and to comprehend the thoughts and ideas articulated to you by others. Although this may seem obvious, learning to communicate this way is not done easily. Learning to communicate is a lifelong process that improves with practice. Good communication should not be about winning, losing, competing, or having the last word. A conversation that depends on having the last word results in less meaningful and sometimes harmful communication. When communication becomes competitive, clarity and accuracy are usually compromised. A communication style that involves both the speaker and the listener creates a reciprocity that is meaningful for both individuals.

Gender and Communication Styles

Gender and role models influence how our personal communication style develops. Most people identify with same gender role models and emulate same gender communication patterns. The way we learn to speak and express ourselves is based on our earliest role models, usually our parents and others who are closest to us. The way we speak says much about us, and can identify regional, ethnic, cultural differences, and even level of education. According to John Gray, the author of *Men are from Mars, Women are from Venus*, when it comes to communication, men and women are often not even on the same planet![1]

Men are often competitive in their communication patterns, especially with other men. In such conversations, they focus on an issue, trying to have the last word or making the most important point, possibly getting angry, saying what they think, and not too concerned if they hurt the other man's feelings. Women are often more **affiliative** in their communication patterns, tending not to initiate conflict, and usually trying not to hurt the feelings of others. However, some women whose feelings are hurt by a difficult conversation are not able to forgive and forget easily. Women may take statements said in anger more personally than men, and because of their affiliative nature, must resolve any real or imagined hurtfulness before a healthy level of communication can resume.

Effective Communication

In modern American life, we are bombarded with auditory and visual stimuli. We watch television, listen to music, talk, text, tweet, and check e-mail on our cell phones. We organize our lives on our personal digital assistants, and send and receive e-mail on our computers. This communication may occur without much thought, quickly and in small increments. In addition to all of this, we also have face-to-face conversations. In the corporate world this is called "face time," the time spent in one-to-one, personal communication with a client, a coworker, or a supervisor. Consider how much face time you spend with the important people in your life, those with whom you have a daily relationship. For many people, this time is minimal. A few minutes in the morning and evening, and the rest of the day is filled with work and other life responsibilities. Even for a young couple with no children, an evening at home may find one person on the sofa watching television while the other person is on the computer answering e-mail. As a result of our busy lives and over-stimulation of our senses, many people seem to have forgotten some important fundamentals regarding the art of communication.

The ability to clearly state thoughts and hear exactly what someone else is saying is one of the most important components of a successful relationship. Though we have many communication role models, we eventually develop our own communication style based on environmental and life experiences. Many people reach adulthood as effective communicators. Others have less developed communication skills, making it difficult to communicate clearly in relationships, actually hearing what others are saying. Difficulty with communication may also be due to shyness, lack of confidence, or low self-esteem.

> **Key Terms**
>
> **Communication**: The exchange of thoughts, opinions, or information in speech, writing, or signs.
>
> **Affiliative**: A more submissive communication style that seeks to minimize conflict.

Critical Thinking Question: Describe ways you can improve the way you communicate with those who are important to you.

Being a Good Listener

Effective communication depends on many variables, primarily on taking the time and interest to communicate well and develop good listening skills. For many Americans, our fast-paced lives make us impatient and unwilling to make time to really listen. In our platonic, professional, and intimate relationships, taking the time to listen can enhance connections with others, making our lives more meaningful. In the book *The Art of Relationships* Fritsen points out that when someone really listens to you it is resonating, because there is enthusiasm and energy in the conversation.[2] For most people, communication means learning to speak well. Workplace seminars and college courses in Speech and Oral Communication can help improve speaking and presentation skills. Unfortunately, the emphasis of these courses is almost always on speaking, not listening, producing a population that speaks well but listens poorly. In a friendship that may evolve to an intimate and possibly a sexual relationship, it is important to be more altruistic in communication patterns. If you really want to develop a deeper level of communication, let the other person talk. Be attentive and encourage him or her to speak freely, really listening to what is said. As you listen, periodically ask if you accurately interpreted what was said. As you speak, you should also ask your listener if they understand what you are saying. The box entitled "Two-Way Communication" provides examples of different communication patterns. Can you identify your style?

Two-Way Communication

1. At a dinner party, the host asks a guest if he is enjoying the special dish that was prepared. The guest responds with an "absolutely yes," but picks at his food and leaves most of it on his plate. The host is offended and concerned.

   This is a type of *nonverbal communication*. Although the guest verbally responded yes, his behavior said no.

2. During an argument, Ruth tells John exactly what he is doing wrong in their relationship. She begins each sentence with "you" and proceeds to place total responsibility and blame on him. John is offended. He defends himself, and the argument deteriorates into a shouting match.

   In this communication pattern, Ruth has failed to *take responsibility* and *be accountable* for her role in the relationship. She needs to express her views on what is wrong in the relationship without blaming John. In beginning each sentence with "I" rather than "You," she now owns her feelings, her thoughts, and has assumed responsibility for her part in the relationship. This allows John to respond with his views on the relationship without needing to defend himself.

3. In a group assignment, students are asked to equally divide the tasks of a project. A leader immediately emerges, asking the others to identify their strengths and task preferences. Two students respond clearly, but the third says she will do "whatever" and retreats into silence. The leader makes assignments, asking if everyone agrees they are fair and appropriate. The first two say yes, while the third student just shrugs her shoulders. When they meet next, only the leader and the first two students have completed their assignments. Challenged by the other group members, the third student states that she felt that if she had disagreed it would have upset them, and that no one seemed to want to listen to her, so she felt left out.

   The quiet student is expressing herself with a *non-assertive communication pattern*. She uses body language to express herself and avoids eye contact. Her communication pattern could be improved by practicing direct communication, making eye contact, and communicating one-to-one. The group leader and the other two members might have improved the meeting, had they paid attention to her body language and lack of responsiveness. Providing specific choices for the third student and asking her to express her feelings gives her an opportunity to express herself and make a choice.

4. Amy asks Chad the classic question: "Does this dress make me look fat?" When a question of this nature is asked, the speaker is usually asking for reassurance and does not want an honest answer. Even if Chad were to say, "Do you really want me to tell you the truth?" Amy would probably respond, "An answer like that tells me you think I look fat." Amy is placing Chad in a no-win situation, but there is a solution. Chad can ask Amy how she thinks she looks in the dress. He might ask her to turn in front of a mirror, and as he appraises her, diverts her attention to how she feels. As she expresses herself, he can endorse this. Understanding what Amy wants will help Chad answer her!

   Amy is showing signs of insecurity and low self-esteem. It would benefit her to spend more time focusing on her positive traits and working to improve her self-image. None of us should ask for an honest answer unless we are comfortable receiving it.

5. Phuong is proud of his ability to be effective and productive on the job. He is the leader of a group of coworkers who have a project due by Friday. On Monday, he makes assignments, and one worker responds that he cannot do his assignment, asking for an alternative. Phuong reminds him in a loud voice that this happened with a previous assignment, and suggests the worker simply cannot be pleased. Phuong points out that the group was late on the previous project, saying it was this worker's fault. The worker defends himself, saying his expertise is in a specific field, yet Phuong has given him an assignment outside his field. The worker points out that each group member had trouble completing the work on time, so the responsibility should be shared. Phuong screams at him that his time is being wasted, and that he will do both his and the coworker's jobs himself.

   Phuong is an *aggressive communicator*. He is hostile, loud, and frequently blames others. He is not accountable, using "You" statements to place blame. He does not accept responsibility for own behavior and incomplete work, preferring to blame others. The coworker has correctly identified how the assignments might be better distributed, pointing out that all group members had difficulty completing their assignments the previous week. After Phuong states he will do both jobs, the coworker might ask Phuong to reconsider, and give him an assignment in his field of expertise.

Talking Just to Talk

Talking just to talk is communication without substance. It occurs when we stop caring about whether we are communicating in a meaningful way. Many people have busy lives, and most would appreciate a reduction in meaningless talk. Are you guilty of meaningless conversation? Have you ever listened to yourself and considered if what you are saying is of interest to the other person? Is it meaningful to either of you? For example: A coworker has returned from a trip to Europe and recounts his vacation in great detail. If you have never been to Europe, or are not really curious about it, this may not interest you. A communication opener for the European traveler is to ask a prospective listener if he has been to Europe, then the conversation can be adjusted based on the perceived level of interest. Another lapse in communication etiquette occurs when someone recounts in detail the trials and tribulations of a friend or relative whom you do not know. Not only can this be annoying and inconsiderate, it is probably meaningless to you. The art of good communication involves having a willing listener and a responsible communicator who keeps the conversation interesting for both individuals.

Motivation Maximizer

To determine how well people listen to you as you go about your daily life, conduct a "listening experiment" by trying one of the following:

1. Go into your favorite coffee shop and place an order. For example: "I want a tall mocha coffee with one-half the chocolate and no whipped cream."

   Keep track of how well the server listens and how much you must repeat. There are really only four things to remember, but for someone who does not listen well, only a couple will be heard.

2. Order a sandwich at your favorite delicatessen. For example: "I want a ham and Swiss on rye, toasted, with spicy mustard, no mayonnaise, and sweet pickles."

Did the server hear your order? Did you need to repeat anything? This example is more complicated because there are more things to remember. How much of your order needed to be repeated?

After you conduct one of these listening experiments, or one you thought of on your own, consider whether *you* are guilty of not listening well. It may take some effort, but when someone speaks to you, listen from the beginning so you do not need to ask the speaker to repeat what was said.

There are times when we are busy and distracted, and may be guilty of not listening well. But learning how to listen well makes you a more effective communicator. It is important in the delicatessen, and even more important when communicating with people in your life that you care about. Improving your ability to listen is a skill that can be learned. Your challenge is to take responsibility for better communication and be accountable for listening well.

Open Communication

Open communication requires establishing and maintaining a level of honest communication with a friend, spouse, or partner. It is an agreement allowing the freedom to discuss any topic and makes both individuals accountable for keeping each other informed. Some couples build this into their daily routine by setting aside a time to talk. Discussions may involve thoughts and concerns about the minutiae of daily life, as well as any relationship concerns. Establishing a routine of open, consistent communication provides a safe, comfortable environment to discuss even difficult issues. In open communication, the emphasis is always on avoiding blame. Relationship concerns are addressed as "I" messages, rather than "You" messages. For example, "I need to spend more time with you," rather than, "You never want to spend time with me."[3]

Conflict Resolution

The most reliable path to conflict resolution in a relationship is open communication. Ideally, discussions will be face-to-face, but difficult issues can still be resolved when a face-to-face meeting is not possible. Although it may be useful to involve a third party, only the individuals engaged in the conflict can really find resolution. A third party, possibly a friend or a therapist, can act as a guide by encouraging each person equally and helping to identify solutions. Consider the following guidelines before you attempt to resolve a relationship conflict:

1. Clearly identify and agree on the problem.

2. Work on one problem at a time.

3. Reveal individually what you can and cannot accept or agree to.

4. Jointly explore areas of possible compromise.

5. Ensure that both individuals feel comfortable with what they have given up or gained.

6. Neither individual should attempt to win everything.

7. Neither individual should leave the discussion believing that they have unfairly given up or gained, or not been heard.

8. If one or both individuals become angry, stop the discussion immediately and set a time to reconvene later.

9. Once compromises and decisions are agreed upon, decide on a date to review the issues and determine if appropriate solutions have been found.

10. Before leaving the discussion, partners should state what they think has been agreed to and what is expected of them. Verbal agreement ensures that each partner has been heard and each partner understands expectations.[4]

Conflict resolution only works when there is a sincere mutual interest in resolving the problem. Hurtful, angry remarks are nonproductive, causing unnecessary emotional pain that takes the focus from the real issue. You must also be honest about whether resolving the conflict is important to you. Lack of interest in conflict resolution indicates lack of interest and importance associated with the value of the relationship.

Foundations for Healthy Relationships

Communication is one of the keys to a healthy relationship, but there are other important components, as well. Our personal **self-esteem**, how we feel about ourselves, is important in all relationships. The gender to which

we most closely identify and the gender to which we are most attracted helps to define heterosexual, homosexual, and bisexual orientations. In every relationship, each person plays a role generally influenced by gender, or in response to the dynamics of the relationship. The primary constant in a healthy relationship with another person is the inevitable change that must be addressed as life events continue to evolve.

Self-Esteem

Since we are generally most comfortable with individuals similar to ourselves, couples with similarities are often more successful in long-term relationships. Your **self-concept** reflects your confidence and how you view yourself, which are also factors. If you have a high level of self-esteem and are more **inner-directed**, you have a well-developed sense of autonomy and will be more confident in your relationships. If you have low self-esteem and need validation from others to feel good about yourself, you may be **other-directed**, less autonomous, and generally lack self-confidence.[5]

Because two people with different levels of self-esteem create an inequality that affects every aspect of the relationship, they may be less compatible and have difficulty being mutually supportive. These differences place one person in charge and the other in a subservient role, and while this may initially be mutually acceptable, an unequal balance inhibits relationship growth, and the relationship may erode over time. The person with lower self-esteem needs perpetual reinforcement that becomes the responsibility of the partner with higher self-esteem, who may eventually tire of this role.

The way we develop relationships with others is the result of many factors, including diversity of life circumstances. Opportunities for individual growth and achievement are not equal across ethnic and socioeconomic communities, or even between genders. By the time you reach young adulthood, you occupy a niche in society that reflects your cumulative life experiences. You will have many opportunities to affect your place in society, and education is one avenue for improving your options. As you enjoy academic and other successes, self-esteem and self-confidence improve, and more opportunities become available. If you are accountable for your present circumstances, you can be responsible for improving your future. Your life circumstances depend on the choices you make, and how much responsibility and accountability you are willing to accept for the direction of your life.

> **Key Terms**
>
> **Self-concept**: How you view yourself, your social character, your appearance, and your intellect.
>
> **Self-esteem**: Sense of self-worth; confidence in your own value as an individual.
>
> **Self-directed**: Able to make decisions for oneself; autonomous.
>
> **Other-directed**: Depend on others to make decisions for you; lacking autonomy.

Challenge Question: Describe the effect of self-esteem on a relationship.

Gender Identity

Gender identity refers to the gender with which you most closely identify, male or female. There is not always an apparent delineation, and individuals may not clearly identify with one gender but both, making them **androgynous**. The gender to which a person is sexually attracted indicates sexual preference.

Parents who provide children with toys and games that are gender-specific encourage the gender identity of their children. Some parents may even choose playmates to ensure that girls play with girls and boys play with boys. However, it is normal for young children to have playmates of either gender, and any perceived androgynous behavior is accepted. Children are most likely to self-select their playmates based on common interests and likability, rather than on the gender of the playmate.[6]

> **Key Terms**
>
> **Gender identity**: The gender to which you most closely identify.
>
> **Androgynous**: A blending of male and female behaviors or interests.

The first relationships we develop are with our family, or those with whom we live as children. As we move through life, we form connections beyond our family, to our classmates, friends, extended family members, coworkers, and other professional acquaintances. Relationship networks are a combination of all of these connections,

and will change throughout life. New relationships are formed, some come to an end, and others we keep for a lifetime. Most people will develop a significant intimate relationship with a person with whom they share their life, and our most intimate relationships are influenced by the gender to which we are most sexually attracted. Although the majority of relationships are **heterosexual**, 10% are **homosexual** and 5% are **bisexual**. The characteristics of successful relationships are similar, regardless of sexual orientation.[7]

> **Key Terms**
>
> **Heterosexual**: Sexual attraction to someone of the opposite gender.
>
> **Homosexual**: Sexual attraction to someone of the same gender.
>
> **Bisexual**: Sexual attraction to members of both genders.

Heterosexuality

The majority of relationships are heterosexual, when individuals are attracted to someone of the opposite gender. For most individuals, this is a comfortable and predictable orientation that starts in childhood and is confirmed during puberty, when hormonal and physical changes cause adolescents to become aware of their sexuality. For most people, relationship role models are heterosexual, and for many, a heterosexual lifestyle is comforting and familiar. It involves finding a life partner and may include marriage, having children, and forming a family.

Homosexuality

Approximately ten percent of adult sexual relationships are homosexual, when there is an emotional and sexual attraction to a person of the same gender.[8] For some individuals, the attraction to the same gender occurs at a young age, and by adolescence, hormonal and physical development brings a new awareness of sexuality. For individuals who are homosexual, this is a time when preference for the same gender will be more obvious to them and possibly to others. It is also a time when homosexual attraction may be suppressed because of religious, social, or personal condemnation. Being honest about personal sexuality depends on self-esteem and available social support.

Bisexuality

About five percent of individuals are bisexual, when there is an emotional and sexual attraction to both males and females. Some bisexual individuals may be primarily heterosexual, even married with children, but may occasionally have a homosexual relationship. Other bisexuals may be involved in a heterosexual relationship for years, find that they are attracted to someone of the same gender, and begin a new life as a homosexual. And less frequently, a homosexual individual may decide that he or she is primarily heterosexual and become involved in a heterosexual relationship. Sexual ambiguity may have less to do with sexual orientation and preference and more to do with opportunity, changing life circumstances, and a more accepting social view of bisexuality and homosexuality.

Gender Roles

When two individuals live together, certain relationship roles are established. In a traditional marriage fifty years ago, the husband went to work and the wife remained home to raise the children. Today, gender roles are often dictated by the economic reality that both partners must work, share parenting responsibilities, or depend on others for childcare. It may also be that one partner has an excellent paying job, so one goes off to work and the other stays home with the children. Gender roles are also established in homosexual and bisexual relationships similar to those of husband and wife, although in homosexual relationships, the roles tend to be more egalitarian. Gender roles have many variations, often depending on economic circumstances and whether there are children.

Intimate Relationships

Intimacy in a relationship is characterized by respect, closeness, familiarity, affection, love, and communication. An intimate relationship can be between family members, among friends, or with a romantic partner, and intimacy is the essence of our significant relationships with others.

If an intimate relationship is to develop into a romantic relationship, it progresses through a series of stages. The first stage is to *seek information*, asking friends or acquaintances who know this person, or by questioning the person yourself. The second stage is *experimenting*, getting to know the person by discovering mutual interests. In the book, *In the Company of Others: An Introduction to Communication*, Rothwell indicates that most relationships do not progress beyond the second stage and therefore have no future.[9]

If the relationship continues it reaches the third stage, when it *intensifies*. This may involve spending more time together, openly discussing feelings, and making social introductions to other significant people. The next stage is *merging*, in which the two individuals are recognized as a couple, and may begin using nonverbal signals to express their feelings for each other. *Bonding* is the final stage, in which two people may engage in a symbolic union or marriage. Most successful relationships have shared power, and effective, supportive communication patterns. Bonding does not guarantee continuation of the relationship, and many relationships end prior to this stage because the couple begins to grow apart. Previously shared pleasures are now experienced alone, and some topics of conversation may be avoided because of the potential for conflict. When this happens, the relationship begins to stagnate. Rothwell calls this a treadmill effect: you may have run for miles but you have not gotten anywhere, and the dreaded words, "we need to talk about our relationship," are uttered. Other signs of relationship difficulty may be apparent as one partner begins to avoid the other either physically and/or emotionally. *Termination* is the final step, and Rothwell's work shows that after a relationship has fallen apart, it is difficult to renew and recapture the magic.

Challenge Question: Describe Rothwell's progression of an intimate relationship.

Friendships

Friendships are a vital part of social and emotional development, providing important early connections between you and someone other than a member of your family. Humans are very social—the ability to make friends begins in childhood, and it is normal to develop friendships at a very early age. Almost everyone has at least one good friend—this may be someone with whom you do not live but nonetheless share many aspects of your life, or it could be your spouse or life partner. From childhood to adulthood, we learn how to socially interact with a variety of individuals outside our family. Some of these people will become friends for a short time, and some for a lifetime. There are adults who seem comfortable in any social setting and make friends easily, which indicates they were probably also social as children. Children find friends when there is a mutual interest and attraction: they like each other, want to spend time together, and a bond of trust develops between them that cements the friendship. Trust allows the friendship to grow and develop indefinitely, unless there is a circumstance causing a loss of trust. With children, this could be simply telling a secret you promised not tell. In adult friendships, dishonesty, loss of loyalty, and a lack of genuineness will erode trust, possibly ending the friendship. The elements of a good friendship include honesty and feelings of compassion and caring, which nurtures the relationship and allows it to grow and become stronger, creating a resiliency that protects the relationship during difficult times.[10]

Critical Thinking Question: Identify the characteristics that are important for you in establishing a friendship with someone.

Image of Health in Depth

Shyness

It is estimated that up to 40 percent of adults in the United States are chronically shy, to the degree that it causes difficulty in their lives. Studies indicate that those who are shy have an actual fear of social encounters and tend to avoid social situations. Shyness is considered a social phobia, and those who are shy have difficulty in meeting people, starting or maintaining a conversation, interacting in small groups, and may struggle with any sort of intimacy. Overcoming shyness may be facilitated in a clinical setting, in which shy individuals are assessed to determine the degree of shyness and their most socially difficult situations. They are then exposed to feared situations in a group setting, in which they practice behavioral change in simulated situations with other group members. This role-playing provides a safe environment to learn appropriate social skills. Additional exercises include saying hello to a certain number of people at a social gathering, talking to a sales clerk about the weather, and asking someone to go for coffee. The shy person becomes more confident by participating in these activities, and further improvement occurs with traditional communication training, such as self-disclosure, learning how to accept criticism, to actively listen, and to manage anger.

Shyness can be destructive to self-esteem and result in negative attitudes toward others. It is possible for a shy person to learn behaviors that reduce the feelings of shyness and the fear of social situations, and become an accomplished and willing participant in conversations with others.[11]

Components of a Developing Relationship
Intimacy in adult relationships depends on being mutually honest and ethical, and a willingness to disclose important details about one's personal life to establish a bond of trust. A commitment of time and a sincere interest in the relationship are also required.

Attraction and Dating
During adolescence and early adulthood, physical attraction is often the most important characteristic when initially considering dating partners. But even if the physical

attraction is strong, without a foundation of shared interests, goals, and genuine like for the other person, physical attraction is not enough to form a relationship.

When most people discover an attraction to someone, they begin to work through a mental checklist as they consider the person as a possible partner. It is similar to a reciprocal job interview, with each individual evaluating the other. If you pass the first step, you move to the first date and begin the relationship probationary period. During this time, either person can terminate the relationship without cause and without warning. But when you pass this period, the relationship moves toward beginning a commitment, when you begin to disclose things to one another, developing a level of intimacy.

Critical Thinking Question: How do you conduct your first "job interview" with a potential date?

Image of Health in Depth

Trust, Self-Disclosure, and Lying

In adult relationships, as personal information is disclosed the component of trust becomes extremely important, and honesty is vital. It is counterproductive to the growth, development, or longevity of a relationship to fabricate or embellish details of your life. In order for a relationship to progress, the listener must accept self-disclosures, treat this information with respect and confidentiality, and appreciate your honesty.

Ideally, honest communication builds intimacy in a relationship, even if there are difficult personal disclosures. There is a risk, however, that a difficult personal disclosure may change or end the relationship. Consider what you would do if a person with whom you have had a few dates and are beginning to feel a warm attachment discloses that he or she is addicted to prescription painkillers. This is information you certainly want, but does it change your feelings? Do you want to continue this relationship? Self-disclosure means that you disclose personal information, even if it is difficult and could potentially end the relationship. Intimacy can develop without knowing every detail of someone's life, but there should be a mutual expectation and responsibility to make disclosures completely truthful, so trust can be established from the beginning of the relationship. When omissions become apparent, it creates a feeling of mistrust and causes one to question what else the individual has failed to disclose.

Sternberg's Triangular Theory of Love

Robert Sternberg developed the Triangular Theory of Love to explain the different dimensions of love, including a combination of **intimacy**, **passion**, and **commitment**.[12] According to Sternberg, there are seven forms of love, depending on which of the three triangular components are present. There is also a non-love category, in which none of the components are present.

Key Terms (Sternberg)

Intimacy: Feeling close, connected, and bonded in loving relationships.

Passion: Physical and emotional drives that lead to romance, physical attraction, and sexual consummation in loving relationships.

Commitment: The realization that one feels love in the short term, and the commitment to maintain that love in the long term.

Table 4-1. The Seven Forms of Love

COMBINATIONS OF INTIMACY, PASSION, AND COMMITMENT			
	Intimacy	Passion	Commitment
Non-love			
Liking or friendship	■		
Infatuation		■	
Empty love			■
Romantic love	■	■	
Companionate love	■		■
Fatuous love		■	■
Consummate love	■	■	■

(Source: Sternberg, A Triangular Theory of Love, 1986.)

- *Non-love* is typical of daily casual interactions with people with whom you do not share intimacy, passion, or commitment.

- *lis* is the characteristic found in true friendships, in which a person feels a closeness with another but lacks passion or commitment.

- *Infatuated love* is sometimes described as "love at first sight," and generally includes a strong sexual attraction but lacks intimacy and commitment.

- *Empty love* describes a once strong love that has diminished over time, and intimacy and passion are absent. In cultures in which arranged marriages occur, relationships may begin as empty love, evolving to include intimacy and passion.

- *Romantic love* is essentially *liking*, with a physical component, passion, that bonds romantic lovers emotionally.

- *Companionate love* describes a long-term, committed friendship that may occur in marriages and committed relationships, in which passion is absent but deep affection and commitment remain. The love ideally shared between family members is a form of companionate love, as is the love between close friends.

- *Fatuous love* is a combination of passion and commitment, but lacking in intimacy. An example is a whirlwind courtship and marriage, in which commitment is motivated largely by passion, without the stabilizing influence of intimacy.

- *Consummate love* includes all three elements and is the complete form of love, representing the ideal relationship. Sternberg cautions that the attainment of consummate love is no guarantee that it will last, and that reaching this goal is easier than maintaining it. For example, consummate love may change to companionate love over time, as passion diminishes.

Critical Thinking Question: Consider your current or most recent intimate relationship, and determine which of Sternberg's Seven Forms of Love best describes your experience.

Loving Relationships

Falling in love is an event that may happen once or several times in a lifetime, with the first instance of falling in love often occurring in adolescence. This initial feeling of love is sometimes called **infatuation**, when there is a strong physical and emotional attraction but a relationship has not yet formed. When a relationship is new, the feelings of attraction include excitement when you see your new love, planning ways to spend time together, and eventually declaring your love for them. This is a time of joy if these feelings are reciprocal, but if they are not, it can be a time of emotional trauma.

Falling in love as an adult is initially not much different than during adolescence. It can temporarily turn your world upside down, causing you to be unable to eat or sleep normally or think about anything other than your new love interest. Mutually falling in love is one of the greatest joys of life. Although physical attraction is important, mature adults also consider such factors as respect, admiration, shared values, spirituality, relationship equity, intimacy, and commitment.

Key Term

Infatuation: A strong physical and emotional attraction to another person.

Critical Thinking Question: Evaluate how truthful you are when disclosing information about yourself to another person.

Committed Relationships

Building a committed relationship means that it has evolved to a point where you believe you want to spend the rest of your life with this person. It assumes that there is agreement on common goals and expectations for each person's role in the relationship, and it means you both have a strong feeling of love, intimacy, and commitment. Ideally, you treat each other with respect, have shared values, and intend to have an equal partnership in which one partner does not dominate the other. A committed relationship depends on many variables, possibility beginning with cohabitation, or the decision to marry or form a domestic partnership.[13]

Marriage

For most people, marriage is the consummate committed relationship. We learn about marriage from an early age, observing the marriages of parents, family, and friends. People choose to marry for many reasons, but primarily from the desire to build a lifelong, loving relationship with another person within the framework of a legally binding contract. Although marriage is not the end of personal autonomy, it changes the way we feel about ourselves and creates a personal, social, and legal connection that is reflected in many aspects of our lives.

For most people, marriage is the first step in forming a family. It is a comfortable, socially endorsed living arrangement that for many people provides a nurturing environment that is preferred to singlehood.

Although currently fifty percent of all marriages end in divorce, many people will remarry at some point in their lives. Unless there is an agreement otherwise, monogamy for both partners is an expectation of marriage. As relationships dissolve and separation or divorce occurs, many people actively pursue a new relationship with the goal of a new marriage. **Serial monogamy** refers to those who are monogamous in each marriage or relationship—they may have a succession of marriages or relationships, but are committed to only one person at a time.[14] Some couples may enter into marriage with the agreement of having an open partnership, wherein each individual considers the marriage his or her primary relationship, but both partners have the freedom to occasionally explore a relationship, including sexual intimacy, with someone else. When only one partner is exploring a relationship outside of marriage, it is not an open marriage—this is may be clandestine and is considered an extramarital affair.

Jeremy and Sarah

Jeremy and Sarah have been dating for a few weeks. They are both enjoying the relationship, and the possibility of having a sexual relationship is apparent. Jeremy thinks he has found the love of his life and the mother of his future children. The next time they are together, he asks Sarah to stay overnight. When Sarah shares with him that she wants to be with him, but cannot have sex right now because she has a herpes outbreak, Jeremy is furious. He believes Sarah has led him on and been dishonest. Sarah denies this, saying she has been honest and that the right time to share this difficult information is prior to any sexual activity. She tells him that even if she did not have a current outbreak, she would have told him her herpes status before having sex. She asks if he has ever discussed sexually transmitted infections (STIs) with a partner before having sex. He assures her that he would never ask such a question, that he is careful and has never been exposed to any STIs. Sarah reminds him that STIs continue to spread because people are not comfortable sharing information about them, and just because Jeremy has never been advised does not mean he has never been exposed. She tells Jeremy that she was infected by someone who did not have the courage to tell her, and asked if Jeremy would prefer that she continue the cycle by not telling him. She tells him she has learned about the herpes infectious disease process, and knows when she is at highest and lowest risk of passing it on. She promises that if they become sexually active, he will always know her status. Jeremy spends the next day wondering which would be better—knowing or not knowing. He decides that he loves Sarah, and after reflecting on her courage to tell him about her STI, his opinion of her is even higher. He decides that knowing is better than not knowing and enthusiastically pursues his relationship with Sarah. ■

Key Term

Serial monogamy: Commitment to one person in a current marriage or relationship.

All relationships will suffer setbacks and challenges; the key to overcoming them is based on three simple components: effective communication, cohesion, and flexibility. You have already learned how to improve your communication and handle conflicts. Cohesion involves working together and refers to the balance between being part of a couple and maintaining personal autonomy. There will be times when you and your partner must be apart, and maintaining autonomy is helpful to both partners. If there is commitment and honesty, physical separation is not threatening. Flexibility is your ability to adjust to change and to know how to regain relationship balance. Successful marriages begin in love and personal commitment, and are maintained successfully when each partner works to keep a harmonious balance in the marriage.

Critical Thinking Question: Identify what you consider the pros and cons of marriage.

Image of Health in Depth

Improving the Odds for a Happy Marriage

Observing the interactions between our parents and other adult role models helps us formulate a sense of what we want in our own relationships. We may have observed relationships that were loving, distant, or abusive, and we all have expectations in our personal relationships that may or may not align with those of our partner. You should be aware of what really matters to you before you make a permanent commitment. In her book, *1001 Questions to Ask Before You Get Married*, Monica Leahy provides lists of things to consider that will affect the progress of a relationship.[15] These include:

- Growing up in a traditional family, or one with a divorced or single parent.

- The influence of parents and in-laws on your marriage.

- The time you will spend with your parents and in-laws.

- Past relationships and former marriages.

- Having children and financing a family.

- Religion, race, culture, and politics.

- Expectations for careers.

- Daily lifestyle; sharing responsibilities in your daily routine.

- Financial security and managing money.

- Expectations for sexual intimacy.

- Expectations for emotional intimacy.

- Planning the wedding and the honeymoon.

Cohabitation

Although it may not be true that two can live as cheaply as one, cohabitation is nevertheless a popular living arrangement for all age groups. Cohabitation may allow each partner more freedom and greater autonomy than marriage, and it is usually easier to negotiate a relationship breakup without the legal entanglements of marriage. Some couples prefer a time period of cohabitation to see if they really want to get married. Others may feel constrained by a legal marriage contract, seeing no benefit to marriage and preferring cohabitation. Although not common, there are individuals who have lived happily as partners for years without ever marrying or forming a domestic partnership.[16]

Image of Health in Depth

Common-Law Marriage[17]

Nine states and the District of Columbia recognize common-law marriage, in which two people agree that they are married, live together, and conduct themselves as a married couple. This does not involve a wedding; it is simply a mutual agreement to be married. In most states, the woman takes the man's name, and the couple files a joint tax return. No state recognizes common-law divorce—dissolution of a common-law marriage can only occur by court order.

Domestic Partnerships

Domestic partnerships are a different type of legal partnership arrangement that are similar to marriage, requiring completion of a Domestic Partnership Agreement that allows unmarried heterosexual or homosexual couples to establish a legal connection with each other. There are some legal advantages, such as allowing your domestic partner to be covered by your health insurance, or to be able to visit you in the hospital when only direct family members are allowed. Many companies accept domestic partners for health insurance, death and disability entitlements, and retirement beneficiaries. There is potential legal liability when a domestic partnership dissolves, especially if there is a large disparity in income between the partners. The domestic partner with less income may have a legal claim to a financial settlement if the partnership dissolves.

Same-Sex Partnerships

In the 2000 census, the number of households identifying as gay and lesbian showed a three-fold increase over 1990.[18] This increase may be due to more gay and lesbian households feeling more comfortable identifying as homosexual, because of increasing social acceptance and the willingness of many companies to recognize domestic partners. Though a few states currently allow same-sex marriage, there has been a national debate in recent years regarding same-sex marriage, considered controversial because it deviates from the cultural norm. Efforts to legalize gay and lesbian unions have been compared to the struggle of the civil rights movement, when disenfranchised African Americans had to fight for equal rights under the law. Another comparison has been made to the struggle for women's suffrage, resulting in the Nineteenth Amendment to the U.S. Constitution, giving women the right to vote and serve on juries. In some cases, the issue of gay marriage has been politically divisive, but there has been a steady improvement in the legal rights for gays and lesbians.

Image of Health in Depth

Keeping Your Relationship Strong

As relationships evolve and sustain themselves over the years, some remain healthy and adapt to inevitable change. Others do not, and the relationship may become stagnant and end. Some relationships endure the test of time, though they may not be healthy. This may happen not because the partners have stopped caring for each other, but because they no longer have similar interests. Interests and priorities may have changed, resulting in less time together and less meaningful communication. Although these problems may be avoided and can certainly be addressed, they are not unusual in long-term relationships. Change is inevitable in life, and change in relationships does not necessarily mean relationship destruction. When a couple identifies symptoms of relationship difficulty or change, those in a healthy relationship will begin to address the problem before it gets worse. There are ups and downs even in strong relationships, and it is not unusual to have your feelings toward your partner change. It may be important to focus on the things you used to enjoy about each other, or identify things you used to do together. Some couples in long-term relationships discover a cycle of emotional change, in which they feel they are falling in love with their partner again, after a period of ambivalence. This may be due to rediscovering the qualities in your partner that you found attractive in the first place, or you may find a new attraction to qualities that were not so obvious to you before. In a strong relationship, there may be problems and disagreements, but there is a genuine bond of love and affection between the partners.

Choosing to Stay Single

According to the 2000 census, ten percent of Americans have chosen to remain single, never marrying.[19] This is a conscious choice for many of these individuals. While it is proven that marriage or a committed relationship may benefit your health, lowering the incidence of chronic disease and even increasing life expectancy, some people see being single as an opportunity to pursue individual goals and passions, to invest time in a career and personal interests, and to be solitary whenever the need arises. For others, perhaps the right person was never found. Single people are not necessarily lonely, and most have productive, fulfilling lives.

Image of Health in Depth

Aging and Intimacy

Interest in sex and sexual intimacy are an important part of the lives of many older individuals. The need for intimacy is lifelong, and depending on physical health, sex is an important part of an intimate relationship. Most young people have a difficult time thinking of their parents having sex, and even more difficulty when considering their grandparents' sexual activity. As women age, become menopausal, and produce less estrogen, natural vaginal lubrication decreases and can diminish sexual pleasure, and changes in body size and shape may make them feel less desirable. Men produce less testosterone as they age, and it may take longer to become sexually aroused and have an erection. These difficulties can be easily resolved, and as people live longer, both genders can expect to have satisfying sexual experiences well into old age. Sexual difficulties for an older population can most often be addressed medically, possibly requiring adjustment to existing medications or a prescription for a new medication.[20,21]

Family Life

Considering a Family

Becoming a family can be accomplished in many different ways. The American concept of family has changed over the years, but is generally considered to include at least one child and one or two parents. In the 1950s, the typical family was a two-parent family with one or more children. Today, this family arrangement still exists, but other family combinations may include:

- Single parents with children
- Surrogate parenting
- Blended families
- Same-sex parents

Family planning involves the opportunity to choose to become pregnant or to adopt. Irresponsible or no birth control use can also lead to a family, even though the prospective mother or couple may be unprepared. Ideally, having children is a conscious decision, and at the very least, the mother or couple should consider relationship stability, economic stability, and childcare. Responsible parenting requires a selflessness and responsibility that lasts until the child is 18 and beyond.

Parenting Styles

For most people, parenting brings a measure of joy as well as a measure of concern and anxiety, and a primary concern is to avoid doing anything that will diminish the emotional, psychological, and physical growth of their children. Parenting requires adjustments according to the temperament of the child: a child who is outgoing, assertive, and may anger easily requires different parenting than a shy, withdrawn child. The temperament of a parent is also a factor in parenting styles. There are four types of parenting identified by Diana Baumrind and others, and although parents may exhibit behavior from all four styles, most use primarily one style. These styles are Authoritarian, Authoritative, Permissive, and Uninvolved.

Authoritarian parents are demanding, in charge, and are likely to give orders and expect them to be obeyed. This style restricts autonomy and does not encourage any verbal give-and-take. Children raised with this parenting style tend to have low self-esteem, lack intellectual curiosity, and may be unhappy and withdrawn.

Authoritative parents also have strong views about the behavior of their children, but are more rational, encourage verbal feedback, and share the reasoning for expected behavior. Children in an authoritative home are typically more self-confident, have well-developed social skills, tend to be happy, and are well adjusted.

Permissive parents are warm and accepting of a child's behavior, allow the child much autonomy, and provide little direction or discipline. A permissive parent wants to be their child's best friend, allowing the child to act impulsively and with impunity. Children from a permissive home may be immature, lack impulse control, and perform poorly in school. However, they tend to be happy, with high self-esteem and good social skills.

Uninvolved parents take little interest in their children, are not demanding, and are unresponsive to their children's needs. An extreme case is parental neglect, in which the child receives virtually no attention from the parent. Children of uninvolved parents often have low self-esteem, perform poorly in school, lack impulse control, and are unhappy.[22,23]

Single Parents

Single parenting may be a choice, or may be the result of separation, divorce, abandonment, or the death of a spouse, and may also be the result of an unplanned pregnancy. Regardless of the circumstances, there are typically emotional, financial, and logistical challenges with single parenting. The single parent must provide all emotional support for children, as well as maintain good personal emotional health. The single parent, often the mother, may face severe financial and economic hardship. Keeping a family functioning can be a logistical challenge, since the single parent not only works, but must also ensure the children are cared for. Some single parenting occurs by choice, when an unmarried person chooses to raise a child alone. When single parenting is a choice, the emotional, economic, and financial considerations may not be as problematic.

Challenge Question: Describe some of the challenges faced by a single parent.

Surrogate Parenting

Surrogate parenting involves individuals who are not the child's biological parents. These individuals assume parenting responsibilities because the real parents are unable or unwilling to assume their parenting duties, or because a parent needs childcare help. A person involved in surrogate parenting may be a grandparent, stepparent, aunt, uncle, or other relative, or a family friend, all of whom are willing to share parenting responsibilities, and who are concerned enough for the welfare of the child to devote time for parenting.

Blended Families

Divorce and remarriage often create combined families. A blended family is formed when a couple entering a second marriage brings children into the new family. Though they are combined with a new set of parents, the children in this arrangement are related to only one parent. It is not unusual in blended families to have more children from the new marriage as well, creating a blended family that potentially has children from three different sets of parents.

Same-Sex Parents

Today, many same-sex couples are starting families of their own. For gay men in a committed relationship, this has many possibilities. The couple can adopt an infant or child; they can establish a contract with a surrogate mother, in which the sperm of one partner is used to inseminate the surrogate; or, the couple could use the sperm of one or both partners in vitro with donor eggs, and establish a contract with a surrogate who will have six to eight fertilized eggs implanted into her uterus.

Gay women may also adopt children, but often, one partner chooses to become pregnant by artificial insemination with donor sperm. Current research suggests that children who are raised by same-sex parents are emotionally well adjusted, with no real differences in self-esteem or gender identity from children of heterosexual parents.[24]

Keys to a Successful Family Life

Strong families have similarities allowing for regular growth and sustainability. The components of caring are essential regardless of the family structure, and include:

- An appreciation for each other's strengths and weaknesses.

- Respect for the importance of the family and a commitment to family members.

- Frequent family rituals unique to each family, with the emphasis on spending time together.

- The ability to communicate in a productive way among all family members.

- Providing support for each other as a family during times of crisis.

- Knowing when to get help and resolve problems through counseling or other interventions.[25]

Relationships in Transition

It is not always completely obvious to both individuals that their relationship is changing or in trouble. One partner may start spending more time away from home, using the accepted excuse of longer work hours. But when there are relationship difficulties, a pattern will eventually emerge that may include some or all of the following:

- Less time spent at home and less time together.

- Difficult or limited communication.

- Increasing number of arguments.

- Lack of interest in sex or emotional intimacy.

It is possible that the situation may become intolerable and one partner will move out. The couple can try to identify the primary problem and solve it themselves, or they may try to resolve their differences with the help of a therapist, though in this case, both individuals must be sincerely interested in trying to save the relationship. This is not always the case. A good therapist will recognize this, and may help the individuals see that the relationship is over. If there is violence in the relationship, a different dynamic is involved that will be addressed in Chapter 15.

Challenge Question: What are some of the signs of a relationship in trouble?

Broken Relationships

There are two realities about marriage in America:

1. Ninety percent of people will get married.

2. Fifty percent of all marriages will end in divorce.

It is human nature to want a relationship with another person. Most of us hope for a relationship that includes love, intimacy, passion, mutual support, and most of all, a person who makes us happy, and almost all relationships begin this way. Both individuals profess their love for each other and look forward to a lifetime of blissful intimacy. Then ordinary life events happen, and one or both partners may have difficulty adapting to these changes in a meaningful way. Unresolved differences are the primary reason couples seek marriage counseling, therapy, or life coaching. Unfortunately, therapy is not always successful. Statistically, almost two-thirds of couples that seek counseling show either no improvement after a year of counseling, or their relationship has deteriorated further.[26] Most approaches to relationship therapy require that the couple try to solve problems together, but this is often not a successful approach. Another option is to ask each individual to focus on what is most desirable in a relationship, determining the things you can live with and those that are impossible to accept. Both individuals must determine their fundamental needs for happiness, identifying what they need to be happy in a relationship while maintaining their individuality. The best way to learn about relationships is to be involved in one. The early part of a relationship is usually filled with love, passion, and the feeling that you can't spend enough time with your new love. As the relationship continues, the passion and intimacy may diminish, and for some, expectations and needs for happiness are not adequately met.

Observations of other relationships are the primary influence on behavior in a marriage or partnership—this may be your observation of your parents' relationship, or even the relationships of television personalities. In a relationship, the way you treat your partner, the respect you show, the way you communicate and express your wants and needs, and how you deal with anger are all likely to be influenced by observing others. Some couples pride themselves on never having an argument or even a disagreement; however, this is not necessarily a confirmation of relationship stability, but perhaps more of a statement of pride and endurance. Some families have a history of abuse that can be traced back several generations. Both genders may observe and learn abusive behavior, and both seem programmed and willing to play their part. There is no question that abusive relationships need much more work than non-abusive relationships, but in each, the key to understanding problems starts with understanding the needs of each individual.

Anger in relationships can be initiated by a variety of stimuli, and indicates that some needs are not being met for one or both partners. This anger is not often volatile or explosive, but can be persistent and will eventually cause relationship difficulties. Anger in relationships manifests itself in the interactions between the couple and how they treat each other. Unresolved anger causes gradual disintegration in the level of communication patterns that outwardly appear as disinterest and dislike. This can progress to:

- Limited superficial conversations about the minutiae of living together.

- Communicating only when absolutely necessary.

- Not speaking to each other.

Improvement in communication can only occur after an effort is made to determine the sources of anger. If there is interest by one or both partners to resolve differences, it may be possible that an introspective process of self-discovery will illuminate the sources of anger. This is a difficult process, and must be conducted independently by each partner. It is only after individual sources of anger are identified that the couple can focus on either rebuilding the relationship or choosing to end the relationship.

Jealousy in a Relationship

The facts on jealousy:

- Jealousy is not a statement of love and caring.

- Jealousy is a sign of low self-esteem.

- Jealousy shows a lack of trust in the relationship.

- Jealousy can lead to violence.

- Jealousy destroys relationships.

You are in a jealous relationship if your partner:

- Accuses you of being unfaithful.

- Misinterprets a meaningless conversation with a stranger as seduction or flirting.

- Makes false accusations about your alleged romantic involvement with a coworker.

- Demands to know where you are at all times.

- Checks on you to see if you are where you said you would be.

- Asks you about time that can't be accounted for.

- Makes verbal or physical threats.

- Is violent and has caused you physical or emotional harm.

Divorce and Relationship Termination

Divorce becomes an option when there are irresolvable differences and the couple agrees that divorce is the only option. Divorce is rarely amicable and is often very contentious. In most states, it involves dividing all property and other assets equally, which involves negotiating and occurs most often with legal representation for each partner. If the income levels of the divorcing couple are not equal, a final settlement may involve alimony payments from the spouse with greater income to the spouse with less income. Or, the divorcing couple may agree to a settlement amount at the time of final dissolution that includes a settlement for alimony. When a family is separated by divorce and children are involved, there is additional trauma for everyone. Very often, divorce is the final solution to relationship difficulties that children have probably long been aware of. If a child is under the age of eighteen, the court must make a determination about which parent will assume custody of the child or children. A custody decision depends on many factors, including ability and fitness to be a parent. Often, both parents want custody of children and both are equally able to be successful parents. Various joint custody agreements can be negotiated that may range from equal custody to complete custody for one parent. Children are often in the middle of a custody tug-of-war with their parents; and children may have a strong opinion about which parent they prefer to live with. Ultimately, a judge will make this decision.

Divorce

Putting the Child First

Divorce and custody battles affect children in many ways, and every divorce and custody situation is different. During times of family instability, it is common for children to start doing poorly in school, have emotional outbursts, develop sleep difficulties, or start using drugs. The breakup of their family causes feelings of depression, grief, and anger. Some children even feel that they are somehow to blame. And when a marriage starts to fall apart, the couple begins to invest more time on themselves and their personal crisis, which makes less time available for children. Special care needs to be taken to reduce the effects of divorce on children. Children need to be told about the changes in their family and should be involved in discussions about custody. They should be reassured that the divorce is not their fault. It is also important for parents to avoid using children as negotiating tools for their own self-interests. It is sometimes useful for children to spend time with grandparents or family friends, if it will help bring stability to their daily routine. Children function best in a predictable, safe environment; however, divorce proceedings sometimes make a stable home environment impossible.[27]

Challenge Question: List some things that can help children deal with the prospect of divorce.

Responsibility and Accountability

Accepting that you are responsible for your ability to communicate with others and accountable for the effect your communication style has on all personal relationships affects all aspects of life.

Taking Responsibility for Communication and Relationships

The way we communicate with others is based on life experiences, education, and social environment. Communicating involves learning to speak well and to listen well. The quality of intimate relationships can be evaluated by how effectively we are able to communicate our thoughts and how much effort we give to listening. It is your responsibility to determine the number of individuals with whom you choose to have an intimate relationship. These individuals are usually family members, close friends, and an intimate partner or spouse. It is also your responsibility to improve or maintain the quality of your relationships with important individuals in your life.

Focusing on Accountability

One of the best ways to determine personal accountability in intimate relationships is to evaluate how you think you are viewed by the important people in your life. Are you the kind of person you would like as a friend or intimate partner? Are you always honest and ethical in your dealings with others? Do you ever lie to the people that you care about? Are you guilty of not listening? Only you can answer these questions, and only you can make needed changes. Learning to communicate well and develop intimacy is a lifelong process. It is also something over which you have complete control.

Summary

The Communication Process

- Communication styles include verbal, nonverbal, and meta messages.

- Communication goals include conveying your thoughts clearly and accurately, and comprehending what is said to you.

- They way we learn to speak and express ourselves is based on our earliest role models.

- Men tend to have a competitive communication style, while women are more affiliative.

- Difficulty communicating may be due to shyness, lack of confidence, or low self-esteem.

- The amount of "face time" we spend with the important people in our lives may be minimal.

- Learn to be a good listener by letting the other person talk.

- Talking just to talk is communication without substance.

- Open communication is the freedom and ability to discuss any topic.

- To resolve conflict: Agree on the problem, find areas of compromise, and jointly agree on acceptable solutions.

Foundations for Healthy Relationships

- Level of self-esteem is important in intimate relationships.

- Gender identity is the gender to which you most closely identify.

- Gender roles today are often influenced by economic circumstances.

- Romantic relationships sometimes progress through predictable stages.

- Most successful relationships have shared power and effective, supportive communication patterns.

Intimate Relationships

- Friendships are an important part of social and emotional development.

- Up to 40 percent of adults are chronically shy to the degree that it causes difficulty in their lives.

- Self-disclosure means that you disclose personal information, even if it is difficult and could potentially end the relationship.

- Sternberg's Triangular Theory of Love includes the components of intimacy, passion, and commitment.

- Infatuation is a strong physical and emotional attraction to someone with whom you have not yet formed a relationship.

- A committed relationship assumes there is agreement on common goals and expectations for each person's relationship role.

Committed Relationships

- Marriage is the consummate committed relationship.

- Serial monogamy refers to individuals who are monogamous in each marriage or relationship.

- Cohabitation means living together without any legal rights or commitments.

- Domestic partnerships are a legal arrangement similar to marriage.

- About 10 percent of Americans are single and have never married.

Family Life

- Choosing to become a family involves a variety of parenting arrangements.

- Different parenting styles depend primarily on the temperaments of both parent and child.

- Strong families have similarities that allow for growth and sustainability.

Relationships in Transition

- A pattern different from the norm will emerge when relationship difficulties arise, indicating areas of conflict.

- Ninety percent of Americans will get married, and fifty percent of all marriages end in divorce.

- Unresolved anger in a relationship causes disintegration in communication.

- Jealousy shows a lack of trust and destroys relationships.

- Divorce is an option when there are irresolvable relationship differences.

- A judge ultimately makes decisions about children's custody in a divorce.

Reassessing Your Knowledge

1. What are some keys to becoming an effective communicator? How can you improve your listening skills?

2. Describe the importance of self-esteem and gender identity for healthy relationships.

3. Identify the components of an intimate relationship, from friendship to a committed, loving relationship.

4. Describe the differences between committed relationships, including marriage, cohabitation, domestic partnerships, and same-sex marriage.

5. What are some keys to successful families? Describe some differences in parenting styles.

6. Describe the circumstances that may lead to a divorce. Identify some ways to protect children from the stress of divorce.

To answer these questions, you might choose to work in groups with your colleagues. Check your answers against the written material in the text, and reread those sections where you made errors.

Health Assessment Toolbox

Go Ask Alice
Online answers to questions regarding interpersonal relationships.
http://www.goaskalice.columbia.edu

Gottman Institute
Relationship and Parenting tips and suggestions.
http://www.gottman.com

Snell Multidimensional Relationship Questionnaire
http://www4.semo.edu/snell/scales/MRQ.

htmVocabulary Challenge
Match the term in the left-hand column with its correct definition in the right-hand column.

TERM		DEFINITION
Self Concept	A.	A submissive communication sytle that seeks to minimize conflict
Self esteem	B.	Legal partnership living arrangement
Androgynous	C.	The gender to which you most closely identify
Intimacy	D.	Living together
Serial monogamy	E.	Sense of self-worth, confidence in your value as an individual
Affiliative	F.	Feeling close, connected and bonded in a loving relationship
Gender identity	G.	A strong physical and emotional attraction to another person
Co-habitation	H.	How you view yourself, your social character, your appearance, and your intellect
Domestic partnership	I.	Commitment to one person in a current marriage or relationship
Infatuation	J.	A blending of male and female behaviors or interests

Exploring the Internet

Divorce Support Online
http://www.divorcesupport.com

Family Education Network
http://www.familyeducation.com

Gay and Lesbian Couples Network
http://www.couples-national.org/

Go Ask Alice
http://www.goaskalice.columbia.edu

Mayo Clinic: Family Therapy
http://www.mayoclinic.com/health/family-therapy/
MY00814

National Institutes of Health, Eunice Kennedy Shriver,
National Institute of Child Health and Human Devel-
opment: Adventures in Parenting
http://www.nichd.nih.gov/publications/pubs/adv_in_
parenting/index.cfm

The Gottman Relationship Institute
http://www.gottman.com/

Selected References

1. Gray, J. *Men Are From Mars, Women Are from Venus: A Practical Guide for Improving Communication and Getting What You Want in Relationships.* San Francisco:Harper Collins, 1998.

2. Fritsen, J. The *Art of Relationships: How to Create Togetherness That Works*, Laguna Beach, CA: Insightful Publishing, 2006.

3. Gottman, J. *Why Marriages Succeed or Fail…and How You Can Make Yours Last.* New York: Simon & Schuster, 1994.

4. Ibid.

5. Rotter, J.B. Generalized Expectancies of Internal versus External Control of Reinforcements. *Psychological Monographs*, 80. (Whole No. 609). 1966.

6. Gentile, D.A. Just What Are Sex and Gender, Anyway? A Call for a New Terminological Standard. *Psychological Science*, 4: 120–122, 1993.

7. Hatfield, E., and Rapson, R. *Love, Sex, and Itimacy: Their Psychology, Biology, and History,* Reading, MA: Addison Wesley, 1993.

8. U.S. Census Bureau, 2000.

9. Rothwell, J.D. *In the Company of Others; An Introduction to Communication.* New York: Phillip A. Butcher, 2004.

10. Paul, M. *The Friendship Crisis: Finding, Making and Keeping Friends When You're Not a Kid Anymore.* New York: Rodale, 2004.

11. Zimbardo, P.G. *Shyness*, Reading, MA: Addison-Wesley, 1977.

12. Sternberg, R.J. A Triangular Theory of Love. *Psychological Review*, 93: 119–135, 1986.

13. Kaplan, M., and Maddux, J.E. Goals and Marital Satisfaction: Perceived Support for Personal Goals and Collective Efficacy for Collective Goals. *Journal of Social and Clinical Psychology*, 21(2): 241–252. 2002.

14. Ben-Zeev, A. Is Serial Monogamy Worth Pursuing? *Psychology Today*. October 31, 2008.

15. Leahy, M. *1001 Questions to Ask Before You Get Married*. McGraw-Hill, 2004.

16. Cohan, C.L., and Kleinbaum, S. Toward a Greater Understanding of the Cohabitation Effect: Premarital Cohabitation and Marital Communication. *Journal of Marriage and the Family*, 64(1): 180–192. 2002.

17. National Conference of State Legislatures. Common Law Marriage, 2010.

18. U.S. Census Bureau, United States Census 2000.

19. Ibid.

20. U.S. National Institutes of Health. National Institute on Aging: Sexuality in Later Life. April 20, 2010. Downloaded September 30, 2010.

21. Lindau, S.T., et al. A Study of Sexuality and Health among Older Adults in the United States. *The New England Journal of Medicine*, 357: 762. 2007.

22. Baumrind, D. Child-Care Practices Anteceding Three Patterns of Preschool Behavior. *Genetic Psychology Monographs*, 75, 43–88. 1967.

23. Baumrind, D. Rearing Competent Children. In W. Damon (Ed.), *Child Development Today and Tomorrow*, 349–378. San Francisco: Jossey-Bass. 1989.

24. WebMD. Same Sex Parent Raise Well Adjusted Kids, 2005. Downloaded September, 2010.

25. Fiese, B.H., et al. A Review of 50 Years of Research on Naturally Occurring Family Routines and Rituals: Cause for Celebration? *Journal of Family Psychology*, 16(4): 381–390. 2002.

26. McGraw, P.C. *Relationship Rescue*. New York: Hyperion, 2000.

27. Children and Divorce. American Academy of Child and Adolescent Psychiatry. Downloaded October, 2010 from http://www.aacap.org/cs/root/facts_for_families/children_and_divorce

Image of Health

Sexual Health and Reproduction

SEXUAL HEALTH

- Sexual Anatomy
  - Female Reproductive Organs
  - Male Reproductive Organs
- Sexual Development
  - Puberty: Physical and Hormonal Changes
  - Menstruation, Menstrual Cramping, Amenorrhea
  - Premenstrual Syndrome, Toxic Shock Syndrome
  - Menopause
- Human Sexual Response
  - Human Sexual Response Model (Masters and Johnson)
  - Alternative Female Sexual Response Model (Basson)

SEXUAL BEHAVIOR

- Sexual Diversity
  - Heterosexuality
  - Homosexuality
  - Bisexuality
  - Transgender
- Sexual Stimulation and Intercourse
  - Kissing and Erotic Touch
  - Sexual Intercourse
  - Anal Intercourse
- Sexual Fantasy and Phone Sex
- Abstinence and Celibacy
- Safer Sex
  - Cybersex or Internet Sex

SEXUAL DYFUNCTIONS

- Female Sexual Dysfunction
  - Low Sexual Desire and Sexual Arousal
  - Painful Intercourse
  - Orgasmic Dysfunction
- Male Sexual Dysfunctions
  - Premature Ejaculation
  - Erectile Dysfunction
  - Painful Intercourse

REPRODUCTION

- Conception
  - Normal Fertilization
  - Identical and Fraternal Twins
- Pre-Parenting Behavior
  - Financial Considerations
  - Choosing a Physician
- Infertility
  - Female Infertility
  - Male Infertility
- Infertility Treatments and Options
  - Intrauterine Insemination
  - In Vitro Fertilization
  - Gamete Intrafallopian Transfer (GIFT)
  - Zygote Intrafallopian Transfer (ZIFT)
  - Surrogate Parenting
  - Adoption
- Pregnancy
  - Pregnancy Testing
  - Pregnancy Trimesters

- Prenatal Testing
- Pregnancy Complications
  - Ectopic Pregnancy
  - Spontaneous Abortion
  - Effects of Drugs, Smoking, and Alcohol on the Fetus
  - Premature Labor

LABOR AND BIRTH

- Labor Options
  - Lamaze Technique
  - Leboyer Technique
  - Bradley Technique
- Birthing Options
- Stages of Childbirth
- Birthing Complication
  - Breech Birth
  - Caesarean Birth

AFTER THE BIRTH

- Newborn Screening
- Breast Feeding
- Postpartum Depression
- Sudden Infant Death Syndrome

RESPONSIBILITY AND ACCOUNTABILITY

- Taking Responsibility for Your Sexual Health
- Focusing on Accountability for Your Sexual Health

Student Learning Outcome

LEARNING OUTCOME	APPLYING IT TO YOUR LIFE
For both genders, describe the physical and hormonal changes that occur at puberty.	Identify the effects of these changes on your personal development.
Identify three types of sexual diversity based on sexual orientation.	Describe the sexual behavior and orientation to which you most closely identify.
Identify at least one male and one female sexual dysfunction.	Describe a possible treatment for each dysfunction you identified.
Describe a cause for each example of female and male infertility.	Identify a possible treatment for each example of infertility.
Identify the three stages of a normal childbirth.	List two complications that can affect a normal childbirth.

Assess Your Knowledge

1. The woman's ovum or eggs:
    a. Are produced during puberty.

    b. Exist at birth.

    c. Are continually produced in the ovaries.

    d. Are produced when necessary each month.

2. Sperm are produced in the _____ and stored in the _____.
    a. Scrotum, seminal vesicles

    b. Testes, vas deferens

    c. Seminiferous tubules, epididymis

    d. Epididymis, vas deferens

3. Normal conception takes place in the:
    a. Uterus

    b. Vagina

    c. Fallopian tube

    d. Ovary

4. Fertilization of egg and sperm in a laboratory setting is called:
    a. Intrauterine insemination

    b. In vitro fertilization

    c. Gamete intrafallopian transfer

    d. Zygote intrafallopian transfer

5. At which stage of labor does actual birth occur?
    a. First

    b. Second

    c. Third

    d. Second and third

Answers:

1. b; 2. c; 3. c; 4. b; 5. b.

Sexual Health

Sexual health is determined by many variables, including gender, emotional health, and ethnic, cultural, and socioeconomic factors. The qualities that comprise our sexuality start at **conception**, become obvious at birth, evolve dramatically during adolescence, and continue to change throughout our lives. No two humans, even identical twins, are exactly the same. They may share gender or be members of the same family, but the only constant of our sexuality is our diversity.

Sexual Anatomy

Gender is determined at conception, and sexual anatomy evolves during fetal development. At birth, sexual anatomy is complete but not fully developed. A baby girl has a complete reproductive system, including a **uterus**, **fallopian tubes**, and **ovaries**. A baby boy has a complete urogenital system, with **penis**, **urethra**, **vas deferens**, **prostate**, **Cowper's glands**, **seminal vesicles**, **testes**, **epidydimis**, and **scrotum**. It is not until puberty that sexual anatomy begins to complete its development. In females, hormonal changes cause the ovaries to increase estrogen production, and the pituitary gland to release the follicle stimulating hormone (FSH) and luteinizing hormone (LH), triggering the ovary to release the first egg. This process is called ovulation, which under normal circumstances will occur each month for the next thirty years or more. The first menstruation is called **menarche**. Estrogen also causes the development of breasts, growth of underarm and pubic hair, an interest in personal sexuality, and awareness of sexual attraction.

In adolescent boys, hormonal changes cause the testes to produce more testosterone, possibly resulting in wet dreams, in which ejaculation occurs during sleep. The **seminiferous tubules** in the testes also begin producing sperm, a process that continues throughout life. During adolescence, physical changes for boys include growth of facial, pubic, and body hair, deepening of voice, increased height and weight, increase in size of penis and testicles, and heightened interest in personal sexuality.

Key Terms

Conception: The fertilization of an egg by sperm, marking the onset of a pregnancy.

Uterus: Muscular, expandable organ of the female reproductive system where a fertilized egg implants and develops.

Fallopian tubes: A pair of thin ducts also called oviducts, connecting the ovaries to the uterus. Fertilization usually occurs in one of the fallopian tubes.

Ovaries: The female gonads, which contain eggs and produce hormones.

Testes: The male gonads, which produce sperm and testosterone.

Penis: Dual-purpose male organ that delivers sperm to the vagina and discharges urine from the bladder.

Urethra: In males, a tube that conveys semen and urine. In women, the tube discharges urine from the bladder.

Vas deferens: The excretory duct of the testes that carries sperm and eventually branches into the urethra.

Prostate: A male gland that surrounds part of the bladder and the urethra. It secretes a fluid that neutralizes acid in the urethra.

Cowper's glands: Two pea-shaped nodules located just below the prostate gland, which secrete a fluid that lubricates the urethra and neutralizes acid left by urine in the urethra.

Seminal vesicles: A glandular structure that produces a fluid, which nourishes sperm.

Epididymis: A system of ducts on the posterior of the testes that stores sperm prior to ejaculation.

Scrotum: An external fleshy sac that contains the testes.

Luteinizing hormone (LH): A hormone released from the pituitary gland that initiates the release of estrogen and progesterone into the blood prior to ovulation.

Follicle stimulating hormone (FSH): A hormone released from the pituitary gland that causes the egg to be released from the ovary.

Ejaculation: The discharge of semen during orgasm.

Menarche: The first menstruation in women.

Seminiferous tubules: Long, thread-like tubes found in each of the testicles; the actual site of sperm production.

Challenge Question: What initiates the physical changes that occur at puberty?

Female Reproductive Organs

The female reproductive organs are located in the abdomen and are completely internal. The entire system is present at birth, including over one-half million ovarian follicles that will begin to be released as mature eggs at puberty. The primary components of the female reproductive system includes a pair of ovaries containing ovarian follicles, a pair of fallopian tubes, and the uterus. The fallopian tubes are the approximate diameter of a pencil, about 2.75 to 5.5 inches long, and connect the ovaries to the uterus. The process of ovulation starts when the pituitary gland releases the LH and FSH into the bloodstream, causing the ovaries to release the hormones estrogen and progesterone, which helps prepare the woman's body for possible pregnancy. During ovulation, an egg is released from one of the ovaries and travels down a fallopian tube, a process that takes five or six days. If sperm are present during this period, fertilization will likely occur in the fallopian tube. If the egg is unfertilized, it is absorbed into the nutritive lining of the uterus and is sloughed off during menstruation. Ovulation and menstruation are cyclical, occurring approximately every 28 days. Failure to menstruate, or irregular menses, may result from congenital abnormalities, physical disorders (disease, obesity, malnutrition), emotional or hormonal disturbances, and especially diseases that involve the ovaries, thyroid, or adrenal glands.[1]

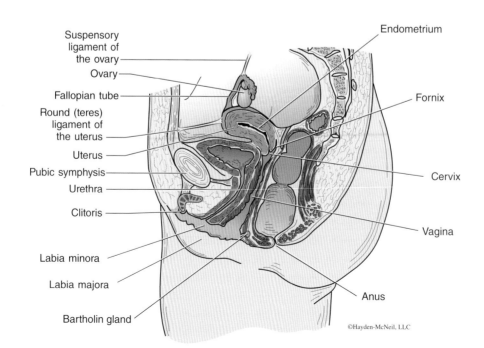

Suspensory ligament of the ovary — Ovary — Fallopian tube — Round (teres) ligament of the uterus — Uterus — Pubic symphysis — Urethra — Clitoris — Labia minora — Labia majora — Bartholin gland

Endometrium — Fornix — Cervix — Vagina — Anus

©Hayden-McNeil, LLC

FIGURE 5-1. Female anatomy.

Critical Thinking Question: Describe the process of ovulation.

Male Reproductive Organs

Male reproductive organs are both internal and external. The genital system shares part of the urinary system, called the urogenital system, which includes the bladder and the urethra. The only part of the urinary tract that aids in reproduction is the urethra. The testes produce the male hormone testosterone, and sperm are produced in the seminiferous tubules, which are located inside the testes. A normal adult male produces approximately 400 million sperm per day, and it takes 74 days for sperm to become fully mature. Mature sperm are stored in the epididymis, a small structure located on the top and back of the testes. The scrotum is a fleshy sac that suspends the pair of testes externally, protecting the testes and epididymis. The ideal temperature for sperm production is 3–5 degrees cooler than normal body temperature. The scrotum will automatically adjust for fluctuations in temperature, relaxing and extending the testes away from the body during hot weather and drawing them close to the body during cold weather. The vas deferens, a conduit for sperm, is a small tube that can be felt through the skin of the scrotum at the back of each of the testes. It travels internally, connecting with the urethra just below the bladder. During sexual arousal, mature sperm congregate in a mass in the epididymis. When ejaculation occurs, sperm travel up the vas deferens and past the seminal vesicles, which release a fluid that nourishes sperm; past the prostate gland, which releases an alkaline fluid that neutralizes residual acid left from urine in the urethra; and past the Cowper's glands, which neutralize acid and secrete a pre-ejaculate fluid that lubricates the urethra. Sperm, seminal fluid, and prostate fluid combine to become semen, the total volume of which is approximately half a teaspoon, and may contain 200–400 million sperm.

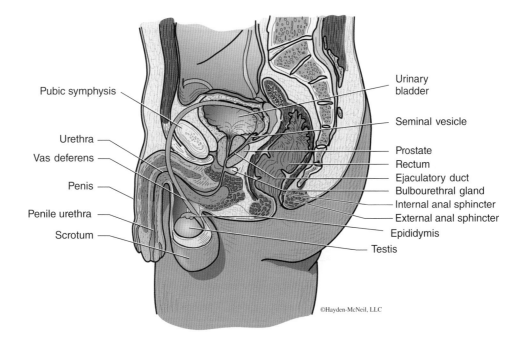

Pubic symphysis

Urethra

Vas deferens

Penis

Penile urethra

Scrotum

Urinary bladder

Seminal vesicle

Prostate

Rectum

Ejaculatory duct

Bulbourethral gland

Internal anal sphincter

External anal sphincter

Epididymis

Testis

©Hayden-McNeil, LLC

FIGURE 5-2. Male anatomy.

Critical Thinking Question: Describe the process that leads up to and culminates with ejaculation.

Sexual Development

Human sexual development begins in the womb. The reproductive system is complete for both genders at birth, but does not begin to develop until hormonal changes initiate this development at puberty, which varies but typically occurs between ages 10–13. Sexual development for girls usually starts slightly earlier than for boys, and it takes less time for girls to reach complete sexual development compared to boys.

Puberty: Physical and Hormonal Changes

Puberty is initiated by a release of the sex hormones testosterone and estrogen. Girls grow to their adult height and reach sexual maturity about four years from the onset of puberty. For girls, puberty usually begins 1–2 years earlier than for boys, and the time period for puberty is approximately four years, compared to six years for boys. An increase in the hormone estrogen causes the initial stages of breast development and the growth of pubic hair. The ovaries and uterus increase in size, and the first menstruation (menarche) occurs at ages 10–12 years. For the next 1–2 years, menstruation may not occur regularly each month and may not include ovulation. Ovulation requires the release of LH and FSH from the pituitary gland, which does not always occur during the early stages of puberty.

For boys, it takes about six years after the onset of puberty to reach adult height and sexual maturity. Increased testosterone causes fundamental changes: at age 12–13, a boy begins to grow more body hair, including the beginnings of facial, pubic, and underarm hair. His voice begins to change to a deeper pitch, and the increase in testosterone causes more muscular and skeletal bulk—he will experience a growth spurt as his bones and muscles continue to increase in size. He begins to produce sperm in the testes and will experience more frequent erections and ejaculations.

Challenge Question: Describe the differences in the developmental time period for boys and girls experiencing puberty.

Menstruation, Menstrual Cramping, Amenorrhea, Toxic Shock

A women's menstruation, the monthly sloughing off of the nutrient-rich layer of blood that has lined the uterus in preparation for a fertilized egg, marks the time of fertility in her life. Starting at age 10–12, this process is repeated each month for the next 30–40 years. Menstruation stops when a fertilized egg implants in the uterus and results in the growth and development of fetus and placenta. It will also stop when a woman's production of estrogen is disrupted; for example, when her ovaries are removed or at menopause, when she stops producing estrogen.

For some women, monthly menstrual cramping may occur a few days before and during her monthly period. This cramping is the result of contractions in the uterus, and seems to be more severe in women with high levels of prostaglandin, a hormone produced in the uterus. **Amenorrhea**, the cessation of menstruation in women, normally occurs during pregnancy or menopause, but can be caused by a severe loss in body weight, such as in **anorexia**, or because of extreme athletic training and competition. Other causes include congenital reproductive abnormalities, metabolic disorders such as obesity and diabetes, and systemic diseases such as syphilis and tuberculosis.

Challenge Question: Describe some of the causes of amenorrhea in young women.

Key Terms

Amenorrhea: Cessation of menstruation.

Anorexia: Psychological eating disorder that causes extreme reduction in caloric intake because of the imagined perception of being overweight.

Premenstrual Syndrome/Toxic Shock

Premenstrual syndrome, or PMS, is a collection of physical, psychological, and emotional symptoms that affect some women 1–2 weeks prior to their monthly period. It is estimated that up to 80 percent of women have at least some of the symptoms of PMS each month.[2] Typical symptoms include abdominal bloating and water retention, breast tenderness, depression, anxiety, irritability, anger, mood swings, fatigue, acne, and insomnia. Although individual symptoms may vary each month, some women experience premenstrual dysphoric disorder (PMDD), with symptoms so severe they are disabling, making it difficult to function in daily life.

Toxic shock is a rare, staphylococcal bacterial infection that can be serious and life threatening. The earliest cases involved women who used super-absorbent tampons and did not change the tampon frequently enough, producing a prime environment in the vagina for a bacterial infection. Currently only about half of current toxic shock cases are the result of tampon use.

Critical Thinking Question: Identify the symptoms of PMS and the difference between PMS and PMDD.

Menopause

Menopause marks the end of fertility for women. It occurs usually between the ages of 45–55, caused when estrogen production diminishes, then ceases altogether. For some, menopause may occur before age forty due to family history, illness, or surgeries.

The symptoms of menopause vary by individual, and may include hot flashes and night sweats, insomnia, vaginal dryness, lack of interest in sex, mood swings, fatigue, depression, difficulty concentrating, aching joints, loss of hair on head, and increased hair growth on face. For years, women were given hormone replacement therapy (HRT) or synthetic estrogen to alleviate the symptoms of menopause. Currently, most doctors do not recommend this treatment due to increased risk of breast cancer. In some women, HRT simply delays the symptoms of menopause, which begin as soon as HRT is stopped.

Human Sexual Response

Emotions, hormones, physical attraction, and physical touch drive sexual response. At puberty, an increase in the hormones estrogen and testosterone causes not only physical developmental changes, but also an increased awareness and interest in sex.

Critical Thinking Question: Identify the factors you think are important in human sexual response.

Human Sexual Response Cycle (Masters and Johnson)

William Masters and Virginia Johnson analyzed the human sexual response cycle, and after eleven years of research on human sexuality, they published their findings in their book, Human Sexual Response.[3] They identified four stages of human sexual response that are experienced by both genders.

During the first stage, the arousal or excitement stage, there is increased blood flow, called vasocongestion, to the genital area. In men, this causes the spongy tissue in the penis to fill with blood, resulting in a partial erection. In women, increased blood flow causes the vagina to lubricate, the outer lips of the labia to swell, and the spongy tissue of the clitoris to fill with blood.

During the second or plateau stage, the reactions from the first stage intensify. The man's penis becomes fully erect as vasocongestion continues, and all spongy tissue in the penis fills with blood. In women, the vagina becomes more lubricated in preparation for penile penetration. For most women, the nipples become hard and erect.

The third stage is orgasm. For men, contractions occur in the ducts and glands of the penis, as well as in the muscles of the pelvis and anus. Male orgasm includes ejaculation, in which semen is ejaculated from the end of the penis via the urethra. Orgasm may occur during sexual activity with a partner, or as a result of **masturbation**. For women, contractions occur in the vagina and the pelvic and anal regions. Inability to reach orgasm during penile penetration may be due to lack of readiness by the female—she may still be in the excitement or plateau stage while her partner is ready for orgasm. It may also be due to a lack of the clitoral stimulus that occurs with most common intercourse positions. For both genders, orgasm produces both an emotional and physiological feeling of intense pleasure.

Key Term

Masturbation: Self-stimulation of the genitals, causing increasing levels of sexual arousal, including orgasm.

The fourth stage is the resolution stage, when the genital areas return to an unstimulated state. For men, there may be a delay before an erection can occur again, depending on factors such as age and physical and psychological health. Most women do not experience a delay, and when properly stimulated, are capable of multiple orgasms.

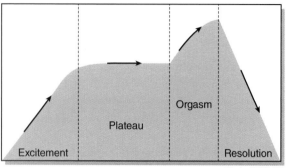

©Hayden-McNeil, LLC

FIGURE 5-3. Sexual response cycle.

Alternative Female Sexual Response Model (Basson)

For some women, intimacy needs that include love, affection, and emotional bonding are more important than the needs for physical sexual arousal and the release of sexual tension. Nurturing those requirements for intimacy and emotional bonding actually initiates sexual desire, possibly encouraging interest in sex for these women.[4] In the Masters and Johnson model, sexual desire initiates the human sexual response cycle, whereas in the Basson model, love, intimacy, and emotional bonding initiates both sexual desire and the human sexual response cycle. The Basson alternate response model is particularly descriptive for women who have been in long-term relationships.

See http://www.arhp.org/uploaddocs/FSRfactsheet.pdf for diagram of the Basson model.

Sexual Behavior

Sexual behavior involves both individual behavior and behavior with a partner. Just as every human is unique, sexual behavior is very personal and unique for each individual. Attitudes about sexual behavior evolve over a lifetime, with parents, peers, culture, and society all impacting how an individual views sexual behavior. Interest in sex is influenced by many factors, including general physical and psychological health, variance in hormone production, partner availability, aging, and cultural and social norms.

Sexual Diversity

Sexual diversity refers to variance in sexual attraction and preference. Although there may be cultural and environmental norms that influence sexual preference, most adults are aware of their personal sexual attraction and preference. Alfred Kinsey was the first to attempt to identify sexual diversity by sexual preference, and purported that gender orientation is not a simple dichotomy, either heterosexual or homosexual. The Kinsey scale shows there is a range of individual preferences regarding adult sexuality, and that many individuals are not exclusively either heterosexual or homosexual.[5,6]

Table 5-1. The Kinsey Scale

RATING	DESCRIPTION
0	Exclusively heterosexual
1	Predominantly heterosexual, only incidentally homosexual
2	Predominantly heterosexual, but more than incidentally homosexual
3	Equally heterosexual and homosexual
4	Predominantly homosexual, but more than incidentally heterosexual
5	Predominantly homosexual, only incidentally heterosexual
6	Exclusively homosexual
X	Asexual

(Source: Kinsey Institute, 1948.)

The many factors that may determine sexual orientation are not completely understood. Most scientists believe it is a combination of biological, hormonal, emotional, and environmental factors.

Heterosexuality

Surveys indicate that the majority of the American population is sexually attracted to the opposite gender. There are many cultural norms in place to encourage a heterosexual lifestyle: it is the primary lifestyle we experience as children, and most individuals eventually emulate the behavior of parents, family, or other role models. The societal norm of heterosexuality provides a comfort level for a lifestyle that is familiar and accepted. Although heterosexuals are attracted to the opposite gender, it is possible to be curious about a relationship with the same gender without being homosexual.

Homosexuality

About ten percent of males and five percent of females identify themselves as being exclusively homosexual. These individuals are sexually attracted to and engage in sexual activity with the same gender. It was not until 1973 that the American Psychiatric Association changed the designation of homosexuality as a psychiatric disorder;[7] prior to that time, homosexuality was considered deviant sexual behavior, and most medical or psychiatric interventions involved attempts to "cure" it. Today, most experts recognize that sexual orientation is not a choice, and therefore it cannot be changed. Some people who are homosexual may hide their orientation to avoid prejudice that exists, or to avoid a personal moral conflict.

Bisexuality

About five percent of the population identifies as being sexually attracted to both genders, and may have sexual experiences with both genders. These relationships are not necessarily concurrent and may be more the result of partner availability than a true bisexual orientation. A person may also identify as primarily heterosexual or homosexual, and have an occasional bisexual relationship.

Transgender and Transsexual

Transgender individuals identify with the opposite gender, perhaps dressing as and assuming the typical mannerisms of that gender. A transsexual believes that he or she is or should be the opposite sex, and may experience both social and emotional difficulty as a result of this conflict. Some transsexuals elect to have sexual reassignment surgery, in which the anatomy is changed from one gender to the other. Sexual reassignment surgery is uncommon and includes extensive psychotherapy and hormonal therapy prior to surgery.[8]

Motivation Maximizer

If your professor asked you to write an anonymous statement about your attitude regarding your personal sexuality, what would you say? At this stage of your life, when most individuals reading this text are young adults, thoughts of sex may not be far from your mind. But how would you describe your sexual self? Look again at the Kinsey scale in this chapter. This scale from zero to six allows for considerable sexual orientation variability. How would you rate yourself at this point in your life? One of the most important components of adult sexual relationships is to have a clear understanding of your personal views regarding sexual orientation, so you can be honest about your own sexuality and accepting of the views of others. Statistically, most individuals identify on the Kinsey scale as zero, exclusively heterosexual. But is this an accurate reflection of your true feelings? Only you know the answer. Accountability and honesty in a sexual relationship begins with accountability and honesty regarding your personal views. If you are accountable for the things you say and the sexual self you project, you can make honest and ethical decisions regarding your sexual relationships. Discussions about sex are difficult in many relationships, as there may be a lack of genuineness and honesty. Be accountable and take responsibility for this very important component of your life.

Sexual Stimulation and Intercourse

Sexual stimulation for both men and women can involve touching, licking, or manipulating any part of the body, but particularly those areas that are known as erogenous zones, such as the nipples and genitals. When an individual becomes sexually aroused, noticeable physiologic changes occur, including heightened tactile sensitivity to erogenous areas, as well as increases in heart rate, blood pressure, and respiration.

> **Key Term**
>
> **Erogenous zones**: Areas of the body that become hypersensitive to touch during sexual arousal.

Erotic Sexual Behavior

Starting in adolescence and continuing through adulthood, it is common for both genders to explore and touch their own genitals, and for most, this will cause a level of sexual arousal. This exploration includes masturbation, during which the genitals are self-stimulated to the point of orgasm, as well as self-exploration of erogenous zones, causing a heightened sense of pleasure and sexual arousal, though not to the point of orgasm.

Erotic sexual behavior can be enjoyed by couples or by individuals. It usually involves either creating visual fantasies or watching erotic media. Masturbation, whether manually, by rubbing the genitalia against objects, or by using stimulating devices such as vibrators, may also be part of eroticism. For some people, cultural, social, or religious beliefs may cause feelings of guilt and make enjoyment difficult or impossible. Knowing your partner, talking with your partner, and understanding your partner's motivation are necessary components to a satisfying sexual relationship.

Oral genital stimulation is often an expansion of erotic touch. Oral stimulation of the penis with the mouth is called **fellatio**. **Cunnilingus** is oral stimulation of the female genitalia. This is a part of foreplay for many couples, and can enhance sexual stimulation prior to intercourse, possibly leading to orgasm for one or both individuals.

Key Terms

Fellatio: Oral stimulation of the penis.

Cunnilingus: Oral stimulation of the labia, clitoris, and vaginal entrance.

Sexual Intercourse

Sexual intercourse is typically the result of sexual arousal that may culminate in orgasm. For partners engaged in sexual intercourse, it is possible to have simultaneous orgasms. However, an orgasm may not occur simultaneously or may not occur at all, and the experience can still be a pleasurable one. Only about one-third of women report having an orgasm during penile penetration, but seventy percent of women are able to achieve orgasm as a result of masturbation.[9] For heterosexual couples, sexual intercourse involves either vaginal or anal penetration by the penis. For gay men, intercourse may involve anal penetration by the penis, mutual masturbation, or use of sexual aids. For lesbian women, sexual intercourse involves mutual manual manipulation of the genitalia with fingers or sexual aids. The stages of the human sexual response cycle from excitement to orgasm are the same for heterosexual couples, gay and lesbian couples, and even for an individual who masturbates to orgasm.

Anal Intercourse

Anal intercourse, practiced by about ten percent of heterosexual couples and fifty percent of homosexual males, is the stimulation and penetration of the anus by the penis, fingers, or with sexual aids. Because the tissue in the rectal passage is very thin, unprotected anal intercourse heightens the risk for transmission of sexually transmitted infections, including human immune deficiency virus (HIV). Use of condoms can make the practice safer, but does not eliminate all risk.

Sexual Fantasy and Phone Sex

Sexual fantasy involves using the creative power of imagination to produce images or thoughts that may be sexual in nature. Some individuals and couples use fantasy and visual and auditory media while masturbating to orgasm; other individuals use fantasy or imagery during sexual intercourse with a familiar partner to increase the excitement of what may have become a potentially normal, predictable event. Thoughts of fantasy are sexually arousing to some people, when the fantasy includes expressions of sexual intimacy that are unlikely to be experienced in reality. This may include fantasy sex with a member of the same gender, a popular media figure, or any individual who is not a realistic sexual partner.

Sexual fantasy can precipitate phone sex, in which two or more consensual adults describe sexual acts or give instructions over the phone. Today, a large industry has evolved allowing individuals to pay a fee to call telephone sex lines. Phone sex is not always anonymous, and may be shared by couples that are separated geographically but enjoy expressing themselves sexually over the phone.

Abstinence and Celibacy

Abstinence usually involves avoiding sexual intercourse with another person for a period of time, though sexually abstinent people may still engage in masturbation. Celibacy is a permanent commitment to abstain from sex. The choice to have sex is personal, but can be greatly influenced by parents, religion, peers, and cultural norms.

Safer Sex

The term "safer sex" began to be used in the early 1980s, when human immunodeficiency virus/acquired immunodeficiency syndrome (HIV/AIDS) was recognized as a fatal sexually transmitted disease. The term refers to sexual penetration when a Co is worn. It is called safer sex because even though a condom does not offer 100 percent protection against pregnancy or transmission of disease or infection, it is safer than not using a condom.

It is difficult for most people to have a discussion about sex, especially early in a relationship. Even when a couple is sexually active, there is often little discussion about personal concerns, likes and dislikes, history of sexually transmitted diseases, or history of sexual abuse. The riskiest behavior involves multiple sex partners, in which the primary interest is having sex, with little interest in forming a relationship. This is sometimes called anonymous sex, and is most widely practiced by homosexual men. Anonymous sex is the main reason HIV/AIDS was initially seen as a gay men's disease in America, because the gay male community was originally most affected. The ability to communicate about sex is ultimately a safety issue, one for which you have personal responsibility.

Just as other risky behaviors may occur under the influence of drugs and alcohol, so does risky sexual activity. It can lead to a variety of negative consequences, ranging from unplanned pregnancy, sexually transmitted infections, and even to charges of molestation and rape.

Casandra's Story

Cassandra was in her first term at the university. She came from a small town and had little experience with the sort of life she was now enjoying. She was living in the dorm, meeting new friends, going to parties most weekends, and having a great time. She was concerned because her new boyfriend was talking about taking their relationship a step further. He did not know that she was a virgin, and that she was scared to death of the suggestions he was making about having sex. To him, this seemed to be an expected part of any relationship.

Cassandra talked with the girls in her dorm about this dilemma. She did not want to mention that she had never had sex, but she wanted to know what they would do if a guy suggested having sex. Her friends told her get on the pill—it is that easy! Cassandra did not even know where to get birth control pills, so she ventured into the Student Health Center on campus.

She got much more information than she expected. The nurse talked about different contraceptive methods, sexually transmitted diseases, and even about Cassandra's right to say no. Cassandra had not even considered *not* agreeing to have sex. After all, she did not want him to think that she was inexperienced or unsophisticated.

That evening, she considered her options. She wondered if sex would improve the relationship she was in, and decided she had not even thought of him much in the past couple of weeks. How would sex change her feelings about him? She thought about what he might say when she said no to sex, and wondered if he would pass comments on to other guys about her being frigid or afraid. Could she stand this kind of insult?

But her concerns were unwarranted. When she told him no, he said that was okay with him and if she changed her mind, he wanted to be the first to know. But in the meantime, they would continue to be friends and spend time together.

Cassandra began to think that it is nice not to feel pressured to have sex, and that she might be seeing this boyfriend further into the future than she had anticipated. ■

Cybersex or Internet Sex

The Internet has provided new opportunities for connecting people, without regard to geographic area. There are many online dating services that allow individuals to exchange information online and arrange for a face-to-face meeting. Although there are many Internet sites that provide legitimate dating services, there is also a darker side of the Internet that includes pornography and sex for hire. The Internet is an anonymous place, where pedophiles can easily troll the sites visited by children. Many have successfully arranged liaisons with children, sometimes in cooperation with the parents. Law enforcement has become more proactive in discouraging this activity by posing as children online, making arrangements to meet, and arresting the pedophile when the meeting occurs. For safety, sharing personal information on the Internet, such as full name and address, should be avoided, and children should be monitored carefully when using the Internet.

Key Term

Pedophiles: Adults who are sexually attracted to children.

Sexual Dysfunction

Sexual dysfunction is a condition in which personal sexual gratification is reduced or lacking completely as a result of a psychological trauma, such as sexual abuse, sexual assault, or rape, or may be due to physical limitation, including chronic diseases such as diabetes, cardiovascular disease, and cancer, as well as the hormonal changes that occur with aging.

Female Sexual Dysfunction

It is common for most women to experience at least one episode of sexual dysfunction at some point in their lives. The symptoms include difficulty with at least one stage of the human sexual response cycle, and may occur **postpartum**, at menopause, or as the result of an illness. Most women's health practitioners do not believe a true sexual dysfunction exists unless it negatively affects a relationship with a partner or causes emotional distress. The symptoms of female sexual dysfunction are low interest in sex, inability to become sexually aroused, lack of orgasm, and pain while having intercourse. Treatment is available for both the physical and psychological causes of female sexual dysfunction.[10]

Key Term

Postpartum: The time period following childbirth.

Low Sexual Desire and Sexual Arousal

Lack of interest in sex may be caused by hormones; for example, when estrogen is diminished at menopause. It may occur postpartum, when a new mother has anxiety about her many new parenting roles. Physical changes or illness may also be a factor: obesity and the resulting poor self-esteem may lead to a lack of comfort with one's own body, causing low interest in sex. Anxiety, depression, or posttraumatic stress syndrome from sexual abuse or rape can cause a decreased or lack of interest in sexual activity. Psychological issues need to be addressed, in addition to investigating the possibility that the cause may be organic.[11]

Painful Intercourse

In younger women, painful intercourse, or **dyspareunia**, may occur when the **hymen** is still intact and the young woman is a virgin. Dyspareunia may also occur when a young woman engaged in sexual intercourse with a male may not have reached full sexual arousal and the vagina is not fully lubricated. The penis may also be too large to be comfortably accommodated by the vagina, even when the woman is fully aroused.

Key Terms

Hymen: A fold of mucous membrane that surrounds and partially covers the external vaginal opening.

Dyspareunia: Painful intercourse.

Painful intercourse for older women may be the result of physical changes caused by a decrease in the hormone estrogen, including a reduction in the size of the labia that surround the clitoris, causing more of the clitoris to be exposed and leading to an unpleasant feeling during sexual activity. The vagina also loses some elasticity, becoming narrower, and the natural lubrication produced during sexual arousal occurs more slowly, and is sometime inadequate. All of these symptoms can be managed and treated, and many menopausal women continue to have satisfying sexual relationships.

Orgasmic Dysfunction

Orgasmic dysfunction means difficulty in achieving an orgasm, even after sufficient stimulation and arousal. If the problem is persistent and frequent, some doctors will prescribe a series of exercises to strengthen the muscles of the pelvis. The most common of these are Kegel exercises, which require that a woman tighten her pelvic muscles as if she were stopping her flow of urine. For some women, strengthening pelvic muscles improves pleasurable sexual sensations.

Male Sexual Dysfunction

The primary male sexual dysfunctions are premature ejaculation, erectile dysfunction, and low interest in sex. The type of sexual dysfunction is sometimes a characteristic of age, but other reasons include relationship problems, depression or anxiety, substance abuse, obesity, diabetes, or other chronic health problems.

Premature Ejaculation

Premature ejaculation refers to ejaculation that occurs before penetration. It may be caused by fatigue, stress, consumption of alcohol, or drug use. It may also happen when a man is inexperienced in sexual activity. For some men, premature ejaculation has been a problem from their earliest sexual activity; for others, it can become a problem even after years of previously satisfying sexual relationships. Men who are experiencing additional stress or anxiety about their relationship or other events in their lives are more likely to experience premature ejaculation. Once a pattern of premature ejaculation is established, it is considered sexual dysfunction. For most men, it causes additional concern and anxiety, possibly exacerbating the problem.

Erectile Dysfunction

Erectile dysfunction (ED), also called impotence, is the inability to achieve or maintain an erection firm enough for sexual intercourse. It is more common in older men, especially men over the age of sixty-five, but is not necessarily part of aging. The most common causes for erectile dysfunction are diseases that affect the nervous and vascular systems, such as diabetes, kidney disease, prostate disease, heart disease, multiple sclerosis, and chronic alcoholism. Treatment for ED usually involves a recommendation for lifestyle changes, such as weight loss, smoking cessation, or an exercise program, and may also involve individual or couple counseling to discover anxieties associated with intercourse. Since 1998, the treatment may also involve oral medications, such as Viagra.

Image of Health in Depth

The Little Blue Pill

Viagra was the first drug approved by the Food and Drug Administration to cause the penis to become erect. It works by enhancing the effects of nitric oxide, a chemical that relaxes smooth muscles and allows for more blood flow to the penis during sexual stimulation. Viagra and two other ED drugs, Cialis and Levitra, belong to a class of drugs called PDE (phosphodiesterase) inhibitors. They are similar in their effectiveness, and must be taken one hour prior to intercourse.

Painful Intercourse

Painful intercourse (dyspareunia) for men has several potential causes: it may be due to a skin disorder on the penis, such as eczema or psoriasis, or possibly caused by Peyronie's disease, a disorder that causes the bending of the penis while erect. Another possibility for uncircumcised males is foreskin that is too tight to retract over the head of the penis during intercourse. **Circumcision** can alleviate this condition.[12]

Key Term

Circumcision: The removal of the foreskin from the head of the penis. It is routinely performed in the United States on male babies. In many other parts of the world, including many European countries, circumcision is not as common.

Reproduction

Responsible sexual behavior provides a choice about pregnancy. Ideally, pregnancy should always be a choice made by the couple or the prospective mother.

Conception

The miracle of life begins when a viable sperm from the male penetrates an egg from the female. The joining of sperm and egg is called conception, which marks the start of a remarkable process that, in approximately nine months, results in the birth of a baby.

Normal Fertilization

In most circumstances, the egg is fertilized in the fallopian tube. After the male ejaculates into the vagina, sperm make their way through the vagina and uterus and into both fallopian tubes. Sperm swim by a method called flagellation, wherein the tail of the sperm whips back and forth, propelling it forward. There are up to 300 million sperm in each ejaculation, but only about 50–200 make it all the way to the waiting egg. As soon as the first sperm penetrates the egg, an enzyme is produced by the egg, making it impenetrable to all other sperm. The egg and sperm combine deoxyribonucleic acid (**DNA**), 23 chromosomes from the male and 23 chromosomes from the female, and a brand-new genetic blueprint is created. This first combination of cellular division produces a zygote, and over the next five to seven days, the zygote makes its way down the fallopian tube to the uterus. It attaches to the rich nutritive layer in the **endometrium**, where is it considered a blastocyst, a mass of about 150 cells. The inner layer of blastocyst cells becomes the embryo, while the outer layer of cells becomes the **placenta**. For the next eight weeks, the embryo continues to grow, and at eight weeks it is considered a fetus. The placenta evolves from blastocyst cells and is attached to the fetus by an umbilical cord. The **amniotic sac**, filled with **amniotic fluid**, surrounds the fetus and the umbilical cord. The health of the fetus depends on the health of the placenta, the umbilical cord, and the amniotic sac.

Challenge Question: Describe the process of normal fertilization.

> **Key Terms**
>
> **DNA**: Deoxyribonucleic acid, the molecular basis of heredity.
>
> **Endometrium**: The mucous membrane lining the uterus that is composed of three layers.
>
> **Placenta**: An organ that connects the developing fetus to the uterine wall to allow nutrient uptake, waste elimination, and gas exchange via the mother's blood supply.
>
> **Amniotic sac**: A thin membrane that forms a sac around the embryo and fetus.
>
> **Amniotic fluid**: The fluid that suspends the embryo and fetus within the amniotic sac.

Identical and Fraternal Twins

Under normal circumstances, the possibility of having twins is primarily determined by genetic history. If you are a twin, or if you have sets of twins in your family, you are more likely to give birth to twins if you choose to become pregnant. Other circumstances that can cause twins or multiple births involve fertility treatments, which are an option for couples that are incapable of conceiving and want a family.

Identical twins are created when an egg is fertilized by one sperm, then divides into two zygotes with identical sets of DNA that share the same gender and every other physical trait. Identical twins are a mirror image of each other, and often seem to share an emotional and psychological closeness throughout life.

Fraternal twins occur when two eggs are penetrated by two sperm. The combination of DNA will be different for each twin, including the sex chromosome that determines gender. This allows for the possibility that twins will be of opposite gender and not identical in their physical characteristics. They go through fetal development together, and are born during the same birthing process.

Critical Thinking Question: Describe the process of conception for both identical twins and fraternal twins.

Pre-Parenting Behavior

Responsible pre-parenting behavior involves a careful consideration of the many consequences that a pregnancy will have on the lives of prospective parents and families. It is much easier if a pregnancy is planned, because it implies that the couple is in agreement about choosing to become parents. If a pregnancy is unplanned, the prospective mother may have the full support of her partner, or she may make all pre-parenting decisions alone or with very little support.

Financial Considerations

The costs of having a baby depend on several factors, including availability of health care facilities, health insurance coverage, hospital costs, or birthing facility costs. It also depends on the birth itself. Even with the cost of an **epidural**, a normal vaginal delivery is less expensive than a **Caesarean section**, but may not be an option for some women. A Caesarean section is more expensive because it is a surgical procedure and requires a hospital stay.

Key Terms

Epidural: A local anesthetic injected into the space between the outer membrane covering the spinal cord and the bones of the spine. It is used during childbirth to help alleviate the pain of a vaginal delivery.

Caesarean section: Abdominal surgical delivery involving multiple incisions through the abdomen and uterus to remove the baby. This also involves an epidural to allow the mother to be conscious and aware, but pain-free during the procedure.

Costs for having a baby depends on how long mother and baby stay in the hospital, as well as if there are any medical complications. A normal, non-complicated delivery in which both the mother and baby are discharged within 24 hours may cost $4,000, while medical complications and longer hospital stays increase these costs to $20,000 or more. Most health insurance providers have adequate maternity care, but there is variability between plans. If you plan to have children and you have a choice of health insurance plans, comparing maternity benefits is advised. Birthing clinics and midwife services are usually much less expensive but may not have adequate medical knowledge or facilities to accommodate a medical emergency during a complicated delivery.

Choosing a Physician

For many women, the choice of a physician for pregnancy is her family practice doctor, who will probably refer her to an obstetrician/gynecologist OB/GYN once the pregnancy is confirmed.

A doctor who specializes in the care of pregnant women is an **obstetrician** who is either a medical doctor or an **osteopath**. An obstetrician has completed further training in obstetrics and gynecology after medical school, specializing in prenatal care and delivery. An osteopath specializes in the manipulation of the muscles and bones but also uses conventional medicine for maternity care and delivery.

If the pregnancy is considered high risk, the patient may be referred to a **perinatologist**, an obstetrician with additional training who specializes in high-risk pregnancies. Women who have had difficulty with past pregnancies or have developed serious problems during a pregnancy may benefit from the care of a perinatologist.

A woman who has a low-risk, uncomplicated pregnancy may request that a **certified nurse-midwife** deliver her baby. A certified nurse-midwife is a registered nurse who has additional professional training in nurse-midwifery. A physician oversees the work of a nurse-midwife and is available should complications arise. Nurse-midwives generally work in nonhospital settings called birthing clinics, and may not be covered by all insurance plans.

> **Key Terms**
>
> **Obstetrician**: A medical doctor (MD) who specializes in pregnancy, labor and immediate post delivery.
>
> **Osteopath**: A doctor of osteopathy (DO) who specializes in maintaining correct relationships between bones, muscles and connective tissues.
>
> **Perinatologist**: A medical doctor (MD) who is an obstetrician that specializes in high-risk pregnancies.
>
> **Certified nurse-midwife**: A person with an AS, BS, or MS degree in nursing and who has also completed specialized training in midwifery.

Infertility

When a couple desiring a pregnancy has difficulty conceiving for approximately one year, infertility in both the male and female is suspected. Infertility has many causes and can affect either gender. Historically, a variety of folklore remedies of dubious scientific validity have been recommended to couples who could not conceive. It was not until the end of the twentieth century that sophisticated options to improve fertility became available.

Female Infertility

One of the most common reasons for female infertility is a problem with ovulation. Hormones control ovulation, and if either the pituitary gland or hypothalamus is not working properly, ovulation will cease. Ovulation can also be erratic because of stress, obesity, excessive weight loss, over exercise, diabetes, and thyroid gland or adrenal gland irregularities.

Age is also a factor. After age 35, becoming pregnant is more difficult. Early menopause that stops ovulation can occur either naturally when eggs stop being released, or as a result of surgical removal of the ovaries. When ovulation stops and the egg is not released, fertilization is impossible.

Conception usually takes place in a fallopian tube, and about 40 percent of infertility issues are caused by blocked fallopian tubes. Some women are born with one or both tubes malformed, and scarring caused by an ectopic pregnancy or endometriosis may also prevent the sperm from reaching the egg. The most common cause of tube blockage is pelvic inflammatory disease (PID), the result of an infection of Chlamydia or gonorrhea. Both of these

sexually transmitted infections rarely present symptoms in women, so there is no indication of infection until PID develops. Since a woman has two fallopian tubes, fertility may still occur in the non-blocked tube. Microscopic surgery can open the tube, but if it has burst, there are no options.

Male Infertility

About fifteen percent of couples are infertile, and in about half those cases, male infertility is the cause. Male infertility is due to low sperm production, misshapen or immobile sperm, blockages in the urethra that prevent the delivery of sperm, or the inability to effectively ejaculate. Illnesses, injuries, chronic health problems, lifestyle choices, and other factors can play a role in male infertility.

Factors that reduce sperm production or cause sperm to develop inappropriately include smoking tobacco or marijuana, excessive alcohol use, diabetes, obesity, and excessive weight loss. Overheating the testicles either by prolonged periods of sitting, tight clothing, or hot baths may also affect sperm production, since sperm are most effectively produced at 3–5 degrees cooler than body temperature.

Treatments depend on the cause and include surgery, medications, and perhaps treating sexual intimacy issues.

Infertility Treatments and Options

About 85 percent of infertile couples can be diagnosed and treated with conventional medical therapies. If conventional therapies do not work, other therapies, including **assisted reproductive technology (ART)**, are the next option.

> **Key Term**
>
> **Assisted reproductive technology (ART)**: Includes all fertility treatments wherein both eggs and sperm are handled. It does not include artificial insemination (sperm only) or medically inducing egg production (egg only) unless the intention includes egg retrieval.

Intrauterine Insemination

Intrauterine insemination, also called artificial insemination, involves introducing sperm through a small, flexible catheter inserted through the vagina and into the uterus, where the sperm are expelled. The woman is given fertility drugs to produce multiple eggs and is carefully monitored to ensure the procedure occurs at the time of ovulation. Sperm are separated from the other components of semen and stored. When ovulation is imminent, an intrauterine insemination procedure is performed.[13]

In Vitro Fertilization (IVF)

In vitro fertilization (IVF), conception outside the womb that usually occurs in a laboratory, is the oldest clinical fertility technique. Fertility drugs are given to stimulate the production of multiple eggs. Eggs are extracted and combined with sperm in laboratory setting resulting in the creation of human embryos. Two or more embryos are transferred into the uterus using a thin catheter that passes through the vagina and cervix. Multiple embryo transfer improves the chances of implantation and pregnancy, and also improves the chances for multiple births, which may or may not be desired. This procedure is often used by women with blocked fallopian tubes and in women under age 35, and results in a live birth about 30–35 percent of the time.[14]

Image of Health in Depth

Louise Brown: The First Test Tube Baby

The first successful in vitro fertilization procedure occurred in 1978, and resulted in the birth of Louise Brown in Bristol, England. Louise's mother had blocked fallopian tubes and after nine years of attempting to become pregnant, she became part of a new experimental procedure. This procedure involved using a laparoscope to remove an egg from the mother's ovary, combine it with sperm from the father in a laboratory test tube, and after two days, placing the fertilized egg in the mother's uterus. Throughout the pregnancy, many concerns were expressed about the health of a baby conceived outside the human body. Louise Brown was born on July 25, 1978, a healthy baby girl.

Gamete Intrafallopian Transfer (GIFT)

Gamete intrafallopian transfer (GIFT) involves extracting mature eggs from the ovary and transferring them to the fallopian tube along with sperm. This procedure may be used when sperm count is low or ovulation is irregular. Fertility drugs are given to stimulate the production of multiple eggs, and the eggs are transferred to the fallopian tube. Some couples prefer this method because

if successful, conception still takes place in the fallopian tube, not in a laboratory. Since multiple eggs are transferred, multiple births are a possibility.

Zygote Intrafallopian Transfer (ZIFT)

Zygote intrafallopian transfer (ZIFT) may be used if the fallopian tubes are completely blocked, preventing sperm from ever reaching an egg. Fertility drugs are given to stimulate multiple eggs, eggs are removed from a woman's ovaries and fertilized in a laboratory, and after the in vitro procedure, a fertilized egg is placed in an unblocked part of the fallopian tube via laparoscopic procedure. The fertilized egg travels from the fallopian tube to the uterus, where it implants in the endometrium.

Surrogate Parenting

Surrogate parenting involves a contract with a woman who will become pregnant and give birth to a baby for another person. The surrogate may work independently or through an agency. Couples who use a surrogate mother have usually exhausted their options for creating their own pregnancy. In many cases, sperm from the father is used so that the genetic composition of the baby represents at least one parent.

Adoption

Adoption is always an option for an infertile couple. It requires a court order that names an individual or individuals as having legal parenting rights. There are adoption agencies worldwide that can facilitate the adoption of a baby from almost any country, and there are hundreds of children in the United States that are available for adoption. The most difficult children to place for adoption are older children, those with special needs, babies born to mothers addicted to drugs, and those born with HIV. Adoption is sometimes the result of surrogate parenting, when grandparents who are raising grandchildren legally adopt, or foster parents decide to adopt children in their care.

Pregnancy

Responsible sexual behavior makes pregnancy a choice made by sexually active individuals. Parents of any age must consider that having a baby involves years of physical, emotional, and financial nurturing, requiring a commitment of time that changes the lives of everyone involved who cares for a new baby.

There are several early signs of pregnancy, and each woman's experience will be slightly different. The most obvious indication is a missed menstrual period. Once an egg is fertilized, ovulation ceases and so do monthly menstrual periods. Some women have a light monthly menstrual-like bleeding during pregnancy, but the amount of blood is far less than a normal monthly period. Other early symptoms include fatigue; breasts that are sore or tender to touch; nausea, especially in the morning; and increased urination.

Pregnancy Testing

Pregnancy testing kits work by detecting the presence of human chorionic gonadotropin (hCG) in urine. After conception and implantation in the uterus, the embryo begins to make hCG, which becomes detectable in urine in about two weeks. Human chorionic gonadotropin is also later produced by the placenta. Its primary role is to preserve the disintegration of the corpus luteum of the ovary that makes progesterone, a hormone required for a successful pregnancy.[15]

Key Term

Human chorionic gonadotropin (hCG): A hormone produced during a pregnancy, first by the embryo and later by the placenta. Its purpose is to maintain production of progesterone.

Challenge Question: Describe how a pregnancy testing kit confirms a pregnancy.

Pregnancy Trimesters

Pregnancy is divided into trimesters of approximately 13 weeks each. The first trimester starts from the point of conception. The fertilized egg begins to divide rapidly, and at this stage is called a zygote. After about 5 days, the zygote becomes a blastocyst and attaches to the uterine wall. By the end of the second week after conception, the blastocyst becomes an embryo. The embryo continues cellular division at a spectacular rate, concentrating on the framework for all major systems of the body, especially the nervous system and the circulatory system. By the end of the first trimester, the foundation for all major body systems is in place, and the embryo is now considered a fetus. The heart is beating, fingers and toes are formed, and gender is usually apparent. The tiny fetus is only three inches long and weighs less than one ounce.

During the second trimester, the new mother's physical appearance begins to indicate that she is pregnant. Breasts become larger, waist thickens, and for most women, the nausea and other side effects of early pregnancy begin to diminish. The fetus continues to grow, completing the development of most body systems. By the end of the second trimester, the baby is twelve to fifteen inches long and weighs between one to two pounds. The fetus has a fifty percent survival rate if premature birth occurs at this point.

Most fetal growth occurs during the third trimester. From week 33, the baby is gaining one-half pound per week until birth occurs at around week forty. This final rapid weight gain is important for the health of the newborn. Babies born prematurely who do not experience this final fetal growth spurt may have serious complications.

Prenatal Testing

There are several types of prenatal testing that are used to determine the risk of birth defects such as **Down syndrome**, **spina bifida**, **cystic fibrosis**, or **cleft palate**. Non-invasive tests, such as **ultrasonography** or maternal serum screens, are usually preformed first. Ultrasonography or ultrasound involves diagnostic imaging to determine structural abnormalities in the fetus. A common maternal serum screen is **alpha-fetoprotein screen**, wherein the mother's blood is tested to determine the level of alpha-fetoprotein in her blood. If these levels are high, it may be an indication that there is a problem with the fetus or the placenta. In this case, a more invasive procedure such as **amniocentesis** may be performed, in which a syringe is used to withdraw amniotic fluid from the amniotic sac. Amniotic fluid is a replica of the genetic blueprint for the developing fetus, and will indicate if there are birth defects—the risk for which increases with the age of the mother. Placental tissue shares the same genetic characteristics as the fetus, and in chorionic villus sampling, a small sample of the placenta is extracted and tested. Chorionic villus sampling can be performed earlier in the pregnancy, usually after the tenth week, whereas amniocentesis is not performed until at least the fourteenth week.

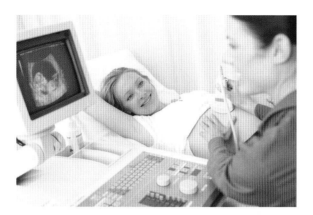

Key Terms

Down syndrome: A congenital condition characterized by mental retardation, upward slanting eyes, broad short skull, broad hands with short fingers, and little muscle tone.

Spina bifida: A congenital condition in which the spinal column is not completely sealed, allowing for protrusion of the meninges and possibly the spinal cord.

Cystic fibrosis: A hereditary disease that causes difficulty with digestion and breathing, due to excessive mucus accumulation in airways.

Cleft palate: A congenital separation of the roof of the mouth and sometimes the lip.

Ultrasonography: A pregnancy ultrasound that uses sound waves to observe fetal development in the womb.

Alpha-fetoprotein screen: A prenatal blood test to determine the level of maternal alpha-fetoprotein (AFP) in a pregnant woman. A high level of AFP is a marker for spina bifida.

Amniocentesis: The extraction of amniotic fluid from the amniotic sac surrounding the fetus to screen for genetic abnormalities.

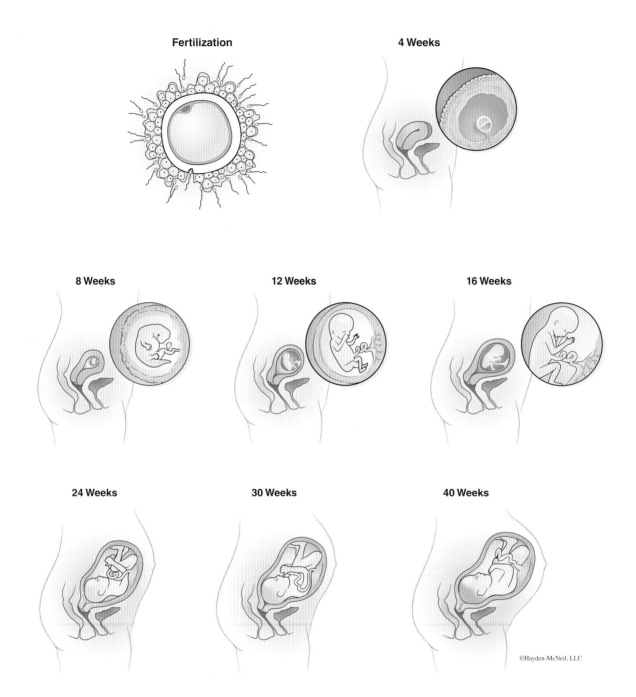

FIGURE 5-4. Fetal development over several weeks.

Pregnancy Complications

A difficult pregnancy is more likely for a woman with one or more of the following characteristics: older than thirty-five, of poor general health, a history of or addiction to drugs and alcohol, HIV positive, a history of sexually transmitted diseases, previous high-risk pregnancy, overweight or underweight, or has diabetes. Multiple risk factors increase the likelihood of a difficult pregnancy. Perinatology, or maternal fetal medicine, is a subspecialty of obstetrics in which treatment is performed by medical professionals who are trained to care for both fetus and mother in higher-than-normal-risk pregnancies. A perinatologist may be necessary if the fetus has a known abnormality, or if the mother has a condition that may affect the fetus.[16]

Ectopic Pregnancy

An ectopic or tubal pregnancy takes place outside the uterus, usually in the fallopian tube. Instead of implanting in the endometrium of the uterus, the fertilized egg attaches to the wall of the fallopian tube, where development progresses until the fallopian tube can no longer accommodate the growth. This mass of cells is abnormal, unable to grow into a normal fetus. Indications of ectopic pregnancy are lower abdominal pain, unusual bleeding, and a positive pregnancy test. Without treatment, about one-half of ectopic pregnancies are resolved by spontaneous tubal abortion. In other cases, especially if the fallopian tube has ruptured or is about to rupture, a laparoscopic surgery is performed to remove the mass of cells from the fallopian tube. Ectopic pregnancy may be caused by older age of the mother, smoking, history of pelvic inflammatory disease, use of fertility drugs, and prior fallopian tube damage from infection, such as sexually transmitted infections. After an ectopic pregnancy, future pregnancies depend on whether the fallopian tube was removed or repaired. Only a small percentage of women who experience ectopic pregnancy are infertile.[17]

Spontaneous Abortion

Spontaneous abortion, also called miscarriage, refers to any pregnancy that ends spontaneously before the fetus is able to survive outside of the uterus. Spontaneous abortions most often occur during the first trimester, but may occur up to the twentieth week of pregnancy; after the twentieth week, pregnancy losses are called preterm deliveries. Once fetal heart rate is detected, the risk diminishes to about five percent. There is an increased risk for spontaneous abortion if women are older than thirty-five, smoke cigarettes, or have lupus or diabetes. Other risks include hormonal irregularities such as Cushing's syndrome and thyroid disease, sexually transmitted diseases such as herpes, and uterine structural abnormalities such as fibroid cysts.[18]

Effects of Drugs, Smoking, and Alcohol

Using drugs, smoking, and drinking alcohol all affect the developing fetus and increase the risk of spontaneous abortion and abnormal fetal development. Any substance inhaled, injected, drunk, or consumed enters the mother's blood and is circulated to the fetus. The level of risk depends on the type of drug and frequency of use.

A considerable amount of research shows the damage caused to the fetus by maternal alcohol use. Fetal Alcohol Disorder Syndrome (FADS) is a group of symptoms that include mental retardation, birth defects, abnormal facial features, cognitive impairment, and vision and hearing problems. The effects of fetal alcohol syndrome will be present throughout the life of the child. However, these effects can be avoided entirely if the mother chooses not to drink during pregnancy.[19]

Marijuana use has been shown to reduce sperm count in men and cause irregular menstrual periods in women, and there is some evidence that marijuana also affects sperm motility and penetration of the egg. Long-term affects do not seem to be as severe as fetal alcohol disorder syndrome; however, the tetrahydrocannabinol (THC) in marijuana is not blocked by the placenta, and virtually all THC will enter the fetus. Tetrahydrocannabinol is a known psychoactive substance that affects the brain. Though the effect on the brain of a developing fetus is not known, the effect on an adult brain can range from analgesic to hallucinogenic, depending on the amount and concentration.[20]

Smoking while pregnant reduces the amount of oxygen the fetus receives, increasing the risk of spontaneous abortion, premature birth, and stillbirth. Children born at full term to smoking mothers are more likely to have lower birth weight than those born to nonsmokers, and may be at more risk for sudden infant death syndrome.[21]

Premature Labor

Premature or preterm labor may occur after week twenty, or up to three weeks prior to the expected delivery date.

Contractions in the uterus cause the cervix to dilate earlier than normal and can result in a premature birth. Contractions in premature labor can often be stopped, so it is important for women to recognize the symptoms and seek medical help, allowing the fetus to continue to grow and develop in the uterus.

Labor and Birth

Labor may start a few weeks or a few hours before birth, beginning with "lightening": when the baby settles lower in the pelvis, moving closer to the birth canal. Located at the cervix, the mucus plug accumulates throughout the pregnancy and is discharged when the cervix begins to dilate. This may happen up to two weeks before delivery, or immediately prior to birth. Labor contractions are experienced differently by each woman, and may even differ for the same woman with successive pregnancies. It is generally described as similar to strong menstrual cramps, causing a dull ache in the lower back and lower abdomen. The uterus contracts in a wavelike motion from top to bottom that lasts from 30–90 seconds, occurring 15–20 minutes apart. During uterine contractions, the abdomen becomes hard, and is soft between contractions. For natural childbirth, various birthing techniques teach women to breathe, relax, and concentrate during contractions. As birth becomes imminent, contractions are stronger and more frequent; contractions that start too early increase the risk of a premature birth. False labor, sometimes called Braxton-Hicks contractions, is actually a tightening of the abdomen that can usually be relieved by changing position. Braxton-Hicks contractions do not intensify or become more frequent, as contractions do in true labor.

The rupture of the amniotic membrane, when the "water breaks," means delivery may occur within the next 24 hours. However, even during labor the amniotic membrane does not rupture naturally for all women, and may be ruptured by the delivery room doctor in the hospital. Contractions continue and the cervix dilates until completely dilated at ten centimeters, when the baby is about to be born.

Critical Thinking Question: Describe the progressive changes that occur in labor that indicate birth is imminent.

Labor Options

There are many natural childbirth options, most involving both parents taking classes to learn how to best assist the birthing process.

Lamaze

The Lamaze technique recommends that labor begin on its own, without inducement. A spouse or partner is present, there is no routine medical intervention, and women are free to move around during labor. Birth occurs in a sitting position and mothers and babies are not separated at birth. Newborns have unlimited access to breastfeeding.[22]

Leboyer Method

The Leboyer method was designed to minimize the trauma to a newborn baby, but may also reduce the stress of childbirth for the mother. This method advocates a quiet, dimly lit birthing environment and emphasizes natural birth, with no extra effort with pushing and no use of forceps on the baby's head to help pull the baby from the birth canal. After delivery, the baby is placed on the mother, and the umbilical cord is not cut until it stops pulsing. The Leboyer method also recommends placing the new baby in a warm bath to simulate the environment in the womb.[23]

Bradley Technique

The Bradley technique is a twelve-week natural childbirth course that teaches families how to have a successful natural birth. The class encourages the bonding between the parents and baby, emphasizing the importance of the partner coach to assist in pain management relaxation techniques during labor. Drugs are not used unless the pregnancy becomes complicated. Unlike other methods, Bradley classes include information about a possible **episiotomy**, and the conditions under which a Caesarean delivery may be necessary.[24]

Key Term

Episiotomy: A surgical incision used to enlarge the perineum during childbirth to facilitate delivery.

Birthing Options

Birthing options depend on the health of both the mother and the fetus. If the pregnancy has been normal and healthy, more birthing options are available. If the pregnancy is considered high risk, the birth should take place in a hospital setting with a neonatal intensive care department.

Pregnant women have many non-hospital birthing facility settings from which to choose. Women who choose birthing centers prefer an environment that feels comfortable and more like their home. Birthing centers are not able to administer an epidural, use labor induction devices, or administer drugs, and there are no surgical alternatives such as Caesarean deliveries. A birthing center is also not able to give long-term care, and most new mothers and infants are discharged within twelve hours.

In birthing clinics and hospitals, midwives may take the place of doctors. There are various certification levels, from certified nurse-midwives to self-taught lay midwives. Most midwives work in hospitals, where they are able to refer patients to other health care professionals if the pregnancy becomes complicated. Lower cost is the primary advantage of using a midwife, which may be an appropriate choice for low-risk pregnancies.

Stages of Childbirth

It is generally recognized that there are three stages of childbirth, with levels of progress within each stage. The rupture of the amniotic membrane initiates the beginning of the actual birth, but because not all women experience "water breaking," it is not recognized as an actual stage.

The first stage is divided into three parts: early labor, active labor, and transition. During early labor, the cervix begins to dilate, contractions begin, and the cervical mucus plug is expelled. Early labor may last several hours or even a few days, especially for first-time mothers. Active labor begins when contractions increase in frequency, intensity, and duration, and the cervix dilates up to 7 centimeters. Active labor usually lasts between three and eight hours, but may be much shorter for subsequent deliveries. The cervix dilates completely to 10 centimeters and contractions increase in strength and frequency during transition, which may last between 15 minutes and 3 hours. Women who choose to have an epidural for pain relief usually do so at this point.

In the second stage, the baby is delivered. This may take a few minutes or several hours. Some birthing protocols include encouraging the mother to push once the cervix is completely dilated, while natural birth protocols allow for the birth to happen in its own time, requiring the mother to push only when it feels right to do so. Crowning occurs when the top of the baby's head is visible, and when the baby's head exits the vagina, the rest of the baby will soon follow. Health care professionals ensure that the airway is clear and the umbilical cord is free. Immediate placement of the baby will depend on the birthing facility.

The third stage of labor is the expulsion of the placenta, which usually occurs within five to ten minutes after the birth of the baby. In a traditional hospital setting, the umbilical cord is clamped and cut while it is still pulsing and attached to the placenta. Natural birthing methods recommend the umbilical cord not be cut until it stops pulsing, since the baby is still deriving nutrients and oxygen from the placenta.[25]

Birthing Complications

Childbirth is a potentially complex process that may result in a variety of complications. If childbirth takes place in a hospital, both the fetus and mother can be carefully monitored. The options for facilitating a difficult birth will depend on factors such as a premature birth, abnormally long labor, position of the baby, or any detected abnormalities.

Breech Birth

A breech birth occurs when the baby is positioned with feet or bottom toward the birth canal, rather than head first. It is not unusual for babies to be in breech position early in the pregnancy and return to a headfirst position toward the end of pregnancy. Because of the risks involved to the baby, the usual protocol for a breech birth is to perform a Caesarean delivery. With a vaginal delivery, the risks of injury to a breech baby include compressing the umbilical cord, which deprives the baby of oxygen and causes nerve and brain damage, or separating the hip socket from the femur.

Caesarean Birth

A Caesarean delivery, also know as a C-section or Caesarean section, is a surgical procedure in which incisions are made through the abdomen and uterus to deliver one or more babies. A C-section is usually preformed if the life of the fetus or mother is at risk, or if the fetus or mother are too fatigued to continue with labor. The risks of Caesarean delivery are the same as for any major operation, including postoperative infections, excessive blood loss, adhesions, or hernias.

After the Birth

Immediately after the birth of a baby, screening tests are conducted and breastfeeding begins.

Newborn Screening

Within the United States, the comprehensiveness of newborn screening varies from state to state. At minimum, newborn babies are screened for a number of genetic disorders that may not be obvious at birth. A typical test involves taking a few drops of blood from the baby's heel and sending the blood sample to a screening lab for testing. Parents are notified if there is a problem or a need to retest. Infant screening can detect serious life-threatening conditions before symptoms begin.

Breastfeeding

Most health care professionals recommend breastfeeding for at least the first six months of the baby's life. For the baby, breast milk provides complete nutrition as well as immunity to many infections. For the new mother, breastfeeding helps bonding with the new baby, delays the return of normal ovulation, and lowers the risk of breast and ovarian cancers. Breastfeeding is not recommended for women who have HIV or active tuberculosis, or for those who use drugs and alcohol.[26]

Postpartum Depression

The birth of a baby can trigger many feelings, which may include joy and excitement but may also include anxiety and depression. After giving birth, some new mothers have mood swings and crying spells called the "baby blues," but these symptoms usually subside within a couple of weeks. Other new mothers experience more intense feelings of depression for a longer period of time, called postpartum depression. Symptoms include insomnia, irritability, loss of appetite, fatigue, feelings of inadequacy, difficulty bonding with the baby, and thoughts by the mother of harming herself or the baby. There is no single cause for postpartum depression, but physical changes that include hormonal changes, feeling overwhelmed, and adjusting to the demands of a new baby are all possible causes. Treatment may include counseling, antidepressants, or hormone therapy.[27]

Sudden Infant Death Syndrome

The unexplained death of an infant less than one year old is called Sudden Infant Death Syndrome (SIDS). The causes are usually sleep related, and it is most common in infants between two and four months old. Since placing a baby on its stomach for a nap or to sleep increases the risk of SIDS, babies should always be placed on their back to sleep. The sleeping surface should be a firm mattress with a fitted sheet; loose bedding, pillows, quilts, and soft toys should be kept away from the baby's face. The baby should not be allowed to become too hot during sleep from too much clothing or a room that is too warm. Other risk factors include premature or low birth weight; babies born to mothers who smoke or use drugs; African-American, American-Indian or Native-Alaskan babies; and exposure to environmental tobacco smoke.[28]

▼

Responsibility and Accountability

Taking Responsibility for Your Sexual Health

If you are accountable for your actions, you assume responsibility for the decisions you make regarding your sexual health. This reflects your honesty and integrity as you form relationships that may include sexual intimacy, and involves decisions you make regarding relationships, family planning, pregnancy, and parenting. Being responsible for your sexual health involves making decisions about some of the most important things in life.

Focusing on Accountability for Your Sexual Health

Choices made about personal sexuality affect many aspects of life. Most of these choices concern self-care and are entirely up to you. Your sexual orientation, knowledge of sexual intimacy issues, and willingness to communicate with a partner make you accountable for personal sexual health. Choices about whether to be sexually active, form a sexual relationship, or become a parent are all measures of adult accountability.

Summary

Sexual Health

- The qualities that comprise sexuality start at conception.

- The female hormone estrogen and male hormone testosterone cause sexual development at puberty.

- Ovulation occurs when an egg is released from an ovary.

- Fertilization normally occurs in the fallopian tube.

- Menstruation is the monthly sloughing off of the nutritive layer in the uterus.

- An adult male produces 400 million sperm per day, and it takes 74 days for sperm to mature.

- Sperm are produced in the seminiferous tubules in the testes.

- Boys generally start puberty later and develop more slowly than girls.

- Premenstrual syndrome (PMS) is a collection of physical, psychological, and emotional symptoms that affect some women 1–2 weeks prior to their monthly period.

- Menopause is the end of fertility for women, when estrogen production slows and ovulation stops.

- Masters and Johnson identify the human sexual response cycle as including four phases: excitement, plateau, orgasm, and resolution.

- The Basson sexual response model identifies women's intimacy and emotional bonding needs as a way to initiate sexual desire and response.

Sexual Behavior

- The Kinsey scale shows a range of diversity for sexual preference, from heterosexual to homosexual.

- Most of the American population identifies as heterosexual, or being sexually attracted to the opposite gender.

- About 10 percent of males and 5 percent of females identify as being exclusively homosexual.

- Erogenous zones are areas of the body that become hypersensitive during sexual arousal.

- Masturbation is self-stimulation of the genitals, causing sexual arousal, including orgasm.

- Fellatio is oral stimulation of the penis.

- Cunnilingus is oral stimulation of the labia, clitoris, and vaginal entrance.

- Abstinence is the avoidance of sexual intercourse with another person for a period of time.

- Celibacy is a permanent commitment to abstain from sex.

- Safer sex refers to penetration by the penis when a condom is worn.

Sexual Dysfunctions

- Sexual dysfunction is indicated by difficulty with at least one stage in the human sexual response cycle.

- Male sexual dysfunctions include premature ejaculation, erectile dysfunction, and low interest in sex.

Reproduction

- Conception occurs when a sperm from the male penetrates an egg from the female.

- Conception normally takes place in the fallopian tube.

- After conception, the fertilized egg is considered a zygote. After 5–7 days, it moves from the fallopian tube to the uterus, when it is considered a blastocyst.

- The inner layer of blastocyst cells becomes the embryo; the outer layer of cells becomes the placenta.

- The embryo continues to grow, and at 8 weeks it is considered a fetus.

- Identical twins occur when an egg is fertilized by one sperm, then divides into two zygotes with identical sets of DNA.

- Fraternal twins occur when two eggs are fertilized by two sperm, resulting in different sets of DNA.

- A Caesarean section is an abdominal surgical delivery.

- A doctor who specializes in the care of pregnant women is an obstetrician/gynecologist, or OB/GYN.

- Female infertility is caused by lack of ovulation, blocked fallopian tubes, and older age of the prospective mother.

- Male infertility is caused by low sperm production, misshapen or immobile sperm, blockages in the urethra, and the inability to effectively ejaculate.

- Assisted reproductive technology (ART) includes all fertility treatments in which both sperm and eggs are handled.

- Pregnancy testing kits work by detecting the presence of human chorionic gonadotropin (hGC) in the urine.

- Pregnancy is divided into trimesters of approximately 13 weeks each, with most fetal growth occurring in the third trimester.

- Prenatal testing is done to determine the risk of birth defects.

- An ectopic pregnancy is a pregnancy outside the uterus, usually the fallopian tube.

- Spontaneous abortion, also called miscarriage, refers to a pregnancy that ends spontaneously before the fetus is able to survive.

Labor and Birth

- Labor involves contractions of the uterus and dilation of the cervix in preparation for birth.

- There are three stages of childbirth, with birth occurring in the second stage.

- Expulsion of the placenta occurs during the third stage of childbirth.

After the Birth

- Newborn babies are screened for a number of genetic diseases that may not be obvious at birth.

- Breastfeeding is encouraged for at least the first six months.

- Postpartum depression affects some women after giving birth when they have difficulty coping with the demands of a new baby.

- Sudden Infant Death Syndrome (SIDS) is the unexplained death of an infant less than one year old.

Reassessing Your Knowledge

1. What are the major changes that occur for each gender at puberty? At what ages does this happen, and how long is the process?

2. Describe the four parts of the Masters and Johnson human sexual response cycle. How is the Basson sexual response model different?

3. What are the most common sexual dysfunctions for men and women?

4. Describe the process of reproduction from conception to birth.

5. Identify some labor and birthing options for a prospective new mother.

6. Describe why breastfeeding is important for at least the first six months after birth. Why do some women experience postpartum depression?

Health Assessment Toolbox

Planned Parenthood, Questions and Answers with Dr. Cullins
http://www.plannedparenthood.org/health-topics/ask-dr-cullins-6602.htm

The Kinsey Institute: Advancing Sexual Health and Knowledge Worldwide
http://www.kinseyinstitute.org/

Kinsey Confidential: Sexual Health Information from the Kinsey Institute
http://kinseyconfidential.org/

Male Health Center: Not for Men Only
http://www.malehealthcenter.com/

Vocabulary Challenge

Match the term in the left-hand column with its correct definition in the right-hand column.

TERM		DEFINITION
Ovaries	A.	Organ that nourishes the fetus
Testes	B.	Tube that carries sperm
Vas deferens	C.	Tube that links the ovary to the uterus
Fallopian tube	D.	Female gonads
Hereosexual	E.	Pregnancy outside the uterus
Homosexual	F.	Stages of fetal development
Ectopic pregnancy	G.	Sexual attraction to the opposite gender
Pregnancy trimesters	H.	Abdominal surgical delivery
Caesarean birth	I.	Sexual attraction to the same gender
Placenta	J.	Male gonads

Answers
D; J; B; C; G; I; E; F; H; A.

Exploring the Internet

American Association of Sex Educators, Counselors, and Therapists
http://www.aasect.org

Center for Young Women's Health
http://www.youngwomenshealth.org

Dr. Drew
http://www.drDrew.com

Go Ask Alice
http://www.goaskalice.columbia.edu

The Kinsey for Research in Sex, Gender and Reproduction
http://www.kinseyinstitute.org/

Male Health Center
http://www.malehealthcenter.com

Sexuality Information and Education Council of the United States
http://www.siecus.org/

Selected References

1. Katz V.L., Lentz G.M., Lobo R.A., and Gershenson, D.M., eds. *Comprehensive Gynecology*. 5th ed. Philadelphia, PA: Mosby Elsevier. Chap 42, 2007.

2. Grady-Weliky, T.A. Premenstrual Dysphoric Disorder. *New England Journal of Medicine*, 2003.

3. Masters, W.H., and Johnson, V.E. *Human Sexual Response*, New York: Bantam Books. 1966.

4. Basson, R. Sexual Desire and Arousal Disorders in Women. *New England Journal of Medicine*. 2006.

5. Kinsey, A., and Pomeroy, W. *Sexual Behavior in the Human Male*. Philadelphia, PA: WB Saunders Co. 1948.

6. Kinsey, A., and Pomeroy, W. *Sexual Behavior of the Human Female*. Philadelphia, PA: WB Saunders Co. 1954.

7. Cabaj, R.P., and Stein, T.S., Eds. *Textbook of Homosexuality and Mental Health*. Washington, DC: American Psychiatric Press. 1996.

8. Diagnostic and Statistical Manual of Mental Disorders, Fourth Edition. American Psychiatric Association, Washington DC, 2000.

9. Hite, S. *The Hite Report: A Nationwide Study of Female Sexuality.* New York: Seven Stories Press,, 1976.

10. Brotto, L.A., et al. Women's Sexual Desire and Arousal Disorders. *Journal of Sexual Medicine*, 7: 586. 2010.

11. Basson, R. Women's Sexuality and Sexual Dysfunction. In: Gibbs R.S., et al. *Danforth's Obstetrics and Gynecology.* 10th ed. Philadelphia, Pa.: Lippincott Williams & Wilkins. 742. 2008.

12. Taylor F.L., et al. Peyronie's Disease. *Urological Clinics of North America*, 34: 517. 2007.

13. Mayo Clinic. *Intrauterine Insemination.* Mayo Foundation for Medical Education and Research, 2010.

14. American Pregnancy Association. *In Vitro Fertilization: IVF.* Online, 2007.

15. WebMD. *Health and Pregnancy: Human Chorionic Gonadotropin (hCG).* 2008.

16. Johns Hopkins Medicine. Department of Gynecology and Obstetric, Maternal Fetal Medicine (High Risk Pregnancies), downloaded 080110. http://www.hopkinsmedicine.org/gynecology_obstetrics/specialty_areas/obstetrics_services/services/maternal_fetal_medicine_high_risk_pregnancies/

17. WebMD. Women's Health, Ectopic Pregnancy. Reviewed March, 2010. Downloaded from http://women.webmd.com/pregnancy-ectopic-pregnancy

18. MedicineNet. Miscarriage (Spontaneous Abortion). July, 2010.

19. National Institutes of Health, Department of Health and Human Services. Fetal Alcohol Spectrum Disorders, July 2007. http://www.nih.gov/about/researchresultsforthepublic/FetalAlcohol.pdf

19. Lester, B.M., and Dreher, M. Effects of Marijuana Use During Pregnancy on Newborn Crying. *Child Development*, 60(23/24): 764–771. 1989.

20. Ibid.

21. Centers for Disease Control and Prevention (CDC). What Do We Know About Tobacco Use and Pregnancy. June 11, 2007.

22. Lemaze, F. *Painless Childbirth: The Lamaze Method*, Pocket Books, 1965.

23. Leboyer, F. *Birth Without Violence*, Rochester, VT: Healing Arts Press. 2002.

24. Bradley, R.A., and Ingraham, E. *Natural Childbirth the Bradley Way.* Dutton, 1985.

25. Labor and Birth. The National Women's Health Information Center. Downloaded January 9, 2009, from http://womenshealth.gov/Pregnancy/childbirthandbeyond/laborandbirth.cfm

26. National Institutes of Health. Eunice Kennedy Shriver National Institute of Child Health and Human Development. *Breastfeeding.* 2009.

27. Depression During and After Pregnancy. National Institutes of Health. Downloaded March 10, 2010, from http://www.womenshealth.gov/faq/depression-pregnancy.cfm

28. Moon, R., et al. Sudden Infant Death Syndrome. *Lancet*, 370: 1578. 2007.

Image of Health

Family Planning

REASONS TO PREVENT PREGNANCY

- Age
- Finances
- Partnership
- Commitment

SAFETY AND EFFECTIVENESS OF BIRTH CONTROL

- Birth Control Safety
- Long Term Use
- Reversibility
- Rates
  - Theoretical Effectiveness
  - Typical Use Effectiveness
  - Continuation Rate
  - Contraceptive Failure Rate

OPTIONS FOR PREVENTING PREGNANCY

- Abstinence, Fertility Awareness, and Other Noninvasive Methods
  - Abstinence
  - Lactational Amenorrhea Method
  - Fertility Awareness Methods
  - Withdrawal and Douching
  - Spermicides

BARRIER METHODS

- Condom Methods
  - Male Condoms
  - Female Condoms
- Methods that Cover the Cervix
  - Contraceptive Sponge
  - Cervical Cap
  - Diaphragm
- Intrauterine Device

HORMONAL METHODS

- Oral Contraceptives
  - Estrogen and Progestin Pills
  - The Mini Pill
- Contraception Skin Patch
- Vaginal Contraception Ring
- Implantable Contraception
- Injectable Contraception
- Emergency Contraception
  - Plan B—The Morning-After Pill

PERMANENT BIRTH CONTROL METHODS

- Tubal Ligations
- Vasectomies
  - Things to Consider before Sterilization

FUTURE FOR BIRTH CONTROL

- The Career Pill
- The Male Pill

IF PREGNANCY OCCURS

- Viewing Your Options
  - Abortions
  - Concerns with Abortions
- Types of Abortions
  - Surgical Abortions
  - RU-486
  - Abortion Complications

RESPONSIBILITY AND ACCOUNTABILITY

- Your Responsibility and Your Partner's Responsibility
- Focusing on Accountability

Student Learning Outcomes

LEARNING OUTCOME	APPLYING IT TO YOUR LIFE
List and describe reasons to prevent pregnancy.	Consider how a pregnancy would affect you at your current stage of life.
Describe how the safety and effectiveness of birth control is measured.	Consider the concerns you may have about the safety and effectiveness of different birth control methods.
Describe the different methods used to prevent pregnancy.	Be able to discuss how each of these methods works to prevent pregnancy, and identify the type best suited for you.
Explain the differences between Plan B and RU-486.	Identify places you could purchase Plan B, should you ever need it.
Understand how tubal ligation and vasectomy work to permanently prevent pregnancy.	List considerations you may have before choosing either a tubal ligation or vasectomy.

Assessing Your Knowledge

1. On average, raising a baby from birth to age one costs about:
    a. $3,500
    b. $5,300
    c. $10,200
    d. $15,400

2. Long-term use of oral contraceptives in women has been linked to:
    a. No health risks in nonsmoking women
    b. Increased risk of breast cancer
    c. Increased risk of endometrial cancers
    d. Increased risk of ovarian cancer

3. The intrauterine device:
    a. Is no longer available in the U.S.
    b. Is a permanent method of birth control
    c. Can be used for up to one year without risk
    d. Is available in either 5-year or 10-year use options

4. Plan B—The Morning-After Pill:
    a. Causes abdominal contractions to prevent a blastocyst from embedding in the uterus
    b. Is available only with a prescription
    c. Works to prevent sperm from fertilizing an egg
    d. Induces an abortion

5. The most frequently occurring abortion in the U.S. is:
    a. Dilation and curettage
    b. Manual aspiration
    c. Partial birth abortion
    d. Vacuum aspiration

Answers:
1. c, 2. a, 3. d, 4. c, 5. d

Family Planning

Infanticide was the most common method of birth control in pre-industrial societies. It was considered easier, less risky, and less painful than other methods that had been used. Because food was not always available in sufficient quantities and starvation was not unusual, population control helped alleviate the burden on the food supply. When infanticide became illegal at the beginning of the 18th century, women resorted to abortion methods—men were seldom involved in the practice. Originally, abortion was attempted using various potions that ranged from herbal teas to mashed ants, to turpentine, castor oil, and quinine water in which a rusty nail had been soaked.[1,2]

Since those early methods, women have attempted to terminate pregnancies by extreme exercise, heavy lifting, hot baths, and even shaking. Unplanned pregnancies are still prevalent today, even though there are many alternatives for prevention, including over-the-counter and prescription products.

Today, more women die in childbirth than from abortion methods and birth control measures. The desire and perhaps the need to control family size still persists, with as many varying views as there are methods.

In March 1905, President Roosevelt criticized birth control and condemned the move toward smaller families as decadent, and as a sign of moral disease. In contrast, early suffragists promoted voluntary motherhood, and saw celibacy and abstinence as the optimum method of birth control. During the late 1870s, sex outside of marriage was considered immoral, and even within marriage was considered immoral if not used strictly for reproduction. However, these attitudes have changed greatly over the last century.

For some, birth control is appropriate for family planning: a method is selected and if used successfully, pregnancy occurs only when planned. For others, birth control violates religious, moral, or cultural beliefs, and is considered abhorrent in any form.

Unwanted pregnancies may occur for those who use birth control but do not commit 100 percent to its practice, or for those who do not use the method correctly. Even without user error, contraceptive methods have failure rates. In either case, decisions about maintaining or terminating a pregnancy may arise.

For those who opt not to practice any method of birth control, a large family can compromise resources. Some argue that this burden may then extend to the supporting government agencies of the state in which the family lives.

All of these concerns promote research into more effective birth control methods, and more understanding of the disparate views on this issue.

Reasons to Prevent Pregnancy

Because being a parent lasts a lifetime, choosing to become pregnant is not a short-term decision. There are many reasons to prevent pregnancy, and this section examines the most prominent.

Age

Most of the research on age and pregnancy involves pregnancy complications in older women, though younger mothers tend to have different pregnancy complications. Statistically, the younger parents are at the time of conception, the less chance the child has of success in life. Parents younger than 18 are typically not financially or emotionally mature enough to handle the responsibility of parenthood. Very young mothers often do not seek medical care during their pregnancies, and therefore do not know how to best manage a pregnancy. This lack of information and knowledge can result in a pregnancy with more complications, resulting in a birth with more difficulties.

Older mothers face a different set of possible complications. Women are born with all the eggs they will ever have, and as women age, their eggs age with them. After age 35, women have reduced fertility rates because their eggs are not as viable. Historically, women married at earlier ages and had children before they were 30 years old. Today, more women are postponing their pregnancies. Between 1991 and 2001, first births in women from 35–39 years of age increased 36 percent, and among women 40–44 years old, they increased 70 percent.[3] Nevertheless, advanced maternal age has been shown to be an independent risk factor for adverse outcomes in pregnancy, including birth defects, which are more common in the pregnancies of older women.[4] This includes children born with Down syndrome, exhibiting varying degrees of mental retardation as well as physical birth defects.

FIGURE 6-1. Child with Down syndrome.

Post-menopause introduces another set of complications, since women who hope to become pregnant at this stage must take **fertility drugs** or use methods of **artificial insemination**. Fertility treatments increase the likelihood of multiple births, and advanced age may make it more difficult to manage a multiple birth pregnancy, as well as to care for multiple babies after delivery.

Key Terms

Down syndrome: A chromosomal condition caused by the presence of all or part of an extra 21st chromosome.

Fertility drugs: Drugs that treat infertility by causing women to ovulate.

Artificial insemination: A procedure in which sperm is inserted directly into the uterus.

Finances

The medical costs of managing a pregnancy in the U.S. varies by state, as well as by the availability and scope of health insurance. In 2004, the average total cost of pre-natal care and hospital delivery was $7,600,[5] while a **Caesarean section** with complications averaged $15,500.[6] If a baby requires neonatal intensive care, costs for the infant average $2,000 per day.[7]

Key Term

Caesarean section: A major surgery where a baby is removed from the mother's uterus via an incision in the abdomen.

In the first year of life, a family can expect their new baby to cost about $10,200. The cost to raise a child born in 2009 to age 17 is estimated to be over $222,000 for a middle-income family.[8] If you are considering a pregnancy, also consider the costs and whether this is a responsible decision for you at this time in your life. If you do not want to become a parent, consider whether you are doing everything possible to prevent a pregnancy.

Critical Thinking Question: Describe some concerns for a forty-year-old woman who desires a pregnancy.

Partnership

Managing a pregnancy, having a baby, and raising a child can be a full-time job. And for a single person, the work-load and the financial and emotional burdens are more complicated. In a relationship, having a baby can be one of the more stressful events in a couple's life together. Therefore, an important part of planning a pregnancy must include evaluating the relationship and considering how having a baby will affect it.

Commitment

When an unplanned pregnancy occurs, several significant questions occur to the prospective parents, including:

- Am I ready to become a parent?

- Am I ready to commit to this child's other parent?

- Is this the best time for us to become parents?

- How will this affect the plans I/we have for our lives?

These are common questions for prospective parents. But in addition, is this the best time for this baby to be born?

FIGURE 6-2. Commitment is life-long.

For planned pregnancies, these questions would have been addressed in advance of the decision to become pregnant. While choosing to have a child means a lifetime commitment to everything that is wonderful about raising a child, it also means a lifetime commitment to all that can be expensive, worrying, stressful, and frustrating about raising a child. When you make this this *lifetime commitment*, you are making a promise to do your very best, perhaps even sacrificing some of your desires and interests for your child.

Critical Thinking Question: What characteristics do you have that mark your readiness—or lack of readiness—for parenthood?

If you are not ready to make the commitment to become a parent, you should evaluate and consider your birth control options.

Safety and Effectiveness of Birth Control

While the use of birth control can be very beneficial, it is not without consequences. These consequences range from medical safety to the potential impact of an unplanned pregnancy.

Birth Control Safety

With few exceptions, all birth control methods carry some risks. However, these risks are always lower than those associated with a pregnancy and delivering a child. Evaluating birth control options should include how lifestyle behaviors might impact the safety of the option you select. For example, smoking will increase the risk of high blood pressure and stroke if you choose **oral contraceptives** (OCs). Or if you have a latex allergy, the use of latex condoms will result in more serious problems for you than for someone who is not allergic. It is the responsibility of the user to consider the risks that may be associated with any method of birth control, and to make the necessary lifestyle changes to limit this risk.

Key Term

Oral contraceptives (OCs): A variety of hormonal compounds in pill form that prevent ovulation, thereby preventing pregnancy.

Long-Term Use

Some birth control methods are only used at the time of **coitus**. Others, such as OCs, are taken daily for as long as the woman chooses not to conceive. Still others are inserted or injected by a physician for a prescribed length of time.

Key Term

Coitus: Sexual intercourse.

In healthy, nonsmoking women, long-term use of OCs incurs very few health risks. In fact, studies have shown that women who use OCs for more than ten years have an 80 percent reduction in risk for developing **endometrial** and **ovarian cancer**.[9,10] Since some women who take OCs may not use an additional protective barrier method, they are still at risk for infection from **human papilloma virus**, which can cause cervical cancer, as well as for any other sexually transmitted infections (STIs) or human immune-deficiency virus (HIV).

> **Key Terms**
>
> **Endometrial cancer**: A cancer that occurs in the endometrial lining of the uterus.
>
> **Ovarian cancer**: A malignant tumor located on the ovary.
>
> **Human papilloma virus**: A virus that affects the skin and mucous membranes of humans and some animals. Over 100 types of the virus have been identified, and some are known to cause cervical cancer.

There are currently two **intrauterine devices** (IUDs) available in the U.S. One is effective for five years, the other for ten years. Although both cause some initial complications, neither method has been associated with any long-term health problems.

Implantable contraceptive inserts are placed under the skin, where they function as effective birth control devices for specific periods of time. Since the implant contains the same hormone as some OCs, the associated risks are the same.

> **Key Term**
>
> **Intrauterine device**: A plastic device inserted into the uterus as a contraceptive.

Reversibility

After evaluating the safety of a birth control method, the next critical component is its reversibility. How will this method affect your ability to conceive when you decide to stop using it, and how quickly will you return to your pre-use **fertility** state?

> **Key Term**
>
> **Fertility**: The ability to reproduce.

Since women often do not know how fertile they are before electing to use contraception, there are many common misconceptions regarding the reversibility of birth control. When some women who have used OCs decide to become pregnant but have difficulty conceiving, they often assume their use of OCs is the cause. With only two exceptions—Depo-Provera and increasing age—once a woman stops using a birth control method, her ability to conceive returns to its original level.[11]

Rates

Every birth control method is evaluated to determine its effectiveness in preventing pregnancy. Effectiveness rates include typical use rates, rates that are generated when the method is tested under perfect circumstances, rates to determine how many people continue to use the method, and finally, how often the method actually fails.

Theoretical Effectiveness

Theoretical effectiveness refers to how effective the method is when used *exactly* as directed. Realistically, this is often not the case. The effectiveness of OCs is based on being taken at the same time every day. However, any method that requires an action by the user can be compromised. Birth control methods that are injected or inserted by a physician usually match their theoretical effectiveness rate, because effectiveness does not depend on the patient.

FIGURE 6-3. Knowing how effective your method of birth control is will help you avoid an unplanned pregnancy.

Typical Use Effectiveness

The most common reason for a **contraceptive** method to fail is user error. Diaphragms are forgotten, condoms slip, OCs are taken at random times or missed altogether, or the user elects to "go with the moment," forgoing a planned method. As you consider a method of contraception, think about how methodical you are, how committed you are to preventing pregnancy, and how easy each method is to use.

> **Key Term**
>
> **Contraceptive**: Any agent that prevents conception.

Continuation Rate

The effectiveness and ease of use of a contraceptive can also be measured by its continuation rate, which shows the percentage of those who continue to use the method after a specified period of time. A method with a high continuation rate indicates that it is successfully preventing pregnancy, and that the user is comfortable with the method.

Contraceptive Failure Rate

Contraceptive failure rate indicates the percentage of women who unintentionally became pregnant during the first year of using the method. "Image of Health in Depth: Contraceptive Efficacy" shows the failure rates of methods with typical use and with perfect use. The final column shows the method's continuation rate.

Challenge Question: Describe why there is a difference between theoretical effectiveness rates of contraception and actual effectiveness rates.

Image of Health in Depth

Contraceptive Efficacy

Percentage of women experiencing an unintended pregnancy during the first year of typical use and the first year of perfect use of contraception, and the percentage of women who continue use at the end of the first year. United States.

METHOD	PERCENT OF WOMEN EXPERIENCING AN UNINTENDED PREGNANCY DURING THE FIRST YEAR OF USE		PERCENT OF WOMEN CONTINUING USE AT ONE YEAR
	TYPICAL USE	PERFECT USE	
No method	85	85	
Spermicides	29	18	42
Withdrawal	27	4	43
Fertility awareness-based methods	25		51
Standard days method		5	
Two-day method		4	
Ovulation method		3	
Sponge use: **parous** women	32	20	46
Sponge use: **nulliparous** women	16	9	57
Diaphragm	16	6	57
Condoms			
Female (Reality)	21	5	49
Male	15	2	53
Combined pill and progestin-only pill	8	0.3	68
Evra patch	8	0.3	68
NuvaRing	8	0.3	68
Depo-Provera	3	0.3	56
IUDs			
ParaGard (copper T)	0.8	0.6	78
Mirena (LNG-IUS)	0.2	0.2	80
Implanon	0.05	0.05	84
Female sterilization	0.5	0.5	100
Male sterilization	0.15	0.10	100

(Source: Trussell, J. Contraceptive efficacy. In Hatcher R.A., Trussell J., Nelson A.L., Cates W., Stewart F.H., Kowal D. *Contraceptive Technology: Nineteenth Revised Edition*. New York NY: Ardent Media, 2007.)

Key Terms

Emergency contraceptive pills: Treatment initiated within 72 hours after unprotected intercourse, reducing the risk of pregnancy by at least 75 percent.

Lactational amenorrhea method: Breastfeeding a newborn that results in amenorrhea, a highly effective, *temporary* method of contraception.

Parous women: Women who have given birth.

Nulliparous women: Women who have never given birth.

Challenge Question: Describe how to evaluate a birh control method.

Options for Preventing Pregnancy

There are many options available to help prevent pregnancy. When evaluating your choices, consider that pharmaceutical companies are continually exploring new contraceptive devices and medications. Research and development are ongoing, and this section covers only those available in 2010. The range of options for birth control begin with **abstinence** and continue through **sterilization**.

Key Terms

Abstinence: The act or practice of refraining from sexual intercourse.

Sterilization: Any surgical procedure intended to eliminate the ability to reproduce.

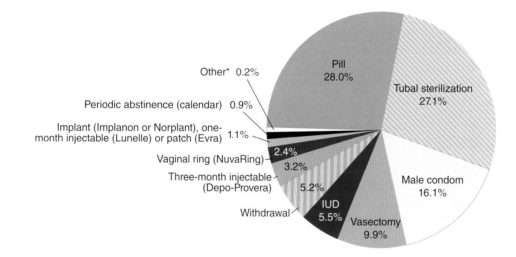

FIGURE 6-4. Facts on contraceptive use in the United States, among women ages 15–44.

(Source: Guttmaches Institute, June 2010.)

Abstinence, Fertility Awareness, and Other Noninvasive Methods

Methods that do not alter a woman's hormonal cycle, such as abstinence and fertility awareness, are often considered to be natural methods. They are immediately reversible with no long-term effects; unfortunately, they may not be as reliable as other methods.

Abstinence

Although there is research showing many individuals using various methods of contraception, smaller groups who consciously use abstinence as a method of pregnancy and/ or disease prevention have not been extensively analyzed. A study presented at the 2003 meeting of the American Psychological Society (APS) found that over 60 percent of college students who had pledged virginity during their middle school or high school years had broken their vow to remain celibate until marriage.[12] However, the study did not indicate how many of these broken vows constituted one single instance, as opposed to how many abandoned abstinence altogether. A different study conducted in Texas showed that abstinence-only programs did not actually change sexual behavior.[13]

Lactational Amenorrhea Method

Women who choose to breastfeed may enjoy the added bonus of birth control. During lactation, women may experience amenorrhea, or failure to menstruate, and may not ovulate. Like all other methods in typical use, the **lactational amenorrhea method** is not 100 percent effective. If you are breastfeeding and do not wish to become pregnant, talk with your doctor about a birth control method that is suitable for lactating women.

FIGURE 6-5. Breastfeeding may induce amenorrhea and reduce the chance of pregnancy.

Fertility Awareness Methods

There are four different types of **fertility awareness methods**, and the most frequently used is the calendar method. With this method, it is assumed that ovulation will always occur 14 days before the onset of the next menstruation. Women abstain from vaginal intercourse during this fertile period, generally considered to extend from day 10 through day 18 of the menstrual cycle. However, many variables can affect ovulation, including stress, exercise habits, nutrition, and fatigue, and therefore, this method has a high failure rate with typical use.

The second type of fertility awareness, known as the standard days method, is for women whose menstrual cycle lasts between 26 and 32 days. Intercourse must be avoided from day 8 to day 19 of the cycle.

The temperature method, the third method of fertility awareness, requires that a woman take her temperature each day before getting out of bed. Ovulation causes a slight increase in body temperature, between 0.4°F and 0.8°F, and women are generally most fertile two to three days before the change in body temperature. Since the egg is viable for about 24 hours and sperm are viable for about three days in the reproductive tract, those using this method should abstain from intercourse for three days prior to the anticipated rise in temperature until at least the third day after the temperature has risen. To improve accuracy, women are advised to chart their temperature changes for at least three months before using this method.

The fourth method is the mucus method or Billings method. During most of her cycle, a woman's vaginal mucus is cloudy and tacky. A few days before ovulation it becomes clear, slippery, and appears slightly elastic. When this occurs, the woman has entered her most fertile phase. Using the cervical mucus method may be unreliable if vaginal infections occur or if vaginal products are used.

There are no medical side effects or risks for any of these methods, they are generally acceptable to most religious practices, and each is immediately reversible. The primary disadvantage is that they are very ineffective in typical use.

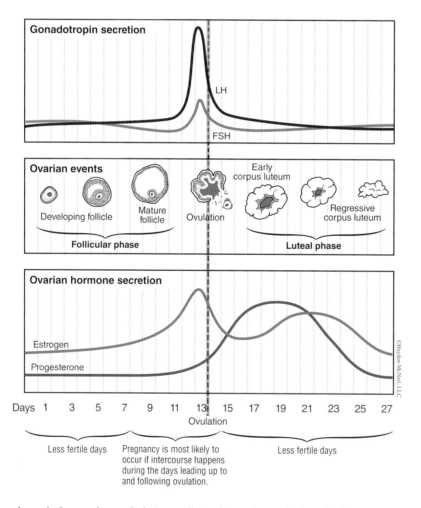

FIGURE 6-6. A woman's ovulation cycle can help to predict safer and unsafe days for intercourse.

Withdrawal Method and Douching Method

The withdrawal method, also called **coitus interruptus**, has been used for centuries. It requires withdrawing the penis from the vagina prior to ejaculation. But because there can be a release of sperm prior to ejaculation, this method is not very effective or reliable.

Advantages to the withdrawal method are that it is without negative health consequences, it is immediately reversible, and its cost is negligible. Disadvantages are that many men cannot control their ejaculation completely, and pre-ejaculate can never be controlled.

Douching uses a variety of liquids to "wash out" the vagina after intercourse. Using pressure, the liquids are forced into the vaginal canal, and then allowed to run out. However, as those liquids are forced upward, so is any ejaculate in the vagina. Research also shows that sperm may reach the uterus almost immediately after ejaculation, avoiding the douching liquid entirely. Regular douching has been associated with a higher incidence of **pelvic inflammatory** disease, and because of this risk and its lack of effectiveness, douching offers no contraceptive advantages.

Key Terms

Fertility awareness method: A set of practices in which a woman uses one or more of her primary fertility signs to determine the fertile and infertile phases of her menstrual cycle.

Coitus interruptus: The act of withdrawing the penis prior to ejaculation during sexual intercourse.

Pelvic inflammatory disease: An inflammation of the female pelvic organs, most commonly the fallopian tubes, usually as a result of a bacterial infection.

Spermicides

Spermicides are sperm-killing products available in foam, cream, jelly, film, or suppository form. They are inserted deep into the vagina before intercourse, and/or may be used with another contraceptive method, such as a condom or diaphragm. Spermicidal foam requires an insertion tool to ensure that it reaches the base of the cervix. Depending on the product, spermicides must either be applied immediately or must be in place for fifteen minutes prior to intercourse. These products work both by acting as a barrier to the uterus and by killing sperm.

Spermicides are readily available, easy to use when applying the correct technique, and their effect is immediately reversible. Used alone, the effectiveness of spermicides is very low.

Key Term

Spermicide: A substance that kills sperm.

Critical Thinking Question: Why do fertility awareness methods have such low effectiveness rates?

Barrier Methods

Barrier methods help prevent sperm from reaching the egg. With typical use, effectiveness for these methods ranges from 68 percent to 85 percent, and they have the advantage of being immediately reversible. The choice of barrier will determine if it is available over the counter, or if it requires a prescription.

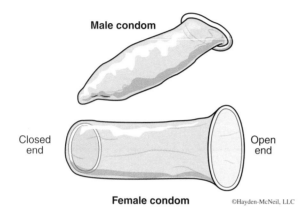

FIGURE 6-7. Condoms are one of the oldest methods of birth control.

Condom Methods

Condom methods either cover the penis to contain the ejaculate, or enclose the vaginal canal in a pouch that will keep the ejaculate from entering the uterus. Both methods are designed to prevent sperm from reaching an egg.

Male Condoms

Male condoms were one of the first effective methods of preventing pregnancy. Made of either latex or polyurethane, condoms are thin sheaths rolled over the erect penis before it enters the vagina or other orifice. They are easy to use, inexpensive, and very effective—if used consistently and properly, they can prevent pregnancy and HIV. In the first year of use, typical failure rate is just 15 percent but if the condom is used correctly, the failure rate drops to just 2 percent.

Latex condoms are thicker than polyurethane, allowing less sensitivity and heat transference, which some may consider a disadvantage. Since spermicides and lubricants create the sensation of moisture and increase heat transference, applying one of these products to the penis before the condom is worn can improve sensitivity. Since polyurethane condoms allow more heat transference, they are considered more sensitive. Though polyurethane condoms have been approved by the FDA as an effective method of preventing pregnancy and the transfer of HIV in people allergic to latex, latex condoms are still considered the optimum barrier.

Both latex and polyurethane condoms help protect against pregnancy, and in 2001, the Centers for Disease Control and Prevention convened a panel of experts to determine the effectiveness of condoms in preventing sexually transmitted infections (STIs). The panel determined that latex condoms, when used properly and consistently, are effective against preventing the transmission of HIV, as well as the transmission of gonorrhea in men. Although the panel did not believe there was enough evidence to state that condoms are effective in protecting against other STIs, they did state that the condom is the most effective prevention method overall. Only abstinence or a mutually exclusive, disease-free relationship is more effective at preventing STIs.

The "lamb skin" condom is a third type of male condom. Though the earliest condoms were made from animal skins, lambskin condoms are actually made from the membranes of sheep intestines. These condoms are extremely thin, allowing greater sensitivity than either latex or polyurethane condoms. They are effective against pregnancy, but they are *not* effective against the transmission of HIV or any other sexually transmitted infection.

Female Condom

The **female condom** is a polyurethane pouch with flexible rings at each end. It is inserted deep into the vagina before sexual activity, with the ring at the closed end up against the cervix, where the cervical muscles hold the ring in place. The ring at the open end remains outside the body, and after the condom is inserted, an application of spermicide is placed into the pouch to provide both moisture and an additional barrier. Ejaculated sperm collect inside the pouch, preventing them from entering the vagina. In its first year of typical use, the female condom has a 21 percent failure rate, but with perfect use, the failure rate can be reduced to just 5 percent.

This method allows women to share the responsibility for preventing pregnancy *and* HIV transmission. Female condoms are readily available at supermarkets and drugstores, and because they are made from polyurethane, they can be used by people who are allergic to latex. Female condoms can be used with both oil-based and water-based lubricants. They have no effect on a woman's natural hormone cycle, and contraception via condoms is immediately reversible. And unlike the male condom, the female condom stays in place regardless of whether a man maintains his erection.

The disadvantages for female condoms include reduced sensitivity, and possibly a sound that some users say is created as the pouch moves during intercourse. Although prices vary, female condoms generally cost more than male condoms. Like the male condom, they can only be used once.

Critical Thinking Question: What can be done to make condom use more attractive for a man?

> **Key Terms**
>
> **Male condom**: A sheath usually made of either latex or polyurethane that covers the penis during sexual intercourse, used as a contraceptive method and/or STI preventative.
>
> **Female condom**: A polyurethane pouch inserted into the vagina prior to sexual intercourse, helping to prevent pregnancy and transmission of STIs.

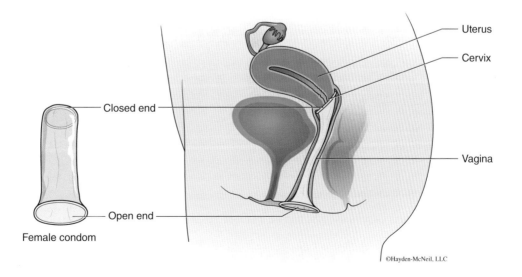

©Hayden-McNeil, LLC

FIGURE 6-8. Correct insertion of the female condom is necessary to achieve highest effectiveness.

Methods that Cover the Cervix

For pregnancy to occur, sperm must swim up the vaginal canal and travel through the cervix, the opening to the uterus, and move up either fallopian tube from the uterus. Condoms collect ejaculate to prevent sperm from entering the uterus, while contraceptive methods that cover the cervix work by blocking the entrance to the uterus.

Contraceptive Sponge

The contraceptive sponge combines a barrier method with a spermicide to help prevent pregnancy. Before use, water is applied to the sponge until it is thoroughly wet, then the sponge is inserted into the vagina at the base of the cervix prior to sexual activity. In the first year of typical use, the sponge has a failure rate of about 16 percent in women who have never had a child, 32 percent in women who have experienced childbirth. The sponge can be inserted as early as 12–24 hours before sexual activity, so it does not interrupt foreplay. Other advantages include its immediate availability and ease of use, and it can be used with a condom as an additional barrier method. After sexual activity, the sponge must be left in place for six hours.

However, the sponge does not protect against any STI, including HIV. Other disadvantages include the possibility of sponge use resulting in yeast infections, and in rare instances, **toxic shock syndrome** has occurred.

Challenge Question: Identify three different barrier methods that use a spermicide.

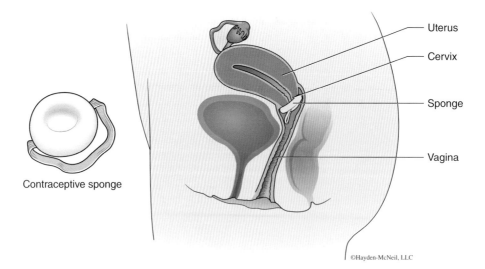

Contraceptive sponge

Uterus

Cervix

Sponge

Vagina

©Hayden-McNeil, LLC

FIGURE 6-9. The female sponge is easy to use and can be inserted 12–24 hours before onset of sexual activity.

Cervical Cap

The **cervical cap**, made of either latex or silicone, is a barrier type of birth control that fits snugly over the cervix, blocking the entrance to the uterus. It is available only through a health care provider, who determines both the size and type of the cap suitable for the patient.

Before insertion, a spermicide is applied to the rim of the cap to provide added proection. The cap can be inserted into the vagina hours before sexual activity occurs, so it does not interrupt foreplay. Once ejaculation has occurred, the cap must be removed within 48 hours. The cap should be washed in warm, soapy water before storage, and can be reused.

Three types of cervical caps are available in the U.S. Lea's Shield is a one-size-fits-all cap made of silicone; Prentif is made of latex and is available in four sizes; and FemCap is available in three sizes and is made of silicone.

Cervical caps may provide some protection against STIs. In typical use, failure rates for women who have given birth are about 32 percent, and 16 percent for women who have never had a child. Reversibility is immediate, and using the cap does not interfere with a woman's hormonal cycle.

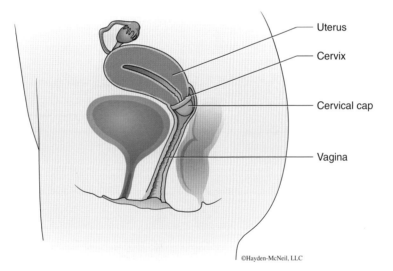

Uterus

Cervix

Cervical cap

Vagina

©Hayden-McNeil, LLC

FIGURE 6-10. The Insertion of the female cap.

Diaphragm

Made of either soft latex or silicone with a spring molded into the rim, the **diaphragm** is a cervical barrier method of birth control. Because the cervical opening must be measured to determine the correct size of diaphragm and the patient must be taught correct insertion technique, a physician's prescription is required. Prior to insertion, a spermicide is applied around the edge of the rim and a teaspoonful of spermicide is placed inside the dome. The diaphragm is then squeezed together and inserted deep inside the vagina, where it covers the cervix. It can be inserted up two hours prior to sexual activity, and must remain in place for 6–8 hours after the last ejaculation. For multiple acts of intercourse, an additional teaspoonful of spermicide should be inserted into the vagina before each ejaculation. Like the cervical cap, after removal the diaphragm must be washed in warm, soapy water, then stored carefully, as it can be reused.

The diaphragm is available in different sizes so that it precisely covers the cervix. If the female experiences a weight change of ten pounds or more, cervical dimensions may change and she will need to be fitted for a new diaphragm. Women should also be refitted after a pregnancy of 14 weeks or longer.

In typical use, the failure rate of the diaphragm is about 16 percent. Its contraceptive effects are immediately reversible, the hormonal cycle is not affected, and it may be reused for 1–3 years. Some women experience urinary tract infections with diaphragm use, and very rarely, toxic shock syndrome may occur.

Challenge Question: Describe the differences between the sponge and the diaphragm.

Key Terms

Contraceptive sponge: A contraceptive method that combines a barrier and spermicide to prevent conception.

Toxic shock syndrome: A rare but potentially fatal infection, usually caused by bacteria.

Cervical cap: A thimble-shaped cup that fits over the cervix, used with a spermicide to prevent conception.

Diaphragm: A barrier method made of latex or silicone and used with spermicide, designed to cover the cervix and prevent conception.

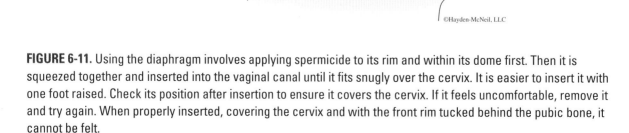

©Hayden-McNeil, LLC

FIGURE 6-11. Using the diaphragm involves applying spermicide to its rim and within its dome first. Then it is squeezed together and inserted into the vaginal canal until it fits snugly over the cervix. It is easier to insert it with one foot raised. Check its position after insertion to ensure it covers the cervix. If it feels uncomfortable, remove it and try again. When properly inserted, covering the cervix and with the front rim tucked behind the pubic bone, it cannot be felt.

The Intrauterine Device (IUD)

Placed in the uterus, the **intrauterine device** (IUD) is the world's most widely used method of reversible birth control.[14] Used primarily in China and India, it is both a barrier method and a hormonal method, since it blocks a fertilized egg from embedding in the uterus, and its progestin coating may damage or kill sperm.[15]

Unfortunately, because of past problems with one type of IUD that was withdrawn from the market in 1975, it has not been widely used in the U.S. The two types of IUDs that are available today have been shown to be safe and effective, and doctors are careful in determining patients for whom IUD use is appropriate.

The IUD is a small, T-shaped plastic device that is either wrapped in copper or contains progestin, and inserted into the uterus by a health care professional. Depending on the type, it is effective for 5–10 years, but can be removed sooner if the woman decides to become pregnant.

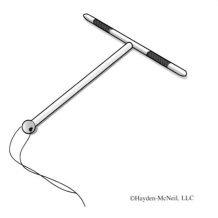

©Hayden-McNeil, LLC

FIGURE 6-12. A physician inserts the IUD.

After insertion, a small plastic string tied to the end of the IUD is suspended through the cervix. Women can check that the IUD is in place by feeling for this string, and it is also used by health care professionals for removal of the IUD.

The Levonorgestrel IUD (LNg IUD) releases levonorgestrel, a form of progestin. This type appears to be slightly more effective at preventing pregnancy than the copper IUD, and may also have a lower risk of pelvic inflammatory disease. The Levonorgestrel IUD is left in place for about five years, preventing fertilization by damaging or killing sperm and irritating the lining of the uterus where a fertilized egg would implant and grow. In addition, the LNg IUD makes the mucus in the cervix thick and sticky so sperm cannot pass through to the uterus. The hormones in the LNg IUD also relieve menstrual cramping and irregular menstrual bleeding.

The copper IUD works by producing a fluid that is toxic to sperm, making the uterus and fallopian tubes inhospitable for fertilization. This IUD is more commonly used in the U.S., is highly effective at preventing pregnancy, and can be left in place for ten years.

Advantages for both types of IUD are that once inserted, pregnancy prevention requires no additional thought. And since IUDs last for at least five years, they are very cost effective. They can be used by women who are breastfeeding, and most women also experience reduced menstrual cramps and spotting. Additionally, the LNg IUD reduces menstrual bleeding by about 90 percent after the first few months of use, possibly even preventing menstrual flow entirely. Studies have shown that the use of LNg IUDs may prevent endometrial cancer, and reduce the risk of pelvic inflammatory disease and ectopic pregnancy. In typical use, the Copper T, sold as the ParaGard, has a failure rate of .8 percent, while the rate of the LNg IUD, sold as the Mirena, is .2 percent.

In a very small number of users, around one in 1,000, the IUD may puncture the uterus. Although this is very rare, it almost always occurs during insertion. About 2–10 percent of IUDs are expelled from the uterus into the vagina during the first year of use. Another disadvantage is that IUDs offer no protection against STIs.

Image of Health in Depth

Things to Consider When Choosing a Birth Control Method

Choosing to become sexually active is a decision that requires both responsibility and accountability. Sexual intercourse does not necessarily improve a relationship, nor will it guarantee its longevity. However, if you decide to become sexually active, your next decision should be the birth control method you will use to prevent pregnancy. Remember, it can take just one act of unprotected intercourse to become pregnant. This can be the first time you ever have sex, or it can occur after you have been sexually active for a long time. The time to make decisions about pregnancy is before it occurs. Here are some things to consider when choosing the best method of birth control for you.

- *Spontaneity of sex*. Will you be more comfortable with a method that does not interrupt foreplay, or will you be just as comfortable interrupting sexual activity temporarily to apply your birth control method?

- *Availability of method*. Will you be comfortable seeking the advice of a physician and requiring a prescription for your birth control method? Physician-prescribed methods are usually far more effective, but if you prefer an over-the-counter method, consider how easy it is to access, how long it remains effective, whether it has to be stored in any particular way, and your level of comfort using it.

- *Ease of use of method*. For some methods, such as the diaphragm and cervical cap, a health care provider must train the patient to ensure the device is inserted properly. The diaphragm and female condom require added spermicide to increase their effectiveness in preventing pregnancy. Male condoms must be removed immediately after ejaculation, and other barrier methods within specific time frames. Some methods must be inserted into the vaginal canal, so you should be comfortable with that procedure. Consider all of these details and your comfort with them when selecting your method.

- *Reversibility of method*. Most people want birth control for only a specific period of time. When that time has ended, they want their ability to conceive to return to its original, pre-contraception state. Most methods allow this, but using Depo-Provera may cause fertility to be inhibited for up to a year after the injections have stopped.

- *Cost of method*. Birth control can be expensive, although never as costly as pregnancy or raising a child. The cost of the method could also be shared between the partners.

- *Responsibility for the method*. Do you consider birth control to be the responsibility of the man, the woman, or of both partners? As you select your method, consider how you will engage the support of your partner.

Hormonal Methods

Hormonal methods are based on the knowledge that pregnancy prevents a woman from ovulating. During pregnancy, a woman releases both progesterone and estrogen from the corpus luteum in amounts high enough to suppress ovulation. Hormonal methods contain progestin, a laboratory-made compound similar to progesterone, and estrogen, preventing ovulation the same way the corpus luteum does during pregnancy.

Oral Contraception

Oral contraceptives first became available in the early 1960s. In addition to preventing ovulation, OCs inhibit the movement of sperm by thickening the cervical mucus and altering the lining of the uterus. In the unlikely event that an egg is fertilized, the change in the uterus makes it inhospitable for implantation. Many different types of OCs are available today, and all products containing estrogen and/or progestin require a physician's prescription. Users receive a prescription for one year of contraception, and must return to the physician for an annual pelvic exam in order to obtain a new prescription.

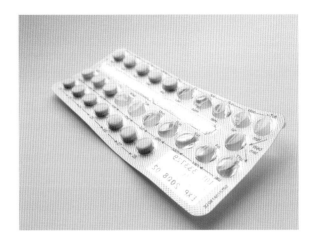

FIGURE 6-13. Introduced in the 1960s, birth control pills are highly effective at preventing pregnancy when taken according to directions.

Estrogen and Progestin Pills

The combination pill, the most common type of OC, contains both estrogen and progestin, though different brands contain varying amounts of estrogen and progestin. The estrogen and progestin are in sufficient quantity to cause the corpus luteum to suppress ovulation, as it does during pregnancy. Each one-month packet usually contains 21 active pills and seven inactive pills. An active pill containing estrogen and progestin is taken each day for 21 days. This is followed by seven days of inactive (usually sugar) pills, during which time the woman will experience a light menstrual period. With perfect use, the combined pill has a first-year failure rate of just .3 percent, while typical use results in a 5 percent failure rate.[14]

In 2003, an extended cycle combined pill called Seasonale became available. Seasonale is taken for 84 consecutive days, followed by inactive pills for seven days, during which time a light menstrual bleeding occurs. This reduces the number of periods a woman experiences, from 13 per year to just four per year. Spotting and light bleeding are quite common during the first months of using Seasonale.

More recently introduced is YAZ, a combination oral contraceptive that acts as a contraceptive, treats the significant emotional and physical symptoms of premenstrual syndrome that some women experience, and also helps treat moderate acne. YAZ contains 24 active pills, which contain both estrogen and progestin, followed by four inactive pills. The most frequent side effects of YAZ

include intermittent spotting, headaches, and nausea. Because the ingredients may increase potassium, women with kidney, liver, or adrenal disease should not use YAZ, as it could lead to more serious health problems.

Combination pills have a very effective contraceptive rate, provide predictability of menstruation cycles, reduce menstrual flow and cramping, and the contraceptive effects are reversible almost immediately after it is stopped. Additional medical advantages include the reduced risk of anemia, ectopic pregnancy, and endometrial, ovarian, colon, and rectal cancers, as well as reduced incidence of pelvic inflammatory disease.[17] A major disadvantage is that OCs do not provide any protection from sexually transmitted infections. In addition, pills containing estrogen may cause swollen breasts, and some women experience a reduced sex drive, irregular spotting, depression, headaches, and migraines. Although infrequent, some women may also develop **chloasma**, or large, brown freckles on the face.

Serious side effects have been reported in a small number of women, usually those who smoke and/or have a history of circulatory disease. These side effects include blood clots and an increased risk of stroke. Oral contraceptive users may be more prone to high blood pressure, blood clots in the arms and legs, and possibly benign liver tumors that may rupture and bleed.

Key Term

Chloasma: Brown patches on the facial skin.

The Mini Pill

Another type of OC taken daily contains only progestin. This synthetic form of progesterone has fewer side effects than pills containing estrogen, but is associated with more irregular bleeding patterns. Progestin-only pills are often called mini-pills, and two varieties are currently available in the United States. Failure rates appear to be about the same as combination oral contraceptives. The primary disadvantage is the disruption of the menstrual cycle, but less common side effects include headache, breast tenderness, nausea, and dizziness.

All OCs are immediately reversible, and do not provide any protection from STIs or HIV. Before deciding to take the pill, read "Image of Health in Depth: Questions to Ask Your Physician about the Pill."

Image of Health in Depth

Questions to Ask Your Physician About the Pill

1. Am I a good candidate for the pill, and would a lower dose pill work for me?

2. What side effects have others experienced on the brand recommended for me?

3. When are side effects serious enough for me to schedule a doctor visit?

4. What should I do if I forget to take a pill?

5. If I choose to take the pill, how often should I come in for regular check-ups?

Contraceptive Skin Patch

In 2001, the FDA approved the first contraceptive skin patch. OrthoEvra is a thin, 1 3/4-inch square patch applied to the skin that slowly releases estrogen and progestin into the bloodstream. Each patch is worn continuously for one week, and then a new patch is applied. This occurs for three consecutive weeks, and during the fourth week, no patch is worn and the woman has her menstrual period. The patch can be worn on the upper arm, abdomen, buttocks, or upper torso, though not on the breasts. It remains in place during bathing and swimming, but if it should fall off for more than a day, the user should begin a new three-week cycle of patches. When a patient starts using a patch for the first time, a backup method of contraception should be used for the first week.

The patch works the same as OCs, with similar disadvantages. With perfect use, the failure rate for the patch is very low, 0.3 percent, with typical use failure rate at 8 percent. The contraception reversibility for the patch is almost instantaneous. The patch is not as effective in women who weigh more than 180 pounds, and it does not provide any protection against STIs or HIV.

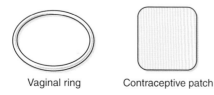

Vaginal ring   Contraceptive patch

FIGURE 6-14. The patch is small and skin toned. The vaginal ring is inserted into the vagina and left in place for three weeks.

Vaginal Contraceptive Ring

Also introduced in 2001, the vaginal contraceptive ring works in the same way as OCs and the contraceptive skin patch.[18] Two inches in diameter and containing both estrogen and progestin, the ring is inserted into the vagina during the first five days of menstruation, and left in place for three weeks. When it is removed at the end of the third week, the woman begins her next menstrual cycle. At the end of the fourth week, a new ring is inserted.

During the very first cycle with the ring, backup contraception other than a diaphragm must be used. Alternate contraception should also be used if the ring is removed for more than three hours.

Sold as the NuvaRing, it offers the same advantages and disadvantages as OCs, except for a lower incidence of nausea. In a small percentage of users, there is some vaginal discharge, irritation, and **vaginitis**. The perfect use rate is 0.3 percent, typical use has a failure rate of 8 percent, and reversibility for the NuvaRing is immediate. The ring may not be as effective in women who are overweight, and like contraceptive patches and birth control pills, the ring does not provide protection from STIs or HIV.

Key Term

Vaginitis: Inflammation of the vagina.

Implantable Contraception

Implantable contraceptives have been available in other countries for decades. They were first introduced in the U.S. in 1990 as Norplant, which consisted of six thin, flexible tubes that contained progestin only. Typically inserted in the fatty tissue of the woman's upper arm, Norplant provided effective contraception for five years. Unfortunately, there were some unpleasant side effects, and as a result of complaints and lawsuits, Norplant was ultimately removed from the market.

In the U.S. today, women can choose from Jadelle or Implanon as implantable contraceptives. Implanon became available in 2006, and provides birth control for three years. Like OCs, Implanon works by releasing progestin to prevent the release of an egg, changes the mucus in the cervix, and alters the lining of the uterus. Inserted by a physician, Implanon, one tiny rod about 1.5 inches by 0.08 inches, has a failure rate of less than 1 percent.

Once inserted, it provides immediate and continuous birth control, making it more attractive to those who tend to forget to take OCs, insert the NuvaRing each week, or change patches. The most common side effect with Implanon is irregular periods: some women bleed more, others less, and some do not bleed at all. This is similar for all progestin-only birth control methods, and is the most common reason women opt not to use the device. About 1 percent of women will experience mood swings, weight gain, headache, acne, and depression.

©Hayden-McNeil, LLC

FIGURE 6-15. Jadelle implantable contraception.

The same company that produced Norplant manufactures Jadelle. Clinical trials have shown Jadelle has a failure rate of just 0.3 percent over three years, and 1.1 percent if left in place for five years. It consists of two tiny rods, each 1.7 inches long and 0.09 inches in diameter. As with Implanon, it is inserted in the fatty tissue on the underside of a woman's arm, releasing progestin to prevent ovulation, and has similar side effects. In the U.S., Jadelle has been approved for three-year use since 1996.

Injectable Contraception

Depo-Provera has been on the market since the 1960s. This progestin-only birth control provides contraception for three months, is 99.7 percent effective, and with typical use is more effective than the pill. Injections are needed every 11–13 weeks, and it begins working immediately. With Depo-Provera, many women have lighter periods and some do not bleed at all. The most severe side effect is calcium loss, and the longer this contraceptive is used, the more calcium loss occurs, increasing the risk of **osteoporosis**. In addition, the reversibility rate of Depo-Provera can be up to 12 months.

Key Term

Osteoporosis: A bone disease caused by calcium loss that leads to an increased risk for fractures.

Emergency Contraception

Emergency contraception refers to those methods used after unprotected sexual intercourse or when a method has failed, such as if a condom breaks. These methods are not for regular use, and should only be used in emergency situations. Some argue that this form of contraceptive is actually an **abortifacient**, since it may inhibit implantation of a fertilized egg. Emergency contraception works primarily by inhibiting or delaying ovulation and by altering the transport of sperm and eggs. If sperm are unable to reach the fallopian tubes, conception is unlikely to occur. If sperm are in the fallopian tubes but ovulation has not occurred and is delayed by emergency contraception, conception cannot occur.

Key Term

Abortifacient: Any agent or substance that induces an abortion.

Emergency contraception can be used immediately, or up to five days after intercourse. This form of contraception is *not* as effective as other birth control methods, and does not provide any protection from STIs or HIV.

Motivation Maximizer

As you read through the options for preventing pregnancy, some men may assume that they don't have to worry about it, since almost all women are on the pill. They may even assume that being on the pill means the woman has been checked for sexually transmitted infections. Both assumptions are wrong. Most college women are in fact not on the pill, and those who use OCs have an annual exam to check for cervical cancer, not for sexually transmitted infections. If your partner is on the pill, are you absolutely certain she takes it at the same time every single day, or does she sometimes forget?

Some women have already had a scare in which they wait and hope for their menstrual flow to start, convincing themselves they are late because of stress, because of exams, because of anything but pregnancy.

Some couples rely on condoms, but they sometimes forget or choose not to use them. After all, they tell themselves, it is just once. What is the likelihood of getting pregnant or contracting an STI when you don't use a condom just this one time? Each and every time you have unprotected sex, your risk stays about the same.

Some women already know the outcome of such thoughts, having had the experience of an unplanned pregnancy. Those who opted to terminate a pregnancy or entered into an adoption may still be dealing with the emotional trauma of those decisions. Those who maintained the pregnancy may be dealing with the added pressures of child expenses, babysitting, and other complications of having a baby while in college. This happened because they neglected to be responsible and ensure an adequate birth control method was used every time.

How difficult would it be to add a condom to your routine every time you choose to have sex? For about $1, you can help ensure that you do not have an unplanned pregnancy, as well as reducing your exposure to any possible sexually transmitted infections. For that $1, you also help ensure that your career dreams and goals will materialize. Assume responsibility now rather than having to be accountable later, trying to answer the question: What do we do now?

Plan B—The Morning-After Pill

Plan B is not an abortion pill; it does not work if the consumer is already pregnant, if a fertilized egg has already embedded in the uterus. This pill works by either preventing ovulation, preventing sperm from reaching an egg, or by preventing a fertilized egg from implanting in the uterus. It is an emergency contraceptive used when contraception has failed, when you have had unprotected sex, or when a sexual assault has occurred. It is not a substitute for routine birth control, and Plan B offers no protection from HIV or STIs.

Plan B contains levonorgestrel, one of the same hormones found in birth control pills. It should be taken within 72 hours after unprotected sex, working better the sooner it is taken. When used as directed, Plan B is considered safe for most women, with no serious side effects. Common side effects include nausea, stomach pain, headache, dizziness, and breast tenderness. After using Plan B, some women experience spotting, or have a lighter or heavier period than normal. If a period is more than a week late, it is important to have a pregnancy test done.

Although it is FDA approved, Plan B is controversial; some doctors will not prescribe it, and some pharmacists will not fill prescriptions for it. It is available for women over 18 years of age without a prescription, but in most states, all women under 18 require a prescription.

Critical Thinking Question: If you discover you are going to become a parent within the next eight months, what changes would this cause you to make in your life?

FIGURE 6-16. Pregnancy is optional. You can choose to prevent pregnancy.

Permanent Birth Control Methods

Permanent birth control methods, or sterilization, include **tubal ligation** for women and **vasectomy** for men. Each is highly effective at preventing pregnancy, and generally, those who have already had all the children they plan to have may choose sterilization.

Key Terms

Tubal ligation: A surgical procedure in which the fallopian tubes are cut or tied to prevent conception.

Vasectomy: A surgical procedure in which the ducts that carry sperm from the testes are cut and tied so that no sperm can pass.

Tubal Ligation

Female sterilization involves preventing the egg from entering the fallopian tubes, either by blocking or by severing the tubes. Ovulation and menstruation still occur, so a woman will experience her usual monthly hormonal cycle. However, eggs are absorbed into the abdominal cavity, rather than being released into the fallopian tubes.

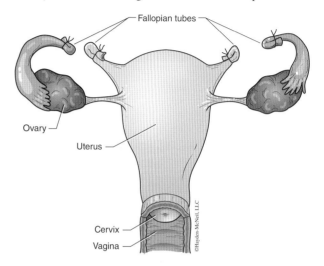

FIGURE 6-17. Tubal ligation should be considered a non-reversible form of birth control.

The most common procedure for tubal ligation is known as a laparoscopy, where a **laparoscope** is inserted into a small cut about 1 cm long, made near the navel. Carbon dioxide gas is pumped in to help move the abdominal wall, providing easier access to the fallopian tubes. A second incision is made near the pubic hairline, and the surgical instruments necessary to either cut or cauterize the tubes are inserted. The procedure can be performed in 20 to 30 minutes under general anesthesia, spinal anesthesia, or local anesthesia with sedation, and is frequently performed after a vaginal or cesarean delivery. Minor complications occur in about 6–11 percent of cases, making female sterilization a little riskier than male sterilization, and it costs about four times more than a vasectomy. The potential complications for women include wound infection, pain, and bleeding. Serious side effects are rare, and the death rate for the procedure is very low. The possibility of failure is less than one in 200 women, or 0.4 percent, becoming pregnant in the first year after sterilization.

> **Key Term**
>
> **Laparoscope**: A long, thin, telescope-like surgical instrument used to view interior parts of the body.

Vasectomy

A vasectomy is a minor operation typically performed in a doctor's office, and the patient remains awake during the 30-minute procedure. Before the surgery, a local anesthetic is used to numb the scrotum, and one or two small cuts are made. The vas deferens are lifted up, cut, and tied or sealed with an electric current. The small openings in the scrotum are then closed with stitches, and the patient returns home and can go back to normal work the next day. He is not considered sterile until there are no active sperm in three separate ejaculate samples over the course of a few weeks. The samples are checked for active sperm at the physician's office.

Another type of vasectomy does not require an incision. After the anesthetic, the skin of the scrotum is pierced and gently stretched so that the tubes can be reached and blocked. No stitches are required, and there are fewer complications than with scalpel procedures. This type of vasectomy accounts for about one third of all those currently performed in the U.S.

A vasectomy merely blocks sperm from moving through the vas deferens. There is still ejaculate, and all other pre-vasectomy conditions remain the same: there is no change in sex drive, erection function, or any hormonal activity. Sperm are still produced, but are absorbed into the body.

Although there have been major improvements in surgical techniques, success rates with vasectomy reversal procedures are still very low. Some men consider sperm banking in the event they decide to father a child after a vasectomy; however, sperm banking, like egg banking, is not a fertility insurance plan. It is expensive, and banked sperm and eggs cannot be guaranteed to produce a pregnancy at an unknown time in the future.

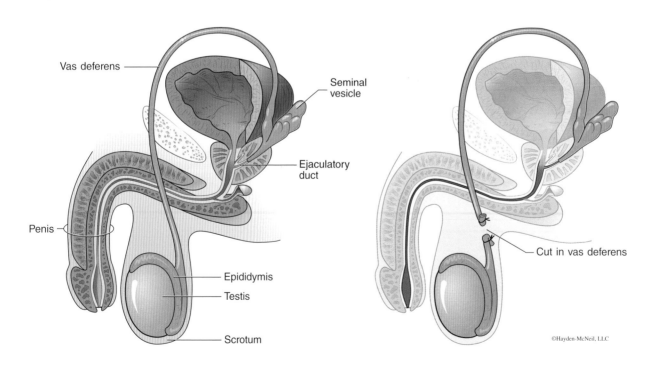

Vas deferens

Seminal vesicle

Ejaculatory duct

Penis

Cut in vas deferens

Epididymis

Testis

Scrotum

©Hayden-McNeil, LLC

FIGURE 6-18. The vas deferens before and after a vasectomy.

Complications with vasectomies are rare, but include infection at the surgical site and minor post-operative discomfort. Significant complications are even more rare, and may include swelling around the incision or inside the scrotum, bruising, and sperm granulomas, which occur when sperm leak from the vas deferens into the surrounding tissue, causing asymptomatic lumps. In some cases, sperm granulomas may require surgical treatment.

Although vasectomy is cheaper than tubal ligation, with fewer side effects and complications, vasectomies are still performed less frequently.

Things to Consider before Sterilization

If you are thinking about sterilization, it is important to consider all possible future scenarios. The following is a list of things to consider.

- Before becoming sterilized, consider using or having your partner use a long-term birth control method, such as an IUD or contraceptive implant.

- If you are thinking about becoming sterilized because you and your partner have as many children as you want, or because you both have decided you do not want children, consider whether this view would change if you were with a different partner.

- If you have considered banking sperm and eggs, and feel prepared to become sterilized, consider how you might feel if these banked eggs and sperm were ineffective and did not result in pregnancy. Would your sterilization still be acceptable to you?

- Consider that you might change your mind as you age. Quite often, the views we have at one age are different later in life.

- Always view sterilization as an irreversible procedure from which there is no recourse.

Image of Health in Depth

College versus Parenthood

The cost of raising a child to post-baccalaureate degree is approximately $450,000. Having a baby during college will impact your future earnings, and the more we learn, the more we can expect to earn. But what is a four-year college degree worth in the marketplace?

Among full-time, year-round workers between the ages of 25–34, white, black, and Hispanic four-year college graduates earn an average of 60 percent more than high school graduates from the same demographic groups. This results in an increased annual income of about $15,000. For Asian Americans, the difference is higher, at about 80 percent.

Amortized, the cost of raising a child until she or he completes a four-year degree is about $20,450 per year. Therefore, perhaps a responsible financial decision is to postpone pregnancy until you have completed your college education and are earning those extra dollars!

The Future for Birth Control

Current research suggests that future birth control pills for women may also prevent STIs, help prevent cancer, and even extend a woman's fertility.[19]

The Career Pill

Canadian researchers are currently studying what is termed a "career pill." Although this innovative concept is still at least 15 years in the future, it may eventually allow women to postpone or delay ovulation from their teens, and resume it when they are ready to reproduce. Such a pill may also delay the onset of menopause.

The Male Pill

The hormone-free male pill, which prevents the ejaculation of sperm, may be on the market in five years. Intended as a single dose taken a few hours before having sex, the male pill affects contraction of the muscles that control ejaculation, resulting in a dry ejaculation. According to researchers at King's College London, it is not expected to interfere with performance or orgasm sensation.[20]

In the U.S., researchers are also developing an injectable contraceptive for males, given every two months. The contraceptive contains both testosterone and progestin and works by suppressing sperm production.

Challenge Question: As a woman, would you feel protected against pregnancy if your partner told you he was on the pill? Or might you continue to use your chosen method of birth control, just in case? For men, how would you feel about having to remember to take the pill?

If Pregnancy Occurs

Other than sterilization, there is no birth control method available that can guarantee complete effectiveness against pregnancy. Part of the reason is user error, or failure to use a birth control method. But even if use is managed effectively, the methods themselves are not without failure. So if a pregnancy occurs, what comes next?

Viewing Your Options

Immediately after unprotected sex, steps can be taken to prevent pregnancy. This should always be your first option. Once a pregnancy is established, choices will become harder to make, and the options are more costly. Choices include terminating the pregnancy, carrying the pregnancy to term, giving the child up for adoption, or choosing to raise the child.

Abortion

By definition, an abortion is the expulsion of an embryo or fetus before it has developed sufficiently enough to survive. A pregnant female who has had a miscarriage has technically had a spontaneous abortion. Abortion usually refers to pregnancies terminated by mechanical or chemical means, and in this section, the term abortion will be used to mean deliberately induced expulsion of an embryo or fetus.

Various methods of abortion have been in place throughout history. Abortion was legal in the U.S. until the mid-1800s, when the **Comstock Act** made it illegal. This act also made contraception illegal, and it was not until 1965

that a Supreme Court ruling overturned a law prohibiting the use of contraception by married couples. Soon after this landmark decision, four states repealed abortion laws.

The most widely known ruling relative to abortion is Roe vs. Wade. In this 1973 decision, the Supreme Court struck down a Texas law banning abortion. Since that landmark ruling, there have been at least eleven more court decisions on abortion. The most recent took place in 2003, when President Bush signed the Partial Birth Abortion Ban Act, in which Congress declared that when a physician punctures the skull of a fetus to collapse it so that it can be more easily expelled, it is an unnecessary, inhumane procedure. When allowed, this procedure was generally used to preserve the health of the mother, and at the time was the only viable medical option. Today, the Supreme Court has upheld the Partial Birth Abortion Ban Act.

Key Term

Comstock Act: The Comstock Act (1873) is a United States federal law that made it illegal to send any "obscene, lewd, and/or lascivious" materials through the mail, including contraceptive devices and information.

Concerns with Abortion

There is possibly no other medical issue on which people differ so vehemently as that of abortion. Pro-life advocates believe that a fertilized egg must be viewed as a human being, and that its termination is murder. The pro-choice view is that a distinction must be made between the stages of embryonic and fetal development, in order to determine when life begins. For some, the view is that if the fetus cannot be sustained outside of the uterus, then life has not begun, and a woman maintains the right to choose what to do with her own body.

Pro-life proponents argue that women have a choice with contraceptive options, and pregnancies can therefore be prevented. Pro-choice advocates counter this argument citing contraceptive failure rates, lack of funds for contraception, and issues of rape-induced pregnancies.

There is no easy answer to this issue. If a couple decides that an abortion is the best alternative, they must then consider the potential medical and emotional consequences that this might entail.

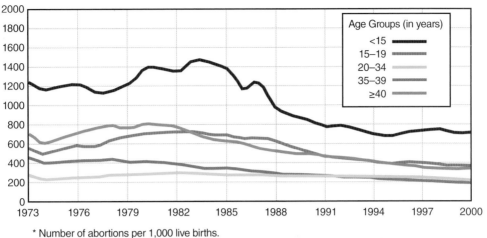

* Number of abortions per 1,000 live births.
** For 1998–1999, data are from 48 reporting areas, and for 2000, from 49 reporting areas.
Data obtained from cdc.gov.

FIGURE 6-19. Abortion ratio* by age group of women who obtained a legal abortion—selected states, United States, 1973–2000.**

Types of Abortion

Abortions are either surgical or medically induced. Surgical abortions are performed far more frequently and account for about 98 percent of all terminated pregnancies. However, medical abortions, involving the use of such drugs as mifepristone, may soon surpass surgical abortions.

Surgical Abortions

Prior to the sixth week of pregnancy, manual vacuum aspiration can be performed. In this procedure, the cervix is dilated and the contents of the uterus are removed, using a hand-held syringe. Between the sixth and twelfth weeks, suction curettage or vacuum aspiration is the most common surgical method for ending a pregnancy. In this procedure, the cervix is dilated, and a suction curette is inserted into the uterus. The curette is attached to rubber tubing connected to an electric pump. Suction is applied, and the uterus is scraped of any remaining tissue. This procedure is completed in less than ten minutes, and there is a low risk of complications. Following both procedures, the woman bleeds to shed any remaining uterine lining.

Between the twelfth and 24th week of pregnancy, dilation and evacuation (D & E) can be used. During a D & E, dilators gradually open the cervix overnight. The uterus is then emptied the next morning, using surgical instruments and an aspirating machine. This type of abortion is very rare, accounting for only about 1 percent of all abortions in the U.S.

RU-486

RU-486 is the commonly used name for an artificial steroid that blocks the progesterone needed to continue a pregnancy. Its generic name is mifepristone, and it is sold under the brand names Mifeprex and Early Option. RU-486 is a drug that when taken alone results in an abortion about 60 percent of the time. To increase the rate of abortion, a second drug is taken 48 hours later. This second drug, prostaglandin, causes the uterus to contract and expel the embryo. Misoprostyl is the generic name for the prostaglandin drug, which is sold as Cyotec.

An RU-486/mispoprostyl abortion takes from two days to four weeks, and requires at least three physician visits. At the first visit, the patient undergoes a pelvic exam, and the side effects and risks are explained. These include cramps, nausea and vomiting, dizziness, diarrhea, and heavy bleeding. If excessive bleeding should occur, the patient is advised to seek emergency medical care immediately. At the end of the first visit, the patient signs a consent form.

At the second visit, the patient is examined to determine if the embryo is still in place. If it is, the RU-486/misoprostyl combination is prescribed. This can be given orally or via a vaginal suppository. The third visit occurs about 14 days later, to ensure the embryo and placenta have been expelled completely and that bleeding has ended or is controlled.

RU-486 should not be used if it has been more than 49 days since the last period. The FDA has also warned that RU-486 should not be used under any of the following conditions:

- You have an IUD.

- You have an **ectopic pregnancy**.

- You have problems with your adrenal glands.

- You take blood-thinning medication.

- You have a bleeding problem.

- You take certain steroid medications.

- You cannot return for the final two visits.

- You cannot easily get emergency medical help if needed.

- You are allergic to either mifespristone or misoprostyl.

Although RU-486 and the follow up drug, misoprostyl, are both approved in the U.S., they may not be easy to get. Some doctors believe that a surgical abortion is less risky, while others oppose the use of these two drugs on either moral or religious grounds. Some opt not to prescribe the drug because of the counseling that is involved, as well as from the concern that patients may not return for all follow-up visits.[21]

The drug costs about $270 for the three-pill regimen. With the added cost of physician visits and laboratory work, this could make an RU-486 abortion more costly than a surgical abortion.

Key Term

Ectopic pregnancy: A pregnancy that develops outside the uterus, usually in the fallopian tubes.

Abortion Complications

There are few medical and emotional complications from abortions. In 1988, the United States Surgeon General conducted an extensive review to determine whether abortion resulted in either positive or negative impacts on mental health. He concluded that neither could be shown. Of course, this does not mean that no one has ever suffered emotionally as a result of the procedure, nor does it mean that no one has ever experienced emotional relief. It simply means that apparently, the majority of women experience neither.

Medical complications may include infection and bleeding, and in some rare cases, the abortion is not complete and the patient must undergo a repeat curettage. There is no evidence to suggest that an abortion increases the risk for any form of cancer, subsequent infertility, spontaneous abortions in future pregnancies, premature delivery, or low-birth-weight babies.

Image of Health in Depth

Roe vs. Wade

Roe vs. Wade was the 1973 landmark case resulting in the Supreme Court decision to legalize abortion. Based on the argument that laws against abortion violated a constitutional right to privacy, the decision overturned all state and federal laws outlawing or restricting abortion. This case remains one of the most controversial and politically significant in U.S. Supreme Court history.

Roe vs. Wade began when Norma McCorvey, claiming pregnancy as a result of rape, filed suit against an abortion injunction in Texas. (Today, Ms. McCorvey has stated that the rape claim was false.) Roe reached the U.S. Supreme Court on appeal, and on January 22, 1973, the court voted with a 7–2 margin to strike down Texas abortion laws.

Jessica's Story

Jessica became sexually active when she was a junior in high school. Now in her first year of college, she considers herself to be much brighter, more informed, and more adult. She looks back on her high school behavior and is amazed at how lucky she was—no STIs or unplanned pregnancies, though she did little to prevent either. She has been dating a freshman for a few weeks and knows they are getting close to having a sexual relationship, but Jessica is committed to ensuring her safety and her plans to finish college. One night, she tells her boyfriend about the lectures regarding sexually transmitted infections in her health class. He seems very bored by this. Jessica reels off statistics about STIs and tells him of the approximate one million unplanned pregnancies that occur each year. She asks what he would do if he got someone pregnant. He jokes and says it's not likely to be her, since they are not sexually active. But Jessica pushes and says, "But what if?" "Well," he says, "most girls are on the pill, right?" Jessica says that she is, but what if it fails? No one plans a car crash, but they still occur. And because of that, we all wear seat belts and have air bags to add to our protection. No one thinks this is too much protection; it is just accepted. The boyfriend thinks about this and understands that Jessica is suggesting that being on the pill may not be enough. It might be a seat belt, but maybe they need an airbag, too! They laugh about the analogy, but agree that birth control is important, and that each of them must assume responsibility. After all, adding a condom to the birth control package also helps reduce the risk of STIs! ∎

Responsibility and Accountability

As a college student, you may frequently be overwhelmed with the responsibilities you face. Failure to deal with any of your responsibilities may lead you to accept the resulting accountability. But when it comes to the responsibility involved with sexual activity, the resulting accountability can include emotional, medical, and financial costs. With so much at stake, thinking ahead is very important.

Your Responsibility and Your Partner's Responsibility

A responsible adult will think carefully before engaging in any sexual activity. The responsibility will include not only thinking about protection against STIs and pregnancy, but also about any emotional consequences of this action.

The responsibility to protect oneself regarding sexual behavior rests with each individual. If you are sexually active, it is *your* responsibility to protect yourself from STIs and unplanned pregnancy. If your partner tells you that she or he is using a safe method of birth control, the partner is ensuring self-protection. Although this protection might transfer to you, it does not relieve you of ensuring your own safety and protection. It is also your personal responsibility to understand your emotional expectations and determine whether they will be met.

Focusing on Accountability

The two major consequences of sexual activity are contracting an STI or addressing an unplanned pregnancy. Both can be 100 percent avoided with responsible planning and decision-making. If you engage in unprotected sex and a pregnancy results, what do you think you would do? Perhaps you have already faced this decision in the past—are you comfortable with that choice today? Would it have been better if you had prevented the pregnancy? Accountability for an unplanned pregnancy can result in huge expenses, both financially and emotionally. The time to consider this is before engaging in sexual activity. You are in college with the hope of improving your future opportunities—being accountable for an unplanned pregnancy could end your college plans.

Summary

Reasons to Prevent Pregnancy

- In the U.S., birth control was viewed as immoral as late as 1902.

- Being younger or being older can impair pregnancy outcome.

- Raising a child to age one costs about $10,000.

- Partnerships and commitment need to be reviewed carefully before becoming pregnant.

Safety and Effectiveness of Birth Control

- For smoking women, OCs carry increased risk.

- Allergies to latex cause problems with some types of condoms.

- Theoretical effectiveness refers to how effective a product is when used exactly according to directions and without any user error. Typical effectiveness, or in use effectiveness, is the rate that occurs during the first year of use.

- Reversibility refers to how quickly a user returns to the same fertile state she had before using the birth control product.

- Continuation rate is the number of people who continue to use a contraceptive method after a specified period of time.

Options for Preventing Pregnancy

- Fertility awareness methods for birth control include the calendar method, the standard day's method, the temperature method, and the mucus method, or Billings Method. Withdrawal and douching are also used as birth control methods, but with even lower prevention rates than seen with fertility awareness methods.

- Barrier methods include condoms, diaphragms, cervical caps, contraceptive sponges, and IUDs. They work by preventing the sperm from reaching the egg.

- Hormonal methods include OCs, skin patches, vaginal contraceptive rings, implantable methods and injectable methods. They prevent the female from ovulating each month.

- RU-486 blocks the action of progesterone needed to continue a pregnancy.

- Emergency contraception (Plan B) is used after unprotected sex. It works by inhibiting or delaying ovulation or by altering the transport of sperm and eggs.

Permanent Birth Control Methods

- Permanent birth control methods are either tubal ligation for women or vasectomy for men.

- Other than sterilization, no birth control method can guarantee its effectiveness against pregnancy.

- If pregnancy occurs, choices range from abortions, to adoptions, or to parenthood.

- Most abortions are conducted in the first 12 weeks of pregnancy.

- There are few medical or psychological issues that result from abortion.

Reassessing Your Knowledge

1. Describe the differences between natural, hormonal, and barrier methods of birth control. List any advantages or disadvantages each method may have.

2. Discuss factors that should be considered when choosing a birth control method.

3. Describe what is generally meant by the term "miscarriage" and what is generally meant by the term "abortion." Identify the three different types of abortion, and describe what happens in each.

4. Articulate the difference between Plan B and RU-486.

To answer these questions, you might choose to work in groups with your colleagues. Check your answers against the written material in the text, and reread those sections in which you made errors.

Health Assessment Toolbox

Sexual Health—What Birth Control Method Is Right For You?

This site asks a series of questions to help you with birth control choices.

http://www.womenshealthmatters.ca/centres/sex/.../birthcontrol.html

Getting on Birth Control Pills without Getting off Your Budget

Learn how much it costs for contraceptive pills, from the initial physician exam to the monthly cost of birth control, and learn where less expensive options may be available.

http://www.estronaut.com/a/cost_of_pill.htm

Healthy Women

Learn how contraception works, and the advantages and disadvantages of each method.

http://www.healthywomen.org/healthtopics/contraception

Expenditures on Children by Families, 2006

This site reviews the cost of raising a child from birth to age 17.

http://www.cnpp.usda.gov/Publications/crc/crc2009.pdf

Planned Parenthood

The Planned Parenthood site offers information on birth control, emergency birth control, and abortion **options.**

http://www.plannedparenthood.org/

Vocabulary Challenge

Match the term in the left-hand column with its correct definition in the right-hand column.

TERM		DEFINITION
Abortion	A.	The use of breastfeeding as a contraceptive method
Lea's shield	B.	Inflammation of the vagina
Career pill	C.	An inflammation of the female pelvic organs, most commonly the fallopian tubes, usually as a result of bacterial infection
Pelvic inflammatory disease	D.	Any agent or substance that induces an abortion
Abortifacient	E.	Sexual intercourse
Lactational amenorrhea method	F.	A rare but potentially fatal infection usually caused by bacteria
Coitus	G.	The expulsion of an embryo or fetus before it is developed sufficiently enough to survive
Toxic shock syndrome	H.	Barrier method that covers the cervix to help prevent conception
Diaphragm	I.	A pill in the development stage that will delay the onset of ovulation
Vaginitis	J.	A one-size cervical cap made of silicone

Answers

G, J, I, C, D, A, E, F, H, B.

Exploring the Internet

At this site, users can use interactive tools to learn more about menstrual suppression, and how to choose a birth control method.

http://www.arhp.org/topics/contraception

About.com

Offers a simple method to help females calculate the day they ovulate.

http://infertility.about.com/library/blcalovulate.htm

About.com

Offers helpful information on how to talk with your partner about birth control.

http://contraception.about.com/od/talkingaboutbirthcontrol/ht/TalktoPartner.htm

Planned Parenthood offers a variety of information about sexuality and birth control.

http://www.plannedparenthood.org/

The American Pregnancy Helpline

Offers a series of questions to help you determine if you are ready to become a parent.

http://www.thehelpline.org/unplanned-pregnancy/parenting/am-i-ready-to-be-a-parent/

Selected References

1. Himes, N. *Medical History of Contraception*. Gamut Press Incorporated. 1963.

2. Devereux, G. *A Typological Study of Abortion in 350 Primitive, Ancient and Pre-Industrial Societies*, Ed. Harold Rosen. NY: The Julian Press. 1954.

3. Heffner, L.J. Medical Biology: On Advanced Maternal Age in Humans. *New England Journal of Medicine*. 351: 1927. 2004.

4. Jolly, M., Sebire, N., Robinson, S., and Regan, L. The Risks Associated with Pregnancy in Women Aged 35 Years and Older. *Human Reproduction*, 15(11): 2433–2437. 2000.

5. Machlin, S.R. and Rohde, F. *Health Care Expenses for Uncomplicated Pregnancies*. Research Findings No. 27. August, 2007.

6. Merrill, C., and Steiner, C. *Hospitalizations Related to Childbirth*, 2003. HCUP Statistical Brief #11. August 2006. Agency for Healthcare Research and Quality, Rockville, Md. http://www.hcup-us.ahrq.gov/reports/statbriefs/sb11.pdf

7. *Care of Children and Adolescents in U.S. Hospitals*. HCUP Fact Book No. 4. AHRQ Publication No. 04-0004, October 2003. Agency for Healthcare Research and Quality, Rockville, MD. http://www.ahrq.gov/data/hcup/factbk4/factbk4.htm

8. Lino, M. (2010). Expenditures on Children by Families, 2009. U.S. Department of Agriculture, Center for Nutrition Policy and Promotion. Miscellaneous Publication No. 1528-2009.

9. Emons, G., Fleckenstein, G., Hinney, B., Huschmand, A., and Heyl, W. Hormonal Interactions in Endometrial Cancer. *Endocrine-Related Cancer*; 7(4): 227–242. 2000.

10. Modan, B., Harge, P., Hirsh-Yechezkel, G., et al. Parity, Oral Contraceptives, and the Risk of Ovarian Cancer Among Carriers and Non-Carriers of BRCA1 or BRCA2 Mutation. *New England Journal of Medicine*, 345(4): 235–240. 2001.

11. Speroff, L., and Darney, P.D. Injectable Contraception, *A Clinical Guide for Contraception*. 4th Ed. Philadelphia: Lippincott Williams & Wilkins, 201–220. 2005.

12. Lipsitz, A., Bishop. P., and Robinson, C. *Virginity Pledges: Who Takes Them and How Well Do They Work?* American Psychological Society 15th Annual Convention. 2003.

13. Tanne, J.H. Abstinence only Programmes Do Not Change Sexual Behavior, Texas Study Shows. *British Medical Journal* 330(7487): 326. 2005.

14. Ozalp S.S. Copper Containing, Framed Intrauterine Devices for Contraception. T*he WHO Reproductive Health Library*; Geneva: World Health Organization. 2006.

15. d'Arcangues, C. Worldwide Use of Intrauterine Devices for Contraception. *Contraception*, 75: S2–S7. 2007.

Chapter 6

16. Birth Control Methods. The National Women's Health Information Center. U.S. Department of Health and Human Services. Office on Women's Health. Women's health.gov. Downloaded June 29, 2010, from http://www.womenshealth.gov/faq/birth-control-methods.cfm

17. Burkman, R., et al. Safety Concerns and Health Benefits Associated with Oral Contraception. *American Journal of Obstetrics and Gynecology*, 190(4 Suppl): 5–22. 2004.

18. Johansson, E.D., and Sitruk-Ware, R. New Delivery Systems in Contraception: Vaginal Rings. *American Journal of Obstetrics and Gynecology*, 190(4 Suppl): 54–59. 2004.

19. The Future of Birth Control. Medicine.net. Downloaded July 1, 2010, from http://www.medicinenet.com/script/main/art.asp?articlekey=52189 on.

20. Medical News Today: Male Contraceptive Pill. Downloaded November 13, 2007, from www.medicalnewstoday.com/articles/57550.php

21. Raine, T, R., et al. Direct Access to Emergency Contraception Through Pharmacies and Effect on Unintended Pregnancies and STIs. *Journal of the American Medical Association*, 293(1): 54–62. 2005.

Unit Three

Taking Charge of Physical
Health

UNIT THREE

Image of Health

Nutrition

ELEMENTS OF NUTRITION

- The Energy in Food
- Carbohydrates
  - Simple Carbohydrates
  - Complex Carbohydrates
  - The Glycemic Index
  - Fiber
- Proteins
  - The Structure of Proteins
  - Recommended Intake of Protein
  - High Protein Diets
- Fats
  - Saturated Fats
  - Unsaturated Fats
  - Recommended Intake of Fat

MICROELEMENTS OF NUTRITION

- Vitamins
  - Recommended Intake of Vitamins
- Minerals
  - Recommended Intake of Minerals
- Antioxidants and Phytonutrients
- Water

GUIDELINES FOR HEALTHY EATING

- 2010 Dietary Guidelines for Americans
- Specific Populations and the Recommendations
- Dietary Reference Intakes
- Daily Recommended Values

HEALTHY DIETARY PLANS

- The USDA Pyramid
- The Harvard Pyramid
- The Mediterranean Pyramid
- The Vegetarian Pyramid

CHALLENGES TO HEALTHY EATING

- Restaurant Choices
- Fast Food Eating
- Beverage Choices
- Packing It to Go

CONSUMER ISSUES IN NUTRITION

- Organic Foods
- Genetically Modified Foods
- Irradiated Foods
- Food Allergies
- Food Intolerances

CHOOSING A DIET BASED ON HEALTH DECISIONS

- Diet to Reduce Disease Risk

RESPONSIBILITY AND ACCOUNTABILITY

- Taking Responsibility for Nutrition
- Focusing on Accountability

Student Learning Outcomes

LEARNING OUTCOME	APPLYING IT TO YOUR LIFE
Describe the six major nutrients and their purposes.	How balanced is your current diet regarding these nutrients?
Describe the differences between the USDA pyramid and the Harvard Healthy Eating Pyramid.	Select a pyramid to meet your nutritional and health goals, and develop an eating plan based on that pyramid.
Describe some challenges faced when eating away from home.	Identify ways you can still maintain a healthy diet when eating away from home.
Describe what is meant by organic foods, genetically modified foods, and irradiated foods.	What steps can you take to improve your nutrition, based on your knowledge of organic foods, genetically modified foods, and irradiated foods?
Differentiate between food allergies and food intolerances.	Identify any symptoms of food allergis or food intolerances you have.

Assessing Your Knowledge

1. An example of a simple carbohydrate is:
   a. Fruit juice
   b. White bread
   c. Shredded wheat cereal
   d. Both (a) and (b) are simple carbohydrates

2. Complex carbohydrates differ from simple carbohydrates in that they:
   a. Provide immediate energy
   b. Contain only four grams of carbohydrates
   c. Provide sustained energy
   d. Cause blood sugar levels to spike quickly

3. There are _____ essential amino acids
   a. 6
   b. 8
   c. 12
   d. 14

4. Which of the following are examples of complete proteins?
   a. Milk, lima beans, and whole wheat spaghetti
   b. Whole wheat foods, eggs, and cheese
   c. Poultry, beef, and pork
   d. Both (b) and (c) are correct

5. Examples of monounsaturated fats include:
   a. Butter, corn oil, and safflower oil
   b. Corn oil, safflower oil, and olive oil
   c. Safflower oil, peanut oil, and olive oil
   d. Canola oil, olive oil, and peanut oil

Answers:

1. d; 2. c; 3. b; 4. c; 5. d.

Elements of Nutrition

Eating is one of life's greatest pleasures, and should be a positive part of each day. Did you eat breakfast this morning? Do you remember what you had for dinner last night? Although many people make an effort to eat well, those who consistently make poor nutritional choices will eventually be accountable for those choices. Choosing to eat well requires that you know how to make informed decisions about food, and that you have access to appropriate food choices.

Your knowledge about nutrition will help you make informed, responsible decisions. This chapter will help you understand the basic components of nutrition, and how to make good food choices to improve your nutritional habits.

Nutrition is the act or processes by which we consume and utilize food. **Nutrients** are the components, or building blocks, of nutrition. Some are essential and must be obtained from outside the body, while others are made within the body. The major nutrients are carbohydrates, fats, proteins, vitamins, and minerals. Water is also essential, though it does not supply any nutrients or calories. Table 7-1 lists the six classes of essential nutrients.

Table 7-1. Six Classes of Essential Nutrients

NUTRIENT	PURPOSE	SOURCES
Carbohydrates	The body's favorite energy source. Carbohydrates supply energy to the cells in the brain, the nervous system, and blood, and supply energy to muscles during activity.	All grains, cereals, breads, fruits, vegetables, and milk.
Proteins	Proteins form the structure of muscles, bones, blood, enzymes, and hormones. They are used to build and repair cell tissue, aid growth, regulate water and acid-base balance, and can be used for energy if carbohydrates and fats are unavailable.	Meat, fish, poultry, eggs, milk, legumes, and nuts.
Fats	Fats are used to insulate, protect, and supply energy, and also for the absorption of fat-soluble vitamins.	Most animal products contain fat. Fat is also found in some nuts, seeds, fish, grains, and vegetables.
Vitamins	Vitamins facilitate cellular metabolism.	Fruits, vegetables, and grains, and some are found in meats and dairy.
Minerals	Minerals aid in growth and maintenance of tissue and act as catalysts in the release of energy.	Found in most food groups.
Water	Water comprises 50–60 percent of the human body. It transports chemicals, regulates temperature, facilitates removal of waste products, and provides a medium for chemical reactions.	Found in fruits, vegetables, and liquids.

The Digestive Process

The digestion of nutrients begins in the mouth, where salivary enzymes work to break down food. During this process, food becomes warmer and is lubricated with saliva, making it easier to continue its passage through the **gastrointestinal tract**.

The stomach releases gastric enzymes, creating an acidic environment that turns food into a liquid mass called **chyme**, which moves from the stomach to the small intestine. Only about twenty percent of food nutrients are released from the stomach to the bloodstream. **Carbohydrates** are the first to be absorbed, while protein takes longer to reach the chyme stage, and fats longer still.

The small intestine does the bulk of the digestive work, combining chyme with enzymes and secretions from the pancreas, liver, and gall bladder. Eighty percent of nutrients pass through the walls of the small intestine and into the blood.

Undigested chyme enters the large intestine, where it becomes concentrated and absorbs liquid in preparation for excretion. Very few nutrients are absorbed into the blood from the large intestine.

Key Terms

Nutrient: Any element or compound necessary for or contributing to an organism's metabolism, growth, or other functioning.

Gastrointestinal tract: The gastrointestinal tract is the system of organs that takes in food, digests it to extract energy and nutrients, and expels the remaining waste.

Chyme: The thick semi-fluid mass of partially digested food that is passed from the stomach to the intestinal tract.

Carbohydrate: One of the main dietary components that includes starches, sugar, and fiber.

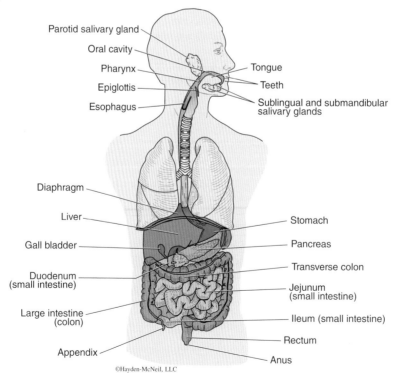

©Hayden-McNeil, LLC

FIGURE 7-1. Digestive system.

The Energy in Food

Energy in food is expressed in terms of calories. A **kilocalorie** (Kcalorie) is the amount of heat needed to raise the temperature of 1 kilogram (kg) of water 1 degree Celsius. One **calorie** is 1/1,000 of a kilocalorie, and in common usage, it is a unit of energy derived from food or drink.

Only three of the essential nutrients provide calories:

- Fats provide 9 calories per gram.

- Carbohydrates provide 4 calories per gram.

- Proteins provide 4 calories per gram.

Alcohol also supplies energy at 7 calories per gram. Although this is not an essential nutrient, it is a factor in evaluating total calories consumed.

Key Terms

Kilocalorie: 1,000 calories, or the energy needed to raise the temperature of 1 kilogram of water one degree Celsius.

Calorie: A unit of energy, or 1/1,000 of a kilocalorie.

The other three nutrients, minerals, vitamins, and water are also essential, but do not provide calories.

Challenge Question: Name the nutrients that contain calories and identify the number of calories per gram that each nutrient contains.

Carbohydrates

More carbohydrates are required in diets than other nutrients, because they are the body's preferred energy source. Carbohydrates come from starches, sugars, and fiber, and all come from plant-based sources. Most experts agree that about 45–65 percent of total calories should come from carbohydrates.[1] For a 2,000 calorie per day diet, this is 225–325 grams of carbohydrates each day.

A steady infusion of carbohydrates provides energy for all body cells, including the brain. Carbohydrates are quickly converted to chyme in the stomach and gradually released into the bloodstream from the intestinal tract, where they are used for immediate energy, converted to **glycogen** or into fat for storage.

Glycogen, the body's main source of stored energy, is stored in muscle tissue and the liver. Excess glucose in the bloodstream is converted into glycogen and stored. For the 8–12 hours after finishing a meal, glucose derived from glycogen is the primary source of blood glucose used by the body. Once the liver and muscles are saturated with glycogen, remaining unused blood glucose is converted to fat for storage.

FIGURE 7-2. This represents about 200 grams of carbohydrates.

Carbohydrates are found in all grains, grain products, **legumes**, nuts, and in all fruits and vegetables. Fruits, vegetables, legumes, and nuts also supply essential vitamins and minerals, fiber, and important **phytonutrients** that may be linked to disease prevention, a reduction in inflammatory diseases, and improved health. Grain carbohydrates may also contain vitamins, minerals, fiber, and phytonutrients, but the nutrient density is based on whether the grain has been refined.

Carbohydrates are classified as either simple or complex, depending how many sugar units are in each molecule.

Challenge Question: What is the function of carbohydrates in the body?

Simple Carbohydrates

Simple carbohydrates are either monosaccharides or disaccharides, meaning one or two molecules of glucose bonded together. These carbohydrates are quickly digested and can raise blood sugar levels very quickly. Examples of simple carbohydrates are sodas, jams, jellies, candy, and sugar. Fruits, fruit juices, and milk are also primarily simple carbohydrates, but they may also provide vitamins, minerals, and fiber. Americans eat more than 152 pounds of caloric sweeteners each year, resulting in over 275,000 calories per year from sugar sources.[2] Table 7-2 identifies some of the sources of sugar most people consume.

Table 7-2. Sugar in Common Foods

FOOD	SERVING SIZE	SUGAR
Angel food cake	4 ounces	7 teaspoons (tsp) sugar
Cheese cake	4 ounces	2 tsp sugar
Chocolate cake (iced)	4 ounces	15 tsp sugar
Iced cupcake	1	6 tsp sugar
Strawberry shortcake	1 standard serving	4 tsp sugar
Brownie (no icing)	¾ ounce	4 tsp sugar
Ginger snaps	1 cookie	13 tsp sugar
Chocolate éclair	1	7 tsp sugar
Iced cream puff	1	25 tsp sugar
Ice cream	1/8 quart	23 tsp sugar

Image of Health

Making Better Choices

Which is better for you: Brown sugar, honey, or white sugar?

Brown sugar, honey, and white sugar are all simple carbohydrates, but which is better for you? In terms of nutritional value, they are identical and equal in terms of calories, and none contains enough of any other element to make it a better choice. Brown sugar is white sugar with molasses added to it. White sugar is nutritionally the same, whether it is raw or processed. Honey is a liquid product made from pollen by bees, consisting mostly of fructose, glucose, and water, and it does not spoil. Nutritionally, honey is the same as sugar, but common folklore still erroneously assumes it to be a better choice. The trace amounts of any vitamins it contains are too small to be beneficial.

Complex Carbohydrates

Complex carbohydrates are polysaccharides, meaning they are long chains of glucose molecules bonded together. They are nutritionally dense, supplying energy, vitamins, minerals, and sometimes fiber. Table 7-3 compares the nutrient values in some common foods. Notice that complex carbohydrates are more likely to contain protein and have a lower fat content.

Complex carbohydrates, like their nutritionally simple counterparts, supply just four calories per gram, but within those four calories comes a nutritional powerhouse. They take longer to digest and are released more slowly into the bloodstream, providing a sustained energy source. Examples of complex carbohydrates include cereals; rice; breads and pastas; vegetables, such as potatoes and corn; and some fruits, such as bananas and dates.

Critical Thinking Question: Why are complex carbohydrates usually better than simple carbohydrates in human nutrition?

Table 7-3. Complex vs. Simple Carbohydrates*

FOOD	SIMPLE OR COMPLEX?	PROTEIN	FIBER	VITAMINS AND MINERALS?	FAT	CALORIES
1 slice whole wheat bread	Complex	3 grams	2 grams	Yes, because they occur naturally in whole wheat	1.6 grams	69
1 Poptart	Simple	2 grams	1 gram	Yes, because it is made with enriched flour	5.3 grams	204
1 cup Batman cereal	Simple	2 grams	1 gram	Yes, because it is made with enriched flour	1.1 grams	106
1 cup 100 percent shredded wheat biscuits	Complex	5 grams	6 grams	Yes, because they occur naturally in whole wheat	.9 grams	107
1 apple	Simple	0 grams	3 grams	Yes, because they occur naturally	0 grams	72
1 fruit roll-up	Simple	0 grams	0 grams	Only if added by the manufacturer	0 grams	52
1 cup cooked whole wheat spaghetti	Complex	7 grams	6 grams	Yes, because they occur naturally	.8 grams	172
1 cup cooked enriched semolina spaghetti	Complex	7 grams	2 grams	Yes, because they have been added	.6 grams	196

*Food analysis done using MyPyramid.gov

Roxanne's Story

Roxanne is desperate to lose weight. Swimsuit season is coming, and she is also the maid of honor for her best friend's wedding. She seeks the advice of her friends and is persuaded to try a low carbohydrate diet. They tell her this is the secret to weight loss, and if she simply gives up those fattening carbohydrates, her weight will drop miraculously. Roxanne is motivated and determined. For a week, she avoids as many carbohydrates as she can. She no longer eats cereal, fruit, and toast for breakfast; instead, she eats just two eggs. She gives up bread and eats slices of turkey and a salad for lunch. For dinner, she restricts herself to chicken breasts served with another salad and broccoli. She craves a baked potato, some rice, or some pasta, but she is determined to stick with this diet.

At the end of the week, the miracle has happened and her weight has dropped. She is convinced that low carbohydrate diets are the key to success and tells her nutrition professor her exciting news. Unfortunately, the professor is not astounded or impressed. She asks Roxanne to list what she normally eats for a week, and a long list is developed.

Then she asks Roxanne to list what she ate during the last week, and a very short list is created. The professor shows Roxanne that her weight loss was due primarily to calorie reduction, but explains she is giving up mostly good calories rather than nutritionally weak calories. She advises Roxanne that reducing any calorie source in her diet will cause weight loss, but since carbohydrates are essential, continuing with this diet will cause her energy level to drop, her intake of vital vitamins and minerals will be reduced, and she will consume fewer phytonutrients that can aid immunity and help prevent diseases.

But the worst news of all is that most of Roxanne's apparent weight loss is water weight. Carbohydrates need water for digestion; therefore, body cells do not store as much water if carbohydrates are not consumed. The professor asks Roxanne if her objective is to lose water, lose muscle, or to lose body fat. Of course Roxanne wants to lose fat, so her professor helps her develop a calorie-reduced, nutritionally sound diet that includes exercise and that can be maintained. ∎

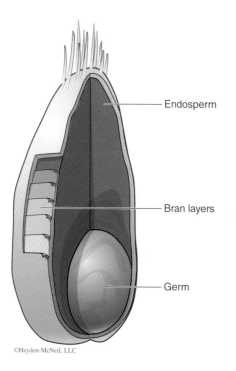

Endosperm

Bran layers

Germ

©Hayden-McNeil, LLC

FIGURE 7-3. Grain kernel.

Complex carbohydrates that come from grains can be further broken down into either whole grains or refined grains. The grain kernel consists of three layers, as depicted in Figure 7-3. The outer layers, called bran, contain naturally occurring fiber, B vitamins, up to 80 percent of the grain's minerals, and other phytonutrients. The inner layer is the endosperm, or the starch in the grain. The endosperm also contains some B vitamins, as well as protein. The center of the grain holds the germ containing B vitamins, vitamin E, trace minerals, and healthy unsaturated fats, together with phytonutrients and antioxidants.

When a grain is refined, the bran and germ are extracted, reducing the nutrient content by 25 percent to 90 percent. If the grain is wheat, the remaining endosperm is ground into a fine powder. Manufacturers must then use vitamins and minerals to "enrich" the product to a specific government standard. This enrichment, sold as enriched wheat flour, usually does not provide any fiber, nor does it reach the original level of nutrients contained in the entire grain of wheat. If the entire kernel of wheat is used, the manufacturer will list 100 percent whole wheat flour. Enriched flour products or refined carbohydrates contain the same number of calories as their whole grain counterparts, but they are lower in fiber and essential nutrients. Whole grains take longer to chew and to digest, and they are released more slowly from the intestinal tract, causing a lower spike in blood glucose levels and helping to maintain feelings of **satiety** longer.

Key Term

Satiety: State of having enough, or more than enough, food.

The Glycemic Index

Consumption of any form of carbohydrate causes changes in insulin delivery and blood glucose levels. Insulin is a hormone the body uses to convert food to energy, and blood glucose levels indicate how much sugar is currently in the bloodstream.

Simple carbohydrates tend to cause a rapid spike in blood sugar levels, while complex carbohydrates cause a more moderate effect. The glucose response of a food is measured by the glycemic index, ranking 50 grams of sugar or white bread with a value of 100 on the index, and comparing 50 grams of other common foods to that measure. The glycemic response is the level to which blood glucose rises in reaction to a particular food. People with particular health concerns, such as Type I diabetes, are often advised to consume foods with lower glycemic index values.

For the average person, it may be difficult to base a diet on the glycemic index, since the body's response to food is affected by food preparation, other foods that may be present, and the health of the individual. People who are less fit and overweight tend to have higher blood sugar values. Table 7-4 lists the glycemic index on 50 grams of some common foods compared with 50 grams of white bread.

Table 7-4. Glycemic Index of Common Foods

FOOD	AVERAGE GLYCEMIC INDEX	FOOD	AVERAGE GLYCEMIC INDEX
1 slice of bread (50 grams)	100	Pound cake	54
Cookies	79	Popcorn	72
Hamburger bun	61	Rice cakes	78
Fruit Loops	69	White rice	69
Corn Flakes	81	Brown rice	50
Coca-Cola	63	Instant rice	69
Waffle	76	Whole milk	27
Apple	38	Non-fat milk	32
Banana	51	Orange	42
Mango	51	Pear	38
Baked beans	48	Canned kidney beans	28
Lentils	29	Pinto beans	39
Peas	48	Pop-tarts	70
Spaghetti, durum	38	Spaghetti, whole wheat	37
Peanuts	14	French fries	75

These values are just a guide. The glycemic index (GI) of foods can vary greatly and the impact of food can be influenced by factors other than GI value.[3]

Fiber

Non-digestible carbohydrates are called **fiber**. Because digestive enzymes cannot break down most fiber, it passes through the intestinal track and is eliminated through the bowel. Some types of fiber are broken down into acids and gases, causing intestinal gas. Fiber is only found in complex carbohydrates, but because it cannot be digested, fiber does not contribute calories.

The Food and Nutrition Board has identified two types of fiber: dietary fiber, which occurs naturally in plant foods, and functional fiber, a non-digestible carbohydrate that has either been synthesized in a laboratory or extracted from a natural source. Total fiber always refers to the sum of both dietary and functional fiber.

Challenge Question: What is the difference between dietary fiber and functional fiber?

Dietary fiber comes from all plant foods and can be broken down into two types. Viscous fiber, previously known as soluble fiber, is found in fruits, legumes, barley, and oats, and has been shown to lower blood glucose and cholesterol.[4] Foods containing viscous fiber are released more slowly into the bloodstream from the intestinal tract. Within the intestine, these fibers bind with cholesterol so that when fiber is excreted, cholesterol is also excreted, rather than being transported into the bloodstream.[5]

The second type of fiber is cellulose fiber, also called insoluble fiber. It is found in whole wheat, grains, cereals, and nuts. Unlike viscous fiber, cellulose fiber does not dissolve and is excreted completely, and allows bowel movements to pass easily and occur more regularly.[6]

Critical Thinking Question: What health benefits does fiber provide?

Current recommendations suggest that adult males under age 50 should consume about 38 grams of total dietary fiber per day, and adult women under age 50 should consume about 25 grams each day. Over the age of 50, men should consume about 30 grams per day and women about 21 grams per day.[7] Despite these recommendations, the typical American eats only about 15 grams of dietary fiber each day. The best sources of fiber are fruits and vegetables, nuts, legumes, and whole grains—and not only are these good sources of fiber, they also supply an abundance of vitamins, minerals, and phytonutrients. "Image of Health in Depth: Fiber and Health" describes ways that fiber has been shown to ward off certain diseases, and dispels myths about things fiber cannot do.

Image of Health in Depth

Fiber and Health

A high intake of fiber has been associated with a reduced risk of cardiovascular diseases.[8,9] Cardiovascular disease (CVD) is the leading killer of Americans, caused by the inability of cholesterol-blocked arteries to deliver enough oxygenated blood to the heart. In a Harvard study, a high intake of fiber was shown to reduce the risk of CVD by up to forty percent.[10] Low fiber intake has been linked with metabolic syndrome, a constellation of factors that increases the chances of developing heart disease and diabetes, including high blood pressure; high insulin levels; excess weight, especially around the abdomen; high levels of triglycerides; and low levels of high-density lipoprotein (HDL), the good cholesterol.[11]

Several studies suggest that a higher intake of fiber may help to reduce plaque buildup in coronary arteries.[12] Researchers have shown that replacing refined flours with whole grain flour reduces the risk of Type II diabetes in men.[13] Primarily caused by excess weight and low levels of physical activity, Type II diabetes has reached epidemic proportions in the United States, and major studies have shown that diets low in fiber and high in foods with a high glycemic index double the risk for Type II diabetes.[14] A high-fiber diet may reduce or eliminate diverticular disease, a painful colon disease affecting about one third of people over the age of 45. In a long-term study of male health professionals, those who ate a diet high in insoluble fiber were shown to reduce their risk of diverticulitis by about forty percent.[15] Fiber, particularly that found in whole grains, has also been shown to reduce constipation and make bowel movements easier to pass. Constipation is the most commonly reported gastrointestinal problem and could be alleviated by making small dietary changes.[16]

If you are considering adding more fiber to your diet, start slowly, as increased fiber may initially cause some gastrointestinal discomfort. Whole foods are the best source for fiber—using high fiber supplements increase fiber, they may not contain vitamins, minerals, and phytonutrients. There is also some evidence that fiber only works to reduce the risk of disease when it is part of a whole food.[17]

Table 7-5. Fiber in Common Foods

FOOD	GRAMS OF FIBER
1 cup of oatmeal, regular or quick	4
1 cup of raisin bran	8
½ cup peas	5
1 banana	3
1 slice whole wheat bread	2
1 cup kidney beans	8
1 medium-sized pear	4
1 cup broccoli	3

> **Key Term**
>
> **Fiber**: The non-digestible component of plant foods.

Proteins

Proteins are complex organic compounds that form the main structure of muscles, organs, and glands. Every living cell and all body fluids, except bile and urine, contain protein. The body is about 20 percent protein by weight. The cells of muscles, tendons, and ligaments are maintained with dietary protein and proteins are used to build and repair cell tissue and to provide some energy.

The Structure of Proteins

Proteins are made up of **amino acids**, and if they are not present in the right balance, the body's ability to use protein will be affected. If amino acids needed for protein synthesis are limited, body protein may be broken down to obtain them. Because protein deficiency affects all organs and is of particular concern during childhood, adequate intake of high-quality protein is essential for health.[18] Table 7-6 lists the common amino acids found in foods. Eight of the amino acids are considered essential for adults because they must be obtained from food, and arginine and histidine are also essential amino acids for children.[19] The other ten amino acids can be made by the body and are referred to as non-essential amino acids. Some lists of amino acids will include selenocysteine and pyrrolysine, which are unclassified amino acids.[20]

> **Key Term**
>
> **Amino acids**: The building blocks of protein.

Table 7-6. The Amino Acids

ESSENTIAL	NONESSENTIAL
Isoleucine	Alanine
Leucine	Asparagine
Lysine	Aspartate
Methionine	Cysteine
Phenylalanine	Glutamate
Threonine	Glutamine
Tryptophan	Glycine
Valine	Proline
Arginine*	Serine
Histidine*	Tyrosine

*Arginine and histidine are considered essential in children because the metabolic pathways that metabolize these proteins are not fully developed. (Source: Vaughn's summaries Amino Acids Summary Table 2003, 2004)

A single food that contains all eight essential amino acids, such as animal products and some soybeans, is considered a complete protein. Incomplete proteins, such as plant proteins, lack one or more of the essential amino acids, or are low in protein value. However, incomplete proteins can be combined to provide all the essential amino acids. For instance, rice is low in isoleucine and lysine, while beans provide those amino acids. Combining rice and beans, therefore, provides all the essential amino acids, as does combining any grain with nuts or beans. Eating a combination of these foods throughout the day will ensure an adequate supply of protein. Although combining plant foods provides all essential amino acids, only animal products contain heme iron, which is derived from hemoglobin and is found in red meats, fish, and poultry. The iron found in plant foods, such as lentils and beans, is called non-heme iron, and is added to iron-enriched and fortified foods. Heme iron is better absorbed than non-heme iron, but most of the iron in the human diet comes from non-heme iron.[21]

Recommended Intake of Protein

The Institute of Medicine recommends that adults get a minimum of 0.8 grams of protein per kilogram of body weight. For adults who weigh 160 pounds, this is about 58 grams of protein.

Average protein consumption in the American diet is adequate, and excess protein may actually be harmful, increasing the risk of dehydration, and liver and kidney damage. If protein is from an animal source, it also contains saturated fat and cholesterol. A diet high in saturated fat and cholesterol has been linked to coronary heart disease, stroke, hypertension, and cancers of the prostate, breast, and colon.[22] Excess protein cannot be stored, and offers no advantage to health or physical performance. Once the body has received sufficient protein, excess protein is either metabolized and excreted or converted into fat. During the metabolic process for protein, different chemicals are released, including **nitrosamines**, some that have been shown to be carcinogenic in laboratory animals. Research suggests that humans are susceptible to their carcinogenic properties.[23]

Key Term

Nitrosamines: Any of a class of organic compounds present in various foods and other products, and found to be carcinogenic in laboratory animals.

Challenge Question: What is the recommended daily requirement for protein for an adult?

Image of Health in Depth

Soy Protein—Facts and Myths

In October 1999, the Food and Drug Administration (FDA) approved a statement to be used on labels of soy-based foods to promote their heart-healthy benefits. The agency reviewed research from 27 studies showing soy protein's value in lowering levels of total cholesterol and low-density lipoprotein (LDL, or "bad" cholesterol). Soy is an excellent addition to a healthy diet, but is not necessarily a complete protein. Soybeans are dependent upon the conditions in which they are grown, and most are deficient in one or more essential amino acids, though some farmers now enrich the soil to prevent this. Soy grown in this manner is generally used for animal consumption to increase growth rate. Soy that is sold for human consumption may not have come from enriched soil, and may not be a complete protein.

Other claims about soy protein's ability to help with menopause or prostate cancer are not supported by scientific research. After peanuts, soybeans cause more allergic reactions than any other food.

High Protein Diets

In order to operate at peak performance, the human body needs an appropriate balance of carbohydrates, proteins, fats, vitamins, minerals, and water. Deviating from this balance for a short time probably will not cause any health problems, but long-term maintenance of a diet that restricts, eliminates, or even greatly increases one of the necessary nutrients can prove damaging. In some parts of the world, protein deficiency causes major health problems, whereas in America, too much protein is consumed, which can also increase health disease risks. High protein animal-based foods will increase the risk for coronary heart disease, as well as renal, bone, and liver abnormalities.[24] Diets high in protein may also cause **ketones** to be released into the bloodstream, which could lead to **ketoacidosis**, lowering appetite and energy and possibly causing nausea.[25] In severe cases, ketoacidosis can result in death. If protein replaces refined carbohydrates, it may facilitate weight loss. Emerging research shows that dietary protein may satisfy hunger longer than carbohydrates or fats.[26]

Challenge Question: Why do high protein diets result in quick weight loss?

> ### Key Terms
>
> **Ketones**: Substances made when the body breaks down fat for energy. Normally, the body receives energy from carbohydrates in the diet. However, if carbohydrates are inadequate, stored fat is broken down and ketones are released into the bloodstream. Ketones are also released when blood sugars remain high for extended periods of time.
>
> **Ketoacidosis**: Occurs when the body depends on fat for energy, and is unable to utilize the ketones being produced. Excess ketones in the blood spill over into the urine, pulling body fluid with them. Untreated, this condition can lead to coma and even death.

Fats

Fats, also called lipids, are necessary for healthy skin and hair, insulating body organs, maintaining body temperature, and for cellular metabolism. Fats are necessary to store and transport the fat-soluble vitamins A, D, E, and K, and improve the taste and texture of food. Fats contain 9 calories per gram, providing the largest amount of energy per gram of all the nutrients.

Moderate consumption of appropriate fat, between 20–30 percent total calories, is essential for health, though overconsumption can be harmful.[27] When too many fat calories are consumed, the excess is converted into **tryglycerides** in the liver, which make up about 95 percent of body fat. The remaining 5 percent is comprised of cholesterol. High tryglyceride and cholesterol levels lead to **atherosclerosis**, a narrowing of the arteries and other forms of heart disease.

All fats are made up of carbon and hydrogen atoms. Hydrogen causes the fat to become harder at room and body temperature, and the amount of hydrogen a fat cell carries determines the density of the fat. Fats are either saturated or unsaturated. **Saturated fats** are generally hard at room temperature and are considered the most harmful type of fat to consume. Unsaturated fats are either **monounsaturated** or **polyunsaturated**, depending on how many hydrogen atoms they contain, and are considered to be more beneficial to health.

Saturated Fats

Saturated fats contain all the hydrogen their chemical structure allows. With the exception of tropical oils such as palm and coconut oil, saturated fats are derived from animal sources—all meats and dairy products contain saturated fat and cholesterol. Less than 10 percent of total fat should come from saturated fats, with the remainder from poly- and monounsaturated fats.

Saturated fats have been shown to increase the risk of coronary diseases, cancers, diabetes, and obesity, and to contribute to high blood **cholesterol** levels.[28,29] Cholesterol is an essential fat produced by the liver and absorbed from the foods we eat. Some types of cholesterol can build up on arterial walls, narrowing the blood passageway and causing atherosclerosis.

Unsaturated Fats

Unsaturated fats come from plant-based sources, formed when there are one or more double bonds in the fatty acid chain. Hydrogen atoms are eliminated when double bonds form, making the fat more liquid. Unsaturated fats are either polyunsaturated or monounsaturated—polyunsaturated fats are fatty acids with more than one double bond. Corn, safflower, sesame, soybean, and sunflower oils are high in polyunsaturated fat, as are the oils from many nuts and seeds.

Monounsaturated fats contain only one double-bonded carbon atom in the chain, and are more liquid than the polyunsaturated fats. Canola, olive, avocado, and peanut oils are high in monounsaturated fat.

Key Terms

Triglycerides: The chemical form, and a harmful form, in which most fat exists in the body.

Atherosclerosis: A common form of arteriosclerosis, in which fatty substances form a deposit of plaque on the inner lining of arterial walls.

Saturated fat: A fat that contains all of the hydrogen atoms it can carry. Animal-based fats and tropical oils are saturated fats.

Monounsaturated fats: A fat that has only one double-bonded carbon atom. Some plant-based fats, including canola, olive, and peanut oils, are monounsaturated.

Polyunsaturated fats: A fat that has more than one double-bonded carbon atom. Most plant-based fats are polyunsaturated.

Cholesterol: A soft, waxy substance found among lipids (fats) in the bloodstream and in all body cells.

Table 7-7. Percentages of Saturated, Polyunsaturated and Monounsaturated Fats in Common Vegetable Oils

TYPE OF FAT	SATURATED FAT	POLYUNSATURATED FAT	MONOUNSATURATED FAT
Canola oil	7	31	62
Olive oil	14	8	77
Peanut oil	18	34	48
Avocado oil	10	14	71
Safflower oil	6	15	79
Soybean oil	15	60	25
Palm kernel oil	86	2	12
Coconut oil	92	2	6
Corn oil	13	61	25

Numbers do not add up to 100 since all fats contain other fatty substances in small quantities.[31]

Recommended Intake of Fat

Almost all medical authorities agree that less than 30 percent of total calories should come from fat, and the majority of fat calories should come from unsaturated fats. For someone on a 2,000 calorie a day diet, this would allow about 600 fat calories a day, or about 67 grams of fat.

Both polyunsaturated and monounsaturated fats may lower blood cholesterol level when used in place of saturated fats. Table 7-7 lists the percentages of saturated, polyunsaturated, and monounsaturated fat in common vegetable oils.

Trans Fatty Acids

Small quantities of trans fatty acids (TFA) are found in animal products such as beef, pork, and the butterfat in butter and milk, and are also formed when unsaturated oil is partially hydrogenated to make margarine, shortening, or cooking oil. Partially hydrogenated oils provide about three quarters of the TFAs in the U.S. diet. Trans fatty acids increase the risk of coronary artery diseases by raising total blood cholesterol and low-density lipoprotein levels in the blood.[30]

Critical Thinking Question: Why are saturated fats more harmful than unsaturated fats?

Microelements of Nutrition

Though necessary for life, some important components of nutrition do not supply calories. Vitamins, minerals, and phytonutrients, all of which can be found in foods, are these necessary microelements of nutrition.

Vitamins

Vitamins, organic compounds that are either water- or fat-soluble, are essential for normal health, growth, and the proper functioning of cells. The fat-soluble vitamins are A, D, E, and K, and can be stored in the body in fat cells. Vitamin C and the chain of B vitamins are water-soluble and cannot be stored in sufficient quantity, and must be consumed daily. A diet that includes plenty of vegetables, grains, and fruit, with smaller amounts of dairy and meat products, ensures sufficient dietary vitamins. With the exception of vitamin A, vitamin deficiency is not common in the U.S. Vitamin toxicity, the result of excessive consumption of a fat-soluble vitamin, is also rare. Table 7-8 lists some of the health benefits and sources for vitamins.

Recommended Intake of Vitamins

Although all vitamins can effectively be consumed in food, more than half the population also takes one or more vitamin supplements. Most of these supplements are unneeded and do not offer any disease-reducing benefits.[30] Many medical authorities suggest that vitamin supplementation is necessary only during pregnancy, for those on severely restricted diets, those who lack sufficient sunlight exposure, or those who do not tolerate milk and dairy products. Table 7-9 lists recommended intakes for vitamins.

Critical Thinking Question: Why do water-soluble vitamins need to be consumed daily?

Minerals

Minerals are inorganic elements essential for normal body function and cell metabolism. Less than 100 mg/day are required for trace minerals, while major minerals are needed at greater than 100 mg/day. Table 7-10 lists the major minerals, sources, and dietary functions.

Trace minerals include iron, iodine, cobalt, chromium, copper, fluorine, manganese, molybdenum, selenium, and zinc. All trace minerals are toxic at high levels, and some—arsenic, nickel, and chromium—have been linked in carcinogenesis. With the exception of iron, zinc, and iodine, mineral deficiencies are rare. Infants have a higher deficiency risk because of their rapid growth and potentially poor dietary habits. Toxicity in adults usually occurs as a result of excess intake in products that are touted as protecting against chronic diseases.

Recommended Intake of Minerals

Table 7-12 shows the recommended daily intake of minerals, along with the levels at which toxicity may begin.

Antioxidants and Phytonutrients

Antioxidants are a classification of several organic substances, including vitamins C, E, and A, the mineral selenium, and a group known as carotenoids. Carotenoids are pigments that give fruits and vegetables their color, and are thought to help prevent or postpone heart disease, stroke, and cancer, although research has failed to prove this when antioxidants are taken as supplements.[31]

At the molecular and cellular levels, antioxidants serve to deactivate certain particles called free radicals. In humans, free radicals usually come in the form of the oxygen molecule, and the oxidation process for the oxygen molecule can sometimes be carcinogenic. Free radicals are the natural by-products of many processes within and among cells, and are also created by exposure to various environmental sources, such as tobacco smoke and radiation.

Free radicals may cause damage to cellular walls, certain cellular structures, and genetic material within cells. Over a long period, such damage may become irreversible and may lead to diseases such as cancer.[32] Antioxidants eliminate free radicals at the cellular level within the body, before they cause harm.[33] Sources for antioxidants include sweet potatoes, carrots, spinach, cantaloupe, and mangoes. The effect of antioxidants is seen in populations where whole foods containing them are eaten. The benefits are not seen in people who consume antioxidatnt supplements.

Table 7-8. Health Benefits and Sources for Vitamins

VITAMIN	SOME KNOWN HEALTH BENEFITS	SOURCES
Vitamin A	Maintains normal vision, essential for immune system, necessary for growth.	Liver, chicken, milk, yogurt, cheese, eggs, and carrots.
Vitamin D	Helps to maintain constant levels of calcium in blood. Important in insulin and prolactin secretion, muscle function. Vital for kidney and parathyroid gland function, and necessary for healthy bones.	Milk, fortified cereals, and other grain products.
Vitamin E	Protects vitamin A from oxidation during digestion. Enhances immune system and inhibits carcinogens from reaching target site.	Almonds, wheat germ, peanuts, and peanut butter.
Vitamin K	Helps coagulate blood; helps build bones.	Swiss chard, kale, parsley, brussel sprouts, and other greens.
Vitamin B-1	Vital for healthy nervous system and nerve transmission. Essential in converting glucose to energy.	Wheat germ, pork, whole grains, dried beans, seeds, and nuts.
Vitamin B-2 (Riboflavin)	Essential for metabolizing carbohydrates and fats. Involved in the formation of red blood cells.	Dairy products, meat, poultry, whole grains, and some greens.
Vitamin B-6 (Pyridoxine)	Necessary for immune system function, essential in making certain amino acids.	Fish, poultry, pork, eggs, and whole grains.
Vitamin B-12 (Cobalamin)	Works with folic acid to produce red blood cells.	Dairy products, meat, poultry, whole grains, and some greens.
Vitamin C (Ascorbic acid)	Activates liver-detoxifying system, inhibits formation of carcinogenic compounds, enhances function of key white blood cells, vital to bones, healing of wounds, and iron absorption.	Guavas, red and green peppers, citrus fruits, cantaloupe, kiwis, broccoli, and other foods.
Biotin	Key role in metabolizing fats, carbohydrates, and proteins.	Liver, cauliflower, eggs, cheese, salmon, and spinach.
Choline	Helps maintain central nervous system.	Synthesized by the body.
Folic acid (Folate, B vitamin)	Used by body to break down and synthesize amino acids. Recommended for women of childbearing age; helps prevent neural tube birth defects.	Lentils, cooked collard greens, papaya, chick peas, strawberries, oranges, and other foods.
Niacin (B-3)	Enhances body to use carbohydrates, fats, and proteins. Aids nervous system and digestive tract, promotes healthy skin.	Beef, liver, peanuts, chicken, tuna, corn grits, salmon, and peanut butter.
Pantothenic acid	Necessary for adrenal cortex function.	Organ meats, lobster, poultry, lentils, split peas, and other foods.

(Source: Food and Nutrition Board, National Academy's Institute of Medicine.)

Table 7-9. Dietary Reference Intakes (DRIs): Recommended Intakes for Vitamins

VITAMIN	RECOMMENDED DIETARY ALLOWANCES (RDA) OR DIETARY REFERENCE INTAKES (DRIS)
Vitamin A	RDA: Men 900 mcg; Women 700 mcg
Vitamin D	AI: 5–10 mcg*
Vitamin E	RDA: 15 mg
Vitamin K	AI: Men 120 mcg; Women 90 mcg*
Vitamin C	RDA: Men 90 mg; Women 75 mg; Smokers 125–110 mg
Choline	DRI: Men 550 mg; Women 425 mg
Thiamin (B1)	RDA: Men 1.2 mg; Women 1.1 mg
Riboflavin (B2)	RDA: Men 1.3 mg; Women 1.1 mg
Niacin (B3)	RDA: Men 16 mg; Women 14 mg
Pantothenic acid	AI: 5 mg*
Vitamin B6	RDA Men 1.3–1.7 mcg; Women 1.3–1.5 mcg
Folic acid/Folate	RDA: 40 mcg
Vitamin B12	RDA: 2.4 mcg

* Adequate intakes are shown when there is insufficient science to establish an RDA.
(Source: Food and Nutrition Board, National Academy's Institute of Medicine.)

Table 7-10. Functions and sources of Major Minerals

MAJOR MINERAL	FUNCTION	SOURCE
Calcium	Necessary for teeth, bones, blood plasma, and other body fluids, where it influences nerve transmission, clotting, and muscle contraction.	Dairy products and green leafy vegetables; vitamin D is required for calcium absorption.
Phosphorus	Bone and tooth formation; phosphorus is found in every human cell.	Dairy products.
Magnesium	Necessary for carbohydrate and protein metabolism; cell reproduction and smooth muscle action.	Nuts, soybeans, and cocoa.
Sodium	Necessary for fluid balance, cell permeability, and muscle function.	Table salt, milk, and spinach.
Potassium	Necessary for fluid and electrolyte balance and heart muscle activity; also required for carbohydrate metabolism and protein synthesis.	Grains and bananas.
Chlorine	Aids in digestion.	Table salt.
Sulfur	Necessary for energy metabolism, enzyme function, and detoxification.	Meat, eggs, and legumes.

(Source: Food and Nutrition Board, National Academy's Institute of Medicine.)

Table 7-11. Functions and Sources of Minor Minerals

MINOR MINERAL	FUNCTION	SOURCE
Iron	Needed for the formation of hemoglobin, the oxygen-carrying compound in red blood cells.	Meats, eggs, dark, green leafy vegetables, legumes, and whole grains. Some refined grains are enriched with iron.
Iodine	Necessary for cellular metabolism, normal thyroid function, and the production of thyroid hormones.	Sea fish and sea salt, cod liver oil. Small amounts occur in milk, meat, vegetables, and cereals.
Cobalt	Helps prevent anemia.	Green leafy vegetables, meat, liver, milk, oysters and clams.
Manganese	Helps convert protein and fat to energy, promotes normal bone growth, and maintains healthy reproductive, nervous, and immune systems.	Avocados, nuts, seeds, tea, raisins, pineapple, spinach oranges, leafy vegetables.
Molybdenum	An essential minor mineral whose precise function is not clearly understood. It may be used to treat rare, inherited disorders such as Wilson's disease.	Beans, dark green leafy vegetables, eggs, grains, legumes, whole grains.
Selenium	The antioxidant properties of selenium help prevent cellular damage from free radicals.	Content in foods depends on where goods were grown. In the U.S. meats and bread are common sources along with unblanched brazil nuts.
Zinc	Necessary for cell reproduction, and tissue growth and repair.	Meat, seafood, liver, eggs, milk and whole grain products.

(Source: Food and Nutrition Board, National Academy's Institute of Medicine.)

Table 7-12. Recommended Intake of Minerals

MINERAL[1]	WOMEN		MEN	
	MINIMUM	MAXIMUM	MINIMUM	MAXIMUM
Boron	NK*	20 mg	NK	20 mg
Calcium	1,000 mg	2,500 mg	1,000 mg	2,500 mg
Chromium	25 mcg	NK	35 mcg	NK
Copper	900 mcg	10,000 mcg	900 mcg	10,000 mcg
Fluoride	3 mg	10 mg	4 mg	10 mg
Iodine	150 mcg	1,000 mcg	150 mcg	1,000 mcg
Iron	18 mg	45 mg	8 mg	45 mg
Magnesium	310 mg	350 mg	400 mg	350 mg
Manganese	1.8 mg	11 mg	2.3 mg	11 mg
Molybdenum	45 mcg	2,000 mcg	45 mcg	2,000 mcg
Nickel	NK	1.0 mg	NK	1.0 mg
Phosphorus	700 mg	4,000 mg	700 mg	4,000 mg
Selenium	55 mcg	400 mcg	55 mcg	400 mcg
Vanadium	NK	1.8 mg	NK	1.8 mg
Zinc	8 mg	40 mg	11 mg	40 mg

*NK: Not known; [1] Daily intakes are only shown for persons aged 18–50. If your age is outside this parameter, your dose may be different.
(Source: Food and Nutrition Board, National Academy's Institute of Medicine.)

Phytonutrients, a group of non-nutritive plant chemicals, protect and prevent diseases within plants. There are more than a thousand known phytonutrients, and research has indicated that they can protect humans against diseases. Some known phytonutrients include lycopene, found in tomatoes; flavanoids, found in fruits; and isoflavones, found in soy. Though they are not necessary to sustain life, health and even longevity may be improved by eating foods containing phytonutrients.[36]

Eating more fruits and vegetables is the best way to obtain both antioxidants and phytonutrients.

Water

All cells and organs need water to function. The body can maintain for weeks without food, but cannot survive without water for more than a few days. Water makes up between 50–60 percent of body weight, is the basis of saliva, serves as a lubricant for fluids surrounding the joints, regulates body temperature through perspiration, and helps prevent and alleviate constipation by moving food through the intestinal tract.

The larger and more active a person is, the more water they require. The standard daily recommended water intake is between 48 and 64 ounces. Although this is usually prescribed as "glasses of water," much of the water needed can be found in fruits, vegetables, and water-based drinks.

Motivation Maximizer

Jon is overwhelmed. He was overwhelmed after reading the nutrition chapter, and now after the lecture, he thinks there is nothing he can eat that will not cause him some issue or harm. He also comments to friends that trying to eat the way he should would cost a fortune.

Sound familiar? Most people feel this way when faced with a large amount of information. What can you do to change your eating habits that will be cost effective and nutritionally sound, but not cause you to be in the kitchen or the grocery store for half of your day?

Start with a plan. How much money do you spend on food? Consider all the food you buy, from coffees and candies to popcorn at the cinema. You will probably find that between eating out, snacking, and eating at home, you are spending far more than you realize. With your dollars in mind, think about your favorite foods and how you can make them healthier. If pizza is on this list, try ordering it with twice as much tomato sauce, more vegetables, and half as much cheese. Order hamburgers with ketchup and mustard but without any special sauces, and ask for extra tomatoes, lettuce, and onions. There is no way to make French fries a healthy food choice, so eat them only very occasionally. Start each day with a whole grain cereal, low-fat milk, and some fruit. Non-branded cereals, sold in bags rather than boxes, are usually much cheaper. When you go food shopping, have a menu plan so you can purchase appropriate foods. If you cook dinner, make enough for leftovers for the following night. Examine the deli section in your grocery store, and consider learning how to make salads that you could package for lunch. Seasonal fruits and vegetables are usually cheaper, and often on sale. If you dislike preparing food, buy convenience vegetables that are already chopped, or frozen vegetables that you can microwave. Combine this with a zip top can of tuna or chicken, and you have a healthy, inexpensive lunch. Remember that fueling your body with the right foods has many benefits, including more energy and more brainpower.

Guidelines for Health Eating

There are many tools available to make choosing healthy foods easier. The Dietary Guidelines are designed to promote health and reduce the risk for disease, and the Daily Reference Intakes are standards to help prevent nutritional deficiencies.

2010 Dietary Guidelines for Americans

Every five years, the Department of Health and Human Services (HHS) and the United States Department of Agriculture (USDA) publish a document promoting improved dietary habits to reduce the risk for major chys. The guidelines contain the following key points:

- Consume a variety of nutrient-dense foods and beverages within and among the basic food groups, and choose foods that limit saturated and trans fats, cholesterol, added sugars, salt, and alcohol.

- Maintain body weight; balance calorie intake with calorie expenditure.

- Engage in regular physical activity.

- Eat at least two cups of fruit and 2.5 cups of vegetables each day. Eat at least three or more ounces of whole grain products daily, and consume about three cups of fat-free or low-fat milk or equivalent milk products.

- Consume less than 10 percent of your calories from saturated fats, and keep cholesterol at less than 300 mg per day. Avoid trans fats as much as possible.

- Choose fiber-rich fruits, vegetables, and whole grains.

- Consume less than one teaspoon of salt each day, and choose to eat potassium-rich foods such as fruits and vegetables.

- If you drink alcohol, do so in moderation and with safety in mind.

- To avoid microbial food illnesses, keep foods at the correct temperature and all food surfaces clean.

Because of the high rate of chronic disease in America today, the dietary guidelines Web site includes plans for health concerns in specific populations.

The Dietary Guidelines for Americans
http://www.health.gov/dietaryguidelines/

Along with published information, other dietary tools are available. Most packaged food must comply with a food labeling code mandating that ingredients be listed on the product.

Daily Reference Intakes

From 1941 until 1989, Americans used the **recommended dietary allowances** (RDAs) to determine certain nutrient requirements. RDAs were retired in 1989, and the Food and Nutrition Board of the National Academy of Sciences introduced the **daily reference intakes** (DRIs).

There are four types of DRI reference values, including **estimated average requirement** (EAR), **recommended dietary allowance** (RDA), **adequate intake** (AI), and the **tolerable upper limit intake** (UL). These values are used when determining safe and appropriate amounts of vitamins and minerals.

Key Terms

Estimated average requirement (EAR): A daily nutrient intake value estimated to meet the requirement of half of the healthy individuals in a life stage and gender group; used to assess dietary adequacy and as the basis for the RDA.

Recommended dietary allowance (RDA): The average daily dietary intake level that is sufficient to meet the nutrient requirements of nearly all (97 to 98 percent) healthy individuals in a particular life stage and gender group.

Adequate intake (AI): A recommended intake value based on estimates of nutrient intake by a group (or groups) of healthy people that are assumed to be adequate; used when an RDA cannot be determined.

Tolerable upper intake level (UL): The highest level of daily nutrient intake that is likely to pose no risk of adverse health effects for almost all individuals in the general population.

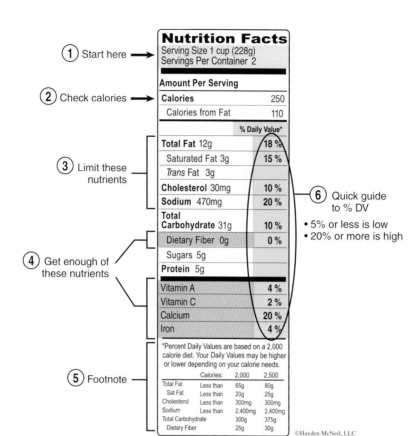

1. Pay attention to the serving size, and consider how many servings you will eat. Consuming more or less will increase or decrease all the nutritional values and calories.

2. A serving has 250 total calories, 110 calories or almost half of which come from fat. For total calories, 40 are considered low, 100 are considered moderate, and more than 400 per serving is high.

3. The first nutrients listed are in yellow to indicate "Limit These Nutrients." The nutrients identified in blue represent nutrients that often deficient, such as fiber, vitamin A, vitamin C, calcium, and iron.

4. The Percent Daily Value (% DV) provides recommendations for key nutrients based on a 2,000-calorie diet. It helps you determine whether the food is high or low in this nutrient.

5. The footnote refers to the daily values (DVs) for a 2,000- or 2,500-calories-per-day diet. The % DV reflects the percentage of this ingredient compared to the recommended percentage.

Daily Recommended Values

The Food and Drug Administration uses daily recommended values (DRV) on food labels, rather than daily recommended intake (DRI). The DRV is not a recommended intake of a nutrient, but is intended as a reference point to help consumers determine their overall daily dietary intake based on a calorie-specific diet. The DRV for energy-producing nutrients (fat, carbohydrate, and protein) is based on the number of calories consumed per day. For labeling purposes, 2,000 calories has been established as the reference for calculating percent daily values. For example, the DRV for fat, based on a 2,000-calorie diet, is 65 grams. A food that has 13 grams of fat would show a DRV of 20 percent.

Daily recommended values are also used to regulate food claims. A food label claiming high fiber would need to contain 20 percent or more of the DRV for fiber, or 5 grams or more. Daily recommended values for energy-producing nutrients are always calculated as follows:

- 20–30 percent of calories from total fat.

- 10 percent of calories from saturated fat.

- 50–60 percent of calories from carbohydrates.

- 10 percent of calories from protein (the DRV for protein applies only to adults and children over 4).

- 11.5 grams of fiber per 1,000 calories.

Healthy Dietary Plans

Although there are many food plans available, not all of them support the optimal health you may want to achieve. Some offer fast weight loss, but if maintained, may compromise health. Others lack specific necessary food groups, or are not based on substantiated scientific research. When choosing a plan, ensure that it includes all the major food groups, and that it does not promise "quick fixes" or "fast weight loss." Choose reliable dietary plans supported by reputable authorities and based on scientific research that has been published in known medical journals.

The USDA MyPyramid

MyPyramid food guidance system is an interactive Web site where users provide age and gender information, and receive specific dietary guidelines in pyramid format. For children, the site contains games to help promote healthful eating and exercise. Within the pyramid, food is broken down into five groups, and dietary recommendations are based on calorie intake and exercise.

**MyPyramid Food Guidance System
http://www.mypyramid.gov**

Physical activity is promoted and guidelines are provided for achieving diet and exercise goals.

FIGURE 7-4. Key consumer messages include:

- Grains: Make half of your grains whole grains

- Vegetables: Eat a variety of vegetables

- Fruits: Focus on fruits

- Milk: Get your calcium-rich foods

- Meat and beans: Go lean with protein

Within MyPyramid, food groups are broken down as follows.

Grains

The pyramid differentiates between whole grains and other grains. Grains are emphasized as the food group low in fat and rich in complex carbohydrates and dietary fiber. Based on an average number of calories consumed by adults in the U.S. (2,000 calories), MyPyramid suggests six servings from the grains group. The following foods would be a single serving from this group:

- one slice of bread (whole grain is a better choice than refined breads)

- one cup of dry cereal

- One half cup of cooked cereal, rice, pasta, or other grain product

- one six-inch tortilla

- one small muffin or half of a small bagel

Aside from providing complex carbohydrates and fiber, the grains group supplies vitamins and minerals.

High-fat and high-sugar foods, such as doughnuts and pastries that contain grains, are not good choices for this group.

Vegetables

On a 2,000-calorie diet, individuals are advised to eat five half-cup servings of vegetables each day. Vegetables provide vitamins, minerals, phytonutrients, some carbohydrates, and fiber. Choose a variety of colors in order to achieve the various benefits each vegetable provides. Examples include:

- one half cup of cooked or raw vegetables

- one cup of raw salad greens or cooked leafy greens, such as cabbage, kale, or collard greens

- one cup of vegetable juice (generally, juices do not contain fiber)

Fruits

Like vegetables, fruits are rich in vitamins, some minerals, phytonutrients, fiber, and carbohydrates. On a 2,000-calorie diet, four one half-cup servings of a variety of fruits are recommended. Generally, one small piece of fruit, about the size of a baseball, is considered a half-cup serving. Examples include:

- one half cup of fresh grapes

- one half cup of canned or frozen fruit (choose naturally sweetened as opposed to those packed in syrup)

- one small apple, orange, or banana

- one quarter cup of dried fruit, such as raisins or cranberries

- one half cup of 100 percent fruit juice

Milk

The milk group includes milk, yogurt, cheeses (except cream cheese), and lactose-free or lactose-reduced dairy products. Emphasis is placed on reduced-fat or non-fat over full-fat varieties. Skimmed (non-fat) and reduced-fat milk contains the same ingredients as whole milk, except the fat has been removed or reduced. Milk products provide calcium, protein, and carbohydrates, and fortified products also supply vitamin D. On a 2,000-calorie diet, the recommendation is three servings from this group. The following are examples of a serving:

- one cup of milk

- one individual, standard container of yogurt

- one and one-half ounces of natural cheese, or about one and one-half slices of processed cheese

- one half cup of ricotta cheese

Although ice cream would fit in this group, it can be high in fat and sugar and contains less calcium than milk. One single scoop of ice cream equals about one third cup of milk, so it is not a good choice.

Meat, Poultry, Eggs, Beans, and Nuts

This group supplies protein, certain B vitamins, iron, and zinc. It is the one area of the diet that most Americans consume in excess. For someone consuming about 2,000 calories a day, the recommendation is five and one half ounces of protein-rich (or its equivalent) foods. Examples of an equivalent single serving include:

- one egg

- one tablespoon peanut butter

- one ounce of cooked meat, poultry, or fish (select lean cuts—an average-sized boneless chicken breast weighs about three and one-half ounces)

- one-half ounce of nuts or seeds

- one quarter cup of cooked legumes or tofu

Fats and Oils

The final group on MyPyramid is fat and oil, either added to foods or used for cooking. For a 2,000-calorie diet, the recommendation is six teaspoons of added fat per day. One tablespoon of salad dressing or mayonnaise is the equivalent of one teaspoon of oil or soft margarine. When selecting from this group, choose cooking oils that are unsaturated, such as canola, olive, corn, and safflower oils. Choose margarines that contain mostly unsaturated fats and do not contain any trans fats.

The Harvard Healthy Eating Pyramid

Researchers at the Harvard School of Public Health found fault with the USDA MyPyramid, claiming it was based on unsound science that failed to reflect the wealth of current available health and diet information. Although Harvard supports the new MyPyramid in some respects, some researchers still believe it does not contain enough information to help make informed choices about diet and long-term health. One of the Harvard concerns with the USDA MyPyramid recommendations is that half of the grains eaten can come from refined starch. Another is that meat is grouped with poultry, fish, and beans, even though numerous studies show that replacing red meat with poultry, fish, beans, and nuts provides a number of health benefits.[37,38] Harvard researchers also state that the recommended milk servings on MyPyramid have not been shown to be beneficial in preventing osteoporosis, and may even increase ovarian and prostate cancers.[39,40,41]

Faculty members at Harvard developed the Healthy Eating Pyramid, which resembles the USDA MyPyramid, but reflects current research that has reshaped the definition of healthy eating. The base of the Healthy Eating Pyramid is exercise and weight control. Whole grain foods should be eaten at every meal, and plant and vegetable oils are promoted. The Healthy Eating Pyramid suggests that vegetables be eaten in abundance, and fruit eaten each day. Nuts and beans are promoted before other protein sources, such as fish, poultry, and eggs, which are recommended for consumption a maximum of twice each week, if at all. The Harvard Healthy Eating pyramid suggests just 1–2 servings of dairy or a calcium supplement, and recommends that everyone take a multivitamin pill each day. According to this pyramid, refined grains, red meat, butter, sweets, and even potatoes should be used sparingly.

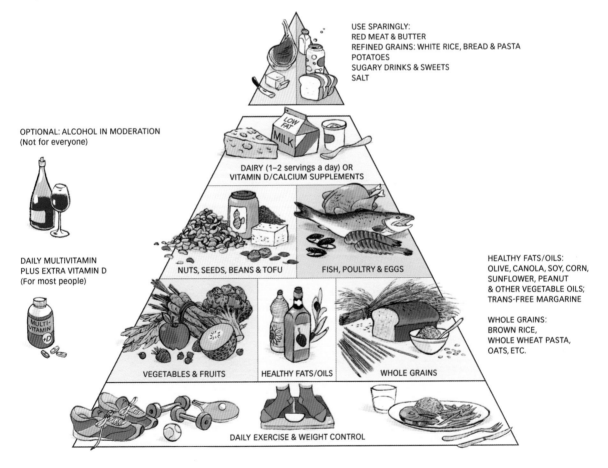

FIGURE 7-5. Harvard Healthy Eating Pyramid.

The Mediterranean Pyramid

Although medical services were limited in the early 1960s, chronic disease rates in Crete and much of the rest of Greece and southern Italy were among the lowest in the world, while life expectancy was among the highest. Dietary behaviors were examined, and as a result, the Mediterranean Pyramid emerged. Although this pyramid suggests food types, quantity of calories is not suggested, as this is dependent on calorie expenditure. The population was more active in the 1960s, and this may have been a contributing factor to lower disease rates and longevity.

The Mediterranean Pyramid places exercise at its base, then promotes whole grains, fruits, vegetables, and nuts. Dairy, meats, and fish are limited.

Mediterranean Diet Pyramid
A contemporary approach to delicious, healthy eating

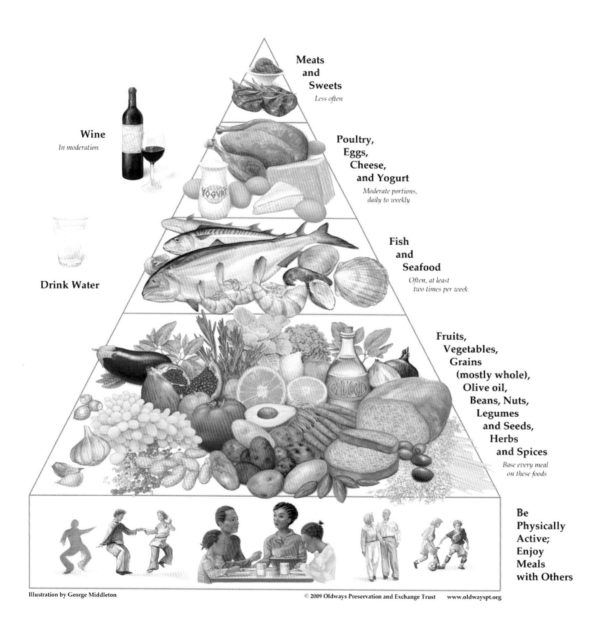

Illustration by George Middleton   © 2009 Oldways Preservation and Exchange Trust   www.oldwayspt.org

FIGURE 7-6. Mediterranean Diet Pyramid.

Copyright © 2009 Oldways Preservation & Exchange Trust, www.oldwayspt.org. Used with permission.

The Vegetarian Pyramid

The Vegetarian Pyramid replaces foods in the protein group with meat alternatives, such as legumes, nuts, soy, and seeds. As part of a healthy diet that includes whole grains, these foods contribute the necessary amino acids to provide complete proteins. The main advantage is that they do not provide the cholesterol and saturated fat found in the animal-based protein group.

The Traditional Healthy Vegetarian Diet Pyramid

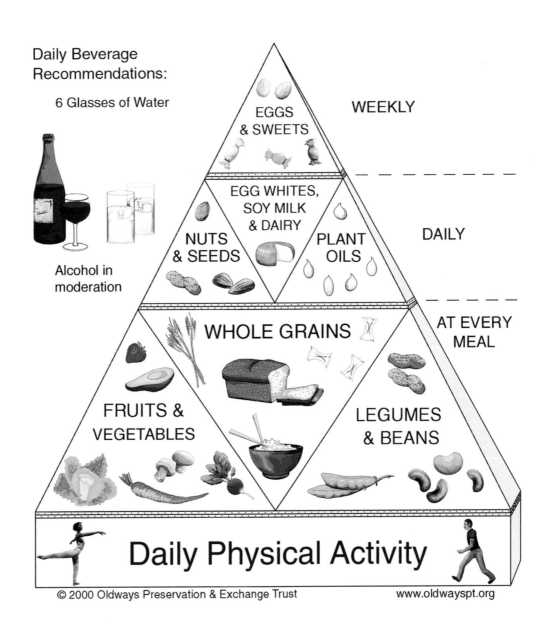

FIGURE 7-7. Vegetarian pyramid.

Image of Health in Depth

Dietary Types

Omnivores: Omnivores generally eat animal-based foods and vegetation.

Vegetarians: Vegetarians generally eat dairy and eggs (lacto-ova vegetarians), and may eat fish. They do not eat other animal products.

Vegans: Vegans do not eat or use anything that comes from an animal. This diet can be difficult to follow, since it involves reading all food labels to ensure no animal products are included. The vegan diet requires careful planning to ensure that all nutrients are consumed.

One other dietary plan, the Dash Eating Plan, is for those with high blood pressure. Table 7-13 shows food groups and serving sizes for this plan.

Table 7-13. The Dash Eating Plan

TYPE OF FOOD	NUMBER OF SERVINGS FOR 1,600–3,100 CALORIE DIETS	SERVINGS ON A 2,000 CALORIE DIET
Grains and grain products (include at least three whole grain foods each day)	6–12	7–8
Fruits	4–6	4–5
Vegetables	4–6	4–5
Low-fat or non-fat dairy foods	2–4	2–3
Lean meats, fish, poultry	1.5–2.5	2 or less
Nuts, seeds, and legumes	3–6 per week	4–5 per week
Fats and sweets	2–4	Limited

The Dash Eating Plan is recommended by the National Heart, Lung and Blood Institute, The American Heart Association, the 2005 Dietary Guidelines for Americans, and the U.S. guidelines for treatment of high blood pressure.

Image of Health in Depth

Eating for Diabetes

About 8.3 percent of the population, or 25.8 million people, have diabetes. The American Diabetes Association does not endorse one specific diet plan for those at risk for developing diabetes, or for those living with the disease. Rather, emphasis is placed on specific food choices. For those at risk for or who have Type II diabetes, the guidelines call for 14 grams of fiber per 1,000 calories, with whole grains making up half of the grain intake. Emphasis is placed on nutrient rich foods, weight loss, and exercise.

For people with Type I diabetes, the guidelines are more specific, recommending carbohydrates from fruits, vegetables, whole grains, legumes, and low-fat milk. Emphasis is placed on eating fiber-rich foods and keeping saturated fats to less than 7 percent of total calories. The guidelines also call for eating at least two servings of non-fried fish each week, and reducing cholesterol intake to 200 milligrams per day.

American Diabetes Association
More information, with recipes, can be found at **http://www.ada.org.**

Critical Thinking Question: What steps can you take to improve your nutritional habits?

Challenges to Healthy Eating

With our fast-paced lives and the wealth of nutrition information available, it can be difficult to focus on and maintain a healthy nutritional plan. The key to success is to try to plan ahead. Food prepared at home, with less added fat, oil, salt, and sugar, is usually better than pre-packaged or restaurant food. However, more appropriate choices can also be made outside of the home.

Restaurant Choices

At one time, eating in restaurants was a luxury for special occasions. Today, many Americans may eat in restaurants more than once a week, with choices such as all-you-can-eat buffet diners, and family-style and upper-scale restaurants. Buffet diners usually offer lower quality foods in greater quantities at a reduced cost. Though this may seem financially appealing, it is a poor choice because for many people, an all-you-can-eat buffet encourages overeating.[42] Family restaurant menus tend emphasize fried foods, which can be produced quickly and kept warm for long periods. Additionally, desserts at family restaurants focus on ice cream and pies made with large amounts of fat and sugar. Upper-scale restaurants may not improve dietary choices much, although foods at these restaurants are generally served in more reasonable quantities, and fresh vegetables may be available and cooked appropriately.

When choosing to eat in a restaurant, select a restaurant that offers soups and salads, and ask for vegetables with your meal. When possible, ask for butter to be replaced with olive oil. If servings are large, ask for a box so you can immediately pack half of the serving to take home. If fresh fruit is not available, try splitting one small dessert.

Fast Food Choices

Healthy food choices at fast food restaurants are limited, but some general rules can help you make better choices.

1. Choose broiled chicken over hamburger.

2. Avoid cheese and special sauces.

3. Ask for extra tomatoes, lettuce, and onions.

4. Choose a smaller size and avoid the "supersizing" temptation.

5. If possible, choose fruit slices or a salad over French fries.

6. In sandwich shops, ask for extra vegetables and have the sandwich served on whole grain bread, if available.

Pizza restaurants may offer the choice of reducing the cheese while increasing the tomato-based sauce, making a healthier option for pizza. Limit pepperoni and sausage, as both are preserved meats high in saturated fat and **carcinogens**. Research has shown that preserved meats are more heart-dangerous than red meats.[43] Vegetarian pizzas are more commonly available, and may be something you will enjoy.

Key Term

Carcinogen: An agent known to cause cancer.

Choosing Beverages

The primary function of beverages is to provide a water-based product. If that water comes packed in sugar and/or fat, the benefit is minimal. Soda is a calorie-dense way to take in fluids. Diet sodas may be marginally better, but water is still the optimal choice. Some beverages sold in specialty coffee shops contain as much fat and as many calories as those found in a full meal. Fruit juices are high in calories, and are not filling. If weight gain is an objective, pure fruit juice can help, but if calorie control is important, fruit juices are not a good choice. When choosing milk, select the lowest fat content available and avoid calorie-dense, flavored milk beverages.

Packing It to Go

In order to avoid the temptation of cheap, easy-to-access fast food, consider packing food for work and school. Choose foods that do not require refrigeration, or pack them with an ice pack. You can also choose to freeze fresh fruit or vegetable juice and use this as the cooling agent in your lunch bag. Foods that require refrigeration must be maintained at less than 40°F, and heated foods at 140° or higher. Soft foods are easily damaged, so select apples over bananas, and pack sandwiches in plastic containers to protect them. As you plan your meal, remember to include at least one fruit and two vegetable servings.

Consumer Issues in Nutrition

Along with an abundance of nutrition science, there are also new developments in agricultural methods. Some of these methods increase crop productivity and some increase shelf life, and both may reduce the end cost of the product.

Organic Foods

The National Organic Program of the USDA has established standards and guidelines for organic food. No claims are made to suggest that organic foods may be better for human nutrition, or that non-organic foods are harmful. Farmers who emphasize the use of renewable resources and the conservation of soil and water to enhance environmental quality for future generations produce organic food. Organic meat, poultry, eggs, and dairy products come from animals that are given no antibiotics or growth hormones. Organic food is produced without the use of most conventional pesticides, fertilizers made with synthetic ingredients or sewage sludge, bioengineering, or ionizing radiation. Before a product can be labeled organic, a government-approved inspector must certify the farm that produces the food to ensure the farm meets USDA organic standards. Due to the limited supply of organic foods, they tend to be more costly and more difficult to find.

Genetically Modified Foods

Genetic modification (GM) is a technology that alters the genetic makeup of animals, plants, or bacteria with the intent to improve the end product. Combining genes from different organisms is known as recombinant **deoxyribonucleic acid** (DNA) technology, and the resulting organism is said to be either genetically modified, genetically engineered, or transgenic. Genetically modified products include medicines and vaccines, foods and food ingredients, feeds, and fibers. In 2003, about 167 million acres grown by 7 million farmers in 18 countries were planted with transgenic crops, primarily herbicide- and insecticide-resistant soybeans, corn, cotton, and canola.

Plans for future genetic modifications include bananas that produce human vaccines against infectious diseases such as hepatitis B, fish that mature more quickly, fruit and nut trees that yield years earlier, and plants that produce new plastics with unique properties.

Foods that have been genetically modified are controversial, but have not resulted in any known negative effects. Genetic modification technology may result in higher crop yields and lower cost, making foods more available to everyone.

> **Key Term**
>
> **Deoxyribonucleic acid (DNA)**: A material present in nearly all living organisms that carries all genetic information.

Irradiated Foods

Irradiating foods can eliminate disease microorganisms, in much the same way pasteurization can kill bacteria and other parasites that would cause foodborne diseases. Irradiation is done in one of three ways:

1. Gamma rays (in use for 30 years to sterilize medical equipment).

2. Electron beam (E-beam food sterilizers have been in use for 15 years).

3. X-ray (the most recent technology for food irradiation).

Irradiated foods do not change in nutritional value, nor do they become dangerous as a result of the process. Ray energy is absorbed as it passes through the food, then loses energy. Treated food is warmed slightly, and some treated foods may taste marginally different. Irradiation kills living cells in food, which can be beneficial in that it prolongs shelf life. The safety of irradiated foods has been endorsed by the World Health Organization, Centers for Disease Control and Prevention, the USDA, and the FDA.

Food Allergies

A food allergy is an immune response to a food that the body mistakenly believes is harmful. Although a person could be allergic to any food, eight foods constitute 90 percent of all food-allergic reactions: These foods are peanuts, soy, milk, eggs, tree nuts, fish, shellfish, and wheat. There are many possible allergic reactions to these foods, from mild stomach irritation to life-threatening consequences.

Image of Health in Depth

Food Additives

Food additives are vital to our food supply. They may prevent food from spoiling, improve the nutritional value of foods, add a pleasing color and taste, and allow many foods to be available year round in great quantity.

Although most people think of food additives as chemical compounds, something as simple as baking soda or vanilla is also a food additive.

The five main reasons for additives are:

1. To maintain product consistency. Anti-caking agents, stabilizers, and emulsifiers provide food with either free-flowing capability, or a uniform texture, to prevent separation.

2. To maintain or improve nutritional value. Vitamins and minerals are added to many common foods to improve their nutritional value.

3. To prevent bacterial contamination and food-borne illnesses. Preservatives postpone or prevent product spoilage caused by mold, bacteria, fungi, or yeast. Antioxidants are used to prevent fats and oils in baked goods and other foods from becoming rancid.

4. To provide leavening or control acidity/alkalinity. Yeast is an example of a leavening agent that causes bread and biscuits to rise during baking. Other additives help modify the acidity or alkalinity of foods for best flavor, taste, and color.

5. To enhance flavor or generate desired color. Many spices and natural and synthetic flavors are added to foods to improve their taste or make their color more appealing. For example, margarine is generally an off-white color before a yellow food dye is added to it.

The Food and Drug Administration oversees food additives, and all must be generally regarded as safe. Generally Regarded As Safe (GRAS) substances are those whose uses are recognized as safe by experts, based on either their extensive history in food or on published scientific evidence. Manufacturers may request the FDA review a substance to determine whether it is GRAS.

Food Intolerances

Food allergies and food intolerances generally overlap. A food allergy can become life threatening, while food intolerance is the body's inability to digest a specific food, passing through the intestinal tract only partially digested. Examples of such intolerances are lactose and gluten intolerance. Lactose intolerance can result in gastrointestinal cramping and diarrhea, while gluten intolerance can result in Celiac's disease. Gluten is found in wheat, rye, and barley products, and can also be found in stamp and envelope adhesive and in medicines and vitamins. Celiac's disease causes damage to the small intestine, where foods cannot be properly digested, and the affected person, although eating normally, becomes malnourished.

Choosing a Diet Based on Health Decisions

Dietary choices are one of the ways to be responsible and accountable for personal health. Some dietary choices may reduce the risk of disease, while other choices may avoid the onset of disease altogether.

Diet to Reduce Disease Risk

The disease process is complicated. In order for a disease to occur, many factors must be in place. Nor does disease prevention occur with one simple step. With careful management of other potential risk factors, eating appropriate foods within an acceptable calorie intake may reduce the risk of certain chronic diseases. The traditional Western diet, which is high in meat, dairy, and other fats, while low in fruits, vegetables, and whole grains, may increase the risks for heart disease, cancer, and Type II diabetes in both men and women. Many people who eat a traditional Western diet also exercise less. The effect of exercise is unclear, but regular exercise may offset additional weight caused by excessive calorie intake.

It is generally accepted that improving diet and exercise and being a nonsmoker reduces risk for heart disease, while poor dietary choices, being sedentary, and smoking increase risks.

Ultimately, the choice is yours. Poor diet may undermine your health, and excess calorie intake will lead to obesity. Choosing a diet based largely on plant foods and mono- and polyunsaturated fats will likely improve health and reduce risk of some diseases. "Image of Health in Depth: Food and Cancer Risk" provides information from the American Cancer Society (ACS) on the link between food and cancer risk.

Image of Health in Depth

Food and Cancer Risk[44]

FOOD OR BEVERAGE	POSSIBLE BENEFITS AND ADVICE
Alcohol	People who drink alcohol have a higher incidence of cancers of the mouth, larynx, pharynx, esophagus, liver, and breast. The ACS recommends no more than two drinks per day for men and one drink per day for women. (A drink is defined as 12 ounces of beer, five ounces of wine, or 1.5 ounces of liquor.)
Diets rich in fruits and vegetables containing antioxidants	Antioxidants, when consumed as part of a whole food, may protect against some cancers. Taking antioxidant supplements has not been shown to be protective, and may be harmful.
Aspartame	The sweetener aspartame has not been shown to increase risk for any form of cancer.
Beta-carotene	In a large study, beta-carotene supplements were given to smokers, and were found to increase the risk for lung cancer. The ACS advises that beta-carotene not be taken as a supplement, but only as part of a whole food.
Bioengineered food	Studies have shown no increased risk of cancer from bioengineered foods.
Calcium	Several studies suggest calcium-rich foods may reduce the risk of colon-rectal cancers. Supplements containing large amounts of calcium were shown to increase the risk for polyp formation, which is a precursor to colon-rectal cancer, and to increase the risk for prostate cancer. The ACS advises calcium be restricted to 1,000 mg a day for people aged 19–50, and for those over 50, restricted to 1,200 mg daily.
Coffee	Although consuming coffee may increase the risk for fibrocystic breast lumps (a non-cancerous breast disease), no association has been found between cancer and coffee consumption.
Fats	All fats increase your risk for obesity, and being obese increases risk for a variety of cancers. Saturated fats have been shown to increase risk for cardiovascular diseases and certain cancers, while omega-3 fatty acids have been shown to reduce the risk of cancers.
Garlic	Ongoing studies have yet to show a link between cancer reduction and garlic consumption.
Preserved meats	Since they contain known carcinogens, preserved meats may increase the risk for colon-rectal cancers. To reduce your exposure to known carcinogens, all meats cooked in smoke or salted should be avoided.
Soy	Ongoing studies have yet to show a link between soy consumption and cancer reduction.

Diseases with a Dietary Influence

Osteoporosis is a decrease in bone density, resulting in fractures that occur easily. The disease develops over many years without any symptoms or discomfort, until either a fracture occurs or bone density is tested. Calcium and phosphorous form the hard substances in bone and are essential during the growing years. When combined with regular weight-bearing activity, eating a balanced diet that provides adequate calcium may help reduce the risk of osteoporosis.

One of the biggest predictors of Type II diabetes is increased body weight. Maintaining adequate calorie intake helps reduce the risk of obesity, which has been linked to cardiovascular diseases and some cancers.

Hypoglycemia is a disease in which the pancreas produces too much insulin, resulting in low blood sugar. With low blood sugar, a person may become confused, irritable, weak, and dizzy. Eating regular, balanced meals and maintaining weight helps reduce hypoglycemic episodes.

Over a lifetime, a person eats about 85,000 meals. These meals provide needed energy, nutrients, and enjoyment that enhance life. Keeping your food choices within a healthy framework will help reduce your risk of disease, and may increase your healthy years life expectancy.

▼

Responsibility and Accountability

This chapter focused on making more informed choices in food selection. With this knowledge, you can make better decisions regarding what you eat, and as a result you may reduce your risks of certain diseases.

Taking Responsibility for Nutrition

Preferring certain foods to others is learned behavior. You can relearn food enjoyment by choosing to try healthier foods. Being responsible in your food choices will be very beneficial to you, and may influence those close to you to try more nutritious food, as well. The choices you make each day will impact your health in the coming years, and will have an immediate influence on your energy and brain aptitude today. More than likely, there have been times you have said that the reason you don't feel well or are not managing your life well is because you are not taking care of basics, such as eating, exercise, and sleep. When you make the effort to make better basic health choices, you feel better. If you make healthier foods an automatic choice for yourself, you are choosing to become healthier.

Focusing on Accountability

Being accountable means you are willing to answer for the consequences of your actions and choices. It is easy to say you will be accountable when that accountability is in the future. But if someday you are told that you could have reduced your risk of a certain disease had you made better choices, will you still think your past choices were worth it? Choosing healthier foods is one way to maintain your health, keeping your health care costs down, which is beneficial to you and to society as a whole. When you make healthier choices, it does not mean you can never eat pizza or ice cream, or that your only food choices should be eggplant and tofu. It means making healthier choices more frequently than unhealthier choices. You have the knowledge now. All that remains is putting it into action.

Summary

Elements of Nutrition

- Nutrients are the components of nutrition, including carbohydrates, proteins, fats, vitamins, minerals, and water.

- Energy in food is expressed in calories. Fats provide 9 calories per gram, and protein and carbohydrates each provide 4 calories per gram weight.

- Carbohydrates, the body's preferred source of energy, can be either simple or complex. Unused carbohydrates are converted and stored first as glycogen, then as fat.

- Fiber is a non-digestible form of carbohydrate that is essential to health.

- Protein is used by the body to build and repair cell tissue. They are comprised of amino acids, eight of which are essential and must be obtained from foods. Foods containing all eight essential amino acids are called complete proteins.

- Fats are either saturated or unsaturated, and are used by the body to insulate and protect, as well as for some chemical reactions, and is also used as an energy source. Unsaturated fats are healthier choices than saturated fats, which can clog arteries.

- Cholesterol is a waxy substance made by the human body when animal products are consumed, and is implicated in a variety of diseases.

Micro Elements of Nutrition

- Vitamins are organic compounds that are either water-soluble or fat-soluble. They are essential for health, growth, and the normal functioning of cells. Most foods contain one or more vitamins.

- Minerals are inorganic compounds that are essential for normal body function and cell metabolism.

- Antioxidants are organic substances that may prevent or postpone heart disease, stroke, and cancer.

- The human body is 50–60 percent water by weight. Humans can maintain longer without food than without water.

Guidelines for Healthy Eating

- The Dietary Guidelines were established to promote health and reduce the risk for disease.

Healthy Dietary Plans

- There are several options for healthy dietary plans, including the USDA MyPyramid, the Harvard Healthy Eating Pyramid, the Mediterranean Pyramid, and the Vegetarian Pyramid.

Challenges to Healthy Eating

- Restaurant and fast food choices present difficulty when trying to eat a healthy meal. Careful selection and moderate consumption will help.

- Beverages may be calorie dense and nutritionally limited.

- Packing food to go helps reduce the temptation to buy cheap, easy access foods. Packed foods need to be maintained at specific temperatures to ensure food safety.

Consumer Issues in Nutrition

- Consumer issues in nutrition range from organic food choices to genetically modified foods, irradiated foods, and food additives.

- Food allergies can be life threatening, while food intolerances result when food is only partially digested.

- Selecting a healthful diet may help reduce the risk of some diseases, such as osteoporosis and diabetes.

Reassessing Your Knowledge

1. Describe the components of nutrition, and identify what function each provides, where they are found, and how many calories are contained in a gram of each.

2. What are the Dietary Guidelines, and how do they help us choose a more healthful diet?

3. Compare and contrast the health benefits between two different dietary pyramids.

4. Consider ways you can choose to make eating on campus healthier while keeping it affordable.

5. How do organic foods help sustain the environment?

To answer these questions, you might choose to work in groups with your colleagues. Check your answers against the written material in the text, and reread those sections where you made errors.

Chapter 7

Health Assessment Toolbox

MyPyramid

This site offers personalized eating plans and interactive tools to help you assess your diet.

http://www.mypyramid.gov

The Healthy Eating Pyramid

The Harvard Pyramid offers a research-based approach to healthier eating, with an emphasis on exercise.

http://www.hsph.harvard.edu/nutritionsource/what-should-you-eat/pyramid/

The DASH Diet

The DASH diet is based on the research studies—Dietary Approaches to Stop Hypertension—and has been proven to lower blood pressure, reduce cholesterol, and improve insulin sensitivity.

http://dashdiet.org/dash_diet_book.asp

Journal of the American College of Cardiology: Diets and Cardiovascular Disease—An Evidence Based Assessment.

This review examines several dietary approaches to cardiovascular health and evaluates the available scientific evidence regarding these diets.

http://content.onlinejacc.org/cgi/content/full/45/9/1379

Vocabulary Challenge

Match the term in the left-hand column with its correct definition in the right-hand column.

TERM		DEFINITION
Chyme		A. Fiber that naturally occurs in food
Glycogen		B. A bioactive plant substance that is non-nutritive but considered to have a beneficial effect on health
Dietary fiber		C. Thick semi-fluid mass of partly digested food that is passed from the stomach to the intestinal tract
Functional fiber		D. An immune response to food that the body mistakenly believes is harmful
Antioxidants		E. A polysaccharide that is stored in the liver and muscle tissue for energy needs
Nutrient		F. An inability to process a specific food
Phytonutrients		G. Fiber that has been synthesized in a laboratory or extracted from a natural source
Food allergy		H. Any element or compound necessary for or contributing to an organism's metabolism, growth, or other functioning
Nitrosamines		I. Any class of organic compounds present in foods found to be carcinogenic
Food intolerance		J. Organic substances thought to prevent or postpone heart disease, stroke, and cancer

Answers
C; E; A; G; J; H; B; D; I; F.

Exploring the Internet

The American Diabetes Association

The American Diabetes Association Web site provides information on the disease along with nutritional information.
http://www.diabetes.org/

American Heart Association

Tips for shopping and eating out, recipes, and nutrition information.
http://www.deliciousdecisions.org

FDA Center for Food Safety and Applied Nutrition

This site provides food safety, food labeling, food additives, and dietary supplements information.
http://www.fda.gov/Food/default.htm

The Tufts Health and Nutrition Newsletter

Tufts University publishes a monthly newsletter that offers information on current research in nutrition, health, and exercise.
http://www.tuftshealthletter.com/

Smart Nutrition Starts Here

This government Web site provides online access to government information on food and human nutrition for consumers.
http://www.nutrition.gov

Nutrition for Everyone

Vitamins and Minerals: This site provides vitamin and mineral fact sheets.
http://www.cdc.gov/nutrition

Food Safety

Your Gateway to Federal Food Safety Information: FoodSafety.gov is the gateway to food safety information provided by government agencies.
http://www.foodsafety.gov/

The Vegetarian Resource Group

At this site, vegetarianism is promoted as the healthy, environmentally correct, and ethical way to eat.
http://www.vrg.org/

The National Cancer Institute

Eating, Before, During, and After Cancer Treatments: This user-friendly Web site offers appropriate help for those who have cancer, or who are supporting someone with cancer.
http://www.cancer.gov/cancertopics/coping/eatinghints

Digestive Disorders Health Center

This WebMD site offers information on a variety of digestive disorders with helpful nutrition hints.
http://www.webmd.com/digestive-disorders/features/crohns-disease-54-tips-to-help-you-manage

National Digestive Disease Clearing House Lactose Intolerance

A government site that provides educational materials to increase knowledge and understanding about digestive diseases.
http://digestive.niddk.nih.gov/

The Food allergy and Anaphylaxis Network

This site works to build awareness about food allergies.
http://www.foodallergy.org/

Selected Reference

1. Office of News and Public Information. Report Offers New Eating and Physical Activity Targets to Reduce Chronic Disease Risk. National Academy of Sciences. Dowloaded August 22, 2010, from http://www8.nationalacademies.org/

2. Profiling Food Consumption in America. Agricultural Fact Book: Chapter 2; page 20. Source: USDA's Economic Research Service. 2000.

3. Foster-Powell, K., et al. International Table of Glycemic Index and Glycemic Load Values. *American Journal of Clinical Nutrition*, 76: 5–26. 2002.

4. Schafer, G., Schenk, U., Ritzel, U., Ramadori, G., and Leonhardt, U. Comparison of the Effects of Dried Peas with Those of Potatoes in Mixed Meals on Postprandial Glucose and Insulin Concentrations in Patients with Type 2 Diabetes. *American Journal of Clinical Nutrition,* 78(1): 99–103. (PubMed) 2003.

5. Ripsin, C.M., Keenan, J.M., Jacobs, D.R., Jr., et al. Oat Products and Lipid Lowering: A Meta-Analysis. *JAMA*, 267(24): 3317–3325. 1992.

6. Cummings, J.H. The Effect of Dietary Fiber on Fecal Weight and Composition. *Fiber in Human Nutrition*. 3rd ed. Boca Raton: CRC Press, 183–252. (PubMed) 2001.

7. Institute of Medicine. *Dietary, Functional, and Total Fiber. Dietary Reference Intakes for Energy, Carbohydrate, Fiber, Fat, Fatty Acids, Cholesterol, Protein, and Amino Acids.* Washington, DC: National Academies Press; 265–334. 2002.

8. Pereira, M.A., O'Reilly, E., Augustsson, K., et al. Dietary Fiber and Risk of Coronary Heart Disease: A Pooled Analysis of Cohort Studies. *Archives of Internal Medicine*, 164(4). February 23, 2004.

9. Estruch, et al. Effects of Dietary Fiber Intake on Risk Factors for Cardiovascular Disease in Subjects at High Risk. *Journal of Epidemiology Community Health*, 63: 582–588. 2009.

10. Rimm, E.B., Ascherio, A., Giovannucci, E.L., Spiegelman, D., Stampfer, M.J., and Willett, W.C. Vegetable, Fruit, and Cereal Fiber Intake and Risk of Coronary Heart Disease among Men. *JAMA*, 275: 447–451. 1996.

11. Mckeown, N.M., Meigs, J.B., Liu, S., et al. Carbohydrate Nutrition, Insulin Resistance, and the Prevalence of the Metabolic Syndrome in the Framingham Offspring Cohort. *Diabetes Care*, 27(2): 538–546. February, 2004.

12. McKeown, N.M., Meigs, J.B., Liu, S., Wilson, P.W., and Jacques, P.F. Whole-Grain Intake Is Favorably Associated with Metabolic Risk Factors for Type 2 Diabetes and Cardiovascular Disease in the Framingham Offspring Study. *American Journal of Clinical Nutrition*, 76: 390–398. 2002.

13. Fung, T.T., Hu, F.B., Pereira, M.A., et al. Whole–grain Intake and the Risk of Type 2 Diabetes: a Prospective Study in Men *American Journal of Clinical Nutrition*, 76: 535–540. 2002.

14. Schulze, M.B., Liu, S., Rimm, E.B., Manson, J.E., Willett, W.C., and Hu, F.B. Glycemic Index, Glycemic Load, and Dietary Fiber Intake and Incidence of Type 2 Diabetes in Younger and Middle-aged Women. *American Journal of Clinical Nutrition*, 80(2): 348–356. 2004.

15. Aldoori, W.H., Giovannucci E., Rockett, H.R.H., Sampson, L., Rimm, E.B., and Willett, W.C. A Prospective study of Dietary Fiber Types and Symptomatic Diverticular Disease in Men. *Journal of Nutrition*, 128: 714–719. 1998.

16. Cummings, J.H. The Effect of Dietary Fiber on Fecal Weight and Composition. In: Spiller GA, ed. *Fiber in Human Nutrition*. 3rd ed. Boca Raton: CRC Press, 183–252. 2001.

17. Fiber. Oregon State University, Linus Pauling Institute, Micronutrient Information Center. Downloaded July 14, 2010, from lpi.oregonstate.edu/infocenter/phytochemicals/fiber

18. Report of the Dietary Guidelines Advisory Committee on the Dietary Guidelines for Americans, 2010. USDA Center for Nutrition Policy and Promotion. Downloaded July 14, 2010, from http://www.cnpp.usda.gov/DGAs2010-DGACReport.htm

19. Young, V.R. Adult Amino Acid Requirements: the Case for a Major Revision in Current Recommendations. *Journal of Nutrition,* 124(8 Suppl): 1517S–1523S. 1994.

20. Fürst P., and Stehle, P. What Are the Essential Elements needed for the Determination of Amino Acid Requirements in Humans? *Journal of Nutrition.* June, 2004.

21. Hurrell, R.F. Preventing Iron Deficiency Through Food Fortification. *Nutrition Review,* 55: 210–222. 1997.

22. Johns Hopkins Medicine Health Alerts. Nutrition and Weight Control Special Report. *Diet and Longevity—A Dietary Arsenal Against 8 Serious Disorders*. February 7, 2006.

23. Scanlon, R.A. The Linus Pauling Institute Newsletter, Oregon State University. Fall/Winter, 2000.

24. Sachiko, T.; St. Jeor, R.D., Howard, B.V., PhD, PhD; T. Elaine Prewitt, RD, DrPH; Vicki Bovee, RD, MS; Terry Bazzarre, PhD; Robert H. Eckel, MD; Dietary Protein and Weight Reduction. A Statement for Healthcare Professionals From the Nutrition Committee of the Council on Nutrition, Physical Activity, and Metabolism of the American Heart Association. *Circulation*. 104: 1869–1874. 2001.

25. Chen T.Y., Smith W, Rosenstock J.L., Lessnau K.D. A Life-threatening Complication of Atkins Diet. *Lancet*; 367:958. 2006.

26. C de Graaf, T Hulshof, JA Weststrate and P Ja. Short-term Effects of Different Amounts of Protein, Fats, and Carbohydrates on Satiety. *American Journal of Clinical Nutrition*, Vol 55, 33–38. 1992.

27. World Cancer Research Fund. Food, Nutrition, Physical Activity, and the Prevention of Cancer: A global perspective. *American Institute of Cancer Research*. Washington, DC:2007.

28. Lefevre M., Champagne C.M., Tulley R.T., Rood J.C. and Most M.M. Individual Variability in Cardiovascular Disease Risk Factor Responses to Low-fat and Low-saturated-fat Diets in Men: Body Mass Index, Adiposity, and Insulin Resistance Predict Changes in LDL Cholesterol. *American Journal of Clinical Nutrition*, 82 (5): 957–963, November 2005.

29. Sabate, J., Oda, K., and Ros, E. Nut Consumption and Blood Lipid Levels: A Pooled Analysis of 25 Intervention Trials. *Archive Internal Medicine*, 170(9): 821–827. May 10, 2010.

30. USDA Nutrient Database for Standard Reference (Release 1L), the National Sunflower Oil Association, and the Flax Council of Canada. *Nutrition Action Newsletter*, July–August, 2002.

31. Allison, D.B., Denke, M.A., Dietschy, J.M., Emken, E.A., Kris-Etherton, P.M., and Nicolosi, R.J. Trans Fatty Acids and Coronary Heart Disease Risk. Report of the Expert Panel on Trans Fatty Acids and Coronary Heart Disease. *American Journal of Clinical Nutrition*, 62: 655S–708S. September, 1995.

32. Neihouser, N.L., Wassertheil-Smoller, S., Thompson, C., et al. Multivitamin Use and Risk of Cancer and Cardiovascular Disease in the Women's Health Initiative Cohorts. *Archives of Internal Medicine*, 169(3). February, 2009.

33. Stranges, S. Effects of Selenium Supplementation on Cardiovascular Disease, Incidence and Mortality: Secondary Analysis in a Randomized Clinical Trial. *American Journal of Epidemiology*, Vol 163: 694–699. April 15, 2006.

34. Zidenberg-Cherr, Sheri. Trace Elements and Free Radicals in Oxidative Diseases *American Journal of Clinical Nutrition*, 62: 847–848. Oct 1995.

35. Dekkers, J.C., van Doornen L.J.P., and Kemper H.C.G. The Role of Antioxidant Vitamins and Enzymes in the Prevention of Exercise-Induced Muscle Damage. *Sports Medicine* 21: 213–238, 1996.

36. *Phytochemicals in Health and Disease*. edited by Yongping Bao and Roger Fenwick. New York: Marcell Dekker Inc. 2004.

37. He, K., et al. Accumulated Evidence on Fish Consumptions and Coronary Heart Disease Mortality: A meta-analysis of Cohort Studies. *Circulation*, 109: 2705–2711. 2004.

38. Nicholls, S.J., et al. Consumption of Saturated Fat Impairs the Anti-Inflammatory Properties of High-density Lipoproteins and Endothelial Function. *Journal of the American College of Cardiology*, 48(4): 715–720. 2006.

39. Owusu W., Willett W.C., Feskanich D., Ascherio A., Spiegelman D., and Colditz G.A. Calcium Intake and the Incidence of Forearm and Hip Fractures Among Men. *Journal of Nutrition*; 127:1782–87. 1997.

40. Feskanich D., Willett W.C., Stampfer M.J., and Colditz G.A. Milk, Dietary Calcium, and Bone Fractures in Women: a 12-Year Prospective Study. *American Journal of Public Health*, 87: 992–997. 1997.

41. Bischoff-Ferrari H.A., Dawson-Hughes B., Baron J.A., et al. Calcium Intake and Hip Fracture Risk in Men and Women: A Meta-Analysis of Prospective Cohort Studies and Randomized Controlled Trials. *American Journal of Clinical Nutrition*; 86:1780–1790. 2007.

42. Wansink, B., Painter J.E. , and North J. *"Bottomless Bowls: Why Visual Cues of Portion Size May Influence Intake,"* Obesity Research, 13:1, 93–100. NAASO—The Obesity Society. 2005.

43. Micha R., Wallace S., Moxaffarian, D. Red and Processed Meat Consumption and Risk of Incident of Coronary Heart Disease, Stroke, and Diabetes Mellitus. A Systematic Review and Meta-Analysis. *Circulation*. May 17, 2010.

44. American Cancer Society: Guidelines on Nutrition and Physical Activity for Cancer Protection. *CA: A Cancer Journal for Clinicians*, 52: 92. 2002.

Image of Health

Physical Fitness

WHAT IT MEANS TO BE PHYSICALLY FIT

- Components of Fitness
  - Cardiorespiratory Fitness
  - Muscular Strength and Muscular Endurance
  - Flexibility
  - Body Composition
  - Endurance Training: Aerobic vs. Anaerobic
- Benefits of Fitness
  - Physical Health
  - Mental Health
  - Social Health

KEYS TO IMPROVING PERSONAL FITNESS

- Commitment
- Motivation
- FITT: Frequency, Intensity, Time, Type
- Rate of Perceived Exertion Scale (RPE)
- Circuit Training and Cross Training
- Mind-Body Exercise
  - Yoga
  - Pilates
  - Tai Chi

DRUGS AND SUPPLEMENTS

- Steroids, Human Growth Hormone, and Creatine
- Protein Supplements
- Stimulants

INJURY PREVENTION

- Overload and Over-Training
- Heat and Cold
- Warming Up and Cooling Down
- Rest and Recovery
- RICE
- Hydration and Sports Drinks
- Staying Injury Free

RESPONSIBILITY AND ACCOUNTABILITY

- Taking Responsibility for Physical Fitness
- Focusing on Accountability

Student Learning Outcomes

LEARNING OUTCOMES	APPLYING IT TO YOUR LIFE
Describe what it means to be physically fit.	Assess your current level of physical fitness.
List the five components of fitness established by the American College of Sports Medicine (ACSM).	Describe the ACSM components you have incorporated into your own life.
Identify some of the benefits of exercise.	Describe how you might personally benefit from an exercise program.
Identify some different types of exercise programs.	Determine the type of exercise program that would be best for you.
Describe some of the keys to injury prevention.	Identify steps you will take to minimize the risk of injury while exercising.

Assess Your Knowledge

1. Physical fitness is:
    a. Your medical history.

    b. Your ability to relax and be in the moment.

    c. Your ability to engage in physical activities for work or play.

    d. Your ability to lead group exercises.

2. The components of fitness established by the ACSM are:
    a. Cardiorespiratory fitness, muscular strength, muscular endurance, flexibility, body composition.

    b. Cardiorespiratory fitness, aerobic fitness, anaerobic fitness, flexibility, endurance.

    c. Cardiorespiratory fitness, anaerobic fitness, fat-to-lean ratio, body composition, endurance.

    d. Cardiorespiratory fitness, flexibility, endurance, fat-to-lean ratio anaerobic fitness.

3. The FITT exercise model includes:
    a. Frequency, interval, target, time.

    b. Frequency, intensity, total, target.

    c. Frequency, intensity, time, type.

    d. Frequency, interval, total, type.

4. Mind/body exercise refers to the link between:
    a. Emotional health and spiritual health.

    b. Meditation and competitive athletics.

    c. Yoga and pilates.

    d. Physical health and psychological health.

5. The acronym RICE refers to:
    a. Rest, ice, compression, elevation.

    b. Recovery, injury, compression, emergence.

    c. Reaction, intensity, competition, event.

    d. Reduction, injury, compound, elevation.

Answers:

1. c; 2. a; 3. c; 4. d; 5. a.

Physical Fitness

Physical fitness is a dimension of wellness determined by many variables, including age, gender, and physical ability or disability. There are several ways to determine personal level of fitness. Although rarely a formal evaluation, personal fitness can be measured by how you compare to others in your **peer group** and by your ability to accomplish daily tasks, including performing the physical duties required for your work or engaging in physical activities for recreation.

Key Terms

Physical fitness: The ability to exercise at a moderate to vigorous level on a regular basis without great fatigue.

Peer group: Individuals who are equal in age, education, and social class.

Many people take physical fitness for granted, and expect to perform physically at a reasonable level, even if they have not exercised in years. There is an expectation that you will feel physically well most of the time. If you do not, there is a reasonable explanation.

A more sedentary lifestyle, coupled with a gradual increase in calories consumed year after year, has resulted in a population of Americans in which 66 percent are considered overweight, and 34 percent of those who are overweight are obese.[1] Obesity among adults in the U.S. has not changed since 2003–2004,[2] and in 2008, the National Health Survey found that only 33 percent of men and 29 percent of women engage in regular physical activity, and 36 percent reported no leisure time physical activity at all.[3] Whether you are part of the group who exercise regularly, or the 36 percent that exercises rarely, if ever, this chapter will provide information to help motivate you to start or continue an exercise program.

Critical Thinking Question: What factors determine your personal physical fitness?

One factor in America's reduced emphasis on exercise is that elementary school physical education requirements have changed. Over the years, many schools have reduced or eliminated required exercise or physical education in the curriculum. In addition, those responsible for conducting school exercise programs may have little training in how to manage successful group exercise. Lack of exercise opportunities in schools has produced a population of young people who may not regularly exercise.

Many adults also lead lives that are not very physically demanding. We rarely walk if we can ride or drive, we surround ourselves with labor-saving devices, and exercise has become a special event we must schedule or build into our day.

Because it affects so many parts of our lives, the decline in physical fitness has become a national concern. National fitness determines worker productivity, health care costs, and longevity. Current national longevity projections indicate that for the first time in U.S. history, children may not live as long as their parents. The projected cause is childhood obesity and diabetes, which leads to lifelong obesity and adult diabetes that will shorten lifespan.[4] However, this could be alleviated by a lifetime of exercise.

The human body is designed for recurring daily activity. Without regular movement or exercise, the body begins to atrophy. Muscles become less strong, joints less flexible, and bones less dense. Exercise can be incorporated into daily life at any age, and the benefits are both immediate and long term. If you have already achieved a level of fitness, there may still be room for improvement. If you are a non-exerciser, you can start an exercise regimen and improve your fitness. Physical fitness begins with small steps that lead to small changes, and when combined with motivation can lead to improved fitness.

Image of Health in Depth

Federal Involvement in Physical Fitness

Federal involvement in physical fitness began in 1956, with the first President's Council on Physical Fitness. The American Association of Health, Physical Education, Recreation, and Dance (AAHPERD) created a battery of tests that were administered to schoolchildren to evaluate fitness levels.[5]

Schools across the country became involved in fitness testing, and comparisons were made among schools and between states. There was even a national exercise song, called *Chicken Fat*, developed early in the program that was played in fitness classes as children followed the exercise directions in the song.[6] Pre- and post-fitness testing was done for the first time, and the result of these efforts was improved fitness levels among American children.

The AAHPERD fitness tests continued to evolve, and by 1987, they became resource recommendations to enhance the existing physical education curriculum and supplement daily lesson plans. By 1989, AAHPERD had developed the Physical Best program, encouraging goal setting as part of fitness development.[7] Physical Best Activity guides, software, and modifications for students with disabilities were available to teachers nationwide. Through the years, The President's Council on Fitness evolved into the President's Council on Fitness and Sport, and even today, one of the President's responsibilities is to name the Council chair, usually a well-known sports figure.

The President's Council on Fitness and Sport is a federal mandate to enhance physical activity and sports participation for children and adolescents. Overseen by the Department of Health and Human Services, the intent of the program is to expand national interest in the benefits of regular physical activity, active sports participation, health promotion, and disease prevention.[8] Even with federal mandates, reduced funding for education at the state and local levels has limited physical activity opportunities for many school children.

What It Means to Be Physically Fit

Physical fitness is the ability to perform exercise at a moderate to vigorous level on a regular basis without great fatigue. Exercise-related activity results in many health benefits, including heart and lung function, muscular strength and endurance, flexibility, and improved body composition. In addition, people who exercise regularly, even if they are overweight, have a lower risk of early death.

Components of Fitness

The American College of Sports Medicine (ACSM), as well as several other leading fitness professional organizations, established the following components of fitness for evaluating an individual's physical health: cardiorespiratory fitness, muscular strength, muscular endurance, flexibility, and body composition.

Image of Health

ACSM Guidelines for Healthy Aerobics Activity

• Exercise 3–5 days per week.

• Warm up for 5–10 minutes before aerobic activity.

• Maintain exercise intensity for 30–45 minutes.

• Gradually decrease the intensity of your workout, cooling down, then stretch during the last 5–10 minutes.

Cardiorespiratory Fitness

Cardiorespiratory fitness is the ability of the heart and lungs to work efficiently in supplying oxygen to skeletal muscles during sustained physical activity. When cardiorespiratory fitness is poor, the heart must work harder and may not be able to respond with high enough intensity during an emergency. Poor cardiorespiratory fitness is associated with heart disease, diabetes, colon cancer, stroke, depression, and anxiety. Improving cardiorespiratory fitness through **aerobic** exercise involves any activity that uses large muscle groups and **isokinetic** movement so that heart rate, respiration, and body temperature all increase, improving heart and lung function and increasing the amount of oxygen to the body.

Cardiorespiratory endurance training is sustained aerobic exercise of increasing duration, resulting in a stronger heart and improvement of the entire cardiorespiratory system. A healthy heart pumps more blood with less effort, increasing blood flow to tissues, muscles, and organs. Many exercise activities improve cardiorespiratory fitness, leading to numerous health benefits: weight loss, increased muscle mass, increased metabolism, and improvement in energy levels. For those with elevated blood pressure, there may be a reduction in both systolic and diastolic pressure, and for those with diabetes, blood sugar management will be improved. Most physically fit individuals seem to have better stress management and improved psychological health—and for many, improvement in cardiorespiratory fitness leads to improved body image and self-esteem.

Key Terms

Cardiorespiratory fitness: The ability of the heart and lungs to work efficiently to supply oxygen to skeletal muscles during sustained physical activity.

Aerobic: Literally meaning "with oxygen." Aerobic exercise is continuous, such as running or fast walking, requiring the exchange of oxygen for muscles to perform.

Isokinetic: Exercise that maintains constant tension through movement as muscles shorten or lengthen, in exercises such as running, walking, cycling, or swimming.

Cardiorespiratory endurance training: Sustained large muscle dynamic exercise designed to improve cardiorespiratory fitness.

Muscular Strength

Just as the heart and lungs must be exercised to improve cardiorespiratory fitness, muscles must be exercised to improve **muscular strength**. Muscular strength is the ability of a muscle to exert force against a physical object, and if diminished, muscles become less dense and less able to perform daily activities. For older adults, this may result in muscle cells becoming nonfunctional, having lost their attachment to the nervous system.[11]

Muscular strength can be improved by either **isometric** or **isotonic** exercises. Isometric exercises include any exercise that requires strength to hold a position by pressing against an immoveable object.

FIGURE 8-1. Isometric exercises are frequently part of a yoga practice.

With isotonic exercise, muscles are contracted and shortened through a range of motion, such as a weight training program or when lifting heavy objects during daily activities.

FIGURE 8-2. Isotonic exercises cause muscles to contract and shorten though a range of motion under constant tension.

Muscular Endurance

As you improve muscular strength, **muscular endurance** also improves and allows the muscles to engage in sustained effort while resisting fatigue. The ability of some people to run a 26.2 mile marathon or cycle for 100 miles are examples of muscular endurance.

Some form of weight training is essential for everyone. Building muscular strength and endurance increases the density of muscle tissue, helps reduce the proportion of body fat, and increases the proportion of lean tissue. Increasing muscular strength also increases ligament and tendon strength, and helps improve balance. And since improved balance helps prevent falls, a modified weight training program is recommended for older individuals, as falls are the number one source of unintentional injuries for the elderly.[12]

Flexibility

Flexibility involves being able to move a joint through a full range of motion. Inflexibility will compromise movement and function, possibly resulting in difficulty with everyday activities, such as getting into and out of a car or bending to tie shoelaces. Inflexibility also reduces balance—as less flexible joints age they become stiffer, causing an unnatural body posture that puts stress on joints and muscles. Flexibility can be improved and maintained using stretching exercises, best performed during or following cardiorespiratory activity. Figure 8-3 illustrates a variety of exercises to help improve flexibility.

Because it helps improve body alignment and range of motion, good flexibility is an important part of physical fitness. Flexibility depends on age, heredity, and lifestyle. Muscles, tendons, and ligaments become stronger as the human body adapts to exercise routines. Flexibility can also alleviate incidence of lower back pain and help reduce the muscle and tendon injuries occurring in sports and in daily activities. Unless a stretching routine is also incorporated, strength training could result in some inflexibility.

Key Terms

Muscular strength: The ability of a muscle to exert force against a physical object.

Muscular endurance: The ability of a muscle to engage in sustained effort while resisting fatigue.

Isometric: Strength training that involves holding a position or pressing against an immovable object such as the floor or wall.

Isotonic: Contracting and shortening a muscle through a range of motion under constant tension, such as in weight training.

Flexibility: The ability to move a joint through its full range of motion.

Chest   Upper back   Back of upper arms   Calf   Back of thighs   Back of thighs

Front of thighs   Front of thighs   Outer thighs   Inner thighs   Inner thighs

Lower back   Lower back   Lower back   Torso

FIGURE 8-3. Stretches to improve flexibility.

Body Composition

Body composition is the ratio between lean body mass (muscle, bone, and water) and both essential and nonessential fats. It reflects the way the body stores fat and develops muscle, and is influenced by gender, heredity, ethnicity, and exercise habits. Your skeletal structure, which is hereditary, determines much of your body composition. Smaller skeletal bones support smaller muscles, tendons, and ligaments, while a larger skeletal structure will naturally support larger muscles, tendons, and ligaments. In addition to skeletal size, bone density also differs among ethnicities. African Americans and those of other African ethnicities have a higher bone density than individuals of Asian or Northern-European ethnicity. A high bone density provides a stronger skeletal structure for muscular development and lessens the risk for osteoporosis. Additionally, each gender stores nonessential body fat differently. Men tend to store excess body fat around the waist, which is a risk factor for cardiovascular disease, while women store it around the hips and buttocks with minimal disease risk. Excess or nonessential body fat occurs when the number of calories consumed each day exceeds the number of calories burned. Essential fat is the amount of fat required by all humans for insulation, padding, and hormone production.

Critical Thinking Question: Explain the factors that determine your personal body composition, or fat-to-lean ratio.

It is difficult to determine actual body composition by visual observation. A person who looks obese may have some excess body fat, but may also be very muscular. The ratio, therefore, may actually be more lean than fat. A very thin person may look lean, but in reality may have a body composition ratio that is more fat than lean. The best way to determine actual body composition is to conduct a test using one of the several measurement protocols discussed in Chapter 9, such as hydrostatic weighing or skin-fold caliper testing. Body composition can be improved by appropriate diet and exercise.

Endurance Training: Aerobic versus Anaerobic

Endurance training results from a gradual increase in exercise over time, and can include both weight training and cardioresiratory exercise. Cardiorespiratory endurance exercise is primarily aerobic, as opposed to **anaerobic**.

Aerobic exercise improves cardiorespiratory efficiency and promotes the development of **slow-twitch muscles**. Anaerobic training is short, intense exercise such as sprinting, promoting the development of **fast-twitch muscles**, and is not ideal for endurance training. Improving endurance by training aerobically is a measure of total fitness.

Image of Health in Depth

Competitions for Life

Triathlon. Competitors swim, bike, and run various distances, including the Iron Man distance, which is 1.5-mile swim, 112-mile bike and 26.2-mile run.

Running. Various race events where the distance can vary from 3.1 miles, to a marathon of 26.2 miles, to ultra runs of 50-100 miles.

Ultra Swimming. Examples include swimming around Manhattan, from the California coast to Catalina Island, or across the English Channel.

Ultra Bike Rides. Century rides, where participants ride 100 miles, or the Race Across America, in which participants cycle coast to coast over a few weeks.

Three-Day Breast Cancer Walk. Participants walk 20 miles per day for a total of 60 miles over three days.

All of these events require training over a period of many months, and almost anyone who is physically healthy can train, raise their personal level of fitness, and complete one of these events.

The best way to develop an endurance training program is to establish a goal. Your goal may be to run a 10K or a marathon, to be able to walk long distances in your neighborhood and get more physically fit, to walk or run a specific distance, or perhaps train for a specific event, such as those described in the "Image of Health: Competitions for Life." If you are a college student, you have the opportunity to take an exercise class through the campus recreation or exercise science department. There are also many community programs that are available through the YMCA or other local organizations. The advantage of a class, whether it is on a college campus or at the local YMCA, is that it puts you on an exercise schedule. Even if the class meets only twice per week, it should be enough to keep you on track. If you are a beginning exerciser, it is often difficult to maintain an exercise schedule on your own; it is too easy to put off exercise until later in the day, or later in the week, and soon, you are not exercising at all. There are also programs on the Internet that can help you get started and keep you on a program to progressively improve. Some online training programs also include a coach, usually for a fee, who will help you set goals, give you a training program, counsel you on training, diet, and injury prevention, and encourage your training efforts.

Key Terms

Anaerobic: Literally meaning "without oxygen." Exercise that is explosive and short term, such as sprinting, throwing events in track and field, and heavy weight training, in which muscles depend primarily on oxygen in blood.

Fast twitch muscle fibers: Capable of producing short bursts of strength and speed, but fatigue quickly. Ideal for sprinting.

Slow twitch muscle fibers: Capable of muscle contractions over long periods. Ideal for distance running.

Benefits of Fitness

Physical fitness yields many benefits, including physical health, mental health, and social health. Although the benefits of exercise are well known, many people still do not exercise: only 33 percent of men and 29 percent of women engage in moderate physical activity. Healthy People 2010, Federal goals for American health, established a 50 percent exercise goal for both men and women. Studies show that men are more likely to exercise than women, and people with higher socioeconomic status are more likely to exercise than those of lower socioeconomic status. One of the simplest and cheapest ways to improve total health and well-being is to be more physically active. Choosing to exercise is part of self-care and self-responsibility.

Physical Health

Improving your fitness level at any age has many benefits for total physical health. Fitness allows the body to work more efficiantly, remain strong, resist disease, and provide more energy.

More Efficient Metabolism

Metabolism regulates how the body uses fuel (food). Exercise raises metabolism and allows the body to burn more calories. It is important to exercise consistently, even at less intensity or for a shorter time, than to miss several days of exercise.

Increased Musculature and Bone Density

Exercise, especially weight training, increases muscular development, and weight training as well as any weight-bearing exercise, such as walking or running, improves bone density. Weight training and weight-bearing exercise are especially important for women with a small skeletal structure, since it helps to prevent osteoporosis.

Improved Cardiovascular Functioning

Exercise causes the heart to become stronger and the entire circulatory system to become more efficient. Regular exercise is known to reduce both cholesterol and triglycerides, helping to reduce the incidence of the plaque buildup that clogs arteries.

Reduced Risk for Certain Chronic Diseases

Choosing a lifetime of exercise can reduce the risk of diabetes, cardiovascular diseases, some cancers, and hypertension. Regular exercise helps prevent chronic diseases, because it helps regulate blood fats and insulin for diabetics, improves cardiorespiratory fitness for those with cardiovascular disease, and can also lower blood pressure.

More Energy

The human body responds well to exercise, adapting quickly and raising fitness and energy levels. Increased energy is almost immediately noticeable with an exercise program, which helps motivate people to continue exercising.

Mental Health

Improved Sleep Habits

Exercise works muscles and the cardiovascular system, facilitating more restful sleep and recovery and helping prevent insomnia. It is important to exercise at a level that promotes fitness but does not make you overtired. Restful sleep is promoted by being pleasantly tired from exercise, not exhausted.

Improved Psychological Health

Brain chemical changes occur when exercise produces endorphins, natural mood elevators that help to reduce the incidence of depression. Although all depression cannot be prevented by exercise, in many cases it can be helpful. A change of environment can also cause a positive mood shift: Going for a walk, getting out of the house, meeting an exercise group, or walking at the beach or in a park are all likely to improve mood.

Better Personal Stress Management

Exercise reduces stress for most people. Some types of exercise are particularly good stress relievers, such as yoga, tai chi, or running or walking. You will need to experiment to determine the type of exercise that works best for your stress management. Some individuals notice a reduction in stress when they do an intense aerobic workout, but others may feel more stressed after a difficult workout, finding better stress relief with yoga, or any meditative deep-breathing exercise.

Greater Aptitude for Academic Work

Exercise increases oxygen flow to the entire body, including the brain. Because the brain thrives on oxygen rich blood, cognitive ability can improve with exercise. If you are overwhelmed with papers, tests, projects, or final exams, take a break and go for a brisk walk.

Social Health

Improved Social Connections

Exercise is often done in groups, and can result in new friendships and more social connections. For many people, exercising in a group or with an exercise partner is one of the joys of exercise: it helps with motivation, and the social aspect makes it fun.

Positive Body Image

Exercise leads to weight loss and improved muscle tone and definition. You look and feel better, and this can raise self-esteem. Even a beginning exerciser will notice a difference and as small improvements progress to more noticeable improvements, this positive change is empowering.

Lifelong Exercise

Throughout your working life, exercise can provide many benefits to offset stress, and can also be a hobby to enjoy during your retirement years.

Keys to Improving Personal Fitness

Improved fitness requires motivation, a commitment to exercise, finding an exercise you enjoy, and making time to exercise. No matter what your current level of fitness, it can probably be improved. Even those who have never exercised can begin a program that will result in improved personal fitness.

Commitment

People who exercise regularly do not necessarily have more free time; they have simply made a commitment to exercise. Regular exercisers often find that daily exercise provides increased energy and allows for the accomplishment of more tasks. Finding an exercise activity that is enjoyable will help with personal commitment; setting personal goals and keeping track of accomplishments such as weight loss, body composition, or exercise goals can be empowering and motivating. Once you begin to notice the benefits of exercise, it will become a more important part of your life.

Critical Thinking Question: Describe how you plan to take responsibility for your personal fitness.

Challenge Question: What are the important keys to improving personal fitness?

Beginning and maintaining an exercise program requires identifying the what, when, and how of exercise. The most important decision is choosing exercise you will enjoy, and that realistically fits your lifestyle. The next important decision is making exercise time part of your daily routine. Many of those who exercise regularly do so first thing in the morning; as the day progresses and you become tired and busy, it is too easy to find excuses to skip exercise. Choosing how you will exercise ensures that you have some variety in your exercise program, and changing what you do will keep it interesting and help make it fun. Exercising with a group or a friend is a good way to help you keep on track, plus it allows someone else to help plan your exercise.

Motivation

Making time to exercise depends primarily on personal motivation. Fitness improves physical and psychological health, body composition, and body image, and aids in weight loss. Additional incentive for exercise may be a doctor recommendation to help alleviate a medical condition. Exercise is known to help manage diabetes, blood pressure, and blood cholesterol.

Whatever your motivation, improving fitness requires creating goals and a plan to maintain the fitness you have achieved. This is a lifelong process, but once you have achieved a certain level of physical fitness, it is easier to maintain. Eventually, exercise no longer feels like work, but becomes an enjoyable part of your day. Even if life circumstances keep you from exercising for a period of time, you will find it easier to regain your fitness, having once experienced what it feels like to be physically fit.

Motivation Maximizer

Everyone has only 24 hours in each day. Some people manage to fill their non-sleeping hours with school, work, family, and exercise. It is part of your personal responsibility to determine the most efficient way to fill your 24 hours. If your perception is that there is no time to exercise, there may be even less than you may think—because lack of exercise may result in shortened lifespan. There are many positive reasons for making the time to exercise, rather than finding ways not to. Consider the potential positive outcomes of establishing an exercise routine. Small fitness goals lead to bigger fitness accomplishments.

Critical Thinking Question: Describe a situation that would most likely motivate you to exercise.

FITT: Frequency, Intensity, Time, and Type

The FITT principle is a good model for establishing an effective exercise program. FITT, an acronym for *frequency*, *intensity*, *time*, and *type*, provides a template for beginning to advanced exercisers to track their total fitness, and is essentially a program design that can be manipulated as fitness improves. *Frequency* is the number of times per week that you will exercise; *intensity* refers to how hard you will exercise; *time* is the number of minutes you will spend in an exercise session; and *type* refers to the kind of exercise you will do, such as walking, running, cycling, or swimming.

Frequency

Determining how frequently to exercise depends on fitness level, type of exercise, and fitness goals. To gradually improve your fitness level, an exercise session should occur every other day, or three to four times per week. For a beginning exerciser, it is more important to exercise more frequently for a shorter period of time than less frequently for a longer period. It is not beneficial to make up for a week of missed workouts on the weekend; this can lead to excessive fatigue and overuse injuries. For strength and endurance exercise, muscles should have a day of rest before being worked again, while flexibility exercises can be done each day.

Intensity

Determining intensity correctly is the key to establishing a safe and productive exercise plan. For beginning cardiorespiratory exercise, heart and lungs need to be gradually trained to allow for longer and more difficult workouts. As workload increases, the body requires more blood to the muscles and responds by increasing both heart rate and respiration, moving oxygen-rich blood to the muscles. It is important to keep the intensity of exercise at a rate that allows the cardiorespiratory system to work efficiently. Too much intensity causes the heart and lungs to work harder to keep up; the exerciser will be gasping for breath, will fatigue more quickly, and will recover more slowly. It is better to start with less intensity, allowing the cardiorespiratory system to adjust and gradually improve. There are several sophisticated testing measures to determine cardiorespiratory efficiency, but you can approximate the intensity very accurately by exercising within a target zone for heart rate or by using a perceived exertion scale.

Image of Health in Depth

Determining Your Target Zone for Exercise Intensity

- Determine resting heart rate first thing in the morning, measuring carotid pulse on the side of your neck or radial pulse in your wrist.

- Count how many times your heart beats in a ten-second period, and multiply the number by six to determine resting heart rate (RHR).

- To determine maximum heart rate (MHR), subtract your age from 220.

- Once you know RHR and MHR, you can determine target heart rate (THR) using the following formula for 60 percent intensity: MHR + RHR × .60 − RHR = THR

- Target heart rate for 85 percent intensity: MHR + RHR × .85 − RHR = THR

- Exercising within your range will help to steadily improve fitness level.

Target Heart Rate Examples

- The following example is for a beginning exerciser, twenty years old, with a resting heart rate of 70 beats per minute.

  $220 - 20 = 200 + 70 \times .60 - 70 =$ 172 target heart rate

- The next formula is for a 40-year-old who has been exercising for a year (intermediate exerciser) and has a resting heart rate of 60 beats per minute.

  $220 - 40 = 180 + 60 \times .70 - 60 =$ 162 target heart rate

- And finally, a formula for a 60-year-old, lifelong (advanced) exerciser with a resting heart rate of 50 beats per minute.

  $220 - 60 = 160 + 50 \times .85 - 50 =$ 152.5 target heart rate

In these examples, you may have noticed that as age goes up, recommended target heart rate goes down, since intensity of exercise is determined by both age and resting heart rate. In addition, exercise improves total cardiovascular health, making the heart a more efficient organ and increasing the volume of blood that can be moved with each contraction. When the heart becomes a more efficient pump, fewer contractions are required per minute, resulting in a lower resting heart rate.

Critical Thinking Question: Using the Target Zone for Exercise Intensity formula, calculate your own target heart rate at 60 percent intensity.

Rate of Perceived Exertion Scale (RPE)

The Rate of Perceived Exertion Scale (RPE), also called the Borg rating of perceived exertion, is a numerical measure from 1–10 that helps determine how hard your body is working based on *your perceptions* of increased breathing rate, sweating, and muscle fatigue. Since this is a subjective scale, perceptions will vary day to day, and by each individual. During a workout session, the exerciser assigns a number from 1 to 10, depending on how he or she feels. Once established, the scale can be used to self-monitor a workout to adjust the intensity. The RPE is a way to reach maximum potential in a workout each day, and allows for variability in daily energy.[13]

Determining Intensity for Muscular Strength, Endurance, and Flexibility

Intensity for muscular strength and endurance exercise is determined by the amount of weight lifted or moved, as well as the number of repetitions in a set. For strength training, heavier weights are lifted with fewer repetitions, while for endurance training, lighter weights are lifted with more repetitions. A typical strength-training regimen is three sets of 3–5 repetitions using a specific weight. For endurance training, the typical regimen is three sets of 12–15 repetitions. If the correct weight is used, the muscles used will be almost exhausted with the final lift of the last repetition. Therefore, if improved strength and/or endurance is desired, the amount of weight should be increased when the muscles are able to lift a weight without fatigue.

Flexibility intensity refers to the tension felt when a muscle is stretched. The stretch should be **static**, not moving or bouncing, and held just to the point of resistance. When a muscle is stretched in a pushing/pulling, **ballistic** bouncing motion, injury may result. Stretching should be done after a warm-up or at the end of the exercise routine, when muscles, tendons, and ligaments stretch more easily, with less risk and increased oxygenated blood flow. Stretching muscles prior to a warm-up can result in injury.

Key Terms

Static: A force of tension on a muscle that is being stretched without movement.

Ballistic: A force of tension on a muscle that is being stretched with movement.

Time

The amount of time spent on each exercise session depends on fitness level, fitness goals, and amount of real time available for exercise. For a beginner, an exercise session may be only 10–15 minutes, but when performed 3–4 times per week, it results in 30–60 minutes of weekly exercise. Though this may not initially seem like much

time, it is the beginning of a fitness regimen and as fitness improves, the amount of time spent exercising can be increased. A minimal level of fitness can be maintained with as little as 30 minutes of exercise, 3–4 times per week. Realistically determining the amount of time you have to exercise means evaluating your busy life. When you make exercise a priority, you are more likely to find time for it.

Type

Personal interest, goals, and availability help determine the type of exercise: if you choose exercise you enjoy, you are more likely to stay committed to an exercise program. If your goal is to lose weight and body fat, a less intense cardiorespiratory program of longer duration will be more effective than a short-duration, high-intensity exercise. A high-intensity, short-duration exercise session will improve cardiorespiratory endurance, but will burn less body fat. For example, for a beginning exerciser interested in weight loss, swimming may not be intense enough to generate loss of body fat. Though swimming can improve cardiorespiratory fitness and flexibility, it may not be an optimal choice for weight loss.

For most men, muscle size can be improved with strength training. Some women are concerned that weight training will cause excessive muscular development, a body image some women consider undesirable. However, women typically cannot increase muscle size the same way as men, because compared to men, women have very little **testosterone**, the male hormone required in developing muscle size. Men naturally have more testosterone, larger bodies, and larger muscles, even without weight training.

Key Term

Testosterone: Male sex hormone.

Challenge Question: Name and describe the four components of the FITT principle of exercise.

Wanda's Story
Building Exercise into Life

At the age of thirty, Wanda was grateful for the many successes she had worked hard to achieve. She was a college graduate and worked as an elementary school teacher, a job she loved. She was economically self-sufficient and relatively happy in her life.

Recently, her doctor informed her that she needed to lose weight to reduce the complications of progressive obesity, including both cholesterol and triglyceride levels that were too high. Wanda had never been thin, but in high school she was active in sports, and considered fit by most standards. She also came from a family where no one was thin. She was concerned because both of her parents were obese and had recently been diagnosed with cardiovascular diseases. Wanda had gained weight in college and now could not seem to find time to exercise. She thought

often about exercise and how good she felt when she was more active, but now, when she got home from work she was too tired to exercise, and getting up early was difficult for her.

The visit with her doctor was a wake-up call. When he used the term "progressive obesity," she was shocked to realize he was referring to her. Wanda knew that she was a little overweight, but did not think of herself as obese. Yet according to the BMI table her doctor showed her, she was indeed in the obese range. That evening, Wanda decided to walk around her neighborhood before dinner. The amount of huffing and puffing this required surprised her, and she realized she was definitely out of shape. She resolved to try to walk briskly for at least 20–30 minutes, 3–4 times per week. She reasoned that she could certainly find the time to walk for 30 minutes, but was surprised by all of the excuses she seemed to come up

with when she got home from work. So she decided to take her exercise clothes with her, change before she left her teaching job, and stop at a park on the way home to do her walk. This plan seemed to work much better for Wanda.

After a month, Wanda had walked almost every day after work. It was becoming easier for her, and she was walking faster. Although she did not notice any weight loss, she realized she was finding the walks more enjoyable. She read in a fitness magazine that combining exercise with some dietary changes was the best way to improve fitness and lose weight, so she started taking her lunch to school instead of eating in the cafeteria. After another month, she noticed some weight loss, as well. Other teachers at her school were also noticing, giving her a sense of accomplishment and pride and helping motivate her. Two of her teacher friends became

inspired by the changes they saw in Wanda, and asked if they could join her on her walk after school. Soon, Wanda was leading five of her colleagues on a daily walk, and they were bringing food from home to share at lunch so they could avoid the cafeteria's higher-calorie options.

At her next doctor visit, Wanda was pleased to find that not only had her weight dropped a few pounds, but both her cholesterol and triglyceride levels had dropped, as well. She had more energy, was sleeping better, and was wearing smaller clothes. But for Wanda, the best part was how much she enjoyed her daily walks with her friends. The after-school walking group was now up to ten people, and they had all made so much progress that they decided to train for the 3-day, 60-mile walk for breast cancer. ∎

Warming Up and Cooling Down

Warming up prior to exercise involves elevating heart rate and respiration and increasing circulation in preparation for exercise, and is accomplished when the body begins to sweat lightly. For most people, a warm-up occurs after ten minutes on the treadmill prior to a workout with weights, or a ten-minute walk before starting a run. Because a warm-up helps the body become more flexible and less prone to injury, it is especially important for a beginning exerciser. During a warm-up, blood is circulated to muscles that will be used during exercise, and without a warm-up, muscles may not have enough oxygen to perform efficiently and will fatigue more quickly.

Cooling down allows the body to recover and begin to return to a resting state. It is important especially after strenuous exercise of high intensity and long duration. For example, walking after a hard run helps slow respiration and heart rate, and allows the circulatory changes that occurred with exercise, in which more blood is needed in the muscles, to return to normal.

Circuit Training and Cross Training

Circuit training is a type of exercise that incorporates both weight training and cardiorespiratory fitness. This involves alternating a weight machine, an isotonic workout, with a cardiorespiratory machine such as a stationary bicycle, an isokinetic workout. A typical circuit includes 12–15 weight machines opposite 12–15 stationary cycles. To complete a circuit, an individual moves alternately between a weight machine and a cardiorespiratory machine, spending a specific amount of time on each piece of equipment. Some circuit laboratories use a recorded voice command to designate the time interval on each piece of equipment, and most circuit laboratories have at least two complete circuits with slightly different weight machines. A typical interval is 30 seconds on each exercise station, with a 15-second interval to change exercise stations. Thirty seconds allows for at least 15 repetitions on a weight machine, and 30 seconds of cardiorespiratory workout keeps heart rate up. As fitness levels increase, individuals can progress to completing two or more circuits, as well as increasing weight on the weight machines and adjusting the cycle to require more effort.

FIGURE 8-4. Circuit lab at San Diego City College.

Cross training simply means alternating between different types of exercise. The best example of cross training is the training required for a triathlon, because it involves three very different training efforts: swimming, cycling, and running. Individuals with overuse injuries who want to maintain fitness while the injury heals may also employ cross training. For example, a runner or walker may develop shin splints, a painful condition resulting from an inflammation of the muscles on front of the lower leg. This individual should rest from running or walking, but may be able to cross train in swimming or cycling to maintain cardiorespiratory fitness.

Mind/Body Exercise

Mind/body exercise refers to the link between psychological health and physical health. Although most exercise is useful in managing stress, some types of exercise seem particularly effective. The mind/body connection is also important for athletes to learn how to concentrate and focus during competition, sometimes under extreme pressure. Exercises that are considered mind/body emphasize concentration, breathing, and focus.

Yoga

Yoga is an exercise that requires strength, flexibility, and breath control. It involves concentration and emphasizes being in the moment, blocking out all other thoughts and holding positions with correct body alignment. People who practice yoga are able to manage stress by focusing on their breath and blocking out extraneous thoughts, sometimes called **mindfulness**. There are varieties of yoga, such as Ashtanga, that emphasize body alignment, breathing, and movement, wherein positions are held requiring **isometric** strength. Bikram yoga is performed in a heated

room, and yoga poses flow in a faster sequence. Bikram is a more aerobic, cleansing yoga workout, in which a more intense yoga exercise combined with the heated room causes the practitioner to breathe heavily and perspire profusely. Hatha yoga is a more fundamental form that teaches basic yoga poses with emphasis on breathing and mindfulness. Yoga is an exercise to do independently or as a supplement to other exercises, and because it emphasizes flexibility and isometric strength, it is a good injury prevention exercise.

> **Key Term**
>
> **Mindfulness**: The ability to concentrate on the breath and movement while excluding any extraneous thoughts.

Pilates

Pilates is similar to yoga, involving flexibility, strength, and breath control. Beginning Pilates is done primarily on a mat on the floor, emphasizing concentration and a series of core body poses that strengthen the muscles of the torso and improve spinal alignment. These exercises are influenced by both aerobic exercise and yoga, and practitioners believe that the central aim of Pilates is a fusion of mind and body in order that the body will move with strength, fluidity, and balance. Movement in Pilates is usually continuous, emphasizing breathing to increase the intake of oxygen during exercise. Pilates can also be done with special equipment that allows for more advanced positions that may not be possible on a mat.

Tai Chi

Tai chi is considered a soft martial art. It involves positions that resemble martial arts, but the exercise is done in a series of slow rather than explosive movements. It requires memorizing various positions that are done in a sequence with one movement flowing into the next, so that it looks like one continuous movement. There are many forms of tai chi of varying lengths, with some involving a sequence of over one hundred different positions. It requires concentration to ensure that the sequence is followed. The focus on breathing helps make tai chi a relaxing experience for practitioners.

Challenge Question: Identify some mind/body exercises and describe why they are considered mind/body.

Drugs and Supplements

It is possible that drugs and supplements may enhance human performance, and there are many rumors about athletes who have used a variety of performance-enhancing drugs. Athletes who use drugs or supplements are seeking advantage in sports in which even a slight advantage can make a difference in performance and results. However, use of any of these substances is not without health risks. The typical recreational athlete is less likely to use performance-enhancing drugs such as steroids or human growth hormone, but is more likely to use supplements such as creatine or extra protein, with the expectation that strength and performance will improve.

Image of Health

Drugs and Sports

Marion Jones. The five-time track-and-field Olympic medalist pleaded guilty in 2007 to taking performance-enhancing drugs during the 2000 Olympic Games. Her medals were taken away, her track and field records expunged as if they never existed, and she spent six months in prison for lying to a Federal agent about her drug use.

Floyd Landis. Landis won the Tour de France cycling title in 2006, amid allegations of using performance-enhancing drugs. In 2010, Landis finally admitted to using drugs during the 2006 Tour de France, and accused several other professional cyclists of also using drugs.

Steroids, Human Growth Hormone, and Creatine

Steroids and Human Growth Hormone (HGH) are used by bodybuilders of both genders to increase muscle size more quickly. Steroids are artificial testosterone, typically injected into the blood. In men, long-term use causes testicular atrophy, while in women, steroids cause the advent of some male secondary sex characteristics, such as a deep voice and facial and body hair. Unless a woman takes steroids (artificial testosterone) or HGH (artificial human growth hormone), she will be unable to build muscle like a man. Human Growth Hormone (HGH) is naturally made by the pituitary gland and aids the growth and development of children. After childhood, smaller amounts of HGH are released by the pituitary gland, and

by age thirty, very little HGH is released. Synthetic HGH is injected by some bodybuilders, professional athletes, and individuals who think it will delay aging, and proponents of HGH believe it improves performance and increases muscle size and strength. Steroids and HGH are banned by the World and US Anti-Doping Agency, the Olympic Committee, and most professional and amateur sports leagues. In 2004, the Anabolic Steroid Control Act became federal law, and in 2005, androstenedione, commonly called andro, and seventeen other steroids were made unavailable without a prescription.[14]

A substance found in all skeletal muscles, creatine occurs naturally in foods, especially animal protein, and is essential for the energy production required for muscles to perform. Because more creatine is needed for muscle contractions, creatine levels are elevated with exercise; therefore, non-active individuals will naturally have lower levels of creatine in their blood. Artificial creatine or creatine monohydrate is endorsed by many bodybuilders, who believe it will enhance muscular development. The only negative side effect appears to be dehydration if adequate water is not increased when synthetic creatine is ingested.

Protein Supplements

The average American diet typically includes too much protein. Most individuals need 40–60 grams of protein per day, easily obtained from food, and many people consume well over that amount. Coaches and personal trainers often recommend protein supplements to individuals who are trying to build muscle: building muscle through weight training involves increasing the amount of weight and number of repetitions, until the muscle is completely fatigued on the last repetition. This causes damage to muscle filaments, and rebuilding muscle filaments requires protein. As muscle filaments are damaged and rebuilt, the muscle becomes larger and stronger.

Proponents of protein supplements believe that in order to rebuild damaged muscle filaments, extra protein is needed. These individuals encourage a supplement of one-half to three-quarter grams of protein for each pound of body weight. A 180-pound male typically needs 90 to 135 grams of protein per day, an amount that could be easily obtained from food. However, bodybuilders will often ingest one gram of protein or more for each pound of body weight, or 180 grams of protein or more for a male who weighs 180 pounds. Unfortunately, taking protein supplements or eating excessive amounts of high-protein foods is not without risk.

There are potential health complications from excess protein. It can cause damage to kidneys, reduce calcium in bones, produce an inflammatory response that can clog arteries, and increases the risk of certain cancers. In addition, there are many extra calories in protein supplements. A protein supplement with 100 grams of protein per serving may total 1,000 calories when combined with the other ingredients in the supplement. Few individuals, even strenuous exercisers, can afford to consume 1,000 extra calories without weight gain.[15]

Table 8-1. Protein Requirements of Athletes[16]

TYPE OF ATHLETE	DAILY PROTEIN REQUIREMENTS PER POUND OF BODY WEIGHT
Endurance athlete	.55–.64 grams
Strength and power athlete	.64–.90 grams
Athlete on fat loss program	.72–.90 grams
Athlete on weight gain program	.81–.90 grams (1 gram/lb is widely accepted)

Stimulants

A variety of stimulants have also been used to enhance athletic performance. In the 1980s, at least one professional baseball player used cocaine, believing it improved his abilities. For track athletes and swimmers for whom fractions of seconds can make the difference between first or second place, caffeine has been shown to provide a boost; therefore, high levels of caffeine are now banned by the NCAA due to performance-enhancing effects.[17]

Over time, as equipment, training, and nutrition have improved, athletic performance has also improved. While improvements in equipment, training, and nutrition provide legitimate means of success, the use of stimulants and drugs lacks legitimacy and safety. And because very little research is available, potential damage to health is unknown.

Injury Prevention

Unfortunately, injuries are common among both athletes and recreational exercisers. Although it is impossible to eliminate all injuries, there are several precautions that can minimize injury risk.

Overtraining

The highly motivated new exerciser is likely to attempt to progress too quickly, creating the potential for injury. When people begin noticing the benefits of exercise, they commonly increase the amount and intensity of exercise, with the goal of even faster improvement. However, trying to progress in your exercise routine too quickly may not lead to faster improvement, and can possibly lead to injury. It takes time for the human body to adapt to the stress of exercise, and the amount of time required to adapt is different for everyone, so it is important to be sensible about exercise progression.

Generally, younger people can progress more quickly than older people, but there are other variables to consider, as well: body composition, obesity, anatomical configuration, medical health issues, and chronic diseases. A healthy young person can push himself in an exercise program and improve physical fitness more quickly, while a middle-aged, slightly overweight diabetic individual will need to progress more slowly. Unfortunately for many who are older and out of shape, the prospect of exercise to improve personal fitness seems impossible. However, attempts to improve fitness at any age will almost always have positive results, and will generally make the person feel better. It is not realistic to compare your fitness or exercise progression with another person and expect similar results; it is important to establish a program that works for you. It may initially be slower, with little intensity and less frequency, but if the program works for you, it will lead to improved physical fitness with minimal risk of injury.

Heat and Cold

Exercising in extreme temperatures requires special preparation. If you are running, walking, or cycling in hot weather, it is important to wear clothing that is lightweight, light in color, ideally made from synthetic fabric that will wick moisture from the skin and transfer it to the clothing, where it will evaporate. Sweat-soaked clothing traps heat and can chafe skin, making hot-weather exercise even more uncomfortable. It is important to

hydrate before, during, and after any exercise session, but especially if the weather is hot. Becoming overheated and dehydrated can cause heat stroke or **hyperthermia**, wherein core body temperature may rise to more than 104 degrees, a level that can be fatal.

Precaution should also be taken when exercising in cold weather. For outdoor exercise when the temperature is below freezing, it is important to dress in layers that you can adjust as you become warmer. Because much body heat is lost through the head, it should always be covered in cold weather, and since fingers and toes are likely to get cold fastest, gloves and warm socks should be worn. If it is windy, it will be even colder because of wind chill: a 32-degree day can easily drop to 18–20 degrees with a wind. Every winter, there are cases of exercise-related **frostbite**, especially to the nose, fingers, and toes. A windbreaker jacket will help to insulate you, and a scarf or bandana should be worn so that it can be pulled up over the mouth and nose. Another risk of cold weather exercise is **hypothermia**. This is the opposite of heat stroke, occurring when core body temperature drops below 95 degrees and the body cannot maintain its normal temperature of 98.6 degrees. Because it is often not recognized and symptoms develop slowly, hypothermia can be a very serious condition.[18]

Key Terms

Hydrate: To drink water. Proper hydration is necessary during exercise to prevent dehydration, muscle cramping, and heat stroke.

Hyperthermia (heat stroke): Elevated core body temperature when the body produces more heat than can be dissipated. A core body temperature of 104 degrees or more is considered hyperthermic.

Frost bite: Tissue damage caused by exposure to temperatures below freezing.

Hypothermia: Core body temperature drops to 95 degrees or more as a result of exposure to cold temperatures.

Warming Up and Cooling Down

Warming up prior to exercise is a way to get the body ready for exercise. Regardless of the activity, warming up is a way to prepare the body for greater intensity, and should therefore involve less strenuous effort than the actual exercise. The cool down is a less strenuous effort, allowing the body to recover from a more intense workout. For example, if your primary exercise is walking, warm up by walking slowly for 5–10 minutes, then walk faster for 20–30 minutes, and finish with a cool down of 5–10 minutes of slower walking or some stretching exercises. Warming up and cooling down are effective ways to help the body prepare for and recover from exercise.

Rest and Recovery

Regardless of the type of fitness program you have devised for yourself, it is important to consider how much rest and recovery you need. Younger individuals need less rest and recovery than those who are older, but at any age, the human body needs time to recover after exercise. A beginning exerciser will generally work out every other day, using the non-exercise day for rest and recovery. As fitness improves, many people exercise almost every day, taking one or two days off from more intense exercise each week. The intensity, duration, and even type of the exercise session vary each day, and the days with less intense workouts are the rest and recovery days. Knowing when you need to rest requires that you pay attention to how your body feels. For example, if you are walking or running and have increased the distance, notice if you have any new aches and pains, or if you feel more tired than usual.

Although it is normal to feel a little tired after an exercise session, it is not normal to feel exhausted. If you feel knee or joint pain while exercising, it may be a sign that your body needs more recovery time, or that you need different footwear or a change in exercise terrain. A common classification of sports injuries is the overuse injury. It starts with a minor pain in the foot, knee, hip, elbow, or shoulder, and is usually caused by the repetitive motion of exercise. Continuing to exercise through the pain may cause a progressive injury that can become quite serious, resulting in a chronic injury that becomes troublesome in all future exercise. It is important to rest and let your body recover when you feel pain while exercising, before reaching the point of overuse. Pain that does not resolve after rest may indicate a more serious injury that can't be alleviated by rest alone. If this occurs, it may be time to seek a medical opinion.

Image of Health in Depth

Who to See for an Exercise Injury

Orthopedist. A medical doctor who specializes in the prevention or correction of injuries to the skeletal system and associated muscles, joints, and ligaments.

Podiatrist. A medical doctor who specializes in the diagnosis, treatment, and prevention of injuries or diseases of the human foot.

Chiropractor. A practitioner who treats injuries to the spine and neck by manipulation of the spine.

Massage Therapist. A practitioner trained in the manipulation of soft body tissues for therapeutic purposes.

RICE

The most common practice for treating an exercise-related injury is RICE, an acronym for *rest, ice, compression, elevation.* The first step in treating an injury is to *rest* from exercise. Next, *ice* is applied to the sore or injured area. Securing the ice in a small towel and holding it firmly in place with a flexible bandage around both ice and towel causes *compression. Elevation* involves keeping the injured area elevated for at least twenty minutes. Because ice reduces swelling and increases blood flow, icing an injury promotes healing for soft tissue injuries. Over-the-counter anti-inflammatory analgesics such as aspirin or ibuprofen may also be helpful. Acetaminophen is a good pain reliever, but it is not an anti-inflammatory drug.

Hydration and Sports Drinks

The human body is between 50–60 percent water, and maintaining this volume is essential for good cell metabolism. Dehydration occurs continually, even without exercise, and if water volume drops, metabolic changes cause the heart and other systems of the body to work much harder. The sweat produced during exercise is the body's attempt to cool itself by releasing fluid through the skin, creating a cooling effect when air hits moisture on the skin. Human sweat is composed primarily of water, salt, and minerals, but can include other compounds depending on the diet and health of the exerciser. A person taking medication, using drugs, or drinking alcohol will have trace amounts of these substances in sweat, because all are eventually circulated in the blood and will affect the hydration balance in the body. It is important to drink water before, during, and after exercise, especially in hot weather.

There are a variety of sports drinks on the market. Most include or are mixed with water, and the primary component is simple carbohydrates (sugar), since they provide quick fuel during exercise. One of the most well-known sports drinks is Gatorade, originally developed for the University of Florida football team in 1965. It consists primarily of water, sugar, salts, and minerals, and was the first widely used hydration drink promoting electrolyte balance. **Electrolytes** are body salts and minerals that help regulate hydration in the body and are important for nerve and muscle function. Some hydration drinks also include a small amount of protein, since research shows that a 4:1 carbohydrate:protein ratio improves muscle recovery after exercise. The protein and carbohydrate combination seems to facilitate the release of insulin that helps skeletal muscles absorb glucose.[19] Exercise and recovery drink products are intended primarily for endurance athletes who are exercising for an hour or more each session. If you are a beginning exerciser with a total exercise time of thirty minutes to an hour, hydrating with water is sufficient to keep your body adequately hydrated.

Key Term

Electrolytes: Body salts and minerals that help regulate hydration in the body and are important for nerve and muscle function.

Image of Health

The Risk of Sweating for Weigh Loss

There are some individuals who exercise in sealed latex or rubber-coated clothing to purposely sweat with the intention to lose weight. This technique will cause temporary weight loss due to water loss from dehydration, and is not permanent. Trapping body heat in clothing while exercising raises core body temperature to dangerous levels and may cause heat stroke.

Staying Injury Free

Most lifelong exercisers have experienced an exercise-related injury. Although it is impossible to eliminate the incidence of all injuries, there are a number of choices you can make to reduce the frequency and severity of sports-related injuries.

Choose good footwear that is appropriate for the activity. If you are starting a running or walking program, there are shoes specifically designed to provide good arch support, heel stability, and flexibility that allows you to push off in a forward motion. These shoes are very different from court shoes for tennis or basketball, which are heavier, less flexible, and designed for both forward and lateral mobility. Running long distances in your basketball or tennis shoes causes a heavy foot plant, makes it difficult for you to push off and have a smooth stride, and can lead to shin splints or even a tibial stress fracture.

Take a class or get instruction from an expert who can teach you the fundamentals of your new exercise. Learning how to do something correctly from the beginning can eliminate potential injuries and make the experience more enjoyable. If you are trying a new sport such as tennis or golf, instruction is essential to learn the fundamental skills.

Instruction can be helpful, even for walking and running. Everyone has a different walking and running stride that depends primarily on length of legs, flexibility, and anatomical width of the pelvis. While you are running or walking, see if you can find a stride that is so smooth you can't hear your foot plant for each step. Ideally, you will neither over-stride nor under-stride. Over-striding causes you to land jarringly on your heel and can cause knee and groin pain. Under-striding, in which shorter steps are taken, causes a flat foot plant, a gait that is not smooth, and can cause knee and arch pain. The goal is to smoothly roll from heel to toe and push off with each foot plant.

Paying attention to anything that causes you discomfort can prevent some injuries. A slight knee pain will progress to a greater knee pain that can stop your exercise program. A hot spot in your shoe while walking or running is the first sign of a blister, which can also stop you from exercising. Knee pain can sometimes be alleviated by changing footwear, using **orthotics**, changing your stride, or by additional strengthening exercises. A problem with chronic blisters can usually be solved by buying socks that are smooth and absorbent, and by carefully putting your socks on to eliminate any wrinkles.

Changing your exercise routine can help an overuse injury heal and still allow some exercise benefit. If you are

primarily a runner or walker and suffer from chronic knee pain, you might try cycling or swimming. Either exercise will keep cardiorespiratory fitness levels high, and they are both easier on your body. Swimming is especially good for injury rehabilitation, but in order to really derive cardiorespiratory benefits, you must be fairly skilled at swimming so that you can keep moving for the same amount of time and at the same intensity that you normally run or walk.

Key Term

Orthotics: Inserts for shoes to provide arch support and stability.

Challenge Question: Describe some ways to reduce exercise-related injuries.

Image of Health in Depth

Healthy Feet

Many exercise-related injuries involve problems with feet. When you begin an exercise program and select appropriate footwear, some simple foot care can make all the difference in keeping you injury free. The following are guidelines for healthy feet:

1. Make sure your socks fit. They should fit snugly on your feet, but not so snugly that your toes curl under. You should be able to easily wiggle your toes inside socks and shoes.

2. Lace your shoes tightly enough so that your feet don't move, but not so tightly that you feel the shoe pressing on your arch. Tightly lacing the mid-foot compresses the arch, inhibits flexion, and can cause pain. You should be able to wiggle your toes, and your heel should not slip when you walk.

3. Hot spots on your feet while running or walking indicates a friction point where two surfaces are rubbing together. This is usually caused by improperly fitting socks or shoes, and an unrelieved hot spot will cause a blister. Treatment involves adjusting socks, relacing shoes, or applying an adhesive protector, such as moleskin or a "second skin" spray. Always test new shoes in training prior to a running or walking event.

4. Carefully treat blisters, as poorly treated blisters can lead to infection, including severe bacterial infections such as staphococcus or MRSA. It is usually better not to drain blisters on your feet: the fluid will diminish in a few days, and there is less risk for infection.

5. Trim toenails to avoid toenail loss. If you are wearing athletic footwear and exercising, toenails should be no longer than the end of your toe. You should have about one inch of space between the end of your toe and the inside toe of the shoe. On longer walks and runs, your toes will make contact with the end of the shoe, especially going downhill, and toenails longer than the end of your toe will bump the inside toe of the shoe. When this happens repeatedly over the course of a longer run or walk, the area of the toe underneath the cuticle will be damaged, causing your toenail to turn black, eventually falling off as a new toenail forms underneath. This is a classic runner's experience, but it is completely avoidable.

6. Athlete's foot is a highly contagious fungal infection that is easy to treat. The fungus, thriving in warm, moist environments, is common in public showers and locker rooms where floors are wet. It is important to carefully dry your feet, especially between each toe, prior to putting on shoes and socks. Drying your feet after showering will usually prevent this fungus even if you are exposed. Athlete's foot causes redness and itching, especially between toes, and can progress to visible skin damage. Athlete's foot is easily treated with an over-the-counter anti-fungal cream, but untreated athlete's foot can lead to open sores and a more serious bacterial infection.

7. Plantar fasciitis is an inflammation of the connective tissue that holds the muscles of the foot together. It is an overuse injury caused by overtraining, poor arch support, or by a hard foot plant when the feet make hard contact with the ground on each step. It is most noticeable in the morning when first getting out of bed, because it is painful to walk. The pain is generally on the bottom of the foot under the arch. Icing the injured area, using anti-inflammatory analgesic drugs, and a reduction or change in exercise will alleviate the pain.[20]

Critical Thinking Question: Describe some steps you can take to reduce the risk of exercise-related injuries.

▼

Responsibility and Accountability

Taking Responsibility for Physical Fitness

Becoming responsible for your physical fitness will have many positive outcomes, such as reduced risk of chronic disease, improved mental health, and improved body composition. If you choose not to be responsible for personal fitness, you must be accountable for the possibility of a reduced quality of life and a shortened lifespan.

Although very few adults are on a regular exercise program, even a minimal exercise program has many benefits to improve total health: it can help with weight control, stress management, and insomnia; and can provide you with more energy, a better self-image, and a greater aptitude for academic work. The challenge is to accept the responsibility to improve your level of fitness and build some exercise into your life.

Focusing on Accountability

We are all accountable for the decisions that we make. Choosing whether to exercise has consequences for how well you feel, how you sleep, how you learn, and how you protect yourself from chronic diseases. Exercise is part of self-care and an important part of total health. It is one of the things over which you have complete control, and is a way to improve your quality of life throughout your lifetime.

Summary

What It Means to Be Physically Fit

- Physical fitness is a dimension of wellness and is determined by age, gender, physical ability or disability, and amount of exercise.

- As fitness levels in the United States have declined, obesity has increased.

- National fitness levels determine work productivity, health care costs, and longevity.

- The ACSM components of fitness include cardiorespiratory fitness, muscular strength and endurance, flexibility, and body composition.

- Body composition is the ratio between muscle, bone, and essential and non-essential fats.

- Aerobic exercise improves cardorespiratory fitness.

- Exercise will improve physical, mental, and social health.

Keys to Improving Personal Wellness

- Improving fitness requires motivation, a commitment to exercise, finding an exercise you enjoy, and making time to exercise.

- The FITT principle is a good model for establishing an exercise program.

- Exercising at your target rate ensures that you will improve cardiorespiratory fitness, but will not become injured or over-fatigued.

- Circuit training incorporates both weight training and cardiorespiratory fitness.

- Cross training involves alternating between different types of exercise, such as swimming, cycling, and running.

- Mind/body exercise refers to the link between physical health and psychological health.

Drugs and Supplements

- Drugs and supplements may enhance athletic performance, but many have negative side effects.

- It is better to progress slowly in a fitness program, rather than over-train and risk illness or injury.

Injury Prevention

- Warming up before exercise and cooling down after helps make the body less prone to injury.

- It is important to drink water before, during, and after exercise.

- There are many things you can do to ensure that your feet remain healthy during exercise.

Reassessing Your Knowledge

1. Describe the current level of fitness in the United States.

2. Identify the five components of fitness established by the American College of Sports Medicine.

3. List some of the benefits of exercise.

4. Describe the components of the FITT exercise model.

5. Identify how you can prevent exercise injuries.

To answer these questions, you might choose to work in groups with your colleagues. Check your answers against the written material in the text, and reread those sections where you made errors.

258   Physical Fitness • CHAPTER 8

Image of Health

Health Assessment Toolbox

American Heart Association: Just Move
Physical Activity Program.
http://www.justmove.org/

Interactive Exercise Plan
http://www.myexerciseplan.com/

President's Council on Fitness, Sports and Nutrition
http://www.fitness.gov/

Shape Magazine Virtual Trainer
http://www.shape.com/virtualtrainer/public/index

Exploring the Internet

American College of Sports Medicine
http://www.acsm.org

American Council on Exercise
http://www.acefitness.org

American Heart Association: Just Move
http://www.justmove.org

CDC Physical Activity Information
http://www.cdc.gov/nccdphp/dnpa

Medline Plus: Exercise and Physical Fitness
http://www.nlm.nih.gov/medlineplus/
exercisephysicalfitness.html

World Health Organization (WHO): Move for Health
http://www.who.int/moveforhealth/en/

Vocabulary Challenge

Match the term in the left-hand column with its correct definition in the right-hand column.

TERM		DEFINITION
Cardiorespiratory fitness		A. Heat stroke, when core body temperature is 104 degrees or above
Body composition		B. Contracting a muscle through a range of motion under constant tension, such as in weight training
Aerobic exercise		C. Inability to sleep
Anaerobic exercise		D. To drink water
Insomnia		E. Exercise that incorporates both weight training and cardiorespiratory exercise
Circuit training		F. Fitness level of the heart and lungs
Mind/body exercise		G. Exercise that requires oxygen, such as running or fast walking
Hyperthermia		H. Exercise that links psychological health and physical health
Isotonic exercise		I. Explosive exercise such as sprinting
Hydrate		J. The ratio between fat and lean body mass

F; J; G; I; C; E; H; A; B; D

Answers

Selected References

1. Ogden, C.L., Fryar, C.D., Carroll, M.D., and Flegal, K.M. Division of Health and Nutrition Examination Surveys. Mean Body Weight, Height and Body Mass Index, United States, 1960–2002. 2007.

2. Summary Health Statistics for U.S. Adults: National Health Interview Survey, National Center for Health Statistics, Table 27. 2008.

3. Ibid.

4. Ludwig, D.S. Childhood Obesity: The Shape of Things to Come. *New England Journal of Medicine*, 357(23): 2325–2327. December 6, 2005.

5. Department of Health and Human Services. The Presidents Council on Physical Fitness and Sport, Fiftieth Anniversary, 2006.

6. John F. Kennedy Library and Museum. The Federal Government Takes On Physical Fitness, "Chicken Fat Exercise Song," 1961.

7. President's Council on Physical Fitness, AAHPERD Physical Best Tests, 1989.

8. United States Department of Health and Human Services, The Presidents Council on Fitness and Sports Charter, 2007.

9. ACSM Position Stand: The Recommended Quantity and Quality of Exercise for Developing and Maintaining Cardiorespiratory and Muscular Fitness, and Flexibility in Healthy Adults. *Medicine & Science in Sports & Exercise*, 30(6): 975–991. June, 1998.

10. Corbin, C.B., and Lindsey, R. Concepts in Physical Education with Laboratories, 8th ed. *Times Mirror*, Dubuque, IA, 1994.

11. Snijders T., Verdijk L.B., and van Loon L.J. The Impact of Sarcopenia and Exercise Training on Skeletal Muscle Satellite Cells. *Aging Research Review*, 8(4): 328–338. October, 2009.

12. Kannus, P., Parkkari, J., Koskinene, S., et al. Fall Induced Injuries and Death Among Older Adults. *JAMA*, 281: 1895–1899. 1999.

13. Centers for Disease Control, Physical Activity for Everyone, Borg Rating of Perceived Exertion Scale, 1998.

14. United States Department of Health and Human Services, U.S. Food and Drug Administration, Anabolic Steroid Control Act of 2004.

15. Berning, J.R., and Nelson-Steen, S. *Nutrition for Sport and Exercise*, Jones and Bartlett Learning, 2005.

16. Hargreaves, M., and Snow, R. Amino Acids and Endurance Exercise. *International Journal of Sport Nutrition and Exercise Metabolism*, 11: 133–145. 2001.

17. National Collegiate Athletic Association, 2009–2010 Banned Drugs, 2010.

18. Centers for Disease Control, Winter Weather Facts and Questions, 2009.

19. Niles, Eric S. et al. Carbohydrate-Protein Drink Improves Time to Exhaustion after Recovery from Endurance Exercise. *Journal of Exercise Physiologyonline*, 4(1). January, 2001.

20. American Academy of Family Physicians, Understanding Plantar Fasciiti—Diagnosis and Treatment. WebMD, downloaded July, 2010.

Image of Health

Fundamentals of Weight Management

Student Learning Outcomes

LEARNING OUTCOME	APPLYING IT TO YOUR LIFE
List several methods used to assess body composition.	Using one of these methods, calculate your percentage of body fat and evaluate if you can improve muscle mass, lose or gain weight.
Identify some contributing factors for obesity.	Identify at least two factors that might predispose you to obesity.
Identify the pros and cons of two weight management plans.	Describe a weight management plan you could maintain for a lifetime.
List and describe measures for morbid obesity.	Identify a method you would advise an obese friend to use, and state why.
Describe symptoms and characteristics of eating disorders.	Recognize the symptoms of eating disorders, and identify methods you would use to help a friend with an eating disorder.
Identify the three components of a successful lifelong weight management plan.	List steps you can take to help yourself or a friend maintain a lifelong weight management goal.

Assess Your Knowledge

1. Which of the following diseases increase as a result of the obesity epidemic.
   a. Type II diabetes

   b. Type I diabetes

   c. Chronic gastric disease

   d. General gastric disease

2. The percentage of Americans who are obese is:
   a. 20 percent

   b. 35 percent

   c. 50 percent

   d. 60 percent

3. The phrase "years of potential life lost" or YPLL refers to:
   a. A longevity estimate.

   b. A method for calculating death rates.

   c. The number of years that could have been added to life span if a healthier lifestyle had been followed.

   d. Morbidity tables developed by the Centers for Disease Control.

4. The energy balance equation is:
   a. A balance between disease and wellness.

   b. A balance between calories consumed and calories burned.

   c. A diet that improves energy.

   d. An equation that identifies the best food energy sources.

5. The number of calories that must be burned in order to lose one pound of fat is:
   a. 1,700

   b. 2,300

   c. 3,500

   d. 4,500

Answers:

1. a; 2. d; 3. c; 4. b; 5. c.

Fundamentals of Weight Management

The physical profile of America has changed dramatically during the last 50 years. We have changed from a nation of physically fit individuals to one that struggles with obesity. There are many contributions to this changing profile, but the major reason is that we are consuming too much food for the physical requirements of our daily lives.

The national concern about weight control is a phenomenon of the late twentieth century that continues today. For a variety of reasons, Americans have developed a physical profile, in which six of every ten people are obese. This alarming fact has produced an increase in chronic diseases and created the possibility that for the first time in history, children may not live as long as their parents.[1] It will be up to you to decide if you are already part of the obesity epidemic, if you will join the obesity epidemic, or if you will take charge of your weight and your health and refuse to be part of this epidemic.

Although it is difficult for many people, maintaining a healthy body weight is the result of the behaviors you practice. You are responsible for the quality and quantity of what you eat, and you are accountable for your resulting body size. It is far easier to make changes to your diet and exercise behaviors when you are young, but these changes can be accomplished at any age. In this chapter, you will learn the causes and costs of obesity, be able to assess your own body weight, understand the relationship between excess body weight and disease, and know how to manage your weight successfully. Figure 9-1 breaks down obesity by age group.

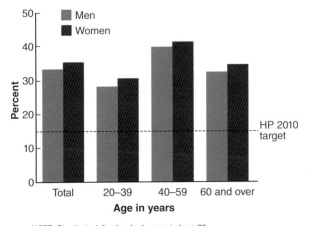

NOTE: Obesity is defined as body mass index ≥30.
SOURCE: CDC/NCHS, National Health and Nutrition Examination Survey.

FIGURE 9-1. Obesity by age group.

Measurement and Assessment of Body Composition

Before you embark on a quest to change your body size, one of the first steps is to accurately assess your current body composition. Determining body composition requires that you identify the percentage of body weight that is primarily fat and the percentage that is lean or muscle tissue. Knowing your fat-to-lean ratio is an important part of weight control, because it will help you plan how to reach your goal. Since excess body fat increases your risk of cardiovascular disease, cancers, and Type II diabetes, knowing your ratio may help motivate you to get in better shape.

The lean part of the human body includes bone, water, connective tissues, organ tissue, and teeth. The remaining mass is body fat. Body fat is further broken down into essential and nonessential fats. **Essential fats** are those that are part of nerves, heart, lungs, brain, liver, and mammary glands, and are crucial for normal body functioning. In men, essential fat makes up between 3–5 percent of body weight; in women, it makes up between 8–12 percent of body weight. **Nonessential fats** are stored body fat, the result of eating too many calories for energy needs.

An **overweight** person is one who has a total body weight, relative to height, above that recommended for the general healthy population. A person is considered **obese** if total body weight is greater than 25 percent for men and 33 percent for women, and Body Mass Index (BMI) is 30 or greater. Although often not considered a problem, being underweight also has disadvantages. **Underweight** is generally defined as having less than a 19.1 BMI for women, and less than a 20.7 BMI for men. Being underweight may be an indicator of an eating disorder, and in extreme cases can lead to cardiac arrest or other organ failure. It inhibits normal body functioning in both genders and can lead to reproductive problems in women.

Key Terms

Overweight: Having more body weight, relative to height, than is recommended for the general healthy population.

Obese: Being at least 20 percent over ideal weight for height, with a BMI greater than 25 percent for men and 33 percent for women.

Underweight: For women, having a BMI of less than 19.1; For men, having a BMI of less than 20.7.

Essential fats: Fats required by the body that must be ingested because they cannot be synthesized.

Nonessential fats: Fats that can be synthesized by the body.

There are many ways to assess body composition and each method has advantages and disadvantages. As you consider which method might be right for you, think about accuracy, availability, and cost.

The Body Mass Index

Currently, the most widely used method to determine health risks caused by weight is the **body mass index (BMI)**. It is based on the assumption that a person's body weight should be proportional to height. However, this method does not differentiate fat weight from lean weight, and can be inaccurate for people who carry a larger amount of muscle mass, people who are shorter, people who are older and losing muscle mass, and people who may be ill. The BMI is determined by dividing an individual's body weight (in kilograms) by the square of their height in meters. The National Institutes of Health (NIH) have established BMI standards to indicate a range of weights, from underweight to extreme obesity.

Key Term

*Body mass index (BMI): A measure of relative body weight, correlating highly with more direct measures of body fat, calculated by dividing total body weight in kilograms, by body height in meters squared.

---

*The Body Mass Index Table is available in the summary at the end of this chapter.

Hydrostatic Weighing

Hydrostatic weighing is considered the most accurate and also the most difficult test to conduct. It involves having the test subject sit on a scale while submerged in a tank of water. The measurement for underwater weight is compared to actual body weight, using a formula that will identify the percentage of body fat. Lean tissue has greater density than fat tissue and fat actually floats, so the more body fat one has, the greater the floating ability and lighter the weight underwater. Hydrostatic weighing is available in some fitness centers, where it is done in either a special hydrostatic tank or in a swimming pool. Its major disadvantage is that it is an inconvenient method to test large numbers of people, and requires special facilities and a trained professional.

Bio-Impedance Testing

Bio-impedance testing involves placing an electrode contact on either a foot or hand of the test subject that emits a very slight electrical pulse. This low-grade electrical pulse produces a reading that differentiates the amount of body fat from total muscle. Although it offers a rough guideline for body fat, its accuracy is affected by hydration, recent exercise, and alcohol and caffeine consumption. It is generally available in health and fitness centers and is less expensive than hydrostatic weighing. It has a fairly high standard error range, so it is not reliably accurate enough for some people.

Skin Fold Measurement Testing

Skin fold assessment involves measuring the thickness of skin folds at several body sites, then applying the results to a formula that determines body fat percentages. In fitness centers or labs where personal trainers are conducting hundreds of skin fold caliper tests, the results will closely match hydrostatic weighing. Less experienced trainers may produce less accurate results, and results can also be affected by the quality of the skin calipers. This method is easy to perform and is usually offered at low or no cost in fitness centers.

BOD POD

The BOD POD is based on the same whole-body measurement principle as hydrostatic weighing. The BOD POD is a large oval cabinet that uses a patented air displacement technology instead of water. The subject sits comfortably inside the BOD POD, while computerized pressure sensors determine the amount of air displaced by the person's body. They are available in some large universities, health clubs, and on cruise ships. This method might be more appropriate for people who have a fear of water, but it is more expensive than other methods.

http://www. bodpod.com/bodycomp

Near Infrared Interactance (NIR)

Near infrared interactance (NIR) is based on the principles of light absorption, reflectance, and near infrared spectroscopy. A probe is placed on the subject's bicep that emits infrared light. The light passes through the fat and muscle of the arm and is reflected back to the probe. The test considers the height, weight, sex, age, frame size, and activity level of the subject, as well as the density measurements obtained. The results indicate both body fat and lean tissue percentages. Although NIR is cost effective, it is not as accurate as skin fold tests.

Dual Energy X-Ray Absorptiometry (DEXA)

Dual Energy X-Ray Absorptiometry (DEXA) is a technology that uses two X-ray energies to measure body fat, muscle, and bone mineral. It takes about 12 minutes to complete, exposure to radiation is minimal and it is considered among the most accurate measurement devices. DEXA is only available in research centers, hospitals and universities.

▶**Critical Thinking Question**: What factors would you consider before determining a method to assess your personal percentage of body fat?

Metropolitan Life Insurance Company Height and Weight Chart

Less invasive methods that are easier to use, and can be used without any training, are available. Among these, the Metropolitan Life Insurance Company Height and Weight Charts and the body mass index have been used to predict morbidity and mortality risks.

Historically, a common measure for determining normal body weight was the Metropolitan Life Insurance Company Height and Weight Chart. It was developed in the 1950s by the Metropolitan Life Insurance Company to determine ideal body weights associated with the lowest mortality for height, weight, and gender. It involves measuring the height and weight of a subject and finding the corresponding height and weight on the chart. The MetLife chart gives a recommended weight range by gender; although easy to use, these charts can be inaccurate for some people. "Image of Health in Depth: Weighing In," shows how recommended weight has increased across time as the population has become more obese.

Image of Health in Depth

Weighing In

The following chart shows how recommended weights have increased over the years as the population became more obese. Note the differences in recommended weight for a 19-year-old male and female between 1971–74 and 1999–2002: a 19-year-old male could weigh 12 pounds more and a 19-year-old female 18 pounds more between 1999–2002 than between 1971–74.

GROUP	1963–65	1971–74	1999–2002
Women 20–74	138*		164*
Men 20–74	165*		190*
Men 19 years	Unavailable	159.7*	172*
Women 19 years	Unavailable	131*	149.3*
Girls 12–17	118*	154.6–162.1	130*
Boys 12–17	125*	152.8–176.9	141*
Boys 6–11	46.7–57.3	46.5–57.6	52*
Girls 6–11	46.4–58	46.5–58.3	54*

* Advance Data, Vital and Health Statistics; No. 347, October, 27, 2004. Weights are in pounds.

Waist-to-Hip Ratio

Research from Tufts University has shown that assessing waist-to-hip ratio calculations offers a more reliable factor than body mass index ratios.[2] Waist-to-hip ratio is determined by dividing your waist measurement by your hip measurement. A waist-to-hip ratio above 0.94 for men and above 0.82 for women is associated with an increased risk for disease and identifies subjects who should reduce their weight.

Total Waist Measurement

A second method is simply to measure your waist, which reveals a stronger assessment of abdominal fat. A total waist measurement of more than 40 inches for men and 35 inches for women is associated with an increased risk for disease.

As Americans continue to gain weight and reduce activity levels, the risk for some diseases and the potential risk for reduced life expectancy are increased. Now that you know how to assess your weight, perhaps you have found yourself to be a little overweight, or you may know that you are more than 20 percent above ideal weight and so are obese. Maybe now is the time to address this issue and take charge of your life again. Weight can be managed, and by the end of this chapter you will know the risks for being overweight and obese, and how to successfully manage your own weight.

Contributing Factors for Obesity

For many obese people, it is not just a simple solution to reduce calorie intake, because there are other factors involved. Obesity appears to be linked to genetics, body shape, childhood obesity, sedentary behavior, and even environmental and cultural influences. Although it is clear that the greatest majority of overweight people eat more calories than are needed, simply reducing calorie intake may not cause lifelong reduction of weight. In most cases, it requires considerable change of lifelong behaviors.

Genetics and Obesity

It might be comforting to think that obesity is caused entirely by genetics, but no such proof exists. The Human Genome project has identified more than 400 genes linked to weight, but how they interact is still a mystery. It may be that genes require a behavioral component to trigger their action. In order for genes to influence weight, they must be combined with either overeating and/or sedentary behavior. Today, studies estimate the genetic contribution to obesity ranges from 25–40 percent.[3]

Body Shape

There are three different body shape classifications: endomorphs, mesomorphs, and ectomorphs. Endomorphs have bigger bones and larger thighs and hips. They usually have a larger percentage of body fat and weight loss is often more difficult for this type. Mesomorphs have an athletic build and gain muscle easily. Most individuals with this body type have fast metabolisms and can lose weight easily. Ectomorphs have a thin, linear appearance and can also lose weight easily. However, this body type has a harder time gaining muscle mass and more body fat.

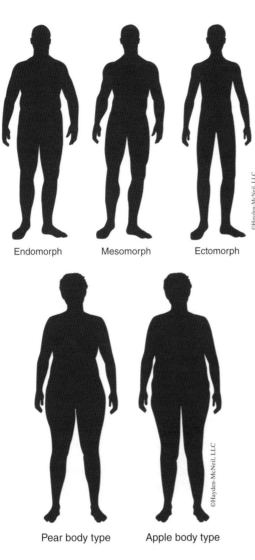

Endomorph   Mesomorph   Ectomorph

©Hayden-McNeil, LLC

Pear body type   Apple body type

©Hayden-McNeil, LLC

FIGURE 9-2. Body types.

Where you carry body fat can be an indicator of disease risk. People with larger abdomens, sometimes called the apple shape, have a higher risk for obesity-related diseases than people with larger hips, the pear shape. The apple shape (also called visceral obesity) is a predictor for cardiovascular disease, because extra fat is stored in the abdomen and is associated with a number of cardiovascular and metabolic disease risk factors. When these risk factors cluster together in an individual, this clustering is referred to as metabolic syndrome and synergistically increases the risk for cardiovascular disease. Pear-shaped individuals store more fat under the skin (adipose tissue), rather than around internal organs. This fat cluster tends to occur in the buttocks and thighs.

Childhood Obesity

Childhood obesity has reached a point today that for the first time in the history of the United States, the current generation of children are not expected to live as long as their parents.[4] The incidence of childhood obesity is so profound, with new increases predicted each year, that the children of today could have life spans shortened by as much as five years. The complications of obesity, diabetes, heart disease, kidney failure, and cancer are likely to occur in these individuals at younger ages. Since more than half of Americans are now considered overweight, being able to predict who might become overweight becomes an important public health issue. In 2002, George Bray showed that obesity in childhood and adolescence can predict obesity in adults.[5] But what predicts childhood obesity?

A good predictor of childhood obesity is parental obesity.[6] Maternal obesity in early pregnancy more than doubles a child's risk of obesity at ages 2–4 years.[7] A more recent study listed the following eight keys to childhood obesity:[8]

- Higher birth weight.

- Spending more than eight hours per week watching TV around three years old.

- Sleeping less than 10.5 hours per night when around three years old.

- Larger than normal size in early life.

- Rapid weight gain in the first year of life.

- Rapid catch-up growth between birth and two years.

- Early development of body fat in the preschool years.

- Childhood obesity by age seven if one or both parents are obese.

Other predictors of childhood obesity include parents' socioeconomic and education status, where the lower the status, the higher the weight.

Children who overeat develop more fat cells. These cells store body fat, and with more fat cells, a greater amount of fat can be stored. It has not been shown that a larger number of fat cells promotes a bigger appetite, and it is unclear whether weight loss reduces the number of fat cells.

Image of Health in Depth

The Myths of Aging and Hormone Imbalance

There are two myths regarding the cause of obesity. The first purports that obesity is simply a phenomenon of aging. The older one gets, the heavier one is. The reality is that although Americans tend to gain weight as they age, it is not part of the aging process. It is true, however, that metabolism slows down as an individual ages, and if eating habits do not also slow down, weight gain will occur. As a person ages, fewer calories are needed and portion sizes should be diminished for weight to remain stable. In addition, as people age, activity level also usually diminishes, and fewer calories are burned.

The second myth is that obesity is caused by hormone dysfunction. Hormones do play a part in the location of fat storage, especially for women. Women experience hormonal changes at puberty, during pregnancy, and at menopause. During puberty, breast development occurs and hips become wider. Although there are great hormonal changes during menopause and pregnancy, neither of these specifically causes weight gain. Rather, the weight gain that occurs is more likely caused by women eating more to fulfill cravings triggered by hormonal changes.

▶Challenge Question: Describe why body shape and body fat distribution can be a predictor for cardiovascular disease.

Sedentary Behavior

Americans worked primarily in agriculture during the early part of our history, and then in factories during the industrial revolution of the late eighteenth and early nineteenth century. By the end of the last century, the U.S. had evolved from an industrial society to a technological society, and became more sedentary. Previous societies exercised as a result of their work endeavors, and many of their daily tasks were labor intensive. Today, many labor-saving devices make living easier, but reduce the number of calories an individual burns. Almost 60 percent of all adults do not engage in any sort of vigorous leisure time physical activity, and only about 25 percent of adults exercise three times each week.[9] Men are more likely to actively participate in an exercise activity than women, but both genders exercise less as they age.[10]

Exercise is one of the easiest and cheapest ways to offset weight, even without changing eating habits. A calorie reduction plan might result in a loss of muscle tissue as well as fat tissue, whereas exercise burns primarily fat tissue and tends to maintain muscle. In addition to reducing weight, exercise strengthens the heart muscle and helps offset the risk of cardiovascular diseases. The American Cancer Society (ACS) has stated that at least thirty minutes of dedicated exercise five or more days each week cuts the overall risk of cancer.[11] Exercise has also been shown to help with recovery from cancer treatments.[12,13]

Despite the health advantages of exercise, most people fail to engage in any form of physical activity. One study has shown that 60 percent of the incidence of overweight children can be linked to excessive television watching.[14] Although a lack of physical activity may not yet have revealed itself to you in excess weight, if you don't take appropriate steps soon, you may be faced with a bigger challenge as you age. One easy way for college students to include physical activity in their lives is by enrolling in an exercise class at the campus.

Image of Health in Depth

Overweight Prevalence
(Data are for U.S. for 1999–2002)

- 64 Percent of adults age 20 years and older are overweight.

- 30 Percent of these adults age 20 years and older are obese.

Source: NHANES Data on the Prevalence of Overweight and Obesity among Adults: United States, 1999–2002.

- 15 percent of adolescents age 12–19 years are overweight.

- 15 percent of children age 6–11 years are overweight.

Source: Prevalence of Overweight among Children and Adolescents: United States, 1999–2002.

Environmental Influences

There are many factors in our daily environment that cause us to overeat more now than in the past. Many people who have busy lives find fast food readily available and low in cost. We are bombarded by advertisements for fast food, and have gradually increased portion sizes for the food we eat.

In the 1970s, Americans spent $6 billion on fast food per year. Thirty years later, that amount had increased to $120 billion! Not only is more food being eaten outside of the home, but food choices and portion sizes have changed. A standard serving of soda has increased from eight ounces to 20 ounces. A serving of French fries has increased from 3 ounces to more than 8 ounces.

In homes, food is served on platters and people help themselves. Research has shown that greater variety of food offered, the more will be eaten, even at home. Another contributor to the obesity epidemic is the success of numerous, all-you-can-eat buffet restaurants. The buffet typically charges a set price and patrons are encouraged to eat all they can. This environment certainly does not inspire portion control.

FIGURE 9-3. Notice the variety of health foods this family is enjoying.

Image of Health in Depth

Comparing Fast Food Choices
Even when eating fast food, it is possible to make informed choices, at least in terms of calories. Note the differences in the following table comparing differences in calories and other nutrients between a Double Whopper with cheese from Burger King and a 12-inch roast beef sandwich from Subway. The standard Subway roast beef sandwich does not include either cheese or mayonnaise. If cheese and mayonnaise are included, total calories for the Subway sandwich will increase to 700 calories. This is still almost 400 fewer calories less than a Double Whopper with cheese.

Choosing reduced-fat or nonfat items has not helped the obesity crisis, nor have sugar-free choices reduced weight. When the fat or sugar is removed from a food, a way must be found to replace either the flavor or the texture of the food. Often, nonfat or reduced-fat foods have similar calories to their full-fat counterparts. If a product is reduced or nonfat, the uneducated consumer may assume that more can be eaten even though calories are not reduced.

NUTRIENTS	TYPICAL FAST FOOD DOUBLE BURGER WITH CHEESE (399 GRAMS)	HEALTHY ALTERNATIVE ROAST BEEF SANDWICH WITH STANDARD VEGETABLES (446 GRAMS)
Total calories	1070	580
Fat calories	630	90
Total fat	70 grams	10 grams
Saturated fat	70 grams	4 grams
Cholesterol	185 grams	30 grams
Sodium	1500 grams	1840 grams
Carbohydrate	53 grams	90 grams
Fiber	4 grams	8 grams
Protein	57 grams	38 grams

Image of Health in Depth

Fat-Free vs. Regular Calorie Comparison

It is possible to lose weight by eating fewer calories and/or by increasing physical activity. Reducing the amount of total fat and saturated fat is one way to limit overall calorie intake. However, eating fat-free or reduced-fat foods isn't always the answer to weight loss. A fat-free food is not necessarily lower in calories; in fact, it could be higher in calories because of added sugars. Calories may also be added when you eat more of the reduced-fat or fat-free food than you would normally eat. The following list of foods and their reduced-fat varieties demonstrates that just because a product is fat-free, it doesn't mean that it is calorie-free.

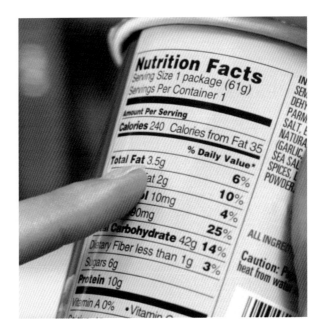

FAT-FREE OR REDUCED FAT	Calories	REGULAR	Calories
Reduced-fat peanut butter, 2 T	187	Regular peanut butter, 2 T	191
Reduced-fat chocolate chip cookies, 3 cookies (30 g)	118	Regular chocolate chip cookies, 3 cookies (30 g)	142
Fat-free fig cookies, 2 cookies (30 g)	102	Regular fig cookies, 2 cookies (30 g)	111
Nonfat vanilla frozen yogurt (<1 percent fat), 1/2 cup	100	Regular whole milk vanilla frozen yogurt (3–4 percent fat), 1/2 cup	104
Light vanilla ice cream (7 percent fat), 1/2 cup	111	Regular vanilla ice cream (11 percent fat), 1/2 cup	133
Fat-free caramel topping, 2 T	103	Caramel topping, homemade with butter, 2 T	103
Low-fat granola cereal, approx. 1/2 cup (55 g)	213	Regular granola cereal, approx. 1/2 cup (55 g)	257
Low-fat blueberry muffin, 1 small (2 1/2 inch)	131	Regular blueberry muffin, 1 small (2 1/2 inch)	138
Baked tortilla chips, 1 oz.	113	Regular tortilla chips, 1 oz.	143
Low-fat cereal bar, 1 bar (1.3 oz.)	130	Regular cereal bar, 1 bar (1.3 oz.)	140

Source: National Heart, Lung, and Blood Institute.

Nutrient data taken from Nutrient Data System for Research, Nutrition Coordinating Center, University of Minnesota.

Economic and Cultural Factors

In America today, there are cultural and economic factors that influence food choices. For a family who is struggling economically, food choices center on quantity and low cost. There may be less concern about healthful eating, and more concern about what tastes good and does not cost much. Fast food is often viewed as a lifesaver for the economically disadvantaged. Families in this group have little time for shopping and food preparation and purchasing low-cost fast foods provides a solution to this problem. As a result, children in families with little money to spend on food learn eating behaviors that exclude fruits and vegetables and emphasize meals heavy in saturated fat, sugar, sodium, and protein. Even economically advantaged children learn at an early age that hamburgers and pizza provide much more eating enjoyment than fruits and vegetables.

College students today often pay for a high-priced education and living costs through low-paying jobs and inadequate student loans. Finding time pressures include attending classes, going to work, and finding time to study and socialize. Time to shop and prepare wholesome food is often difficult, resulting in visits to local fast-food restaurants.

There are also cultural influences that affect eating behavior. Children learn to appreciate certain foods, and these foods become the foundation for lifelong food choices. As adults, we like certain foods because we have always eaten them, and some of these foods have a cultural or ethnic identity. Consider foods associated with the Mediterranean region of the world. Within this area, people eat more fruits, vegetables, nuts, and primarily use non-saturated oils. This diet allows for better weight control management, so there is less obesity in the Mediterranean region and a lower incidence of heart disease compared to the United States.[15] Compare these dietary choices with those of Mexico, where the staple diet includes beans cooked in lard, white rice, animal-based protein choices, and fewer vegetables and fruits. Weight control is more difficult for people eating a traditional Mexican diet.[16]

Some favorite foods can also be considered comfort foods, reminding people of positive feelings experienced as children, or they are foods that were used as rewards for good behavior. As adults, people restore these good feelings through food that provides a sense of comfort. This can lead to an over-consumption of ice cream "rewards" or unhealthy portions of other calorie-laden comfort foods.

The Psychology of Adult Obesity

For obese individuals, psychological health may depend on the level of acceptance or dissatisfaction with personal obesity. For a person who has spent a lifetime as an obese child, adolescent, and adult, the image of being lean may be difficult to imagine. By the time adulthood is reached, there have probably been several attempts at weight loss by individual effort or medical intervention. As a result, the perception of failure regarding weight loss is fairly high. There may be a profound feeling that successful, permanent weight loss is an unrealistic or impossible goal. However, most obese individuals, regardless of weight loss history, will intellectually accept that to lose weight would be a positive accomplishment and good for personal health. These individuals can successfully lose weight, but must accept that permanent weight loss requires permanent behavior modification regarding diet and exercise.

Health Risks of Obesity

There are many health-related risks associated with obesity. In addition to the major health issues linked with obesity described below, excess body fat, particularly in the abdominal area, may also cause sleep apnea, asthma, and complications during pregnancy.

Diabetes

Diabetes is the sixth leading cause of death in the United States, and the incidence is increasing among college aged individuals. It is a disease in which the body either does not produce (Type I diabetes) or properly use the hormone insulin (Type II diabetes) required to metabolize glucose (sugar). Glucose from food stays in the blood, resulting in elevated blood sugar. This affects an estimated 25.8 million people in the United States and another 7 million not yet diagnosed, with a total economic cost of over $130 billion yearly.[17] A major risk factor for Type II diabetes is excess weight. Previously, this disease was only seen in obese people over forty, but with the onset of obesity in children and adolescents, the disease is now being diagnosed at earlier ages.

FIGURE 9-4. Testing blood sugar levels.

High Blood Pressure

High blood pressure is defined as pressure greater than 140/90. Although not all obese individuals have high blood pressure, even moderate weight gain is almost invariably associated with an increase in blood pressure. Conversely, individuals who lose weight show a reduction in blood pressure. Chronic high blood pressure is a disease that causes premature death independently and is a leading risk factor for cardiovascular disease.

Cardiovascular Disease

As early as 1983, long-term studies identified obesity as an independent risk factor for cardiovascular disease, and the Framingham Heart Study showed this risk was even greater for women.[18]

According to the American Heart Association, obesity raises the risk for high blood **cholesterol** and triglyceride levels. In addition, obesity lowers **high-density lipoprotein** (HDL), the good cholesterol, further increasing risk for cardiovascular disease.

Losing body fat by diet and exercise will potentially change overall blood fat profile, reducing overall cholesterol values, raising HDL, and lowering LDL.

Key Terms

Cholesterol: A white crystalline substance found in animal tissue and some foods. A high blood cholesterol level can contribute to coronary artery disease.

High density lipoproteins: A blood constituent involved in the transport of cholesterol and associated with a decreased risk of atherosclerosis and heart attack.

Cancer

In 2002, about 41,000 new cancer cases in the U.S. were linked to obesity,[19] and being overweight reduced cancer recovery rates. In that same year, 14 percent of cancer-related deaths from cancer in men and 20 percent in women were linked with excessive weight and obesity.[20]

▶**Challenge Question**: Describe some of the health consequences for individuals who are obese.

Economic Impact of Obesity

In addition to health risks, rising obesity has a huge financial impact in terms of lost worker productivity, higher insurance rates, and a shorter life span.

Lost Worker Productivity

Overweight people tend to miss more days of work, require more medical care in their lifetimes, and die sooner than individuals of normal weight. These costs affect everyone in the workplace, including increased work effort for those who do not miss work, and increased healthcare costs for employers that eventually are passed on to employees. Employee sick days ultimately increase the cost of the end product for consumers.

Higher Insurance Rates

Medical insurance is structured the same way as car insurance and life insurance, with premiums, deductibles, and claims. The healthy pay for the sick (the good drivers pay for the poor drivers), and the living pay for the dead. As the number of obese people in the U.S. increases, it is inevitable that health care costs will increase. Since obesity is mostly preventable, this cost is also preventable.

▶ **Critical Thinking Question**: Why does health insurance increase as obesity increases?

Shortened Life Span: Lost Opportunities

Finally, the cost of obesity can be measured in **years of potential life lost (YPLL)**. If you die before you achieve your full life expectancy, the difference is known as years of potential life lost. The biggest impact will be the emotional toll on survivors, some of whom will miss work and others who will become seriously debilitated because of grief. But there is another economic impact, as well. National budgets are based on expected numbers of productive workers in the workforce. If that number drops, tax collections are reduced, end product is reduced, and there are fewer people to buy products. The result is higher costs for all.

Key Term

Years of potential life lost (YPLL): Estimates the average time a person would have lived, had they not died prematurely.

Weight Management Principles

Weight management for adults is a personal, continuous endeavor, and decisions about how much you will weigh are entirely up to you. You may choose to eat low-calorie foods and regulate your meals with smaller portions. You may choose to incorporate some exercise, even walking, into your daily life or take the stairs instead of the elevator. Accepting responsibility for personal weight management by making informed choices can lead to personal accountability. In the following section, you will find information that will help you to be more accountable for your own body size and weight.

STATE OF CALIFORNIA
DEPARTMENT OF HEALTH SERVICES

CERTIFICATE OF DEATH
STATE OF CALIFORNIA – DEPARTMENT OF PUBLIC HEALTH

	NAME OF DECEASED – FIRST NAME	MIDDLE NAME	LAST NAME	DATE OF DEATH
DECEDENT'S PERSONAL DATA	John	Peter	Doe	01/03/2010
	SEX: male	COLOR OR RACE: cauc.	MARITAL STATUS: divorced	DATE OF BIRTH: 06/26/1967 — AGE: 42
	USUAL OCCUPATION: contractor	KIND OF BUSINESS OR INDUSTRY: building	BIRTHPLACE: Oklahoma	CITIZEN OF WHAT COUNTRY: United States

CAUSE OF DEATH	IMMEDIATE CAUSE → (Final disease or condition resulting in death)	(A)	Cardiovascular disease
	Sequentially, list conditions, if any, leading to cause on line a. Enter UNDERLYING CAUSE (disease or injury that initiated the events resulting in death) LAST	(B)	Obesity
		(C)	
		(D)	

Understanding Your Metabolism

Metabolism is essentially how your body converts fuel into energy. This process is continuous, and a low level of metabolic activity is required even during sleep. This low level metabolic activity is referred to as **resting metabolic rate**. Metabolism is set at birth by the genetic contribution of parents. As you grow and develop, each individual may develop a different metabolic rate. There can also be great variances in metabolic rates among siblings. Just as you may have inherited obvious physical characteristics from one parent more than the other, your metabolism may closely reflect one parent's more than the other. This results in siblings from the same parents who have very different metabolic rates, even as young children.

Key Terms

Metabolism: The chemical processes occurring within a living cell or organism that are necessary for the maintenance of life. In metabolism, some substances are broken down to provide energy for vital processes, while other substances necessary for life are synthesized.

Resting metabolic rate (RMR): The energy required to maintain vital body functions, including heart rate, respiration, body temperature, and blood pressure, while the body is at rest. RMR accounts for about 55–75 percent of daily energy expenditure (DEE). Food digestion accounts for about 5–15 percent of DEE, while between 10 percent and 40 percent is used during physical activity.

Influences on Metabolism

Metabolism is an internal sensor for weight control and can be stimulated or depressed by your behavior. There are two positive ways to influence your metabolism to burn more calories. The first is to exercise, since daily exercise increases metabolism and burns more calories. The second is to change your body composition fat-to-lean ratio. Lean muscle needs more calories than fat tissue. The more muscle mass your body has, the faster your metabolism will work to burn calories to create more fuel for this muscle mass. Because men have more testosterone, they are more able than women to increase muscle mass. When a muscle becomes stronger, muscle fibers become denser and require more calories to function.

Calorie Expenditure

Estimates of caloric needs are based on gender, body size, fat-to-lean ratio, age, and activity. The following are generalities, and there are exceptions. Men need more calories than women; larger people need more calories than smaller people; individuals with more muscle mass need more calories than individuals who have very little muscle mass; the young need more calories than the old; and those who exercise need more calories than those who do not exercise.

Image of Health in Depth

Metabolic Rate and Calories

On average, a person who weighs 150 pounds will burn about one calorie per minute while at rest. When this person exercises, metabolic rate increases to about 5 calories per minute for the duration of the exercise. After working out, metabolic rate stays elevated at about three calories per minute for up to four hours.

To lose weight, it is most effective to reduce calories *and* to increase exercise. You can estimate your calorie needs using the following guidelines:

1. Sedentary people need about 11 calories for each pound of weight.

2. 2–3 times a week exercisers need about 13 calories for each pound of weight.

3. 5–7 times a week exercisers need about 15 calories for each pound of weight.

As you consider calorie expenditure, remember the following:

1. The faster you move, the more calories are burned, just as you burn more fuel as you drive a car faster.

2. The more effort you put into a movement, the more calories you burn, just as more fuel is is used driving a car up hills.

3. A heavier person burns more calories during any type of movement. It takes more effort to move extra weight.

4. The more muscle or lean weight you possess, the more calories you burn, even at rest.

5. Increasing fitness level increases amount of fat calories burned during most movements.

Since energy expenditure depends on so many factors, identifying how many calories are burned in any given activity is difficult to predict. The key is to find an enjoyable activity so that you will do it longer and more consistently. The longer and more frequently you work out, the more calories you expend.

There are other, less healthy ways to influence metabolism by either artificially stimulating or depressing metabolism. Taking stimulant drugs that affect the central nervous system will raise heart rate, respiration, and blood pressure, and will also speed up metabolism. Stimulant drugs can be illicit drugs such as methamphetamine or cocaine, legal prescription drugs such as diet pills, or herbal supplements like ephedra or nicotine from cigarettes. If you artificially stimulate metabolism with drugs, your body responds by burning more calories. When you stop taking stimulant drugs, your body responds by slowing metabolism.

Long-term, low-calorie dieting will depress metabolism. The metabolic rate slows down to prevent the body from losing too much fat and muscle mass.

▶**Critical Thinking Question**: Describe how metabolism influences weight control and what you might do to influence your own metabolism.

The Energy Balance Equation

An important key for managing your weight is to understand the energy balance equation. This simple equation reflects a balance between the number of calories you take in every day and the number of calories you burn. If you have maintained the same weight for several months, you are eating the right number of calories to maintain that weight. You may be overweight or underweight, but stability in weight indicates a balance between energy expenditure and caloric consumption. In terms of weight loss or gain, the source of calories does not matter. If you eat fewer calories, you will lose weight. Conversely, if you eat more calories than you need, you will gain weight. Of course your choice of calories is important for optimal health, and some foods are more calorie dense than others.

Low nutrient density
High calorie density

High nutrient density
Low calorie density

©Hayden-McNeil, LLC

FIGURE 9-5. Calories vs. weight.

Motivation Maximizer

Making Food Choices for Weight Control

Susan is a typical college student. It seems she does everything at the "too much" level. She is carrying more than a full academic load and she works many hours in order to pay expenses. In addition, she carries too much body weight. When she grocery shops, she chooses only fat-free or sugar-free items and if she is lucky, she manages to get both fat- and sugar-free foods. She assumes this makes them reduced calorie. She eats lunch with her best friend Angela each day and finds it frustrating. Angela can eat whatever she wants and never gains a pound. Susan seems to gain weight by just looking at the plate. Angela is as busy as Susan, and carries a similar load. How does she manage to eat more and not gain weight? Angela explains that she tries to burn calories every chance she gets. She might park in a far corner of the campus so she can walk further, or she will take the stairs instead of the elevator. Each term she takes one physical activity class to commit herself to exercise. She tells Susan that sugar- or fat-free does not mean reduced calories, and that many times, these foods have a similar number of calories to their fat- and sugar-containing counterparts. Susan wonders how difficult it might be for her to change her behavior. Could she find time to exercise? Angela insists that by adding exercise, Susan will gain energy. Could she change her eating habits? Angela insists that there is more pleasure in eating just one chocolate chip cookie than half a dozen cookies that are fat- and sugar-free! And Angela reminds Susan that she must be on campus anyway, and taking a physical activity class is a good stress reliever.

▶**Critical Thinking Question**: What could you do to increase the number of calories you burn in a day?

Set-Point Theory

The set-point theory was developed in 1982, by Bennett and Gurin, to explain why some people do not lose weight when they diet. Bennett and Gurin argued that each person has a specific set-point that dictates how much fat the person should carry. If a person diets, the body makes changes to maintain fat. This might include altering metabolism and increasing hunger levels. Altering the set-point is difficult, but the most promising method is by a sustained increase in physical activity. Although the concept of a set-point might be comforting, there is no proof that it exists.[21]

Gaining Weight

For some individuals, the challenge regarding weight is to maintain or even increase weight. If you are an active young person, especially if you are male, you may need to carefully monitor your diet so that you do not lose weight. Since males tend to be more active than females, increasing weight can be challenging.

Most young people who struggle to gain weight simply do not eat enough. This group needs more food at more frequent intervals. Trying to burn fewer calories is often not an option, because very lean people are often active and exercise is always beneficial, if enough calories are consumed. Nutrient-dense calories will help promote weight gain more quickly. Fruit juices, smoothies, nuts, dried fruits, and peanut butter are examples of foods that are relatively high in calories while also being nutritionally dense.

Image of Health In Depth

Choosing Calories for Weight Gain

Those who want to gain weight still need to eat a healthy diet and include good, calorie-dense food choices, including:

1. Make fruit smoothies with yogurt and fresh fruit.

2. Carry little bags of assorted nuts and dried fruit around with you for snacking.

3. Choose higher calorie foods such as starchy vegetables, dense whole grain breads, and hearty bean soups.

4. Eat avocados and peanut butter and other nut or fruit butters.

5. Eat several times each day rather than just three times, and choose larger portions. Aim for 2–3 calorie-dense snacks each day.

6. Maintain your exercise routine so that metabolism functions efficiently.

Weight Reduction

After reading this section, you will learn how to create a successful personal weight loss plan, if you choose to lose weight.

Ideal Self and Body Image

An important consideration is a personal view of your "ideal" self. Visualization is a powerful psychological tool to help realize accomplishment in many endeavors. You can't "imagine" yourself thin and make it so, but you can have a mental image or picture of what you would like to look like. This mental image is what you hope to accomplish, whether your goal is weight loss or weight gain. As you consider your body image goals, recognize the genetic contributions of your parents as a framework and work within that context to set realistic goals.

Image of Health in Depth

Goal Setting and Weight Loss

Assume that you have decided to lose weight for health benefits, greater self-esteem, or well-being. Perhaps you know others who have tried the latest weight-loss diets and trends, but have not succeeded in losing weight or in keeping it off. How do you make a plan that will succeed? You are more likely to succeed if you set realistic goals and plan adequately. Review the discussion of the Prochaska and DiClemente behavior change model in Chapter 1, using the following steps.

STEP ONE	How much are you currently eating?	Keep track of all food and drink for three days and analyze it for calorie intake using www.mypyramid.gov	You have moved beyond the Prochaska and DiClemente's Precontemplation Stage
STEP TWO	Review your current eating habits and decide where you can make changes.	If you have favorite foods and they are calorie dense, such as fast food, you will need to reduce portion size while considering eating lower calorie-dense foods like fruits and vegetables.	Prochaska and DiClemente's Planning Stage
STEP THREE	Plan your eating!	Keep low-calorie, nutrient-dense foods readily available for those eating impulses. Plan your evening meal before you leave the house in the morning to avoid stopping for fast food. Take your lunch with you to ensure that you eat low-calorie foods that are nutrient dense.	Prochaska and DiClemente Preparation Stage
STEP FOUR	Plan your exercise!	You know when you must be in class and when you must go to work. You do these things because they are planned. Plan when you will exercise and what type of exercise you will do.	Preparation Stage
STEP FIVE	Get a buddy!	Losing weight and exercising with a friend will help keep you motivated.	Prochaska and DiClemente's Action Stage
STEP SIX	Stick with it!	You did not gain all this weight quickly, and you will not be able to lose it all quickly. Plan for gradual weight loss and know that even when you don't see changes, internal changes are taking place that are improving your health.	Action Stage

The number of calories you eat and the number of calories you expend each day determines body weight. The best way to make this a plan for life is to follow a healthy eating plan and begin regular physical activity. You should plan to lose about 1/2 to 2 pounds per week. This means eating between 250 and 1,000 fewer calories per day than needed to maintain weight.

Motivation Maximizer

If your professor were to survey the class for those who have attempted to alter their weight at one time or another, most hands would go up. If you have been unsuccessful at either losing weight or gaining weight, you probably have a good idea of what prevented your success. Perhaps you did not see results quickly enough, or you did not find time to exercise, or maybe you felt that your food choices were too restricted. Whatever the reason, you can do better this time. From your reading, you know how to assess your weight, and you know the most successful way to lose weight—eat fewer calories and expend more calories. Once you make a firm commitment about changing your lifestyle to achieve weight loss, it will happen. You can do it; you want to do it, now you must commit 100 percent to achieving your goals. At any time, that little voice in your head may try to throw you off track, but you make the choices and you make the decisions. Remember, little changes lead to bigger changes; small steps to bigger steps, and with every success, you build on your ability to stay on track. Start today. Make a decision to stock your home with calorie-appropriate foods and get rid of all the high-calorie temptations. Go for a walk this evening, and next semester consider taking an activity class at school. Don't give up. If you have some little lapses, just shake them off and move on. Never let a lapse, become a relapse, become a collapse!

Know Your Caloric Needs

If you are a normal weight non-exercising female, your normal daily caloric intake is about 1,500 calories; if you exercise, it can be as high as 2,200 calories. If you are male and don't exercise you need 2,200 to maintain weight and 2,700 if you exercise. There are about 3,500 calories in one pound of fat. If you reduce your caloric intake by 500 calories per day or exercise and burn the equivalent of 500 calories per day, you will lose 1 pound in a week.

A common misconception in weight management is the actual weight of fat tissue versus muscle tissue. People who diet and exercise but do not see weight loss will often claim that muscle weighs more than fat. A pound of muscle and a pound of fat weigh the same. The difference is the density of the tissue. A pound of muscle is exceptionally dense, whereas a pound of fat is less dense and more expansive. If you do not see weight change and you are exercising, you may still be taking in more calories than you need.

Image of Health in Depth

Nutrition Bars
Nutrition bars are high in calories, developed for active people and for those who have difficulty maintaining weight. Many bars have 200 or more calories. If you are trying to lose weight and are eating nutrition bars as a snack, you should consider a lower calorie snack like fruit, carrots, or celery sticks.

Determining how many calories you need to maintain your desired weight can be discovered through a variety of diet analysis programs found on the Web. Internet Resources listed at the end of this chapter provide sites for this.

Image of Health in Depth

Choose Your Calories Carefully!
Which of the following contains the least number of calories?
1. Eight ounces of regular soda

2. Two fat-free sandwich cookies

3. Two cups of sliced, fresh strawberries

4. Twenty baby carrots

The correct answer is they all contain about 100 calories.

Your new eating habits should take into consideration your likes and dislikes and include a variety of foods to provide enough nutrients and calories. A weight loss plan that restricts portions to a very small size or that excludes certain foods may be hard to maintain, and may not be feasible over time.

As you consider different weight loss plans, ask yourself the following:

1. Does it include all essential food groups?

2. Does it eliminate any particular food group?

3. Does it contain sufficient fiber?

4. Does it include foods and menus that are readily available?

5. Must you buy special foods or products?

6. Is it affordable and easy to prepare?

7. Does it include a behavior modification plan?

8. Does it include an exercise component?

9. Must you have a doctor's prescription?

10. Could you live with this plan for life?

Image of Health in Depth

The Fallacy of Spot Reducing Weight

Trying to lose abdominal fat? You may see advertisements for devices to help you do abdominal crunches, and these ads may suggest that crunches burn body fat. Your friend may tell you to do sit-ups to burn abdominal fat, or leg lifts to burn thigh fat. But, the only way to burn fat is to burn it all over the body. You cannot do any spot reducing. Exercising will increase muscle mass in the area you exercise, and will improve muscle definition so that when you lose the fat, you look better. But exercise cannot be targeted to burn fat in a specific location.

Diets in the News

The central theme of *Image of Health* is to encourage readers to take responsibility and be accountable for personal health. The following selection of popular diets is not an endorsement for a particular diet. You should be able to critically evaluate each of these diets, now that you understand the fundamentals of metabolism and the energy balance equation.

Diets are continually being promoted, and people do lose weight on some of them. Any diet that reduces the number of calories consumed will cause weight loss. Consider that most of these diets are a temporary fix and may not result in long-term weight loss. Individuals who lose weight and keep it off almost always do so by reducing calories from foods that they have always eaten. Diets that work either decrease calories, increase exercise, or both.

Table 9-1. Comparison of Calories Among Major Diets

BOOK	CALORIES	CALORIE SOURCE	CLAIMS	POINTS TO CONSIDER
Eat More, Weigh Less by Dean Ornish, MD	1,500	80 percent carbohydrates, 15 percent proteins, 5 percent fat, 40 g fiber	Fat free is key to weight loss.	Without a dietician's help, it is hard to maintain with so little fat. Fat provides flavor and texture to our food.
Sugar Busters by Steward, Andrews, and Balart	1,600	35 percent carbohydrates, 25 percent proteins, 40 percent fat, 20 g fiber	Refined carbohydrates cause weight gain by raising blood sugar.	There is little scientific evidence to support this claim.
Dr. Atkins' Diet Revolution by Robert Atkins, MD	1,800	15 percent carbohydrates, 30 percent proteins, 55 percent fat, 10g fiber	Only carbohydrates make you fat. Eliminate them and your body burns fat.	There is little scientific evidence to support this claim. If you eliminate some calories, no matter what the source, your body must find energy from another source.
Protein Power by Michael and Mary Dan Eades	1,700	15 percent carbohydrates, 25 percent proteins, 60 percent fat, 50 g fiber	Limits carbohydrates, lowers insulin, and insulin causes obesity.	This claim has been refuted by scientific research. It would be hard to maintain this diet, since carbohydrates are ubiquitous. A diet with 60 percent fat will increase your risk for heart disease. The diet does not allow for individual variation.
The Zone by Barry Sears	1,000	40 percent carbohydrates, 30 percent proteins, 30 percent fat, 50g fiber	Claims the FDA 60:15:30 ratio of carbohydrates, protein, and fats causes weight gain. Changing to his 40:30:30 plan will result in weight loss.	The ratio is not the problem; the number of calories is the problem! Notice how few calories you eat on this diet! Any time you reduce calories, you lose weight!
Dieting with the Duchess by Weight Watchers	1,400	55 percent carbohydrates, 25 percent proteins, 20 percent fats, 25 g fiber	Food choices based on point system. Eat only the required points and you lose weight.	An easy-to-maintain calorie reduction method, with appropriate choices. This has been shown to produce long-term success.
The South Beach Diet by Arthur Agatston, MD	No calorie count is specified, but calories are greatly reduced in the first two weeks by eliminating carbohydrates and fruit.	Emphasizes healthy fats, and allows only low glycemic index carbohydrates. No bread, potatoes, fruits, corn, carrots, rice, or cereal in first two weeks, and strongly discouraged even after the initiation phase.	Claims foods that are high on the glycemic index result in more weight gain.	The diet restricts many healthful food choices and there is no evidence to support that high glycemic index foods lead to more weight gain. Exercise is not promoted.

As you consider each of these diets, note the number of calories allowed. Most of the diets also increase fiber intake. Fibrous foods may cause you to feel more satisfied, possibly resulting in eating less. Some of the diets presented greatly restrict carbohydrates making them very low in fiber. It would be difficult to find 50 grams of fiber in a diet that restricts carbohydrates, since fiber is only found in plant-based foods.

A Weight Loss Diet for Everyone

There are hundreds of books on dieting available. The only weight loss diet that works is one that reduces calories and increases calorie expenditure by exercising. If these two components are present, the plan is likely to work. A better plan for healthy eating is one that is comprised of **nutrient dense** calories from all essential food groups, combined with an exercise plan you can adhere to. However, a new, healthy eating plan will not work unless you become responsible for what you eat, responsible for exercising, and accountable when you lapse. If you do lapse, just remember the days when you were successful and get back on track.

> **Key Term**
>
> **Nutrient dense**: Food that contains a large number of nutrients relative to the amount and size of the food.

▶**Challenge Question**: If a diet is successful at causing weight loss, what key element must be present?

Medical Treatment Options

For those who have serious obesity and are unable to lose weight, medical intervention may be necessary. Options may include obesity drugs, and possibly surgery for those with morbid obesity.

Obesity Drugs

Drug companies are following the obesity epidemic with great interest. Of particular interest to drug companies are the approximately 70 million American adults who have a body mass index (BMI) of 30 or more. These individuals are the bulk of the obesity epidemic, and their projected health care estimates are expected to reach almost 2 trillion a year.[22]

The interest by drug companies in developing obesity drugs is not new. Amphetamines were once widely prescribed for obesity, and they work as long as the patient continues to take the drugs. Amphetamine drugs are effective because they artificially raise metabolism, causing the patient to burn more calories. However, once these stimulant drugs are stopped, metabolism slows and the individual gains weight. Most researchers realized that to effectively treat obesity, a non-amphetamine approach was more desirable, and research efforts branched out in many directions.

There are almost a dozen new drugs in the development stage for obesity. Most drugs being developed are geared toward chemically causing the human body to signal **satiety** to the brain, retard fat digestion in the intestine, improve fat metabolism, or depress appetite. Most obesity prescription drugs are designed for short-term use only, and each has side effects. A recently FDA approved weight-loss drug is Alli, marketed by GlaxoSmithKline. The drug comes with a companion book that promotes calorie control and exercise and emphasizes that weight loss is not easy and requires lifestyle changes. Alli works by inhibiting absorption of up to one-fourth of dietary fat. Since long term, slow, endurance activity together with calorie reduction is advocated, how much weight loss is due to Alli versus the behavior change is unknown.

> **Key Term**
>
> **Satiety**: State of having enough or more than enough food.

Extreme Measures for Morbid Obesity

For individuals who have reached a weight gain level that is considered morbidly obese, there are surgical options.

Morbid obesity is defined as a person with a BMI over 40. Surgical options may be considered when the individual is at least 100 pounds overweight and conventional weight loss attempts have been unsuccessful.

> **Key Term**
>
> **Morbid obesity**: Defined as having a BMI over 40.

The following surgical procedures are extreme measures that have risks for the patient, as with any surgery. With gastric bypass and stomach stapling, the patient faces a lifetime of eating small, mostly liquid-based meals. Liposuction has a history of risk from excessive bleeding and from infection, although the current procedure is greatly improved.

Gastric Bypass Surgery

A gastric bypass procedure is used almost exclusively on individuals who are morbidly obese. It involves stomach stapling to reduce the size of the stomach so that it has a capacity of only one or two fluid ounces. This smaller stomach pouch is reconnected at a point midway along the small intestine. The larger pouch of the stomach is reconnected at a point farther down the small intestine, allowing for the introduction of gastric juices necessary for digestion. Gastric bypass is effective because very little food can be eaten at one time, and the food that is eaten has less opportunity to be absorbed in the small intestine. Gastric bypass patients take vitamin and mineral supplements to ensure they are not nutritionally deficient.

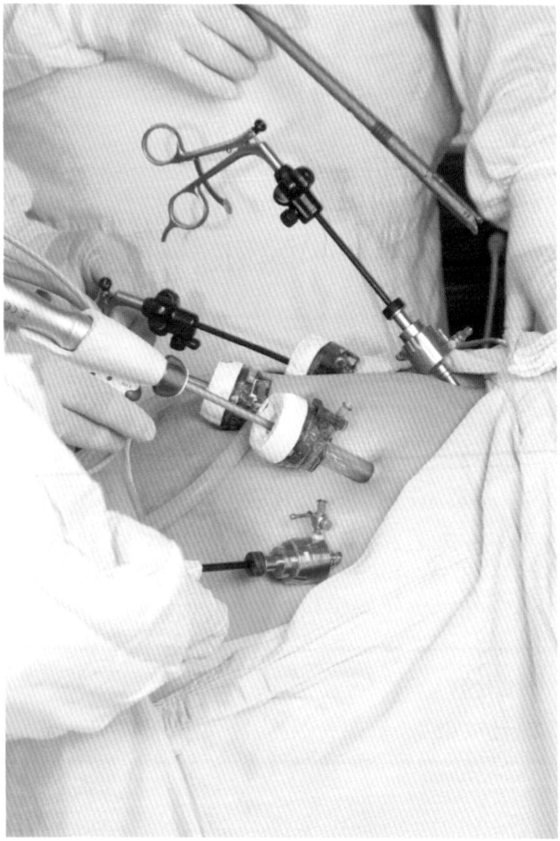

Stomach Stapling

Stomach stapling drastically limits the amount of food that can be eaten at one time, and also slows the passage of food. The procedure involves stapling the stomach to form one side of a small pouch, the bottom of which is constricted by a saline-filled band that encircles part of the outside of the stomach. A small hole is made in the bottom of the constricted pouch, allowing food to flow into the remainder of the stomach and the rest of the gastrointestinal track. This procedure alone is not as effective as gastric bypass, however, it effectively makes the stomach smaller, limiting the amount of food and calories that can be absorbed.

▶**Challenge Question**: What is the difference between gastric bypass surgery and stomach stapling?

Liposuction

The most popular and less expensive surgical fat-reduction procedure is liposuction. The patient is awake during the procedure and can communicate with the surgeon. Liposuction is for individuals who are minimally overweight, it is not a procedure for the morbidly obese. Considered cosmetic surgery, liposuction can effectively remove fat deposits from areas such as hips, thighs, and stomach. Even with liposuction, individuals will still need to change eating habits and maintain a regular physical exercise routine in order to maintain the benefits of liposuction.

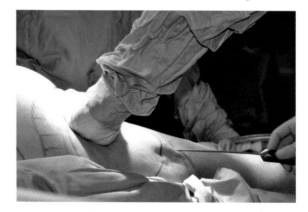

FIGURE 9-7. Liposuction.

FIGURE 9-6. Gastric bypass surgery.

Eating Disorders

Food is essential and ideally it is part of daily life that brings pleasure and enjoyment. It should not be an anxiety-producing or depressing event. You must be accountable for your eating and know that eating behavior may be affected by your emotional state. Over a lifetime, an average person eats about 85,000 meals. When food begins to dominate thought patterns, there is potential for extreme behaviors that include absence of eating as well as overeating.

The three major eating disorders are anorexia, bulimia, and binge eating. Personality characteristics across all three disorders typically include being extremely fearful of becoming fat and a compulsive need to have strict control over calorie intake. Women suffering from eating disorders come from white, middle- to upper-class families, and are generally high achievers, though they may be lacking positive self-esteem. It is uncommon for men to have a restricted calorie eating disorder.

Anorexia

Anorexia is a psychological disorder in which there is a preoccupation with being thin, to the degree that personal identity about body image and thoughts about food become irrational. The typical anorexic is a woman who is a high achiever and needs to have personal self-control of her life. Losing control in any area of life is alarming to the anorexic, and controlling food can be a balm that restores a sense of well-being and feeling in control. In the early stages, a borderline anorexic begins to strictly limit eating. Most who are diagnosed as anorexic also become avid exercisers and may exercise several hours a day. This combination of low caloric intake and extreme exercise can cause enormous weight loss, to the point that hospitalization is required. Hospital treatment includes a regimen of high-calorie food infusion, usually a combination of intravenous total parenteral nutrition (TPN), and oral feeding. Additional treatment is needed to begin to heal the psychological trauma associated with an anorexic perception of eating, food, and body image.

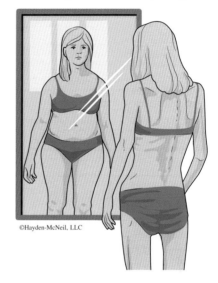

©Hayden-McNeil, LLC

Khali's Story

Anorexia and the High Achiever

Khali was a high achiever. She came from an upper middle-class family and excelled in school, at sports, and in her dance class. She became concerned about her weight when she was not selected for a lead role in a dance production. Initially, Khali just tried to restrict what she ate, but she did not think she was getting results fast enough. She increased her exercise routine and continued to reduce her food intake, and soon began to take laxatives to rid herself of anything she did eat. Soon, she was eating just a half dozen lettuce leaves, a quarter cucumber, and five grapes a day. She drank copious amounts of diet soda to help her feel full. She had a difficult time staying awake, and one day, fell asleep in class. She did not wake when the class period ended. After waking her, the instructor expressed concern for Khali's health and asked if she was eating enough. Khali insisted it was a virus. In another class, a week later, Khali lost consciousness and fell out of her chair. She was taken to a hospital, diagnosed as anorexic, and was admitted to the hospital in critical condition.

For Khali, there was a happy ending. Intravenous fluids were begun, and soon she was participating in psychotherapy to help her understand her condition. Gradually, she was able to eat small meals without fear of weight gain, and before she left the hospital she could see her real self in a mirror, and not the distorted, larger-than-life image she had seen.

Many anorexics are not as lucky. Some die, and some suffer cardiac arrest and although they survive them, they may be left in a vegetative state. Help is available, so if you or someone you know suffers from anorexia or bulimia, get help. Go to your college health services, or your college psychology or health department. Or look into http://www.pale-reflections.com/, a program on the World Wide Web. ∎

Binge Eating and Bulimia Nervosa

Binge eating and **bulimia nervosa** are related eating disorders and may trigger the onset of anorexia. Binge eating does not necessarily lead to bulimia, but both behaviors can have serious health implications. Spontaneous binge eating is extreme loss of portion control. The individual eats large amounts of food, much more than would be considered normal, producing rapid weight gain. The progression from binge eating to bulimia nervosa is often precipitated by concern about weight gain. The individual continues to binge eat followed by vomiting (purging) the consumed food, and some may also use laxatives to eliminate foods. Bulimia causes damaged tooth enamel from the acids in vomit, a gag reflex when one tries to eat normally, and difficulty with regular bowel movements when laxatives are removed.

▶**Challenge Question**: What are the major differences between anorexia, binge eating, and bulimia?

Key Terms

Anorexia: An eating disorder characterized by a preoccupation with body weight; fear of gaining weight resulting in self-starvation.

Binge eating: An eating disorder characterized by episodes of severe overeating.

Bulimia nervosa: An eating disorder characterized by recurrent episodes of excessive eating, followed by purging foods through vomiting and/or the use of laxatives.

Maintaining Ideal Weight

Whether your weight-loss goal is to gain weight or lose weight, eventually you will arrive at your ideal weight. Your goal now is to maintain this weight for a lifetime. Although there will always be small fluctuations in weight, it is possible to maintain your weight long term by taking responsibility for your personal lifelong eating plan, and by being accountable for what you eat and how much you exercise.

Lifelong Weight Control

There are many individuals who are able to maintain ideal body weight for a lifetime. This requires an ability to be in tune with your body, so that adjustments in diet and exercise are made to maintain ideal weight. When small weight gain occurs, it is easier to make small adjustments to return to ideal weight rather than allow substantial weight gain to occur before action is taken. The same is true for those who have a difficult time maintaining weight. It is easier to make adjustments by eating calorie-dense foods more frequently when weight loss is first noticed, rather than to wait until substantial weight loss has occurred. These choices are really part of self-care, and are the responsibility of each individual.

Holiday and Vacation Eating

Many individuals complain about weight gain during holidays or while on vacation. These are events over which you have complete control, and the same principles of responsibility and accountability must be employed. *Just because food is available, even if it is special food, you are not required to eat it!* This does not mean that you need to deprive yourself, it just means that you must exercise some control. You should enjoy holiday and vacation food, but excess eating does not necessarily improve enjoyment. It is better to eat slowly and savor what you are eating rather than to eat these foods compulsively. One dessert on a vacation cruise is fine; trying all of the desserts is not responsible decision making. Your knowledge about portion control and calorie density will help you to make better decisions during holidays and vacations.

After weight loss, long-term weight management can be difficult for some. Lapsing back to old eating habits or choosing not to exercise as frequently can quickly reverse weight loss accomplishments. For most people, maintaining ideal weight is a lifelong personal responsibility. In early stages of weight loss an individual may be frequently reinforced for successful efforts, but this will diminish across time. It may be necessary for some people to build in rewards for their accomplishments, and it may help if family members and social networks remember that this is a long-term change and continue to provide support and encouragement.

Ultimately, weight control is a matter of calories eaten versus calories spent. If too much food is eaten, "spending" more by burning calories with exercise will help offset this. The rewards will be a lifetime without the higher risk of cardiovascular disease, cancers, and diabetes, and a lifetime with possibly higher personal self-esteem and satisfaction with body image.

On the journey to appropriate weight management, it is best to avoid hunger by planning low-calorie meals and snacks throughout the day.

The three major components of a successful lifelong weight management plan are:

1. Recognizing that you have control over what you eat.

2. Recognizing that you can choose to make time to exercise.

3. Ensuring that the calories you consume are equal to the calories you spend if you want to maintain your current weight.

Like any difficult or important accomplishment, personal weight management may not be easy and it may take a long time to return to desired weight. Ideally, there should be no set time limit for an ultimate weight loss goal. However, short-term weight loss goals such as losing weight for a wedding or special event can be motivating.

Since everyone is different in terms of body type and metabolism, all weight management programs should be individually planned. There should be initial weight loss (or weight gain) goals, nutritional goals, and exercise goals established that could be fairly easily attained, so that some success is recognized that will be motivating. Since this is a lifelong undertaking, lifestyle choices regarding diet and exercise should be established so that individuals can picture themselves making new positive choices for a lifetime. As goals are reached, new goals are set with an undefined time frame for reaching an ultimate weight management solution.

Responsibility and Accountability

Taking Responsibility for Your Weight

Being thin is not the answer to the obesity crisis unless you have an appropriate fat-to-lean body composition. Some thin people still have more body fat than their overall weight requires. Overweight individuals who exercise regularly may be healthier than some thin individuals.

Focusing on Accountability

Responsibility for weight begins with assessing your eating and exercise habits. Eating the appropriate number of nutrient-dense calories that include a large variety of fruits and vegetables, some whole grains, and adequate amounts of protein and dairy is the first step to weight management. Adding in moderate-intensity exercise on most days of the week will help assure your weight remains stable, even during holiday seasons. Your personal accountability is shown when you look in the mirror. If you don't see a lean individual, you need to step back and evaluate your eating and exercise habits. Don't become discouraged. Weight management is a lifelong project, and with reasonable goals, one that you can achieve.

Summary

Measurement and Assessment of Body Composition

- Body mass index (BMI) is a table to indicate percentage of body fat based on height and weight.

- Hydrostatic weighing involves submersion in a tank of water or a swimming pool to determine percentage of body fat.

- Bio-impedance testing uses a low-grade electrical pulse that measures percentage of body fat.

- Skin fold measurement for body fat assessment requires determining various skin fold measurements using a caliper and applying the results to a formula.

- The BOD POD uses air displacement and works in a way similar to hydrostatic weighing.

- Near infrared interactance (NIR) uses infrared spectroscopy to determine percentage of body fat.

- Dual energy X-ray absorptiometry (DEXA) uses X-ray energies to measure percentage of body fat.

- The MetLife height and weight chart was historically used to determine if individuals were overweight.

- Waist-to-hip ratio is a good predictor of body mass.

- Total waist measurement reveals an assessment of abdominal fat, a predictor for chronic diseases.

Contributing Factors for Obesity

- The propensity to be overweight or obese is partly due to genetics.

- There are several body shapes that are predictors of obesity and/or disease risk.

- Obese children are projected to have a shorter lifespan.

- Sedentary behavior is a phenomenon of the late 20th century.

- Environmental influences such as the availability of fast food is a contributor to the obesity epidemic.

- Many adults who are obese have been obese since childhood.

Health Risks of Obesity

- The risk for diabetes increases for those who are obese at any age.

- Even moderate weight gain can cause high blood pressure.

- Being obese increases both cholesterol and triglyceride levels and risk for cardiovascular diseases.

- Obesity is a risk factor for cancer.

Economic Impact of Obesity

- Obesity lowers worker productivity.

- Obesity raises insurance rates for everyone.

- Those who are obese die sooner, measured as years of potential life lost (YPLL).

Weight Management Principles

- Metabolism is how effectively your body burns fuel (food).

- Metabolism can be positively increased by exercising and changing body composition from fat to more lean (more muscle).

- Calories are expended even at rest. The more active you are, the more calories burned.

- The energy balance equation refers to the balance between calories ingested and calories burned. If the balance is equal, weight is stable.

- Set-point theory explains why some people do not lose weight on a diet. There is no evidence that set-point theory has validity.

- Gaining weight requires eating nutrient dense foods more frequently.

Weight Reduction

- It is good to have a future image of yourself after successfully completing a weight loss program.

- Weight loss is a behavior change that requires changes to lifestyle.

- You should have realistic idea about the number of calories that should be ingested daily.

- There are many diets available but the only diets that work are those that promote eating a regular, balanced diet that reduces calories and incorporates exercise.

- Medical treatment options for obesity involve obesity drugs, gastric bypass surgery, and stomach stapling.

- Liposuction is a cosmetic procedure that is not for the morbidly obese.

Eating Disorders

- Anorexia, bulimia, and binge eating are psychological disorders that primarily affect over-achieving white, middle- to upper-socioeconomic class women.

- A person with an eating disorder will greatly reduce the amount of food ingested or will overeat, vomit ,and use laxatives after eating.

- Individuals with an eating disorder are often avid exercisers in an effort to burn calories.

Reassessing Your Knowledge

1. What diseases are associated with obesity?

2. Why does obesity have a financial impact on all of us?

3. What factors do you think have contributed to the obesity epidemic?

4. How can metabolism be influenced?

5. What are the factors to consider when evaluating a diet?

To answer these questions, you might choose to work in groups with your colleagues. Check your answers against the written material in the text, and reread those sections where you made errors.

Vocabulary Challenge

Match the term in the left-hand column with its correct definition in the right-hand column.

TERM		DEFINITION
Metabolism		A. An eating disorder characterized by self-starvation
Body Composition		B. State of obesity with a BMI of 40 or more that is a risk factor for longevity
Anorexia		C. The chemical processes that occur within a human body in order to maintain life
Basal Metabolic Rate		D. Cosmetic surgical procedure to remove excess body fat
Body Mass Index		E. The ability to maintain a healthy body weight by balancing calorie consumption and expenditure
Morbid Obesity		F. The ratio between fat to lean within the body
Liposuction		G. A surgical procedure to reduce the ability of the stomach to absorb nutrients
Weight Management		H. The rate at which the body uses energy at rest to maintain vital functions
Gastric Bypass Surgery		I. An eating disorder characterized by recurrent episodes of binge eating and vomiting
Bulimia		J. A measure of body weight relative to height to estimate percentage of body fat

C; F; A; H; J; B; D; E; G; I.

Answers

Applying What You Have Learned

1. How can you help educate friends and family members to understand the components of a healthful diet that can result in weight loss?

2. How can you influence the food choices available in your college cafeteria?

3. What criteria would you use to identify someone who might suffer from anorexia or bulimia nervosa?

4. What percentage of body fat-to-lean mass do you carry? How can you improve your ratio?

Health Assessment Toolbox

Athletes and Body Weight
http://www.ag.arizona.edu/pubs/health/az1384.pdf

American Heart Association Guidelines
For Weight Management for Healthy Adults
http://216.185.112.5/presenter.jhtml?identifier=1226

Aim for a Healthy Weight
http://www.nhlbi.nih.gov/health/public/heart/obesity/lose_wt/risk.htm

Choosing a Safe and Successful Weight Loss Program
http://win.niddk.nih.gov/publications/choosing.htm

Health: The Best Ways to Gain Weight
http://www.bbc.co.uk/health/healthy_living/your_weight/reaching_gain.shtml

Portion Distortion
Do you know how portion sizes have changed in the last 20 years:
http://hp2010.nhlbihin.net/portion/

American Diabetes Association
http://www.diabetes.org/

Weight Loss and Exercise
http://www.diabetes.org/

Analyzing Your Diet
http://www.choosemyplate.gov/tools.html

Exploring the Internet

Duke University Diet and Fitness Center
One of the country's oldest and most successful weight loss centers, Duke University takes a complete approach to the issue of weight management. This site provides information about nutrition, stress, fitness, and weight management.
http://www.dukedietcenter.org

National Eating Disorders Association
This national non-profit organization provides support, referrals, information and prevention.
http://www.edap.org

National Association of Anorexia Nervosa and Associated Disorders
http://www.anad.org

Ask the Dietician
Find answers to questions about being over or underweight, healthy eating habits and a healthy body calculator.
http://www.dietician.com

American Diabetes Association
This site provides excellent information for people living with diabetes and people wanting to avoid diabetes. The site contains appropriate recipes and information on weight loss and exercise.
http://diabetes.org

American Heart Association
Take a brief quiz and receive a free cookbook. You will also learn your body mass index and find heart attack and stroke symptoms, as well as information on reducing your risk of chronic diseases.
http://www.americanheart.org

Nutrition Analysis Tools and System
This site provides easy ways to determine your caloric needs, and your calorie expenditure during activity.
http://nat.crgq.com

USDA Nutrient Data Laboratory
This easy-to-use site provides a nutrient breakdown of foods.
http://www.nal.usda.gov

USDA MyPyramid

The most popular government Web site now has over one million users. At this user-friendly site, you can determine your precise nutritional needs and then input and analyze your diet in comparison to it.

http://www.mypyramid.gov

Web MD Evaluation Site

At this site, you can evaluate all of the more popular diets.

http://www.webmd.com/diet/

Morbid Obesity Surgery Evaluations

This site explains the numerous surgical morbid obesity procedures.

http://www.ucsfhealth.org/conditions/obesity/diagnosis.html

Selected References

1. Olshansky, S.J., Passaro, D.J., Hershow, R.C., Layden, J., Carnes, B.A., Brody, J., Hayflick, L., Butler, R.N., Allison, D.B., and Ludwig, D.S., A Potential Decline in Life Expectancy in the United States in the 21st Century. *New England Journal of Medicine*, 352(11): 1138–1145. 2005.

2. See, R., Abdullah, S.M., McGuire, D.K., et al. The Association of Differing Measures of Overweight and Obesity with Prevalent Atherosclerosis: The Dallas Heart Study. *Journal of American College Cardiology*. published online August 6, 2007. doi:10-1016/j.jacc.2007.04.066.

3. Bouchard, C. Genetics of Human Obesity: Recent Results from Linkage Studies. *The Journal of Nutrition*, 127(9): 1887S–1890S. September, 1997.

4. Ludwig, D.S. Childhood Obesity—the Shape of Things to Come. *New England Journal of Medicine*, 357(23): 2325–2327. December 6, 2005.

5. Bray, G. Predicting Obesity in Adults from Childhood and Adolescent Weight. *The American Journal of Clinical Nutrition*, 76 (3): 497–498. September 2002.

6. Schneider, M.B., and Brill, S.R. Obesity in Children and Adolescents. *Pediatrics in Review*, 26: 155–162. 2005.

7. Whitaker, R.C. Predicting Preschooler Obesity at Birth: the Role of Maternal Obesity in Early Pregnancy. *Pediatrics*, 114(1): 29–36. July, 2004

8. Reilly, J.J., Armstrong, J., Dorotsty, A.R., Emmett, P.M., Ness, A., Rogers, I., Steer, C., and Sherriff, A. Early life risk factors for obesity in childhood: A cohort study. *British Medical Journal*, Eov1 (20 May), 38470.670903. 2005.

9. *Healthy People 2010*. Behavioral Risk Factor Surveillance System (BRFSS) 2001; Active Community Environments, U.S. Department of Health and Human Services.

10. Eyler, A.A. Environmental Policy and Cultural Factors Related to Physical Activity. *The Women's Cardiovascular Health Network*. CRC Press, 2002.

11. Byers T., Nestle M., McTiernan A., et al. American Cancer Society Guidelines on Nutrition and Physical Activity for Cancer Prevention: Reducing the Risk of Cancer with Healthy Food Choices and Physical Activity. *CA: A Cancer Journal for Clinicians*, 52: 92–119. 2002.

12. Friedenreich C. M., and Courneya, K. S. Exercise as rehabilitation for cancer patients. *Clinical Journal of Sport Medicine*, 6(4), 237–244. 1996.

13. Courneya, K.S., Mackey, J.R.., and Jones, L.W. Coping With Cancer—Can Exercise Help? *The Physician and Sports Medicine*. 28(5). May, 2000.

14. Tremblay, M.S., and Willms, J.D. Is the Canadian Child Obesity Epidemic Related to Physical Inactivity? *International Journal of Obesity*, 27: 1100–1105. 2003.

15. Schröder, H.M., Vila, I., Covas, J., and Elosua, R. Adherence to the Traditional Mediterranean Diet is Inversely Associated with Body Mass Index and Obesity in a Spanish Population. *The American Society for Nutritional Sciences, The Journal of Nutrition,* 134: 3355–3361. December, 2004.

16. Carrera, P.M., Gao, X., Tucker, K.L., A Study of Dietary Patterns in the Mexican-American Population and Their Association with Obesity. *Journal of the American Dietetic Association,* 107(10): 1735–1742. October, 2007.

17. Fox, C., Pencina, M.J., Meigs, J., et al. Trends in the Incidence of Type 2 Diabetes Mellitus from the 1970s to the 1990s. The Framingham Heart Study. *Circulation*. June 19, 2006.

18. Hubert, H.B., Feinleib, M., McNamara, P.M., and Castelli, W. Obesity as an Independent Risk Factor for Cardiovascular Disease: a 26-year Follow-up of Participants in the Framingham Heart Study. *Circulation*, 67: 968–977. 1983.

19. Polednak, A.P., Trends in the Incidence Rates for Obesity-associated cancers in the U.S. *Cancer Detection and Prevention*, 27(6): 415–421. 2003.

20. Calle, E.E., Rodriguez, C., Walker-Thurmond, K., and Thun, M.J. Overweight, Obesity and Mortality from Cancer in a Prospectively Studied Cohort of U.S. Adults. *New England Journal of Medicine*, 348(17): 1625–1638. 2003.

21. Bennett, W. and Gurin, J. *The Dieter's Dilemma: Eating Less and Weighing More*. Basic Books, 1982.

22. Wang, Y., Beydoun, M.A., and Liang, L. Will All Americans Become Overweight or Obese? Estimating the Progression and Cost of the U.S. Obesity Epidemic. *Obesity*, 2323–2330. July, 2008.

23. Dansinger, M.L., Gleason, A.J., Griffith, J., Selker, H.P., and Schaefer, E.J. Comparison of the Atkins, Ornish, Weight Watchers, and Zone Diets for Weight Loss and Heart Disease Risk Reduction. *Journal of the American Medical Association*, 293: 43–53. 2005.

24. Ogden, C.L., Fryar, C.D., Carroll, M.D., and Flegal, K.M. Division of Health and Nutrition Examination Surveys. Mean Body Weight, Height and Body Mass Index, United States, 1960–2002.

25. Raynor, H.A., and Epstein, L.H. Dietary Variety, Energy Regulation and Obesity. *Psychological Bulletin, 2001*, 127(3): 325–341. October 27, 2004.

Body Mass Index Table

(Source: Ratings from National Heart, Lung and Blood Institute. 1998. *Clinical Guidelines on the Identification, Evaluation, and Treatment of Overweight and Obesity in Adults: The Evidence Report*. Bethesda, MD National Institutes of Health.)

Underweight
Healthy Weight
Overweight
Obese

Weight (lbs)	Height (in)																		
	58	59	60	61	62	63	64	65	66	67	68	69	70	71	72	73	74	75	76
	4'10"	4'11"	5'0"	5'1"	5'2"	5'3"	5'4"	5'5"	5'6"	5'7"	5'8"	5'9"	5'10"	5'11"	6'0"	6'1"	6'2"	6'3"	6'4"
100	21	20	20	19	18	18	17	17	16	16	15	15	14	14	14	13	13	13	12
105	22	21	21	20	19	19	18	18	17	16	16	16	15	15	14	14	14	13	13
110	23	22	22	21	20	20	19	18	18	17	17	16	16	15	15	15	14	14	13
115	24	23	23	22	21	20	20	19	19	18	18	17	17	16	16	15	15	14	14
120	25	24	23	23	22	21	21	20	19	19	18	18	17	17	16	16	15	15	15
125	26	25	24	24	23	22	22	21	20	20	19	18	18	17	17	17	16	16	15
130	27	26	25	25	24	23	22	21	20	20	20	19	19	18	18	17	17	16	16
135	28	27	26	26	25	24	23	23	22	21	21	20	19	19	18	18	17	17	16
140	29	28	27	27	26	25	24	23	23	22	21	21	20	20	19	19	18	18	17
145	30	29	28	27	27	26	25	24	23	23	22	21	21	20	20	19	19	18	18
150	31	30	29	28	27	27	26	25	24	24	23	22	22	21	20	20	19	19	18
155	32	31	30	29	28	28	27	26	25	24	24	23	22	22	21	20	20	19	19
160	34	32	31	30	29	28	28	27	26	25	24	24	23	22	22	21	21	20	20
165	35	33	32	31	30	29	28	28	27	26	25	24	24	23	22	22	21	21	20
170	36	34	33	32	31	30	29	28	27	27	26	25	24	24	23	22	22	21	21
175	37	35	34	33	32	31	30	29	28	27	27	26	25	24	24	23	23	22	21
180	38	36	35	34	33	32	31	30	29	28	27	27	26	25	24	24	23	23	22
185	39	37	36	35	34	33	32	31	30	29	28	27	27	26	25	24	24	23	23
190	40	38	37	36	35	34	33	32	31	30	29	28	27	27	26	25	24	24	23
195	41	39	38	37	36	35	34	33	32	31	30	29	28	27	27	26	25	24	24
200	42	40	39	38	37	36	34	33	32	31	30	30	29	28	27	26	26	25	24
205	43	41	40	39	38	36	35	34	33	32	31	30	29	29	28	27	26	26	25
210	44	43	41	40	38	37	36	35	34	33	32	31	30	29	29	28	27	26	26
215	45	44	42	41	39	38	37	36	35	34	33	32	31	30	29	28	28	27	26
220	46	45	43	42	40	39	38	37	36	35	34	33	32	31	30	29	28	28	27
225	47	46	44	43	41	40	39	38	36	35	34	33	32	31	31	30	29	28	27
230	48	47	45	44	42	41	40	38	37	36	35	34	33	32	31	30	30	29	28
235	49	48	46	44	43	42	40	39	38	37	36	35	34	33	32	31	30	29	29
240	50	49	47	45	44	43	41	40	39	38	37	36	35	34	33	32	31	30	29
245	51	50	48	46	45	43	42	41	40	38	37	36	35	34	33	32	32	31	30
250	52	51	49	47	46	44	43	42	40	39	38	37	36	35	34	33	32	31	30
255	53	52	50	48	47	45	44	43	41	40	39	38	37	36	35	34	33	32	31
260	54	53	51	49	48	46	45	43	42	41	40	38	37	36	35	34	33	33	32
265	56	54	52	50	49	47	46	44	43	42	40	39	38	37	36	35	34	33	32
270	57	55	53	51	49	48	46	45	44	42	41	40	39	38	37	36	35	34	33
275	58	56	54	52	50	49	47	46	44	43	42	41	40	38	37	36	35	34	34
280	59	57	55	53	51	50	48	47	45	44	43	41	40	39	38	37	36	35	34
285	60	58	56	54	52	51	49	48	46	45	43	42	41	40	39	38	37	36	35
290	61	59	57	55	53	51	50	48	47	46	44	43	42	41	39	38	37	36	35
295	62	60	58	56	54	52	51	49	48	46	45	44	42	41	40	39	38	37	36
300	63	61	59	57	55	53	52	50	49	47	46	44	43	42	41	40	39	38	37

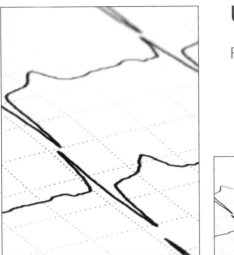

Unit Four

Protecting Yourself from Disease

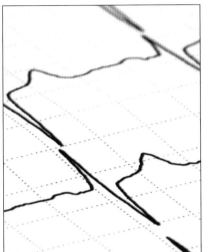

Image of Health

Cardiovascular Disease

Student Learning Outcomes

LEARNING OUTCOME	APPLYING IT TO YOUR LIFE
List and describe the modifiable risk factors for heart disease.	Identify strategies you will use to reduce your risk for heart disease.
Identify two types of strokes.	Describe how you can reduce your stroke risk.
List healthy values for total cholesterol, and HDL and LDL cholesterol.	Determine your blood cholesterol values, and plan how to improve them or maintain them in the normal ranges.
Know appropriate values for systolic and diastolic blood pressure.	Have your blood pressure measured and determine if you are at risk for hypertension.
List and describe various forms of heart disease.	Identify one type of heart disease and methods you can use to reduce its development.

Assess Your Knowledge

1. De-oxygenated blood enters the heart via the:
   a. Aorta
   b. Vena cava
   c. Left ventricle
   d. Right ventricle

2. Oxygenated blood leaves the heart via the:
   a. Aorta
   b. Vena cava
   c. Right atria
   d. Septum

3. Contracting pressure in the heart is called:
   a. Diastole
   b. Systole
   c. Blood pressure
   d. Hypertension

4. Another name for blood fat is:
   a. Glucose
   b. Lipids
   c. Trans fat
   d. Septum

5. Angina is:
   a. A non-reversible form of heart disease.
   b. Chest pain caused by excess oxygen.
   c. Abdominal pain caused by inadequate oxygen.
   d. Chest pain caused by inadequate oxygen.

Answers:
1. b; 2. a; 3. b; 4. b; 5. d.

Cardiovascular Disease

Dr. Robert Jarvik, inventor of the artificial heart, estimated that the average healthy heart beats more than two billion times in a lifetime. The body's entire six quarts or 5.6 liters of blood is pumped completely through the body each minute. It works when you sleep; it works harder when you are stressed or anxious; it works harder still when you exercise. Your heart never rests, and you don't want it to! But how often do you think about it? You may look at the amount you weigh and think your body would be better if you lost or gained a few pounds. You may look at your skin and think it could improve if you used sunscreen. But how often do you concern yourself with one of your body's most major organs—your own heart?

The Heart: Life and Death

The American Heart Association (AHA) estimated that in 2006, more than 81 million Americans had some form of heart disease, accounting for one in every 2.9 deaths, and 831,272 lost lives. More than 151,000 of these deaths were people under age 65. However, though heart disease remains the nation's number-one cause of death, survival rates have improved. Between 1996 and 2006, death rates from **cardiovascular disease** (CVD) declined 29.2 percent, and in the same ten-year period, the actual number of deaths declined 12.9 percent.[1] The estimated direct and indirect cost of CVD in the United States in 2008 was $448.5 billion.[2]

As you read, your heart continues to work with no effort from you; however, how *well* it works depends a great deal on choices you make. This chapter will enable you to make informed decisions about your lifestyle, and help you make the right choices to reduce your risk of CVD.

Your Heart: The Number-One Organ

The heart is about the size of a clenched fist, weighing between seven and fifteen ounces. It is a hollow, muscular, conical-shaped organ comprised of four chambers, located slightly to the left of the center of the chest. The upper chambers of the heart are the left and right **atria**, the lower chambers are the left and right **ventricles**, and a wall of muscle known as the **septum** separates the left and right sides. The strongest and biggest chamber is the left ventricle, and even though its walls are only one half-inch thick, it produces a contraction that forces blood through a valve and into your body.

Key Terms

Cardiovascular disease: The term used to describe various forms of disease related to the heart and blood vessels.

Atria: The two upper chambers of the heart where blood collects before exiting through a valve to the ventricles.

Ventricles: The two lower chambers of the heart that pump blood through arteries to the lungs and the rest of the body.

Septum: A wall of muscle that separates the left and right sides of the heart.

The right side of the heart, consisting of the right atrium and right ventricle, collects oxygen-poor blood as it returns from circulating around the body, then pumps it into the lungs through the pulmonary artery. The lungs refresh the blood with oxygen and return it to the heart via the left atrium, which empties oxygen-rich blood into the left ventricle. From there, blood is pumped into the body via the **aorta**. Each heart chamber has a one-way valve that prevents blood from flowing back into it. When the chamber contracts, the valve at its exit opens, then closes again when the contraction is completed. Each contraction or beat, called **systole**, pumps blood out of the heart. Initially, the right atrium contracts as it receives blood through the **vena cava**, the largest vein in the body. As this contraction occurs, blood is pumped to the right ventricle, which contracts to push blood from the heart into the lungs. **Diastole**, the pressure that exists when the heart rests, occurs between contractions, allowing the heart to refill with blood. Oxygenated blood returns to the heart from the lungs, moving with each contraction through the pulmonary veins into the left atrium, then into the left ventricle, pumping blood to the rest of the body in a process known as **systemic circulation**.

Challenge Question: Describe how blood is returned from the body and pumped through the heart.

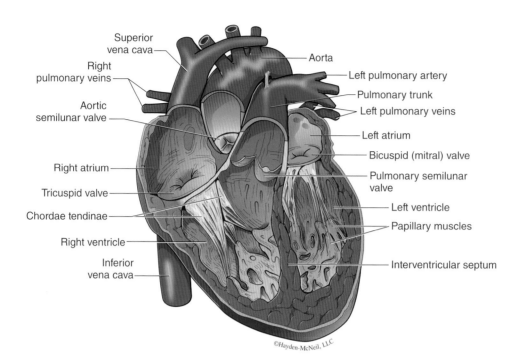

FIGURE 10-1. The human heart.

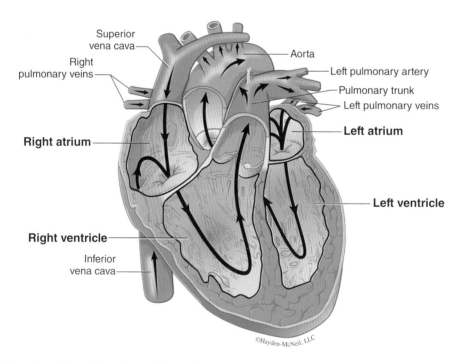

FIGURE 10-2. Direction of blood flow through the atrium and ventricles.

Key Terms

Aorta: The largest artery in the body; delivers oxygen-rich blood from the heart to the body.

Systole: The contraction phase or working phase of the heart.

Vena cava: The largest vein in the body; delivers oxygen-poor blood to the atria.

Diastole: The relaxation phase between contractions of the heart.

Systemic circulation: The circulation of blood from the heart to the rest of the body.

The heartbeat is controlled by an electrical pulse sent from the **sinoatrial node**, in the upper wall of the right atrium. Unless the brain signals danger, exhaustion, or exercise, this pulse occurs at a steady, even rate. Veins, arteries, and capillaries are responsible for the movement of blood to and from the heart and throughout the body. Veins have thinner walls than arteries and return oxygen-depleted blood to the heart. Arteries have thicker, more elastic walls that expand and contract as needed for blood circulation. Capillaries are the smallest extremities of arteries—just one cell thick—and deliver oxygen-rich blood to the tissues in exchange for oxygen-poor blood and waste products, which return to the heart through the veins. Blood circulates completely through the body in just one minute.

In **pulmonary circulation**, the right side of the heart collects oxygen-poor blood from the veins and pumps it into the lungs, where it picks up oxygen and releases carbon dioxide. After blood is oxygenated in the lungs, it moves through the left side of the heart and is pumped into the body through the aorta via systemic circulation.

___

Challenge Question: Into which chambers does de-oxygenated blood flow?

___

Key Terms

Sinoatrial node: The pacemaker of the heart.

Pulmonary circulation: The circulation of blood between the heart and the lungs.

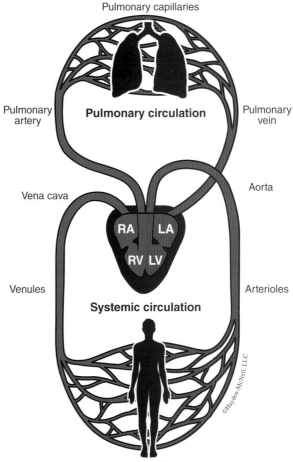

FIGURE 10-3. Direction of blood flow through atrium and ventricles.

Cardiovascular Disease Risk Factors

There are two categories of risk factors for CVD: lifestyle factors that can be changed or modified, and those that cannot be changed, including gender, ethnicity, heredity, and age.

Major Modifiable Risk Factors

The AHA has identified six major risk factors for cardiovascular disease that can be changed by behavior modification.

Tobacco Use

Twenty percent of all CVD deaths can be attributed to smoking. Tobacco use is the number one preventable cause of CVD in the U.S., and risks are increased as use is increased. A person who smokes one pack a day doubles the risk of heart attack over nonsmokers of the same age; smoking two or more packs a day triples this risk. When a smoker suffers a heart attack, he is 2–3 times more likely to die than if he were a nonsmoker.[3] On average, adults who smoke cigarettes die 14 years earlier than nonsmokers.[4]

Women who smoke increase their risk even more if they also take birth control pills. A female smoker taking birth control pills is 32 times more likely to suffer a heart attack, and 20 times more likely to suffer a stroke than a nonsmoking female on birth control pills.

There are several physiological problems caused by smoking. Nicotine is a central nervous system stimulant, increasing blood pressure and heart rate. Smoke contains carbon monoxide, which displaces oxygen in the bloodstream and as a result, oxygen-poor blood is transported around the body, causing all parts of the body to suffer. Because oxygenated blood is necessary to produce **high-density lipoproteins** (good cholesterol), smoking increases **low-density lipoproteins** (bad cholesterol) and **triglycerides**, causing **platelets** in the blood to become sticky, which promotes clots. Smoking also causes fats to be deposited onto arterial walls more quickly, increasing the risk for CVD.

Secondhand smoke has been classified as a known cause of cancer in humans. It is responsible for approximately 3,400 lung cancer deaths and 46,000 heart disease deaths in adult nonsmokers in the U.S. each year.[5,6,7]

Key Terms

High-density lipoproteins (HDL): A blood constituent involved in the transport of cholesterol and associated with a decreased risk of atherosclerosis.

Low-density lipoproteins (LDL): A plasma protein that is the major carrier of cholesterol in the blood. High levels are associated with atherosclerosis.

Triglycerides: Chains of high-energy fatty acids that provide much of the energy needed for cells to function.

Platelets: Any of the numerous small, round cell fragments in the blood that aid in clotting.

Obesity

Obesity is now a global epidemic in both children and adults. In addition to being an independent risk factor for CVD, it is also associated with type II diabetes, hypertension, certain cancers, sleep apnea, increased risk of

morbidity and **mortality**, and reduced life expectancy.[8] Obesity causes changes in lipid profiles, blood pressure, and blood-glucose levels, and predisposes the individual to cardiac complications such as coronary heart disease, heart failure, and sudden death. The epidemic of obesity began in the 1980s, and the prevalence of overweight adults continues to increase.[9] Obesity is measured by **body mass index** (BMI). For people 18–85 years of age, a BMI of 23–25 is considered optimal for whites, and 23–30 for black individuals.[10] A BMI from 25–29.9 is considered overweight, while over 30 is considered obese. Abdominal obesity is also a risk for CVD.[11]

Key Terms

Morbidity: State of ill health or disease.

Mortality: Risk of death.

Body mass index: Body weight in kilograms divided by height, squared, in meters, resulting in a number correlated with body fat.

Critical Thinking Question: Describe why being overweight is a risk factor for CVD.

High Blood Cholesterol

Cholesterol and other fats in the blood are influenced by diet, activity level, tobacco use, genetic predisposition, age, and ethnicity. Overall cholesterol values are a possible indicator for CVD: values less than 200 mg/dl of blood are considered a lower risk for CVD, while values between 200 and 239 mg/dl are borderline high. At above 240 mg/dl, a person has twice the risk of a coronary heart disease as someone whose level is below 200 mg/dl.[12] There are several types of lipoproteins, but of primary interest for cardiovascular health are low-density lipoproteins (LDL) and high-density lipoproteins (HDL).

Low-density lipoprotein are often called bad cholesterol, because they are associated with **atherosclerosis**, a common form of **arteriosclerosis**. These two degenerative conditions affect the health of the arteries. Healthy arteries are normally flexible, strong, and elastic, but low-density lipoproteins cause the arteries to thicken, lose elasticity, and reduce blood flow, resulting in atherosclerosis. When blood vessels become constricted, there is a risk of **myocardial infarction** (heart attack), stroke, and **peripheral vascular disease**.

> **Key Terms**
>
> **Atherosclerosis**: A common form of arteriosclerosis in which fatty substances form a deposit of plaque on the inner lining of arterial walls, restricting blood flow.
>
> **Arteriosclerosis**: Degenerative changes in the arteries, characterized by thicker vessel walls, accumulation of calcium, and consequent loss of elasticity and lessened blood flow.
>
> **Myocardial infarction**: An interruption of blood flow to the heart causing part of the heart muscle to die. Commonly called a heart attack.
>
> **Peripheral vascular disease**: Any disease or disorder of the circulatory system outside of the heart and brain.

In 2003, The American Heart Association (AHA) and the National Institutes of Health (NIH) released new guidelines for LDL levels. These guidelines, shown in Table 10-1, are based on the goal of decreasing death rates from cardiovascular diseases.

Table 10-1. Cholesterol Values

TOTAL CHOLESTEROL INTERPRETATION	
	mg/dl
Desirable	<200
Borderline high	200–239
High	>239
LDL CHOLESTEROL—THE "BAD" CHOLESTEROL	
Optimal	<100
Near/above optimum	100–129
Borderline high	130–159
High	160–189
Very high	>189
HDL CHOLESTEROL—THE "GOOD" CHOLESTEROL	
low (undesirable)	<40
high (desirable)	>60

(Extracted from National Cholesterol Education Program, NIH Publication 05-3290; Revised June 2005.)

High-density lipoproteins carry cholesterol from all parts of the body to the liver. HDL is considered good cholesterol, since the liver breaks down cholesterol and excretes it out of the body via the bile duct.

Lifestyle changes can help improve cholesterol levels. Eliminating saturated and trans fats from the diet, and replacing them with smaller amounts of monounsaturated and polyunsaturated fats, can improve HDL levels. Adding soluble fiber foods and, for those that do not have any issues with alcohol, one to two glasses of red wine each day also improves HDL levels. Aerobic exercise has been shown to reduce overall cholesterol level and increase HDL levels; smoking cessation will reduce both total cholesterol and LDL, and helps increase HDL; and weight loss and ideal body weight maintenance also improve cholesterol values by increasing HDL.

Challenge Question: Why is low-density lipoprotein considered bad cholesterol?

Critical Thinking Question: How does secondhand smoke increase the risk for CVD?

Hypertension (High Blood Pressure)

Because there are no symptoms, hypertension (high blood pressure) is sometimes called the silent killer, and it is a leading cause of CVD and **stroke**.

Blood pressure is essential for circulating blood. Many things can cause blood pressure to increase, including exercise and excitement, but these short-term bouts of high blood pressure are not harmful. However, sustained high blood pressure is damaging to arteries, and is also a stroke risk.

> **Key Term**
>
> **Stroke**: A stoppage of blood flow to the brain.

Blood pressure is measured with a stethoscope and a sphygmomanometer, or blood pressure cuff, producing a measurement in milliliters of mercury. The cuff is wrapped around the upper arm and inflated to produce pressure. As the cuff is deflated, the pressure in the arteries can be measured. The systolic pressure is heard first, followed by the resting diastolic pressure. Systolic pressure is always higher, since this is the contraction of the working heart. Normal systolic pressure in a healthy adult is about 115 millimeters of mercury, and normal diastolic pressure is about 75 millimeters of mercury. The two numbers are expressed as systolic over diastolic, or 115/75. Table 10-2 shows classifications of blood pressure.

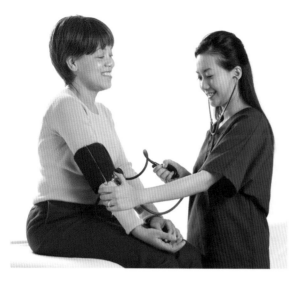

High blood pressure is caused as blood flow meets resistance in the arteries due to atherosclerosis, or by an increased output of blood from the heart caused by excitement or exercise. Atherosclerosis narrows the passage through the arteries, and the heart must work harder to circulate blood through these narrower vessels. This strains and subsequently weakens both the heart and the arteries.

Over time, hypertension damages vital organs and increases the risk for a heart attack, congestive heart failure, stroke, kidney failure, and blindness. Unfortunately, in about 90 percent of cases the specific cause of hypertension is unknown, but it is thought to be a combination of genetic, environmental, and behavioral factors. Environmental factors include any form of pollution that reduces oxygen to the lungs; behavioral factors include smoking, obesity, sedentary lifestyle, stress, and high-fat and high-salt diets. The remaining 10 percent of cases of hypertension are caused by a second underlying illness, and are referred to as secondary hypertension.

Almost one in every three people has hypertension. Risk increases with age, although it can occur in children, as well. Some women experience hypertension during pregnancies, but this is typically resolved when the baby is delivered. Women using oral contraceptives are up to three times as likely to suffer from hypertension as other women.

Table 10-2. Blood Pressure Classifications for Adults 18 and Older

CATEGORY	SYSTOLIC (MM HG)		DIASTOLIC (MM HG)
Normal	less than 120	and	less than 80
Prehypertension	120–139	or	80–89
HYPERTENSION			
Stage 1	140–159	or	90–99
Stage 2	160 or higher	or	100 or higher

Challenge Question: What are the symptoms of high blood pressure?

Sedentary Lifestyle

Since the heart is a muscle, the only way to keep it strong and efficient is to exercise. Despite the evidence about the benefits of exercise, most people do not exercise enough. Women are less likely to exercise than men, and as people age, they are less likely to exercise. Ethnicity and **socioeconomic status (SES)** also seem to influence exercise habits; for example, whites of higher SES status appear more likely to develop a regular exercise routine.

Many people may say they do not have time to exercise. However, those who exercise regularly are not working fewer hours, attending fewer classes, or less involved with family and social life. The only difference is the decision to make exercise an important part of life.

> **Key Term**
>
> **Socioeconomic status (SES)**: A combined measure of an individual or a family's economic and social position relative to others, based on income, education, and occupation.

Diabetes

In the U.S., 25.8 million people have diabetes and another 57 million have pre-diabetes. Most diagnosed diabetics have type II diabetes, a disease commonly considered preventable. Diabetes and pre-diabetes include an increased risk for heart disease: for those with type I diabetes, controlling blood sugar, consuming a low-fat diet with plenty of fruit and vegetables, and exercising regularly can help offset this risk. For those with type II diabetes, weight loss, exercise, and appropriate diet will reduce the need for medications and also reduce the risk of heart disease.

Dietary changes, weight loss, and exercise may prevent those with pre-diabetes from becoming diabetic, thereby reducing the risk of heart disease.

Critical Thinking Question: What methods would you use to improve blood sugar control for someone with diabetes?

Image of Health in Depth

Staying Healthy

Have you noticed some common themes when it comes to improving your health? Many are risk factors that can be modified—for example, you probably know you should stop smoking and start exercising. But why? Because smoking reduces the amount of oxygen in your blood, and exercise increases it. Appropriate weight and body fat levels are another common theme: the heavier you are, the harder every organ in your body must work. Higher body fat levels, particularly in the abdomen, are associated with higher risks for CVD. The last common theme is diet. Without a doubt, eating more vegetables and fruit and reducing your intake of fats will improve all aspects of your health. Four simple things: stop smoking, start exercising, and maintain an appropriate weight and diet. Which one of these are you ready to accept as a challenge?

Non-Modifiable Risk Factors

Non-modifiable risk factors are those that cannot be changed, such as age, ethnicity, gender, and heredity. Although these factors can't be altered, responsible decisions about health and accountability for lifestyle behaviors will help reduce health risks.

Age

As with any other part of the body, the condition of the heart deteriorates with increasing age. This deterioration can be stalled using responsible lifestyle behaviors, but eventually, advancing age will affect your heart. About 70 percent of all heart attack patients are age 65 or older, and about 80 percent of those who have a heart attack after this age will die as a result. For those over 55, the risk of stroke doubles with every passing decade.

Ethnicity

African Americans have higher rates of hypertension, heart disease, and stroke than all other ethnic groups, which may be due to SES and level of education. Generally, members of lower socioeconomic groups are more likely to smoke, live sedentary lifestyles, and have poor dietary habits. However, increased rates of hypertension in people of color may not be solely dependent on socioeconomic status, and researchers are still working to determine causal factors. The known factors are that blood pressure may be improved by smoking cessation, regular exercise, normal weight, and a healthy diet. With a responsible approach to lifestyle, ethnic minorities may be able to reduce their risk of hypertension, heart disease, and stroke.

Gender

Cardiovascular disease is the leading cause of death for both men and women. Men generally have a higher risk of hypertension, though at around age 55, women begin to experience the same risk—until this age, women may be protected by the hormone estrogen. However, smoking, diabetes, and abnormal blood lipids negate the protective factor estrogen provides. For men and women, changing risky lifestyle factors affords protection.

The American Heart Association's Go Red Campaign has helped women learn and respond to risk factors, since risk factors and symptoms of CVD are often different from those of men. In men, plaque is distributed in clumps within the arteries, while plaque in women is more evenly distributed throughout the arterial walls, which may be misinterpreted as normal in an angiographic study. Additionally, rather than experiencing chest pain, most women instead experience flu-like symptoms and a sudden onset of weakness prior to a heart attack. Women also wait longer to go to an emergency room when having a heart attack, and because characteristic chest pain is less frequent in women, doctors may not immediately recognize the presence of a heart attack.

Heredity

Unfortunately, no single gene has been identified as the cause of CVD; rather, it appears as though a cluster of genetic factors is responsible. Combining these genetic factors with lifestyle risk factors such as high blood cholesterol, smoking, poor diet, and poor exercise compounds the risk.

Having a family member diagnosed with early onset **coronary artery disease (CAD)** prior to age 60 increases your risk by about seven times, and the risk is even higher if the family member is younger and/or female. An inherited risk factor cannot be changed, but with careful monitoring of heart health and by practicing heart healthy behaviors, the risk can be greatly reduced.

Key Term

Coronary artery disease (CAD): A narrowing of the small blood vessels that supply oxygen and blood to the heart. CAD is also called coronary heart disease (CHD).

Challenge Question: List and describe the non-modifiable risk factors for heart disease.

Contributing Risk Factors

Other modifiable risk factors have been identified as contributing to CVD risk. These include triglyceride levels and factors relating to your personal psychological profile, particularly a tendency toward anger and hostility.

Triglyceride Levels

Triglycerides are the blood fats obtained from food and also produced by the body. If associated with high blood cholesterol, high triglyceride levels can predict heart disease, particularly in combination with other risk factors, such as diabetes and obesity. Although the role of triglycerides is not fully understood, physicians usually recommend a full lipid screening (blood fat screening) to include both types of cholesterol and triglyceride values. As with high cholesterol, triglyceride values can be decreased with exercise, dietary changes, weight loss, and smoking cessation. The National Cholesterol Education Program (NCEP) advises that normal triglycerides are less than 150 mg/dl, while a level over 200 mg/dl blood is considered high.

Key Term

Lipid: Organic compound comprised of fat and found in the blood.

Stress

Although it seems logical to assume that stress can cause or accelerate heart disease, scientific research does not clearly indicate that this is the case. People experience and respond to stress in different ways, and it is difficult to measure both the amount of stress experienced and the individual stress response given. It may be that stress causes other risk factors to be magnified, or that when people experience ongoing stress, eating behavior is affected, they may exercise less, smoke, and pay less attention to their general state of health.[13] Heart disease occurs when various risk factors occur together—no single factor is responsible, but managing individual factors may help reduce risk.[14]

Social Factors

Certain social factors, such as isolation and low socio-economic status, seem to increase both heart disease risk and survival. Isolated people are less likely to survive a myocardial infarction than people who have emotional support, even with similar levels of medical care. In addition, socioeconomic status may increase risk simply because less educated people are more likely to engage in fewer heart healthy behaviors. Certain personality types also accrue a higher risk: hostility and anger, particularly in men, increase the risk for earlier onset heart disease due to earlier development of atherosclerosis.[15]

Image of Health In Depth

Are You Angry Enough to Cause Heart Disease?

Cynical people who are quick to anger and who tend to be hostile and argumentative are more likely to develop heart disease. This may be because anger, hostility, and even arguments initiate the stress response in the body, leading to increased blood pressure, heart rate, and stress hormones. A cynical, mistrusting attitude seems to be a predictor for heart disease, an idea studies have supported for over thirty years.

In 2007, Duke University researcher Dr. Redford Williams developed a brief hostility test. According to published research, answering yes to five or more of the following statements suggests you are extremely hostile. Finding ways to be easygoing and good-natured can reduce your risk of CVD.

1. I often get annoyed at checkout cashiers, or at the people in front of me in line.

2. I usually keep an eye on the people I work with and live with to make sure they are doing what they should.

3. I often wonder how homeless people can have so little respect for themselves.

4. I believe that most people will take advantage of you if you let them.

5. The habits of friends or family members often annoy me.

6. When I am stuck in traffic, I often start breathing faster and my heart pounds.

7. When I am annoyed with people, I really want to let them know it.

8. If someone does me wrong, I want to get even.

9. I like to have the last word in any argument.

10. At least once a week, I have the urge to yell at someone or even hit him or her.

Stimulant Drugs and Alcohol

Cocaine and **methamphetamine** are stimulant drugs that can increase blood pressure and heart rate, causing significant heart health problems, such as myocardial infarction, stroke, and sudden cardiac death. The risks involved with these stimulants are not associated with the amount of the drug used, its administration route, or the frequency of use.[16] While alcohol, when consumed in moderate amount, has been shown to be heart protective in some studies, it also increases blood pressure, and when consumed in large quantities can increase the risk for heart failure and stroke.

Key Terms

Cocaine: An illicit drug made from coca leaves, used for its stimulant and euphorigenic properties.

Methamphetamine: A manmade substance used in medical treatments for hypotension and narcolepsy, and also used illicitly as a stimulant.

Other Factors

Metabolic syndrome is a cluster of conditions that when combined, increases the risk for CVD, stroke, and diabetes.[17] These conditions, including obesity, high blood pressure, elevated triglycerides, low levels of HDL, and resistance to insulin, seem to synergize to amplify risk. High levels of homocysteine, a common amino acid, have also been linked to increased risk for CVD.[18] Because homocysteine is found in animal products, reducing consumption of meat may result in lower levels. Testing for homocysteine levels is very expensive and is not routinely performed or covered by insurance.

Image of Health in Depth

Homocysteine Levels and Oxidized LDL Particles

Homocysteine is an amino acid produced in the body as a by-product of eating meat. Elevated levels of homocysteine (>15 micromoles per liter of blood) may be associated with atherosclerosis and an increased risk of heart attacks, strokes, blood clot formation, and possibly Alzheimer's disease. Normal levels are between 5–15 micromoles/liter; levels above 100 are considered severe. The consumption of foods containing folic acid, and to lesser extent vitamins B6 and B12, may lower homocysteine levels. However, to date there is no research confirming that high homocysteine levels leads to the prevention of heart disease.

Normal LDL in plasma is not oxidized. Oxidation is believed to contribute to the development of atherosclerosis, occurring when free radicals in the blood increase existing LDL cholesterol.[19] Although a certain amount of LDL is needed for normal cell function, it can be a risk for oxidized LDL when there is too much. **Oxidized LDL** tends to initiate the development of atherosclerosis and also inhibits white blood cell activity. Since oxidized LDL occurs as a result of free radicals, it follows that supplementation with antioxidants may reduce the level, though recent studies have not supported this assessment.

Key Term

Oxidized LDL particles: A low-density lipoprotein containing free radicals that can react with tissues, causing damage.

Studies on lipoprotein (a) and coronary heart disease have produced inconclusive results. Lipoprotein (a) consists of a portion of LDL combined with a protein, the exact function of which is unknown. Although there has been a clear association shown between lipoprotein (a) and heart disease, the exact extent to which it might be causal is still unknown. There is no treatment for lipoprotein (a) in blood plasma.[20]

Inflammation is one cause of atherosclerosis, and one form in particular that influences atherosclerosis is the inflammatory response caused by C-reactive protein.[20] Adding a screening for C-reactive protein to lipid tests may help identify those who are at an increased risk for CVD.

In the last decade, several new risk factors for atherosclerosis have been identified, including those listed above. In addition, two infectious agents have been linked with coronary heart disease: Herpes viruses and *Chlamydia pneumoniae* have been shown to initiate and accelerate development of atherosclerosis in animal models. If this is confirmed in human subjects, these two agents may be considered causal in the development of atherosclerosis. Several intervention trials have been underway since 2002, to determine if antibiotics and vaccinations will work to prevent infections.[22]

Motivation Maximizer

What role have you chosen?

Are you a victim or a victor? If you perceive that problems in your life are caused by situations that are out of your control, if you think you have more bad luck than others, if you believe nothing will ever change no matter what actions you take, then you see yourself as a victim. And bad things often happen to victims because they do not assume responsibility, nor hold themselves accountable for what happens to them. But if you are a victor, you are a take-charge person. You create your own luck and you change the things in your life that are not right for you. Everyone can *choose* whether to be a victor or a victim, and often, people switch between the two roles depending on the situation.

Most Americans will die of CVD, and many will die too young, possibly because they choose to play the role of victim relative to their health. They think nothing can be done to increase life expectancy or prevent disease, and that everyone must die from something. This attitude removes responsibility from the person, but the consequent accountability will prevail.

Of course, you can choose to be a victor and make daily changes to protect your heart health. In doing so, there will be a cumulative effect to other aspects of your health. Consider how easy it might be to find time to walk, or eat some vegetables, or reduce your overall calories, if you need to lose weight. Look around you: thousands of people make little changes every day. You can join this group and become a victor, or you can continue in the victim role. It really is up to you!

The Many Forms of Cardiovascular Disease

Cardiovascular disease has been the leading cause of death in the U.S. since the 1900s, and affects all of us one way or another. Most people think of myocardial infarctions (heart attacks) when they think of this disease, but it comes in many forms: atherosclerosis, heart disease and myocardial infarctions, congenital heart disease, peripheral arterial disease (PAD), rheumatic heart disease, and heart valve problems are the most prevalent.

Atherosclerosis

The main form of arteriosclerosis is atherosclerosis, which occurs when endothelial cells (cells that line arteries) are damaged. The damage to these cells is due to a number of factors, including smoking, hypertension, high homocysteine levels, and deposits of oxidized LDL particles.

Damaged arteries become inflamed, attracting LDL, platelets, and other cells that build up, creating deposits and causing the arterial walls to bulge. These deposits, called **plaque**, make it difficult for the arteries to expand and contract as necessary, reducing blood flow and raising blood pressure. Narrowed arteries are more likely to become blocked by blood clots, resulting in a deprivation of oxygen to organs and systems at the end of the blocked artery. If this occurs in the brain, a stroke results; if it occurs in the heart, it results in a heart attack. Coronary arteries—those that supply blood to the heart—are particularly vulnerable to plaque build-up, causing coronary artery disease. **Peripheral artery disease** occurs when an artery in a limb is narrowed or blocked, causing pain, lack of circulation, and tissue damage, and may require that the limb be amputated.

Major risk factors for atherosclerosis include smoking, sedentary lifestyle, hypertension and high blood cholesterol, diabetes, and family history. This progressive but reversible disease often begins in childhood.

Key Terms

Plaque: A fatty deposit inside an arterial wall; a characteristic of atherosclerosis.

Peripheral artery disease: A disease in which arteries become narrowed or blocked, causing a reduced supply of oxygenated blood to parts of the body.

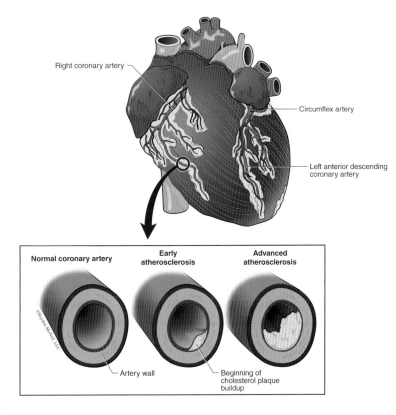

FIGURE 10-4. Blocked coronary artery showing reduced blood flow.

Coronary Artery Disease

Coronary artery disease (CAD) is the leading cardiovascular disease, occurring when coronary arteries become blocked by plaque. Since these arteries supply the heart muscle with oxygenated blood, when a blockage occurs, part of the heart will not receive enough oxygenated blood for normal heart functioning, potentially resulting in a myocardial infarction. Plaque is made of fat, cholesterol, calcium, and other substances. Coronary artery disease is caused by a variety of factors, including smoking, high amounts of fats and cholesterol in the blood, hypertension, and either insulin resistance or diabetes, leading to high amounts of sugar in the blood.

A common symptom of CAD is **angina**, a chest pain or discomfort that occurs when the heart does not get enough oxygen-rich blood. Symptoms of angina will be more severe with exercise or in extreme cold weather. If the CAD is causing **heart failure**, it may be accompanied with shortness of breath. Each of these symptoms gets more severe as the plaque continues to narrow arteries.

Silent CAD occurs when there are no symptoms. In this case, it may not be diagnosed until after a myocardial infarction, heart failure, or an **arrhythmia** is detected.

An arrhythmia is a problem with the rate of rhythm of the heartbeat. During an arrhythmia, the heart may beat too fast, called **tachycardia**, or too slow, called **bradycardia**.

When the heart beats either too fast, too slowly, or erratically, it may not be able to pump enough blood around the body. This can damage the brain, heart, and other organs.

Arrhythmias are caused by smoking, heavy alcohol consumption, certain central nervous stimulants (cocaine and amphetamines), certain prescription and OTC drugs, and caffeine.

Most arrhythmias are harmless, and many do not show symptoms. When signs and symptoms do occur, they generally include:

- Palpitations—feeling that your heart is skipping a beat, or beating too hard or too fast.

- An irregular heartbeat.

- Feeling pauses between heartbeats.

More serious symptoms include anxiety, dizziness, fainting or nearly fainting, sweating, shortness of breath, and chest pain.

Key Terms

Angina: Chest pain or discomfort when the heart does not receive enough oxygen-rich blood.

Heart failure: A condition in which the heart cannot pump enough blood to the body. It is caused either by inadequate amounts of blood reaching the heart, or inadequate force to pump the blood.

Arrhythmia: An irregular heartbeat, in which the heart skips beats or beats too fast. Some arrhythmias can cause the heart to stop beating, leading to sudden cardiac arrest.

Tachycardia: A fast heart rate.

Bradycardia: A heartbeat of less than 60 beats per minute that is physiologically inadequate for the patient. (In some patients, a heart rate of less than 60 is adequate.)

Critical Thinking Question: What is the difference between arteriosclerosis and atherosclerosis?

Image of Health in Depth

Warning Signs of a Heart Attack

- Chest discomfort. Most heart attacks involve discomfort in the center of the chest that lasts more than a few minutes, or that deminishes, then resumes. Symptoms are uncomfortable pressure, squeezing, fullness, or pain.

- Discomfort in other areas of the upper body that may include pain or discomfort in one or both arms, the back, neck, jaw, or stomach.

- Shortness of breath with or without chest discomfort.

- Other signs may include breaking out in a cold sweat, nausea, or lightheadedness.

- The most common heart attack symptom in women is chest pain or discomfort. But women are somewhat more likely than men to experience some of the other common symptoms, particularly shortness of breath, nausea/vomiting, and back or jaw pain.

Warning Signs of a Stroke

- Sudden numbness or weakness of the face, arm, or leg, especially on one side of the body.

- Sudden confusion, trouble speaking or understanding.

- Sudden trouble seeing in one or both eyes.

- Sudden trouble walking, dizziness, loss of balance or coordination.

- Sudden, severe headache with no known cause.

Extracted and modified from American Heart Association, 2008.

Sudden Cardiac Arrest

Also known as sudden cardiac death, **sudden cardiac arrest** is caused by a malfunction in the sinoatrial node that controls heart contractions, causing the heart to stop beating. When this occurs, blood cannot flow to the brain and other organs. This differs from a myocardial infarction, in which blood flow is blocked to part of the heart muscle. Sudden cardiac arrest results in death in about 95 percent of cases, most within minutes of early symptoms.

Key Term

Sudden cardiac arrest: A condition in which the heart suddenly and unexpectedly stops beating.

Image of Health in Depth

Saving a Life

In 2005, the AHA changed its guidelines for non-trained rescuers when faced with a collapsed cardiac arrest victim. The AHA now recommends that *only* chest compressions take place immediately, rather than traditional cardiopulmonary resuscitation, which uses both rescue breathing and compressions. The first six minutes after cardiac arrest are the most critical for rescue, and some concerns were presented regarding mouth-to-mouth rescue breathing causing vital time to be lost. If only chest compressions are given, professional rescuers are ten times more likely to find a treatable victim. Lay rescuers are taught to give two rescue breaths to a non-responsive victim, then begin chest compressions by pushing the breastbone down about two inches (one inch for children) and then releasing. Compressions should be delivered hard and fast, at a rate of about 100 compressions per minute.

Ideally, it is better for all adults to be trained in CPR, so that skills can be practiced before an emergency occurs.

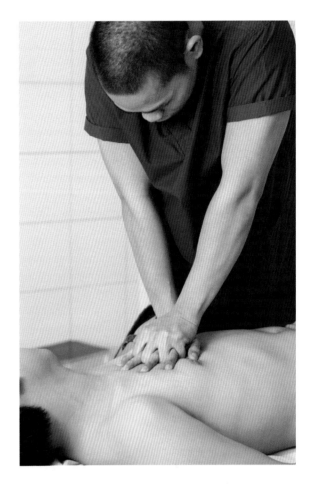

Congestive Heart Failure

Congestive heart failure is a progressive disease usually caused by a series of diseases that impair the pumping action of the heart, including hypertension, long-term alcohol abuse, disorders with heart valves, and less frequently, arrhythmia. Congestive heart failure is diagnosed when the heart is unable to pump adequately to meet the needs of the body.

Symptoms of congestive heart failure vary, but typically include a diminished capacity for exercise, shortness of breath, and swelling in the extremities. Treatment includes lifestyle modification, medications, and possibly a mechanical therapy such as a pacemaker or a heart transplant.

Other Cardiovascular Diseases

Some forms of CVD are **congenital**—present at birth—though symptoms may not appear until later in life. Other symptoms develop over time, affecting the structure and function of the heart.

Congenital Heart Disease

Congenital heart disease, a defect in one or more structures of the heart or blood vessels that occurs during fetal development, affects approximately 8–10 of every 1,000 children. It is responsible for more deaths in the first year of life than any other birth defect, and about one-half million adults in the U.S. have a congenital heart disease.

In most cases, the cause of the disease is unknown. However, factors such as genetic or chromosomal abnormalities, taking certain medications during pregnancy, alcohol or drug abuse during pregnancy, or viral infections during the first trimester increase the risk.

Some of these defects may heal themselves during growth and development, while others require treatment, and some will need monitoring throughout life. Treatment may involve medications, or possibly surgery. The risk of death from congenital heart disease has decreased over the past thirty years, from about 30 percent to less than 5 percent in most cases today.

Rheumatic Heart Disease

Rheumatic heart disease is the most serious complication of **rheumatic fever**, which develops in children and adolescents following sore throat infections, typically caused by an untreated or poorly treated **streptococcal infection**. Symptoms of rheumatic heart disease and the damage it may cause vary greatly. In some cases, a heart valve either doesn't close or open fully, and eventually, damaged heart valves can lead to serious and disabling problems with heart circulation. One hundred years ago, rheumatic heart disease was a leading cause of death in people aged 5–20 years. But with the advent of antibiotics to treat streptococcal infections, rheumatic fever is now uncommon among children, so the incidence of rheumatic heart disease has decreased significantly.

Key Terms

Congenital: Existing at birth.

Rheumatic fever: An inflammatory disease affecting many of the body's connective tissues, especially those of the heart, joints, brain, and skin.

Streptococcal infection: A bacterial infection that results in sore throat, fever, pain, redness, and swelling of the throat and tonsils. Symptoms can be mild to severe, and the condition is contagious.

Cardiomyopathy

Cardiomyopathy causes the heart cavity to become enlarged and too weak to pump efficiently. Blood flows more slowly through an enlarged heart, so blood clots are more likely to form.

This serious condition occurs when the heart muscle becomes inflamed and doesn't function normally. Primary cardiomyopathy cannot be attributed to a specific cause but secondary cardiomyopathy is caused by hypertension, heart valve disease, CAD, congenital defects, or viral infections.

Heart Valve Disease

Heart valves work to control the flow of blood within the heart. They lie at the exit to each of the four heart chambers and maintain a one-way flow of blood through the heart. Blood flows from the right and left atria into ventricles through the open tricuspid and mitral valves. Once the ventricles are full, the valves close, preventing back flow. As the ventricles contract, the pulmonic and aortic valves are forced open and blood is pumped into the pulmonary artery toward the lungs, aorta, and the rest of the body. When the contraction is complete, the valves close.

There are several types of heart valve disease. Some occur when a valve does not close completely or does not close at all. Others are as a result of a valve being too small or too hard, and structural issues within the valve cause still other heart valve diseases. Each of these types can be congenital or occur later in life. Treatment involves protecting valves to minimize further damage, and repairing or replacing valves.

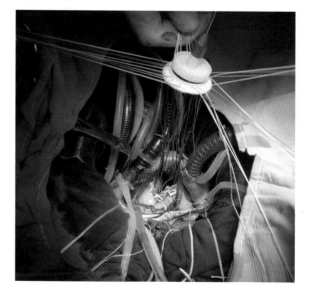

FIGURE 10-5. Prosthetic heart valve surgery.

Stroke

Stroke is the third leading cause of death in the U.S., and a leading cause of disability. The two main types of strokes are **ischemic strokes**, which occur in 80–85 percent of strokes, and **hemorrhagic strokes**. Ischemic strokes are caused when a blood vessel in the brain becomes so narrow or clogged that not enough oxygenated blood can reach the brain. As with CAD, these blockages are caused by plaque, which may be the result of smoking, high blood fats, and hypertension. The plaque may block only very small blood vessels within the brain, or may occur in larger blood vessels in the neck or in arteries leading to the brain. **Emboli** or travelling clots can also cause ischemic strokes.

Hemorrhagic strokes occur when the wall of a blood vessel becomes weak and blood leaks into the brain, causing damage to brain cells and resulting in less blood moving beyond the hemorrhage. If the hemorrhage is large, unrelieved pressure builds and damages other parts of the brain. Hemorrhagic strokes are caused by uncontrolled hypertension, weak spots in blood vessel walls called **aneurysms**, and infrequently by the rupture of a triangle of thin-walled blood vessels, present at birth.

Key Terms

Ischemic stroke: A stroke caused by an inadequate supply of oxygen-rich blood reaching part of the brain, resulting in death of brain cells.

Hemorrhagic stroke: A stroke caused by the rupture of a blood vessel in the brain, often due to an aneurysm.

Emboli: A mass that travels through the bloodstream, lodges in a blood vessel, and stops blood flow. Examples of emboli are a detached blood clot, a clump of bacteria, and foreign material such as air.

Aneurysm: A burst artery caused by weakening of the vessel wall.

Cedric's Story

Cedric won't make it to class this week. He received a call last night telling him his father had been rushed to the hospital following a heart attack. His father is just 51 years old.

On the plane ride home, Cedric thought about his father, about what might have caused this event and what could have been done to prevent it. His father had stopped smoking a couple of years ago, but was quite overweight. His mother would nag Cedric and her husband about their weight and food choices, and they would laugh at her. After all, Cedric's grandfather had lived to be almost 91 and died of cancer. His father never saw himself as a heart disease risk, though his blood pressure was high. Cedric believed himself to be in the same safe group, and along with his father he drank too much, didn't exercise, and ate whatever looked good at the moment. As he travelled home, he remembered how he had promised his mother to change when he went off to college. That had not happened.

In the taxi on the way to the hospital, Cedric got the call he had been dreading. His father had died. Devastated, Cedric remembered laughing with his dad as they ate pizza, and joking with his mother that yes, he would "start exercising just as soon as he had more time." Cedric wondered about his blood pressure. He had no idea what it was, and could not even remember the last time he went to a doctor. Although his father had smoked a couple of packs of cigarettes each day, Cedric only smoked when he was out with friends, and did not consider this a risk for anything except a good time.

At the hospital, Cedric consoled his mother as best he could. She kept asking what she should have done, how she could have helped protect her husband. Cedric had to tell her it was not her fault. It was his father's responsibility to eat better, exercise, lose weight, and take care of himself. As he said this, he wished he had done more to influence his dad. It was too late for that, but Cedric knew it was not too late for him. He would make the changes, becoming active in protecting his heart and all other aspects of his health.

If only he and his dad had been able to start these changes together. ∎

Diagnosis and Treatment of Cardiovascular Disease

Diagnostic and treatment techniques and methods continue to improve in the fight against CVD. The most important aspect of heart health is *preventing* disease before it occurs. Early diagnosis improves recovery and rehabilitation.

Diagnostic Tests for Heart Disease

Diagnosis depends on the symptoms a patient has experienced, as well as on evident risk factors. Generally, the first step in discovering heart disease is an **electrocardiogram** (ECG), which measures heart rate and indicates whether the heart is functioning normally. Following an ECG, a physician may recommend an **ejection fraction** to determine how much blood is pumped out by the left ventricle. Normal, healthy hearts eject from one-half to two-thirds of the blood in a chamber, and less than this indicates that the heart is not working efficiently. An additional **echocardiography** or echo test may be used to determine how thick the heart muscle is and how well it pumps. This safe and painless test uses sound waves that bounce off the heart, creating sonogram images of chambers and valves.

Other common tests include an **angiography**, exercise stress test, and blood tests. During an angiography, a patient is sedated and dye is injected into the coronary arteries through a catheter placed in the groin or arm. As the dye moves through the arteries, doctors can observe any blockages, possibly leading to an **angioplasty** procedure. In an angioplasty, a small catheter with a tiny inflatable balloon at its end is inserted through the catheter in the groin or arm. The balloon is inflated, expanding the arterial wall and stretching the plaque across the expanded area to allow greater blood flow. Angioplasties do not prolong or save lives; rather, they reduce discomfort for patients.

Exercise stress tests record the heart's activity during exercise to see whether the heart responds normally to the stress of exercise. Blood samples are taken to determine the levels of such substances as sodium and potassium (electrolytes), albumin and creatinine. Abnormally high levels of these substances may indicate strain on the body's organs caused by heart failure.

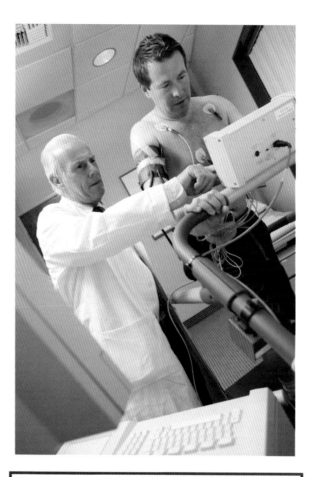

Key Terms

Electrocardiogram: A quick, painless test that records the electrical activity of the heart.

Ejection fraction: A test to measure the volume of blood pumped out by the left ventricle.

Echocardiography: A procedure that sends ultrasound waves into the chest to create moving pictures of the heart and valves.

Angiography: A technique in which dye is injected to determine the movement of blood through vessels and organs, particularly the heart.

Angioplasty: A technique to widen a narrowed or obstructed artery as a result of atherosclerosis. Tightly folded micro-balloons are inflated with water pressure at the site of the blockage to compress plaque and widen the vessel.

Medical Treatments for Heart Disease

Today, there are a large number of prescription drugs used to treat heart disease: some reduce blood pressure, others reduce blood cholesterol, and some thin the blood so it moves more readily through the body. Some patients, after a myocardial infarction or who may have risk for heart disease, are advised to take one baby aspirin (81 mg) each day as a blood thinner.[23] Many heart disease patients are on a variety of medications that must be taken at specific times throughout the day.

Another procedure to relieve a blocked coronary artery is **coronary bypass graft surgery** (CABG), in which blood is diverted around a blocked artery using a graft. Different types of grafts may be used, depending on where the blockage occurs. One common graft is taken from the mammary arteries, also called the **thoracic arteries**, which have been shown to have the best long-term results. Sections of the mammary artery are used to bypass a blocked artery. Saphenous veins taken from the leg of the patient are also used: small sections of the vein are removed, then sewn to divert blood around a blockage, as illustrated in Figure 10-6.

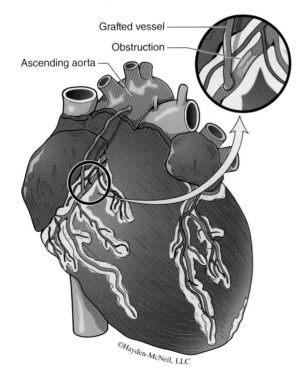

Grafted vessel

Obstruction

Ascending aorta

©Hayden-McNeil, LLC

FIGURE 10-6. Bypass surgery.

> **Key Terms**
>
> **Coronary bypass graft surgery**: A surgical procedure in which arteries or veins from other parts of the body are grafted onto coronary arteries to bypass blockages and improve blood flow.
>
> **Thoracic arteries**: Also known as internal mammary arteries, these arteries supply the anterior chest wall and breasts with oxygenated blood.

Since arrhythmias are a common cause of sudden death, patients with tachycardia or bradycardia may be treated with a defibrillator (electric shock therapy) to establish a normal heart rate. Further treatments may involve medications to maintain a constant, regular heartbeat and in some cases, a pacemaker is inserted into the patient. This device uses electrical pulses to prompt the heart to beat at a normal rate. Most pacemakers contain a sensor that activates only when the heartbeat is abnormal.

Following treatment, most arrhythmia patients undergo cardiac rehabilitation, wherein patients receive instruction on exercise safety and how to maintain a heart healthy lifestyle.

Diagnostic Tests for Strokes

Testing for strokes include imaging, brain electrical activity tests, and blood flow tests. Imaging tests include computed tomography (CT or CAT) and magnetic resonance imaging (MRI).

Computed tomography scans produce detailed images of the brain, eyes, and bones of the skull, providing information on the cause, location, and extent of a stroke. Magnetic resonance imaging tests uses a magnetic field to produce a graphic image of the brain. These images can show the location and extent of brain damage and can distinguish between a **transient ischemic attack**, and an **ischemic stroke**, and bleeding that causes a **hemorrhagic stroke**.

In order to measure how the brain handles different sensory information, electrical activity tests are used. An electroencephalogram (EEG) is the most commonly used measurement device, in which electrodes are placed on the scalp to pick up electrical impulses and results are printed out as brain waves.

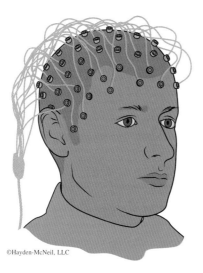

©Hayden-McNeil, LLC

FIGURE 10-7. Patient undergoing an EEG.

Blood flow tests use ultrasound technology to show the flow of blood through the brain. During these tests, a probe is placed in an artery, and the amount of blood flow is measured. Angiography is also used in the brain, in which a special dye is injected and tracked as it passes through vessels.

Key Terms

Transient ischemic attack: A mini-stroke caused when insufficient blood reaches part of the brain.

Ischemic stroke: The most common type of stroke, caused by an interruption of blood flow to the brain.

Hemorrhagic stroke: A stroke caused by the rupture of a blood vessel in the brain.

Medical Treatment for Strokes

Stroke patients often receive similar medicines to heart disease patients, including medicine for high blood pressure and high cholesterol, as well as blood thinners. The treatment that follows a stroke is determined by the extent of brain damage. Some patients may lose their mobility on one side of the body, or the ability to talk, see, or hear. Strokes can occur at any time in a person's life, although most occur in the elderly. Rehabilitation may involve learning how to speak, sit, or stand again, exercise classes, feeding classes, and classes to generate memory activity.

Protecting Against Cardiovascular Disease and Stroke

Cardiovascular disease kills more people than any other disease, but many of these deaths could be postponed, as could death caused by stroke. Taking responsibility for simple lifestyle changes helps reduce risk, and will help recovery if either of these diseases occurs.

Avoid or Stop Tobacco Use

About 35 percent of all smoking-related deaths in the U.S. are from CVD.[24] This translates to about 140,000 people dying each year unnecessarily. Smokers are 2–4 times more likely to develop some form of CHD than nonsmokers, and are 2–3 times as likely to die from it.

Women are not excluded: cardiovascular disease is the leading killer for women. The risk increases dramatically for women who smoke, and their survival rates diminish as a result of smoking.[25]

Smokers are not the only ones who die from tobacco use. Secondhand smoke causes the premature deaths of an estimated 46,000 people from secondhand smoke induced heart disease each year.[26]

If you smoke or use tobacco products, quitting will improve your health. See Chapter 13 for information on quitting. If you do not smoke, continuing to avoid tobacco use and exposure to secondhand smoke will help protect you from CVD. Working within your community to reduce the public areas where smoking is allowed will help prevent secondhand smoke from causing risks for you and others.

Follow a Heart Healthy Diet

To help reduce your risk of CVD, the National Institutes of Health recommend following a heart healthy diet that has:

- Less than 8–10 percent of daily total calories from saturated fat.

- Thirty percent or less of daily total calories from fat.

- Less than 300 milligrams of dietary cholesterol a day. (One egg yolk contains about 217 milligrams of cholesterol.)

- Less than 2400 milligrams of sodium per day. (One tablespoon of soy sauce contains about 1,000 mg sodium; one four-inch bagel contains about 450 mg sodium.)

- Just enough calories to achieve or maintain a healthy weight and reduce your blood cholesterol level.

Poor diet is one of the two most common risk factors for heart disease. A wide range of factors, including social, cultural, economic, and even geographical factors, influences dietary habits. Fresh fruits and vegetables may not be available during certain seasons, or they may be too expensive. Frozen and canned produce is a good alternative.

Fat intake has been clearly established as a risk factor, but the protective effects of certain food choices, diets, or dietary changes are not as clear. Gradually substituting foods containing saturated fat to foods with unsaturated fat helps reduce heart disease risk, provided that the total intake of fat is kept within healthy limits.[27] Reducing both the intake of foods containing salt and the addition of salt to foods helps keep blood pressure in check.[28] It is not difficult to make responsible choices, and it does not mean you can never again eat some of your favorite foods. It simply means ensuring that your diet primarily emphasizes vegetables, fruits, whole grains, and low-fat foods.

Exercise Regularly

Along with the identified risks from diet, physical inactivity is another major risk factor for heart disease. Even small amounts of exercise will reduce risk, so beginning slowly will be beneficial. Working toward exercising for thirty continuous minutes most days of the week will provide the most benefits. In starting an exercise routine, choose something you will enjoy—you will be more likely to make it part of your lifestyle. Chapter 8 offers guidelines on how to begin and maintain an exercise routine, another responsible choice you can make today.

Maintain a Healthy Weight

The greater your weight and percentage of body fat, the more work is required of your heart, so keeping weight and body composition within acceptable guidelines will reduce extra effort for the heart. In Chapters 7, 8, and 9, you learned how nutrition, fitness, and weight management work together. Being lean but not fit is not as protective to your heart, nor is being lean but not eating a heart-healthy diet. All three factors work together to help reduce the risk of CVD.

Managing Stress

Since stress is an inevitable and necessary part of life, eliminating it is not possible. However, it is possible to manage stress. The impact of stress on heart disease is influenced by personality type.[29] You can have a very stressful life, but if your personality type is low-key, laid-back, and unaggressive, your heart may not suffer from it. That same stressful life for a cynical, hostile personality can result in the onset of heart disease. From Chapter 3, you learned methods for coping with stress; you know that how you react to stress is a choice, and that you control your reaction. If you get frustrated waiting in line, what could you do to reduce the frustration? Certainly, you know that being frustrated does not make the line move faster. So, what benefits do you think you get from these feelings? Most people will answer that there are no benefits, so you must consider why you are allowing this feeling to occur.

Working on managing stress more efficiently and developing a less hostile, less cynical personality will help you reduce your risk of CVD.

Control Blood Pressure

High blood pressure is both a leading risk factor for CVD, as well as being an independent disease that can cause death. Although not all high blood pressure can be controlled without medication, it can be improved with some lifestyle changes. The main steps in reducing blood pressure are to quit smoking, reduce body weight, exercise, and improve diet. The DASH diet, described in Chapter 7, has been specifically developed to help reduce blood pressure. Most Americans consume more than the recommended maximum of 2,400 mg of sodium per day, and reducing or even eliminating added sodium in the diet is an important preventive step. It is even more important for older Americans, and for all African Americans. If lifestyle changes do not reduce blood pressure enough, there are several effective drugs available. Keeping your blood pressure below 140/90 is one way to reduce your risk of heart disease.

Monitor Cholesterol Levels

Blood cholesterol should be tested at certain intervals, depending on age, health, and other conditions. Older people and those with chronic diseases such as diabetes may need to have their cholesterol monitored at least annually. Younger, healthier individuals may need to monitor cholesterol every few years, unless advised by a physician to have it checked more frequently. If blood cholesterol is very high, appropriate steps including dietary changes, exercise, and even oral medications may be necessary to bring it into the normal range.

Challenge Question: What are the optimum values for blood cholesterol?

Critical Thinking Question: What could a person do to help bring down blood cholesterol values?

Control Diabetes

High blood sugars increase the risk for CVD in both type I and type II diabetics. If you have diabetes, keeping blood sugar values within appropriate ranges is essential. As you have learned, type II diabetes may be preventable by keeping weight in appropriate ranges, by eating a heart healthy calorie controlled diet, and by exercising. Type I diabetes can be managed with insulin infusion, exercise, and carbohydrate control, helping to keep blood sugars managed within appropriate ranges.

Living Heart Smart

Living heart smart is not difficult, but it does require responsible decision-making. Simple acts like parking further away from your destination so that you walk more, or choosing a low fat entrée rather than a fried entrée, are examples of living heart smart. It is up to you. Every little bit helps, and is a small step toward heart health.

Unfortunately, most heart attack victims do not have any warning signs before a heart attack, and one in four victims have normal cholesterol levels. One in three heart attacks are fatal within the first hour. After ensuring you live a heart healthy life, your next protective step is to be proactive for your heart health. You must recognize and react to symptoms of chest pain and a heart attack. Identify and treat your risk factors. You owe it to yourself and the people you care about to be heart healthy and heart protective. As Benjamin Franklin said, "an ounce of prevention is worth a pound of cure."

▼

Responsibility and Accountability

In this chapter, you have learned the risk factors for heart disease, the various types of heart disease, and the treatments for and ways to protect yourself from heart disease. To protect yourself, you must make informed choices each and every day, make decisions based on knowledge and science, and establish control by choosing to live a heart healthy lifestyle.

Taking Responsibility for Your Heart

Without a doubt, your heart health is your responsibility. But in recognizing this, are you living proactively to protect your heart health? You can answer yes to this question if you consciously elect to live a heart-healthy life on a daily basis. This morning, did you make nutritional choices that would protect your heart health? Yesterday, did you exercise? Did you monitor your blood pressure the last time you had access to a blood pressure monitoring device? You are being responsible if you answered yes to these questions. In general, you must recognize that much is under your control if you continually make choices to improve your heart health.

Focusing on Accountability

Most people want to avoid paying the price of accountability for not protecting their heart health. If you enjoy living a sedentary life today, perhaps smoking, or perhaps eating more pizza and fast food than healthy foods, do you think the cost will be worth it? At some point, everyone is held accountable for decisions they make. Thinking that you will change all this when you finish college, or get married, or start a career, does not protect you. Making changes today begins the protection.

Living responsibly and being accountable does not mean living a dull or boring life. It means making decisions based on what you want to get from your life and for how long you want that life to continue. It is under your control.

Summary

Cardiovascular Disease Risk Factors

- The heart is a muscular, cone shaped organ weighing between 7–15 ounces. It is comprised of four chambers, right atrium, right ventricle, left atrium and left ventricle.

- Modifiable risk factors include tobacco use, obesity, hypertension, high cholesterol levels, sedentary behavior and diabetes.

- Non-modifiable risk factors include age, ethnicity, gender and heredity.

- Contributing risk factors include triglyceride levels, stimulant drug use and alcohol intake, social factors, metabolic syndrome and others.

The Many Forms of Cardiovascular Disease

- Atherosclerosis is a leading form of arteriosclerosis. It often begins in childhood and is a leading cause of CVD and is a potentially fatal disease.

- Coronary heart disease includes angina, myocardial infarction, arrhythmias, and sudden cardiac death.

- The two major types of strokes are ischemic and hemorrhagic.

- Hypertension is often asymptomatic and is an independent disease as well as a significant risk factor for CVD.

- Congestive heart failure develops in relation to hypertension, myocardial infarctions, and aging.

- Other cardiovascular diseases include congenital diseases, valve disorders, rheumatic heart disease, cardiomyopathy, and peripheral artery disease.

Diagnosis and Treatment of Cardiovascular Disease

- Angiograms, angioplasty, electrocardiograms, and echocardiograms are all used to help diagnose heart disease.

- Diagnostic techniques for stroke include imaging, electrical activity tests, and blood flow tests.

Protection Against Cardiovascular Disease

- Tobacco use is a leading cause of CVD. Never starting to use tobacco or stopping smoking provides protection.

- Eating a heart healthy diet that focuses on fruits, vegetables, and low-fat and low-sodium foods helps protect and ensure heart health.

- Exercising aerobically most days of the week for thirty continuous minutes helps build a strong, healthy heart.

- Maintaining body weight in the recommended ranges eases the burden on your heart.

- Working on more effective stress management and having a less hostile, cynical personality will help protect heart health.

- Maintaining normal blood pressure and normal blood cholesterol enhances heart health.

- People with diabetes need to keep blood sugars as close to the normal range as possible.

Reassessing Your Knowledge

1. What are the leading modifiable and non-modifiable causes of CVD?

2. What steps could be taken to help reduce the causes and onset of CVD on your campus?

3. Describe the symptoms of a myocardial infarction. What should you do if you witness a person experiencing these symptoms?

4. Describe the process of atherosclerosis and an appropriate treatment method.

5. List and describe several steps you can take each day to help protect your heart health.

6. Identify acts of heart health irresponsibility that are evident on your campus.

To answer these questions, you might choose to work in groups with your colleagues. Check your answers against the written material in the text, and reread those sections where you made errors.

Health Assessment Toolbox

Heart Attack—Coronary Heart Disease—Metabolic Syndrome Risk Assessment

At this site, you can assess your risk of having a heart attack or dying from coronary heart disease in the next 10 years.
http://www.heart.org/HEARTORG/Conditions/ HeartAttack/HeartAttackToolsResources/Heart-Attack-Risk-Assessment_UCM_303944_Article.jsp

Diabetes Risk Test

This site provides information and a simple tool to assess your risk for pre-diabetes or type II diabetes.
http://www.diabetes.org/site-map.html

Stroke Risk Assessment

At this site you can estimate your stroke risk in comparison to others in your age group.
http://strokecenter.stanford.edu/consent.html

Each of these sites offers assessment tools, but does not offer to diagnose, evaluate or treat any medical condition. Please see your licensed medical physician for any aspect of your health that concerns you.

Vocabulary Challenge

Match the term in the left-hand column with its correct definition in the right-hand column.

TERM		DEFINITION
Angioplasty		A. A permanent arterial dilatation usually caused by weakened vessel walls
Echocardiography		B. A technique to widen a narrowed or obstructed blood vessel as a result of atherosclerosis
Systolic pressure		C. A quick, painless test that records the electrical activity of the heart
Diastolic pressure		D. A plasma protein that is the major carrier of cholesterol in the blood. High levels are associated with atherosclerosis
Low-density lipoprotein		E. Organic compound comprised of fat
High-density lipoprotein		F. A procedure that sends ultrasound waves (like sonar) into the chest to create moving pictures of the heart
Lipid		G. A blood constituent involved in the transport of cholesterol and associated with a decreased risk of atherosclerosis and heart attack
Emboli		H. The relaxation or resting phase of the heart
Aneurysm		I. The contraction or working phase of the heart
Electrocardiogram		J. A blood clot that travels through the bloodstream, lodges in a blood vessel, and blocks it

B; F; I; H; D; G; E; J; A; C

Answers

Exploring the Internet

American Heart Association

Provides information on all aspects of heart health and protection.

http://www.americanheart.org

American Stroke Association

Information and resources for stroke victims, family members, and caregivers.

http://www.strokeassociation.org/STROKEORG/

Your Guide to Lowering Your Blood Pressure with DASH

This National Institutes of Health site provides information on lowering salt and sodium in your diet and how to use food labels, and provides recipes for a week of appropriate meals.

http://www.nhlbi.nih.gov/health/public/heart/hbp/dash/index.htm

Exercises to Keep Your Heart Healthy

WebMD offers exercises to keep a healthy heart and prevent heart failure.

http://www.webmd.com

Understanding Stroke—The Basics

From symptoms to treatment to prevention, this reliable guide from WebMD offers expert advice.

http://www.webmd.com

Selected References

1. American Heart Association. Cardiovascular Disease Statistics. Downloaded April 26, 2010, from www.americanheart.org

2. Heart Disease and Stroke Statistics, Update. American Heart Association, 2008.

3. Tobacco-Related Mortality, Fact Sheet. Downloaded April 26, 2010, from www.cdc.gov/tobacco

4. Centers for Disease Control and Prevention. Annual Smoking-Attributable Mortality, Years of Potential Life Lost, and Economic Costs—United States, 1995–1999. *Morbidity and Mortality Weekly Report*, 51(14): 300–303. 2002.

5. Centers for Disease Control and Prevention. Smoking-Attributable Mortality, Years of Potential Life Lost, and Productivity Losses—United States, 2000–2004. *Morbidity and Mortality Weekly Report*, 57(45): 1226–1228. 2008.

6. U.S. Department of Health and Human Services. *The Health Consequences of Involuntary Exposure to Tobacco Smoke: A Report of the Surgeon General.* Atlanta: U.S. Department of Health and Human Services, Centers for Disease Control and Prevention, Coordinating Center for Health Promotion, National Center for Chronic Disease Prevention and Health Promotion, Office on Smoking and Health, 2006.

7. California Environmental Protection Agency. *Environmental Tobacco Smoke: A Toxic Air Contaminant.* Sacramento: California Environmental Protection Agency, Air Resources Board, 2006.

8. Poirier, P. Obesity and Cardiovascular Disease: Pathophysiology, Evaluation, and Effect of Weight Loss. An Update of the American Heart Association Scientific Statement on Obesity and Heart Disease *Circulation*, 113: 898–918. 2006.

9. Flegal, K.M., Carroll, M.D., Ogden, C.L., and Johnson, C.L., Prevalence and Trends in Obesity Among US Adults, 1999–2000. *JAMA*, 288: 1723–1727. 2002.

10. Zieske, A.W., Malcolm, G.T., and Strong, J.P., Natural History and Risk Factors of Atherosclerosis in Children and Youth: the PDay Study. *Pediatric Pathology and Molecular Medicine*, 21: 213–237. 2002.

11. Ysuf, S., Hawken, S., Ounpuu, S., Dans, T., Avezum, A., Lanas, F. et al. Effect of Potentially Modifiable Risk Factors Associated with Myocardial Infarction in 52 Countries. *Lancet*, 364: 937–952. 2004.

12. National Cholesterol Education Program. Third Report of the Expert Panel on Detection, Evaluation and Treatment of High Blood Cholesterol in Adults (Adult Treatment Panel III). Downloaded May 10, 2010, from http://hp2010.nhlbihin.net/atpiii/calculator.asp

13. Greenwood, D.C., Muir, K.R., Packham, and Madeley, R.J., Coronary Heart Disease: a Review of the Role of Psychosocial Stress and Social Support. *Journal of Public Health*, 18(2): 221–231.

14. American Heart Association. Heart Disease and Stroke Statistics–2008 Update. Dallas, TX: AHA, 2008.

15. Boyle, S.H., et al. Hostility, Anger and Depression Predict Increases in C3 over a 10-Year Period. *Brain Behavior Immunity*. doi:10.1016/j.bbi.2007.01.008. 2007.

16. Granger, Christopher. Director, Cardiac Arrest Unit, Duke University Medical Center. What Is the Relationship Between Cocaine and Heart Disease? Broadcast Interview, ABC, February 6, 2008.

17. Langenberg, C., Bergstrom, J., Scheidt-Nave, C., et al. "Cardiovascular Death and the Metabolic Syndrome: Role of Adiposity-signaling Hormones and Inflammatory Markers." *Diabetes Care*, 29(6): 1363–1369. 2006.

18. de Jager. J., Dekker. J.M., Kooy, A. et al. Endothelial Dysfunctions and Low Grade Inflammation Explain Much of the Excess Cardiovascular Mortality in Individuals with Type 2 Diabetes. The Hoorn Study." *Arteriosclerosis, Thrombosis and Vascular Biology*, 26: 1086. 2006.

19. Frei, B. Cardiovascular Disease and Nutrient Antioxidants: Role of Low-Density Lipoprotein Oxidation. *Critical Review of Food Science and Nutrition*; 35(1–2): 83–98. 1995.

20. Danesh, J., MBChB, D.Phil; Collins, R. MBBS, MSc; and Peto, R., FRS. Lipoprotein(a) and Coronary Heart Disease: Meta-Analysis of Prospective Studies. *Circulation*, 102(10): 1082–1085. September 5, 2000.

21. Pasceri, V., Willerson, J.T., and Yeh, E.T.H. Direct Pro-inflammatory Effect of C-Reactive Protein on Human Endothelial Cells. *Circulation,* 102: 2165–2168. 2000.

22. Leinonen, M., Saikku, P., Evidence for Infectious Agents in Cardiovascular Disease and Atherosclerosis. *Lancet Infectious Diseases*, 2(1): 11–17. January, 2002.

23. Berger, J.S. Aspirin as Preventive Therapy in Patients with Asymptomatic Vascular Disease. *JAMA*, 303(9): 880–882. 2010.

24. A Report From the American Heart Association Heart Disease and Stroke Statistics–2008 Update. *Circulation, 2008*, 117: e25–e146. January 29, 2009.

25. U.S. Department of Health and Human Services. The Health Consequences of Smoking: A Report of the Surgeon General. Office on Smoking and Health, 2004 [accessed April 30, 2010].

26. Centers for Disease Control and Prevention. Smoking and Tobacco Use. April 2009.

27. Howard, B., et al. Low Fat Diet and Risk of Cardiovascular Disease. *JAMA*, 295(6): 655–66. 2006.

28. Sachs, F., Moore, T., Appel, L., et al. A Dietary Approach to Prevent Hypertension: A Review of the Dietary Approaches to Stop Hypertension (DASH) Study. *Clinical Cardiology*, 22(S3): 6–10.

29. Frasure-Smith, N., and Prince, R. The Ischemic Heart Disease Life Stress-Monitoring Program: Impact on Mortality. *Psychosomatic Medicine*, 47(5): 431–445. 1985.

Image of Health

Cancer and Chronic Diseases

UNDERSTANDING CANCER

- The Risk of Developing Cancer
- Cancer Disease Process
- Diagnosing Cancer

COMMON CANCERS

- Lung Cancer
- Breast Cancer
- Colorectal Cancer
- Female Reproductive Tract Cancers
- Male Reproductive Tract Cancers
- Pancreatic Cancer
- Leukemia
- Skin Cancers

THE THREAT OF CANCER

DIABETES

- Type I Diabetes
- Type II Diabetes
- Gestational Diabetes
- Preventing Diabetes

RESPIRATORY SYSTEM DISORDERS

- Asthma
- Allergies
- Chronic Obstructive Pulmonary Disease

DIGESTIVE DISORDERS

- Inflammatory Bowel Disease
- Irritable Bowel Syndrome
- Diverticulosis and Diverticulitis
- Other Digestive Disorders

RESPONSIBILITY AND ACCOUNTABILITY

- Taking Responsibility for Your Cancer Risk
- Focusing on Accountability

Student Learning Outcomes

LEARNING OUTCOME	APPLYING IT TO YOUR LIFE
Describe how cancer develops, and list lifestyle risk factors that influence its development.	Identify behaviors you may practice that are risky for cancer, and consider ways you will eliminate them.
Identify two common cancers that affect young adults—one male cancer and one female cancer.	Describe two self-screening tests that can be conducted to detect early-stage cancer.
Differentiate between type I, type II, and gestational diabetes, and know risk factors for each type.	Evaluate yourself and your family members for diabetes risk, and identify ways these risks can be minimized.
List and describe the symptoms of respiratory system disorders.	Identify behaviors that you or family members may have that influence risk for contracting a respiratory system disorder.
Describe and identify symptoms for at least one type of digestive disorder.	Identify a digestive disorder that you have or have had, and consider ways you can reduce the likelihood of its reoccurrence.

Assess Your Knowledge

1. The most frequently occurring cancer is:
   a. Skin cancer
   b. Lung cancer
   c. Breast cancer
   d. Prostate cancer

2. The lymphatic system:
   a. Joins muscles and tendons.
   b. Integrates with the pulmonary system to support respiration.
   c. Is part of the immune system.
   d. Enables blood to flow away from the heart.

3. Rates of new cancer diagnosis and deaths have:
   a. Increased in recent years.
   b. Decreased in recent years.
   c. Remained constant across time.
   d. Fluctuated dramatically.

4. Which form of diabetes can probably be prevented?
   a. Type I diabetes
   b. Type II diabetes
   c. Both types can be prevented
   d. Neither type can be prevented

5. Chronic obstructive pulmonary disease:
   a. Is primarily caused by smoking and can be cured.
   b. Is primarily caused by environmental pollution and can be cured.
   c. Is primarily caused by smoking and cannot be cured.
   d. Is primarily caused by environmental pollution and cannot be cured.

Answers:

1. a; 2. c; 3. b; 4. b; 5. c.

Cancer and Chronic Diseases

Of all diseases, people perhaps fear cancer the most. Some may view cancer as unavoidable or incurable, but the truth is quite different. Although approximately one in every two men and one in every three women will be diagnosed with some form of cancer during their lifetimes, more than half will recover completely. Cancer is not just one disease; it is many diseases that share similar attributes. Cancer can now be detected and diagnosed much earlier, which greatly improves survival rate. Treatments and surgeries for cancer continue to improve each year, also improving the outlook for cancer patients. Today, there are even vaccinations that can help prevent certain cancers, and other cancers are now considered preventable with appropriate lifestyle changes.

Cancer remains the second leading cause of death in the United States causing about 25 percent of all deaths. Other chronic diseases, such as diabetes and respiratory and digestive disorders, may affect as many as forty million people in the U.S.

In this chapter, you will learn how to reduce your risks of dying from cancer and other chronic diseases. Accurate knowledge is the key to prevention, and with early detection and appropriate treatment, you can become more accountable for your own health outcomes.

Understanding Cancer

The term "cancer" describes diseases in which abnormal cells divide without control, are able to invade other tissues, and can spread through the blood and **lymphatic systems**. There are more than 100 types of cancer, each named for the organ or type of cell in which they begin. The most frequently occurring is skin cancer, and most forms of skin cancer are easily prevented or treated and cured. Understanding what causes cancer will help you learn to be more responsible in protecting yourself from this disease.

> **Key Term**
>
> **Lymphatic system**: Part of the immune system, the lymphatic system is interconnected spaces and vessels between body tissues and organs, by which lymph circulates throughout the body.

Rates of new cancer diagnoses and rates of death from all cancers have declined significantly in recent years. In 2010, the estimated number of new cancer cases was 1,529,560, not including non-melanoma skin cancers. The anticipated 2010 death rate was 569,490.

Table 11-1. U.S. Incidence and Mortality Rates from Cancer Cases diagnosed in 2004–2008[1]

RACE/ETHNICITY	INCIDENT RATE* FOR MEN	DEATH RATE* FOR MEN	INCIDENT RATE* FOR WOMEN	DEATH RATE* FOR WOMEN
All Races	541.0	225.4	411.6	155.4
White	543.6	222.5	423.0	155.0
Black	626.1	296.5	400.4	180.6
Asian/Pacific Islander	347.7	134.2	297.0	94.1
American Indian/ Alaskan Native	338.0	183.7	309.0	138.0
Hispanic	360.2	150.5	287.5	102.3

*All rates are per 100,000 of that population. Death rates are for 2003–2007.

The Risk of Developing Cancer

Cancer death rates are declining, though not as quickly as heart disease death rates. For both diseases, smoking is a primary cause. The heart works to repair itself once smoking stops, but smoking-induced cancers cause gene mutations that cannot be reversed, making these cancers more difficult to treat.

Many of the leading forms of cancer can be prevented, or the risks greatly reduced. The American Cancer Society has estimated that, with proper use of sun protective clothing and sunscreens, 90 percent of skin cancers can be prevented. Avoiding both smoking and exposure to tobacco smoke can prevent about 87 percent of lung cancers, and risk for many other cancers can be reduced with appropriate dietary choices, weight management, and regular screenings. Only about 5 percent of cancers can be linked to heredity—most cancers are caused by gene damage or mutation across a lifetime. In January 2006, the National Cancer Institute estimated that about 11.4 million Americans with prior history of cancer were still living. Of this number, many were cancer free and considered cured, some cases were managed by treatments, and others were in remission.

Table 11-2. New Cancers in Men and Women: 2010 Estimates

MEN	WOMEN
Prostate (28%)	Breast (28%)
Lung, bronchus (15%)	Lung, bronchus (14%)
Colon, rectum (9%)	Colon, rectum (10%)
Urinary bladder (7%)	Uterine corpus (6%)
Melanoma of the skin (5%)	Thyroid (5%)
Non-Hodgkin lymphoma (4%)	Non-Hodgkin lymphoma (4%)
Kidney and renal pelvis (4%)	Melanoma of the skin (4%)
Oral cavity and pharynx (3%)	Kidney and renal pelvis (3%)
Leukemia (3%)	Ovary (3%)
Pancreas (3%)	Pancreas (3%)

(Extracted from American Cancer Society, Inc. 2010. Surveillance and Health Policy Research.)

The risk of cancer is determined in part by lifestyle choices. Smoking, the primary cause of cancer, remains the number-one cause of preventable death in the U.S. Obesity and poor dietary choices affect the development of colon, stomach, and renal cancers. Lifestyle choices

including self-examinations and medical screenings have the potential to save more than 100,000 people each year.[2]

Cancer is non-discriminating: anyone can get cancer, and risk increases with age. About 78 percent of all cancers are diagnosed in people aged 55 or older, which may be the result of internal factors within cells as they age, or the prolonged exposure to external factors, such as tobacco, chemicals, and sunlight.

▶**Challenge Question**: What percentage of cancers is diagnosed in people under age 55?

Cancer Disease Process

Cancers always start in cells, the basic units of life. Under normal circumstances, cells grow and divide in controlled ways, and when they die are replaced with new cells. The DNA (deoxyribonucleic acid) in the cell may occasionally become damaged, and the cell behaves aberrantly: it may not die when it should, and new cells form when they are not needed. This overgrowth of cells is called **hyperplasia**, and some of these cells may become abnormal, called **dysplasia**. With time, a mass of tissue with no physiological purpose, called a **tumor**, may develop. Many **benign** or noncancerous tumors are similar in composition to surrounding cells, but are encapsulated in a protective membrane that prevents them from invading nearby tissue. They only become dangerous when their presence interferes with some aspect of body function, such as when a benign tumor blocks a blood vessel, interrupting flow of blood. If this interrupted blood flow leads to the heart or brain, serious complications can occur, including death. **Malignant** tumors are those that are cancerous, and since they are not encapsulated, they are able to invade other parts of the body. When this happens, the cancer has **metastasized**.

▶**Critical Thinking Question**: What prevents a benign tumor from invading nearby organs and tissues?

> **Key Terms**
>
> **Hyperplasia**: An abnormal multiplication of cells.
>
> **Dysplasia**: An abnormal change in cellular structure.
>
> **Tumor**: A mass of cells that may be benign or malignant.
>
> **Metastasize**: The movement of cancerous cells in the body from the original location to a new location.

Tumors may result from both external factors (tobacco, chemicals, radiation, and infectious organisms) and internal factors (inherited mutations, hormones, immune conditions, and mutations that occur from metabolism). These **causal** factors may act together, or in sequence, to promote or initiate **carcinogenesis**. After exposure to external factors, it can take ten years or more before cancer is detectable.

> **Key Terms**
>
> **Causal**: Implying a cause.
>
> **Carcinogenesis**: Production of cancer.

Diagnosing Cancer

Cancer is diagnosed based on its spread, called "staging." The staging is referred to as TNM: the extent of the primary tumor (T), the presence or absence of regional lymph node development (N), and the presence or absence of distant metastases (M). When these stages are determined, a second level of staging occurs, ranking from I to IV. A staging of I refers to early stage, and IV to advanced stage. Survival rates are based on TNM and stage number. Between 1999 and 2005, the five-year survival rate of all cancers was 68 percent, representing an 18 percent improvement in survival.[3]

Techniques to diagnose specific cancers vary by type of tissue. Suspected breast cancer may be diagnosed by taking a **biopsy** of tissue from the area. Leukemia may be diagnosed by taking a blood sample to determine the white blood cell count. Scanning, spinal tap, X-ray, or angiogram, among other methods, may diagnose brain cancers.

Image of Health In Depth

Types of Cancers

Cells grow at different rates in different types of tissue. The type of tissue in which a cancer originates determines the type of cancer.

Carcinomas form in epithelial tissues, including the skin, the lining of the intestines, body cavities, the surface of body organs, and outer portions of glands. About 80–90 percent of all cancers begin in epithelial tissues, because these tissues are frequently shed and replaced.

Sarcomas are found in connective tissue, such as bones, tendons, cartilage, and muscle, as well as in fat tissues.

Leukemia is a cancer of blood that originates in bone marrow or the lymphatic system.

Lymphomas originate in the lymph nodes or glands.

> **Key Term**
>
> **Biopsy**: The process of removing tissue for examination.

Table 11-3. Leading Cancer Deaths in Men and Women

MEN	WOMEN
Lung, bronchus (29%)	Lung, bronchus (26%)
Prostrate (11%)	Breast (15%)
Colon, rectum (9%)	Colon, rectum (9%)
Pancreas (6%)	Pancreas (7%)
Liver and intrahepatic bile duct (4%)	Ovary (5%)
Leukemia (4%)	Non-Hodgkin lymphoma (4%)
Esophagus (4%)	Leukemia (3%)
Non-Hodgkin lymphoma (4%)	Uterine corpus (3%)
Urinary bladder (3%)	Liver and intrahepatic bile duct (2%)
Kidney and renal pelvis (3%)	Brain and other nervous system (2%)

(Source: American Cancer Society. Cancer Facts & Figures 2010. Atlanta: American Cancer Society; 2010.)

Common Cancers

The incidence of different cancers has been tracked, showing an increase or decrease in rates over time. The biggest change is seen in lung cancer, with rates increasing to match the increasing rate of smoking by both genders. The term "epidemic" has been used to describe the increase in lung cancer rates for women—in 1930, it was the seventh most lethal cancer in women; today, more women die of lung cancer than breast, ovarian, and uterine cancers combined.[4]

Table 11-4. Estimated New Cancer Cases and Deaths by Sex for All Sites, U.S., 2010

SITE	MALE NEW CASES	MALE ESTIMATED DEATHS	FEMALE ESTIMATED NEW CASES	FEMALE ESTIMATED DEATHS
Oral cavity and pharynx	25,420	5,430	11,120	2,450
Digestive system	148,540	79,010	125,790	60,570
Respiratory system	130,600	89,550	110,010	71,120
lung cancer	116,750	86,220	105,770	71,080
Breast	1,970	390	207,090	39,840
Ovary			21,880	13,850
Prostate	217,730	32,050		
Genital system	227,460	32,710	83,750	27,710
Urinary system	89,620	19,110	41,640	9,440
Uterus			43,470	7,950
Brain and other nervous system	11,980	7,420	10,040	7,720
Endocrine system	11,890	1,140	35,040	1,430
Lymphoma	40,050	11,450	33,980	10,080
Leukemia	24,690	12,660	18,360	9,180

(Extracted from American Cancer Society. Cancer Facts and Figures, 2010. Atlanta: American Cancer Society; 2010.)

Lung Cancer

Lung cancer, a carcinoma, remains the leading cause of cancer death for both men and women, and is the second most common non-skin cancer diagnosed in both genders. Since 1987, more women have died from lung cancer than breast cancer. Due to the invasive nature of lung cancer, early detection has not resulted in greater survival rates. Symptoms may include:

- A persistent cough

- Sputum streaked with blood

- Chest pain

- Voice change

- Repeated episodes of pneumonia or bronchitis

Smoking remains the most important risk factor for lung cancer, and risk increases with quantity and duration of cigarette consumption. Other risk factors include exposure to secondhand smoke, radon, asbestos, and air pollution. Besides chest X-ray and sputum cytology, there is currently no routine screening for lung cancer. In 2002, a study was launched to assess whether screening high-risk individuals using spiral computed tomography (CT) scans and standard chest X-rays would result in detecting lung cancer. It is anticipated that results from the study will take eight years to analyze, and results were expected during 2010.[5]

The type and stage of lung cancer determine the treatment, which may include surgery, chemotherapy, radiation therapy, targeted therapy, or a combination of treatments. Lung cancer is difficult to control with current treatments, so patients are often advised to participate in a clinical trial in which new cancer drugs are tested. Because treatments can result in secondary issues such as pain, shortness of breath, and pneumonia, patients often receive **palliative** care to improve quality of life. Lung cancer cannot be cured; the goal of treatment is to prevent metastastis.

The one-year survival rate for lung cancer increased from 35 percent in 1975–1979 to 42 percent in 2000–2005, the increase is likely due to improvements in surgical techniques and combination therapies. The five-year survival rate for all stages of lung cancer is only 15.6 percent; however, if the lung cancer is localized when diagnosed, the five-year survival rate increases to 52 percent.[6]

Key Term

Palliative care: Care provided to reduce symptoms and manage pain.

Prostate Cancer

Excluding skin cancer, the most frequently occurring cancer in men is prostate cancer, which is also the second leading cause of cancer deaths. About 16 percent of all men will develop prostate cancer, and risk increases with age. Risk also increases for men if a first-degree relative—father, brother, or son—had prostate cancer. Other risk factors include diet and lifestyle. African-American men are 61 percent more likely to develop this disease than Caucasian men, and are 2.5 times more likely to die from it.

Most prostate cancers are diagnosed before symptoms develop, through either a prostate-specific antigen screening test (PSA) or a digital exam.[7] Symptoms for prostate cancer include a need to urinate frequently, difficulty urinating, painful urination, and weak or interrupted urine flow. Other symptoms include blood in the urine or semen, difficulty with erections, painful ejaculation, and frequent pain in the lower back.

Prostate cancer is relatively slow growing. It may be present for years before it is large enough to detect, and even longer before it spreads beyond the prostate. Treatment for the disease may include a prostatectomy (removal of the prostate), radiation therapy, chemotherapy, and hormone therapy. Some prostate cancers may never progress, so treatment may not be used. Though survival rates for prostate cancer are high, survivors do face challenges that include recurrence, treatment complications, and quality of life for survivors.

Motivation Maximizer

Is it really worthwhile to try to reduce risk factors for cancer? After all, everyone has to die of something. Not all smokers get lung cancer, so why should a smoker quit? And sometimes nonsmokers get lung cancer, so is there a point to all of this?

Ask anyone who has been diagnosed with cancer if there is a point, and you will hear a resounding yes. You may argue that you enjoy certain behaviors that increase your risk, and you may claim to enjoy them so much it would be worthwhile to continue even if you one day receive a cancer diagnosis.

This is what Nurit thought when she smoked during her college years, and has smoked off and on for about 15 years. Today, in her third year after a lung cancer diagnosis, she not only fights the disease, but must also fight to stop blaming herself. She wishes she had never smoked, or wishes she had stopped sooner.

Oliver heard about testicular self-tests in high school, but never bothered with them. When he was diagnosed with testicular cancer and had one testicle removed, he wondered why he had not cared enough about himself to perform a self-test.

Over 6 million people worldwide die from cancer each year. If everyone adopted prevention practices, more than one half of these cases could be prevented.[8] There are no guarantees: you may practice prevention and still be diagnosed with a cancer later in life. You may continue your risky behaviors and never have a diagnosis, though the odds are not in your favor. Practicing prevention greatly reduces the likelihood of developing cancer. People buy lottery tickets that may have a one in a million chance of winning—yet they buy them because think they could win. By practicing prevention, the chance of winning against cancer is far higher than one in a million.

Breast Cancer

Breast cancer is the most frequently occurring cancer in women. Although incidence rates are dropping, perhaps due to reduced use of hormone replacement therapy (HRT), an estimated 207,090 invasive breast cancer cases were expected to occur in 2010, and about 1,970 of these cases will be in men. The most important risk factor for breast cancer is age. Risk is increased by inherited genetic mutations. Modifiable risk factors include being overweight or obese, physical inactivity, and consumption of one or more alcoholic beverages a day. Reproductive factors that increase risk are a long menstrual history, never having children, having the first child after age 30, and recent use of oral contraceptives. Protective factors appear to be maintaining normal weight, breastfeeding, and moderate or vigorous physical activity.

The earliest sign of breast cancer is often an abnormality detected on a mammogram. A **mammogram** can detect a tumor long before it can be felt by the woman or by a health care provider. Less common symptoms include persistent changes to the breast, such as thickening, swelling, distortion, tenderness, and spontaneous discharge. Breast pain is usually the result of benign conditions, and is not a symptom of breast cancer.

Image of Health In Depth

Genetic Risk

Having a first-degree relative that has had breast cancer increases the risk, as do inherited genetic mutations in the BRCA1 and BRCA2 genes.[9] These cancer-causing mutations account for approximately 5–10 percent of all breast cancer cases, and there is an increased prevalence of this mutation in women of Ashkenazi Jewish descent. Since the mutation is found in less than 1 percent of the population, routine screening is not recommended. Nonetheless, women with a strong family history and/or ovarian cancer might consider counseling to determine if genetic testing is appropriate. If a woman is identified as a carrier, removal of the breasts and/or ovaries decreases the risk of cancer considerably. However, simply carrying the gene does not guarantee breast cancer will develop.

Treatment for breast cancer may involve a **lumpectomy** (surgical removal of the tumor) or **mastectomy** (removal of the breast), with removal of some of the underarm lymph nodes. Treatments may also include radiation therapy, chemotherapy, and hormone therapy.

Chapter 11

Key terms

Lumpectomy: Surgical removal of a tumor.

Mastectomy: Surgical removal of the breast.

Breast Screenings

To detect breast cancer before it causes symptoms, screenings are performed. If symptoms occur, breast cancer is more likely to have spread. The American Cancer Society (ACS) has changed its recommendations for screenings and now recommend that all women have their personal screening exam checked by a health care provider. For those aged 20–39, a clinical breast exam performed by a health care provider should be done every three years, and in this age group, monthly breast self-exams should be performed. For women over 40, an annual mammogram is recommended, along with a yearly clinical breast exam and monthly self-exams.

Breast self-exams should be conducted about one week after a period. Palpate the breast and note any changes that may have occurred, including lumps and thickening. Performing the exam in the shower may be the most convenient method. Self-exams are conducted by pressing firmly with the pads of fingertips over the entire breast in a circular fashion. Check the entire breast tissue, including under the armpit.

Breast Self-Examination

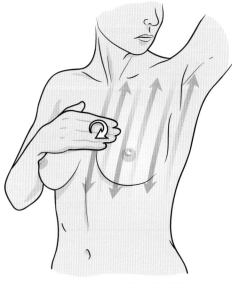

©Hayden-McNeil, LLC

Long-term survival rates for women who undergo lumpectomy followed by radiation therapy are similar to those after mastectomy. The five-year survival rate for localized breast cancer is about 98 percent. This drops to 84 percent if the cancer has spread regionally. Metastasized breast cancer survival rates are 23 percent, and continue to decline after five years.[10]

Colorectal Cancer

Colorectal cancer is the third most common cancer in both men and women. An estimated 102,900 new cases of colon cancer and 39,670 new cases of rectal cancer are anticipated in 2010. Even though these numbers may seem large, incidence rates continue to drop due to an increase in screening for colorectal polyps, which can result in detection and removal of polyps before they progress to cancer. Screening may be done several ways, and health care providers may elect to use one or more of the following:

- Fecal occult blood test: This test checks for hidden blood in fecal matter.

- Sigmoidoscopy: In this test, the rectum and lower colon are examined using a lighted instrument called a sigmoidoscope. During the test, precancerous and cancerous cells may be found and either removed or biopsied. A thorough cleansing of the lower colon is necessary before this procedure.

- Colonoscopy: This is the most effective scanning tool. The day before the procedure, patients are given a medication that facilitates emptying the entire colon and bowel. Under a mild tranquilizer, the entire colon is examined using a colonoscope. Precancerous and cancerous growths can be detected and either removed or biopsied, including growths in the upper part of the colon not examined in a sigmoidoscopy.

Other tests may include a digital rectal exam and various forms of X-ray.

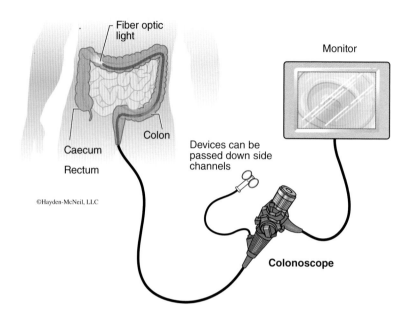

©Hayden-McNeil, LLC

Early stage colorectal cancer is usually **asymptomatic**. Advanced disease symptoms include rectal bleeding, blood in the stool, a change in bowel habits, and painful cramping in the lower abdomen.

As with most cancers, risk increases with age. More than 90 percent of colorectal cancer cases are diagnosed in people over age 50. Risk also increases with inherited genetic mutations, a family history of colorectal cancer, and a personal history of chronic inflammatory bowel disease. Modifiable risk factors include obesity, physical inactivity, smoking, heavy alcohol use, a diet high in red or processed meats, and an inadequate intake of fruits and vegetables. Studies have shown that overweight men and women are more likely to die from colorectal cancer.

Incidence and survival rates vary across ethnic groups. Black Americans are more likely to be diagnosed with colorectal cancer and more likely to die from it than are white Americans. Lack of access to regular screenings that can detect early stage precancerous conditions or cancer may greatly increase the chance of prevention or survival.

Table 11-5. Colorectal Cancer Incidence and Death Rates by Race

RACE/ ETHNICITY	MALE		FEMALE	
	INCIDENCE	DEATH	INCIDENCE	DEATH
All Races	59.2 per 100,000 men	22.7 per 100,000 men	43.8 per 100,000 women	15.9 per 100,000 women
White	58.9 per 100,000 men	22.1 per 100,000 men	43.2 per 100,000 women	15.3 per 100,000 women
Black	71.2 per 100,000 men	31.8 per 100,000 men	54.5 per 100,000 women	22.4 per 100,000 women
Asian/ Pacific Islander	48.0 per 100,000 men	14.4 per 100,000 men	35.4 per 100,000 women	10.2 per 100,000 women
American Indian/ Alaska Native	46.0 per 100,000 men	20.5 per 100,000 men	41.2 per 100,000 women	14.2 per 100,000 women
Hispanic	47.3 per 100,000 men	16.5 per 100,000 men	32.8 per 100,000 women	10.8 per 100,000 women

(Extracted from U.S. National Institutes of Health; National Cancer Institute. Surveillance Epidemiology and End Results. 2003–2007.)

Surgery is the primary form of treatment for colorectal cancer. If the cancer has not spread, this may be curative; however, if cancer has spread to the bowel or lymph nodes, chemotherapy and radiation therapy may be used.

With the advent of more sophisticated screening tests, preventing colorectal cancer is becoming a greater possibility. Early prevention steps include maintaining weight through diet and exercise, smoking abstinence, and reduced alcohol intake. For those with a history of non-modifiable risk factors, early onset of screening may be advised. For others, screening should begin at age 50.

> **Key Term**
>
> **Asymptomatic**: Not showing or producing symptoms of a disease or medical condition.

Image of Health In Depth

Childhood Cancers

Although rare, more than 10,700 cases of cancer are anticipated in children in 2010. An estimated 1,340 children will die, with about one third of these deaths caused by childhood leukemia. Early symptoms are rare and nonspecific. Regular medical check-ups may help detect early stage cancers, and parents should also be alert for unusual thickening of skin or lumps, loss of energy, pain, headaches with vomiting, vision changes, and weight loss.

The most common childhood cancers are leukemia and brain cancers. Treatment is determined by the type of cancer and includes surgery, chemotherapy, and radiation. Survival rates continue to improve, averaging about 80 percent when death rates from childhood cancers are combined.

Female Reproductive Tract Cancers

Ovarian cancer accounts for about 3 percent of all cancers in women and causes more deaths than any other reproductive tract cancer. Early symptoms are usually nonspecific, but may include abdominal swelling, bloating, pelvic pain, and loss of appetite. As with other cancers, risk increases with age. Estrogen replacement therapy, heavier body weight, and family history of breast and ovarian cancer also increase risk. Pregnancy and the use of oral contraceptives may reduce risk. There is no recommended early screening test for ovarian cancer.

Cervical cancer is most frequently diagnosed in women between 35 and 55 years of age. Many of these women were likely exposed to **human papilloma virus** (HPV) in their teens or twenties. Most cases of HPV resolve without treatment, but the virus remains for some women, and cervical cancer could develop as a result.

> **Key Term**
>
> **Human papilloma virus**: One of the most commonly spread sexually transmitted infections, sometimes leading to genital warts.

Since the introduction of **pap tests** as part of a regular gynecological screening, incidence of cervical cancer, which begins with cells that become dysplastic, has declined. Treatment is usually 100 percent successful for cervical dysplasia, but left untreated, cancer may develop and spread to the bladder, intestines, lungs, and liver.

Risk factors for cervical cancer include early onset of sexual activity, multiple partners, sex with a partner who has multiple partners, and daughters born to mothers who took DES to prevent miscarriage.

Symptoms include continuous vaginal discharge, abnormal bleeding, and periods that become heavier or last longer than usual. Symptoms of advanced stage cervical cancer may include loss of appetite, weight loss, fatigue, and pelvic and back pain. A number of screening tests and treatments are available, and radiation may be used if the cancer has metastasized.

Image of Health in Depth

Preventing Cervical Cancer with Vaccination

In 2006, the Food and Drug Administration approved a new vaccine that prevents infection against the four leading HPVs that cause cervical cancer. Known as Gardasil, this vaccine is administered between the ages of 9 and 26, and is the first vaccine known to prevent any type of cancer. Gardasil is given as three injections over six months. It protects against two types of HPV that cause 75 percent of cervical cancer, and two more types that cause 90 percent of genital warts. In boys and young men between the ages of 9–26, Gardasil helps protect against 90 percent of genital warts cases. Although it may not fully protect everyone, and does not prevent all forms of cervical cancer, it is a step toward providing young men and women with a prophylactic against HPV, which in turn reduces the risk for cervical cancer in women. More recently, the FDA approved Cervarix as an alternate to Gardasil.

Key Term

Pap test: A test to detect cancerous or precancerous cells of the cervix allowing for early diagnosis of cancer.

▶**Challenge Question**: What are the most common childhood cancers and what is their combined survival rate?

Male Reproductive Tract Cancer

Testicular cancer is the most common form of cancer among men aged 15–34. This form of cancer is readily treatable, even when the cancer spreads. Symptoms for testicular cancer may include a lump or enlargement in a testicle, a feeling of heaviness in the scrotum, dull ache in abdomen or groin, and a general feeling of being unwell. Testicular cancer generally only affects one testicle.

Risk factors include a family history of testicular cancer, abnormal testicle development, and an undescended testicle. Testicles typically descend before birth, but if this does not happen, some boys require surgery to relocate the testicle to the scrotum. The disease is more common in white men than other ethnicities.

Testicular cancer is diagnosed with ultrasound as well as blood tests, which can identify tumor markers in blood that are normally occurring substances, but become elevated in certain situations. If cancer is suspected, surgery is performed to remove the testicle. In older men, seminoma, a nonaggressive carcinoma that is particularly sensitive to radiation, usually develops. Nonseminoma tumors tend to develop in younger men and can spread rapidly. These more aggressive cancers are treated with radiation and chemotherapy. A man's risk during his lifetime of developing testicular cancer is about 1 in 271. An estimated 8,480 new cases were expected in 2010, and 350 will die from this cancer. Practicing monthly testicular exams increases early detection and survival rates.

Image of Health in Depth

Testicular Self-Exam

The best time to examine the testicles is after a warm shower or bath. The heat causes the scrotum to relax and move away from the body.

1. The exam is performed to detect any signs of swelling on the skin or scrotum.

2. Using the index and middle fingers, hold the testicle and gently roll your thumb over the area. It is normal for one testicle to feel slightly larger than the other, and some men may feel the spermatic cord that leads upward from the epididymis at back of the testicle. A testicular exam performed once per month will allow for changes to be more easily detected.

3. If a lump or unusual swelling is detected, see a doctor as soon as possible. A testicular exam should be part of a routine physical exam.

Pancreatic Cancer

Located behind the stomach, the pancreas is an organ that secretes enzymes that aid in digestion, as well as hormones that regulate the metabolism of sugars.

Symptoms of pancreatic cancer generally don't occur until the disease has advanced and may include:

• Upper abdominal pain that may radiate to the back.

• Yellowing of skin and whites of eyes.

• Loss of appetite.

- Weight loss.

- Depression.

Risk factors for pancreatic cancer are similar to those for other cancers, including smoking, being overweight or obese, older age, family history of pancreatitis, pancreatic cancer, and certain genetic syndromes. Pancreatic cancer occurs more frequently among blacks than whites.

Diagnosing pancreatic cancer involves an ultrasound, a **computed tomography scan (CT scan)**, **magnetic resonance imaging (MRI)**, or tissue biopsy. Once diagnosed, the physician will determine treatment based on staging. Very few pancreatic cancers are resolved with surgery; most patients undergo radiation and chemotherapy. A new emerging area of cancer treatment is targeted drug therapy: drugs target specific abnormalities within cancer cells, blocking the chemicals that signal the cancer cells to grow.

Incidence rates for pancreatic cancer have been stable in men since 1981, but have been increasing in women by about 1.7 percent per year since 2000, Perhaps due to increased smoking among women. The five-year survival rate is about 5.5 percent.

> ### Key Terms
>
> **Computed tomography scan (CT scan)**: Also called a CAT scan, this radiologic scan produces cross-sectional images of a part of the body onto a computer screen.
>
> **Magnetic resonance imaging (MRI)**: Magnetic resonance imaging is an imaging technique that uses electromagnetic radiation to obtain images of soft tissue in the body.

Leukemia

Leukemia is cancer of the blood, originating in bone marrow or the lymphatic system. Leukemia incidence rates are similar to those for pancreatic cancer: white men and women have a higher incidence than other races, and the five-year survival rate is almost 54 percent.

Higher radiation exposure increases the likelihood of leukemia. Generally, there are no early symptoms, and those that occur are often mistaken for other illnesses. Symptoms include fever, chills, and flu-like symptoms. In addition, anemia may occur, causing paleness, weakness, fatigue, and shortness of breath. Some leukemia patients bleed easily from minor cuts, have frequent infections, loss of appetite, and weight loss. Diagnosis includes blood tests, bone marrow biopsy, and in some cases, a spinal tap and chest X-rays.

Not all cases of leukemia progress to a critical stage. However, if treatment is necessary, it includes either oral or intravenous chemotherapy.

Skin Cancer

Basal cell carcinoma rarely metastasizes, and accounts for more than 90 percent of all skin cancer in the U.S. In 2006, more than 2 million people were treated for basal cell carcinoma. Sun exposure, tanning beds, and aging are the most important risk factors, with lighter-colored skin at higher risk than darker skin tones. Basal cell carcinoma is most often treated with curettage, which involves cutting out the cancerous cells, followed by desiccation, which is the application of an electric current to control bleeding and kill remaining cancer cells.

Squamous cell carcinoma is the second most frequently occurring skin cancer, and is also highly curable. Like basal cell carcinoma, it is caused by exposure to sun and tanning beds, but unlike basal cell carcinoma, this type of cancer can metastasize. Treatment is determined by the size of the cancerous area, and may include curettage and desiccation, surgical excision, cryosurgery (freezing), and Mohs micrographic surgery. In the Mohs method, microscopic excisions are made and then checked under a microscope during surgery. More excisions are made, until a sample is shown to be free of all cancerous cells.

Melanoma is the most dangerous type of skin cancer because it can metastasize, and is the leading cause of death from skin diseases. It involves cells called melanocytes, which are responsible for skin and hair color. Early symptoms are recognized in a mole or growth by one or more of the following signs:

- *Asymmetry*: One half of the abnormal area is different from the other half.

- *Borders*: The lesion or growth has irregular sides.

- *Color*: Color changes from one area to another, with shades of tan, brown, and black. White, red, and blue are sometimes present.

- *Diameter*: The trouble spot is typically larger that the size of a pencil eraser.

> **Key Term**
>
> **Melanoma**: Skin cancer that is the leading cause of death for skin diseases.

Surgery is the first form of treatment, and may be followed by radiation or chemotherapy. Risk factors for melanoma include family history of the disease, red or blond hair and fair skin, multiple birthmarks, freckling on back, three or more blistering sunburns before age 20, three or more years spent in long periods outdoors in the summer as a teenager, and development of precancerous marks.

If detected early, melanoma can be cured. Preventative measures include limiting sun exposure, using a sun protection factor (SPF) of at least 30 SPF prior to exposure, avoidance of tanning devices, and wearing sun protective clothing.

Seen is melanoma with a uneven, ragged, border. The ABCDE test is used for detection of melanomas: A—Asymmetry B—Border C—Color D—Diameter E—Elevation/ Evolution. Credit: National Cancer Institute/Photo Researchers, Inc.

Melanoma, with coloring of different shades of brown, black, or tan. Credit: National Cancer Institute/Photo Researchers, Inc.

 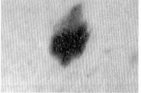

Malignant (cancerous) melanoma on the waist of a 47-year-old woman. A malignant melanoma is a type of skin cancer that arises from the melanocytes, the cells that produce the pigment (melanin) that gives skin its color. The main cause of melanoma is exposure to ultraviolet radiation in sunlight. It is an aggressive cancer that often spreads (metastasizes) to other parts of the body. Treatment is with surgical excision of the melanoma. Credit: Dr P. Marazzi/Photo Researchers, Inc.

Dysplastic nevus. Credit: Biophoto Associates/Photo Researchers, Inc.

▶**Critical Thinking Question**: How would you evaluate a mole for cancer warning signs?

The Threat of Cancer

Cancer can be frightening, but most people never receive a cancer diagnosis. After reading about cancer, some feel more threatened and anticipate that any symptom they have may indicate cancer. Though this is highly unlikely, a visit to the doctor will resolve this worry. The causes of some cancers are unknown, while for others, certain behaviors are a risk factor. Being responsible for your health by eating a healthful diet, drinking in moderation, if at all, exercising regularly, and not smoking are steps that can help reduce the risk of cancer. Practicing breast, testicular, and skin self-exams will help identify any potential cancer problems in early stages. A medical practitioner may also recommend screenings for cervical and colorectal cancer.

Image of Health In Depth

Cancer Warning Signs

Warning signs for cancer have been developed by various cancer organizations. The following is a list from the American Cancer Society. As you read through the list, remember that each sign can be suggestive of cancer or of other health issues, and only a licensed medical practitioner can diagnose accurately.

Change in bowel or bladder habits.

A sore that does not heal. This may also be indicative of diabetes.

Unusual bleeding or discharge.

Thickening or lump in breast or elsewhere.

Indigestion or difficulty swallowing.

Obvious change in wart or mole.

Nagging cough or hoarseness.

The acronym **CAUTION** is used to make remembering the warning signs easier.

Diabetes

Once a fatal disease, diabetes became manageable in the 1930s when its cause was identified. At that time, only one type of diabetes was recognized; today, there are three major types of diabetes. Diabetes occurs when the body ceases to produce insulin, produces too little insulin, or does not use insulin efficiently. Insulin is needed to move blood glucose into cells for energy production; without insulin, blood glucose levels become abnormally high. In the short-term, **hyperglycemia** does not cause organ damage but does cause fatigue, weakness, excessive urination and thirst, blurry vision, and vulnerability to infection. Long-term hyperglycemia damages blood vessels, resulting in **neuropathy**, eye damage that can lead to blindness, reduced kidney function, and foot damage that can lead to amputation. Hyperglycemia also raises blood pressure, narrows the arteries, and interferes with cholesterol control, that may double the risk for heart attack and stroke compared to someone with normal blood sugar levels.[11]

Key Terms

Hyperglycemia: Blood glucose values over 160 mg/dl. Normal blood sugar values are less than 100 mg/dl.

Neuropathy: Damage to the nerves of the peripheral nervous system.

Type I Diabetes

This rapid onset disease may affect as many as three million people in the United States.[12] Previously called juvenile onset diabetes or insulin-dependent diabetes, it is most frequently diagnosed in children between the ages of 2 and 15, but may be diagnosed at any age. In type I diabetes, the islet cells in the pancreas cease to produce insulin. Left untreated, patients can lapse into a coma and die. Treatment for type I diabetes involves lifelong infusion with insulin. The insulin dose must correlate with the carbohydrates that are eaten, to ensure that blood glucose levels remain as close to normal as possible. This can be done with frequent daily injections, or with insulin infusion therapy using an insulin delivery pump. Patients must check blood sugar several times each day to ensure it stays within normal ranges—if blood sugar drops too low, the patient will experience **hypoglycemia**, with symptoms that include sweating, rapid change in mood, and inability to follow or engage in conversation. Hypoglycemia is caused when the patient either infuses or injects too much insulin, or does not eat enough carbohydrates for the insulin dose. It is treated with any fast-acting sugar, such as orange juice, milk, or even candy; if left untreated, hypoglycemia may lead to seizures.

At the opposite end of the scale, type I diabetics may become hyperglycemic if they do not infuse enough insulin for their food intake. Over time, hyperglycemia can result in renal failure, loss of sight, amputations, and nerve failure. Mortality rates for people with diabetes are higher than for non-diabetics; diabetics have lower survival rates for diseases, and lower life expectancy than do non-diabetics.[13]

The cause of type I diabetes is not clearly understood. Although it may be prevalent in some families, a causative gene has not been identified. Some patients experience a viral illness prior to their **diagnosis**, and as the body identifies and destroys the agents causing this illness, it may mark insulin-producing cells and destroy them. Because of this, type I diabetes is considered an autoimmune disease.

Marc's Story

At age 15, Marc began to experience extreme thirst and fatigue. Since he was on the swim team, the symptoms seemed normal. He was not eating less but was losing weight, though he assumed this was because of his intense exercise schedule. One day, he commented to his parents that he was having trouble seeing the board at school. They encouraged him to sit closer, but when he said he was already in the front row, they made an appointment to see the doctor.

Diagnosed with type 1 diabetes, Marc's life was about to change in ways no one could anticipate. He and his family attended classes to learn how to determine how many grams of carbohydrates were in a meal, and how to match that to units of insulin that would be injected. Marc had to alter the dose based on how much he exercised, since exercise caused the insulin to be used more efficiently. But within a few days of insulin treatment, Marc was feeling fine again. Although with diabetes it was difficult to consider everything he wanted to eat, Marc was doing a good job managing his disease.

One day at his part-time job, Marc injected his insulin as he was about to leave for the lunchroom. Unexpectedly, his supervisor asked him to postpone lunch for an hour because of a business rush. About 45 minutes later, Marc was having a seizure on the floor due to hypoglycemia. An ambulance was called, and Marc learned the hard way that insulin does not wait on food. Had any of Marc's co-workers been able to recognize his symptoms of hypoglycemia, the episode might have been avoided. They later told him he had been sweating and not following directions, saying he had become belligerent. Marc could also have avoided the seizure by drinking milk, a sugared soft drink, or orange juice as soon as he knew his lunch was going to be postponed. If that was not available, he could have eaten a candy bar or a chocolate bar to maintain his blood glucose levels. He could even have told his supervisor that postponing lunch was not an option for him.

Today, everyone knows someone with diabetes. Would you recognize hypoglycemia in someone you know that has type 1 diabetes? Would you know what to do? ∎

Type II Diabetes

Previously called adult-onset diabetes or non-insulin dependent diabetes, this disease may account for about 90–95 percent of all diagnosed cases of diabetes, representing about 15 million people. Estimates suggest another 5.7 million people have type II diabetes, but have not been diagnosed.[14]

People with type II diabetes still produce insulin, but do not produce enough or cannot efficiently use the insulin that is produced. Over time, the resulting high blood glucose levels cause dehydration, excessive urination, and damage to the nerves and small blood vessels of the eyes, kidneys, and heart. This predisposes the patient to **atherosclerosis**, which may lead to heart attack and stroke.

> ### Key Terms
>
> **Hypoglycemia**: Blood glucose values that fall below 70 mg/dl. Symptoms include sweating, rapid change in mood, and inability to follow or engage in conversation, and left untreated, may lead to seizures.
>
> **Hyperglycemia**: Blood glucose values over 160 mg/dl. Long-term hyperglycemia results in weight loss, and can lead to renal failure, blindness, and amputations.
>
> **Atherosclerosis**: A common form of arteriosclerosis in which fatty substances form a deposit of plaque on the inner lining of arterial walls.

Although anyone can get type 2 diabetes, those at highest risk are individuals who are overweight or obese, have family members with the disease, or had **gestational diabetes**, as well as individuals with **metabolic syndrome**. Previously, this disease was seen primarily in those over 40, but with the obesity epidemic, children, teens, and young adults are now being diagnosed. Symptoms for this disease, which may include increased thirst, increased hunger (especially after eating), dry mouth, nausea, vomiting, frequent urination, and fatigue, progress slowly and are often not noticed. As symptoms progress, patients will experience blurred vision, numbness in hands and feet, and impaired healing of wounds. Like type I diabetes, this disease also requires lifelong treatment, involving careful weight management and a nutritionally balanced diet and exercise program. Some patients may require insulin by injection, but most cases are managed with oral medications that cause insulin to be used more effectively. Patients who maintain weight within a normal range and maintain an exercise program may be able to manage the disease without medication.

Uncontrolled type II diabetes, in which blood sugar remains elevated, may result in complications that include **retinopathy**; kidney damage; poor blood circulation, which inhibits wound healing; and nerve damage, which causes decreased sensation in the feet and when combined with poor blood circulation, increases the risk for amputations.

FIGURE 11-5. Obesity is a leading risk factor for type II diabetes.

Key Term

Gestational diabetes: High blood sugar levels that occur during pregnancy. About 40 percent of women who develop gestational diabetes will later develop type II diabetes.

Metabolic syndrome: A cluster of problems including high cholesterol with high LDL and low HDL levels, high triglycerides, and high blood pressure.

Retinopathy: A general term that refers to some form of non-inflammatory damage to the retina of the eye. Untreated, it can lead to blindness.

Gestational Diabetes

Gestational diabetes occurs during pregnancy, more frequently in African Americans, Hispanic/Latino Americans, and American Indians, and is also more commonly seen in obese women and in women with a family history of diabetes. The disease results in glucose intolerance during pregnancy, causing hyperglycemia. Treatment is necessary to bring maternal blood sugar levels into a normal range to avoid complications for the fetus. About 5–10 percent of women with gestational diabetes are diagnosed with type 2 diabetes immediately after the pregnancy.[15]

Critical Thinking Question: Differentiate between type I and type II diabetes.

Preventing Diabetes

There are several clinical trials in progress to prevent type I diabetes, but as of 2010, no known prevention exists.

Type II diabetes and gestational diabetes can be prevented by keeping weight in normal range, consuming a nutrient dense diet, and exercising regularly. In 2003–2006, almost 26 percent of U.S. adults aged 20 years or older had **impaired fasting blood glucose** levels, a rate that jumped to over 34 percent in adults over age sixty. Considered a prediabetes condition, progression to the disease is not inevitable. Weight loss and exercise that maintains blood glucose levels in the normal range may prevent or delay diabetes.

Key Term

Impaired fasting blood glucose: In impaired fasting blood glucose, the blood glucose is between 100–125 mg/dl. Normal fasting blood glucose levels are below 100 mg/dl and values over 125 mg/dL indicate diabetes.

▶**Challenge Question:** What methods can you use to avoid type II diabetes?

Respiratory System Disorders

The respiratory system is made up of organs that facilitate breathing, including the nose, pharynx, larynx, trachea, bronchi, and lungs. If any of these organs fails to perform efficiently, respiration will be compromised. This might be caused by an acute condition, such as a common cold, or a chronic condition such as asthma.

Asthma

Asthma is a lung disease that inflames and narrows the airways, causing wheezing, chest tightness, shortness of breath, and coughing. Because airways are swollen, they become sensitive to some substances that are inhaled, causing muscles around the airways to tighten and reducing the flow of air. Cells in the airways may begin to produce excessive mucus, making the airways even narrower.

Asthma cannot be cured, but the disease can be managed. Its cause is unknown, but risk is increased in people who have an inherited tendency to develop allergies, who have asthmatic parents, certain respiratory infections during childhood, and/or exposure to some viral infections in infancy or early childhood.[16]

Since asthma can be life threatening, it is important to treat symptoms early. Treatment involves long-term control, which helps to reduce inflammation, and immediate onset medications, which relieve symptoms that may flare up. With time, patients learn what might cause an asthma attack, and can work to avoid those situations.

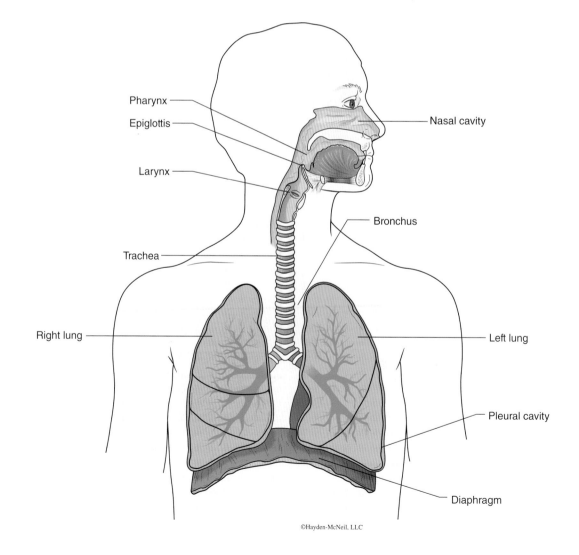

Allergies

Genetic and environmental factors both play a role in allergies. An allergic response occurs when an immune response is over-sensitive, resulting in a variety of symptoms that depend on the allergen and the person. Common inhaled allergens include dust, pollen, mold, and pet dander, and often cause a stuffy nose, itchy nose and throat, mucus production, and coughing or wheezing. Food allergies can result in nausea, vomiting, abdominal pain, diarrhea, or even a severe, life-threatening reaction.

FIGURE 11-6. Some environments can be difficult for people with allergies.

Treatment for allergies begins with avoiding allergens. If medication becomes necessary, antihistamines and decongestants may be used. For an acute allergic reaction, epinephrine can be life saving when given immediately.

Chronic Obstructive Pulmonary Disease

The two main forms of chronic obstructive pulmonary disease (COPD) are emphysema and chronic bronchitis. Smoking is the leading risk factor for COPD, and risk increases with increased smoking. Exposure risk factors include secondhand smoke, pollution, and certain gases or fumes in the workplace. Not smoking prevents most cases of COPD. There is no cure, and because symptoms develop slowly, some people may be unaware they have the disease. Currently, between 3 and 7 million are diagnosed with COPD, but estimates suggest that in the U.S., more than 16 million people may have undiagnosed COPD.[17] People with COPD suffer years of progressive breathing discomfort and disability, with the number of deaths at approximately 100,000, and increasing.[18] The goal for COPD treatment is to impede the progress of the disease. The first step is to stop smoking and/or avoid inhaling smoke or pollution. Some patients are treated with inhalers that dilate the airways, some may need inhaled steroids to reduce lung inflammation, and in severe cases, steroids may be administered by mouth or intravenously.

Emphysema begins with shortness of breath during any type of exertion, and eventually, the patient will be short of breath even at rest. The disease progresses to include difficulty breathing, coughing and wheezing, and excess mucus production. Because of breathing difficulties, patients may have a bluish tint to the skin caused by oxygen depleted blood.

Bronchitis symptoms are similar to COPD, and include coughing, wheezing, shortness of breath, mucus production, chest discomfort, and fatigue. Acute bronchitis may follow a cold and result in a nagging, lingering cough. Chronic bronchitis can develop without first having acute bronchitis. Its primary cause is tobacco smoke exposure, so the first step in treatment is avoiding this exposure. Bronchitis is also treated with antibiotics.

▶**Challenge Question:** What are the two most common forms of chronic obstructive pulmonary disease?

Digestive Disorders

Digestive disorders affect 60 to 70 million people in the U.S., and in 2004, there were 236,164 deaths attributed to the various disorders.[19,20] Digestive disorders include inflammatory bowel disease, irritable bowel syndrome, diverticular disease, gallstones, hemorrhoids, and others.

Inflammatory Bowel Disease

Nearly one million people have Crohn's disease or ulcerative colitis, the two major forms of inflammatory bowel disease. Causes are unknown, and the diseases may be difficult to differentiate. There is no cure, but medications are available to control symptoms.[21] In some cases, surgical removal of part of the intestine may be necessary.

People with Crohn's disease have chronic inflammation of the gastrointestinal tract. Although the disease can occur at any age, it usually occurs between the ages of 15–35. Risk factors include a family history of Crohn's, Jewish ancestry, and smoking. Symptoms range from mild to severe and occur randomly. They may include abdominal pain, fatigue, loss of appetite, persistent watery diarrhea or constipation, and pain with bowel movements.[22]

Crohn's disease is diagnosed by a variety of tests, including CT scan of the abdomen, magnetic resonance imaging (MRI) of the abdomen, and colonoscopy. Ulcerative colitis is caused by inflammation of the rectum. Symptoms may include rectal bleeding, abdominal pain, and diarrhea, and in some cases, the disease process may subside after a long history of inflammatory symptoms. Treatments include medication, and in some instances, surgery.

Irritable Bowel Syndrome

Irritable bowel syndrome (IBS) is one of the most commonly diagnosed diseases in the U.S. It affects about 1 in every 5 people, more women than men, and more than half the cases are diagnosed before age 35. Symptoms vary, but generally include abdominal pain, bloating, and general discomfort. Since IBS presents a significant diagnostic challenge, physicians base diagnosis on a complete medical examination and history of symptoms.[23] Avoiding foods that cause flare-ups may ease symptoms. Medications are an important part of treatment, but perhaps 70 percent of people with IBS do not receive treatment, and there is no cure. Irritable bowel syndrome is not linked to ulcerative colitis or Crohn's disease, and it does not lead to cancer.

Diverticulosis and Diverticulitis

A diverticulum is a small pouch in the lining of the colon or large intestine. When these small pouches bulge outward through weak spots, the condition is known as diverticulosis. It occurs in about ten percent of people over age forty, increasing to 50 percent of the population over age sixty.[24] When the condition becomes inflamed, it is called diverticulitis.[25]

Although a cause has not been identified, the dominant theory is that **diverticular disease** may result from a low-fiber diet. The disease is very rare in countries that eat high-fiber, non-processed foods. Most people with diverticulosis do not experience any symptoms, though when symptoms occur, they may include discomfort or pain in the lower abdomen. The most common symptom of diverticulitis is abdominal pain, usually on the left side.

The pain is severe and comes on suddenly, worsening over several days. Left untreated, diverticulitis can lead to bleeding, infections, and small tears and blockages in the colon. These symptoms will require treatment to prevent serious illness.

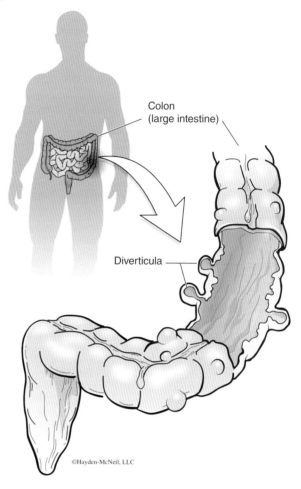

Colon (large intestine)

Diverticula

©Hayden-McNeil, LLC

Pain medications may help relieve symptoms, and a high-fiber diet is often prescribed to reduce attacks. Sometimes an attack may be severe enough to require a hospital stay and intravenous antibiotics. If the patient does not respond to treatment, surgery may be required to remove a section of the intestine.

The National Institute of Diabetes and Digestive and Kidney Diseases is conducting ongoing research for better treatments, cures, and causes of digestive disorders.

> **Key Term**
>
> **Diverticular disease**: Bulging pouches in the colon or large intestine that may become inflamed.

Other Digestive Disorders

The gall bladder is a small sac located below the liver in the right upper abdomen. It secretes a liquid called bile, which is made in the liver, stored in the gall bladder, and helps the body digest fats. If the stored liquid hardens, it breaks into small, pebble-like substances known as gallstones. The cause of gallstones is not understood, but family history, being overweight, a diet high in fat and cholesterol, and being female may influence their formation. As gallstones move into the bile duct, they create blockages that lead to steady pain in the abdomen, in the back between the shoulder blades, and under the right shoulder. If there are no symptoms, treatment is not required, but if a patient has frequent gallstone attacks, surgery may be required to remove the gallbladder.

Hemorrhoids refer to a condition where the veins around the anus or lower rectum become swollen and inflamed. This is caused by straining to move stool out of the rectum, and may occur as a result of pregnancy, aging, chronic constipation, and anal intercourse. Although not dangerous or life threatening, hemorrhoids can be very uncomfortable, causing itching and resulting in blood visible on stool, on used toilet paper, or in the toilet bowl. Most hemorrhoidal symptoms go away within a few days. By age fifty, about one half the population has experienced hemorrhoids. Treatment includes tub baths several times a day during outbreaks, as well as the use of a hemorrhoidal cream.

Responsibility and Accountability

The threat of cancer and other chronic diseases is part of life; however, the diseases themselves may not be an inevitable part of your life. By practicing prevention and performing or having regular screenings, you can reduce your risk.

Taking Responsibility for Your Cancer Risk

Simply by learning about different diseases, you have become more responsible. In some cases, you have learned what steps you can take to reduce your risks, and to recognize early symptoms. Although this may seem overwhelming, making appropriate choices will help. Focus on big risk factors you may have, and work on those one at a time. Smoking, being overweight or obese, poor dietary choices, and sedentary behavior are leading risk factors for many diseases. These are all things that can be changed if you choose to become responsible.

Focusing on Accountability

Accountability is the willingness to be answerable for consequences of actions and choices you make. Your choices can be very costly, especially when the consequences include diseases such as cancer and type 2 diabetes. Not all cancers are preventable, of course, but are you doing everything you can to reduce risk for those that are preventable? Is a suntan worth the risk of melanoma to you? Is smoking worth the risk of lung cancer, as well as other cancers? Remember, with accountability, the cost is not always assumed by the individual; some may be passed on to the family and the community. Costs will include not only finances, but also time and emotional costs, which may be even more expensive. Make the right choices now, in order to reduce your risk of facing this accountability later.

Summary

Understanding Cancer

- About 1 in every 2 men and 1 in every 3 women will be diagnosed with cancer in their lifetimes. More than half will recover.

- Cancer describes cells that grow abnormally and spread through the blood and lymphatic systems.

- Cancer types include carcinomas, sarcomas, leukemia, and lymphomas.

- Risk for cancer increases with age. Consuming alcohol in moderate amounts, if at all, eating a healthful diet, maintaining normal weight, exercising regularly, and not smoking all may help reduce cancer risk.

- Tumors are collections of cells that are benign or malignant.

- Cancer is diagnosed based on its spread, called staging. The extent of the primary tumor, the presence or absence of lymph node development, and whether the cancer has metastasized are all considered when identifying stage.

Lung Cancer

- Lung cancer is the leading cause of death from cancer for both men and women.

- Prostate cancer is the most frequently occurring cancer in men; breast cancer is the most frequently occurring cancer in women.

- Basal and squamous cell cancers are highly curable, while melanoma is the most dangerous form of skin cancer.

- Skin cancer warning signs include asymmetry, irregular border, change in color, or diameter bigger than a pencil of a mole or growth.

- The acronym CAUTION is used to remember common warning signs for cancer.

- Early prevention steps, practicing self-examination, and regular medical screenings for cancer can help with earlier diagnosis and better prognosis.

Diabetes

- There are three major types of diabetes: type I, type II, and gestational diabetes.

- Type I diabetes occurs when the body no longer makes insulin. Patients must be treated with insulin by injection or infusion for life. This disease cannot be prevented.

- Type II diabetes occurs when the body makes either too little insulin, or does not use insulin efficiently. Risk factors include being overweight or obese, having had gestational diabetes, and having family members with type II diabetes. It is treated with weight loss, oral medications, and sometimes insulin by injection.

- Gestational diabetes results in glucose intolerance during pregnancy, and is usually seen in women who are overweight or have a family history of diabetes.

- Complications for uncontrolled diabetes include loss of sight, nerve failure, kidney failure, and amputations.

Respiratory System Disorders

- Asthma is an incurable respiratory disease that causes wheezing, chest tightness, shortness of breath, and coughing.

- An allergic response occurs when the immune system is over-sensitive, resulting in different symptoms depending on the allergen and the person.

- The two main forms of COPD are emphysema and chronic bronchitis. Smoking is the leading risk factor.

- The goal of treatment for COPD is to impede disease progression. It is not curable.

Digestive Diseases

- Digestive diseases are numerous.

- Inflammatory bowel disease is not curable. Crohn's disease and ulcerative colitis are the two major forms.

- Irritable bowel disease is one of the most frequently diagnosed diseases in the U.S., affecting about 20 percent of the population. There is no cure.

- Diverticulosis occurs when small pouches called diverticula bulge outward through weak spots in the colon or small intestine.

- Diverticulitis occurs when the diverticula pouches become inflamed and cause pain.

- Severe cases of diverticulitis with acute pain and complications may require hospitalization. Surgery may be necessary if the patient does not respond to treatment.

- Gallstones occur when bile stored in the gallbladder hardens.

- About fifty percent of the population experiences hemorrhoids by age fifty.

Reassessing Your Knowledge

1. Cancers are named after the type of tissue from which they originate. What are these types, and in what tissue do most cancers occur?

2. List the leading three cancers for men and women, and identify symptoms and prevention strategies for each.

3. List the symptoms, treatment, and possible complications of type I and type II diabetes.

4. Describe risk factors for asthma and list symptoms and treatments.

5. Identify one major digestive disorder and describe symptoms.

To answer these questions, you might choose to work in groups with your colleagues. Check your answers against the written material in the text, and reread those sections where you made errors.

Health Assessment Toolbox

Harvard Center for Cancer Prevention: Your Disease Risk
This risk assessment provides tips for preventing common cancers as well as assessing your personal risk.
http://www.harvard.edu/

The American Institute for Cancer Research
This site provides information on cancer prevention based on lifestyle and nutrition.
http://www.aicr.org

American Academy of Dermatology
This site provides a wide range of materials on the prevention of skin cancers.
http://www.aad.org

Diabetes Risk Test
American Diabetes Association. This site provides a simple tool that can help you determine your risk for having pre-diabetes or type II diabetes.
http://www.diabetes.org>Diabetes Basics> Prevention

AHRQ Innovations Exchange—Child Asthma Risk Assessment Tool
This risk assessment provides a personal risk assessment for a child with asthma.
http://www.innovations.ahrq.gov/content. aspx?id=2114

Vocabulary Challenge

Match the term in the left-hand column with its correct definition in the right-hand column.

TERM		DEFINITION
Palliative care		A. A cancer prevention vaccine
Hyperplasia		B. Blood glucose values over 160 mg/dl
Sarcoma		C. Production of cancer
Cervarix		D. A cancer that begins in skin or tissues that cover internal organs
Hypoglycemia		E. Care provided to reduce symptoms and manage pain
Carcinoma		F. Nerve damage in the peripheral nervous system
Biopsy		G. A cancer that begins in bone, cartilage, fat, muscle, blood vessels or other connective or supportive tissue
Neuropathy		H. Blood glucose levels below 70 mg/dl
Hyperglycemia		I. The process of removing tissue for examination
Carcinogenesis		J. An abnormal multiplication of cells

Exploring the Internet

National Cancer Institute

This site provides information on clinical trials and a comprehensive database of cancer treatment information.

http://www.cancer.gov

American Institute on Cancer Research

This site focuses on changing lives to save lives.

http://www.aicr.org

American Diabetes Association

The American Diabetes Association offers support, answers to questions and information on living with diabetes.

http://www.diabetes.org

Asthma Information and Treatment Options

Information and treatment options for people living with asthma.

http://www.asthma.com

Allergies: Is it a cold or is it an allergy?

This National Institutes of Medicine site offers information on allergies from substances that cause allergies to risk factors for allergies.

http://www.nlm.nih.gov/medlineplus/allergy.html

Food Allergies and Intolerances

Nutrition and Health Issues. Provides access to food allergy resources.

http://www.nal.usda.gov/

Lung Diseases—Respiratory Disorders

This university website provides an overview of respiratory diseases.

http://www.rush.edu/rumc/page-1098994230985.html

National Digestive Diseases Information Clearinghouse.

Educational materials to increase knowledge and understanding about digestive diseases.

http://digestive.niddk.nih.gov/

Selected References

1. Altekruse, S.F., et al (eds). *SEER Cancer Statistics Review*, 1975–2007, National Cancer Institute. Bethesda, MD. November, 2009.

2. Centers for Disease Control and Prevention. Although Most People Getting Screened for Two of the Nation's Deadliest Cancers, Thousands of People Died Last Year Because They Weren't Screened for Colon or Breast Cancer. CDC Vital Signs. July 6, 2010.

3. American Cancer Society. Cancer Facts & Figures 2010. Atlanta: American Cancer Society, 2010.

4. International Early Lung Cancer Action Program Investigators. (2006). Women's Susceptibility to Tobacco Carcinogens and Survival after Diagnosis of Lung Cancer. *Journal of the American Medical Association*, 296: 180–184. 2006.

5. National Cancer Institute. National Lung Cancer Screening Trial. Downloaded September 22, 2010, from U.S. National Institutes of Health: www.cancer.gov

6. American Cancer Society. Cancer Facts & Figures 2010. Atlanta: American Cancer Society, 2010.

7. Draisma, G., Etzioni, R., Tsodikov, A., et al. Lead Time and Overdiagnosis in Prostate-Specific Antigen Screening: Importance of Methods and Context. *Journal of the National Cancer Institute,* 101(6): 374–383. March 18, 2009.

8. Stein, C.J., and Colditz, G.A. Modifiable Risk Factors for Cancer. *British Journal of Cancer,* 90: 299–303. 2004.

9. Infante, M., Duran, M., Lasa, A., et al. Two Founder BRCA2 Mutations Predispose to Breast Cancer in Young Women. Breast Cancer Research and Treatment. *Dordrecht*, 122(2): 567. July, 2010.

10. American Cancer Society. Cancer Facts & Figures 2010. Atlanta: American Cancer Society, 2010.

11. Klein, R., Hyperglycemia and Microvascular and macrovascular Disease in Diabetes. *Diabetes Care*, 18(2): 258–268. February, 1995.

12. Juvenile Diabetes Research Foundation International. Facts Sheets: Type 1 Diabetess (Juvenile Diabetes) Facts. Statistics. Downloaded September 27, 2010, from http://www.jdrf.org/index.cfm?page_id=102585

13. Gu, K., Cowie, C.C., Harris, M.I. Mortality in Adults with and without Diabetes in a National Cohort of the U.S. Population, 1971–1993. *Diabetes Care*, 21(7): 1138–1145. July, 1998.

14. Centers for Disease Control and Prevention. National Diabetes Fact Sheet: General Information and National Estimates on Diabetes in the United States, 2007. Atlanta, GA. 2008.

15. Ibid.

16. U.S. Department of Health & Human Services. National Institutes of Health, National Heart, Lung and Blood Institute. Diseases and Conditions Index. Asthma. Downloaded September 27, 2010, from http://www.nhlbi.nih.gov/health/dci/Diseases/Asthma/Asthma_Causes.html

17. Stang, P., Lydick, E., Silberman, C., Kempel, A., and Keating, E.T. The Prevalence of COPD: Using Smoking Rates to Estimate Disease Frequency in the General Population. *Chest*, 117: 354S–359S. 2000.

18. Croxton, T.L., Weinmann, G.G., Senior, R.M., and Hoidal, J.R. Future Research Directions in Chronic Obstructive Pulmonary Disease. *American Journal of Critical Care Medicine,* 165: 838–844. 2002.

19. National Institutes of Health, U.S. Department of Health and Human Services. Opportunities and Challenges in Digestive Diseases Research: Recommendations of the National Commission on Digestive Diseases. Bethesda, MD: 2009. NIH Publication 08–6514.

20. Everhart, J.E., ed. *The Burden of Digestive Diseases in the United States*. Bethesda, MD: National Institute of Diabetes and Digestive and Kidney Diseases, U.S. Dept of Health and Human Services, 2008.

21. Foong, K.,S., Patel, R., Forbes, A., et al. Anti-Tumor Necrosis Factor-Alpha-Loaded Microspheres as a Prospective Novel Treatment for Crohn's Disease Fistulae. Tissue Engineering Part C: Methods. *Larchmont*, 16(5): 855. October, 2010.

22. Pimental, M., Hwang, L., Melmed, G.Y., et al. New Clinical Method for Distinguishing D-IBS from Other Gastrointestinal Conditions Causing Diarrhea: The LA/IBS Diagnostic Strategy. *Digestive Diseases and Sciences*, 55(1): 145. January, 2010.

23. Fass, R., Longstreth, G.F., Pimental, M., et al. Evidence- and consensus-based practice guidelines for the diagnosis of irritable bowel syndrome. *Archives of Internal Medicine*, 161(17): 2081–2089. September 24, 2001.

24. Bogardus, S.T. What Do We Know About Diverticular Disease? A Brief Overview. *Journal of Clinical Gastroenterology*, 40: S108–S111. 2006.

25. Ibid.

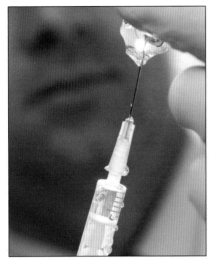

Image of Health

Infectious Diseases

THE INFECTIOUS DISEASE PROCESS

- The Chain of Infection
- The Disease Process
  - Incubation
  - Prodromal Stage
  - Clinical Stage
  - Recovery Stage
  - Dormancy Stage

PREVENTING INFECTION

- Barriers
- Immune Response
- Lymphatic System
- Allergies
- Immunizations
- Naturally Acquired Passive Immunity
- Artificially Acquired Passive Immunity
- Artificially Acquired Active Immunity

COMMON PATHOGENIC INFECTIONS

- Vectors
  - Insects
  - Animals
  - People
  - Water
  - Food
- Bacterial Infections
  - Streptococcal Infection
  - Staphylococcal Infections
  - MRSA
  - Pneumonia
  - Meningitis
  - Toxic Shock Syndrome
- Fungi
- Protozoa
- Helminthes (Worms)
- Prions
- Viral Infections
  - Common Cold and Influenza
  - Hepatitis A, B, and C
  - Mononucleosis
  - Measles
  - Mumps
  - Chickenpox
- Retroviral Infections
- Autoimmune Diseases

SEXUALLY TRANSMITTED INFECTIONS

- Human Papilloma Virus—HPV
- Herpes Simplex Virus II
- Chlamydia
- Gonorrhea
- Syphilis
- Parasitic Infections
- Hepatitis B
- Human Immunodeficiency Virus—HIV

EMERGING INFECTIONS

- Hantavirus Pulmonary Syndrome
- Avian Influenza H1N1
- Severe Acute Respiratory Syndrome—SARS

RESPONSIBILITY AND ACCOUNTABILITY

- Taking Responsibility for Infectious Diseases
- Focusing on Accountability

Student Learning Outcomes

LEARNING OUTCOME	APPLYING IT TO YOUR LIFE
Describe the disease process and how a common cold is transmitted.	Describe how knowledge of the disease process can improve your health.
Identify at least one infection caused by a bacteria and one infection caused by a virus.	Identify the importance of knowing the difference be tween a viral and bacterial infection in terms of treatment.
Describe the infectious disease process for a sexually transmitted infection (STI).	List the things you would do if you suspect or know you have a STI.
Identify some of the emerging infections that have been in the news.	Know how to decrease your risk for becoming infected by an emerging infection.
Describe how the human body protects itself against infectious pathogens.	Identify some events or situations in your life that may put you at risk for acquiring an infectious disease.

Assessing Your Knowledge

1. Fighting bacterial infections was made easier by the discovery of:
   a. Penicillin

   b. Anthrax

   c. Acyclovir

   d. Methicillin

2. The chain of infection starts with:
   a. A pathogen housed in a reservoir

   b. A mode of transmission

   c. A susceptible host

   d. A portal of exit

3. Which of the following is a viral infection?
   a. Meningitis infection

   b. Measles infection

   c. Staphylococcal infection

   d. Toxic shock infection

4. Getting a vaccine to prevent an infection is a form of:
   a. Naturally acquired immunity

   b. Passively acquired immunity

   c. Artificially acquired immunity

   d. Independently acquired immunity

5. A retroviral infection such as lupus or human immunodeficiency virus (HIV) causes an autoimmune response in which:
   a. The body attacks its own organs, tissues, and cells.

   b. The body creates an appropriate immune response to the retrovirus.

   c. The body will go through the infectious disease process and then create its own immunity to the retrovirus.

   d. The body will shut down some of its cellular defense mechanisms in order to isolate the retrovirus.

Answers:

1. a; 2. a; 3. b; 4. c; 5. a.

The Infectious Disease Process

We are surrounded daily by bacteria, viruses, and other agents that have the potential to cause infection—in fact, there are millions of bacteria on our skin and in our environment. Fortunately, only one percent of bacteria are harmful, and the majority are necessary not only for balance in our eco-environment, but also for our bodies to function properly. An *Escherichia coli* (*E. coli*) bacterium discovered in contaminated hamburger has been in the news for causing food poisoning illness in hundreds of people. Yet a type of *E. coli* is present in our own intestines, helping to digest food. We are surrounded by microorganisms that will never cause disease and infection, and they are essential to the earth's flora and fauna, and for all living creatures.

You are responsible for protecting yourself from infection, and for understanding the disease process to help avoid infecting others. In this chapter, you will learn which infectious agents are harmful, and also learn responsible behaviors to reduce your risk of infection.

Challenge Question: Considering that there are millions of bacteria, identify the approximate percentage that are harmful.

From young ages, most of us have some knowledge of infectious disease. As children, we learn we can catch a cold or flu from another person, and that a cut or scrape that is not kept clean can lead to a painful infection. We learn this from observation or personal experience, and as adults, our general knowledge of infectious disease evolves as new types of infections and treatments are discovered. For example, while it is common knowledge today that hand washing breaks the chain of infection, during the Civil War 150 years ago, doctors and surgeons did not wash their hands prior to surgery, or even use clean instruments. Surgical tools were used on multiple patients without cleaning, and because the link between unclean wounds and infection was not understood, keeping wounds and dressings clean was not practiced. In the 1860s, there were no antibiotic drugs to treat infections, which resulted in many amputations and deaths that would have been unnecessary today. While antibiotic drugs are now commonly used for bacterial infections, the first antibiotic, penicillin, was not discovered until the early twentieth century, and was not widely available to the general U.S. population until the 1940s.

Much was learned during the twentieth century about the infectious disease process, including that proper treatment and cure depend on correctly identifying the infectious disease agent. Today, because we are globally interconnected, we are much more susceptible to infections that can spread rapidly from city to city, state to state, and country to country. An infection that spreads throughout a region such as a state is called an **epidemic**; a **pandemic** is an infection that spreads throughout a continent, or even throughout the world.

Key Terms

Epidemic: An infection that spreads rapidly throughout a region such as a state.

Pandemic: An infection that spreads continentally or even globally.

Chain of Infection

The process of infection requires several steps, often called the chain of infection. There are similarities among the components of the process, and there must be a susceptible host available to be infected, such as a plant, animal, or human. There must also be a **pathogen** present, a reservoir to nourish the pathogen, a means for the pathogen to exit the reservoir, a mode of transmission, and a portal of entry to the susceptible host. For HIV, the susceptible host is human, and the chain of infection has the following components:

Pathogen = HIV.

Reservoir = Blood, semen, vaginal secretions, breast milk of an infected human being.

Portal of Exit = HIV exits the human via blood, ejaculating semen, vaginal secretions, or breast milk.

Mode of Transmission = Sexual intercourse, blood transfusion, infected syringes, or in breast milk.

Portal of Entry = Ejaculate enters rectum or vagina; vaginal secretions enter urethra at tip of penis, or transmitted into another vagina or rectum; infected blood is infused or injected into susceptible host; babies are infected by ingesting infected breast milk.

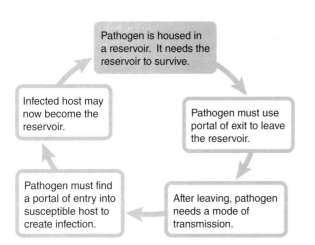

FIGURE 12-1. The chain of infection begins with a pathogen housed in a reservoir. The pathogen exits the reservoir via a portal. It then needs a mode of transmission, followed by a portal of entry into the susceptible host. If any one of these steps is missing, the pathogen cannot infect.

Key Term

Pathogen: A disease-causing organism.

The Disease Process

Once a pathogen has entered the blood of a host and the infection has entered the body, the disease process of illness begins. This process will vary depending on the disease, but generally includes the following stages.

Incubation Stage

The incubation stage occurs when the pathogen attempts to overcome the natural immune response of the body, continuing to multiply and infecting cells. Though there are typically no symptoms, the individual may nevertheless be contagious. It is also possible that during the incubation stage, the immune system will be successful in stopping the progress of the infection, and illness will not occur.

Prodromal Stage

The prodromal stage follows incubation. During this stage, the host or infected person may not look or even feel ill, but the pathogen is multiplying within the body. During the prodromal stage, hosts may travel or go to work or school, perhaps infecting others with whom they come in contact. Sometimes, the host may be aware of being in the prodromal stage: with herpes simplex virus II, commonly called cold sores, the host feels an itching, tingling sensation where the outbreak will occur. However, these symptoms are not evident to others, even though the host is highly infectious during this time.

Clinical Stage

During the clinical stage, symptoms arise as the result of infection. If specific symptoms can be determined as belonging to a particular disease, diagnosis is possible during this stage. Many infections have general symptoms, such as fever, nausea, aching joints, and muscles, and headache, making specific diagnosis difficult. At this stage, infection from one person to another is still possible, and with some infections, highly likely.

Recovery Stage

The symptoms of infection are declining and the person begins to feel well during the recovery stage. People sometimes return to normal activity, but recovery is not complete. The immune system may still be compromised and a relapse is possible. Adequate sleep, drinking plenty of fluids, and eating sufficient nutritional calories can aid the recovery stage.

Dormancy Stage

Some infections are always present after they have entered the body, but in a noninfectious or dormant state. Under certain conditions such as extreme stress or even another infection, the dormant infection can become active.

Preventing Infection

A healthy human body is very resilient in fighting infectious disease. The effectiveness of prevention depends primarily on whether the systems of the body are working effectively, or if they have been compromised. There is much you can do to take responsibility for reducing the incidence of infections for yourself and others.

Barriers

The initial large, effective protector is human skin, which acts as a barrier to pathogens. When there is a break in the skin or if it has been penetrated by a bite, cut, or needle stick, there is greater risk for infection because a portal of entry has been created. Additionally, the lungs defend against pathogens using **cilia**, tiny hair-like structures in the respiratory tract that expel foreign particles by initiating the cough and sneeze reflex. Enzymes in body fluids such as tears and mucus can also destroy or weaken pathogens.

Pasteurizing milk and chlorinating water keeps these liquids safe, and disinfectants kill most pathogens on surfaces. Storing foods at the correct temperature and cooking them to the correct temperature reduces the risk of food-borne disease. Insect and rodent control and eradication prevent or limit certain diseases. Individuals can use masks, condoms, and cover their own mouths when coughing to reduce the spread of infection. Vaccinations, medical testing and treatment, and quarantine when necessary also act as barriers in the spread of infectious diseases.

Key Term

Cilia: Small hair-like organelles that beat in waves to move protozoans, liquids, dust, pollens, and mucus out of the respiratory tract.

Image of Health in Depth

Hand Washing and Antibacterial Soap
There is no documented evidence that hand washing with antibacterial soap is more effective than hand washing with regular soap—using either antibacterial or regular soap breaks the chain of infection, and is an important protocol for reducing some infections.[1] Infections are frequently spread hand to hand, so ensuring that hands are clean is important in deterring infection. With influenza and the common cold, the hands become contaminated if people cover coughs and sneezes. Coughing or sneezing into the crook of the elbow or into your shoulder prevents this, reducing the risk of hand-to-hand infection.

Immune Response

When the human body recognizes a foreign pathogen or **toxin**, it initiates an immune response at the cellular level. Anything that causes the immune system to respond is called an **antigen**, and when the body recognizes and verifies that an antigen is not part of the body, it forms **antibodies**. Antibodies are special proteins specific to the antigen, weakening or destroying it. The body produces antigens primarily in response to bacteria, or to the toxins produced by bacteria.

Other pathogens, including viruses and some bacteria, are combated primarily by special white blood cells called **lymphocytes** and **macrophages**. Lymphocytes have the ability to specifically target a pathogen and remember it, should it enter the body in the future. The two major types of lymphocytes are B cells and T cells, named for their origin in the bone marrow and thymus gland. Both B and T cells can specifically repel an unwanted pathogen and create a memory cell that will recognize it in the future. Helper T cells, killer T cells, and suppressor T cells work together to rid the body of unwanted microbes. Macrophages are **phagocytic**, capable of surrounding and consuming an unwanted microbe, thereby destroying it.

When the body is harmed or fighting an infection, cells in the injured area release **histamine**, which initiates an inflammatory response, resulting in heat and swelling, and causing blood to flow to the injured area. Other cells, especially lymphocytes and macrophages, circulate to the area to combat the infection or injury. White blood cells attacking an infection may lead to pus, a collection of dead white blood cells, at the site.

Critical Thinking Question: Describe the immune response your body will initiate in the presence of a bacterial pathogen.

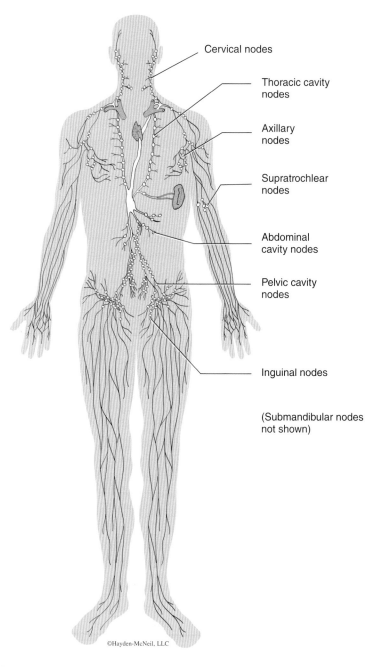

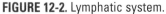

FIGURE 12-2. Lymphatic system.

Lymphatic System

The lymphatic system, a complex system that defends the body from pathogenic microbes, is a major part of the immune response, consisting of the spleen, thymus glands, bone marrow, appendix, tonsils, lymph nodes, and a network of vessels that circulate lymph fluid. White blood cells produced in the bone marrow destroy unwanted pathogens by filtering the destroyed microbes in the lymph nodes. Separate from the blood circulatory system, the lymphatic system filters and keeps lymph fluid levels normal by circulating it between the tissues and eventually to the bloodstream.

Key Terms

Antigen: Any substance that causes the immune system to produce antibodies.

Antibodies: Proteins specific to an antigen, usually bacteria that can destroy or weaken it.

Histamine: A chemical released in the blood that dilates blood vessels and causes heat and swelling at the site of an infection. It also can produce an inflammatory reaction in response to excessive antibodies, created as a result of an allergic reaction to a substance.

Lymphocytes: Special white blood cells that can specifically target a pathogen for destruction, and remember it in case it enters the body in the future.

Macrophages: Special white blood cells that form at the site of infection to destroy pathogens.

Phagocyte: A cell that can destroy a pathogenic microbe by surrounding and consuming it.

Toxin: A poison or harmful substance in the body.

Challenge Question: Name the components of the lymphatic system.

Allergies

In some people, the body apparently overreacts to an antigen by overproducing its antibodies, releasing histamine and causing an allergic reaction that can include rashes, difficulty breathing, excessive mucus production, and tissue swelling. Allergic reactions are sometimes seasonal, occurring in the spring in response to pollens, flowers, and grasses. Treatment usually involves **immunotherapy** or allergy shots that can suppress the offending antibodies.

Key Term

Immunotherapy: Treatment of disease by inducing, enhancing, or suppressing immune response.

Immunizations

Immunizations are vaccines given to provide immunity for certain infections. A vaccine is made from a non-living or weakened version of a pathogen that when injected into the body will cause the body to produce antibodies against a future infection. Vaccines are recommended for most individuals, and are required for children entering the school system in the U.S.

Image of Health in Depth

Vaccine-Peventable Diseases

Anthrax

Cervical Cancer

Diphtheria

Hepatitis A

Hepatitis B

Haemophilus influenzae type b (Hib)

Human Papillomavirus (HPV)

H1N1 Flu (Avian Flu)

Influenza (Seasonal Flu)

Japanese Encephalitis (JE)

Lyme Disease

Measles

Meningococcal

Monkeypox

Mumps

Pertussis (Whooping Cough)

Pneumococcal

Poliomyelitis (Polio)

Rabies

Rotavirus

Rubella (German Measles)

Shingles (Herpes Zoster)

Smallpox

Tetanus (Lockjaw)

Tuberculosis

Typhoid Fever

Varicella (Chickenpox)

Yellow Fever

Recommended Immunization Schedule for Persons Aged 0 Through 6 Years—United States • 2011
For those who fall behind or start late, see the catch-up schedule

Vaccine ▼ Age ▶	Birth	1 month	2 months	4 months	6 months	12 months	15 months	18 months	19–23 months	2–3 years	4–6 years
Hepatitis B[1]	HepB	HepB			HepB						
Rotavirus[2]			RV	RV	RV[2]						
Diphtheria, Tetanus, Pertussis[3]			DTaP	DTaP	DTaP	see footnote[3]	DTaP				DTaP
Haemophilus influenzae type b[4]			Hib	Hib	Hib[4]	Hib					
Pneumococcal[5]			PCV	PCV	PCV	PCV				PPSV	
Inactivated Poliovirus[6]			IPV	IPV	IPV						IPV
Influenza[7]					Influenza (Yearly)						
Measles, Mumps, Rubella[8]						MMR		see footnote[8]			MMR
Varicella[9]						Varicella		see footnote[9]			Varicella
Hepatitis A[10]						HepA (2 doses)				HepA Series	
Meningococcal[11]										MCV4	

Range of recommended ages for all children

Range of recommended ages for certain high-risk groups

1. **Hepatitis B vaccine (HepB).** (Minimum age: birth)
   At birth:
   • Administer monovalent HepB to all newborns before hospital discharge.
   • If mother is hepatitis B surface antigen (HBsAg)-positive, administer HepB and 0.5 mL of hepatitis B immune globulin (HBIG) within 12 hours of birth.
   • If mother's HBsAg status is unknown, administer HepB within 12 hours of birth. Determine mother's HBsAg status as soon as possible and, if HBsAg-positive, administer HBIG (no later than age 1 week).
   Doses following the birth dose:
   • The second dose should be administered at age 1 or 2 months. Monovalent HepB should be used for doses administered before age 6 weeks.
   • Infants born to HBsAg-positive mothers should be tested for HBsAg and antibody to HBsAg 1 to 2 months after completion of at least 3 doses of the HepB series, at age 9 through 18 months (generally at the next well-child visit).
   • Administration of 4 doses of HepB to infants is permissible when a combination vaccine containing HepB is administered after the birth dose.
   • Infants who did not receive a birth dose should receive 3 doses of HepB on a schedule of 0, 1, and 6 months.
   • The final (3rd or 4th) dose in the HepB series should be administered no earlier than age 24 weeks.
2. **Rotavirus vaccine (RV).** (Minimum age: 6 weeks)
   • Administer the first dose at age 6 through 14 weeks (maximum age: 14 weeks 6 days). Vaccination should not be initiated for infants aged 15 weeks 0 days or older.
   • The maximum age for the final dose in the series is 8 months 0 days
   • If Rotarix is administered at ages 2 and 4 months, a dose at 6 months is not indicated.
3. **Diphtheria and tetanus toxoids and acellular pertussis vaccine (DTaP).** (Minimum age: 6 weeks)
   • The fourth dose may be administered as early as age 12 months, provided at least 6 months have elapsed since the third dose.
4. **Haemophilus influenzae type b conjugate vaccine (Hib).** (Minimum age: 6 weeks)
   • If PRP-OMP (PedvaxHIB or Comvax [HepB-Hib]) is administered at ages 2 and 4 months, a dose at age 6 months is not indicated.
   • Hiberix should not be used for doses at ages 2, 4, or 6 months for the primary series but can be used as the final dose in children aged 12 months through 4 years.
5. **Pneumococcal vaccine.** (Minimum age: 6 weeks for pneumococcal conjugate vaccine [PCV]; 2 years for pneumococcal polysaccharide vaccine [PPSV])
   • PCV is recommended for all children aged younger than 5 years. Administer 1 dose of PCV to all healthy children aged 24 through 59 months who are not completely vaccinated for their age.
   • A PCV series begun with 7-valent PCV (PCV7) should be completed with 13-valent PCV (PCV13).
   • A single supplemental dose of PCV13 is recommended for all children aged 14 through 59 months who have received an age-appropriate series of PCV7.
   • A single supplemental dose of PCV13 is recommended for all children aged 60 through 71 months with underlying medical conditions who have received an age-appropriate series of PCV7.
   • The supplemental dose of PCV13 should be administered at least 8 weeks after the previous dose of PCV7. See *MMWR* 2010:59(No. RR-11).
   • Administer PPSV at least 8 weeks after last dose of PCV to children aged 2 years or older with certain underlying medical conditions, including a cochlear implant.

6. **Inactivated poliovirus vaccine (IPV).** (Minimum age: 6 weeks)
   • If 4 or more doses are administered prior to age 4 years an additional dose should be administered at age 4 through 6 years.
   • The final dose in the series should be administered on or after the fourth birthday and at least 6 months following the previous dose.
7. **Influenza vaccine (seasonal).** (Minimum age: 6 months for trivalent inactivated influenza vaccine [TIV]; 2 years for live, attenuated influenza vaccine [LAIV])
   • For healthy children aged 2 years and older (i.e., those who do not have underlying medical conditions that predispose them to influenza complications), either LAIV or TIV may be used, except LAIV should not be given to children aged 2 through 4 years who have had wheezing in the past 12 months.
   • Administer 2 doses (separated by at least 4 weeks) to children aged 6 months through 8 years who are receiving seasonal influenza vaccine for the first time or who were vaccinated for the first time during the previous influenza season but only received 1 dose.
   • Children aged 6 months through 8 years who received no doses of monovalent 2009 H1N1 vaccine should receive 2 doses of 2010–2011 seasonal influenza vaccine. See *MMWR* 2010;59(No. RR-8):33–34.
8. **Measles, mumps, and rubella vaccine (MMR).** (Minimum age: 12 months)
   • The second dose may be administered before age 4 years, provided at least 4 weeks have elapsed since the first dose.
9. **Varicella vaccine.** (Minimum age: 12 months)
   • The second dose may be administered before age 4 years, provided at least 3 months have elapsed since the first dose.
   • For children aged 12 months through 12 years the recommended minimum interval between doses is 3 months. However, if the second dose was administered at least 4 weeks after the first dose, it can be accepted as valid.
10. **Hepatitis A vaccine (HepA).** (Minimum age: 12 months)
    • Administer 2 doses at least 6 months apart.
    • HepA is recommended for children aged older than 23 months who live in areas where vaccination programs target older children, who are at increased risk for infection, or for whom immunity against hepatitis A is desired.
11. **Meningococcal conjugate vaccine, quadrivalent (MCV4).** (Minimum age: 2 years)
    • Administer 2 doses of MCV4 at least 8 weeks apart to children aged 2 through 10 years with persistent complement component deficiency and anatomic or functional asplenia, and 1 dose every 5 years thereafter.
    • Persons with human immunodeficiency virus (HIV) infection who are vaccinated with MCV4 should receive 2 doses at least 8 weeks apart.
    • Administer 1 dose of MCV4 to children aged 2 through 10 years who travel to countries with highly endemic or epidemic disease and during outbreaks caused by a vaccine serogroup.
    • Administer MCV4 to children at continued risk for meningococcal disease who were previously vaccinated with MCV4 or meningococcal polysaccharide vaccine after 3 years if the first dose was administered at age 2 through 6 years.

(Source: CDCP – 2011 Recommended immunization schedules for persons aged 0–18 years. United States, 2011. *Morbidity Mortality Weekly Report* 57(51): Q1–Q4 Centers for Disease Control and Prevention, 2011. Recommended adult immunization schedule—United States, 2011 *Morbidity and Mortality Weekly Report* 57(53): Q1–Q4)

Recommended Immunization Schedule for Persons Aged 7 Through 18 Years—United States • 2011

For those who fall behind or start late, see the schedule below and the catch-up schedule

Vaccine ▼ Age ▶	7–10 years	11–12 years	13–18 years
Tetanus, Diphtheria, Pertussis[1]		Tdap	Tdap
Human Papillomavirus[2]	see footnote [2]	HPV (3 doses)(females)	HPV Series
Meningococcal[3]	MCV4	MCV4	MCV4
Influenza[4]	Influenza (Yearly)		
Pneumococcal[5]	Pneumococcal		
Hepatitis A[6]	HepA Series		
Hepatitis B[7]	Hep B Series		
Inactivated Poliovirus[8]	IPV Series		
Measles, Mumps, Rubella[9]	MMR Series		
Varicella[10]	Varicella Series		

Range of recommended ages for all children

Range of recommended ages for catch-up immunization

Range of recommended ages for certain high-risk groups

1. **Tetanus and diphtheria toxoids and acellular pertussis vaccine (Tdap).** (Minimum age: 10 years for Boostrix and 11 years for Adacel)
   - Persons aged 11 through 18 years who have not received Tdap should receive a dose followed by Td booster doses every 10 years thereafter.
   - Persons aged 7 through 10 years who are not fully immunized against pertussis (including those never vaccinated or with unknown pertussis vaccination status) should receive a single dose of Tdap. Refer to the catch-up schedule if additional doses of tetanus and diphtheria toxoid–containing vaccine are needed.
   - Tdap can be administered regardless of the interval since the last tetanus and diphtheria toxoid–containing vaccine.
2. **Human papillomavirus (HPV).** (Minimum age: 9 years)
   - Quadrivalent HPV vaccine (HPV4) or bivalent HPV vaccine (HPV2) is recommended for the prevention of cervical precancers and cancers in females.
   - HPV4 is recommended for prevention of cervical precancers, cancers, and genital warts in females.
   - HPV4 may be administered in a 3-dose series to males aged 9 through 18 years to reduce their likelihood of genital warts.
   - Administer the second dose 1 to 2 months after the first dose and the third dose 6 months after the first dose (at least 24 weeks after the first dose).
3. **Meningococcal conjugate vaccine, quadrivalent (MCV4).** (Minimum age: 2 years)
   - Administer MCV4 at age 11 through 12 years with a booster dose at age 16 years.
   - Administer 1 dose at age 13 through 18 years if not previously vaccinated.
   - Persons who received their first dose at age 13 through 15 years should receive a booster dose at age 16 through 18 years.
   - Administer 1 dose to previously unvaccinated college freshmen living in a dormitory.
   - Administer 2 doses at least 8 weeks apart to children aged 2 through 10 years with persistent complement component deficiency and anatomic or functional asplenia, and 1 dose every 5 years thereafter.
   - Persons with HIV infection who are vaccinated with MCV4 should receive 2 doses at least 8 weeks apart.
   - Administer 1 dose of MCV4 to children aged 2 through 10 years who travel to countries with highly endemic or epidemic disease and during outbreaks caused by a vaccine serogroup.
   - Administer MCV4 to children at continued risk for meningococcal disease who were previously vaccinated with MCV4 or meningococcal polysaccharide vaccine after 3 years (if first dose administered at age 2 through 6 years) or after 5 years (if first dose administered at age 7 years or older).
4. **Influenza vaccine (seasonal).**
   - For healthy nonpregnant persons aged 7 through 18 years (i.e., those who do not have underlying medical conditions that predispose them to influenza complications), either LAIV or TIV may be used.
   - Administer 2 doses (separated by at least 4 weeks) to children aged 6 months through 8 years who are receiving seasonal influenza vaccine for the first time or who were vaccinated for the first time during the previous influenza season but only received 1 dose.

- Children 6 months through 8 years of age who received no doses of monovalent 2009 H1N1 vaccine should receive 2 doses of 2010-2011 seasonal influenza vaccine. See *MMWR* 2010;59(No. RR-8):33–34.
5. **Pneumococcal vaccines.**
   - A single dose of 13-valent pneumococcal conjugate vaccine (PCV13) may be administered to children aged 6 through 18 years who have functional or anatomic asplenia, HIV infection or other immunocompromising condition, cochlear implant or CSF leak. See *MMWR* 2010;59(No. RR-11).
   - The dose of PCV13 should be administered at least 8 weeks after the previous dose of PCV7.
   - Administer pneumococcal polysaccharide vaccine at least 8 weeks after the last dose of PCV to children aged 2 years or older with certain underlying medical conditions, including a cochlear implant. A single revaccination should be administered after 5 years to children with functional or anatomic asplenia or an immunocompromising condition.
6. **Hepatitis A vaccine (HepA).**
   - Administer 2 doses at least 6 months apart.
   - HepA is recommended for children aged older than 23 months who live in areas where vaccination programs target older children, or who are at increased risk for infection, or for whom immunity against hepatitis A is desired.
7. **Hepatitis B vaccine (HepB).**
   - Administer the 3-dose series to those not previously vaccinated. For those with incomplete vaccination, follow the catch-up schedule.
   - A 2-dose series (separated by at least 4 months) of adult formulation Recombivax HB is licensed for children aged 11 through 15 years.
8. **Inactivated poliovirus vaccine (IPV).**
   - The final dose in the series should be administered on or after the fourth birthday and at least 6 months following the previous dose.
   - If both OPV and IPV were administered as part of a series, a total of 4 doses should be administered, regardless of the child's current age.
9. **Measles, mumps, and rubella vaccine (MMR).**
   - The minimum interval between the 2 doses of MMR is 4 weeks.
10. **Varicella vaccine.**
    - For persons aged 7 through 18 years without evidence of immunity (see *MMWR* 2007;56[No. RR-4]), administer 2 doses if not previously vaccinated or the second dose if only 1 dose has been administered.
    - For persons aged 7 through 12 years, the recommended minimum interval between doses is 3 months. However, if the second dose was administered at least 4 weeks after the first dose, it can be accepted as valid.
    - For persons aged 13 years and older, the minimum interval between doses is 4 weeks.

(Source: CDCP – 2011 Recommended immunization schedules for persons aged 0–18 years. United States, 2011. *Morbidity Mortality Weekly Report* 57(51): Q1–Q4 Centers for Disease Control and Prevention, 2011. Recommended adult immunization schedule—United States, 2011 *Morbidity and Mortality Weekly Report* 57(53): Q1–Q4)

Naturally Acquired Passive Immunity

Naturally acquired passive immunity occurs with the transfer of active antibodies from one person to another. The primary method occurs when the fetus receives antibodies from the mother through the placenta, and continues after birth with breastfeeding. Colostrum, which contains antibodies from the mother, is the first fluid produced by mammary glands after childbirth. Continued breastfeeding ensures naturally acquired immunity until the child's immune system develops.

Artificially Acquired Passive Immunity

Artificially acquired passive immunity is induced by injecting a non-immune person with the blood serum or hemoglobin of an individual who carries antibodies for a particular infection, resulting in temporary immunity. Prior to antibiotic drugs, this was the only method used to treat infectious diseases.

Artificially Acquired Active Immunity

The most common procedure for creating immunity, artificially acquired active immunity involves injecting a person with the antigen for a particular infectious disease, so that the immune system will make antibodies for that disease. Vaccines exist for many bacterial and viral infections, and have resulted in eradicating most childhood infectious diseases in the U.S.

Critical Thinking Question: Describe how a vaccine works to protect against infectious disease.

Common Pathogenic Infections

The world of microorganisms is immense, and is the focus of the field of microbiology. From a general health perspective, an overview of microbiology is necessary in order to understand the precautions and behaviors necessary to reduce the risk of infection.

Consider that it was not until the end of the seventeenth century, with the invention of the microscope, that it was possible to even see microorganisms.[2] Although most microorganisms are harmless, there are six categories that pose the most disease risk for humans: bacteria, fungi, protozoa, helminthes, prions, and viruses. They are called pathogenic because they are able to cause disease, and most are also considered parasitic because they live in or on a host organism, usually causing it harm.

Table 12-1. Top Infectious Diseases Worldwide

DISEASE	APPROXIMATE NUMBER OF DEATHS PER YEAR
Pneumonia	3,884,000
HIV/AIDS	2,777,000
Diarrheal diseases	1,798,000
Tuberculosis	1,566,000
Malaria	1,272,000
Pertussis (whooping cough)	294,000
Tetanus	214,000
Meningitis	173,000
Syphilis	157,000
Many of the 618,000 deaths from liver cancer each year can be tracked to viral hepatitis. The top six diseases cause 90% of all premature deaths worldwide. Overall, infectious diseases kill more than 11 million people each year, representing nearly 19% of all deaths.	

(Source: World Health Organization, 2004. The World Health Report 2004. Geneva: World Health Organization.)

Vectors

There are several ways for humans to get an infection, often involving an infectious partner called a vector—an organism that does not cause the disease itself, but enables the transmission of the infection. Insects, animals, people, water, and food are typical vectors. The common cold or influenza is sometimes considered an airborne illness; however, the vector is not the air itself, but a person who sneezes or coughs into the air, making the virus airborne.

Insects

There are several insects that cause infections, including mosquitoes, fleas, and ticks. According to the World Health Organization (WHO), in sub-Saharan Africa, malaria kills over 1.2 million children each year, most under the age of five years.[3] The vector for malaria is the mosquito, which thrives in warm climates where inadequate irrigation, water systems, sanitation, and waste disposal create an environment for mosquito larvae to flourish. When a mosquito infected with malaria bites a human, the malaria parasite travels to the liver, where it matures and eventually infects blood cells. Symptoms include chills, fever, headaches, sweats, nausea, and vomiting, and may appear in a few days or as long as several months. Many children in malaria-prone areas could be saved simply by covering their beds with mosquito nets.

West Nile virus is transmitted by mosquito bites, and cases have been documented in all U.S. states. For most people there are few symptoms, and no medical attention is required. Mosquitoes become infected by feeding on birds that carry the virus. West Nile virus is considered a seasonal infection that occurs during the summer and fall, and using mosquito repellent and ensuring that clothing covers the skin are the best preventatives. Risk factors for developing a more severe form of West Nile virus include:

- Conditions that weaken the immune system, such as human immunodeficiency virus (HIV), organ transplants, and recent chemotherapy.

- Older age.

- Pregnancy.

West Nile virus may also be spread through blood transfusions and organ transplants, and it is also possible for an infected mother to spread the virus to her child through breast milk.

Fleas, typically those on rats, cause the plague. Millions of people died of the plague in the Middle Ages, when homes were infested with rats carrying the flea, which in turn carried the plague bacterium. According to the World Health Organization (WHO), there are now around 3,000 cases of plague globally per year. Additionally, there are 10–15 cases annually in the United States—specifically in Arizona, Colorado, and New Mexico—caused by flea-infested rats living in or near homes. Individuals infected with the plague have flu-like symptoms and tender lymph nodes. Because it can be treated with specific antibiotics, the fatality rate is only fourteen percent, and effective control of rats has made the plague a fairly rare infectious disease.

Both Lyme disease and Rocky Mountain spotted fever are transmitted by ticks. Lyme disease is carried by the deer tick, a small, brown tick found mostly in the eastern and southern woods of the United States, though some cases have been reported on the west coast. Symptoms of Lyme disease include a red bump on or near the tick bite, fever, chills, headache, fatigue, and enlarged lymph nodes. Another common symptom is a red or pink circular rash that expands up to 15 inches in diameter near the bite site, sometimes referred to as a Lyme disease bull's eye. Rocky Mountain spotted fever is carried by the Lone Star tick, a round, dark brown tick with a white mark on its back. The symptoms of Rocky Mountain spotted fever include nausea, vomiting, muscle pain, joint pain, fever, and eventually a rash.

Ticks can be avoided by wearing long sleeves and long pants, and by using a tick repellent. A ticks looks for hosts who are warm-blooded animals, and will attach to humans, pets, livestock, and wild animals by burrowing its head under the skin of the host, feeding on blood and releasing toxins. Proper tick removal involves carefully extracting the tick with tweezers, ensuring that the head remains intact and is not left under the skin. The sooner the tick is removed, the less chance of infection. Both Lyme disease and Rocky Mountain spotted fever are treated with antibiotics.

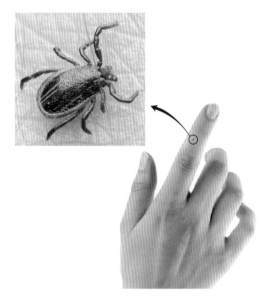

FIGURE 12-3. Deer tick.

Animals

The saliva of dogs, cats, ferrets, and rabbits are known to contain a wide variety of bacteria that can be harmful to humans. About 4.7 million people, most of them children, are bitten by animals in the United States each year.[4] Infections from animal bites are usually bacterial, and can be treated with antibiotics. Rabies is transmitted via the bite of an infected animal, resulting in viral **encephalitis**. Animals in the wild, such as skunks, raccoons, bats, and foxes, transmit most cases of rabies. Rabies infection is rare in the United States, most occurring as a result of raccoon bites. The onset of symptoms occurs sometimes weeks after the bite, which is usually unreported. Treatment should be sought as soon as possible, since an untreated rabies bite can be fatal.[5]

Key Term

Encephalitis: An inflammation of the brain caused by infection, usually a virus. Symptoms include headache, fever, and vomiting, and can become progressively severe to include loss of consciousness, seizures, and death.

People

Passing infections between people, through touch or sexual contact, by sharing common household items such as utensils, by breathing air contaminated by a sick person, or by contact with contaminated blood, is the most common means of transmission for infectious diseases. When coughing or sneezing without covering the mouth and nose, small particles of sputum or saliva are expelled into the air, where they can be inhaled by others. Those at the beginning stage of an infection, such as the common cold or flu, are usually the most infectious. Hosts can be very infectious during the prodromal or beginning stage of infection, even though they are not experiencing symptoms. As a result, the infected person may continue with a normal routine, coming into contact with and infecting many new people. Most infections are spread among people by inhaling infectious pathogens in the air, or by sharing infected utensils, drinks, or food.

Image of Health in Depth

Keeping Your Infection to Yourself

1. Cover your mouth and nose when you sneeze or cough. It is better to cough or sneeze either into a tissue or the crook of your elbow, rather than into your hand.

2. Wash your hands frequently, especially before touching food or another person.

3. Avoid touching your eyes or other mucous membranes.

4. Do not share anything with a sick individual. Keep eating and drinking utensils, towels, and toothbrushes separate.

5. If possible, stay home when you are sick, especially at the beginning stages of an infection when you are most infectious and more likely to contaminate others.

Water

In the United States, most infections from water are caused by parasites in drinking or recreational water. Giardia (giardiasis) is the most common parasitic gastrointestinal infection, found in the intestines and feces of people who become infected by ingesting contaminated water from lakes, streams, swimming pools, and hot tubs. There are 2.5 million cases of Giardia in the U.S. each year.[6] Symptoms include abdominal cramping, diarrhea, nausea, and fatigue, and begin to appear about 7 days to 2–3 weeks after infection. The illness is usually self-limiting, lasting 2–4 weeks. In many untreated patients, however, symptoms of Giardia can last from several months to years, and children with chronic symptoms may fail to thrive.

Cryptosporidiosis (crypto) is a parasite found in the feces of humans and animals. When ingested, the parasite lives in the intestines, causing diarrhea, and even when symptoms stop, the parasites can still be found in the stool of the infected person or animal. Recreational water or well water can easily be contaminated by human or animal fecal sewage containing the crypto parasite, and is then passed on to people or animals that come into contact with this water. To reduce the risk of infection, uncooked food, fruits, and vegetables should be washed carefully prior to eating, and any suspect water should be filtered or boiled. The CDC estimates that there are 300,000 cases of crypto in the United States each year.[7]

Food

Escherichia coli or *E. coli* is a category of bacteria of several different varieties. Depending on the type, symptoms may include urinary tract infections or respiratory illness, including pneumonia, with the most common symptoms being vomiting and diarrhea that may be bloody and severe. *E. coli* infections in the U.S. are caused primarily by infected cattle, with the bacteria living in the gut of the animal before it is released in the feces. When minute amounts of *E. coli*-contaminated feces are ingested in food, unpasteurized milk or apple cider, and soft cheeses made from raw milk, human infection from E. coli may occur. Other cases of *E. coli* infection have been documented in individuals who have eaten undercooked hamburgers, or from eating lettuce that has not been washed. Most infections of *E. coli* are mild, but very young children, the elderly, and those with suppressed immune systems can have severe infections that may become life threatening.

Salmonella is a type of bacteria transmitted by food, water, or infected animals. Once ingested, the bacteria cause fever, nausea, and severe gastrointestinal distress, including bloody diarrhea. The infection can become life threatening when it enters the bloodstream through the intestines. The CDC estimates that there are 1.4 million cases of salmonella infections each year, resulting in 400 deaths.[8]

Image of Health

Protecting Yourself from Salmonella Infections

- Because foods of animal origin may be contaminated with salmonella, uncooked chicken, eggs, and beef should be carefully handled in the kitchen.

- Consuming raw eggs as an ingredient in homemade salad dressing, ice cream, or cookie dough is risky.

- Cross-contamination can be prevented by keeping produce and other ready-to-eat foods separated from areas where uncooked chicken and meat are prepared.

- Thorough washing of hands, kitchen utensils, and cutting boards will alleviate the spread of salmonella infections.

- Consume hamburgers that are completely cooked, so the meat is not pink in the center.

- Raw or unpasteurized milk or dairy products should not be consumed.

- Produce should be thoroughly washed, including melons and other fruits whose skin is not eaten, but that could contaminate the knife used to cut the fruit.

- Those with a salmonella infection should not prepare food or drinks for others.[9]

Bacterial Infections

Bacteria differ from viruses in that they are single-celled organisms that in most cases can survive without a host. Bacteria consist of a single loop of DNA, closely resembling a chromosome, contained in a cell and surrounded by a more rigid cellular wall. Most bacteria are not pathogenic, and survive easily in our environment in water, soil, plants, animals, and people. There are millions of bacteria on human skin and in the digestive tract that are considered "normal flora," essential for healthy digestion and vitamin synthesis. And they are used by the dairy industry to make cheese and yogurt, and by the energy industry to make methane gas. Because genes can mutate and transfer between bacteria, the bacteria are able to respond to external threats. Pathogenic bacteria cause disease either by secreting toxins or by inducing a harmful immune response. Most bacteria that are harmful to humans are transmitted via animals, to whom the bacteria is not harmful, that act as vectors, carrying and passing bacteria to humans. For example, cattle may carry the bacteria for tuberculosis; birds may carry the bacteria for pneumonia; deer and ticks carry the bacteria for Lyme disease; farm animals carry the *E. coli*, salmonella, and campylobacter bacteria that causes food poisoning; fleas on rats carry the bacteria for plague; and farm animals carry the bacteria for anthrax.

Bacteria are also spread from human to human. Sexual activity can introduce pathogenic bacteria from an infected host into an uninfected host. Within the bloodstream, tissue, and organs, the human body is usually aseptic, devoid of bacteria. If bacteria access these areas, infection may result.

Controlling bacterial infections with antibiotics and vaccines was one of the greatest successes of the twentieth century. The rise of antibiotic-resistant infections at the beginning of the twenty-first century is cause for concern with infectious bacteria such as MRSA (methicillin-resistant *Staphylococcus aureus*).

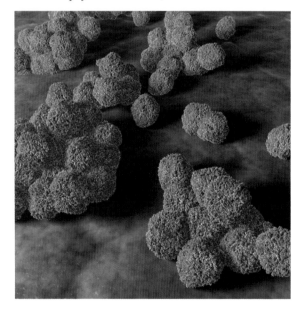

FIGURE 12-4. MRSA.

Critical Thinking Question: Describe why some bacteria are essential.

A MRSA infection is spread by physical contact from an infected person; it is not an airborne disease. There are only a few available antibiotics to treat this infection: bactrim and vancomycin have been effective in the past, but a more recent strain of staph is resistant to vancomycin. VRSA, vancomycin-resistant *Staphylococcus aureus*, is difficult to cure, though patients have been effectively treated with antibiotics that may only be available intravenously.[10]

MRSA is virulent and deadly. According to the CDC, in 2005, more people died from MRSA (18,650) than from AIDS (16,000). It is now the leading cause of surgical site infections, pneumonia, and bloodstream infections in nursing homes and hospitals.

You can lower your risk for MRSA infection by frequently washing your hands thoroughly with soap and water. If soap and water are not available, use a hand sanitizer. If you have any cuts, keep them clean, dry, and covered with a bandage. Keep your hands away from your face, and do not share personal items such as towels, razors, tweezers, and toothbrushes.

Streptococcal Infections
Streptococcal infections, or strep infections, are bacterial infections that cause a variety of health problems, including strep throat and skin infections, toxic shock syndrome, and necrotizing fasciitis (flesh-eating disease). In most cases, antibiotics can destroy streptococcal infections; however, with more serious infections, particularly necrotizing fasciitis, surgical removal of infected tissues and fluids may be necessary, along with antibiotic drugs. Strep throat is transmitted from an infected individual via saliva or nasal droplets. Though it is highly contagious, it is easily treated with antibiotics.

Staphylococcus aureus
Staph bacteria (*Staphylococcus aureus*), a group of more than thirty bacteria that can cause many different infections, are found in the nose and on the skin of most adult humans.[11] Under normal conditions, staph bacteria do not cause disease. However, if the skin or body tissues are damaged, a staph infection can occur, and any part of the body can be infected. It is a common hospital infection in patients with surgical wounds or burns and can lead to **sepsis**, circulatory collapse, and death.[12]

MRSA

An antibiotic-resistant staph infection, methicillin-resistant *Staphylococcus aureus* (MRSA) is resistant to methicillin and similar drugs, such as penicillin. The usual environment for MRSA infections is hospitals and convalescent homes, where infected individuals are either very ill or the elderly. Open wounds from surgery, bedsores, and catheters are primary MRSA infection sites. About ten percent of infections are community-based, and risk of illness varies depending on the community.

> **Key Term**
>
> **Sepsis**: Infection of circulatory blood, also called blood poisoning. Symptoms are elevated heart rate, body temperature, and respiration, all of which are indications of an infection. Sepsis can lead to organ failure and death.

Antibiotics are used to treat staph infections. Simple, over-the-counter triple-antibiotic creams are used for most staph skin infections. If the infection is severe, oral antibiotics are used, and more serious infections are treated in hospital with intravenous antibiotics. The type of antibiotic used depends on the type and location of the infection, as well as the known susceptibility of a particular strain of staph to the antibiotic. Penicillin and similar drugs, such as methicillin and amoxicillin, are usually very effective in treating staph infections.

Pneumonia

Bacteria, virus, or fungus can cause pneumonia, which causes more deaths globally than any other infectious disease, including AIDS, malaria, or tuberculosis.[13] Pneumonia can be prevented with vaccination, and treatment with antibiotics or antiviral drugs is usually successful. Transmission is caused by breathing air that has been contaminated with small-infected droplets exhaled by an infected person during sneezing and coughing. The symptoms of pneumonia resemble a cold, but progress to a fever that may be as high as 104 degrees. Symptoms may also include a severe cough and production of discolored, possibly bloody sputum. The onset of symptoms may be less severe, including a progressive cough, headache, and muscle fatigue. Diagnosis usually involves a chest X-ray to identify possible fluid in the lungs, and sputum may be analyzed to determine if the pneumonia is bacterial, viral, or fungal so appropriate drug therapy can be prescribed. In 2006, 1.2 million people were hospitalized with pneumonia in the U.S., and over 55 thousand died from the disease.[14]

Challenge Question: Identify three possible pathogens for pneumonia, and describe the mode of transmission.

Meningitis

Meningitis is an inflammation of the meninges, the membranes surrounding the brain and spinal cord. It is caused by either a virus or bacteria, and is sometimes triggered by other diseases, such as **lupus**. The symptoms of meningitis can be mild flu-like symptoms to severe symptoms including muscle weakness, seizures, and dementia. Diagnosis is made by a lumbar puncture, wherein cerebral fluid is removed from around the spinal column and analyzed to determine the pathogenic nature of the meningitis. Either antibiotic or antiviral drugs may be used for treatment, depending on whether the cerebral fluid showed the presence of bacteria or virus. Bacterial meningitis is contagious, spread through respiratory and throat secretions in the saliva, possibly exchanged by kissing. The bacteria are usually not airborne and cannot be transmitted by breathing the air near an infected individual.

> **Key Term**
>
> **Lupus**: An autoimmune disease that can impair the function of the joints, kidneys, heart, brain, skin, or blood.

Toxic Shock Syndrome

Toxic shock syndrome (TSS), caused by either the *Streptococcus* or *Staphylococcus aureus* bacteria, was first identified in the 1980s among menstruating women who developed severe bacterial infections leading to fever, shock, multiorgan dysfunction, and in some cases, death.[15] Most infected women reported using super-absorbency tampons, but some cases of TSS have been seen post-surgery in non-menstruating women. Only about 7 percent of TSS is seen in men, usually following a surgical event. Incidence of TSS has declined since the FDA mandated standardized labeling on tampon products. Additionally, the industry has begun making tampons less absorbent, and packaging now also contains information indicating that tampons should be changed more frequently.[16]

Image of Health in Depth

Completing the Prescribed Antibiotic Dose

Antibiotics only treat bacterial diseases, certain fungal infections, and parasites—they do not work against viral diseases. Taking antibiotics unnecessarily will not make you feel better, and can create antibiotic resistance. Antibiotic treatment is structured to wipe out all of the pathogenic bacteria. Although symptoms may improve within a few days, some of the offending bacteria may still be thriving. Stopping medication at this point allows the bacteria to proliferate, and may help them develop resistance to the antibiotic. When bacteria become resistant to the first line of defense, the risk of complications and even of death increases. In the U.S., thousands of people die annually from antibiotic-resistant bacterial infections contracted in hospitals, caused primarily by repeated and improper use of antibiotics. If this continues, costs to treat bacterial infections will continue to increase, and treatment may take much longer.[17]

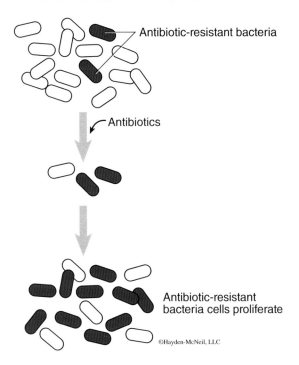

Antibiotic-resistant bacteria

Antibiotics

Antibiotic-resistant bacteria cells proliferate

©Hayden-McNeil, LLC

FIGURE 12-5. Bacterial cell showing resistance to antibiotics.

Fungi

Fungi are organisms that absorb food from organic matter. About 50 of the many thousands of fungi types cause disease in humans, including skin disease, lung disease, and diseases in mucous membranes. Fungi, including molds and yeasts, have a cellular structure very similar to a human cell, making them harder to recognize by the human immune system. Molds and yeasts differ from fungi in their method of reproduction, a process called budding. Fungal spores are inhaled from soil or decaying plants, or are transmitted from animals, bird droppings, or other humans. Inhaled fungal spores cause pneumonia and lung infections, and are most prevalent in tropical regions. A fungus transmitted from another human can develop on the skin, nails, and hair, causing ringworm and athlete's foot, both of which are easy to treat. Under certain conditions, yeasts normally found in the mouth and gut of humans can overgrow, often in response to antibiotic treatment, causing thrush in the mouth or vaginal yeast infections. Although self-treatments are available for vaginal yeast infections, the product may not be effective against the type of yeast that has proliferated, possibly causing the infection to become more severe. Only a medical practitioner can accurately diagnose the infection and prescribe the proper medication.

Fungal infections are particularly harmful for those with immune deficiency diseases, which make them more susceptible to opportunistic infections. One fungus, coccidioidomycosis, causes valley fever, a systemic disease that may be severe, even life threatening.

Though some may be harmful, there are beneficial uses for yeasts and molds, as well. One type of yeast converts sugars into carbon dioxide under aerobic conditions, allowing bread to rise prior to baking. The same yeast under anaerobic conditions allows sugar to be converted to alcohol, the basis for making alcoholic beverages. Yeasts are also used to help make vaccines, notably the hepatitis B vaccine, as well as the first antibiotic drug penicillin, which was originally made from the mold *Penicillium notatum*.

Protozoa

Protozoa are single-cell organisms that can live either externally or internally in humans. Most are not harmful to humans, but the few pathogenic protozoa are difficult for the immune system to recognize and combat. Because their vectors live in the tropics, that is where pathogenic protozoa thrive. Protozoa can be found in water and are transmitted by insects. The most common insect-borne pathogenic protozoa are *Plasmodium*, which infect and spread malaria to humans. There are four types of *Plasmodium*, and depending on the type, these *Plasmodium* cause a variety of illnesses, from flu-like symptoms and fever to brain and organ failure and death. The most common water-borne pathogenic protozoa are Giardia, which infect the gut of animals and humans, causing diarrhea and dehydration. Although not life threatening for adults, Giardia can be serious for children.

An amoeba is a water-borne protozoan that causes dysentery and abscesses in the brain, liver, and lungs, called amoebic dysentery. Less common but very pathogenic protozoa, found in Africa and South America, cause sleeping sickness. These protozoa multiply in the blood of humans and cattle, affecting the central nervous system and leading to coma-like symptoms and death. There are no vaccines to protect against infections involving pathogenic protozoa, and immunity cannot be acquired.

Helminthes (Worms)

Worms, multicellular organisms that are the largest of the pathogens, can grow up to several feet in length. They are extremely difficult for the human immune system to expel, but the immune response is typically perceptible. Fortunately, there are only a few varieties that affect humans. Though they do not multiply once inside the body, they can grow substantially, and a person can be infected with several worms at once.

Three types of worms affect humans—roundworms (nematodes), tapeworms (cestodes), and flukes (trematodes)—causing an enormous amount of disease and suffering in much of the world, including Asia, Middle East, Africa, South America, and the Mediterranean. Most roundworms require an intermediate host as a vector, such as a fly, flea, or mosquito, which carry the worm larvae. When the vector bites the host, the larvae are injected into the blood, where they remain as they develop into worms. Worms may cause the lymphoderma seen in **elephantiasis**, blindness when the worm inhabits the eyes, and cirrhosis and liver failure when in the liver. The Guinea worm, a nematode found only in Africa, lives in standing water and in tiny fleas. Humans ingest the water and fleas, and the larvae reproduce in the intestines. After

about a year, a mature Guinea worm, which may be three feet long, makes its way toward the surface of the skin in the extremities, causing swelling and a painful burning blister. Eventually, the worm will exit the blister, but this may take days and cause a great deal of pain. To sooth the pain, infected people wade in water where the worm will release a new generation of millions of larvae. The flea eats the larvae in the water, and the cycle begins again.

There are no vaccines for worms and few available drugs for treatment. Drug treatment often has extreme side effects, and may make an already ailing patient even more ill.[18]

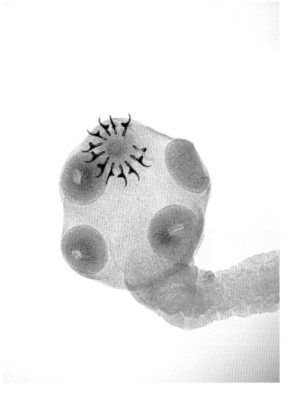

FIGURE 12-6. Tapeworm.

Key Term

Elephantiasis: A parasitic worm infection that blocks the lymphatic system, causing limbs to swell so much they resemble parts of an elephant. The prognosis is good for mild, early infections, but it is fatal for heavy parasitic infections.

Image of Health in Depth

The Carter Center Guinea Worm Eradication Program

Humans are the only host for the Guinea worm. In 1986, when the Carter Center began a campaign to eradicate the Guinea worm, there were 3.5 million cases in Africa and Asia. In 2009, there were 3,190 cases in four African countries, and it is poised to be the next infection after smallpox to be eradiated. Dr. Ernesto Ruiz-Tiben, the director of the Guinea Worm Eradication Program, has said, "Hopefully, Guinea worm will be the first parasitic disease ever eradicated. If and when that happens, we will have done it without a drug and without a vaccine to treat or prevent the disease. If we can do that, it will be one of the greatest achievements in public health."

Prions

Prion refers to an infectious protein, and has only recently been recognized as the cause of the disease bovine spongiform encephalopathies (BSE), or mad cow disease. The disease was first discovered in the United Kingdom (UK), in cows that had been fed meat and bone meal containing BSE-infected products. The infected food came from sheep infected with scrapie, a prion disease of sheep. Although the spread of pathogenic prions is usually animal-to-animal, there is strong evidence that it has occurred in humans. This new variant of prion disease has been called **vCreutzfeldt Jakob disease** (vCJD), a rare, degenerative, fatal brain disorder.

The CDC believes that BSE infection is caused by eating contaminated cattle products or, as in three cases that occurred in the UK, through blood received from an infected, asymptomatic donor. Of the three cases identified in the U.S., two of the patients had moved here from the UK, and were likely infected there. The third person had been born and raised in Saudi Arabia before moving to the U.S., and it is thought that contaminated meat from Saudi Arabia caused his infection.

In 2009, the FDA issued a regulation banning the feeding of sheep meat and by-products to cattle. There are feed-testing programs in place to ensure that herds are no longer fed products that violate the regulation.

Key Term

vCreutzfeldt Jakob Disease: A variant fatal form of classic Creutzfeldt Jakob disease, caused by consumption of contaminated meat products. Classic CJD is a human prion disease that results in death, usually within one year of diagnosis. Classic CJD occurs when normal prion proteins spontaneously transformation into abnormal prions. CJD is a very rare disease, occurring in approximately one in every one million people.

Viruses

Viruses are the smallest of all known pathogens. They depend on the host to provide nutrients for metabolism and multiplication, meaning that unlike most other pathogens, a virus cannot survive outside the host. The structure of a virus is variable, consisting of a protein coat inside which is a **genome** of either **RNA** or **DNA**, though not both. In addition, a lipid envelope may or may not be present, and if present, the lipid envelope surrounds the protein coat. Because of this variable structure, the way a virus multiplies depends on whether the genome is RNA or DNA, and if there is a lipid envelope. When the virus exits the host cell and enters the bloodstream, the lipid envelope is acquired. The virus will not destroy the host cell when exiting, and the envelope protects the virus long enough for it to move through the bloodstream to another site in the body. If it cannot acquire a lipid envelope, the virus exits the cell by rupturing and destroying the cell, causing damage to cells and tissues. No matter how a virus exits a cell, in order to multiply it must enter another cell, which it accomplishes by first attaching to a receptor on the cell surface. For some viruses the cell surface receptor is known, but for most, it is not. The cell surface receptor that has likely received the most attention is the **T cell**, since it is a receptor for **HIV**. "Image of Health in Depth: Viruses Sorted by Genome and Presence or Absence of Lipid Envelope" outlines some of the more common viruses, indicating whether they are DNA or RNA, and with or without a lipid envelope.

Key Terms

Genome: The complete set of genetic material of an organism.

RNA: Ribonucleic acid, a substance in living cells that carries instructions for the synthesis of proteins.

Deoxyribonucleic acid (DNA): A material present in nearly all living organisms that carries all genetic information.

T cell: Also called CD4 cells, part of the immune response that responds to infection.

HIV: Human immunodeficiency virus, the virus that causes AIDS (acquired immunodeficiency syndrome).

Challenge Question: Describe how the presence or absence of a lipid envelope affects the disease process of a virus.

Classifying a virus by whether it has an envelope and whether it has an RNA or DNA genome is the first step in creating a vaccine. For example, the flu vaccine is developed from the envelopes of the flu virus, allowing the body to recognize the virus and begin producing antibodies to fight infection. Because the vaccine is made from the envelope, the virus is not live and will not produce disease. Due to the large number of viruses and their ability to mutate into new viruses, developing viral vaccines is a complicated process.

Image of Health

Viruses Sorted by Genome and Presence or Absence of a Lipid Envelope

RNA VIRUSES WITH LIPID ENVELOPE	RNA VIRUSES WITHOUT LIPID ENVELOPE
Influenza and colds	Colds
Measles	Polio
Mumps	Hepatitis A
Hepatitis C	
HIV human immunodeficiency virus	
Yellow Fever	
Hanta Virus	
Ebola Virus	
DNA Viruses with Lipid Envelope	**DNA Viruses without Lipid Envelope**
Herpes simplex virus	Colds
Small pox	Warts
Hepatitis B	

Common Cold and Influenza

The common cold and influenza are the viruses that most often affect college students. These viruses are highly contagious and easily transmitted from touching another person, drinking from a glass contaminated by a sick individual, or breathing air that contains the virus. Sitting next to a coughing, sneezing person on an airplane or in a classroom increases the possibility of becoming infected with a virus. The flu virus is more serious than a cold virus—it infects the lungs, and symptoms may be severe, especially in individuals with compromised immune systems. Flu symptoms include fever, cough, sore throat, headache, muscle soreness, and fatigue. Gastrointestinal illness, such as nausea, vomiting, and diarrhea, are less common. Though the term "stomach flu" is sometimes used to describe gastrointestinal illness, it is usually caused by other microorganisms, such as the bacteria *E. coli* or salmonella. Although the flu is not usually life threatening, there have been worldwide influenza pandemics. The most famous of these occurred in 1918, when influenza caused over 50 million deaths.

Image of Health in Depth

Is It a Cold or the Flu?

SYMPTOM	COLD	FLU
Fever	Rarely	Common, temperatures between 100°F and 102°F lasting 3–4 days
Headache	Rarely	Usual
General aches and pains	Slight	Usual and often severe
Fatigue and weakness	Quite mild	Can last up to 2–3 weeks
Extreme exhaustion	Rarely	Usual and prominent
Stuffy nose	Common	Occasionally
Sore throat	Common	Occasionally
Chest discomfort, cough	Mild to moderate hacking cough	Common and can become severe
Complications	Sinus congestion or earache	Bronchitis, pneumonia; can be life threatening
Prevention	None	Annual vaccination; Symmetrel, Tamiflu, or Flumadine (antiviral drugs)
Treatment	Only temporary relief of symptoms with over-the-counter (OTC) drugs	Symmetrel, Flumadine, Relenza, or Tamiflu within 24–48 after onset of symptoms

(Abstracted from WebMD—Cold and Flu Health Center, Is it a cold or the flu?)

Critical Thinking Question: What can you do to limit your chances of becoming infected with the common cold virus?

Hepatitis A, B, and C

Hepatitis A, B, and C are viral infections that inflame the liver, affecting its function. Hepatitis A virus can be ingested when saliva is exchanged (e.g., kissing), or more commonly when minute amounts of human fecal waste are consumed, which can occur in day care centers, at home, in restaurants where conditions are not sanitary, and when hand washing does not occur after restroom use.

Hepatitis B is transmitted by sexual activity, sharing needles among drug abusers, accidental needle sticks, and blood transfusions involving a person with Hepatitis B. There are also cases of Hepatitis B infection from tattooing, body piercing, and sharing razors or toothbrushes where contaminated blood is present.

Hepatitis C is found almost exclusively among drug abusers who share needles or because of accidental needle sticks in hospitals, and rarely is caused by transfusion of contaminated blood.

Many people infected with Hepatitis A, B, or C have no symptoms. If symptoms are present, they may include nausea, vomiting, fever, fatigue, and abdominal pain. In rare cases, the symptoms may include jaundice (yellow tint to the skin and yellow whites of eyes), dark urine, and fever. The type of treatment depends on the severity of symptoms: if the symptoms are mild, treatment involves maintaining adequate fluid intake and using over-the-counter (OTC) analgesics to relieve symptoms. In acute hepatitis, with symptoms that may include vomiting and abdominal pain, the liver becomes impaired and cannot process drugs normally, making drug therapy difficult. A poorly functioning liver can allow drugs to build up in the blood, reaching a toxic level. Alcohol should also be avoided because it is toxic to the liver, making proper liver function even more difficult. Preventing dehydration is important in acute hepatitis, possibly requiring hospitalization with intravenous fluids.

Mononucleosis

One of the most common, worldwide human viruses, mononucleosis is caused by the Epstein-Barr virus (EBV), a member of the herpes virus family. Sometimes called the kissing disease, it is readily transferred in saliva, as well as by sharing eating or drinking utensils, and by breathing air contaminated by an infected person. Most adults have been exposed to EBV as children and have developed immunity. In 35–50 percent of cases among adults, there are symptoms of fever, sore throat, and swollen lymph glands.[19] Very few normally healthy individuals who are exposed to EBV become ill.

Andre and Immunity

Andre was a good student who decided to take more than a full load of classes in order to graduate early. He also needed to work part time to pay some of his expenses, and it was important for him to spend time with his girlfriend. Andre decided he would make a schedule to help him manage his time so that he could accomplish everything.

He started getting up at 5 a.m. to study before classes. This was difficult for him because he usually went to bed at 11:30 p.m. or later, but he forced himself to stay on schedule. His heavier class load required more work than he anticipated, and he started falling behind in some classes. He also started losing weight because he was too busy to think about eating, and seemed constantly exhausted. His girlfriend was also making more demands on his time, causing him to become even more tired.

Halfway through the term, Andre became ill with what he thought was influenza. This was new for him, since he was rarely sick. He missed a week of classes and work before going back, but he was still not well and was very behind in his classes. When midterm grades came, he discovered his overall B+ average was now a C–. He had lost even more weight when he was sick, and now had little energy. He was depressed because he could not keep up in his classes, his girlfriend broke up with him, and he felt so tired he wished he could sleep for a week. Andre struggled for the rest of the term, but became ill again during finals. He missed some of his finals and took incomplete grades in half his classes.

Andre finally went to the college health center, where he was diagnosed with Epstein-Barr virus. He learned that his immune system had become compromised due to lack of sleep, poor nutrition choices, and poor stress management. Health center staff explained that normally, he would have been resistant to the virus.

Andre may have been infected by his girlfriend, since many healthy people can carry and spread the virus intermittently throughout their lives. For this reason, transmission of the virus is almost impossible to prevent. Had Andre taken better care of himself, he likely would have simply experienced a sore throat for a day or two, and then recovered. ∎

Critical Thinking Question: What could Andre have done differently to reduce his chances of infection?

Measles

Measles is a highly contagious virus primarily affecting children. Symptoms include a high fever, rash that lasts more than three days, cough, runny nose, and red eyes. Inhaling air contaminated by the coughing and sneezing of an infected person spreads the disease. When exposed to the virus, the infection rate is more than ninety percent. Although incidence of death from measles in the U.S. is low, there are 200,000 deaths worldwide from measles each year.[20]

Death from this disease is caused by opportunistic infections, such as pneumonia or encephalitis, that take advantage of compromised immune systems. The measles vaccine was developed in 1968, and today, only two percent of children immunized after their first birthday will get the disease. Prior to 1968, there were 3–4 million cases of measles each year in the U.S., resulting in 500 deaths. Anyone who has ever had measles has lifetime immunity to the disease.

Image of Health in Depth

The Measles Vaccine and Autism

In 1998, the *Lancet*, one of the most respected medical journals, published a small study conducted by Dr. Andrew Wakefield and associates, who concluded that the study results indicated that the measles, mumps, rubella vaccine (MMR) caused autism. The study was heavily criticized because it breached fundamental principles of research medicine. Dr. Wakefield was accused of showing callous disregard for the suffering of children by taking blood samples from them at his son's birthday party; the parents of the 12 children in his study had paid him 50,000 in British pounds (about $80,000) to prove that the MMR vaccine caused autism. In 2000, the Centers for Disease Control and the National Institutes for Health reviewed all evidence and determined that there is no scientific evidence to support this claim. The American Academy of Pediatrics also reviewed the Wakefield study, and in 2001, it published a policy statement that the MMR vaccine does not cause autism.[21] Dr. Wakefield was investigated for three years by the General Medical Council in Great Britain, and was subsequently removed from the medical register. The *Lancet* retracted the full article.

Mumps

Caused by the mumps virus, mumps infection is rare in the U.S. because children receive the MMR vaccine. For most individuals infected with mumps, symptoms are mild or non-existent, and may include fever, headache, muscle aches, fatigue, and swollen and tender salivary glands under the ears. Rare complications in adult men include inflammation of the testicles and brain; in adult women, inflammation of the brain, ovaries, and breasts, and spontaneous abortion in early pregnancy. In rare cases, both genders will experience permanent deafness.

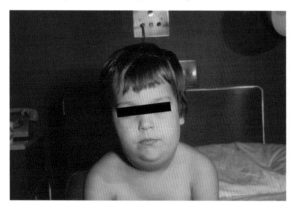

FIGURE 12-7. Child with mumps.

Chickenpox

Varicella zoster virus infection causes chickenpox, which presents as a skin rash with blister-like sores, typically on the face, scalp, and trunk, and some individuals will also have fever. Chickenpox is highly contagious and is spread by coughing, sneezing, and direct contact with skin blisters. Since 1995, a vaccine for chickenpox has been included in the MMR vaccination protocol. This new vaccination, now called MMRV, is given in two doses, and is a live, attenuated vaccine that produces immunity to chickenpox in 80–90% of all vaccinated children. In addition, the vaccine prevents serious illness in almost all vaccinated individuals. Adults who become infected with chickenpox are more at risk for infectious complications, which may include bacterial infection of the skin, swelling of the brain, and pneumonia.

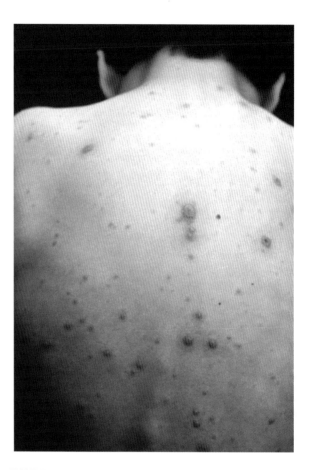

FIGURE 12-8. Adult with chickenpox.

Retroviral Infections

Retroviruses have the RNA genome and a lipid envelope, as well as the enzyme reverse transcriptase, causing synthesis of a complementary DNA molecule by using the virus RNA as a template. There is no cure for diseases caused by a retrovirus, because the immune system attacks the host and cannot defend against the disease.

When a retrovirus infects a cell, it injects its RNA into the cell, along with the reverse transcriptase enzyme, effectively causing the cell to start making the retrovirus. The human body has no effective defense for retroviruses, and there is no cure for any retroviral infections. Cellular defenses force the antibodies to fight the retrovirus, but they are not effective. Although most retroviruses infect animals, the most common retrovirus that affects humans is HIV, human immunodeficiency virus. Classifying a retrovirus involves identifying the antibodies in the blood that are trying to combat it. For example, a test for HIV involves a blood test that measures the level of antibody response to HIV. If antibodies for HIV are present, the individual has tested positive for HIV infection.

The retrovirus HIV causes acquired immunodeficiency syndrome (AIDS), in which the T cells of the immune system are destroyed and immune function is impaired. In America, HIV/AIDS was first identified in homosexual men in 1981, when patients presented serious but rare lung infections and skin tumors. The virus is found in the blood and body fluids of infected individuals, and infection is most likely from sexual contact, sharing needles, or when passed from infected mother to child. Infected mother-to-child transmission, called perinatal transmission, can occur during pregnancy, labor and delivery, or breastfeeding. This transmission is the most common cause of HIV infection in children, and is considered the source of all childhood AIDS cases in the U.S. Since 1994, HIV+ pregnant women and their newborns are given an antiviral medication (zidovudine) that reduces the risk of this transmission.[22]

Sexual transmission of HIV through vaginal, anal, and oral sex can be men to men, men to women, women to men, and women to women. Treatment for HIV involves an antiviral drug therapy protocol that has effectively prolonged and improved the quality of life for infected individuals.[23] Since 1985, studies have shown that sexual transmission of HIV is 100 percent preventable. Choosing to abstain from sexual intercourse until you are in a committed monogamous relationship with a disease-free individual, or choosing to use condoms with every act of sexual intercourse, will help prevent this disease, and responsibility falls on both sex partners. HIV infection has no symptoms, and if you become infected, the cost of accountability is lifelong.

Autoimmune Diseases

Autoimmune diseases are those that cause the body to have an inappropriate response to infection: instead of a normal immune response, the body attacks its own organs, tissues, and cells. There is no known cause for autoimmune disease, but affected individuals appear to have a hereditary predisposition to certain diseases. There are two types of autoimmune diseases: those that attack a single area of cells or tissue, and those that are systemic, such as lupus and rheumatoid arthritis, which damage many parts of the body. Lupus can affect the joints, kidneys, heart, brain, skin, or red blood cells, affecting tissues and organs and impairing function. Rheumatoid arthritis attacks the joints, causing pain, stiffness, loss of mobility, and eventually joint deterioration. Autoimmune

diseases that attack a single area include type I diabetes, affecting the pancreas; Graves's disease, affecting the thyroid; Crohn's disease, affecting the gastrointestinal tract; and Addison's disease, affecting the adrenal glands. There is no cure for any autoimmune disorder, and treatment depends on the severity of the disease, the frequency of symptoms, and the general health of the patient.

Sexually Transmitted Infections

One in four college students today has some type of sexually transmitted infection (STI): if you choose to be sexually active, it is important to know your risks for STIs. Individual responsibility for sexual behavior is part of self-care, and it is important to be accountable for not only your own sexual health, but for those with whom you engage in sexual activity. Sexually transmitted infection is seldom intentional; it usually occurs because a partner has no symptoms and does not think he or she is contagious. The only way to protect completely against STIs is to abstain from sex—both male and female condoms provide some protection, but cannot be 100% guaranteed. Of the almost 20 million new STI infections each year, almost half are among 15–24-year-olds.[24]

The type of sexual activity determines the degree of risk for some STIs. Although oral sex is an effective birth control measure, it is a risky sexual practice if one partner has human papilloma virus (HPV), herpes simplex virus (HSV), or gonorrhea, since each can be orally transmitted. Vaginal and penis-to-rectum intercourse both transmit STIs; in fact, penis-to-rectum may have higher risk. The rectal membrane is thin and may be easily torn, allowing ejaculate to more easily enter the recipient, passing blood back to the donor through the penis. "Image of Health In Depth: Sexually Transmitted Infections" shows the number of cases of a variety of STIs.

Challenge Question: What percentage of the 20 million new STIs each year are the 15–24-year-old age group?

Image of Health

Sexually Transmitted Infections—2008

INFECTION	RATE OR NUMBER
Chlamydia	1,210,523 new infections in 2008. This is the highest number of infections ever reported for any disease in the U.S.
Gonorrhea	336,742 new cases.
Syphilis	431 new cases. Syphilis may soon be eradicated in the U.S.
Chancroid	25 new cases, but this maybe under-reported.
Human papilloma virus	35 percent of all infections are in those age 14–19 years old. 29 percent are in those age 20–29 years old. 13 percent are in those age 30–39 years old. 11 percent are in those age 40–49 years old.
	6.3 percent are in those age 50–65 years old.
Herpes simplex virus	As with any viral infection, actual numerical counts are hard to achieve due to lack of diagnosis. But based on the number that do present, rates have decreased from a 21 percent infectious rate to a 17 percent infectious rate in those age 14–49 years of age.

(Source: Centers for Disease Control, Sexually Transmitted Diseases Surveillance, 2008.)

With the exception of HPV, there are no vaccines for STIs, nor can immunity be acquired. Each time an individual is exposed to an STI, an infection is possible. Any person can become infected with an STI any time they have unprotected sexual intercourse. This can be the first time, or any subsequent time. However, risk of exposure will increase if number of partners increases. Because there are some common STIs that do not present symptoms for either gender, it is possible to become infected and not realize it.

Motivation Maximizer

Who Is Responsible for Sexually Transmitted Infections?

Assume that you have sex with someone and a few days later are experiencing symptoms you do not understand. After a visit to the local health care center, you are told you have a sexually transmitted infection. You are distraught, overwhelmed, and angry! You contact your last partner, who vehemently denies any responsibility. Could this have come from someone you had sex with months ago, or is it this most recent partner? Some infections can take a month or more before presenting symptoms, but most new cases of an STI are from the most recent partner. Did this partner know of their infection? In almost all cases, the unfortunate answer is yes, they did. They may have thought they were not infectious, but you now know they were.

So, who is responsible for your infection? You are. If you choose to be sexually active and decide not to use a condom, you assume responsibility for anything that passes between you and your partner, ranging from bacteria and virus to lice and sperm. It is your responsibility to protect yourself.

And who is accountable for your infection? You show accountability when you choose to seek treatment, and not to engage in sexual activity unless you know you are infection-free. Condoms can cost as little as twenty cents each, and for twenty cents, you can greatly reduce the risk of both lifelong and short-term infections and pregnancy.

The sexual anatomy for males and females provide natural barriers to disease. The environment in the vagina is acidic, making it inhospitable to infectious microorganisms. The urethra in both genders is frequently flushed with urine that is also highly acidic, making it a less likely place for infection. But in spite of natural barriers, STIs persist. Birth control pills, although highly effective for pregnancy prevention, can change the environment in the vagina from more acidic to more alkaline, making susceptibility to infection more likely. The urethra in females is short compared to males, and women are more likely to have bladder infections than men. Men infected with an STI who are not treated can develop an infection of the urogenital system, affecting the urethra, bladder, vas deferens, and testicles. In women, the urinary system is separate from the reproductive system, but allows for the possibility of separate infections.

Human Papilloma Virus (HPV)

Human papilloma virus is an incurable STI. It is caused by one of the more than one hundred different human papilloma viruses, fifteen of which also cause cervical cancer. It is estimated that 80 percent of women and 50 percent of men will become infected with one or more of the varieties of genital HPV at some point in their lives. The most common HPV infections can be prevented with the HPV vaccine, but it is fully effective only if administered before a female has been exposed to any types of HPV. The vaccine does not protect against all the types of HPV that cause cervical cancer, so it is imperative that women continue to get annual pap smears. The vaccine is currently only available to those 9–26 years of age.

Most people who become infected with HPV are not aware of the infection, and in 90 percent of cases, the body's own immune system will clear the infection within two years. Some types of HPV cause genital warts, and in rare cases, these warts can occur in the throat as a result of oral sex. Warts can be small or large, flat or raised, and will appear within weeks or months of sexual contact with an infected partner. Warts can be treated but not completely eradicated, and there will always be a risk for passing on the infection. Protecting yourself from HPV is not difficult. You can choose not to have sex, but if abstinence is not a viable option, choosing to always use a condom will reduce, but not eliminate, your risk of infection. Twenty million Americans currently have HPV, and 6 million new cases are reported each year.[25]

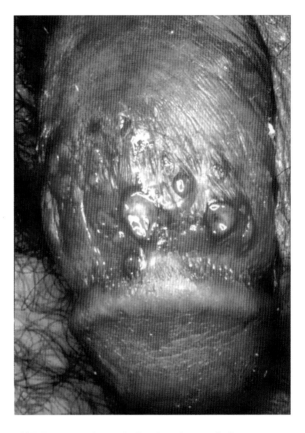

FIGURE 12-9. male genitalia showing genital warts.

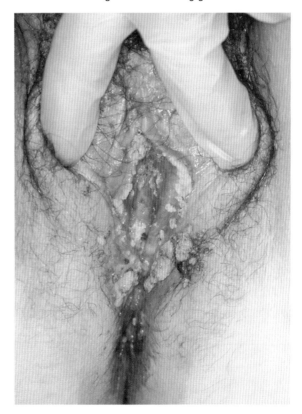

FIGURE 12-10. female genitalia showing genital warts.

Herpes Simplex Virus 2 (HSV2)

Herpes simplex virus two (HSV2), also known as genital herpes, is another STI for which there is no cure. A herpes infection starts within about 14 days after exposure, when the skin begins to itch and becomes red, during the highly infectious prodromal stage. Soon, blisters form, then break, becoming painful ulcerated lesions. In a few weeks, these lesions will crust over and eventually heal. Blisters form at the site of infection, which may be the penis, vagina, rectum, or mouth. Herpes simplex virus one (HSV1), called non-genital herpes, causes fever blisters or cold sores on the mouth and is transmitted by physical contact, usually kissing, with someone who has an active outbreak of HSV1. However, by having oral sex with an individual who has active HSV1 in or on his/her mouth, HSV1 can also be transmitted to the genitals.

Antiviral medications can reduce the number and duration of outbreaks. Once an outbreak of herpes occurs, the virus permanently remains in the infected individual. It becomes dormant, and it may be months or years before another outbreak. Outbreaks are often associated with stress and can sometimes arise as the result of other infections, including those that impair immune response. A CDC press release in March, 2010, indicated that about 1 in every 6 Americans between the ages of 14 and 49 is infected with HSV2. It is one of the most common sexually transmitted infections, and the report showed that HSV2 prevalence is nearly twice as high in women than men, and more than three times higher in blacks that whites. As with other STIs, biological factors may cause women to be more susceptible.[26]

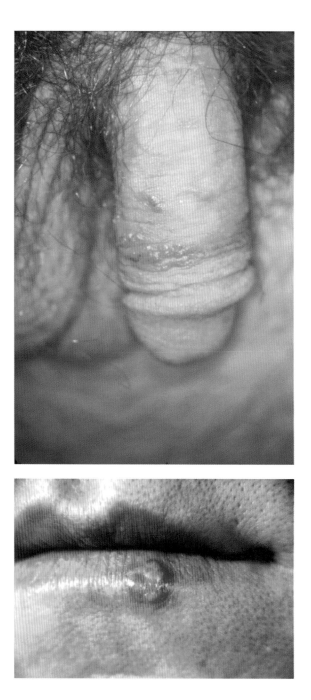

FIGURE 12-11. genital herpes (HSV2) and oral herpes (HSV1).

Chlamydia

Chlamydia trachomatis is the most commonly reported STI, with over 1.2 million new infections reported annually.[27] Though chlamydia is an easily detected and treated bacterial infection, screening remains problematic, since most infected individuals do not show symptoms. Untreated, it can lead to a number of reproductive health problems in women, including infertility and pelvic inflammatory disease (PID), which can cause pain in the abdomen, **ectopic** pregnancy, and infertility. In men, an untreated chlamydia infection can cause urethritis, an inflammation of the urethra, and epididymitis, an inflammation of the epididymis. Either is painful, and can potentially cause sterility.

The highest rate of infection is found among adolescents, with non-Hispanic blacks disproportionately affected. It has been suggested that infection rates may drop if sexually active individuals were examined annually for chlamydia; for women, this could be part of the annual pap smear test. Lack of awareness of testing, social stigma, and barriers to finding and treating sex partners compounds the problem.

Key Term

Ectopic pregnancy: Growth of a fertilized human embryo outside of the uterus, usually in the fallopian tube. Untreated sexually transmitted diseases may cause scar tissue in the fallopian tube, potentially resulting in ectopic pregnancy. Treatment involves removing the embryo from the fallopian tube, which can result in sterility.

Gonorrhea

Gonorrhea is the second most reported STI, with a slightly higher infection rate among young women than young men. Many cases of gonorrhea go undiagnosed and untreated, and the long-term complications for both genders are similar to chlamydia. The most common class of antibiotics used to treat gonorrhea was changed in April 2007, due to resistance to the antibiotic drug. A new category of antibiotics, cephalosporins, is now used to treat gonorrhea, with no resistance noted.[28] Centers for Disease Control estimates that more than 700,000 persons get new gonorrheal infections each year, but only about half of these are reported to the CDC.[29]

Most men experience symptoms with gonorrhea that include a burning sensation when urinating, or a white, yellow discharge from the penis. Some men also have painful or swollen testicles. Symptoms usually appear within 2–5 days of infection, but may take as long as 30 days to appear. In men, gonorrhea can causes epididymitis, and left untreated, this can lead to sterility.

Most women do not experience symptoms. If they do, the symptoms are mild and usually mistaken for a bladder infection. If left untreated, serious complications can arise in women, regardless of the presence or absence of symptoms. Gonorrhea is another common cause of PID in women, with about one million women developing PID each year in the U.S.

Syphilis

After a decline in infection rate for over ten years, syphilis infections increased to over 36,000 cases in 2006, with the largest increase in male-to-male sexual contact. Although the infection rate for women is low compared to men, there was also an increase among women, as well as in congenital syphilis, in which transmission is from mother to infant.[30] Syphilis is highly infectious, but easily treated by antibiotics during the primary and secondary stages. Incubation for syphilis can last from 10 to 90 days before symptoms appear. The primary stage can last from three to six weeks, during which a **chancre** appears at the site of the infection—usually the penis, vagina, rectum, or mouth. The chancre is painless, does not itch, and heals without treatment, but the bacterium that causes syphilis is still active in the host.

The secondary stage is also highly infectious, and may last from four to six weeks. Symptoms include a rash on the palms and bottoms of feet, hair loss, sore throat, and sometimes skin lesions on the genitals that resemble genital herpes. Because the rash is on the palms of the hands, the infection can be transmitted by casual contact. The signs and symptoms of secondary syphilis will resolve with or without treatment, but without treatment, the disease will progress to the latent stage and possibly the late stage of syphilis.

In the latent stage, primary and secondary symptoms have disappeared. The bacterium continues to reside in the host, who is no longer contagious, and the stage may last for years.

Late-stage syphilis occurs in about 15 percent of people who are untreated, and can occur as long as 10–20 years after the initial infection. In this stage, damage occurs to internal organs, including the brain, eyes, heart, blood vessels, liver, bones, joints, and eyes. Symptoms include difficulty coordinating muscle movements, paralysis, gradual blindness, and dementia, and the damage may be so severe that it results in death.[31]

> **Key Term**
>
> **Chancre**: A sore or ulcer that is painless but highly infectious, appearing at the location where the syphilis bacteria (spirochete) enter the body.

Emerging Infections

Because of the ease with which infections can be transmitted, the spread of infectious diseases around the world has increased in the twenty-first century. The global population easily spreads disease—the world economy is interconnected, with goods and services exchanged among many nations. This interconnectedness creates potential for exposure to pathogens from all parts of the world, transmitted primarily by people, animals, plants, insects, and water. For individuals who travel outside of the United States, some protection is afforded by ensuring that personal immunizations are current for world travel. Water-borne infections can be limited by drinking only bottled water where local water sources may be contaminated. In spite of these precautions, exposure to pathogenic organisms remains a possibility, and infections persist.

Hantavirus Pulmonary Syndrome

The Hantavirus was first identified in the United States in 1993. It is a deadly disease transmitted by rodents, when spores from urine and feces are inhaled from contaminated air. Few cases of Hantavirus occur in the U.S., mostly in western states, and almost all affect children. Hantavirus causes severe respiratory distress requiring mechanical ventilation; antiviral drug treatment has been ineffective. Strict rodent control around areas inhabited by humans is the most effective prevention.[32]

Avian Influenza—H1N1

Avian influenza, also known as bird flu or A influenza virus, is carried by wild birds, though it is not infectious to them. Domestic birds such as chickens, turkeys, and ducks become contaminated when they come in contact with fecal excretions from wild birds. The disease causes multiple organ failure in domestic birds, and can lead to death in 90 percent of infected birds within 48 hours. There are several types of A influenza viruses found in birds, and three that currently affect humans.

Most original cases of A influenza that affected humans were the result of contact with contaminated domestic poultry. More recently, one of the A influenza viruses, H1N1, has caused much more illness and death among humans worldwide, and was considered a pandemic.

In the United States, infection with H1N1 reached epidemic proportions, and the Centers for Disease Control recommends that U.S. residents are vaccinated with the H1N1 vaccine.

Severe Acute Respiratory Syndrome—SARS

Severe acute respiratory syndrome (SARS) is a respiratory illness that reached pandemic proportions in 2003 in Asia, Europe, and North and South America. Caused by a corona virus called SARS-CoV, it is transmitted in the air when an infected person coughs or sneezes, and the infected droplets in the air are inhaled by another person. The symptoms include typical influenza symptoms, and most cases result in pneumonia. Although there are still cases worldwide, there has not been a large outbreak of SARS since 2003.[33]

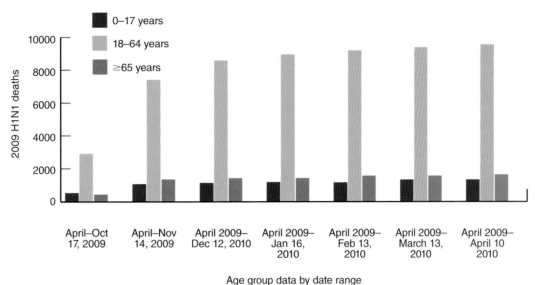

CDC estimates of 2009 H1N1 deaths in the U.S. by age group

FIGURE 12-12. H1N1 deaths.

(Source: CDC, *Morbidity and Mortality Weekly Report*, Dec. 25, 2009.)

Responsibility and Accountability

Is it a personal responsibility to prevent contamination with an infectious disease, and is it possible to prevent infection?

Taking Responsibility for Infectious Diseases

From your reading, you now know that there are many things you can do to reduce your risks, ranging from vaccinations to hand washing. Merely washing hands thoroughly every time the bathroom is used would help reduce the spread of many types of infections. Being responsible includes covering all coughs and sneezes, to ensuring you maintain your health optimally so you recover more quickly when you do become infected. Practicing either abstinence or safer sex by using a condom with every single act of intercourse also shows responsibility.

Focusing on Accountability

For most infections, accountability means becoming ill and having to deal with the unpleasantness of becoming sick. But if you are infected with a sexually transmitted infection (STI), your accountability begins there and goes further. If you are infected with an STI, it is because someone else (and you) did not behave responsibly. If the infected individual was accountable, the person would advise someone in advance that sexual intimacy is not possible at this time. We are comfortable telling people we cannot see them because we have a cold. Within the HIV+ community, this comfort has extended to being able to talk partners about being positive or negative, thus reducing the spread of this virus. If this same attitude could spread to the other STIs, they could be greatly reduced and in some cases even eradicated. Is now a good day to start?

Summary

The Infectious Disease Process

- Only 1 percent of bacteria are harmful, and most are required for our ecosystem and our bodies to function well.

- An *epidemic* is the spread of infectious disease to a region, while a *pandemic* is a worldwide spread of infection.

- The chain of infection requires a susceptible host, but starts with a pathogen housed in a reservoir.

- The disease process includes the following stages: incubation, prodromal, clinical, recovery, and dormancy.

Preventing Infection

- One of the most effective barriers to infection is human skin.

- The human immune response allows the body to make antibodies to fight a particular infection.

- White blood cells called lymphocytes and macrophages can target and destroy a pathogen.

- B cells and T cells are lymphocytes that can repel an unwanted pathogen, as well as remember it in the event of a future infection.

- The lymphatic system is separate from the blood circulatory system and can defend the body from pathogenic microbes.

- Immunizations are vaccines that provide immunity for certain infections and are considered artificially acquired active immunity.

Common Pathogenic Infections

- A vector does not cause disease itself, but enables the transmission of infection. Insects, animals, people, water, and food are all vectors.

- Bacteria are single-cell organisms that can survive without a host.

- MRSA is a bacterium that is resistant to methicillin and other penicillin-like drugs.

- Fungi cause infections that are transmitted from spores that are inhaled, or from person to person contact.

- Protozoa are single-cell organisms that live both inside and outside the human body. Plasmodium is a common protozoan that causes malaria.

- Helminthes or worms are difficult for the human immune system to combat and usually cause a noticeable immune response.

- Prions are proteins that cause spongiform encephalopathy or mad cow disease.

- Viruses are the smallest of the known pathogens and require a host for both metabolism and multiplication.

- Viruses cause the common cold and influenza.

- Hepatitis A, B and C are all caused by viruses.

- Mononucleosis is cause by the Epstein-Barr virus.

- Measles, Mumps and Chickenpox are all caused by a virus.

- Autoimmune diseases cause the body to have an inappropriate response to infection where the body attacks its own organs, tissues and cells.

- HIV is a retrovirus that causes the immune system to attack the host.

Sexually Transmitted infections

- More than 10 million new sexually transmitted infections (STIs) occur in the 15–24-year-old age group each year.

- Certain strains of HPV cause cervical cancer.

- There is no cure for herpes simplex virus one or two.

- Chlamydia, gonorrhea, and syphilis are all common in the 15–24-year-old age group.

- Ectopic pregnancy is the growth of a human embryo outside the uterus, usually in the fallopian tube.

Emerging Infections

- Emerging infections include Hantavirus, avian influenza (H1N1), and severe acute respiratory syndrome (SARS).

Reassessing Your Knowledge

1. What are the most common infection-causing agents?

2. Why can most bacterial diseases be treated and cured, but with viral diseases, only symptoms can be treated?

3. What are the top three infectious diseases worldwide and how can the number of infections for these diseases be reduced?

4. Name two autoimmune diseases and describe why they cannot be cured.

5. Identify the two most common bacterial sexually transmitted infections and the two most common viral sexually transmitted infections. What risks are associated with these infections?

To answer these questions, you might choose to work in groups with your colleagues. Check your answers against the written material in the text, and reread those sections in which you made errors.

Health Assessment Toolbox

Mayo Clinic
The Mayo Clinic provides information and tools for healthy living.
http://www.Mayoclinic.com

Sexually Transmitted Diseases (STDs)
Planned Parenthood. Information about each of the common sexually transmitted diseases and how you can get diagnoses and treatments.
http://www.plannedparenthood.org/health-topics/stds-hiv-safer-sex-101.htm

Travelers' Health
View travel related health information about infectious diseases.
http://wwwnc.cdc.gov/travel

Springtime Allergies
How to nip them in the bud.
http://www.mayoclinic.com/health/springtime-allergies/AA00060-

Vocabulary Challenge

Match the term in the left-hand column with its correct definition in the right-hand column.

TERM		DEFINITION
Pathogen	A.	An infection that spreads rapidly throughout a region
Antigen	B.	Special white blood cells that can specifically target a pathogen for destruction, as well as remember it in case it enters the body in the future
Naturally acquired passive immunity	C.	Special white blood cells that form at the site of infection to destroy pathogens
Lymphocytes	D.	Injecting a person with the antigen for a particular infectious disease so that the immune system will make antibodies for that disease
Macrophages	E.	A disease-causing agent
Cilia	F.	A worldwide spread of infection
Pandemic	G.	Any substance that causes the immune system to produce antibodies
Phagocyte	H.	A cell that can destroy a pathogenic microbe by surrounding and consuming it
Artificially acquired passive immunity	I.	Small, hair-like organelles that beat in waves to move protozoans, liquids, dust, pollens, and mucus out of the respiratory tract
Epidemic	J.	Immunity occurs with the transfer of active antibodies from one person to another

Answers
E, G; J, B; C, I; F, H; D, A

Exploring the Internet

World Health Organization

The United Nations public *health* arm. Monitors disease outbreaks, assesses health systems, and provides leadership for global health matters.

http://www.who.int

Centers for Disease Control and Prevention

The United States organization charged with collecting health information about disease outbreaks and mortality and morbidity records, and providing leadership in national health matters.

http://www.cdc.gov

Emerging and Re-emerging Infectious Diseases

Information about research related to emerging and re-emerging infectious diseases.

http://www.niaid.nih.gov/topics/emerging/Pages/Default.aspx

Vaccines

Homepage for Vaccines and Immunizations

http://www.cdc.gov/vaccines/

Autoimmune Disorders

The Medline Plus Medical Encyclopedia

http://www.nlm.nih.gov/medlineplus/encyclopedia.html

National Foundation for Infectious Diseases

Organization dedicated to educating the public and healthcare professionals about causes, treatment, and prevention of infectious diseases.

http://www.nfid.org/

National Institute of Allergy and Infectious Diseases

Institute provides answers to frequently asked questions, fact sheets, and research aimed at developing better ways to diagnose, treat, and prevent many infections.

http://www.niaid.nih.gov

Centers for Disease Control—Seasonal Influenza

Information on current outbreaks.

http://www.cdc.gov/flu

Selected References

1. Aiello, A.E., Marshall, B., Levy, S.B., Della-Latta, P., Lin, S.X. and Larson, E. "Antibacterial Cleaning Products and Drug Resistance." Centers for Disease Control. October, 2005.

2. Ford, B.J., and van Leeuwenhoek, A. Microscopist and Visionary Scientist, *Journal of Biological Education*, 24(4): 293–300. 1989.

3. World Health Organization, Children and Malaria, Geneva, Roll Back Malaria Global Initiative, 2007. (http://www.rbm.who.int).

4. Gilchrist, J., Gotsch, K., Annest, J.L., et al. Non-Fatal Dog Bite Related Injuries Treated in Hospital Emergency Departments, 2001. *Mortality and Morbidity Weekly Report*, 52(26): 605–610. July 4, 2003.

5. Blanton, J.D., Robertson K., Palmer, D., and Rupprecht, C. Rabies "Surveillance in the United States during 2008," *Vet Med Today: Public Veterinary Medicine*, 235(6). September 15, 2009.

6. Centers for Disease Control, Division of Parasitic Diseases, National Center for Zoonotic, Vector-Borne, and Enteric Diseases, 2009.

7. Ibid.

8. Voetsch A.C., Van Gilder T.J., Angulo F.J., et al. FoodNet Estimate of the Burden of Illness Caused by Nontyphoidal *Salmonella* infections in the United States. *Clinical Infectious Diseases,* 38(Suppl 3): S127–34. 2004.

9. Salmonellosis, Division of Parasitic Diseases, National Center for Zoonotic, Vector-Borne, and Enteric Diseases, 2009.

10. National Center for Preparedness, National MRSA Educational Initiative, Detection, and Control of Infectious Diseases (NCPDCID), Division of Healthcare Quality Promotion (DHQP), 2008

11. Melissa Conrad Stöppler, MD. Staph Infection (*Staphylococcus aureus*). Medicinenet.com, 2010.

12. Screening for Sepsis Could Save Lives. *Archives of Surgery*, July, 2010.

13. Centers for Disease Control. Pneumonia Can Be Prevented—Vaccines Can Help. Downloaded July 27, 2010, from http://www.cdc.gov/Features/Pneumonia/

14. Centers for Disease Control, National Center for Immunization and Respiratory Diseases (NCIRD), National Center for Preparedness, Detection, and Control of Infectious Diseases (NCPDCID), and National Center for Zoonotic, Vector-Borne, and Enteric Diseases (NCZVED). 2010.

15. U.S. Public Health Services. Addressing Emerging Infectious Disease Threats. A Prevention Strategy for the United States. Atlanta: Centers for Disease Control and Prevention, 1994.

16. Schuchat, A., and Broome, C.V. Toxic Shock Syndrome and Tampons. *Epidemiological Review*, 13: 99–112. 1991.

17. Centers for Disease Control, National Center for Immunization and Respiratory Diseases, Division of Bacterial Diseases, Know When Antibiotics Work, June 2009.

18. Playfair, J., and Bancroft, G. *Infection and Immunity.* Oxford University Press Inc., New York, 2008.

19. Centers for Disease Control, National Center for Infectious Diseases, Epstein-Barr Virus and Infectious Mononucleosis, May, 2006.

20. World Health Organization, Global Measles Deaths Drop by 74%, December, 2008.

21. National Institute of Child Health and Human Development, National Institutes of Health, Autism and the MMR Vaccine, 2006.

22. CDC. HIV/AIDS Surveillance Report, 2005. Vol. 17. Rev. ed. Atlanta: U.S. Department of Health and Human Services, CDC: 1–54. 2007.

23. Kilmarx, P. Acquired Immunodeficiency Syndrome. In: Heymann, D.L., editor. *Control of Communicable Diseases Manual*, 19th Edition. Washington, D.C.: APHA Press, 2008.

24. Weinstock, H, Berman, S., and Cates, W. Sexually Transmitted Diseases among American Youth: Incidence and Prevalence Estimates, 2000. *Perspectives on Sexual and Reproductive Health*, 36(1): 6–10. 2004.

25. Centers for Disease Control, Division of STD Prevention, Genital HPV Prevention—CDC Fact Sheet, November, 2009.

26. U.S. Department of Health and Human Services. National Center for HIV/AIDS, Viral Hepatitis, STD, and TB Prevention. Press release March 9, 2010.

27. Centers for Disease Control, Chlamydia Prevention: Challenges and Strategies for Reducing Disease Burden, Public Health Grand Rounds, May 20, 2010.

28. Ibid.

29. Centers for Disease Control and Prevention. Gonorrhea Fact Sheet. Division of STD Prevention (DSTDP).

30. Centers for Disease Control, Syphilis, Sexually Transmitted Diseases Surveillance, 2008.

31. Ibid.

32. Centers for Disease Control, *Morbidity and Mortality Weekly Report*, December 25, 2009. http://www.cdc.gov/mmwr/preview/mmwrhtml/mm5850a3.htm

33. Centers for Disease Control. *Severe Acute Respiratory Syndrome*, 2005. http://www.cdc.gov/ncidod/sars/factsheet.htm

Unit Five

Substance Use and Abuse

Chapter 13

Tobacco and Alcohol

Chapter 14

Drugs and Addictive Behavior

UNIT FIVE

Image of Health

Tobacco and Alcohol

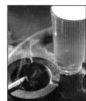

TOBACCO

- Components of a Cigarette
  - Nicotine
  - Tar
  - Carbon Monoxide
  - Arsenic
- Other Forms of Tobacco
  - Cigars and Pipes
  - Clove Cigarettes
  - Beadies
  - Hookahs
  - Spit (Smokeless) Tobacco
- Major Health Hazards of Smoking
  - Cancers
  - Cardiovascular Disease
  - Smoking and Pregnancy
  - Other Conditions Caused by Smoking

- Smoking and Society
  - Tobacco Farming Cost and Gains
  - Smoking on College Campuses
- Smoking Cessation
  - Cessation Symptoms and Expectations
  - Smoking Cessation Options

ALCOHOL

- Understanding Alcohol
  - Ingredients in Alcohol
  - Alcohol Concentration
  - Metabolizing Alcohol
  - Blood-Alcohol Concentration
- Effects of Alcohol
  - Alcohol-Impaired Driving
  - Alcohol and Relationships

- Binge Drinking
- Alcohol and Health
  - Alcohol and the Heart
  - Alcohol and Cancer
  - Alcohol and Pregnancy
  - Alcohol and Other Drugs
- Alcoholism
  - Alcohol Abuse
  - Alcoholism
  - Treating Alcohol Problems

RESPONSIBILITY AND ACCOUNTABILITY

- Taking Responsibility for Tobacco and Alcohol
- Focusing on Accountability

Student Learning Outcomes

LEARNING OUTCOME	APPLYING IT TO YOUR LIFE
List the major ingredients in tobacco, and describe their affects on health.	Identify ways to reduce or eliminate exposure to tobacco smoke on your campus and in your community.
Identify the top leading cause of preventable death in the U.S.	Be able to discuss how these preventable deaths influence health care and lost productivity costs, and consider ways to reduce this expense.
Differentiate between the years of potential life lost (YPLL) with tobacco versus alcohol.	Identify ways to minimize or eliminate the possibility of a tobacco- or alcohol-caused death for you and for those you care about.
Define binge drinking, and list symptoms of alcohol poisoning.	When drinking with friends, describe steps you can take to ensure that no one binge drinks or risks alcohol poisoning.
Describe methods that can be used in your community to reduce the number of people who drive under the influence of alcohol.	What steps can you proactively take to ensure you do not drive or ride with someone who has been drinking?

Assess Your Knowledge

1. Approximately what percentage of all deaths in the U.S. are caused by tobacco?
    a. 16 percent
    b. 33 percent
    c. 50 percent
    d. 60 percent

2. _____ is the addicting agent in tobacco, while _____ is the disease-causing agent.
    a. Tar, nicotine
    b. Carbon monoxide, nicotine
    c. Nicotine, tar
    d. None of the above is correct

3. Hookah smoking is not addicting.
    a. True
    b. False

4. How many people are estimated to die each day due to tobacco exposure?
    a. 750
    b. 1000
    c. 1,200
    d. 1,500

5. There is more alcohol in 1.5 ounces of 80-proof liquor than in a standard 12-ounce bottle of beer.
    a. True
    b. False

Answers:

1. a, 2. c, 3. b, 4. b, 5. b

Tobacco

Nearly everyone knows that tobacco kills hundreds of thousands of people each year. In the twentieth century, tobacco killed 100 million people worldwide.[1] In February 2008, the World Health Organization (WHO) warned that unless urgent action is taken, one billion people will die of tobacco related causes in this new century. Tobacco is generally considered a socially sanctioned drug, despite costing the U.S. more than $97 billion in health care and lost productivity each year.[2] In 2008, 20.6 percent of the population smoked cigarettes.[3] About 14 percent more smoke cigars, almost 1 percent smoke pipes, and over 3 percent use smokeless tobacco, making tobacco the most widely abused substance in the U.S.[4]

Each year, more people die of tobacco-related causes than from homicides, fires, car accidents, AIDS, illicit drugs, alcohol, and suicides combined.[5] Smoking causes one in every six deaths in the U.S., and about one half of those who continue to smoke will die because of this deadly habit.[6] What is it that makes tobacco so hazardous to health?

Components of a Cigarette

The cigarette has been viewed as perhaps the best drug delivery system of all. An addictive agent tightly compressed and bound in an attractive slim package, easily acquired, carried, and ready for smoking wherever allowed. Within that package are more than 4,000 chemicals, including nicotine, tar, carbon monoxide, and arsenic.

Nicotine

Nicotine is the addicting stimulant in tobacco. Like caffeine, nicotine is an alkaloid made from carbon, hydrogen, and nitrogen. It is found in tobacco plants that are harvested, dried, and mixed with other ingredients to produce cigarettes. Nicotine enters the body through inhaled smoke, and is readily diffused through skin, lungs, and mucous membranes. Within ten seconds of inhaling smoke, nicotine reaches the brain, and causes the smoker to feel mildly stimulated. However, the effect does not last very long—although the smoker inhales about 1 milligram (mg) of nicotine per cigarette, six hours later only about .031 mg of that remains in the body.[7]

Once in the body, nicotine causes a release of adrenalin, which increases heart rate and blood pressure and promotes rapid shallow breathing. This produces the same effect as the alarm stage of the stress response, though there is no stressor. From Chapter 3, you know that this stage is designed to help you "run from or fight" a situation perceived as dangerous. To help with this response, the body releases glucose, cortisol, and adrenaline to fuel potential running or fighting; however, when you smoke there is no external danger. In addition to promoting a stress response, nicotine may inhibit the release of insulin required to infuse the cells with glucose. As a result, smokers may experience **hyperglycemia**, or high blood sugar.[8] The only real danger is the addictive potential that nicotine has on the body.

> **Key Term**
>
> **Hyperglycemia**: High blood sugar.

Nicotine attaches to neurons in the brain, altering brain chemistry by releasing abnormal amounts of dopamine. Under normal conditions, the brain releases, then reabsorbs the dopamine, causing a person to feel content and happy. It is usually released in response to a feeling of comfort and pleasure received when enjoying the company of others, or after eating a good meal. Though nicotine causes the release of abnormal amounts of dopamine and gives the smoker intense feelings of pleasure, the tobacco smoke blocks the reabsorption of dopamine.[9] With repeated smoking, brain chemistry changes and inadequate levels of dopamine are released relative to pleasurable situations. This causes the smoker to feel irritable and depressed, and only another cigarette will temporarily relieve these feelings. Nicotine also constricts blood vessels restricting circulation, resulting in the body being deprived of oxygenated blood. For a pregnant woman, this results in her unborn infant receiving a reduced supply of oxygen.

Challenge Question: How does nicotine stimulate the alarm stage of the stress response?

In first-time use, smokers sometimes develop **nicotine poisoning**, causing dizziness, light headedness, rapid and erratic pulse, clammy skin, nausea, vomiting, and diarrhea. These symptoms diminish as tolerance is achieved, usually within 1–3 cigarettes. Most other drugs require months or years to develop such a **tolerance**. Though the pleasure of smoking is lost to the habitual smoker, smoking continues because of the addiction to nicotine.

Challenge Question: How does nicotine affect brain chemistry?

Tar

The many chemicals that are added to tobacco are referred to as tar. Tar is the brown, tacky substance that accumulates in the filter of a cigarette, as well as in the smoker's body. Tar causes a smoker's teeth to become yellow and brown, and can stain the fingers where cigarettes are held. But these are only minor cosmetic problems: the health effects of tar are numerous, including lung damage as **cilia** are destroyed, lung cancer, emphysema, heart disease, stroke, bronchitis, oral cancers, impaired immunity, and death.

In May 2009, the District of Columbia (Washington, D.C.) Circuit of Appeals court ruled that cigarette companies were intentionally misleading smokers by promoting them as "light" and "low-tar." In this ruling, it was determined that manufacturers were falsely suggesting that light and low-tar cigarettes were less harmful, when in fact, no cigarette can be made safer or less harmful.[10] All cigarettes, when used as intended, cause disease and death.

Key Terms

Nicotine poisoning: Symptoms of dizziness, light headedness, rapid, erratic pulse, clammy skin, nausea, vomiting, and diarrhea often experienced by beginning smokers.

Tolerance: When more of a drug is needed to reach the expected effect.

Cilia: Minute, hairlike organelles that beat in waves to move protozoans, liquids, dust, pollens, and mucus out of the cells.

Image of Health In Depth

Tar—Cigarettes' Most Dangerous Ingredient

In 1996, one of the first scientific studies proving cigarettes cause lung cancer was published in *Science*.[11] The study showed that cigarette tar contains benzo[a]pyrene, which inhibits the lungs from preventing the growth of cancerous cells. For the smoker, this may result in cancer, though tobacco companies claimed that no scientific research existed to prove tobacco products actually caused cancer. Since 1996, hundreds of research studies have been published, showing that among other things, tar paralyzes cilia, depresses the immune system, and causes chronic bronchitis, emphysema, and periodontitis, a gum disease that results in loss of teeth.

Tar includes all of the toxic chemicals found in cigarettes. High-tar cigarettes may have as much as 22 mg of tar, while medium-tar cigarettes contain from 15–21 mg, and low-tar cigarettes 7 mg or less. Unfortunately, the lower amount of tar does not protect the smoker. The level of tar is determined by tests that measure tar as it leaves the cigarette—the machines used in these tests withdraw from the cigarette at equal rates. However, smokers vary in how deeply they inhale, how long they hold the smoke in their lungs, and how frequently they inhale, and each of these behaviors determines how large a dose of toxic chemicals the smoker receives. In addition, the reduced tar cigarettes have tiny holes perforated into the filter. When the cigarette is attached to the machine that measures tar concentrate, the pinholes are unobstructed, allowing it to escape without measurement. When a smoker inhales from a cigarette, lips and fingertips may cover the holes, preventing any loss of toxins.[12] Smokers who switch to "lighter" cigarettes tend to change the way they smoke so that they receive the same hazardous chemicals in the same concentration. They may inhale more deeply, hold the smoke in longer, inhale smoke more frequently, and/or smoke more cigarettes.

Critical Thinking Question: Why does smoking a low-tar, low-nicotine cigarette not benefit an addicted smoker?

The lungs and bronchial passageways are lined with tiny protective hairs called cilia, which continuously beat to trap damaging particulates that are breathed into the lungs. The continuous movement of the cilia causes the foreign material to be moved up and out of the throat, protecting the fragile tissue in the lungs.[13] Coughing completes the process as it evacuates these particles in sputum. Smoking inhibits this process in two ways: first, smoking reduces the coughing response; and second, smoking initially affects the rate at which the cilia beat.[14] With continued smoking, the cilia act as though paralyzed, allowing debris to reach and thereby damage lung and bronchial passageway tissues.

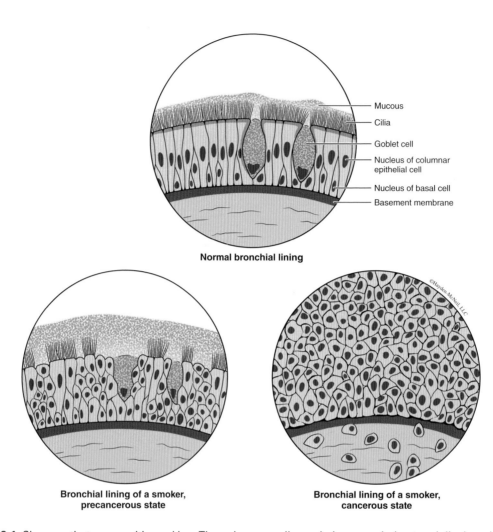

FIGURE 13-1. Changes that occur with smoking. The columnar cells are being crowded out and displaced by more layers of basal cells. Fewer cilia are present and the remaining cilia are not functioning well. Tobacco chemicals are toxic to cilia by first slowing them down, then paralyzing them and finally destroying them.

Carbon Monoxide

Carbon monoxide (CO) poisoning is the leading cause of accidental poisoning deaths in America, yet it is part of the smoke voluntarily inhaled by smokers. Carbon monoxide is odorless, tasteless, and colorless. Symptoms of CO poisoning include headaches, nausea, and fatigue, but these early symptoms are often ignored. Enough carbon monoxide can cause brain damage and death. The amount in a cigarette is not quite high enough to cause death, though it does cause harm by interfering with **hemoglobin** transport.

Oxygen is carried in the blood by hemoglobin, and having oxygenated hemoglobin ensures sufficient oxygen for all cell activity. Carbon monoxide has an affinity for

hemoglobin, and when blood is exposed to both oxygen and CO, hemoglobin prefers carbon monoxide to oxygen, resulting in oxygen deficient blood. Carbon monoxide causes shortness of breath, increased heart rate, increased risk of atherosclerosis, and heart failure, and health risks are increased in those that already have underlying medical conditions.

Challenge Question: What is the purpose of cilia in the lungs?

Arsenic

Tobacco farmers use pesticides to protect tobacco plants. Some of these pesticides contain arsenic that is absorbed into the tobacco leaves and is measurable within tobacco after harvesting. Arsenic is a known carcinogen linked to several cancers including bladder, skin, liver, kidney, and lung cancer. The low levels of arsenic exposure in cigarette smoke may change skin tone, and can cause corns and small warts. Arsenic is found in both **mainstream** and **side-stream smoke**.

Small amounts of arsenic are highly toxic yet smokers willingly inhale arsenic with the smoke in their cigarettes. Nonsmokers also inhale arsenic in environmental smoke.

Key Terms

Hemoglobin: Red blood cells that transport oxygen.

Mainstream smoke: Mainstream smoke is a combination of smoke inhaled and exhaled by the smoker.

Side-stream smoke: Side-stream smoke refers to the smoke from a burning cigarette. This smoke has not been filtered by the smoker and so represents a major threat to non-smokers. Combined with mainstream smoke, side-stream smoke becomes environmental tobacco smoke.

Other Forms of Tobacco

Some individuals use alternate forms of tobacco, ranging from cigars to smokeless tobacco. Unfortunately, some smokers quit cigarettes but move to other forms of tobacco, believing them to be safer. In addition, those who use chewing tobacco may also smoke cigarettes when they cannot chew. However, no form of tobacco is safe.

Cigars and Pipes

Former cigarette smokers usually still inhale the smoke when they switch to either cigars or pipe smoking. Both cigar and pipe tobacco contains more nicotine and more tar than cigarette tobacco, and many of the same toxins, chemicals, and carcinogens are in both. Cigar and pipe smokers have a higher risk of oral cancers, but if the smoke in not inhaled, then the risk of lung cancer, respiratory diseases, and cardiovascular diseases may be reduced.

Clove Cigarettes

When tobacco is mixed with chopped cloves, it becomes a clove cigarette, or a "kretek" or "chicarta." Clove cigarettes contain the same hazardous components as regular cigarettes. In addition, eugenol, also found in cloves, works as an anesthetic, possibly impairing the ability of the respiratory system to defend itself against foreign particles. Eugenol may also suppress the coughing reflex, allowing smoke to remain in the lungs longer and do more damage. Clove cigarettes are equally as addicting as other forms of tobacco.

Beadies

Beadies are small Indian cigarettes often flavored with chocolate, mint, clove, or fruit. Sometimes called bidis, these cigarettes can contain four times the nicotine and twice the tar of U.S. cigarettes. Like clove cigarettes, beadies are still tobacco, just packaged a little differently. Like standard cigarettes, they may increase risk or cause all of the diseases mentioned previously.

Hookahs

Although hookahs come in many styles and materials, they all have the following components:

- A bowl where the tobacco is placed and heated, usually with charcoal or other burning embers.

- A vase or smoke chamber, partially filled with water.

- A pipe or stem, connecting the bowl to the vase by a tube. The tube carries the smoke down into the water.

- A hose with a mouthpiece, through which the smoke is drawn from the vase.[15]

Hookah popularity is promoted by the media, retailers, and by the prevalence of hookah cafes and bars. Often portrayed as the safe alternative to cigarette smoking, hookah users may lack knowledge about potential health hazards and dangers of hookah smoking. Some users believe that if they smoke a hookah daily, they are being safer than daily cigarette smokers. This is untrue, since hookah smokers tend to have smoking sessions that last from 45 minutes to over an hour. During this time, many toxic substances are inhaled.

Hookah smoke contains carbon monoxide, nicotine, tar, and heavy metals.[16] Researchers have identified that the health problems associated with hookah use include lung, oral, and bladder cancer, cancer of the esophagus and stomach, heart disease, and respiratory problems. In addition, hookah smoke is addictive, and since the pipe is shared, there is risk of transmitting infectious diseases such as herpes, tuberculosis, and hepatitis.[17] Hookah smoke also affects the fetus of pregnant women in a way similar to regular cigarettes. Children exposed to hookah smoke may suffer respiratory ailments, ear infections, asthma, and sudden infant death syndrome.[18]

Spit (Smokeless) Tobacco

The two major forms of spit tobacco are snuff and chewing tobacco, which are used by about 6.5 million people in the U.S. Mixing tobacco leaves into a coarse paste and adding flavor makes snuff. Users place small amounts between the cheek and gum, where it is sucked. Chewing tobacco contains shredded tobacco leaves that are pressed into small plugs, or cakes. Users chew small amounts to release the nicotine. Both types cause an increase in saliva production, resulting in excessive saliva that must be either swallowed or spit out. Both spit tobacco and snuff are hazardous to health, delivering the equivalent amount of nicotine of 2–3 cigarettes in a 30-minute chewing session. Health issues such as **leukoplakia**, which can lead to oral cancers, **gingivitis**, and gum recession can occur. Oral cancers, including cancer of the lip, tongue, cheek, floor and roof of the mouth, and cancers of the throat and larynx are the most serious health concerns. Spit and snuff users become addicted to nicotine and frequently resort to cigarette smoking when spitting is not possible.

Critical Thinking Question: How do spit and chewing tobacco compare to smoking cigarettes? Is one less addictive and less health hazardous than the other?

Key Terms

Leukoplakia: A disorder of mucus membranes characterized by white patches on the tongue and inner cheeks that can become cancerous.

Gingivitis: Inflammation of the gums.

Major Health Hazards of Smoking

There is no doubt that smoking cigarettes leads to early onset of several diseases, and may result in early death. Smoking causes lung and other cancers, cardiovascular diseases, respiratory conditions, erectile dysfunction, and prenatal conditions, among other side effects.[19] Using alternate forms of tobacco promotes a host of other diseases and causes numerous health risks. Many of those who smoke believe they will quit before any health consequences occur, or that by the time they suffer any ill health effects, there will be better treatments or even cures. Of course, this is a gamble. And if the gamble is lost, the cost can be death or disability.

Cancers

A smoker is 23 times more likely to die of lung cancer than a nonsmoker, and since smoking causes about 87 percent of lung cancers, eliminating smoking would greatly reduce the incidence of lung cancer.[20] Smokers are inclined to note that some nonsmokers also die from lung cancer. This is true—in fact, about 15 percent of lung cancer cases are in nonsmokers, resulting in 3,000 deaths per year. However, research has fully established that exposure to secondhand smoke can cause lung cancer and heart disease in nonsmokers.[21] Research has also shown that there is no risk-free level of exposure to tobacco smoke, nor any risk-free level in smoking or using tobacco products.[22] Tobacco smoke is a known **carcinogen**, causes deoxyribonucleic acid (DNA) damage, and promotes the initiation and growth of tumors. The DNA damage causes the body to be unable to repair itself, allowing tumors to grow unchecked and become malignant. Any form of smoke that enters the lungs can also paralyze or destroy cilia, the first stage of defense within the respiratory system. Damage to the cilia has

serious consequences for people with impaired immune systems.[23] Unfortunately, lung cancer is hard to detect at an early stage, and difficult to treat at any stage. Five-year survival rates are based on the type of lung cancer, ranging from 5 percent to 17 percent.[24]

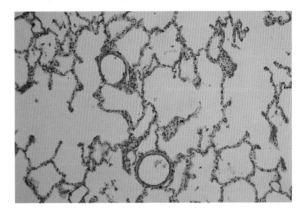

FIGURE 13-2. Healthy lung tissue.

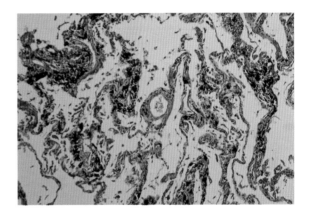

FIGURE 13-3. Lung tissue with cancer.

Tobacco smoking is also responsible for most cancers of the larynx, oral cavity, pharynx, esophagus, and bladder, and is also a cause of kidney, pancreatic, cervical, and stomach cancers, as well as being implicated in acute myeloid leukemia.[25]

Even though cancer is the most likely cause of a death for a smoker in the U.S., worldwide, smokers are more likely to die sooner from cardiovascular disease.[26]

Sean's Story

Sean began smoking when he was 15. He tried it just to see what it was like and at first only smoked around others who smoked. He always thought he would be able to stop anytime he wanted. As of today, he has been smoking for 14 years. He tries to cut down, but something always comes up and he goes back to his usual smoking habits.

Although Sean knows smoking can cause early onset of many diseases, his attitude is that he will quit before he is affected by any of them.

Recently, Sean began dating someone new. She seems to be the perfect match for him, and he is even thinking about this being a long-term relationship. Once, the word "marriage" even popped into his head when he thought of her. There is just one little problem: Sean is having problems with sex. Sometimes he cannot get an erection; other times, he cannot maintain an erection; and sometimes, he cannot postpone his ejaculation. He is sure nerves are causing this to happen—it has never happened before and does not happen often now, but it is happening in this relationship, which he cares a great deal about.

Sean recently saw a magazine cover that indicated erectile dysfunction could be caused by smoking. He searched the Internet to try to find a way to dispute this. Smoking could not possibly be doing this to him! But there it was in clear, definite terms: smoking can lead to erectile dysfunction and impotence.[19] Of all the things he might have worried about concerning smoking, this was never on the list.

And now, of all the reasons he thought might trigger him to stop smoking, this has become number one on the list. One day at a time, one cigarette at a time, Sean has determined that he will not allow tobacco to affect his sex life. ∎

Key Term

Carcinogen: A substance known to cause cancer.

Cardiovascular Disease

Table 13-1 shows the six major independent risk factors for **cardiovascular disease** (CVD), and cigarette smoking is by far the most dangerous. The Surgeon General has called it the leading preventable cause of disease and death in the United States, outranking all others on the top ten causes of preventable death. When diagnosed with cardiovascular disease, tobacco users are more likely to die of it, and die sooner than if they had not used tobacco.

Independently, cigarette smoking increases the risk for **coronary heart disease** (CHD), as well as increasing blood pressure and the tendency for blood to clot, and decreases exercise tolerance.[26]

Women who smoke and use oral contraceptives greatly increase their risk of CHD when compared with nonsmoking women using oral contraception.

Smoking also increases risk for high cholesterol by decreasing high-density lipoprotein (good cholesterol). Atherosclerosis, chronic obstructive pulmonary disease, emphysema, chronic bronchitis, heart attack, and stroke are all more likely to occur in a smoker than in a same-aged nonsmoker.

Table 13-1. Major Independent Risk Factors for Cardiovascular Disease (CVD)

TOBACCO SMOKING	Smoking increases the risk for CVD 2–4 times over that of a nonsmoker.
HIGH BLOOD CHOLESTEROL	As blood cholesterol rises, so does risk of coronary heart disease. When combined with other risk factors, such as smoking and high blood pressure, this risk increases even more.
HIGH BLOOD PRESSURE	An independent risk factor for stroke, heart attack, and kidney disease, but when high blood pressure is present with obesity, smoking, high blood cholesterol, or diabetes, the risk of heart attack or stroke increases significantly.
PHYSICAL INACTIVITY	Sedentary lifestyle is a risk factor for coronary heart disease. Physical activity can improve blood cholesterol, blood pressure, weight management, and diabetes.
OBESITY AND OVERWEIGHT	Excess body fat, particularly when stored in the abdomen and waist area, increases development of heart disease and stroke, even without other risk factors being present.
DIABETES MELLITUS	Diabetes seriously increases risk for CVD. Though keeping blood sugars within the normal range helps reduce the risk, about 75 percent of people with diabetes die from CVD.

(Source: American Heart Association, Risk Factors and Coronary Heart Disease.)

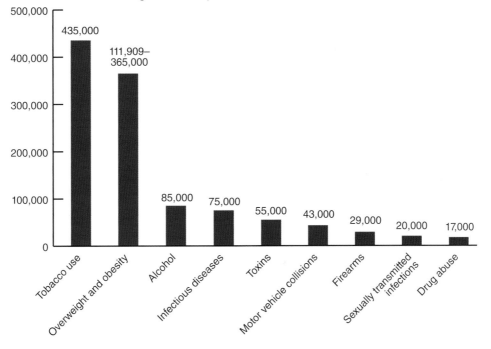

FIGURE 13-4. Leading causes of preventable death in U.S.[27]

> **Key Terms**
>
> **Cardiovascular disease**: Diseases that involve the heart or blood vessels.
>
> **Coronary heart disease**: Heart disease characterized by atherosclerotic build-up that blocks blood flow to the heart muscle, resulting in a myocardial infarction.

Cigarette smoking increases the risk for CHD independently, but when combined with other factors, the risk is magnified. Smoking increases blood pressure, decreases exercise tolerance, and increases blood clotting. The relative risk is higher in people under 50 rather than those over 50 years of age.

Respiratory Conditions

In addition to causing cancers and cardiovascular disease, smoking also causes **chronic obstructive pulmonary disease** (COPD).

The two major forms of COPD are chronic **bronchitis** and **emphysema**. Chronic bronchitis, a condition in which the bronchial tubes become inflamed, swell, and produce mucus, is far more common in smokers than nonsmokers. Chronic bronchitis is progressive, producing coughing and spitting up mucus in attempts to clear the bronchial passageways.

Emphysema patients also experience coughing when trying to clear airways of mucus. Those with emphysema also suffer from **dyspnea** (shortness of breath), fatigue, wheezing, and frequent respiratory infections. Chronic obstructive pulmonary disease symptoms develop slowly, and affected individuals may be unaware that they are developing this non-curable disease. The lungs will eventually be destroyed as lung tissue destruction continues. The only treatments are smoking cessation and bronchodilators. In severe cases, steroids may be prescribed to reduce inflammation, but this is not always effective.

Key Terms

Chronic obstructive pulmonary disease: A group of health conditions resulting in blocked airways and difficulty breathing.

Bronchitis: Inflammation of the bronchial tubes, resulting in coughing from increased mucus production.

Emphysema: Destruction of the lungs over time, as bronchial tubes collapse.

Dyspnea: Shortness of breath caused by mild activity.

Smoking and Pregnancy

For women who smoke and become pregnant, all of the risks are passed to their unborn child. Babies born to smoking mothers may be premature, are typically of lower birth weight, with a smaller head circumference. Smoking may also cause spontaneous abortions, **congenital heart defects**, and **sudden infant death syndrome** (SIDS).

Prenatal smoke exposure also raises fetal blood pressure and increases fetal risk of stroke and heart attack.

Key Terms

Congenital heart defects: Structural problems with the heart present at birth.

Sudden infant death syndrome: The unexpected and sudden death of an infant less than one year of age in which autopsy does not show a cause of death.

Other Conditions Caused by Smoking

A study conducted by the University of California reported that 100,000 U.S. fires were smoking related. Fires caused by smoking result in millions of dollars annually in property destruction. In addition, drivers who are reaching for, lighting, or extinguishing a cigarette are two to three times more likely to have an accident than a nonsmoking driver.

When a smoker inhales deeply from a cigarette, he loses about a minute of life for each minute of smoking. All smokers will die sooner than nonsmokers, they spend about one-third more time on sick leave than nonsmokers, and they have a higher rate of acute and chronic diseases than people who have never smoked. There is no known benefit to smoking tobacco.

Challenge Question: What are the six leading causes of preventable death in the U.S.?

Table 13-2. Smoking Attributable Mortality

CANCERS	CARDIOVASCULAR DISEASES	RESPIRATORY CONDITIONS	RESIDENTIAL FIRES	PERINATAL CONDITIONS
160,848	128,497	103,338	736	776

(Source: Mortality and Morbidity Weekly Report, November 14, 2008/57(45);1226–1228. Smoking Attributable Mortality, Years of Potential Life Lost and Productivity Losses—United States, 2000–2004.)

Smoking and Society

In the early 17th century, European immigrants first introduced tobacco to American society. Soon after, its value as a commodity was realized, and the southern Atlantic region became a major tobacco growing area.

Tobacco Farming Costs and Gains

There is often speculation that reducing tobacco production will negatively impact the U.S. economy. However, the tobacco industry itself is reducing the number of employees by importing tobacco from other countries, by improving production in factories, and by moving operations outside of America to reduce costs. More jobs are lost this way than by any attempt to reduce smoking or by government-mandated health measures.[28, 29]

In 2006, the tobacco industry spent $12.6 billion per year in advertising and promotion. The cost of tobacco to society is measured in several ways, including the cost of **years of potential life lost (YPLL)**. According to a report published in the Mortality and Morbidity Weekly Report, smoking-attributable illnesses resulted in 5.1 million years of potential life lost in the U.S. in 2000–2004, $96 billion in direct medical costs, and $96.8 billion in lost productivity.[30] Smokers also increase the cost of health insurance for everyone, increase costs to employers because smokers use a higher number of sick days, and smokers have lower worker productivity. Health costs are estimated at about $10.28 for every pack of cigarettes sold. Although tobacco raises about $13 billion in tax revenues, this cost does not cover even the Medicaid payments of $23.5 billion for tobacco-related illnesses that are passed on to tax payers.[31]

Key Term

Years of potential life lost (YPLL): Estimates the average time a person would have lived had they not died prematurely.

Image of Health In Depth

Tobacco Facts and Figures

In 2006, the tobacco industry spent $12.6 billion on advertising and promotion.

- During that year, $34 million was spent each day.[32]

- 46 million people over 18 years of age are current smokers.

- 20 percent of high school students are current smokers.

- Each day, about 1,000 people under age 18 become daily smokers.

- Each day, about 1,800 people over age 18 become daily smokers.

- About 70 percent of smokers want to quit, and 40 percent try to quit each year.[33]

- Annually in the U.S., cigarette smoking costs $97 billion in lost productivity, and $96 billion in health care expenditures.

- Secondhand smoke costs more than $10 billion in health care expenditures.[34]

- From 2000–2004, an estimated 1,200 people died each day as a result of smoking or exposure to secondhand smoke.[35]

Critical Thinking Question: How do the economic benefits of tobacco production compare to the health care costs for tobacco use?

Smoking on College Campuses

College students may be particularly vulnerable to begin smoking or to increase a habit that has already started. For many, college represents the first experience of living away from home, and being independent from parental influence. College presents new stressors, including time management, as well as concerns about money, grades, and social relationships. Each of these may impact the decision to begin or maintain smoking.

Many students consider themselves "social smokers," meaning they only smoke with other people. They may smoke less frequently and less intensely, and do not consider themselves at risk for addiction.[36] But even occasional smoking carries the risk of addiction. Most college students smoke for one or more of the following reasons: a tendency toward risk taking, depression, social norms that tolerate smoking, and a lack of self-efficacy to resist peer pressure.[37] Of course, viewing oneself as a "social smoker" is a bonus for tobacco companies. As long as the product is viewed by smokers as not harmful, less harmful, or a product that the user controls, it increases sales, as well as the propensity for addiction as these social smokers continue to smoke.

Today, it is not unusual for college campuses to be entirely smoke free, and in some cases this is influenced by the student population.

Critical Thinking Question: If your campus still allows tobacco smoking, even if only in certain areas, what could you do to help create a smoke-free campus?

Motivation Maximizer

This box is about smoking cessation. If you don't smoke, should you read it? Yes, if you know someone who smokes; yes, if go into areas where smoking is allowed; and yes, if you care about the cost you bear because of tobacco. If you do smoke and don't want to quit, should you read this? The only answer to that question is that it will not cost you anything but a few moments of time, and it may help you change your mind.

Becoming active in curtailing smoking environments benefits everyone. Nonsmokers benefit due to less exposure, and smokers benefit because it reduces their ability to smoke. Does your college campus allow smoking? If it only allows smoking in certain outdoor areas, how is the smoke restricted? Must nonsmokers walk by this area? Must those who are trying to quit walk by this area? Maybe a complete ban on smoking would be beneficial for everyone.

When you go to a park, a beach, or a concert, is smoking allowed? If it is, how does it influence children? If you are a smoker, how might childhood exposure to smoking have influenced you to start smoking? How might it affect the amount you smoke?

Society regulates almost anything that can either cause societal problems or create risks for society. There are driving speed limits to help reduce accidents, save lives, and save gasoline. Warning signs are mandated where there might be exposure to risk. To ensure safety, the city you live in might control where pedestrians are allowed to cross the street. Your college campus may restrict use of bicycles or skateboards in certain areas to make the campus safer.

Yet when it comes to tobacco, which causes more preventable deaths than anything else, there are often no regulations. Opponents may claim that if the government is allowed to control tobacco more than it already does, there may next be an effort to control the purchase of fast food or jogging at night. These are not original ideas; they are propagated by the tobacco industry to make us concerned about government intervention, so that the tobacco industry is protected. There is no safe use of any amount of any tobacco product—all are intended to addict the user.

When you think about smoking or smokers' rights, perhaps your first thought should be that tobacco companies evaded responsibility by promoting a product known to be addictive and deadly. And if you smoke, remember, the tobacco companies encourage you to continue until disease or death causes you to stop. However, you are accountable for your smoking behavior.

Smoking Cessation

Mark Twain's famous quote, "Quitting smoking is easy. I've done it a thousand times," is perhaps the bane of a smoker's life. To quit means you need to understand the difficulties and gather all the necessary resources to ensure success. Smoking causes not only physical addiction, but also psychological addiction.

Cessation Symptoms and Expectations

When you stop smoking, the first symptoms are physical and mental withdrawal, as you react to the loss of nicotine. Mentally, you have lost your crutch. When you are stressed, you will need to find an alternate coping method. When you are bored, you will need to find another way to relieve boredom. Plan for this, and know how you will cope when it happens. Consider tracking what causes you to light up, and think about ways to avoid these situations. Withdrawal symptoms may include dizziness, anxiety, irritability, sleep disturbances, and concentration problems. Some people experience headaches, fatigue, depression, and a change in appetite patterns. With so many negative consequences to quitting, you may think it is hardly worth it. Although these symptoms begin within a few hours of your last cigarette and peak at about the third day, they will gradually subside. During this phase, make sure you have a support group that will help you stay on track. Stay away from other smokers, and restrict your activities to those that disallow smoking.

List your reasons for quitting. Each time you get an urge to smoke, read your list. It may include immediate health benefits, longer life expectancy, lower risk of cancers and heart disease, and perhaps becoming more socially acceptable because you don't smoke. And, of course, there is the money you will save when you are no longer buying cigarettes.

Remind yourself of the physical benefits of not smoking. Within three months of not smoking, your circulation and lung function improves. Between 1–9 months of not smoking, cilia will regain normal function in your lungs, and coughing and shortness of breath will decrease. By one year, your risk of coronary heart disease becomes half that of a smoker. The longer you remain a nonsmoker, the more the risks of smoking are reduced, until after fifteen years, your risk for heart disease is the same as that of a nonsmoker.

Becoming a nonsmoker is the ultimate goal. You will either choose to quit smoking, or smoking will cause you to die sooner. Either way, you stop smoking. Which way do you want to quit?

Smoking Cessation Options

Quitting smoking is as difficult as quitting a heroin or cocaine addiction.[38] About 70 percent of all smokers actually want to quit, but less than 10 percent are successful after one year. If you are a smoker, you can be in this 10 percent.

Today, smokers can find in-patient and out-patient treatment programs in hospitals and clinics that specialize in addiction recovery. Smoking cessation programs can be expensive, and may not be covered by medical insurance. In some areas, group support meetings similar to Alcoholics Anonymous exist.

Nicotine replacement therapy options now abound. With this method, nicotine is released into the body via transdermal patches, gum, medications, nicotine inhalers, nasal sprays, and even a nicotine hand gel. These products help reduce withdrawal symptoms while the smoker learns to manage without the crutch of tobacco. Although these products contain nicotine and are addictive, they do not contain any of the carcinogens in tobacco. Smokers gradually reduce smoking as they learn new behavioral patterns to reduce dependency on tobacco. Other products are available that effect neurotransmitters in the brain. These products work by inhibiting the reuptake of dopamine, serotonin, and norepinephrine, resulting in greater quantities of these neurotransmitters being available.

Pharmaceutical options have a place in smoking cessation, but many people are able to quit without this added expense. Some smokers have found that sucking on thin slices of lemon or lime helps reduce an urge to smoke. Others find it helps to hold something such as worry beads, or even an elastic band. Find what works for you.

The key to successful smoking cessation remains with the smoker, no matter the method used. If the smoker does not want to quit, there is little chance of success. With determination and commitment, you can become a nonsmoker. If you are a smoker and want to stop, review the behavior change steps in Chapter 1, and develop a plan for yourself. Remember to choose a starting date when there is less stress and anxiety in your life. Let your support group know that you have stopped smoking, and ask them to endorse and encourage you in your goal. Contact the American Cancer Society and see if there is telephone support available in your area. Plan for the withdrawal symptoms, and have a method ready for coping. Each and every moment, remind yourself that with every successful minute, every successful hour, every successful day, you are that much closer to being 100 percent tobacco-free. At the end of this chapter, you will find a list of Web sites that can help you in your goal to become smoke-free.

Alcohol

Humans are not unique in their taste for alcohol. Aristotle wrote about monkeys being captured by leaving out jars of palm wine for them. The monkeys would drink and pass out, making them easy prey. In the *Descent of Man*, Darwin wrote that monkeys also got hangovers. Animals are attracted by the pungent smell of fermenting fruit, but what attracts humans?

Understanding Alcohol

Alcohol is the third leading cause of preventable death in the United States, and resulted in about 2.3 million years of potential life lost (YPLL) in 2001.[39] Each alcohol death costs the victim about thirty years of potential life lost.[40] Understanding what causes these deaths is not simply a matter of looking at drunk driving fatalities, because alcohol can cause death in many other ways.

It is a general misconception to think that everyone drinks, or that drinking is a right of passage into adulthood. About one-third of people over age 21 choose not to drink. This may be because they don't like the taste, have seen too many negative repercussions from alcohol, have medical conditions that inhibit the use of alcohol, or because they are recovering alcoholics. If you have chosen not to drink, resist the pressure that people may place on you to use alcohol. If you do drink, know when not to drink, and when to stop drinking.

Ingredients in Alcohol

Ethyl alcohol is the psychoactive ingredient found in all alcoholic beverages. Hard liquors such as gin, whiskey, rum, brandy, and tequila contain from 35–50 percent alcohol by volume. Table wines contain from 9–14 percent, and fortified wines, which have additional alcohol added to them, contain about 20 percent alcohol. Beers, ales, and malt liquors contain from 3–8 percent alcohol. Alcoholic beverages contain a variety of other ingredients, including grains, potatoes, sugar, malt, and hops.

Alcohol Concentration

The amount of alcohol in a beverage is labeled by its proof value. Proof value is two times the concentration of alcohol in the beverage.

An 80-proof bottle of whisky is 40 percent pure alcohol. When comparing the proof values between different beverages, a 12-ounce bottle of beer, a 5-ounce glass of table wine, and 1.5 ounces of hard liquor are each considered equivalent drinks. Each of these measures contain between 0.5 and 0.6 ounces, or 14–17 grams of pure alcohol. Alcohol contains 7 calories per gram, so the calorie count alone in an alcoholic beverage could range from 98 to 119 calories for one drink. Since most alcoholic beverages contain other caloric ingredients, this number is not the total calorie value of a beverage.

©Hayden-McNeil, LLC

12 oz beer   5 oz wine   1.5 oz liquor

FIGURE 13-5. Each of these drinks contains between 0.5 and 0.6 ounces of pure alcohol.

Image of Health in Depth

Alcohol Ingredients

Look at a bottle of beer. The label may extol its virtues as being made from natural ingredients, with natural carbonation. As with all other alcoholic beverages, it will state the volume of alcohol it contains, and there will be a government warning about drinking while pregnant and or when operating machinery. But the label will not list its actual ingredients. You will not know how many grams of carbohydrates or protein it contains, and you will only know the calorie count if it is being promoted as a low-calorie choice.

For people with allergies, lack of labeling can cause serious allergic reactions. Currently, only sulfites and Yellow Dye Number 5 must be listed. Serving size must be listed on other food products, but not on alcohol. Many people do not know that a 12-ounce bottle of beer contains as much alcohol as a 1.5 ounce shot of hard liquor or a 5-ounce glass of wine.

Today, if you buy a bottle of lemonade, the label will tell you what it contains, allowing you to make an informed decision about whether or how much to drink. But if you buy hard lemonade (a lemonade product containing alcohol), you do not have enough information to make an informed choice.

Metabolizing Alcohol

Alcohol is quickly absorbed, as about 20 percent passes directly into the bloodstream from the stomach, with the remainder mostly absorbed by the small intestine. Carbonated alcoholic beverages are absorbed more quickly, though the presence of food in the stomach can slow alcohol absorption. The liver metabolizes nearly all alcohol. Only about ten percent is metabolized in the stomach, and between 2–10 percent is not metabolized but excreted unchanged through breath, urine, and skin pores. During metabolism, alcohol is converted to acetaldehyde, with the help of an enzyme called alcohol dehydrogenase (ADH). How quickly it is metabolized depends on how much ADH is available in the liver; if ADH cannot keep up with the amount of alcohol entering the liver, alcohol continues to be circulated through the body until enzymes are available. Generally, with normal liver function, the liver metabolizes alcohol at a rate of about one drink per hour (about .5 ounces of alcohol).

Critical Thinking Question: How might listing the ingredients in alcohol affect alcohol sales and use?

Challenge Question: How is alcohol metabolized?

Blood/Alcohol Concentration

Alcohol volume in the blood is measured by blood/alcohol concentration (BAC). Expressed as a percentage, BAC .08 percent and above is the legal drunk limit in all 50 states.

Blood/alcohol concentration is dependent upon the amount of alcohol consumed, versus the rate at which alcohol is metabolized. Alcohol is water-soluble, so the less body fat a person has, the greater the volume of water for the alcohol. Generally, women have more body fat than men, so a 150-pound woman will have a higher BAC than a 150-pound man after the same amount of alcohol. Women also absorb more alcohol than men because they metabolize it less efficiently. Because of a woman's smaller size, higher body fat, and less efficient metabolism of alcohol, she will experience the effects of alcohol much sooner, with lower levels of alcohol consumption. Table 13-3 identifies clinical signs and symptoms at various levels of blood/alcohol concentration.

Table 13-3. Blood/Alcohol Concentration

BLOOD/ALCOHOL CONCENTRATION	APPROXIMATE NUMBER OF DRINKS FOR A 150-POUND MAN	CLINICAL SIGNS AND SYMPTOMS
10–50 mg/dl 0.01-0.05 g/dl	Less than 1 drink and up to 3 drinks	Mild euphoria, decreased inhibitions, diminished attention and poor judgment.
50–100 mg/dl 0.05–0.10 g/dl	3–5 drinks	Euphoria, sedation, impaired co-ordination, decrease sensory response time to stimuli, decreased judgment capacity, slurred speech. Reduced ability to operate machinery. Poor decision-making.
150–300 mg/dl 0.15–0.30 g/dl	7–14 drinks	Confusion, disorientation, impaired balance, slurred speech
250–400 mg/dl 0.25–.40 g/dl	14–18 drinks	Sleep or stupor, muscle uncoordination, markedly decreased sensory response to stimuli, incontinence.
400–500 mg/dl 0.40–0.50 g/dl	18–22+ drinks	Coma, hypothermia, respiratory and circulatory failure, possible death.

Effects of Alcohol

In small doses, alcohol causes a feeling of relaxation. It works as an inhibitory agent, and makes people more social in settings that otherwise might make them uncomfortable or nervous. These are some of the very limited benefits of alcohol, only experienced with moderate drinking.

Alcohol Impaired Driving

Each day in the U.S., 36 people die and 700 more are injured because of alcohol-impaired driving.[41] The annual cost of alcohol-related crashes is more than $51 billion.[42] Male drivers are more likely to be involved in fatal accidents than female drivers, and younger drivers are more likely than older drivers to die in alcohol-related crashes.[43] This may be because males are more likely to drive faster and take risks, and older drivers have more driving experience.

In 2002, the CDC reported that sobriety checkpoints reduce alcohol-related crashes by about 20 percent.

Other suggested methods to reduce impaired driving include reducing the legal limit for BAC from .08 to .05 percent, and aggressively enforcing zero tolerance for drivers under age 21 in all states. Community measures that make it socially unacceptable to drive after any amount of drinking, and immediate revocation of the driver licenses of those who drive while intoxicated also work to reduce driving while impaired or drunk. However, the responsibility rests with the driver. If a person drives to a bar or a party for the evening, that person has already planned how he or she will get home. Plans to restrict alcohol consumption to just one or two drinks often fail—the effects of alcohol are so strong that willpower is reduced, and more drinks may be consumed. Another irresponsible choice is to decide not to drive yourself,

but to ride with a driver who has been drinking. In this situation, passengers may avoid citations for driving while intoxicated, but do not avoid the potential crashes, injuries, and death that may result. Responsible choices include not drinking, arranging for a sober designated driver, using public transportation or hiring a taxi.

Image of Health in Depth

Age and Alcohol

In all 50 states and the District of Columbia, you must be age 21 years or older to purchase or publicly possess beverages that contain alcohol. States that do not comply are faced with a reduction in highway funding. The act, called the National Minimum Drinking Age Act of 1984, does not emphasize that you must be 21 to drink alcohol, and in nineteen states, those under age 21 are permitted to drink alcohol. This confusing act causes problems relative to drinking and driving. In all states, it is illegal to drive with a BAC of 0.08 percent or higher, but legal limits do not define a level beneath which it is safe to operate a machine or vehicle. Alcohol impairment can begin to occur at levels much lower than the legal limit.

For those under 21, the zero tolerance code makes it illegal to operate a motor vehicle with any blood alcohol level. Each year, about 1,900 people under the age of 21 die as a result of drinking and driving, 1,600 die from homicide, 300 from suicide, and hundreds of others due to injuries, falls, burns, and drowning, all occurring in the presence of alcohol. This becomes a total of about 5,000 underage drinkers dying each year.[44]

Alcohol and Relationships

Not all people who drink alcohol become alcoholic, but for some, there are adverse consequences for both the drinker and those who come into contact with the drinker. Problem drinking is used to describe non-dependent drinking that has a negative consequence. Relationship violence problems can arise with problem drinking.[45] Approximately one child in four is exposed to alcohol abuse or dependence in the family.[46]

Problem drinking can result in:[47]

- Violence, including sexual abuse
- Marital or couple conflict
- Infidelity
- Jealousy
- Economic insecurity
- Divorce or relationship termination
- Fetal alcohol effects

It is not surprising that couples that seek counseling often have alcohol problems.

Binge Drinking

Binge drinking is defined as consuming more than five drinks in a row for a male or four drinks in a row for a female, with the primary intention of becoming intoxicated. This carries obvious risks that range from behaving inappropriately, to driving or operating any kind of machinery while intoxicated, to premature death. Alcohol is a toxic substance and when consumed in large quantities, it can cause death. Friends may think the binge drinker has passed out or is sleeping it off, but with alcohol poisoning, respiration can slow to dangerous levels and the heart can stop. See "Image of Health in Depth: Alcohol Poisoning" for how you may be able to help someone who is dangerously drunk.

Image of Health in Depth

Alcohol Poisoning

Alcohol poisoning can occur in anyone, at any age. It is the result of consuming large quantities of anything that contains alcohol. Symptoms of alcohol poisoning include:

- Being confused or in a stupor
- Vomiting
- Seizures
- Slow breathing (less than 8 breaths in a minute)
- Breathing irregularly
- Cyanotic skin-tone (bluish tinge to skin, or very pale skin)
- Hypothermia (low body temperature)
- Unconsciousness (passing out)

Anytime a person passes out and cannot be awakened, emergency help is immediately required. While waiting for help, roll the person onto his or her side to reduce the chance of choking on vomit. Even while asleep, blood alcohol concentration continues to rise as alcohol enters the bloodstream, so do not ever assume that a person can sleep off alcohol poisoning.

If the person is still awake, call 800-222-1222 and you will be directed to the poison control center for your area. You will be instructed on whether to take the person to an emergency room. All calls to this number are confidential. You may also elect to call the emergency telephone number in your area.

When you are with people who are drinking, be alert and pay attention. If there is an emergency, you will need to know how much alcohol a person has consumed, anything they may have eaten, and any other substances that have been ingested.

Never leave a drunk or unconscious person unattended. Do not assume that drinking coffee, walking, dancing, or showering will help them to sober up. Only the liver can process alcohol and detoxify the person, and it works very slowly. If the liver is over-burdened, serious side effects, including death, can occur.

Alcohol and Health

In very small doses, alcohol can have a positive effect on health if there are no issues with alcohol. This can be up to one drink per day for women, and up to two drinks a day for men. In small doses, alcohol appears to increase high-density lipoprotein, the good cholesterol, acts as an anticoagulant, and reduces stress. Each of these effects offers a short-term protection against heart disease for middle-aged and older adults. For younger people, alcohol appears to have minimal, if any, benefit.

Since alcohol consumption is self-reinforcing, it becomes difficult to maintain minimal dosing, and with increasing quantity comes increasing health risk.

Alcohol and the Heart

Moderate consumption of alcohol can be good for heart health, but higher levels can be very damaging. Even drinking more than two drinks per day can raise blood pressure, increasing the risk for stroke or heart disease. When alcohol is being served, food is often present. Happy hours are promoted in some bars, offering free food and lower costs for alcohol drinks. The food choices are usually high in fat, high in salt, and high in calories, all of which can burden the heart. Additionally, cheaper drinks promote more drinking.

Chronic, heavy drinking can lead to heart **arrhythmias**, **cardiomyopathy**, and **anemia**. Heavy drinking is also implicated in the development of coronary heart disease and cirrhosis of the liver.

Key Terms

Anemia: A condition of having less than the normal number of red blood cells or less than the normal quantity of hemoglobin in the blood. The oxygen-carrying capacity of the blood is, therefore, decreased.

Arrhythmias: A problem with the speed or rhythm of the heartbeat, resulting in the heart skipping beats or beating too fast or too slow. Some arrhythmias can cause the heart to stop beating, leading to sudden cardiac arrest.

Cardiomyopathy: Degenerative heart disease in which the heart muscle becomes enlarged, thickens, and weakens.

Alcohol and Cancer

Several types of cancer are associated with alcohol use, including cancers of the mouth, pharynx, larynx and esophagus, liver, and digestive tract. Although it is not yet understood how alcohol causes this risk, it is known that risk increases with the amount of alcohol consumed.[48] Drinking alcohol may reduce the body's ability to absorb folate from foods, and may raise estrogen levels. Alcohol may also act as a solvent, helping other chemicals, such as tobacco smoke, enter cells.

Alcohol and Pregnancy

Alcohol is a teratogen, an agent known to interfere with normal embryonic development. Drinking alcohol during pregnancy can lead to a wide range of both physical and mental defects for the baby—**fetal alcohol spectrum disorders** are a direct result of alcohol consumption during pregnancy. This disorder causes problems in how the child looks, grows, thinks, and acts. Drinking at any time during a pregnancy can cause problems, and it is one of the top preventable causes of birth defects.[49] There is higher risk of miscarriage, premature birth, stillbirth, and low birth weight among babies exposed to alcohol in the womb.

Key Term

Fetal alcohol spectrum disorders: A range of neurological and physical impairments that can affect a child exposed to alcohol in the womb.

Children born with FASDs have facial malformation, growth retardation, and neurodevelopment abnormalities of the central nervous systems (CNS). Since the damage occurs during fetal development, there is no cure.

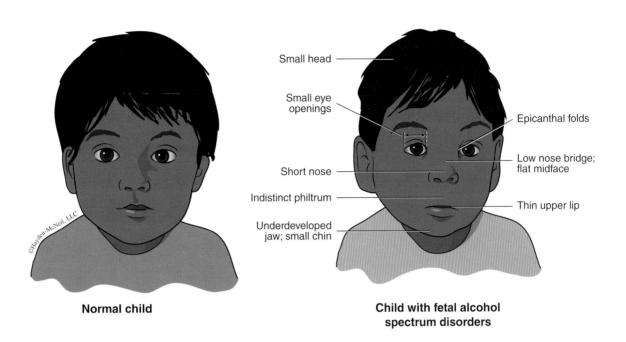

Normal child

Child with fetal alcohol spectrum disorders

Small head

Small eye openings

Short nose

Indistinct philtrum

Underdeveloped jaw; small chin

Epicanthal folds

Low nose bridge; flat midface

Thin upper lip

FIGURE 13-6. Fetal Alcohol Spectrum Disorder.

To ensure the safest outcome for a pregnancy, prospective mothers should cease alcohol consumption before becoming pregnant, and abstain from alcohol during the pregnancy.

Although a male's consumption of alcohol cannot cause FASDs, it does have an impact on sperm development. A woman is born with all the eggs she will ever have; men make sperm throughout life. Since alcohol is circulated in the blood, it will circulate in the testes and may effect the development of sperm, possibly resulting in sperm with deformed heads or tails, limiting their motility.[50] This can reduce male fertility.

Alcohol and Other Drugs

Alcohol is a depressant. When mixed with other depressants, it produces a synergistic effect, in which the combined effects of each drug are greater that the sum of the effects of the two drugs alone.

Mixing alcohol with sedatives such as gamma hydroxybutyric acid (GHB), Rohypnol, tranquilizers, or sleeping pills will multiply the sedative effects of both drugs, possibly causing loss of consciousness, coma, or even death. Using alcohol with marijuana decreases motor control and mental concentration. Acetaminophen combined with alcohol increases the risk of liver damage in chronic, heavy drinkers. There is a higher risk of liver and heart disease in those that combine cocaine with alcohol. For opiate users, adding alcohol can slow down the central nervous system (CNS), cause breathing to slow or stop, and can result in coma or death.

Alcohol is a drug. Like all drugs, it should be used cautiously and with care, if used at all.

Key Terms

Synergistic effect: The combined effect of two drugs become greater than the effect of each drug alone.

Gamma hydroxybutyric acid: An illegal substance that causes drowsiness, dizziness, nausea, and visual disturbances at lower doses, and unconsciousness, seizures, severe respiratory depression, and death at higher concentrations.

Rohypnol: An illegal substance in the U.S. that works as a tranquilizer but is ten times more potent.

Tranquilizers: Drugs designed to calm.

Alcoholism

Most people can drink alcohol and never experience alcohol-related problems. For some, alcohol leads to alcohol abuse, and for others it leads to alcoholism.

Alcohol Abuse

Problem drinkers may not drink everyday. They may not drink large amounts when they do drink, and they may go for weeks without a drink. Signs of alcohol abuse include:

- Problems at work or school, including being late or absent and not doing required work as well as possible.

- Having blackouts where they cannot remember what happened when they were drinking.

- Legal problems as a result of drinking.

- Relationship problems as a result of drinking.

- Causing injury or becoming injured when drinking.

- Exacerbating existing health problems because of drinking.

- Having friends and family members who are worried about their drinking.

An individual who has some or all of these symptoms may consider not drinking alcohol.

Alcoholism

Alcoholism is a condition that occurs when a drinker becomes addicted to and dependent upon alcohol. It is a treatable condition, but does not have a cure. An alcoholic cannot learn to drink socially. Warning signs of alcohol dependence or addiction include:

- Drinking more than planned, or more frequently than planned.

- Drinking more to get the desired effects.

- Avoiding situations where alcohol will not be available.

- Spending a lot of time either drinking or recovering from the effects of alcohol.

- Inability to reduce or stop drinking.

- Continuing to drink even though it has caused personal problems, legal problems, or problems at work or school.

Although this list is not comprehensive and other factors may indicate alcohol dependence or addiction, it is a good starting point. If you think you have an alcohol problem, many agencies and services are available to help.

Treating Alcohol Problems

Withdrawal from alcohol can cause serious complications, including death, for an addicted individual. Symptoms may include feeling sick, vomiting, sweating, nervousness, and tremors. These symptoms usually start about 24 hours after the last drink and become most severe about three days later.

People do not choose to abuse alcohol or become alcoholic, but there are known risk factors. Men are more likely to develop a drinking problem than women. This might be because it is more socially acceptable for men to drink excessively than for women. There is a higher risk of alcohol abuse and dependence if another family member has a drinking problem. The younger you are when you start drinking, the higher your risk for alcohol-related problems later in life.

Although there are many methods for treating alcoholism, treatment methods are influenced by Alcoholics Anonymous (AA). In Akron, Ohio, in 1935, Bill Wilson, a practicing drunk, met Dr. Bob Smith, another alcoholic. Together they talked about their problem with alcohol, and Bill convinced Dr. Bob that alcoholism was a disease, and by working with other alcoholics who wanted to be sober, they could help each other stay sober.

Alcoholics Anonymous is a worldwide organization whose goal is to help people who want to stop drinking. Based on a 12-step program, the organization has had tremendous success in helping people stay sober. Meetings are held in almost every city in the world, at almost every hour. Meetings are free, and the only requirement for attending a closed meeting is the desire to stop drinking.

Other options include in-patient and out-patient medical treatments, which are expensive, and not always covered by health insurance. There are times when the individual is not amenable to treatment, and an intervention may be an option. In this setting, friends and family members work with a professional counselor to initiate a change in behavior in the alcoholic. This may involve confronting the individual, expressing concern regarding drinking behavior, and making recovery options available. If done in a supportive, loving manner, interventions may result in a person agreeing to accept support and stop drinking.

Responsibility and Accountability

In this chapter, emphasis is on two of the legal drugs that cause most of the drug problems in society. Although these drugs may be socially sanctioned, they can have consequences ranging from chronic disease, accidents, and violence, to family break-up and even death.

Taking Responsibility for Tobacco and Alcohol

There is no way to safely or responsibly use tobacco. Any amount is harmful. Frequently, smokers may talk about their rights as a smoker and their freedom to choose whether to smoke. Although all smokers made the choice to try smoking, once addiction occurs, choice is lost and the only benefit is for the tobacco companies. The only responsible choice with tobacco is to not use it, or to stop using it if you are a current tobacco user. It will be hard to stop, but thousands do it every day. Some stop by choice, while others stop due to disease or death.

Most, but not all, people can safely use alcohol in small quantities. When used irresponsibly, alcohol can cause major problems, disease, and death. Being responsible means that the drinker will not drive or operate machinery after any amount of alcohol. Responsibility means the drinker will not combine alcohol with other drugs, and will not influence another person to drink. It means not drinking while pregnant and not serving alcohol to a pregnant woman. Responsibility for underage drinking is not limited to youth. Adults who provide young individuals with alcohol play a large part in the problem of underage drinking. One in four parents think that teens should be allowed to drink when parents are present.[51] Unfortunately, this rite of passage does not ensure safety, and the mandate that parents must be present is often ignored when teens are on their own and choose to drink.

Focusing on Accountability

The Centers for Disease Control and Prevention estimated in 2007 that health care costs associated with smoking were $10.28 per pack. Depending on where you live, a one pack per day habit can cost $1,800 per year.[52] Eventually, all people share the cost of smoking; the smoker bears only partial accountability. Nonsmokers incur the cost both financially, due to increased health care costs, and in some instances are personally affected by disease and death because of secondhand smoke. And we all pay inflated health and life insurance rates to offset the cost of tobacco-induced disease and death.

Accountability for alcohol is also assumed by society as a whole, as well as by those who drink irresponsibly. We pay more for car insurance because of people who cause crashes when they drive drunk. We pay more for health insurance because of alcohol-induced health problems. Being accountable means never driving a motor vehicle or operating machinery after drinking. It means stopping someone from driving if they have been drinking, and it means not serving alcohol to anyone who is underage.

If you want to be both responsible and accountable relative to these two drugs, the options are simple. Do not use tobacco, and avoid those that use it. Drink alcohol only if it is not a problem for you, and drink only in moderate or lower levels. Never drink and drive. You can make the right choice.

Summary

Tobacco

- Tobacco is the most widely abused substance in the U.S., causing one in every six deaths, and is the leading cause of preventable death in the U.S.

- Cigarettes contain more than 4,000 chemicals, including nicotine, tar, carbon monoxide, and arsenic.

- Nicotine is the addicting stimulant in tobacco. Tar refers to the chemicals added to cigarettes.

- Cilia protect the lungs by beating to trap and expel damaging particulates that are inhaled. Smoking paralyzes cilia, allowing debris to reach fragile lung tissue.

- Mainstream smoke is a combination of smoke inhaled and exhaled by the smoker. Side-stream smoke comes from a burning cigarette. Environmental smoke refers to the combination of mainstream and side-stream smoke.

- Other forms of tobacco include cigars, pipes, clove cigarettes, beadies, hookahs, and smokeless forms.

- Tobacco use causes several diseases that may result in early death.

- Tobacco revenue is about $13 billion, but tobacco cost is much higher in terms of medical costs, lost productivity, and years of potential life lost.

Alcohol

- Alcohol is the third leading cause of preventable death in the U.S., resulting in about 2.3 million years of potential life lost in 2001.

- Alcohol is labeled by proof value, which is two times the concentration of alcohol in the beverage.

- The liver metabolizes most alcohol at about the rate of one standard drink per hour.

- Blood/alcohol concentration is the measure of alcohol in 100 milliliters of blood. The legal drunk limit is 0.08 percent in all 50 states.

- Every day, 36 people die and 700 more are injured as a result of alcohol-impaired driving.

- Binge drinking is five or more drinks in a row for men and four or more in a row for women. Binge drinking can result in alcohol poisoning and death.

- Moderate drinking is defined as up to two drinks per day for men and up to one drink per day for women. Moderate drinking can have positive effects on the heart.

- Chronic, heavy drinking can lead to heart arrhythmias, cardiomyopathy, and anemia.

- Alcohol is a teratogen, and drinking during pregnancy can lead to fetal alcohol spectrum disorders.

- Alcohol is a depressant and has a synergistic effect with other depressants.

Reassessing Your Knowledge

1. What impact does nicotine have on brain chemistry?

2. How do other forms of tobacco compare with cigarettes relative to health risks?

3. What diseases are caused by smoking, and what cost does this cause for society?

4. How is alcohol metabolized in the body, and what happens when consumption exceeds metabolism?

5. What are the potential health impacts of alcohol use?

To answer these questions, you might choose to work in groups with your colleagues. Check your answers against the written material in the text, and reread those sections where you made errors.

Health Assessment Toolbox

Smoking Cessation Medications
http://www.drugs.com

CDC's Tips: Tobacco Information and Prevention Source
http://www.cdc.gov/tobacco

Tobacco/Smoking Cessation—National Cancer Institute
http://www.cancer.gov/cancertopics/factsheet/Tobacco

College Drinking Prevention
http://www.collegedrinkingprevention.gov/OtherAlcoholInformation/cutDownOnDrinking.aspx

How to Stop Drinking Alcohol
http://www.webmd.com/mental-health/alcohol-abuse/how-to-stop-drinking-alcohol

Learn About Alcohol Use in Pregnancy
http://www.cdc.gov/ncbddd/fas/

Vocabulary Challenge

Match the term in the left-hand column with its correct definition in the right-hand column.

TERM		DEFINITION
Mainstream smoke		A. Smoke emitted from a burning cigarette
Side-stream smoke		B. A state in which the combined effects are greater than the sum of individual effects
Chronic obstructive pulmonary disease		C. The toxic chemicals found in cigarettes
Synergistic effects		D. Psychoactive ingredient in alcohol
Tar		E. Double the concentration of alcohol in a beverage
Nicotine		F. The addictive stimulant in tobacco
Carcinogen		G. A combination of inhaled and exhaled smoke
Ethyl alcohol		H. Health conditions that block airways and cause difficulty breathing
Proof value		I. A substance known to cause cancer

G; A; H; B; C; F; I; D; E.

Answers

Exploring the Internet

American Cancer Society: Tobacco and Cancer

This site provides information about health issues with smoking and helpful tips for quitting.

http://www.cancer.gov/cancertopics/factsheet/Tobacco/cessation

Mayo Clinic

Information about the health problems associated with smokeless tobacco.

http://www.mayoclinic.com/health/chewing-tobacco/CA00019

Tobacco Free Kids

This site provides information about the economic effects of environmental tobacco smoke and the toll of tobacco in the United States.

http://www.tobaccofreekids.org/

Smoke Freedom

At this site, you can see how much it costs to smoke either cigarettes or beadies.

http://www.costofsmoking.com/

Smoke Free

Here you can learn how stress levels affect your smoking and find information on smoking cessation.

http://www.smokefree.gov/

American Cancer Society

This site provides support, advice, and information on medicines that can help you stop smoking.

http://www.cancer.org/index

Lung Cancer Organization

This site offers a booklet on the progress of treatment of lung cancer.

http://www.lungcancer.org/

Medicinenet

A search for lung cancer at this site provides comprehensive information on the cause of lung cancer, types, signs and symptoms, prognosis, and treatment.

http://www.medicinenet.com

Chronic Obstructive Lung Disease Resources

Extensive information on causes, symptoms and treatment options.

http://www.COPDresource.com

National Heart Lung and Blood Institute

The government's information site on chronic obstructive lung disease.

http://www.nhlbi.nih.gov/health/public/lung/copd/

The Eye Digest

At this site, you can read the literature about cataracts, glaucoma, macula degeneration and other eye diseases.

http://www.agingeye.net/

WebMD

WebMD, one of the more reliable medical information sites on the Web discusses many health issues including eye health. Click on Health A-Z to find the topic that interests you.

http://www.webmd.com

Smoking and Your Baby—American Pregnancy Organization

Facts about smoking during pregnancy and its impact on the unborn child.

http://www.americanpregnancy.org/pregnancyhealth/smoking.html

Erectile Dysfunction—Facts You Need to Know

Provides current, accurate information about erectile dysfunction (ED) including the relationship between smoking and ED.

http://www.nlm.nih.gov/medlineplus/erectiledysfunction.html

Facts About Alcohol Poisoning

Signs and symptoms of alcohol poisoning and what you need to do if you suspect someone has alcohol poisoning.

http://www.collegedrinkingprevention.gov

Binge Drinking

The Harvard School of Public Health Alcohol Study examines the nature, extent, and associated problems with binge drinking.

http://www.hsph.harvard.edu/cas/

Alcoholism

A search of the prestigious Mayo Clinic Web site provides causes, symptoms, risk factors, and other information related to alcoholism.

http://www.mayoclinic.com/

National Institute of Alcohol Abuse

This comprehensive site provides answers to the most frequently asked questions about alcohol.

http://www.niaaa.nih.gov/faqs/general-english/Pages/default.aspx

Alcoholics Anonymous

This is the official site of Alcoholics Anonymous. Here you can find A.A. meetings, information on the Big Book, and A.A. conventions.

http://www.aa.org/

Al-Anon and Alateen

This is the official site of Al-Anon and Alateen providing information for those who have friends and family who are problem drinkers.

http://www.al-anon.alateen.org/

CDC Motor Vehicle Safety

Alcohol impaired driving fact sheet covering the scope of the problem and identifying who is most at risks.

http://cdc.gov/motorviclesafety/index.html

Selected References

1. World Health Organization, WHO Report on the Global Tobacco Epidemic, News Release, World Health Organization. 2008.

2. Kavanagh, K.T. Cost to Society. Downloaded May 27, 2009, from www.tobacco-facts.info/cost_to_society

3. CDC Grand Rounds. *Current Opportunities in Tobacco Control,* 59(16): 487–492. April 30, 2010.

4. Substance Abuse and Mental Health Services Administration. Results from the 2004 National Survey on Drug Use and Health: National Findings. DHHS Pub. No. SMA 05-4062, 2005.

5. Lynch B.S., and Bonnie R.J., editors. Growing Up Tobacco Free—Preventing Nicotine Addiction In Children and Youths, Division of Biobehavioral Sciences and Mental Disorders. Institute of Medicine, National Academy of Sciences. Washington, D.C. p. 3, 1994.

6. Centers for Disease Control and Prevention. Smoking and Tobacco Use—Fact Sheet: Health Effects of Cigarette Smoking. Updated January 2008. Available at: http://www.cdc.gov/tobacco/data_statistics/fact_sheets/health_effects/effects_cig_smoking/

7. How Stuff Works; How NicotineWorks, Meeker-O'Connell, Anne. Downloaded May 27, 2009, from http://health.howstuffworks/nicotine2.htm

8. Research Report Series—Tobacco Addiction. NIDA, Publication No. 98-4342. 1998.

9. Mansvelder, H.D., and McGehee, D.S. Long-Term Potentiation of Excitatory Inputs to Brain Reward Areas by Nicotine. *Neuron,* 27: 349–357. 2000.

10. National Cancer Institute. Risks Associated with Smoking Cigarettes with Low Machine-Measured Yields of Tar and Nicotine. Smoking and Tobacco Control Monograph 13. Bethesda, MD: NCI 2001

11. Denissenko, M.F., Pao, A., Tang, M.S., and Pfeifer, G.P. Preferential Formation of Benso[a]pyrene Adducts at Lung Cancer Mutational Hotspots. *Science,* 274: 430–432. 1996.

12. Ibid.

13. Sleigh, M.A., Blake, J.R., and Liron, N. The Propulsion of Mucus by Cilia. *American Review of Respiratory Diseases,* 137(3): 726–41. March, 1988.

14. Dispinigaitis, P. V. Cough Reflex Sensitivity in Cigarette Smokers. *CHEST.* 123(3). © 2003 American College of Chest Physicians. 2003.

15. Knishkowy, B., and Amitai, Y. Water-Pipe (Narghile) Smoking: An Emerging Health Risk Behavior. *Pediatrics,* 116(1): 113–119. July, 2005.

16. Kiter, G., Ucan, E.S., Ceylan ,E., et al. Waterpipe Smoking and Pulmonary Functions. *Respiratory Medicine,* 94: 891–94. 2000.

17. Chaaya M. El Roueiheb Z., Chemaitelly G.A., Joumana N., and Al-Sahab B. Argileh Smoking among University Students: A New Tobacco Epidemic. *Nicotine and Tobacco Research,* 6(3): 457–463. 2004.

18. Tamin, H., Musharrafieh, U., El Roueiheb, Z., et al. Exposure of Children to Environmental Tobacco Smoker (ETS) and Its Association with Respiratory Ailments. *Journal of Asthma,* 40: 571–76. 2003.

19. Gades, N.M., et al. Association Between Smoking and Erectile Dysfunction: a Population Based Study. *American Journal of Epidemiology,* 161(4): 346–351. 2005.

20. Ries, L.A.G., Eisner, M.P., Kosary, C.L., et al. (eds). SEER Cancer Statistics Review, 1975–2001, National Cancer Institute. Bethesda, MD, 2004.

21. Institute of Medicine Report Brief: Second Hand Smoke Exposure and Cardiovascular Effects: Making Sense of the Evidence. October 2009.

22. National Institute on Drug Abuse, Research Advances, Volume 12, Number 1, January/February 1997.

23. Minna J.D., Neoplasms of the Lung, in Harrison's Principles of Internal Medicine, pt. 5 § 75, at 506–515 (Dennis L. Kasper, MD et al., eds, 16th ed 2005).

24. U.S. Department of Health and Human Services. Targeting Tobacco Use: The Nation's Leading Cause of Death. Atlanta, GA: Centers for Disease Control and Prevention, 2003.

25. Ezzati M., and Lopez A. Estimates of Global Mortality Attributable to Smoking in 2000–2003; *Lancet,* 362: 847–852. September 13, 2003.

26. American Heart Association. Cigarette Smoking and Cardiovascular Diseases. AHA Scientific Position. Downloaded October 26, 2009, from www.americanheart.org/presenter.jh

27. Mokdad A.H., Marks J.S., Stroup D.F., and Gerberding J.L. Actual Causes of Death in the United States, 2000. *JAMA,* 291 (10): 1238–45. March 2004.

28. Tobacco's Impact on the Economy. A Discussion Paper. San Francisco Tobacco Free Coalition and the San Francisco Tobacco Free Project, June 30, 1997.

29. Economic Research Service. Tobacco and the Economy: Farms, Jobs, and Communities. Gale H.F., Foreman L., Capehart T. Agricultural Economic Report No. (AER789) 44 pp, November, 2000.

30. Centers for Disease Control and Prevention Mortality and Mobility Weekly Report. Smoking-Attributable Mortality, Years of Potential Life Lost, and Productivity Losses—United States. 57(45);1226–1228. November 14, 2008.

31. Parish, T.G. Financing Smoking Related Illness and Smoking Cessation in the United States: Can It Be Done? *The Internet Journal of Allied Health Sciences and Practice,* 2(1). January 2004.

32. Federal Trade Commission. Cigarette Report for 2006. Washington, DC: Federal Trade Commission; 2009.

33. Centers for Disease Control and Prevention. Cigarette Smoking Among Adults and Trends in Smoking Cessation—United States. [serial online]. *Morbidity and Mortality Weekly Report,* 58(44): 1227–1232. 2008. [Accessed May 15, 2010].

34. Behan, D.F., Eriksen, M.P., and Lin, Y. Economic Effects of Environmental Tobacco Smoke Report. Schaumburg, IL. Society of Actuaries; 2005 [accessed March 31, 2009].

35. Centers for Disease Control and Prevention. Annual Smoking-Attributable Mortality, Years of Potential Life Lost, and Economic Costs—United States,1997–2001. *Morbidity and Mortality Weekly Report,* 54: 625–628. 2005

36. Moran, S., Wechsler, H., and Rigotti, N. Social Smoking Among U.S. College Students. *Pediatrics,* 114: 1028–1034. 2004.

37. Kear, M.E. Psychosocial Determinants of Cigarette Smoking Among College Students. *Journal of Community Health Nursing,* 19(4): 245–257. Winter 2002.

38. Koop, C.E. The Health Consequences of Smoking: Nicotine Addiction. A Report of the Surgeon General. Center for Health Promotion and Education. Office on Smoking and Health. DHHS Publication No. (CDC) 8808406. 1988.

39. Mokdad, A.H., Marks, J.S., Stroup, D.F., and Gerberding J.L. Actual Causes of Death in the United States, 2000. *JAMA,* 291(10): 1238–1245. March, 2004.

40. Centers for Disease Control and Prevention Alcohol-Attributable Deaths and Years of Potential Life Lost—United States, 2001. *Morbidity and Mortality Weekly Report,* 53(37): 866–870. September 24, 2004.

41. Dept of Transportation (US), National Highway Traffic Safety Administration (NHTSA). Traffic Safety Facts 2008: Alcohol-Impaired Driving. Washington DC: NHTSA, 2009.

42. Blincoe L., Seay A., Zaloshnja E., Miller T., Romano E., Luchter S., et al. The Economic Impact of Motor Vehicle Crashes, 2000. Washington DC: Dept of Transportation (U.S.), National Highway Traffic Safety Administration (NHTSA), 2002.

43. Zador, P.L., Krawchuk, S.A., and Voas, R.B. Alcohol-Related Relative Risk of Driver Fatalities and Driver Involvement in Fatal Crashes in Relation to Driver Age and Gender: an Update Using 1996 Data. *Journal of Studies on Alcohol*, 61: 387–395. 2000.

44. Alcohol Alert. National Institute on Alcohol Abuse and Alcoholism. Number 67. U.S. Department of Health and Human Services, National Institutes of Health. National Institute on Alcohol Abuse and Alcoholism. January, 2006.

45. Roberts, L.J., Roberts, C.F., and Leonard, K.E. Alcohol, Drugs and Interpersonal Violence. In V.B. Van Hasselt and M. Hersen (eds.) *Handbook of Psychological Approaches with Violent Criminal Offenders: Contemporary Strategies and Issues*, New York: Plenum Press.

46. Grant, B.F. Estimates of U.S. Children Exposed to Alcohol Abuse and Dependence in the Family. *American Journal of Public Health*, 90(1): 112–116. 2000.

47. National Institute on Alcohol Abuse and Alcoholism. Alcohol Problems in Intimate Relationships: Identification and Intervention. June, 2003.

48. American Cancer Society. Alcohol Use and Cancer. Downloaded May 19, 2010, from www.cancer.org/docroot/PED/content/PED_3_2xAlcohol_use_and_cancer

49. Maier, S.E., and West, J.R. Drinking Patterns and Alcohol-Related Birth Defects. *Alcohol Research and Health*, 25(3): 168–174. 2001.

50. Passaro, C.T., Little, R.E., Savits, D.A., et al. . Effect of Paternal Alcohol Consumption Before Pregnancy on Infant Birth Weight. *Teratology*, 57: 294–301. 1998.

51. American Medical Association. Teenage Drinking: Key Findings. 2005.

52. United States Marine Corp, National Health Naval Research Center—San Diego, CA.

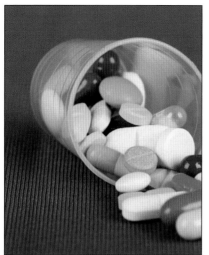

Image of Health

Drugs and Addictive Behavior

DRUG USE

- Who Uses Drugs
- Drug Effects

CATEGORIES OF DRUGS

- Over-the-Counter Drugs
- Prescription Drugs
- Central Nervous System Depressants
- Central Nervous System Stimulants
- Illicit Drugs
  - Marijuana and Hashish
  - Opioids
  - Psychotherapeutic Drugs
  - Cocaine and Crack
  - Hallucinogens: LSD, Peyote, Mescaline, Ecstasy (MDMA)
  - Inhalants

THE PROCESS OF ADDICTION

- Addictive Behavior
- Changes to the Brain
- Drug Progression, Dependence, and Codependence

TREATMENT OPTIONS

- Self-Help Options
- Outpatient and Inpatient Therapies
- Relapse

RESPONSIBILITY AND ACCOUNTABILITY

- Taking Responsibility for Drug Use
- Focusing on Accountability

Student Learning Outcomes

LEARNING OUTCOMES	APPLYING IT TO YOUR LIFE
Describe what it means to be a drug user.	Assess your current level of drug use.
Identify the most popular illicit drug in the U.S. and the population that is most likely to use this drug.	Describe the effect drugs are having on your life.
Identify some of the different effects between stimulant and depressant drug use.	Describe how you might personally react to both stimulant and depressant drugs.
Identify some of the characteristics of addictive behavior.	Determine if you have any characteristics of addictive behavior as a result of drug use.
Describe some of the treatment options for people who are dependent on drugs.	Identify steps you would take to help yourself or someone else who has a drug dependency.

Assess Your Knowledge

1. A prescription drug:
   a. Requires a consent agreement from the patient.

   b. Allows for substitutions at the pharmacy.

   c. Requires a written order from a medical doctor, dentist, or optometrist.

   d. Is the last resort for treatment.

2. The most popular illicit drug in America is:
   a. Heroin

   b. Cocaine

   c. Methamphetamine

   d. Marijuana

3. Drug expectancy is:
   a. The impending arrival of a drug delivery.

   b. An expectation of the drug experience.

   c. Taking drugs during pregnancy.

   d. Frequency of drug use.

4. Marijuana is:
   a. An opioid.

   b. A synthetic drug.

   c. Derived from the hemp plant.

   d. Derived from a cactus.

5. Psychotherapeutic drugs are:
   a. Prescription drugs used in a medical or non-medical way.

   b. A category of drugs sold over the counter.

   c. Another name for hallucinogens.

   d. Drugs used by athletes to gain muscle.

Answers:

1. c; 2. d; 3. b; 4. c; 5. a.

Drug Use

Drug use is certainly prevalent in America, and many people do not realize that some of their daily behaviors are considered drug use. If you start your morning with a cup of caffeinated coffee or tea, you have started your day with a stimulant drug. Millions of individuals drink coffee, and most do so without adverse effects. So is the coffee drinker a drug user? By definition, the answer is yes. Caffeine is considered a **psychoactive** stimulant drug, as it elevates mood in addition to the central nervous system, increasing heart rate, respiration, and blood pressure. Drugs may be **legal**, such as caffeine, or **illicit**, such as marijuana. A **prescription drug** such as OxyContin is legal when used responsibly to relieve pain, but nonmedical use of a **psychotherapeutic drug** is illicit. The psychoactive drugs classified as **hallucinogens** are all illicit. Over the counter (OTC) drugs are available without a prescription and are relatively safe, but when taken in greater than the recommended dose, they can be harmful. Some individuals inhale the fumes of common home or automotive products such as gasoline, spray paint, or glue to get high. Products used in this way are called **inhalants** and are most popular with adolescents. Inhalants can be extremely dangerous, due to the potential to cause respiratory failure and brain damage.[1]

Key Terms

Drug: Any substance other than food that alters the body and its functions.

Psychoactive: A drug that alters mood or behavior.

Legal: Allowed by law.

Illicit: Unlawful, not allowed by law.

Prescription drug: A drug regulated by the Food and Drug Administration (FDA) that requires a written order from a medical doctor or dentist.

Psychotherapeutic drug: Prescription drugs that include pain relievers, tranquilizers, stimulants, and sedatives.

Hallucinogens: Drugs that can cause distortions in time, space, and perceptions.

Inhalants: Common home and automotive products—e.g., gasoline—that produce a toxic vapor that some drug users inhale to get high.

Who Uses Drugs

In 2009, according to the National Survey on Drug Use and Health (NSDUH), an estimated 21.8 million Americans—8.7 percent of the total population over 12 years of age—used illicit drugs. These statistics are the result of the participants' positive responses to a survey about drug use in the previous month.

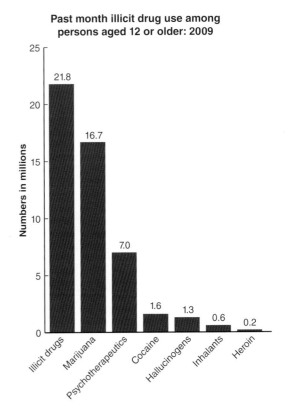

FIGURE 14-1. Drug use in the U.S.

(Source: U.S. Department of Health and Human Services, Substance Abuse and Mental Health Services Administration, September 2010.)

Marijuana, including hashish, was by far the most commonly used illicit drug, with nearly 17 million users. This means over 76 percent of illicit drug users used marijuana as well as other drugs, and marijuana was the only drug used by 58 percent of them. Illicit drugs included in the study were marijuana/hashish, cocaine, heroin, hallucinogens, inhalants, or prescription-type psychotherapeutics used nonmedically. This category shows the number of people who said they had used one or more of these substances in the past month. The hallucinogens included lysergic acid diethylamide (LSD), phencyclidine (PCP), peyote, mescaline, psilocybin mushrooms, and ecstasy (MDMA). In addition to gasoline, spray paint, and glue, inhalants also included nitrous oxide, amyl nitrite, and cleaning fluids. The total rate of illicit drug use in 2008 of 20 million users increased slightly in 2009, to 21.8 million drug users.

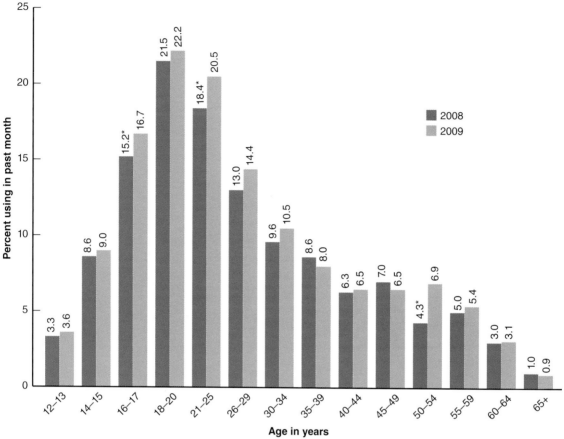

Past month illicit drug use among persons aged 12 or older, by age: 2008 and 2009

Legend: 2008, 2009

Values by age group:
- 12–13: 3.3, 3.6
- 14–15: 8.6, 9.0
- 16–17: 15.2*, 16.7
- 18–20: 21.5, 22.2
- 21–25: 18.4*, 20.5
- 26–29: 13.0, 14.4
- 30–34: 9.6, 10.5
- 35–39: 8.6, 8.0
- 40–44: 6.3, 6.5
- 45–49: 7.0, 6.5
- 50–54: 4.3*, 6.9
- 55–59: 5.0, 5.4
- 60–64: 3.0, 3.1
- 65+: 1.0, 0.9

Y-axis: Percent using in past month
X-axis: Age in years

* Difference between this estimate and the 2009 estimate is statistically significant at the 0.5 level.

FIGURE 14-2. Illicit drug use by age.

(Source: U.S. Department of Health and Human Services, Substance Abuse and Mental Health Services Administration, September 2010. (All material appearing in this report is in the public domain and may be reproduced or copied without permission from SAMHSA.) http://www.oas.samhsa.gov/NSDUH/2k9NSDUH/2k9ResultsP.pdf)

Figure 14-2 illustrates changes in drug using patterns across age groups between 2008 and 2009. Between ages 12 and approximately 34 years old, drug used increased, dropping off at age 35, then increasing again in those age 55–60 years of age, possibly indicating abuse of prescription medications.

Challenge Question: What are the first and second most popular illicit drugs of choice for Americans?

Of the 21.8 million illicit drug users in the United States in 2009, 21.2 million were college-aged students in the 18- to 25-year-old age group. Most illicit drug use in this group involved marijuana, at 18.1 million users.

Psychotherapeutic drugs were the second most popular, followed by cocaine or crack use and hallucinogens. Inhalant use is common among 12–17 year olds, but is not popular among those over 18 years old.

In addition to age, drug use is influenced by gender, ethnicity, and level of education. The ethnic groups most likely to use illicit drugs are American Indians and Alaska Natives, followed by blacks, whites, Hispanics, and Asians. College graduates and those with some college are less likely than those with only a high school education to use illicit drugs.

Xenia's Story

Xenia could not be late again. The professor said one more time and she was out. But she was having a hard time waking up. Of course, she had been up all weekend—and by "up," she meant *up*. Sunday night, she had crashed, and she had not eaten since…when was it? Maybe Friday morning? But she had partied all weekend.

She looked over at her purse and knew there was a small wake-me-up in it. But her rules were that she only used on the weekends…unless there was a party or something, of course. She pulled her purse over and took out the small piece of foil. There was very little left,

but it would give her the jolt she needed.

Thirty minutes later she was flying again as she drove onto the campus. She saw the flashing lights and wondered who the cop was after, but his loudspeaker made it clear she had to stop. "What the heck?" She had done nothing wrong.

At the curb, the campus police officer asked for her various identifications, and she got out her driver's license, student identification, and registration. She could not find her insurance card and could not remember the company name. The officer asked if she had been drinking. She looked at him sullenly. "I never drink

before breakfast—it's a personal rule," she said sarcastically. He was not amused, and he asked her to get out of the car. "You didn't stop at the last stop sign." She argued with him, but wondered which sign he was referring to—she had no idea. He called for backup, and again she wondered what was going on. She could not think clearly, and she told him she was sick. He asked her if she had used any drugs, to which she replied she did not use drugs. The backup car arrived, and the first officer advised that she appeared to be under the influence of a drug. Her pupils were dilated, her reaction time was off, and she was not able to track visually.

At the campus police station, she was assessed for illegal substance use, which showed methamphetamine in her system. Xenia looked at the clock. She had missed the class, and worse yet, she was now going to miss a lot more classes.

On the way to jail, handcuffed in the back of a squad car, she wondered what was going to happen. She was supposed to get a college degree, have a fantastic career, and wonderful future, but she was on her way to jail. She had to wonder whether the drug use was worth it… ■

Critical Thinking Question: Describe some of the reasons for the popularity of inhalants among 12–17-year-olds.

Drug Effects

Individual reactions to drugs are determined by many variables, including gender, body size and weight, metabolism, the presence of other drugs in the body, pregnancy, and to some degree, expectation of drug effects. A drug administered to a person of small body size and weight will have a greater effect than for a person who is larger and weighs more. Metabolic differences can also account for the time it takes for a drug to take effect. To feel its effects, people with faster metabolisms may need more of a drug than a person with a slow metabolism. If other drugs are present in the body, the effect of the new drug may be intensified, or the effect of one or both drugs may be reduced or negated entirely. **Synergism** refers to the effect that occurs when combined drugs have an intensified effect. Sedatives synergize with alcohol, but a tranquilizer drug combined with cocaine will cancel the effect of cocaine.

Taking any drugs while pregnant, particularly during the first trimester, may negatively affect the fetus: the type of drug and frequency of use determines the amount of risk. It is estimated that one in ten women use illegal drugs while pregnant. Because drugs easily circulate to the fetus through the placenta, they can cause birth defects, preterm birth and miscarriage.[2] Combining any OTC drugs, prescription drugs, and/or illicit drugs can be unpredictable and may be very dangerous.

Challenge Question: Identify the variables that account for different individual reactions to drugs.

An individual's reaction to drugs is influenced by the environment in which they are used, as well as by personal drug-using experiences. The user anticipation of the drug experience is called **drug expectancy**, wherein an individual either has direct or observational experience with a particular drug, or expects to feel a certain way when using the drug.[3] In a research study on marijuana, subjects who expected to feel mellow and relaxed tended to have that reaction, while those who expected to become anxious and lack control had a more anxiety-producing experience.[4] The **set** and **setting** regarding drug effects on the individual refers to the mental state of the person (set) and the physical and social environment (setting) of the drug-taking experience.[5] Most of the research on set and setting involved hallucinogenic drugs and heroin, but an individual's mental state and environment also have relevance for other drugs. Drug use has a great deal to do with the mental state of the user, possibly including a need to elevate a depressive mood and relieve pain, anxiety, or boredom. The environment for drug use may be socially comfortable and permissive, or may be anxiety-producing and restrictive. Both set and setting, regardless of the drug, will affect the overall drug experience.

Use of illicit drugs alone, in combination with other prescription or illicit drugs, or with alcohol is risky, as there are so many variables. Because illicit drugs are not regulated, the strength of the drug is unknown. An individual's ability to handle a drug physically, mentally, or emotionally is unknown, even if that individual has used the drug before. It is difficult to evaluate this risk, and therefore difficult to be accountable and responsible regarding illicit drug use.

Challenge Question: Describe drug expectancy.

> **Key Terms**
>
> **Synergism**: Synergism occurs when the effect of one drug enhances the effect of another, or of both drugs being used. If a depressant such as alcohol is combined with another depressant, the depressive effect will be greater.
>
> **Drug expectancy**: The expectation a drug user has in regard to feeling certain effects when using a particular drug.
>
> **Set**: Drug effects based on the mental state of the user.
>
> **Setting**: The physical and social environment of the drug-taking experience.

The effect of drugs is also influenced by the properties of the drug. Pharmacological properties include the amount of drug needed to produce an effect, how long the effect will last, and the chemical characteristics of the drug. A different effect is also seen with the amount of the drug taken. An effect may be experienced at a given dose, but in some instances, increasing the dose will not change the effect. For a drug to have an effect, a **therapeutic level** must be achieved. For some drugs, increasing the dose may cause harmful effects, or even death. The onset of drug activity is known as **time-action** function, referring to the amount of time that must pass before the effect of the drug is experienced, and the amount of time that must pass before the effects are lost.

How a drug is administered will affect how strongly and how quickly the effect of the drug will be felt. Administration methods include oral ingestion, injection, transdermal absorption, and drug inhalation. Generally, swallowing a drug results in the slowest response rate, since the drug must pass through the stomach, and possibly the intestinal tract, before it can be absorbed. Drugs can be injected directly into a vein (intravenous), into a muscle (intramuscular), and subcutaneously (under the skin). Of these methods, intravenous injections cause the drug effect to be realized fastest. Transdermal absorption refers to a drug being absorbed through skin tissue—some birth control methods and analgesics are administered this way. Inhaling a drug, either via smoke or snorting, causes the drug to reach the brain more quickly than any other method.

> **Key Terms**
>
> **Therapeutic level**: The amount of a drug that must be taken to achieve a therapeutic reaction.
>
> **Time-action function**: The amount of time elapsed before the effect of a drug is felt, and the amount of time necessary before the effects have worn off.

Categories of Drugs

There are several ways to classify drugs, including whether they are available over the counter, by prescription, or illicitly. In addition, there are drugs that affect the **central nervous system (CNS)** by either depressing or stimulating it, and drugs that greatly alter mood and perceptions of reality. Some drugs can be used without fear of dependency, but others are known to cause dependency and can lead to substance abuse and addiction. The **Food and Drug Administration (FDA)**, an agency under the federal Department of Health and Human Services, regulates food (human and animal), dietary supplements, drugs (human and animal), cosmetics, medical devices (human and animal), and other products sold in the United States. Part of the FDA mandate is to ensure that prescription and over-the-counter drugs contain what they claim to contain, in the amount specified, and in a form that can be used. These products must also produce the identified beneficial effect, any risks associated with the product must be listed, and benefits must always outweigh risks. Although the FDA oversees dietary supplements, that industry is not required to meet the same standards.

> **Key Terms**
>
> **Central nervous system (CNS)**: Made up of the spinal cord and the brain that controls both somatic and autonomic responses, such as respiration, heart rate, and blood pressure.
>
> **Food and Drug Administration (FDA)**: An agency under the federal Department of Health and Human Services that regulates the approval of all prescription and over-the-counter drugs manufactured and sold in the United States.

Over-the-Counter Drugs

Drugs included in the over-the-counter (OTC) category do not require a prescription from a medical provider, and are available for purchase in pharmacies, grocery stores, and other outlets, as well as via the Internet. More than 300,000 OTC drugs are available, and about 75 percent of the population routinely self-medicates with one or more of these drugs. Over-the-counter drugs are considered safe as long as the user follows directions exactly. If an OTC drug is taken in combination with another drug or with alcohol, or in a greater amount than recommended, there could be serious side effects. The only restricted OTC drug is pseudoephedrine, since it can be used to make methamphetamine. The Combat Methamphetamine Epidemic Act of 2005 requires that pharmacies obtain and record the identity of the purchaser and restrict the quantity allowed for purchase.[6] Oregon is currently the only state to require a prescription for pseudoephedrine. Emergency contraception drugs are OTC drugs for women 17 years and older, but they are prescription drugs for younger women.[7]

Challenge Question: Describe the role of pharmacies in the Combat Methamphetamine Epidemic Act of 2005.

Prescription Drugs

Prescription drugs are those that require a written authorization from a medical doctor, dentist, optometrist, and certain other licensed medical practitioners. There are more than 10,000 prescription drugs available in the United States. From Chapter 2, you know that all prescription drugs receive extensive testing for efficacy and safety. However, as with any drug, there is always an element of risk.

Central Nervous System Depressants

Drugs that depress the central nervous system and slow down the neural activities of the brain are sometimes called "downers." These products slow heart rate, breathing, may reduce blood pressure, reduce response time, and may inhibit critical thinking. They are prescribed for the relief of anxiety and irritability, and to sedate or induce sleep. Depressants drugs include alcohol, barbiturates, benzodiazepines, gamma hydroxybyturate (GHB), marijuana, opioids, and inhalants.

Any depressant drug has the potential to cause death when used in large quantity with the exception of marijuana.

Central Nervous System Stimulants

Drugs that stimulate the central nervous system cause a temporary increase in both mental and physical functioning, including alertness, and are sometimes called "uppers." These drugs may accelerate heart rate and blood pressure, reduce appetite, reduce anxiety, and create a feeling of euphoria and increased energy. Stimulant drugs include amphetamine- and methamphetamine-containing drugs, 3,4-methylene dioxymethamphetamine (MDMA), sold as ecstasy, cocaine, crack, hallucinogens, and caffeine and nicotine. Caffeine and nicotine are considered mild to moderate stimulant drugs, depending on the dose. Amphetamines are prescribed for lethargy and fatigue, to reduce sleepiness, including the symptoms of narcolepsy, to decrease appetite and promote weight loss, and for children diagnosed with Attention-Deficit Hyperactivity Disorder (ADHD). Amphetamines are prescription drugs that are sometimes abused, as they can produce a sense of euphoria and may be addictive. Ecstasy, cocaine, crystal methamphetamine, and hallucinogens are powerful illicit stimulant drugs.

Illicit Drugs

Illicit drugs are a large part of the global economy, with an estimated value of $322 billion each year.[8] The main illicit drugs used worldwide are opiates (mostly heroin); cocaine; marijuana, including hashish; and amphetamine-type stimulants (ATS), such as amphetamine, methamphetamine, and MDMA (ecstasy). The United Nations estimates that 200 million people 15–64 years of age use illicit drugs, with 25 million of them considered abusive users.

Challenge Question: Identify the size of the illicit drug contribution to the global economy and name the number one illicit drug in the world.

Marijuana and Hashish

In the U.S., it is estimated that 2.4 million people age 12 and older used marijuana for the first time in the past 12 months, with most new users younger than 18 years. This early first-time use is one explanation for the 18.1 million marijuana users among 18 to 25-year-olds.[9]

Marijuana is derived from the hemp plant **Cannabis sativa**. The flowers, stems, seeds, and leaves are dried, shredded, and smoked as a cigarette (joint) or in a pipe or hookah. The psychoactive ingredient in marijuana is tetrahydrocannabinol (THC), and when marijuana is smoked, THC passes rapidly from the lungs to the blood stream and the brain. To create maximum absorption through the lungs, users inhale and hold marijuana smoke in their lungs as long as possible before exhaling. Hashish is a more concentrated form of marijuana that can be a sticky dark substance, or it may be a more liquid form, called hash oil. It is usually smoked in a small pipe, mixed with leaf marijuana and smoked in a joint, or is sometimes cooked in foods. Although used in other parts of the world, hashish is rarely used in America.

The THC in marijuana affects the parts of the brain related to memory, concentration, sensory and time perceptions, motor control and feelings of pleasure. Although a marijuana high is pleasurable for many people, it also produces memory loss, makes concentration difficult, and can produce distorted perceptions and lack of coordination.[10] Use of marijuana with alcohol causes a synergistic effect of alcohol-related impairments.[11] The effects of marijuana are felt within ten to thirty minutes, and usually wear off within three hours. Marijuana smoke contains 50–70 percent more carcinogenic hydrocarbons, and the tar in marijuana also contains more carcinogens than cigarette smoke. Because of the way it is inhaled, these carcinogens have greater exposure to the lungs. Inhaling the smoke also increases the amount of carbon monoxide in the bloodstream, and because hemoglobin in blood has a greater affinity for carbon monoxide than oxygen, blood carries less oxygen to all organs and tissues. This results in the heart having to work harder to pump oxygen to these oxygen-starved regions.

Although it is an illegal drug in the United States, there are some medical uses for marijuana. Usually prescribed as Marinol and in tablet form, marijuana can enhance appetite, reduce nausea and vomiting, and reduce muscle pain and spasticity caused by multiple sclerosis.

Critical Thinking Question: Describe why marijuana may inhibit academic success.

Opioids

Opioids are a class of drugs derived either naturally or synthetically from opium, the most popular illicit drug in the world. Pure opium use in the U.S. is virtually non-existent, but natural opium derivatives include morphine and codeine, which are used both medically and illicitly. Morphine is the oldest and most common of the natural opioids, used as an analgesic to relieve severe pain. Codeine is the second most common derivative, used as an analgesic, cough suppressant, and antidiarrheal drug.

Synthetic opioids include the drugs fentanyl, a powerful narcotic analgesic 100 times more powerful than morphine—and methadone, an analgesic used in the treatment of opioid dependence. Natural and synthetic opioids are considered psychotherapeutic drugs, producing a euphoric high. It is estimated that 7 million Americans age 12 years and older use illicit psychotherapeutic drugs each year.[12] Opioid drugs can produce dependence when used illegally or when used with a prescription. When the drug is removed, withdrawal symptoms occur and may include any of the following:

- Agitation
- Anxiety
- Muscle aches
- Increased tearing
- Insomnia
- Runny nose
- Sweating
- Yawning

These symptoms usually start within 12 hours of the last dose, and with time progress to:

- Abdominal cramping
- Diarrhea
- Dilated pupils
- Goose bumps
- Nausea and vomiting

Opioid withdrawal symptoms are very uncomfortable, but not life threatening.

Heroin is considered an opioid because it is made from morphine. It is typically a white or brown powder, though it can be a black sticky substance, and it is usually injected, but can also be smoked or snorted. Heroin, used as a recreational drug, has a high risk for addiction, with nearly 23 percent of individuals who use heroin becoming dependent on it.[13] The Bayer Pharmaceutical Company introduced heroin in 1898 as a morphine substitute for individuals who were addicted to codeine cough suppressants and morphine. Heroin was not thought to be addictive when initially introduced, but it quickly produced a higher rate of dependency than morphine. In 2008, 453,000 Americans age 12 or older had used heroin at least once.[14]

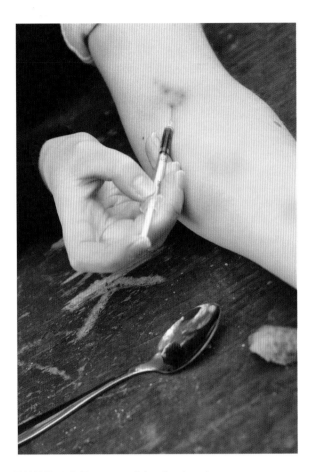

FIGURE 14-3. Drug user injecting heroin.

Aside from reducing or eliminating pain, opioids reduce anxiety and create a feeling of euphoria. As addiction develops, users will forgo most other normal functions so that they can use the drug.

Risks associated with opioid use include fatal overdose, spontaneous abortion, and pulmonary complications, and when injected, there is additional risk of HIV/AIDS, hepatitis, and other infectious diseases. Chronic users may develop collapsed veins, infection of the heart lining and valves, abscesses, and liver or kidney disease.

Psychotherapeutic Drugs

Psychotherapeutic drugs are prescription psychoactive drugs that include pain relievers, tranquilizers, stimulants, and sedatives—prescription drugs that are illicit when used in a nonmedical way. In 2009, there were 2.6 million people age 12 and older that used a psychotherapeutic drug nonmedically for the first time, equating to about 7,000 new users per day, with the average age of 21 years for first use.[15] Pain relievers are the most commonly used drugs, followed by tranquilizers, stimulants, and sedatives. One of the most widely recreationally used drugs in the pain reliever category is oxycodone (trade name Oxy-Contin), an opioid narcotic prescribed to treat moderate to severe pain. Over one-half million individuals used oxycodone nonmedically for the first time in 2009.[16] Side effects with oxycodone abuse include addiction risk, constipation, drowsiness, and shallow respiration. Abusing oxycodone with other drugs can stop breathing and may be fatal.

Barbiturates, including nembutal and amytal, are primarily sedative drugs prescribed for insomnia and anxiety. Because of their potential for both physical and psychological addiction, prescribed barbiturates have been replaced by benzodiazepines, primarily because these are less dangerous in case of overdose. Benzodiazepines, including Valium and Xanax, are depressant medications prescribed for anxiety, panic attacks, and insomnia. This category also includes Rohypnol, known as the "date rape drug," a powerful sedative that impairs motor function and memory and has been used to incapacitate victims of sexual assault.[17] Rohypnol is not legal in the United States, but it is sold in other countries as a treatment for insomnia. Gamma hydroxybutyrate (GHB) is legally available by prescription only, for the treatment of narcolepsy, a sleep disorder. It is an illicit "club drug," frequently used at concerts, parties, and nightclubs, and has also been used as a date rape drug, due to its powerful sedative properties. Despite warnings about the dangers of the drug, some body builders use GHB for the purported increase in human growth hormone it alledgedly provides. Health risks with GHB use include drowsiness, nausea and vomiting, headache, loss of consciousness, loss of reflexes, seizures, coma, and death.

Methamphetamine is a widely used illicit psychotherapeutic stimulant drug that was once prescribed for narcolepsy, depression, alcoholism, arteriosclerosis, and hay fever. It can currently be prescribed for ADHD and obesity under the name Desoxyn. The number of illicit methamphetamine users decreased between 2006 and 2008, but increased in 2009, to over 500,000 users age 12 and older.[18] The drug causes increased heart rate, blood pressure, and metabolism, feelings of exhilaration, energy, and mental alertness. Ongoing use can result in rapid or irregular heartbeat; reduced appetite, leading to weight loss; nervousness; insomnia; and heart failure; and can lead to irritability, delirium, paranoia, and psychosis.

Challenge Question: Identify three psychotherapeutic drugs.

Cocaine and Crack

Cocaine is processed from the leaves of the South American coca plant and has been in use since pre-Columbian times. Historically, the leaves were chewed to reduce fatigue and hunger, promote endurance, and enhance feelings of well-being. In 1855, it was synthesized into a white powder and became available in powder, liquid, and tablet form.

Image of Health in Depth

Cocaine was first synthesized in 1855, but it was not used medicinally until the 1880s. It was highly promoted by famous individuals such as Sigmund Freud, who touted its ability to cure depression and sexual impotence. In the early 1900s, cocaine was widely used by the middle classes and was accepted as a medical treatment for a variety of ailments. Cocaine was also present in the original 1885 formula for Coca-Cola and was an instant success.[19]

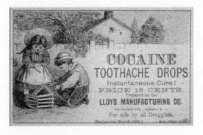

1885 advertisement for cocaine toothache drops.

Today, cocaine is an illicit drug, usually sold as a white powder that can be snorted or mixed with water and injected. Crack cocaine has been processed to make a hard crystal or rock that, when heated, produces vapors that are inhaled. The fastest route of intoxication from cocaine is by either injection or by smoking crack, producing an intense high of fairly short duration, 5–10 minutes. Snorting cocaine does not produce a high of equal intensity to smoking or injecting, but the high lasts longer, from 15–30 minutes. Substance abuse of cocaine and crack is common because the euphoric high is brief and tolerance development for the drug is rapid, encouraging more frequent use of increasing quantity.[20] In 2009, it was estimated that 1.6 million Americans 12 years and older used cocaine or crack, a decline of about ¾ million users from 2006, when it is estimated that there were 2.4 million cocaine users.[21]

Cocaine abuse can lead to heightened temperature, nausea, chest and abdominal pain, respiratory failure, strokes, seizures, and panic attacks.

Hallucinogens

Hallucinogens produce distortions in time, space, and perceptions, and generally include LSD, mescaline, and MDMA. LSD was first synthesized in 1943, and was used as a circulatory and respiratory stimulant. When its hallucinogenic properties became apparent, the United States National Institute of Mental Health funded research studies during the 1960s and 1970s, in order to investigate potential uses for mental health treatments. By 1980, the federal government became concerned that research on LSD was encouraging its use, and discontinued funding. By 1990, when LSD again became popular at certain types of concerts and all-night rave parties, the typical dose was 20 to 80 micrograms, producing a high within 20 to 60 minutes that could last 12 to 24 hours.[22] It causes altered states of perception and feeling; increased body temperature, heart rate, and blood pressure; and persisting perception disorder (flashbacks).

Mescaline is derived from the peyote cactus that grows in southern Texas and Mexico. Because of its bitter taste, mescaline is taken in capsule form, though mescaline powder can also be combined with water and injected. Peyote cactus "buttons" are usually chewed, or they can be boiled to make tea. The taste is extremely bitter and although it can produce a considerable high, it also produces nausea in most people. Other side effects are similar to LSD.

The current most popular hallucinogenic drug is MDMA, sold as ecstasy. Other street names for this drug are Adam, Clarity, Eve, X, and XTC. It is both a stimulant and hallucinogenic drug in pill form, producing distortions in time and space and providing enhanced tactile stimulation. Because ecstasy is an illicit, unregulated drug, there is no consistency in the actual ingredients of each pill. Using MDMA can result in impaired memory and learning, hyperthermia, cardiac and liver toxicity, and renal failure.[23,24,25] Most people who use ecstasy erroneously believe it to be a non-addicting drug. In 2001, a study confirmed that the drug does produce dependence and results in tolerance and withdrawal symptoms.[26]

In 2009, 1.3 million people 12 years and older used hallucinogens, including 760,000 who used ecstasy—an increase of 200,000 ecstasy users, compared to 2008.[27]

Inhalants

Inhalants are industrial, household, and automotive chemicals that can produce psychoactive effects when inhaled. Children and adolescents are the primary abusers of inhalants, since these products are easily available to them. Younger children typically use glue, shoe polish, spray paints, gasoline, and lighter fluid; adolescents commonly use nitrous oxide (whipped cream dispensers, gas cylinders); and adults who use inhalants may use nitrites, also known as "poppers" and include butyl and amyl nitrites, as a sexual enhancer. Inhalants are breathed through the mouth and nose by sniffing or snorting fumes, inhaling fumes from a balloon or plastic bag that contains fumes, or spraying an aerosol directly into the mouth and nose. The practice of inhaling fumes with the intention of getting high is known as "huffing." Intoxication usually lasts just a few minutes, so users often continue huffing, sometimes for hours. In addition to the respiratory distress caused by inhalants, frequent users also suffer from brain damage, hearing loss, bone marrow damage, liver and kidney damage, and limb spasms. In 2009, 600,000 people age 12 and older used inhalants.[28]

FIGURE 14-4. Various types of inhalants.

The Process of Addiction

Just as every human is different in so many ways, the process of drug addiction varies considerably. In the last few years, drug addiction has been recognized as a brain disease, whereas fifty years ago, addictive drug behavior was thought to be a sign of personal weakness, lack of morals, or a propensity to behave outside the usual cultural boundaries of society, allowing for criminal behavior.

Traditional treatment usually involved counseling, more drugs to counter the effect of the abused drugs, and when all else failed, confinement to a drug detoxification or rehabilitation facility. When criminal behavior was involved, detoxification occurred in prison, with little medical intervention. Today, both risk and protective factors for addiction have been developed.

Table 14-1. Examples of Risk and Protective Factors

RISK FACTORS	DOMAIN	PROTECTIVE FACTORS
Early aggressive behavior	Individual	Self-control
Poor social skills	Individual	Positive relationships
Lack of parental supervision	Family	Parental monitoring and support
Substance abuse	Peer	Academic competence
Drug availability	School	Anti-drug use policies
Poverty	Community	Strong neighborhood attachment

(Source: National Institute on Drug Abuse: Drug Abuse and Addiction. Downloaded from http://drugabuse.gov/scienceofaddiction/addiction. html October 29, 2010.)

Addictive Behavior

Drug addiction is a disease that affects both the brain and behavior. Not everyone has the same vulnerability to drugs. There are biological, genetic, and environmental risk factors, plus gender, ethnicity, and stage of development, especially childhood and adolescence.

Although there are many risk factors for drug addiction, no particular risk factor will cause the onset of addictive behavior. Rather, it is the cumulative effect of multiple risk factors that dictates increased risk for addiction. It is estimated that genetic factors account for about 50 percent of vulnerability for addiction, which increases if one or both parents are addicted to drugs, if there was maternal drug use during pregnancy, and if parents suffer from other mental disorders.[29] Drug addiction is a developmental disease that usually begins in childhood or adolescence. Children who are raised in a family where there is drug use, where the home environment is chaotic, and where one or more individuals suffer from mental illness are more likely to use drugs at an early age. The risk increases if their social environment also includes peers who use drugs, or if a person has low self-esteem and poor decision-making skills.

Challenge Question: Identify some of the risk factors for drug addiction.

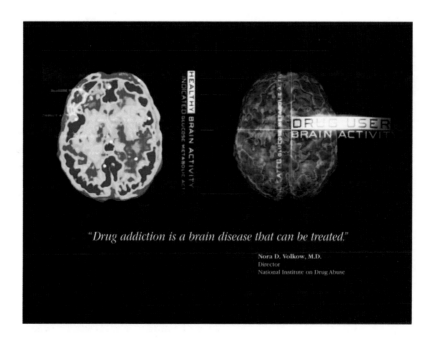

"Drug addiction is a brain disease that can be treated."

Nora D. Volkow, M.D.
Director
National Institute on Drug Abuse

FIGURE 14-5. Healthy brain versus drug user's brain.

(Source: National Institutes of Health, National Institute on Drug Abuse. "Drugs, Brains, and Behavior-The Science of Addiction.")

The decision to take drugs is mostly voluntary, but because drugs change the way the brain works, this can quickly progress to a lack of control, poor decision-making, and destructive and compulsive behavior. This progression can occur at any age, but children and adolescents are particularly vulnerable, since their brains are still developing.

Initially, people take drugs to make themselves feel better, to perform better, or because they are curious about the effects of drugs, and want to experience these effects for themselves. At first, many drugs do produce pleasurable feelings of euphoria. This initial pleasure does not last, however, and when it starts to diminish, the typical protocol for the user is to try more drugs to attempt to reach the pleasure stage again. When drugs cease to have the same euphoric effect, the body and brain have developed a **tolerance** to the drug. More of the drug is then required to try to match the initial feelings of pleasure.

The way drugs are used also indicates degree of risk for addiction. Risk increases if a drug is either smoked or injected, since the drug's effect is almost immediate and the "rush" or euphoric sensation is intense. But the high quickly becomes the low, possibly leading to feelings of depression and lack of self-worth below the threshold of the person's normal feelings.

> **Key Term**
>
> **Tolerance**: When more of a drug is needed to reach the expected effect.

Changes to the Brain

Early drug use is devastating for the developing brain, as it is susceptible to drugs that can alter its development. One critical part of the brain that is still developing during childhood and adolescence is the prefrontal cortex, the part of the brain that controls decision-making, analytical ability, and overall learning ability, and helps modulate emotional development. Early drug use can have immediate effects on brain development and produce changes to the brain that can last a lifetime.

The brain is the most complex organ in the body, consisting of many components that regulate and control all parts of the body. The three main components are the brain stem, the limbic system, and the cerebral cortex, including the prefrontal cortex.

Challenge Question: Why is drug abuse much more devastating for children and adolescents?

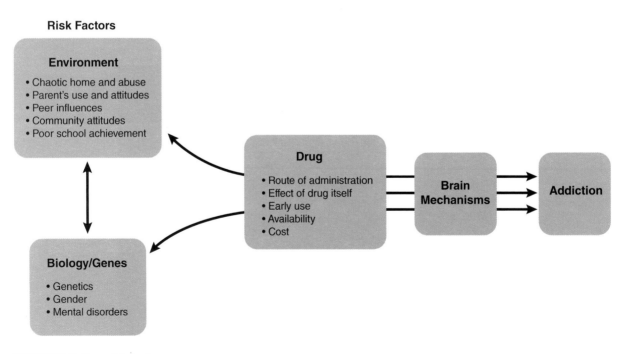

FIGURE 14-6. Drug risk factors.

(Source: National Institute on Drug Abuse (NIDA), The Science of Addiction, Drugs, Brains and Behavior, 2010.)

The **brain stem** controls heart rate, respiration, sleep, and other important functions. The **limbic system** is the reward center of the brain, initiating feelings of pleasure that cause us to want to repeat the behaviors that resulted in these feelings. Drug use can cause the limbic system to over-activate the creation of these intense feelings. Once the reward center is activated, the brain remembers and stimulates the user to repeat the activity, leading to drug abuse. The psychoactive capacities of some drugs also activate both positive and negative emotions in this region. The **cerebral cortex** controls sight, hearing, taste, tactile sensations, and smell, and the prefrontal cortex controls thinking, learning, decision-making, and analytical ability.

Although drugs affect the entire brain, with some drugs, **neurotransmitters** in the limbic system release 2–10 times the amount of **dopamine** than is released with normal pleasurable activity. This changes the pleasure circuits of the brain, producing a powerful motivation to use drugs repeatedly. With recurring drug use, the increase in dopamine will eventually be adjusted by the brain to a lower amount, resulting in depression and listlessness in the drug abuser. As drug using behavior continues, taking drugs becomes a learned behavior impairing cognitive function and resulting in compulsive behavior and addiction.

> **Key Terms**
>
> **Brain stem**: The part of the brain that controls heart rate, respiration, sleep, and other important functions.
>
> **Limbic system**: The reward center of the brain, initiating feelings of pleasure that cause us to want to repeat the behavior, such as eating and sex.
>
> **Cerebral cortex**: The part of the brain that controls sight, hearing, taste, tactile sensations, and smell.
>
> **Neurotransmitters**: Brain chemicals that allow the transmission of signals from one neuron to the next across nerve synapses.
>
> **Dopamine**: A neurotransmitter that plays a major role in drug addiction, as it increases pleasure.

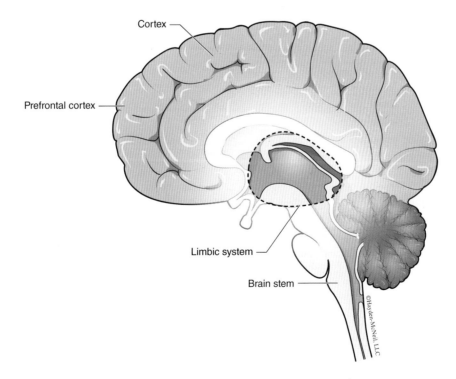

FIGURE 14-7. Three main parts of the brain: cortex (including the prefrontal cortex), limbic system, and brain stem.

Image of Health in Depth

The American Psychiatric Association (APA) Test for Addiction[32]

During the last twelve months:

1. *Have you experienced tolerance to a drug?* Do you need more of the drug or alcohol than previously used to get the same effects?

2. *Have you experienced withdrawal symptoms?* Do you ever use any other substance to prevent withdrawal symptoms?

3. *Have you ever taken more of a drug or alcohol than you had intended?* Did you take the drug for a longer period of time?

4. *Have you tried to reduce or regulate your drug use?* Have you found that you cannot, or that you soon find yourself using at the same level again?

5. *Are you been preoccupied with the drug?* Do you spend a great deal of time obtaining, using, or recovering from the drug?

6. *Have you stopped participating in important social, school, work, or recreational activities?* Is your drug use more important than any of the things that used to give you pleasure?

7. *Have you continued to use drugs in spite of the increasing difficulty drugs cause in your life?* Has your drug use caused relationship, work, and school difficulties? Are drugs causing personal, physical, and mental stress or illness?

Answering yes to three or more questions indicates drug or alcohol dependency, and answering yes to any one question can suggest a risk. Overcoming denial is the first step in recovering. Seeking appropriate help is the second step.

Drug Progression, Dependence, and Codependence

Drug abuse can progressively lead to drug dependence. Risk factors for using drugs include easy access to drugs, family members who use drugs, social acceptance among peers for drug use, low self-esteem, and mental disorders such as depression, anxiety, or bipolar disorders. The progressive stages that may lead to drug dependence include:

- *Experimenting.* When drugs are used recreationally, to be accepted by peers or to defy parents.

- *Regular use.* Drug use causes the individual to miss school or work, avoid family and friends, worry about losing their drug source, establish new friendships with drug users, and develop a tolerance to the drug.

- *Daily preoccupation.* The user stops caring about school, work, family, and friends, and becomes preoccupied with using drugs, obtaining drugs, and may sell drugs to support increased use.

- *Dependence.* The user cannot endure daily life without using drugs. Drug use may be compulsive, causing a lack of control that can result in physical, legal, and financial problems. The user is often estranged from family and friends.[33]

Codependency frequently occurs in families and relationships when one of the individuals is dependent on drugs. Codependency is learned behavior, occurring in dysfunctional families in which there is drug abuse, alcohol abuse, or physical, emotional, or sexual abuse. Codependency involves a partner, spouse, or family member who is a caretaker for the individual who is the source of the abuse, or ill from drug use. This codependent behavior can be compulsive when the caretaker places the needs of the drug dependent person before their own, resulting in a lack of attention for their own needs. In a dysfunctional relationship or family, the attention and concern is on the individual who is dependent, or who is the abuser. Codependent individuals believe that love, security, and approval depend on their ability to take care of this person. They will do more than their share of the work all the time, will do anything to hold on to a relationship to avoid feeling abandoned, often have a lack of trust, have difficulty identifying their feelings, and are hurt when their caretaking efforts are not recognized.[34]

Motivation Maximizer

Should You Use Drugs?

Choosing to use drugs is really a personal decision, and is entirely up to you. You may have accepted responsibility for much of your health and wellness, such as improving your diet, maintaining weight, getting exercise, learning how to manage stress, and knowing the risk factors for chronic diseases. You may also have modified a behavior that has made a positive change in your life, such as quitting smoking. To be accountable for personal drug use means that you identify your current use. Do you smoke marijuana, as do about 20 percent of college-aged students? Do you recreationally use psychotherapeutic drugs, such as OxyContin? Do you spend your free time using drugs recreationally? Does your social life consistently involve experiences with drugs and/or alcohol? If the answer is yes to any of these questions, you may consider how much affect this is having on your life. You may also consider your reasons for attending college.

Is your parental support contingent upon you staying in school? Are you in college because your friends are? Are you mostly interested in the social aspect of college, as a way to meet people and go to parties? Or are you determined to get a college degree? If a college degree is your goal, consider how drug-taking behavior may affect this goal. Although marijuana may relax you and make you feel good, it also inhibits your cognitive abilities. Your ability to read something and remember it, your ability to analytically think through a math or physics problem, your ability to write a paper for an English assignment are all diminished by smoking marijuana. It seems unlikely that smoking marijuana will help you reach your goals when college success is dependent on cognitive abilities. Drug use is a personal decision that must be made by each person. You may be home studying while your friends are out partying and using drugs. Accepting responsibility for personal behavior and being accountable for whether you choose drugs is an important part of self-care. Your future is determined by the choices you make, and the most responsible choices lead to the brightest future.

Treatment Options

There have been many improvements in drug treatment over the past thirty years. Drug addiction is now recognized as a brain disease, a complex illness that affects each individual differently. Although it is true that initial drug use is voluntary, the progression from compulsive abuse to addiction is beyond the ability of the individual to control, even when the consequences are devastating. Controlling an addiction that affects the brain so profoundly is complicated, and to be successful, an individual must have a treatment program that addresses their particular needs. For example, in addition to a drug addiction, the individual may also have a mental or physical illness. Because they are all interrelated, successful treatment must consider the complete physical and mental health of the individual in addition to the drug addiction.

Image of Health in Depth

The National Institute on Drug Abuse: Principles of Effective Treatment

1. Addiction is a complex but treatable disease that affects brain function and behavior.

2. No single treatment is appropriate for everyone.

3. Treatment must be readily available.

4. Effective treatment attends to multiple needs of the individual, not just his or her drug abuse.

5. Remaining in treatment for an adequate period of time is critical.

6. Counseling—individual and/or group—and other behavioral therapies are the most commonly used forms of drug abuse treatment.

7. Medications are an important element of treatment for many patients, especially when combined with counseling and other behavioral therapies.

8. An individual's treatment and services plan must be assessed continually and modified as necessary, to ensure that it meets his or her changing needs.

9. Many drug-addicted individuals also have other mental disorders.

10. Medically assisted detoxification is only the first stage of addiction treatment, and by itself does little to change long-term drug abuse.

11. Treatment does not need to be voluntary to be effective.

12. Drug use during treatment must be monitored continuously, as lapses during treatment do occur.

National Institute on Drug Abuse, 2009.[35]

Self-Help Options

When an individual seeks self-help options for a drug dependency, an important first step for recovery has occurred—acknowledgement that a drug dependency is having a negative impact on life. There are many self-help options, and many are modeled on the 12-step program for alcohol, Alcoholics Anonymous (AA). The AA program provides continuous support, viewing addiction as a disease that requires lifelong abstinence from all substances. Other self-help groups include Narcotics Anonymous (NA), Cocaine Anonymous (CA), Self-Management and Recovery Training (SMART Recovery), and Women for Sobriety (WFS).

Outpatient and Inpatient Therapies

The federal Substance Abuse and Mental Health Services Administration tracks drug treatment admissions for state facilities that are licensed and certified to provide treatment for substance abuse and who receive state and federal funding. The data collected, Treatment Episode

Data Set (TEDS), records admission data, not individual data; therefore, a person who had two treatment episodes in a calendar year is counted as two admissions. In 2007, there were 1.8 million admissions to state and federal drug and alcohol treatment centers. Alcohol accounted for 40 percent of admissions, and four drugs accounted for most of the remainder: opiates (mostly heroin), at 19 percent; marijuana and hashish, 16 percent; cocaine and crack, 13 percent; and stimulant drugs, primarily methamphetamine, 8 percent. Of the 1.8 million admissions, 62 percent received outpatient treatment, 20 percent were admitted to detoxification clinics, and 18 percent entered a residential rehabilitation treatment center.[36] More than one-third of admissions were referred through the criminal justice system, primarily for marijuana and methamphetamine abuse. There are also a large number of private drug rehabilitation treatment centers that are not reflected in federal and state admission data.

Inpatient treatment centers may use drugs during detoxification to help with the withdrawal process. Following detoxification, patients undergo individual and group therapy, must typically attend a 12-step program, and may be involved in family therapy sessions, as well. Length of treatment varies, but most average about 30 days. Following in-patient treatment, recovering addicts are often advised to enter a halfway facility, where they live with other recovering addicts in a supporting, therapeutic environment. This second stage of treatment may last six months or more.

Relapse

Relapse is not uncommon, and it may take many attempts at recovery before the addict becomes resolute in staying drug-free and sober. Addicts often set up their own relapse episodes, as their thinking changes from "I have an addiction problem" to "I don't have a problem and can use drugs recreationally." Along with this denial, addicts may stop attending support group meetings, may cease to interact with someone who is sponsoring their recovery, and may return to situations that foster drug use. Treatment programs emphasize the risk of relapse, working with addicts to develop a plan so they might recognize symptoms and be able to respond appropriately. Without a plan, addicts are more likely to relapse. Relapse prevention requires a reminder to the addict that they are vulnerable, that the disease is lifelong, and it provides redirection to the recovery strategies that have worked for them.

Responsibility and Accountability

Taking Responsibility for Drug Use

It is important to have knowledge about the wide array of drugs, both legal and illicit, that are available to the consumer, and to know the risks and benefits of anything you choose to use. It is your responsibility to follow the directions for prescription drugs and to pay attention to the recommended dose for OTC drugs. The choice to take illicit drugs should include a thoughtful process where you examine the pros and cons of intended drug-taking behavior and consider the possible consequences. Individuals who struggle with substance abuse and addiction began the path to addiction by making the decision to voluntarily take drugs. Taking drugs is a choice that requires both knowledge and responsibility. It is a choice only you can make.

Focusing on Accountability

Accountability for a drug user means you have made the decision to use drugs, and must now accept the consequences for that decision. Many drugs are prescribed for various ailments, requiring accountability for taking the proper dose at the appropriate interval. If you forget to take a prescription or stop the prescription before you should, it shows a lack of accountability. When prescriptions drugs are used for a non-medical reason, there is a lack of accountability for self-care because of the potential for a harmful effect. If the drug user has reached the point at which a drug is abused, it becomes difficult to be accountable, as chemical changes in the brain have made the decision to quit or cut down impossible. However, if an individual who is abusing drugs seeks help, it demonstrates personal accountability for a drug abuse problem.

Summary

Drug Use

- An estimated 2.8 million Americans use illicit drugs.

- The most used illicit drug in the U.S. is marijuana.

- Drugs of choice for 18–25-year-olds are marijuana, psychotherapeutics, cocaine, and hallucinogens.

- College graduates and those with some college are less likely to use illicit drugs than high school graduates.

- Drugs affect people in different ways depending on body size, metabolism, presence of other drugs in the body, pregnancy, and expectation of drug effects.

- Combining drugs is dangerous and may increase the effect of both drugs, cancel the effect of one or both drugs, or cause an unexpected negative reaction.

- Drug expectancy is expecting to feel a certain way, based on personal experience or observation, after taking a drug.

- The "set" is the mental state of the person using drugs.

- The "setting" is the physical and social environment for the drug-taking experience.

- The ability of an individual to handle a drug either physically, mentally, or emotionally is unknown, even if the drug has been used before.

- Stimulant and depressant drugs differ according to how they affect the central nervous system.

Categories of Drugs

- The Food and Drug Administration (FDA) regulates the approval for manufacture and sale of all drugs in the U.S.

- Over-the-counter (OTC) drugs are available without a prescription.

- The Combat Methamphetamine Epidemic Act of 2005 restricts the sale of pseudoephedrine, because it is an ingredient for making methamphetamine.

- The Prescription Drug Marketing Act of 1987 is a federal law that regulates the safety and effectiveness of prescription drugs.

- Prescription drugs require a written authorization from a medical doctor, dentist, optometrist, or limited other medical practitioners.

- Depressant drugs include alcohol, barbiturates, benzodiazepines, gamma hydroxybutyrate (GHB), marijuana, opioids, and inhalants.

- Stimulants include caffeine, nicotine, amphetamines, ecstasy (MDMA), cocaine, crack, and hallucinogens.

- Illicit drugs are a large part of the global economy, with a value of $322 billion each year.

- The psychoactive ingredient in marijuana is tetrahydrocannabinol (THC).

- Opioids are drugs derived either naturally or synthetically from opium, the most popular illicit drug in the world.

- Morphine and codeine are natural opioids.

- The synthetic opioid Fentanyl is 100 times more powerful than morphine.

- Heroin is considered an opioid because it is made from morphine.

- Psychotherapeutic drugs are psychoactive prescription drugs that include pain relievers, tranquilizers, stimulants, and sedatives.

- Methamphetamine is a widely used illicit psychotherapeutic stimulant drug that at one time was prescribed for narcolepsy, depression, alcoholism, arteriosclerosis, and hay fever.

- Cocaine is an illicit stimulant drug that is usually sold as a white powder that can be snorted or mixed with water and injected.

- Crack is cocaine that has been processed to make a hard crystal or rock that when heated, produces vapors that are inhaled.

- Hallucinogens produce psychoactive distortions in time, space, and perception, and include the drugs lysergic acid diethylamide (LSD), mescaline, and ecstasy (MDMA).

- Inhalants are industrial, household, and automotive chemicals that when inhaled can produce psychoactive effects.

The Process of Addiction

- Drug addiction is a disease that affects both brain and behavior.

- Not everyone has the same vulnerability to drugs.

- Risk factors for addiction are biologic, genetic, environmental, plus gender, ethnicity, and stage of development, especially childhood and adolescence.

- The decision to take drugs is voluntary.

- Drugs change the way the brain works, and drug use can quickly progress to a lack of control, poor decision-making, and destructive and compulsive behavior.

- Children and adolescents are vulnerable to addiction because their brains are still developing.

- Tolerance to a drug has developed when more of the drug is needed to get the desired effect.

- Drug use changes the brains of children and adolescents, inhibiting decision- making, analytical ability, overall learning ability, and emotional development.

- The limbic system of the brain is the reward center, initiating feelings of pleasure that are activated when drugs are taken.

- Risk factors for using drugs include easy access to drugs, family members who use drugs, social acceptance among peers for drug use, low self-esteem, and mental disorders such as depression, anxiety, or bipolar disorders.

- Codependent individuals believe that love, security, and approval depend on their ability to take care of the drug abuser.

Treatment Options

- Treatment for drugs must address the particular needs of the addict, including any other mental or physical illness.

- There are many self-help options for drug abuse, most based on the Alcoholics Anonymous (AA) model that requires lifelong abstinence from all substances.

- Living in a halfway house for a period of time may follow inpatient treatment.

- Relapse is not uncommon, and many addicts facilitate their own path to relapse.

Vocabulary Challenge

Match the term in the left-hand column with its correct definition in the right-hand column.

TERM	DEFINITION
Psychoactive	A. Drugs that are made from the juice of the opium poppy
Illicit	B. A drug that alters mood or behavior
Hallucinogens	C. The reward center of the brain that initiates feelings of pleasure
Drug Expectancy	D. Belief that love, security, and approval depend on ability to take care of the drug abuser
Opioids	E. The hallucinogen lysergic acid diethylamide
THC	F. Unlawful; not allowed by law
Psychotherapeutic	G. The expected effect of a drug based on observation or experience
LSD	H. Tetrahydrocannabinol, the psychoactive ingredient in marijuana
Limbic System	I. Psychoactive drugs that include pain relievers, tranquilizers, stimulants, and sedatives
Codependence	J. Drugs that can cause distortions in time, space, and perceptions

Answers:
B; F; J; G; A; H; I; E; C; D

Reassessing Your Knowledge

1. How would you describe the drug-taking behavior of Americans?

2. How would you describe the primary difference between stimulants and depressants?

3. What advice would you give a friend who asked about ecstasy?

4. What changes occur in the brain with drug abuse?

5. What treatment options would you recommend to someone who wants to reduce his marijuana use?

To answer these questions, you might choose to work in groups with your colleagues. Check your answers against the written material in the text, and reread those sections where you made errors.

Health Assessment Toolbox

Club Drugs
Information about drugs classified as club drugs.
http://www.clubdrugs.org/

National Institute on Drug Abuse
http://www.drugabuse.gov/nidahome.html

Office of National Drug Control Policy
http://www.whitehousedrugpolicy.gov/

The National Center on Addiction and Substance Abuse at Columbia University
http://www.casacolumbia.org/templates/Home.aspx?articleid=287&zoneid=32

U.S. Drug Enforcement Administration. Drugs of concern.
http://www.justice.gov/dea/index.htm

Exploring the Internet

Cocaine Anonymous
http://www.ca.org

Codependents Anonymous
http://www.coda.org

Drug Enforcement Administration: Drugs of Abuse
http://www.dea.gov/concern/concern.htm

Marijuana Anonymous
http://www.marijuana-anonymous.org

Narcotics Anonymous
http://www.na.org

National Institute on Drug Abuse
http://www.drugabuse.gov

Substance Abuse and Mental Health Services Administration
http://www.samhsa.gov

Selected References

1. U.S. Department of Health and Human Services, The National Survey on Drug Use and Health (NSDUH), 2006–2008.

2. The American Congress of Obstetricians and Gynecologists, Tobacco, Alcohol, Drugs, and Pregnancy, 2008.

3. Maisto, S., Galizio, M., and Connors, G. *Drug Use and Abuse*. Thompson Learning, Inc. 2008.

4. Orcutt, J. Differential Association and Marijuana Use: A Closer Look at Sutherland (With a Little Help From Becker). *Criminology,* 24: 341–58. May 1987.

5. Zinberg, N. *Drug, Set and Setting*. Yale University Press, 1984.

6. Combat Methamphetamine Epidemic Act of 2005, Department of Justice, Drug Enforcement Administration, Office of Diversion Control, 2006.

7. U.S. Department of Health and Human Services, Food and Drug Administration, Plan B and Plan B One-Step Tablets Information, 2006.

8. United Nations Office on Drugs and Crime, World Drug Report, 2007.

9. U.S. Department of Health and Human Services, Results from the 2009 National Survey on Drug Use and Health, 2010.

10. National Institutes of Health, National Institute on Drug Abuse (NIDA), InfoFacts: Marijuana, 2009.

11. Perez-Reyes, M., Hicks, R.E., Bumberry, J., Jeffcoat, A.R., and Cook, C.E. Interaction Between Marihuana and Ethanol: Effects on Psychomotor Performance. *Alcohol Clinical Experimental Research,* 12(2): 268–76. 1988.

12. U.S. Department of Health and Human Services, Results from the 2009 National Survey on Drug Use and Health, 2010.

13. National Institutes of Health, National Institute on Drug Abuse, NIDA InfoFacts: Heroin. March, 2010.

14. U.S. Department of Health and Human Services, Results from the 2009 National Survey on Drug Use and Health, 2010.

15. Ibid.

16. MedicineNet: Rohypnol, The Date Rape Drug, National Women's Health Center. Downloaded October 13, 2010.

17. U.S. Department of Health and Human Services, Results from the 2009 National Survey on Drug Use and Health, 2010.

18. Pendergrast, M. *For God, Country, and Coca Cola: The Definitive History of the Great American Soft Drink and the Company That Makes It.* Basic Books, 2000.

19. National Institutes of Health, National Institute on Drug Abuse, NIDA InfoFacts: Cocaine. March, 2010.

20. Ibid.

21. U.S. Department of Justice, Drug Enforcement Administration, Office of Diversion Control, D-Lysergic Acid Diethylanmide. 2007.

22. Bolla, K.I., McCann, U.D., and Ricaurte, G.A. Memory Impairment in Abstinent MDMA ("Ecstasy") Users. *Neurology,* 51: 1532–1537. 1998.

23. Nimmo, S.M., Kennedy, B.W., Tullett, W.M., Blyth, A.S., and Dougall, J.R. Drug-Induced Hyperthermia. *Anaesthesia,* 48(10): 892–895. 1993. doi:10.1111/j.1365-2044.1993.tb07423.x. PMID 7902026.

24. Malberg, J.E., and Seiden, L.S. Small Changes in Ambient Temperature Cause Large Changes in 3,4-methylenedioxymethamphetamine (MDMA)-Induced Serotonin Neurotoxicity and Core Body Temperature in the Rat. *Journal of Neuroscience,* 18(13): 5086–5094. PMID 96345. 1998.

25. In-Hei Hahn, MD, FACEP. University Hospital of Columbia, University College of Physicians and Surgeons. Toxicity, MDMA. eMedicine Specialities—*Emergency Medicine.* Downloaded October 29, 2010, from http://emedicine.medscape.co/article/821572-overview

26. Cottler, L.B., Womack, S.B., Compton, W.M., and Ben-Abdallah, A. Ecstasy Abuse and Dependence Among Adolescents and Young Adults: Applicabilityand Reliability of DSM-IV criteria. *Human Psychopharmacology: Clinical and Experimental,* 16(8): 599–606. December, 2001.

27. National Institutes of Health, National Institute on Drug Abuse, NIDA InfoFacts: Cocaine, March, 2010.

28. National Institutes of Health, National Institute on Drug Abuse, NIDA InfoFacts: Inhalants, March, 2010.

29. Ibid.

30. U.S. Department of Health and Human Services, National Institute on Drug Abuse (NIDA), The Science of Addiction, Drugs, Brains and Behavior, 2010.

31. American Psychiatric Association, Diagnostic and Statistical Manual of Mental Disorders, Fourth Edition, Washington D.C.: American Psychiatric Association, 2000.

32. National Institutes of Health, Medline Plus, Drug Dependence, 2010.

33. Mental Health America, Factsheet: Co-dependency, Downloaded October, 2010.

34. U.S. Department of Health and Human Services, National Institute on Drug Abuse (NIDA), Principles of Drug Addiction and Treatment, 2009.

35. U.S. Department of Health and Human Services, Substance Abuse and Mental Health Services Administration, Treatment Episode Data Set (TEDS) Highlights—2007, February, 2009.

Unit Six

Personal Safety and End of Life

Chapter 15
Unintentional and Intentional Injury

Chapter 16
Aging, Death, and Dying

Image of Health

Unintentional and Intentional Injury

PROTECTING YOURSELF

- Increasing Awareness
- Evaluating Risk

UNINTENTIONAL INJURIES

- Home Injuries
  - Falls
  - Poisoning
  - Fires
  - Choking/Airway Obstruction
  - Drowning
- Motor Vehicle Injuries
- Recreational Injuries
- Work-Related Injuries
- Firearm Injuries

INTENTIONAL INJURIES

- Intimate Partner Violence
- Child Abuse and Elder Abuse
- Stalking
- Workplace Violence
- Hate Crimes
- Self-Harm
- Gang Violence
- Homicide

RESPONSIBILITY AND ACCOUNTABILITY

- Taking Responsibility for Injuries
- Focusing on Accountability

Student Learning Outcomes

LEARNING OUTCOME	APPLYING IT TO YOUR LIFE
Describe how to evaluate the level of risk in relationships, home, family, and community.	Evaluate if there is risk in your own relationship, home, family, and community.
Identify the number one cause of home injuries.	Describe how you can improve safety in your own home.
Identify the age group most likely to be involved in a motor vehicle crash.	Describe some ways that you can improve your own safety in a motor vehicle.
Describe some characteristics of communities that promote violence.	Evaluate your own community and determine if there are components that make it unsafe.
Describe why gangs are a concern for public safety.	Evaluate the risk of gangs in your community.

Assessing Your Knowledge

1. What is the number one unintentional home injury?
   a. Falls
   b. Burns
   c. Poisoning
   d. Choking

2. If someone is choking in a restaurant, the first thing you should do is:
   a. Start CPR immediately.
   b. Call 911.
   c. Ask the person if he is choking.
   d. Perform the Heimlich maneuver.

3. Traumatic brain injury (TBI) occurs most frequently in a:
   a. Football game.
   b. Motor vehicle crash.
   c. Horseback riding fall.
   d. Falls.

4. Domestic abuse and assault:
   a. Only occurs in poor socioeconomic communities.
   b. Occurs because the victim provoked the attacker.
   c. Occurs when women are too assertive.
   d. Can occur in every socioeconomic community.

5. In most cases of rape, the rapist is:
   a. A known sexual predator.
   b. Known by the victim.
   c. A stranger to the victim.
   d. Oversexed and can't help his behavior.

Answers:
1. a; 2. c; 3. d; 4. d; 5. b.

Protecting Yourself

Responsibility for unintentional and intentional injuries begins by determining how you can protect yourself. In some cases this is easy, simply being aware and learning how to evaluate risk, and especially how to avoid an **unintentional injury**. But in other situations, particularly relationships or family violence that may result in **intentional injury**, knowing what to do and learning how to evaluate risk is more difficult. Much family and relationship violence results from the dynamics of a **dysfunctional family**. This dysfunction may be the result of many factors, including a history of violence, drugs and alcohol, or mental illness. If your childhood was spent in a dysfunctional family, you may not have been particularly aware of the level of dysfunction as a child. But as an adult, it is important to evaluate and understand the dynamics of your childhood family, since it will affect your adult relationships and family.

Key Terms

Unintentional injury: An injury that occurs without anyone intending harm.

Intentional injury: An injury that occurs when harm is intended.

Dysfunctional family: A family where conflict, misbehavior, and abuse occur continually and regularly, creating a climate that diminishes the emotional and physical health and well-being of family members.

Increasing Awareness

Unintentional injuries can be alleviated in part by increasing awareness of the environment in which you live, in order to make this environment safer for yourself and for those you care about. The types of injuries that are considered unintentional include injuries from motor vehicles, falls, being struck or hit by a person, overexertion, drowning, choking, concussion, fireworks, bicycles, and motorcycles. The most common unintentional injury in almost every age group is falls, though the type of fall and environment where the fall occurs changes as age increases. In childhood and adolescence, falls occur from bicycles, skateboards, ice skates, snowboards, skis, and during sports participation. As age increases, falls are more common in the home, including falling from ladders, in the bath, down the stairs, tripping on rugs, and falling on slippery surfaces such as patios.

Increasing awareness about intentional injuries means recognizing the signs of abuse, including child abuse, relationship abuse, or elder abuse. It means knowing the characteristics of a dysfunctional family so that family violence is recognized and treated as abnormal. Family violence may include physical and sexual abuse, but can also include verbal and psychological abuse. Recognizing and acknowledging destructive behavior may help alleviate intentional injuries, which includes battering, shaking, punching, piercing, cutting, burning, assault, rape, and murder.

Critical Thinking Question: Identify possible sources for both intentional and unintentional injuries in your life.

Evaluating Risk

Falls, the number one unintentional injury, are an inevitable part of childhood. Evaluating risk and employing safety measures can help reduce these incidences: wearing a helmet and other protective equipment offers protection from bicycle falls, skateboard falls, ski and snowboard falls, and from playing contact sports. Wearing seatbelts, driving at the speed limit, employing water safety procedures, and knowing first aid helps reduce risk. Evaluating potential risks in the home and devising safety measures can help alleviate home falls.

Evaluating the risk when there is potential for violence or intentional injury is possible, though it is more difficult because, in a relationship, there is an emotional bond between the abuser and victim. This bond may include love, but is more likely related to control, intimidation, and fear. Risk assessment for violence must also account for other variables, such as drug and alcohol abuse, mental illness, adolescence, and codependency.

Unintentional Injuries

Unintentional injuries are the number one cause of death in the U.S. for individuals age 0 to 44 years.[1] An injury refers to physical damage to the body from an external cause, resulting from a traumatic event or poisoning.[2] Falls are the most common injury for all ages, with the exception of those in the 15- to 24-year age group, wherein being struck or hit by a human, animal, or inanimate object other than a vehicle or machinery is the most common cause.

Motivation Maximizer

Assessing Risk

Many unintentional injuries occur when an individual performs a task or participates in an activity that has considerable risk without acknowledging or evaluating this risk. For example, there has been a 50 percent increase in falls from ladders over the past few years, resulting in more than 2.1 million visits to a hospital emergency room. This usually happens because the ladder is unsafe for the activity or it is used in an inappropriate way.[3]

Assessing risk is part of self-care and personal responsibility. It involves determining the things in your life that have a certain level of risk and planning to reduce that risk. For many college students, one of the major risks is unsafe driving. College students may put car safety maintenance at the bottom of the expenses list; they may drive too fast, drive after drinking, and not insist that all passengers wear seat belts. Each of these risks is easy to control, even eliminate, simply by making responsible choices. One way to motivate yourself might be to ask if you would want your child to make the same choices you have made.

Unintentional injuries are not accidents, and most could be prevented by individual behavior change.

Generally, the ability to accurately evaluate risk is proportionate to age—the older you are, the better able you are to assess risk. This is also influenced by other life responsibilities. As you get older, the decisions you make about risky behaviors do not only affect you, they also affect others. If you are a typical 16-year-old male, the thought of skydiving may be exhilarating. If you are a 36-year-old male with a family, the thought of skydiving may sound like fun, but a personal risk assessment may prevent your participation. This is not about reluctance to have fun, it is about who will take care of your family if you are injured or die in a skydiving incident.

To assess risk in your own life, think about the things you like to do for enjoyment. How many of those things have an element of risk? What can you do to reduce or eliminate that risk? Are you prepared to be accountable for an unintentional injury as a result of your participation in a risky behavior? Who else in your life will be affected if you are injured or die? Only you can answer these questions. Taking responsibility for personal risk and being accountable for risky behavior can greatly reduce the number of unintentional injuries. It can make a big difference in the quantity and quality of your life.

Challenge Question: Describe why unintentional injuries are not accidents.

Home Injuries

Injuries in the home and during recreational activities are not accidents, since most can be prevented. Common injuries that occur in the home are falls, poisoning, fires, choking or airway obstruction, and drowning.

Falls

Each year, falls are the number one cause of nonfatal injuries from childhood through adolescence, with approximately 8000 emergency room visit per day or 2.8 million injured children per year. Some prevention tips are:

1. Ensure playground equipment is safe.

2. Improve home safety with handrails, guardrails, and stair gates.

3. Improve sports safety by ensuring that protective equipment is worn.

4. Supervise young children at home and at play.[4]

Falls among older adults, those age 65 and older, account for moderate to severe injuries, including hip fractures and head trauma. One in three adults age 65 and older experiences a fall each year. Up to 30 percent of individuals who fall suffer severe injuries, and almost half of fatal falls are the result of **traumatic brain injury (TBI)**. In 2008, 2.1 million older adults were treated in emergency departments for nonfatal falls, and almost 600,000 were hospitalized.[5] Falls for older adults are the primary cause of nonfatal traumatic brain injury, accounting for more than 80,000 emergency department visits each year by adults over 65 years. Three out of four of these individuals will require hospitalization.[6]

Key Term

Traumatic brain injury: An injury that occurs when an external force traumatically injures the brain.

Image of Health in Depth

Traumatic Brain Injury

Traumatic Brain Injuries (TBIs) can be mild to severe, occurring when there is a bump or blow to the head, or if there is a penetrating head injury. A mild TBI may have few symptoms, but can include a brief lapse of consciousness, change in behavior or mood swings, headaches, lightheadedness, dizziness, blurred vision, and trouble with memory and concentration. A severe TBI can result in an extended period of unconsciousness and amnesia, and may include repeated vomiting, convulsions or seizures, inability to wake from sleep, slurred speech, loss of coordination, and increased confusion. After initial unconsciousness, a severe TBI can present symptoms weeks or months later, possibly causing lifelong disability.[7]

There are over 1.7 million TBIs each year in the U.S. Some TBIs occur in a motor vehicle crash, so it is imperative to wear a seatbelt while driving or riding in an automobile. Infants and children should be in the back seat, in an approved infant or child safety seat. Wearing a protective helmet while cycling, skiing, snowboarding or skateboarding, and horseback riding can prevent some TBIs.[8]

Challenge Question: Describe the characteristics of a mild TBI.

Poisoning

Poison Control Center Number

In the event of poisoning, call **1-800 222-1222** or **911**

A poison is any harmful substance that can be eaten, inhaled, injected, or absorbed through the skin. Poisoning is the second leading cause of home injury, and most unintentional poisoning deaths are the result of prescription drugs, especially opioid pain medications and benzodiazepines, such as Valium. This poisoning may be the result of an accidental overdose of a prescribed medication, or recreational or nonmedical use of a psychotherapeutic drug. A poisonous substance can be an illicit, prescription, or over-the-counter drug. Cocaine and heroin overdose account for the remainder of unintentional poisoning deaths. About 75 people die in the United States each day as a result of unintentional poisoning, and another 2,000 are treated in a hospital emergency department.[9]

Intentional poisoning occurs either when a person takes a substance to cause self-harm (suicide) or gives a substance with the intent to harm another person (homicide). If the intent is unclear, the poisoning is considered an undetermined intent. About 10 percent of poisoning deaths in 2005 were of undetermined intent.[10]

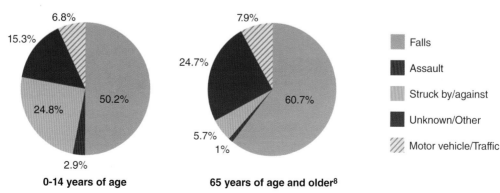

Estimated average percentage of annual traumatic brain injury by external cause, United States, 2002–2006

0-14 years of age: 6.8%, 15.3%, 24.8%, 2.9%, 50.2%

65 years of age and older[8]: 7.9%, 24.7%, 5.7%, 1%, 60.7%

Legend: Falls, Assault, Struck by/against, Unknown/Other, Motor vehicle/Traffic

FIGURE 15-1. Estimated traumatic brain injury in the U.S.

(Source: CDC Traumatic Brain Injury in the United States, PDF page 19. http://www.cdc.gov/traumaticbraininjury/pdf/blue_book.pdf)

Each year, more than 136,000 infants and children from birth to age 19 are treated in a hospital emergency room for poisoning, and over 700 die from the poisoning incident. Many items in the home can be poisonous, and active children often investigate and taste products such as household cleaners, medicines, rodent and ant poisons, and drain cleaners. Removing expired medicine from the home and eliminating access to household chemicals will help to reduce risk. If young children are in the home, the poison control center number should be posted near a phone, and cabinets and cupboards should be locked to prevent child access.

Fires

The number of fatalities from fires has declined over the past several years but deaths from fires is still the third cause of fatal home injury. Cooking causes most residential fires, but most fire-related fatalities are caused by smoke inhalation and toxic gases, not burns. In 2009, there were 377,000 home fires in the U.S., causing 2,565 fatalities and 13,050 injuries. More than half of the fire deaths occurred in homes that did not have smoke detectors.[11]

The risk for home fires can be reduced by following these guidelines:

1. Cook with care. Never leave food unattended while cooking. Keep all flammable items, such as potholders and dishtowels, away from the stove.

2. Do not allow smoking in the home, and never empty burning or hot ashes of any kind into a trash receptacle.

3. Space heaters can ignite bedding and clothing. They should be kept at least three feet away from all flammable materials, and should not be left unattended, as they can overheat and catch fire.

4. Smoke alarms should be installed in every hallway and room, including the basement. They should be tested monthly and their batteries changed at least twice each year.

5. Candles should be placed on a nonflammable tray and never left unattended.

6. A spark guard screen should be placed over the opening of a fireplace, and nonflammable material should be used around the fireplace opening.

7. Every family should have a fire escape plan that they practice. This includes knowing the drop, roll, and crawl routine for exiting. Drop to the floor, roll over the floor if any part of you is on fire, and crawl as low as you can to the exit to avoid smoke inhalation. Agree on a place for family members to meet after escaping a fire.

Choking/Airway Obstruction

Choking and airway obstruction are a frequent cause of home fatalities. Choking can result in an airway obstruction, sometimes called an acute upper airway obstruction, occurring when there is a blockage in the trachea, voice box, or throat. Airway obstructions have occurred with food, peanuts or other nuts, pieces of a balloon, buttons, coins or small toys, all causing an actual physical blockage. An airway obstruction can also occur from allergic reactions to a bee sting, antibiotics, or other medications, possibly causing the throat to swell closed. When the throat constricts due to an allergic reaction and breathing becomes difficult, the person may be experiencing **anaphylactic shock** and will need immediate emergency attention.

Abdominal thrusts, known as the **Heimlich maneuver**, have successfully dislodged foreign objects from the airway. Before performing the Heimlich maneuver, ask the choking person if he can speak. If the person is gasping, wheezing, and cannot speak, proceed with the Heimlich maneuver:

1. The victim will be unable to speak if there is a true airway obstruction.

2. Stand behind the victim. Place your fist, thumb side in, above the victim's navel and grab your fist tightly with your other hand.

3. To force air and a possible foreign object from the windpipe, pull your fist upward and inward in an abrupt motion.

4. Continue with abdominal thrusts until the object is released.

5. If the victim is unconscious, straddle the victim, facing the head, place your fists above the navel, and perform the same abrupt thrust.

Conscious infant:

1. Have someone else call 9-1-1 or local emergency number.

2. Give 5 back blows.

3. If object remains lodged, turn infant over...

4. Give 5 chest compressions.

Conscious adult:

1. Have someone else call 9-1-1 or local emergency number.

2. Give abdominal thrusts (the Heimlich Maneuver)

3. Continue until the object is forced out or victim becomes unconscious.

FIGURE 15-2. First aid for choking.

(Source: www.health.state.ny.us/environmental/cpr/.../first_aid_choking.pdf)

Key Terms

Anaphylactic shock: An allergic reaction that causes circulatory collapse and suffocation due to bronchial and tracheal swelling.

Heimlich maneuver: Emergency procedure to expel an obstruction in the airway of a choking victim.

Challenge Question: What is the first thing to do if you are assisting a choking victim?

Drowning

Drowning is another common unintentional home fatality. In 2007, nearly 4,000 people died as a result of drowning in either a home pool, spa, or in a boating accident. More than 20 percent of drowning victims are children age 14 and younger, and for every child who dies from drowning, four others receive emergency department treatment for nonfatal submersion injuries.[12] Because the brain is deprived of oxygen in a drowning incident, nonfatal injuries can include permanent disabilities, including memory loss, learning disabilities, and a permanent vegetative state. Very young children left unsupervised can drown in bathtubs, buckets, and toilets, and in most home pool drowning incidents, the toddler or child was last seen in the home, with one or both parents present, and had been out of sight fewer than five minutes. Installing secure barriers and fences can help make home pools, spas, and ponds safe. In ninety percent of boating accidents in which a drowning occurred, the victim was not wearing a life vest.[13]

Motor Vehicle Injuries

Unintentional motor vehicle-related injuries are the number one cause of death for individuals ages 1 to 34. Almost 5 million Americans visit a hospital emergency room each year as a result of injuries that occurred in a motor vehicle accident.[14] In 2009, more than 3,000 teens age 15 to 19 years were killed in motor vehicle crashes, and 350,000 were treated in hospital emergency rooms.[15] Young drivers are at particular risk for a motor vehicle crash, as they:

- Lack experience evaluating dangerous driving situations.

- Drive fast and leave little distance between their vehicle and surrounding vehicles.

- Do not always wear a seatbelt.

- Are more likely to drink alcohol and drive than other age groups.

The Graduated Driver Licensing (GDL) program has helped to reduce the rate of fatal teen vehicle crashes. In 2009, there were 3,000 fatalities, dropping from 8,000 per year in 2005.[16] The GDL provides national guidelines that include restrictions in licensing and limitations for driving.

Image of Health in Depth

The Model for a GDL Law

Not all states have the same GDL requirements, but most endorse at least one of the following three possible stages.

Stage 1: Learner's Permit

Drivers should:

- Be at least 16 years old.

- Pass vision and knowledge tests.

- Hold the permit for at least six months.

- Be supervised at all times by a licensed driver who is at least 21 years old.

- Complete basic driver training.

- Complete at least 50 hours of certified driving practice, including nighttime driving.

- Require all vehicle occupants to wear safety belts.

- Be free of at-fault crashes or convictions for at least six months before progressing to the next stage.

- Pass a road test given by an accredited agency before progressing to the next stage.

Stage 2: Intermediate/Probationary License

Drivers should:

- Have a sixth-month minimum holding period.

- Be allowed to drive without supervision during the day. Between at least 10 p.m. and 5 a.m., the driver should be accompanied by a licensed driver at least 21 years old

- Have a limited number of passengers. There should be no teen passengers, with the exception of immediate family members, for the first six months.

- Take and pass an advanced driver's education course during the year.

- Require all vehicle occupants to wear safety belts.

- Be free of at-fault crashes or convictions for at least six months before progressing to the next stage.

Stage 3: Full/Unrestricted License

Drivers should:

- Be at least 18 years old.

- Pass a final road test.[17]

Older drivers are also at risk for unintentional vehicle injuries, especially drivers older than 70 years. However, the fatality and injury rate for older drivers is far less than for teen drivers. After age 75, the rate of fatal crashes increases, though death is often the result of other medical complications due to age. Declining vision and cognitive abilities are the most common reasons for driving difficulty among older Americans. However, older adults are more likely to drive more slowly, drive when the conditions are safest, wear a seat belt, and restrict alcohol use when driving.[18]

Critical Thinking Question: Describe why young drivers are more likely to be involved in a motor vehicle crash than older drivers.

Recreational Injuries

Although recreational activity can improve fitness, coordination, and even self-discipline, it is not without risk. More than 3.5 million children under age 14 sustain a sports or recreational activity injury each year.[19]

Some injuries could be reduced by correctly learning how to perform the activity and by wearing a helmet and other protective equipment. Contact sports such as football, rugby, hockey, and wrestling have a higher rate of injury than individual or noncontact sports. If you are learning a new skill such as skiing or snow boarding, taking a few lessons to safely learn the fundamentals will help reduce injuries. Adolescents and young adults have more recreational injuries than other age groups, for reasons including the following:

- There is difficulty assessing the true risk.

- The potential for fun or a thrill far outweighs the risk.

- There is often significant peer pressure.

- There is a feeling of invulnerability, and that the activity is really safe even though there are legitimate risks.

- The individual is responsible only for himself.

Older individuals are more likely to be better at assessing risk, are less influenced by their peers, and generally try to avoid the potential for an unintentional injury because of work and family responsibilities.

Work-Related Injuries

Over one million people per year take time off work because of a work-related injury. The nature of the injury depends primarily on occupation: laborers who move freight and stock, heavy equipment operators, and tractor-trailer drivers have a high incidence of injury from contact with objects and equipment. Nursing aides, orderlies and attendants, and construction workers have a high incidence of strains and sprains, including back, knee, and other musculoskeletal injuries, as well as overexertion as a result of their work. Retail salespersons have a high rate of repetitive strain injury from contact with equipment, overexertion, and repetitive movement.

Tendinitis and **bursitis** are the two most common repetitive-motion injuries and result from microscopic tears in tissue from continually performing the same action. Tendinitis is an inflammation of a tendon that connects muscle to bone, and is most common in the shoulder, biceps, and elbow. Bursitis is an inflammation of a bursa sac, the small cushions in joints that pad and lubricate the area between tendon and bone. Bursitis can occur in the elbow, knee, hip, and shoulder. Tendinitis and bursitis are painful conditions that can be caused and exacerbated by the motions required for daily work. Some relief can be gained by icing the affected area for 20 to 30 minutes, 2 to 3 times per day, and by eliminating the motion that is aggravating the injury.

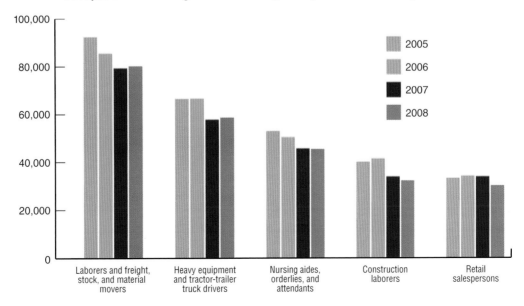

Occupations with a high number of days-away-from-work cases, 2005–2006

FIGURE 15-3. Bureau of Labor Statistics, 2008.[20]

Carpal tunnel syndrome occurs when the **median nerve** in the wrist is compressed from a build up of scar tissue pressing on the nerve. This condition is a common work-related injury for those whose primary work involves using a computer keyboard, working on an assembly line, or using vibrating hand tools. Women are more likely than men to experience carpal tunnel syndrome, primarily due to smaller wrist size. Symptoms are progressive, beginning with tingling, itching, or numbness in the palm of the hand or fingers. It can progress to loss of grip strength, loss of sensation for heat and cold, and chronic pain or numbness of the hand and fingers. Treatment for carpal tunnel syndrome includes physical therapy, reduction of any physical action that may be exacerbating the problem, and anti-inflammatory drugs. If symptoms persist, surgery is performed to release the pressure.[21] Carpal tunnel syndrome can be prevented with correct wrist alignment when using a computer keyboard and by reducing repetitive wrist motion.

Key Terms

Tendinitis: An inflammation of a tendon that connects muscle to bone.

Bursitis: An inflammation of a bursa sac, the small cushions in joints that pad and lubricate the area between tendon and bone.

Carpal tunnel syndrome: Compression of the median nerve in the wrist that can cause tingling, itching, or numbness in the palm of the hand and fingers.

Median nerve: A nerve that extends along the forearm and passes through the wrist, affecting movement and sensation in the hand.

Critical Thinking Question: Identify three types of repetitive motion injuries.

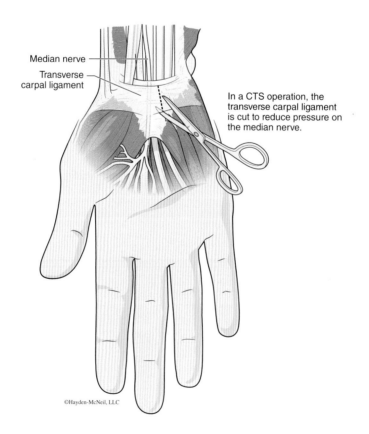

Median nerve
Transverse carpal ligament

In a CTS operation, the transverse carpal ligament is cut to reduce pressure on the median nerve.

©Hayden-McNeil, LLC

FIGURE 15-4. Carpal tunnel surgery.

Lower back pain is a common work-related injury caused by heavy lifting or twisting motions, vibration, and repetitive motion. The spine of the lower back is particularly susceptible to injury, possibly resulting in vertebral disk problems, and nerve or muscle pain. Almost everyone has an occasional episode of back pain severe enough to seek medical attention. Treatment includes icing the injured area, anti-inflammatory drugs, and avoiding the motion that caused the injury. A tendency to have lower back pain usually increases with age, as bone strength, muscular strength, and elasticity decrease. Aging also causes the vertebral discs to degenerate and weaken, allowing for the possibility that a disk could move into the space occupied by the spinal cord, causing more pain.

To improve lower back health:

- Maintain core body strength, including back and abdominal muscles.

- Refrain from lifting objects too heavy for you.

- Lift with knees, keep object close to your body, and pull in stomach muscles.

- Wear low-heeled shoes.

- Sleep on your side on a firm surface.

- Rest your feet on a small stool or stack of books if you must sit for a prolonged period of time.

- Reduce excess weight around the waist that puts a strain on lower back muscles.

FIGURE 15-5. Lifting with legs.

Firearm Injuries

The United States has one of the most heavily armed populations in the world, where almost 40 percent of homes have at least one firearm. In many cases, parents are not aware how much their children know about the location of firearms and ammunition. Although firearms and ammunition must be kept separately and secured with a lock, this is not often the case, placing an increased risk for children and adolescents. Up to one-third of children and adolescents have handled a firearm within the family home.[22]

Firearm safety in the home is most effective when all family members are aware of the existence of firearms and understand safety protocol. Ideally, any firearm should be stored in a locked cabinet or case, with ammunition securely stored in another location. Having a gun in the home increases the risk for adults to be shot fatally or to commit suicide.[23] Regardless of the type of firearm or method of storage, the existance of a firearm in the home appears to increase the risk for suicide among adolescents.[24]

Intentional Injury

Intentional injury refers to an action where an individual purposefully harms another person or harms himself. The National Crime Victimization Survey report from 2009 indicated that 4.3 million people age 12 years and older experienced a crime of violence. These crimes included rape, sexual assault, robbery, aggravated assault and simple assault. The rate of violent crime in the U.S. has declined each year for the past ten years.

Homicide rates have shown little change over the past few years, except in the 18- to 24-year age group, which has the highest homicide rates.

Violent and abusive behavior was not recognized as a public health problem until the 1980s, when homicide and suicide increased dramatically, particularly among adolescents and young adults.[23] From 1950 until 1990, the suicide rate among individuals age 15 to 24 years almost tripled, and homicide rates among 15- to 19-year-old males increased 154 percent from 1985 to 1991. Several government efforts to reduce this trend resulted in the federal Centers for Disease Control and Prevention establishing a Division of Violence Prevention, whose task was to collect evidence on violence and abuse and establish a plan for prevention. One of the first priorities was to understand the risk factors and establish prevention programs in schools and communities, in order to reduce youth violence. These efforts were successful, encouraging a public health approach to other violence problems, such as rape and domestic abuse. As a result of a two-year study that produced data on intimate partner violence, sexual violence, and stalking, Congress passed the Violence Against Women Act in 1994, establishing nationwide rape prevention and education programs. There are now national public health prevention programs for many categories of intentional injury and violence.

Intimate Partner Violence

Intimate partner violence includes rape, physical assault, and stalking by a current or former intimate partner of the same or opposite gender. Although there are incidents of women harming men, most partner violence involves men harming women. One in three women murdered in the U.S. are killed by an intimate partner; for men, the number is one in twenty.[26] The CDC administers and provides support for the Rape Prevention and Education Grant program (RPE) for public health organizations that receive grant money provided by the Violence Against Women Act. Funding supports educational seminars, rape hotlines, and training and development programs for professionals.

Recognizing the signs of domestic abuse is not easy for some people. A relationship may begin with love and kindness, but may eventually change to include abusive behavior. Both the abuser and the abused may make excuses for the behavior for different reasons.

Often in an abusive relationship, the abuser demands control over the victim, forcing the victim to do things she does not want to do, or preventing her from doing things she wants or needs to do. There is a pattern of verbal and psychological abuse in which the abuser demeans the victim, her family and friends, or her personal characteristics. The abuser keeps the victim under control by acts or threats of violence toward the victim, a family member or friend, children, or toward himself by threatening suicide.

Challenge Question: Identify the risk in the U.S. for a woman to be murdered by an intimate partner.

You are in an abusive relationship if your partner does any of the following:

- Calls you names or tells you that you are ugly.

- Embarrasses you in front of children, family, and friends.

- Checks up on you at work, school, or when you are out with friends.

- Does not respect your opinion and makes all decisions.

- Threatens harm or says something bad will happen if you resist his control.

- Prevents you from leaving your house or apartment.

Sharon's Story

Sharon was excited to start college. She was a biology major and had chosen a college known for its Life Sciences department. In her first class, the biology professor divided the class into study groups of four, who would also be her lab partners. One of her lab partners, Lenny, was cute, but she thought he had a girlfriend and did not seem interested in her.

Six weeks into the semester, Lenny told her that he was inviting her and the other lab partners to his off-campus house on Sunday afternoon to study for the midterm exam.

She liked this idea because she enjoyed her lab partners and thought she could get to know Lenny better. Maybe he didn't have a girlfriend after all.

On Sunday, Sharon took the bus to Lenny's house, looking forward to a productive afternoon of studying with her study group friends. When she arrived, only Lenny was there. He told her that the other lab partners couldn't make it and it would just be the two of them. Sharon felt a little uncomfortable being alone with Lenny, but she decided it would be okay. Lenny asked her if she wanted something to drink and

Sharon asked for a soda. Lenny brought the soda and in a short while, Sharon felt the affects of the Rophynol that Lenny had put in her drink. She realized she had been drugged.

A few hours later, Sharon managed to ride the bus back to campus. She knew she had been raped and had some bruises on her face and arms, but could remember little of what happened. She felt betrayed and humiliated and that this was somehow her fault.

The next day she went to class, and Lenny acted as if nothing had happened. This upset

Sharon even more. When a friend asked why she was upset, Sharon told her what happened. Her friend took her to campus police, where she filed a report of rape. She did not go to biology lab that afternoon, but the campus police did. They arrested Lenny on felony charges of rape and assault; he was handcuffed and taken to the local jail in a squad car. Because Lenny used a date rape drug to incapacitate his victim, his future will include even more time in jail. ■

- Slaps or hits you.

- Forces you have sex when you don't want to.

- Forces you engage in oral or anal sexual acts against your will.

- Batters or beats you.

Image of Health in Depth

Rape

According to the federal Department of Justice, rape is forced sexual intercourse, including both psychological coercion and physical force. It is a crime of violence, not a crime of passion. Rape victims are men and women, heterosexual and homosexual.[27] The intent of the rapist is to humiliate, terrify, dominate, and injure the victim.

Date rape occurs when the victim knows the rapist, and a sex act is completed against the wishes of the victim. Rape is a felony in all states, but more than 50 percent of rapes are not reported. Some women do not report a rape because they believe that they were somehow to blame, or they believe they cannot face the demeaning experience of recounting every detail of the rape to the police. Some women are threatened by a rapist and are afraid of retaliation, and some are struggling with the trauma of a rape. They do not want to describe the rape to police or be required to see the rapist in a courtroom. If a rape is attempted, most rape prevention specialists encourage women to scream loudly and often and not to give up, but to fight back and run away if possible.

A rape affects everyone associated with the victim. Husbands or boyfriends believe they failed to protect the victim. Friends and family members witness the aftermath of the trauma as the victim experiences many of the affects of posttraumatic stress syndrome.

What to do if you are raped:

- Do *not* shower or wash.

- Go to the nearest hospital emergency room or campus health center.

- Tell hospital personnel that you have been raped. They will attempt to collect DNA evidence.

- File a police report.

- Press charges.

Child Abuse and Elder Abuse

Child Abuse Hotline

1-800-4-A-CHILD (1-800-422-4453)

Child abuse or maltreatment involves all types of abuse and neglect of a child less than 18 years of age. In 2008, child protective services documented that 772,000 children were victims of maltreatment, and 1,740 children died in the U.S. from abuse and neglect,[28] including:

1. *Physical abuse*: A child is kicked, hit, shaken, punched, or burned.

2. *Sexual abuse*: A child is raped, fondled, or forced to engage in sexual acts.

3. *Emotional abuse*: A child is demeaned, called names, told he/she is worthless, rejected, and threatened.

4. *Neglect*: A child's basic needs are not met including withholding food, clothing, housing, school, and access to medical care.

Children under 4 years are at greatest risk for maltreatment and risk of severe injury and death. A high-risk family environment is one in which there is little social support, and includes drug and alcohol abuse, poverty, and chronic health problems that promote an environment for maltreatment of children. The best strategy for reducing child maltreatment is prevention, by providing parents with support and teaching parenting skills, especially in high-risk environments.

Elder abuse or maltreatment is the abuse of an individual age 60 and older by a caregiver or person the elder trusts. There are six types of elder maltreatment:

1. *Physical*. The elder is slapped, kicked, hit, or burned, resulting in an injury.

2. *Sexual*. The elder is forced to take part in a sexual act without consent.

3. *Emotional*. The elder is called names, is frightened, embarrassed, prohibited from seeing friends and family, and has personal property destroyed.

4. *Neglect*. The basic needs of the elder are neglected, including food, housing, clothing, and medical care.

5. *Abandonment*. The elder is left alone and no one provides care.

6. *Financial*. The elder's money, property, and other assets are illegally confiscated or used.

Approximately one-half million elderly individuals aged 60 or older are victims of maltreatment each year. Maltreatment of the elderly is more likely where there is a lack of social support, and in a home environment where there is drug and alcohol use, emotional and financial dependence on the elder, depression and high levels of stress, some as a result of being a caregiver for the elderly person.

Reducing elder abuse is complex. Caregiver support groups may provide support or respite for caregivers, potentially reducing the potential for harming an elder. Neighbors might reduce the risk by checking on elderly neighbors. Financial risks may be reduced by placing responsibility for the elder's finances with more than one person and by involving a non-beneficiary, such as an attorney.

Challenge Question: Identify some characteristics of child abuse.

Stalking

Stalking includes physically stalking a person, Internet stalking, and bullying. Most stalkers are men who physically stalk someone to control or frighten them. Stalkers invade privacy in the most insidious ways. They will show up unannounced and uninvited to your home, work, school, social event, restaurant, or sports event. Stalkers may break into your home; go through personal items, including your mail; and listen to the phone answering machine, while trying to find out more about your personal life. Stalkers also exhibit signs of compulsive behavior. They are often the former partner or spouse of the victim, though in some instances, the stalker may be unknown to the victim but is nevertheless obsessed by the person.

Stalkers can be verbally and psychologically abusive and can make threats of physical harm. If the stalker harms a person or if the person believes that they are in imminent danger, it is possible to secure a **restraining order**. However, this court order takes time to process, and the stalker must be physically served with the restraining order by a marshal or deputy from the court.

Internet stalking can be on a blog, in an online class, through social networking sites such as Facebook and MySpace, or by unsolicited emails. Stalking on the Internet is especially facilitated by social networking sites,

where personal information may be displayed for friends and family. If a stalker gains access, he or she has the opportunity to know all of the information that has been included on the page. Most social network sites allow users to restrict access to their personal pages and will accept reports of inappropriate behavior.

Bullying, most common in adolescence, occurs when a student or group of students decides they do not like someone, and a campaign of harassment begins. This can be in person, but is often done via cell phone calls and text messaging, personal data assistants (PDAs), and the Internet. In 2009, 19.9 percent of students in grades 9–12 reported that they were bullied, with females bullied slightly more than males.[29] When electronic media is used to embarrass, harass, or threaten others, it is called **electronic aggression**, and is considered a type of violence that has the potential to lead to emotional distress and difficulty in school.

Key Terms

Restraining order: A court order to protect a victim of domestic abuse by prohibiting the abuser from having contact with the victim. If a restraining order is in effect, the abuser will be arrested if contact is made.

Electronic aggression: Using electronic media to embarrass, harass, or threaten another person.

Critical Thinking Question: Describe the ways a stalker can infiltrate your life.

Workplace Violence

Workplace violence is any violent act directed toward a person who is at work or on duty. These violent acts can be physical assaults, threats of assault, harassment, intimidation, or bullying. Between 1992 and 2006, there were 11,613 homicide victims who were killed while at work, for an average of 800 workplace homicides per year. Additionally, an average of 1.7 million people are victims of violent crime while working or on duty in the U.S. The occupations with the highest injury and fatality rates are police officers, corrections officers, and taxi drivers. The federal Bureau of Labor Statistics classifies four types of workplace violence:

1. Violence against a co-worker by an employee, or by a contractor working as a temporary employee.

2. Criminal violence, when the perpetrator has no relationship with the work environment and is involved in robbery, trespassing, or shoplifting.

3. Customer or client violence, when the perpetrator has a relationship with the workplace and becomes violent as a result of that relationship.

4. Domestic violence against an employee in the workplace with whom the assailant has or has had a personal relationship.[30]

Establishing a code of behavior and a method for reporting unacceptable behavior can alleviate some workplace violence. Some violent workplace behavior goes unreported because the victim is afraid of retaliation and in some cases may have been threatened. Employers must have a system in place for addressing the need for an employee to feel safe when reporting abusive or violent behavior.

Challenge Question: Identify the most common occupations for an on the job homicide.

Hate Crimes

A hate crime is committed when a perpetrator selects a victim because of the victim's actual or perceived race, color, religion, national origin, gender, sexual orientation, gender identity, or disability. In 2009, the Hate Crimes Prevention Act (HCPA) was signed into law, providing the Department of Justice the power to investigate and prosecute cases that would be considered hate crimes. The HCPA also requires the Federal Bureau of Investigation (FBI) to track crime statistics based on gender and gender identity.[31]

Self-Harm

Self-harm can take many forms, ranging from self-induced starvation (anorexia), self-cutting and mutilating, inflicting burns intentionally, and suicide.

Cutting refers to intentionally cutting or puncturing fingers, arms, legs, or any body part, resulting in extensive bleeding and emergency medical treatment, including stitches to close self-inflicted wounds. Burning with any

incendiary implement, such as a lighter or cigarette, resulting in second- or third-degree burns is another form of self-harm. Individuals who engage in self-harm may do so for a variety of reasons, including self-punishment for some real or perceived act; as a manifestation of depression; or perhaps as an attention-getting method, a cry for help. It is a serious pattern of behavior that requires both medical and psychotherapeutic intervention. Individuals who are treated in an emergency room for self-inflicted injuries will receive a psychological consultation and referral, but some with self-inflicted injuries will not seek treatment.

The ultimate form of self-harm is to attempt or to commit suicide. In 2007, suicide was a leading cause of death in the U.S., accounting for 34,598 deaths.[32] For each completed suicide, an estimated eleven non-fatal attempts occur, with firearms, suffocation, and poison the most commonly used methods. Most suicides are expressions of extreme distress and are not methods for seeking attention. Suicide is prevalent when mental and substance abuse disorders are major risk factors, so addressing these issues may reduce risk. If you think someone may be suicidal, do not leave the person alone. Seek immediate help, such as campus health services or the nearest hospital emergency room, or call 911 for help. Eliminate access to firearms, poisons, and medications in homes where there is substance abuse or mental disorders.

Table 15-1. Self-Harm Cut/Pierce Nonfatal Injuries and Rates per 100,000. 2006, United States, All Races, Both Sexes, Ages 15 to 24 Disposition: All Cases (CDC, 2006)

SEX	NUMBER OF INJURIES	POPULATION
Both sexes	32,472	42,435,426
Males	14,315	21,844,954
Females	18,157	20,590,472

Gang Violence

Gangs in the United States are increasingly more active in suburban rather than urban areas, and are a concern for public safety. Much gang criminal activity involves drug trafficking, but new gang activity has evolved to include alien and weapons trafficking. In 2008, there were approximately 1 million gang members involved in 20,000 gangs operating in all 50 states and the District of Columbia.[33] Because they engage in violence to protect turf and a drug distribution network, local street gangs are a public threat, committing up to 80 percent of crimes in many communities, including alien smuggling, armed robbery, assault, auto theft, drug trafficking, extortion, fraud, home invasions, identity theft, murder, and weapons trafficking. U.S. gang members regularly cross the U.S.-Mexico border to smuggle drugs and illegal aliens into the United States, and many gangs are developing relationships with foreign-based drug trafficking organizations.[34] Gangs are always recruiting new members from schools, the community, and the Internet.

Risk factors for gang involvement include poor socioeconomic communities, a fragmented family structure, and few community outreach or recreational opportunities. Gangs replace a nonexistent family structure for many young people, both male and female, creating a sense of belonging. Gang members believe they can count on the support of their brother and sister gang members. It is also often a way to improve financial status because of gang involvement in illegal drug trafficking.

Challenge Question: Describe some of the changing demographics of gangs in the U.S.

Homicide

Homicide was the second-leading cause of death for individuals age 10 to 24 years, with 5,686 deaths in 2005.

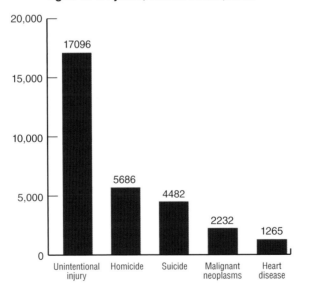

Leading causes of deaths among persons aged 10–24 years, United States, 2005

FIGURE 15-6. Youth violence: national statistics. Five leading causes of deaths among persons age 10–24 years, united states, 2005.[35]

(Source: Centers for Disease Control and Prevention, 2005.)

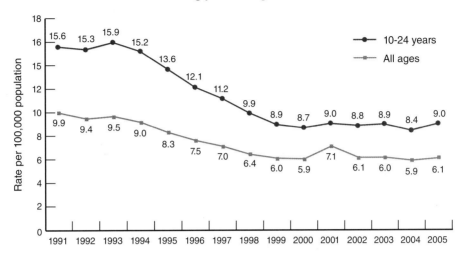

FIGURE 15-7. Firearms were the primary mechanism used in a homicide for both males and females age 10–24 years.

(Source: Centers for Disease Control and Prevention, 2005.)

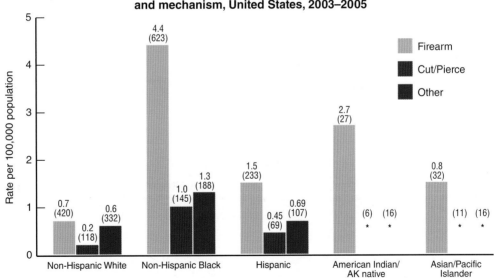

*Race/ethnicity-specific rates and number of deaths (in parentheses) are provided above each bar.
Rates are not presented where the number of deaths are fewer than 20 because they are statistically unreliable.

FIGURE 15-8. Homicide rates among females ages 10–24 years by race/ethnicity and mechanism, United States, 2003–2005.

(Source: Centers for Disease Control and Prevention, 2005.)

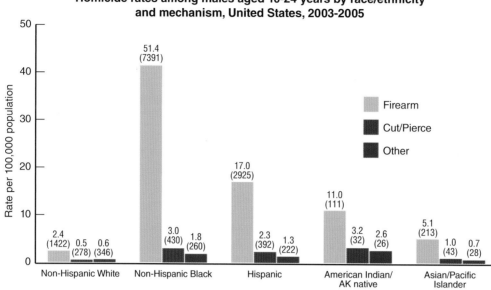

Homicide rates among males aged 10-24 years by race/ethnicity and mechanism, United States, 2003-2005

*Race/ethnicity-specific rates and number of deaths (in parentheses) are provided above each bar.

FIGURE 15-9. Homicide rates among males ages 10–24 years by race/ethnicity and mechanism, united states, 2003–2005.

(Source: Centers for Disease Control and Prevention, 2005.)

▼

Responsibility and Accountability

Taking Responsibility for Injuries

There is much you can do to protect yourself and those you care about from unintentional and intentional injuries. Since unintentional injuries are not accidents, they can be prevented, starting by assessing the risks that exist in your home, school, work, and community. Recognizing the symptoms of an abusive relationship enables you to assess those risks and make changes that are in your own best interest. Identifying potential risk as you enjoy recreational activities will help you reduce the possibility of unintentional injury. Increasing awareness can identify potentially dangerous or unsafe situations in your work and community. Finally, knowing that you are in a high-risk group for a motor vehicle crash should encourage you to be a more responsible driver.

Focusing on Accountability

Once you have identified the risks for injury that may exist in your life, you can be accountable for making necessary changes. If you have identified anything that could cause injury in your home, school, or work environment, you must be accountable for making the changes to reduce that risk. If you know you are in an abusive relationship, you must be accountable for making the necessary changes. If you engage in recreational or sports activities, you must be accountable by using protective equipment. To protect yourself as a driver or passenger in a motor vehicle, you must be accountable by wearing a seatbelt, driving the speed limit, and not driving or allowing someone else to drive while intoxicated.

Summary

Protecting Yourself

- Learning how to evaluate risk to avoid both intentional and unintentional injury.

- Falls are the most common unintentional injury in almost every age group.

- Evaluating risk when there is potential for violence helps reduce intentional injury.

Unintentional Injuries

- Unintentional injury is the number one cause of death for individuals age 0 to 44 years.

- The ability to accurately assess risk usually improves with age and experience.

- Traumatic brain injury (TBI) occurs when an external force traumatically injures the brain.

- Most unintentional poisoning deaths are the result of an accidental overdose of a prescribed medication.

- Cooking causes most residential fires.

- Fatalities from fires are most often from smoke inhalation and toxic gases.

- A choking victim with an airway obstruction can sometimes be assisted by performing abdominal thrusts, known as the Heimlich maneuver.

- Most drowning incidents occur in home pools, spas and boating accidents.

- Motor vehicle crashes are the number one cause of death for individuals age 1 to 34.

- The Graduated Driver Licensing (GDL) program has helped reduce fatal teen motor vehicle crashes.

- Older drivers are less likely to be involved in a motor vehicle crash.

- Over 1 million people per year miss work because of a work-related injury.

- The most common types of repetitive motion injuries are tendinitis, bursitis, carpal tunnel syndrome, and lower back pain.

- Lower back injury is caused by heavy lifting or twisting motions, vibration, and repetitive motion.

- Almost 40 percent of Americans have a firearm in their home.

Intentional Injury

- Intentional injury occurs when a person purposefully harms another individual or harms him/herself.

- The rate of violent crime has declined each year for the past ten years.

- Violent crime is recognized as a public health problem.

- Prevention programs in schools and communities have helped reduce violence.

- One in three women murdered in the U.S. are killed by an intimate partner.

- Domestic abuse is a pattern of verbal, psychological, and physical abuse most often directed against a woman by a man.

- Rape is forced sexual intercourse that includes both psychological coercion and physical force.

- In 2008, 772,000 children were victims of abuse and maltreatment, and 1,740 died.

- Elder abuse is maltreatment to an individual age 60 years or older.

- Approximately one-half million elderly individuals are abused each year.

- A stalker can infiltrate your life physically, emotionally, and through the use of electronic media.

- A court-issued restraining order establishes a boundary of no contact between stalker and victim.

- In 2009, almost 20 percent of students in grades 9–12 reported that they were bullied on campus.

- Violence in the workplace occurs when a person is at work or on duty.

- The occupations with the highest on the job homicide rate are police officers, corrections officers, and taxi drivers.

- A hate crime is committed when a perpetrator selects a victim because of the person's actual or perceived race, color, religion, national origin, gender, sexual orientation, gender identity, or disability.

- Self-harm includes intentionally cutting or puncturing fingers, arms, legs, or any body part that may result in excessive bleeding and medical treatment.

- There are one million gang members involved in 20,000 gangs operating in all 50 states and the District of Columbia.

- Gangs exist in urban and suburban environments and are involved in drug trafficking, as well as alien and weapons trafficking.

Reassessing Your Knowledge

1. Describe how you can evaluate risk in your relationships, home, family, and community.

2. Identify five common home injuries.

3. Identify the characteristics that make younger drivers more at risk for a motor vehicle crash.

4. Describe some characteristics that will confirm that you are in an abusive relationship.

5. Describe the four categories of child abuse.

To answer these questions, you might choose to work in groups with your colleagues. Check your answers against the written material in the text, and reread those sections where you made errors.

Health Assessment Toolbox

Consumer Product Safety
http://www.cpsc.gov/

National Center for Victims of Crime
http://www.ncvc.org/ncvc/Main.aspx

National Center for the Prevention of Child Abuse
http://www.preventchildabuse.org/index.shtml

Rape, Abuse and Incest National Network
http://www.rainn.org/

Safe Kids
Preventing injuries at home, at play, and on the way.
http://www.safekids.org/

Vocabulary Challenge

Match the term in the left-hand column with its correct definition in the right-hand column.

TERM		DEFINITION
1. Unintentional injury	A.	Graduated driver licensing
2. Intentional injury	B.	Work-related injuries that result from performing the same motion
3. Dysfunctional family	C.	An injury that occurs without intending harm
4. TBI	D.	Abdominal thrust to dislodge a foreign object
5. Heimlich maneuver	E.	An injury that occurs when harm is intended
6. Anaphylactic shock	F.	A pattern of conflict and abuse that diminishes emotional and physical health
7. GDL	G.	Using electronic media to bully harass and intimidate
8. Repetitive strain injury	H.	Compulsive unwanted involvement in a person's life
9. Stalking	I.	Traumatic brain injury
10. Electronic aggression	J.	Allergic reaction that restricts circulation and breathing

Answers:
C; E; F; I; D; J; A; B; H; G

Exploring the Internet

Federal Bureau of Investigation
http://www.fbi.gov/

Human Rights Campaign—Hate Crimes
http://www.hrc.org/

National Center for Injury Prevention and Control
http://www.cdc.gov/injury/index.html

National Institutes of Health
http://www.nih.gov/

National Institute for Occupational Safety and Health
http://www.cdc.gov/niosh/

National Highway Traffic Safety Administration
http://www.nhtsa.gov/

U.S. Consumer Product Safety Commission
http://www.cpsc.gov/index.html

U.S. Department of Labor
http://www.dol.gov/

Selected References

1. Chen, L.H., Warner M., Fingerhut L., and Makuc, D. Injury episodes and circumstances: National Health Interview Survey, 1997–2007. *Vital Health Statistics,* 10(241). 2009.

2. Ibid.

3. Trifiletti, L. Ladder Injuries Climbing. *American Journal of Preventive Medicine*, May, 2007.

4. Centers for Disease Control and Prevention, National Centers for Injury Prevention and Control. Protect the Ones You Love: Childhood Injuries are Preventable, 2009.

5. Centers for Disease Control and Prevention, National Centers for Injury Prevention and Control. Falls Among Older Adults: An Overview, 2010.

6. Thompson H.J., McCormick W., and Kagan S. Traumatic Brain Injury in Older Adults: Epidemiology, Outcomes, and Future Implications, *Journal of the American Geriatric Society*, 54(10): 1590–1595. October, 2006.

7. Faul, M., Xu L., Wald, M.M., and Coronado, V.G. Traumatic Brain Injury in the United States: Emergency Department Visits, Hospitalizations and Deaths 2002–2006. Atlanta (GA): Centers for Disease Control and Prevention, National Center for Injury Prevention and Control, 2010.

8. Centers for Disease Control and Prevention, Traumatic Brain Injury in the United States, 2010.

9. Centers for Disease Control and Prevention, National Centers for Injury Prevention and Control. Poisoning inn the United States: Fact Sheet, 2010.

10. Ibid.

11. Centers for Disease Control and Prevention, National Centers for Injury Prevention and Control. Fire Deaths and Injuries: Fact Sheet, 2010.

12. Centers for Disease Control and Prevention, National Centers for Injury Prevention and Control. Unintentional Drowning: Fact Sheet, 2010.

13. Centers for Disease Control and Prevention, National Centers for Injury Prevention and Control. Stay Safe on the Water: National Safe Boating Week, 2010.

14. Centers for Disease Control and Prevention, National Centers for Injury Prevention and Control. Prevention and Control: Motor Vehicle Safety, 2010.

15. Centers for Disease Control and Prevention, National Centers for Injury Prevention and Control. Teen Drivers: Fact Sheet, 2010.

16. Morrisey, M.A., Grabowski, D.C., Dee, T.S., and Campbell, C. The Strength of Graduated Drivers License Programs and Fatalities Among Teen Drivers and Passengers. *Accident Analysis and Prevention,* 38: 135–141. 2006.

17. Mayhew, D.R., Simpson, H.M., Singhal, D., and Desmond, K. Reducing the Crash Risk for Young Drivers. *AAA Foundation for Traffic Safety*. June, 2006.

18. Centers for Disease Control and Prevention, National Centers for Injury Prevention and Control. Older Adult Drivers: Fact Sheet, 2010.

19. National SAFE KIDS Campaign (NSKC). Recreational Injury Fact Sheet. Washington (DC): NSKC. 2004.

20. U.S. Department of Labor, Bureau of Labor Statistics, Nonfatal Occupational Injuries and Illnesses Requiring Days Away From Work, 2008.

21. National Institutes of Health, national Institute of Neurological Disorders and Stroke, Carpal Tunnel Syndrome Fact Sheet, 2009.

22. McNamara, N., and Findling, R. Guns, Adolescents, and Mental Illness, *The American Journal of Psychiatry*. February, 2008.

23. Wiebe, D.J. Homicide and Suicide Risks Associated with Firearms in the Home: A National Case Control Study. *American Emergency Medicine*, 41: 771–782. 2003.

24. Brent, D.A., Perper, J.A., Allman, C.J., et al. The Presence and Accessibility of Firearms in the Homes of Adolescent Suicides. *JAMA*, 266(21): 2989–2995. 1991.

25. Alcohol, Drug Abuse, and Mental Health Administration. Report of the Secretary's Task Force on Youth Suicide. Vol. 1. Washington, DC: US Government Printing Office. 1989.

26. Thompson, M.P., Basile, K.C., Hertz, M.F., and Sitterle, D. Measuring Intimate Partner Violence Victimization and Perpetration: A Compendium of Assessment Tools. Atlanta (GA): Centers for Disease Control and Prevention, National Center for Injury Prevention and Control. 2006.

27. Department of Justice, Bureau of Justice Statistics, Rape Rates. 2010.

28. Centers for Disease Control and Prevention, National Centers for Injury Prevention and Control. Understanding Child Maltreatment: Fact Sheet. 2010.

29. Centers for Disease Control and Prevention, National Centers for Injury Prevention and Control. Youth Violence: Facts at a Glance. 2010.

30. U.S. Department of Labor, Bureau of Labor Statistics, Survey of Workplace Violence Prevention. 2005.

31. Human Rights Campaign, Matthew Shepard and James Byrd, Jr. Hate Crimes Prevention Act, Public Law No. 111–84. October 28, 2009.

32. Centers for Disease Control and Prevention. National Center for Injury Prevention and Control. Web-based Injury Statistics Query and Reporting System (WISQARS): www.cdc.gov/ncipc/wisqars

33. Federal Bureau of Investigation. National Gang Threat Summary. January. 2009.

34. Ibid.

35. Centers for Disease Control and Prevention, National Centers for Injury Prevention and Control. Youth Violence: National Statistics. 2005.

36. Ibid.

Image of Health

Aging, Death, and Dying

THE STAGES OF LIFE

- How Old Is Old?

- Anticipating Aging

- Successful Aging

HEALTH ISSUES AND AGING

- Physical Changes
  - Skin Changes
  - Eyesight Changes
  - Hearing Changes
  - Heart and Lung Changes
  - Changes in Bone Density
  - Urinary Tract Changes
  - Sexual Functioning Changes
- Mental Changes
  - Depression
  - Dementia and Alzheimer's Diseases
  - Memory
- Diseases Affecting the Elderly
  - Independence versus Dependence

COMING TO TERMS WITH THE BEGINNING OF THE END

- The Stages of Dying

- Hospice Care

THE FINAL ACT

- Defining Death

- Final Choices

- The Right to Die

- Final Preparations

- Advance Directions and Living Wills

- Organ Donation

- Surviving Loss

RESPONSIBILITY AND ACCOUNTABILITY

- Taking Responsibility for Your Life

- Focusing on Accountability

Student Learning Outcomes

LEARNING OUTCOME	APPLYING IT TO YOUR LIFE
List and describe five age-related characteristics.	From the list, assess your age based on each characteristic.
Describe three physical age-related challenges.	Identify steps you can take to reduce the onset of age-related challenges.
Describe two mental health challenges faced by the elderly.	Choose an elderly person you know and evaluate his/her mental condition. Consider if you have changed the way you interact with him/her.
Describe the differences in aging based on ethnicity.	Identify ways that these differences can be reduced or eliminated.
List the Kubler-Ross stages of dying.	Consider events in your life, unrelated to death, in which you have experienced these stages.

Assessing Your Knowledge

1. A person who has smoked for several years and is sedentary and overweight might have physical health conditions older than actual age. This is referred to as:
   a. Functional age

   b. Physical age

   c. Biological age

   d. Psychology age

2. The "baby boom" years refers to children born between:
   a. 1946–1965

   b. 1945–1955

   c. 1955–1965

   d. 1950–1960

3. Biological markers refer to:
   a. Birthdays

   b. Changes in mental status

   c. Tools used to assess health

   d. Measurable and quantifiable measures of health

4. Elevated pressure within the eyeball causing impaired vision and possible blindness is caused by:
   a. Cataracts

   b. Glaucoma

   c. Macular degeneration

   d. None of the above

5. Care provided to reduce symptoms and manage pain is known as:
   a. Complimentary care

   b. Palliative care

   c. Hospice care

   d. Routine care

Answers:

1. c; 2. a; 3. d; 4. b; 5. b.

The Stages of Life

In the 1960s, the "hippie" movement and major rock bands proclaimed that you should not trust anyone over thirty. Santana, the Rolling Stones, the Grateful Dead, and the Beatles all viewed and sang about the aging concept with disparity. Today, members of these rock bands are either in or approaching their seventies, and many are still performing successfully. Compared to even fifty years ago, performing rock and roll on stage at age seventy would have been considered a comedy routine. Youth had its place, and the aged had their place.

So, what changed? Is seventy as old today as it was in 1960, or are people today apparently younger? If you had the interest, do you think you will be able to "rock out" at a concert when you are in your seventies? In this chapter, you will learn how you can plan for successful aging, so the later stages of life might be as enjoyable as the years you are living now.

How Old Is Old?

For those who were born in 1900, life expectancy for whites was 47.6 years, and for blacks it was 33 years. For those born in 2003, these numbers have increased to 77.6 years and 72.3 years, respectively. How is being old determined? Is it age-based, ability-based, or a combination? Aging has generally been considered a chronological event that begins at birth. Life begins in the infant stage, progresses into childhood, the teen years, then young adulthood. Middle age is generally considered to begin around age 50, though this number does not represent the middle of life expectancy. Old age is more difficult to define, and has numerous definitions. For some, it starts with becoming a grandparent; for others, retirement; and for those beyond these stages, there may not be a clear definition.

Individuals who study aging are known as gerontologists. **Gerontology** explores the characteristics of aging and how people cope with the process. From this, several age-related characteristics have been defined.

Biological Age: The condition of the person's biological systems. A 35-year-old who does not have the cardiovascular condition to be able to run a few miles might have a biological age older than that of a 65-year-old who can. Biological aging is determined primarily by how well you take care of yourself, though it is also influenced by genetics.

Social Age: How well you match society's expectations for your age. By age 3–4, toddlers should begin to communicate effectively. People in their teens share similar interests and behave in similar ways. Each age has its particular identity, and social age also refers to the role you have in society.

Legal Age: An arbitrary age that allows for certain rights; for example, the legal age required to obtain a driving permit. At age 18, a person is old enough to enter the armed forces and is also considered an adult by the criminal justice system. At age 21, a person is legally allowed to buy and consume alcohol, vote, and serve on a jury. At age 65, a person can receive social security and **Medicare**.

Psychological Age: How you adapt during the aging process determines your psychological age. Psychological age may not be dependent on ability, but rather on perception. Maintaining a positive attitude and being mentally active has been shown to slow psychological aging.[1]

468   Aging, Death, and Dying • CHAPTER 16   Image of Health

Functional Age: How well you and your body function compared to others of a similar age. Certain events, such as reduced bone density and reduced urinary capacity, are anticipated during the aging process. If these events occur earlier or later than expected, functional age will be affected.

Key Terms

Gerontology: The study of the collective and individual processes of aging.

Medicare: Government sponsored health care system for those age 65 or older.

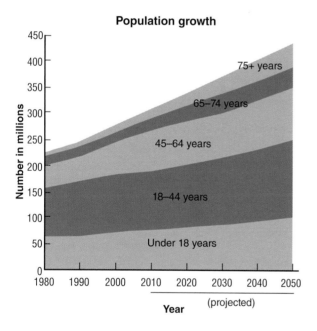

Population growth

FIGURE 16-1. Distribution of the population based on age across time, from 1980 to a projected distribution in 2050.

(Source: CD/NCHS, Mental Health, United States, 2009, Figure 1A. Data from U.S. Census Bureau.)

Older Americans are predominantly white, but the demographics are expected to change in coming years. The number of older black Americans is expected to triple by 2050, beginning at 8–10 percent today and increasing to 24–30 percent. Today, fewer than 4 percent of the aged are Hispanic, but this will increase to 16 percent. Aging among some ethnic minorities may be accelerated by either lack of health care or delays in seeking health care treatment, and onset of chronic diseases is usually earlier in these groups.

Challenge Question: Describe the difference between functional age and biological age.

Critical Thinking Question: What can be done to increase life expectancy among ethnic minorities?

Anticipating Aging

How you view aging will influence how you age. If you view approaching 30 or 40 with dismay and fear, perhaps believing it means you are approaching a less fulfilling life, this could potentially be the life you will build for yourself. If you view it as a further opportunity for growth, new adventures, and different experiences, you will build that life.[2] Anticipating aging refers to the mental attitude you may have about the process. Your opinion about aging is influenced by how you view those much older than you. Do you see them as vital, engaging, productive people who are essential to the social fabric of society, or do you view them as old and unimportant? Some cultures revere the aged, while others do not hold older people in such high esteem.

Views on aging are determined in part by health status and financial security. If asked how long you would like to live, you will probably answer with a specific age, as long as certain conditions are met. For instance, you might want to live into your eighties, as long as you are able to take care of yourself and interact with others. Or you might want both these conditions, as well as financial freedom. Consider the conditions that will be important to you as you age, and think about how responsibly you are planning for them. If good health is one of your conditions, are you already doing everything now to help ensure your future health? If finances are a condition, are you planning today for a secure future? Neither of these events happens randomly, but with planning, success can be achieved. Assess your views in "Image of Health: Viewing the Aging Process."

Image of Health

Viewing the Aging Process

As you answer the following questions, consider your life far into the future.

1. How long would you like to live?

2. What is your vision of the life you will have at that age?

3. Consider your answer to the previous question and compare that vision with the life you have today. How similar are they?

4. What are the keys to your happiness, financial security, and health today?

5. What do you anticipate the keys to happiness, financial security, and health will be when you are 40, 50, 60, 70 years or older?

6. Do you think people in their middle or later years can achieve the same levels of happiness as someone in your age group?

7. Right now, you are working to achieve a college degree or certificate. When completed, you expect that it will lead to a promising career. You are taking the necessary steps toward this goal. As you consider aging, when do you think the planning for that part of your life should begin?

8. What plans should a person make to help assure they are healthy and happy in later years?

Critical Thinking Question: What can you do to ensure you have a healthier older life?

Successful Aging

Between the years 1946 and 1965, more babies were born than at any other time in U.S. history. Referred to as the "baby boom," these children became known as "boomers." Today, the youngest boomers are at least 45 and the oldest are about 65 years of age. As this huge population enters retirement, major changes will occur within society. In 2000, the elderly population numbered about 36 million, and by 2030, the size of the elderly population is expected to double.[3] Not only will 20 percent of the U.S. population be elderly, it is estimated that 55 other countries will have populations in which at least 20 percent are over age 65.[4] This huge increase in the proportion of elderly people to young people will have enormous impact, both socially and economically.[5] As the boomers enter their retirement years, the social security and Medicare systems will be overburdened, and there will not be a large enough population of working people paying into the system to support those taking from the system. Who will support this aging population?

Have these boomers planned for successful aging? What steps does this preparation entail? Planning for successful aging is not much different from planning for a successful life after college: you need to be healthy, you need to have a place to live, you need something to do and someone to do it with, and you need financial security. None of this will change as you age.

As you read this chapter, you will learn how you can improve your chances of successful aging.

FIGURE 16-2. Baby boomers began defining their society in the 1960s.

Health Issues and Aging

In order to be happy, is it first necessary to have health? Or, is it easier to maintain good health and manage ill health if you are happy? Recently, researchers were able to prove that positive emotions have an independent relationship with coronary heart disease.[6] The lead researcher concluded it might be possible to help prevent heart disease by enhancing people's positive emotions. With this in mind, your first focus as you consider your own aging is to reflect on your personal happiness level and what you are prepared to do to maintain or improve it.

Physical Changes

Chronological aging cannot be stopped: year after year, you grow older. However, it may be possible to slow the process so that more people live longer than the average human life expectancy.[7] This process involves improved nutrition, weight management, increased physical activity, and managing all **biological markers** within normal range.

Skin Changes

Skin changes begin around age 30, when collagen deposits in the skin begin to diminish. As a result, soft lines begin to develop, eventually becoming more pronounced with age. The number of age spots increases, particularly in those who have had more exposure to the sun. Ears, nose, and mouth continue to increase in size, while eyes remain the same. This results in the typical look of an aged person, with the nose, ears, and mouth appearing too large proportional to eye size.

Eyesight Changes

Beginning at around age 40, eyesight becomes less acute. The lens of the eye begins to harden and lose transparency. **Presbyopia** occurs when the lens loses its ability to focus. In addition, the pupils shrink, allowing less light to penetrate. These issues combine to cause difficulty with reading. As age progresses, depth perception declines and in later years, color blindness may develop.

FIGURE 16-3. Yone Minagawa died at age 114 as the oldest person in the world.

The risk of **glaucoma** increases by age 40, and most people over age 60 will have some evidence of the disease. It currently affects over two million Americans, and its prevalence will increase to a projected 3 million by 2020.[8] Glaucoma causes pressure to build in the front of the eye, and if untreated, it will damage the optic nerve and may result in blindness.[9] Symptoms begin slowly as peripheral vision diminishes. Many people do not realize they have glaucoma until permanent partial vision loss has occurred. Medicated eye drops lower the pressure and may control the disease, but in some cases surgery to relieve pressure is necessary.[10]

Cataracts are the leading cause of blindness in developing countries. They are also a major public health problem in the U.S., affecting 26.6 million people over age forty. Physical and chemical changes in the eye lens due to normal aging result in a loss of transparency or clarity, causing the formation of a cataract. Smoking, diabetes, and exposing eyes to excessive sunlight increase the risk for developing cataracts. Surgery to remove the cataract is successful in 90 percent of cases.[11]

Macular degeneration is an incurable eye disease whose cause is unknown. In the U.S., it is the leading cause of blindness for those age 55 and older. Of the approximately eight million people who have macular degeneration, two million already have significant loss of vision. It involves the deterioration of the central portion of the retina, resulting in difficulty reading, driving a vehicle, recognizing faces or colors, and seeing objects in fine detail.[12] In 2010, the Federal Drug Administration (FDA) approved the use of micro-sized implantable telescopes to improve vision in patients with end-stage, age-related macular degeneration. The tiny device, called an Implantable Miniature Telescope (IMT), replaces the natural lens, and provides an image that has been magnified more than two times. Clinical results from FDA tests show patients see better and in some cases are able to recognize people and facial expressions that they were previously unable to recognize.

Hearing loss is accelerated when the ears are exposed to loud noise, such as that experienced on a construction site or when listening to loud music.

> **Key Terms**
>
> **Biological markers**: Measurable and quantifiable indicators of health, such as blood pressure, cholesterol level, and blood glucose level.
>
> **Presbyopia**: Lens of the eye loses its ability to focus, making reading difficult.
>
> **Glaucoma**: Elevated pressure within the eyeball, causing impaired vision and possible blindness.
>
> **Cataracts**: Clouding of the lens of the eye, causing blurred vision and eventually blindness.
>
> **Macular degeneration**: Deterioration of the central portion of the retina, resulting in diminished visual difficulties and eventually blindness.

> **Key Terms**
>
> **Presbycusis**: Age-related hearing loss.
>
> **Tinnitus**: A sound in one or both ears that occurs without external stimulus.

Challenge Question: What are biological markers?

Critical Thinking Question: What can be done to inhibit hearing loss?

Hearing Changes

Two types of hearing loss are common in older people. **Presbycusis**, which affects both ears, develops slowly as a person ages. The degree of loss differs from person to person, but hearing aids can help restore sound. **Tinnitus** causes a ringing, roaring, or hissing sound in one or both ears. Although this can occur at any age, it occurs more frequently in older people. There is no cure or treatment for tinnitus, but some patients find that wearing a small earpiece that produces white noise helps them tolerate the ringing, roaring, or hissing.

Heart and Lung Changes

It is unknown whether the prevalence of diseases such as hypertension, coronary artery disease, and heart failure are due to the aging process, or if they occur more frequently in elderly people because of a longer exposure to risk. Cardiovascular aging is a continuous and irreversible process, but the decline rate varies among people primarily due to lifestyle factors. Protective factors include maintaining normal weight, not smoking, engaging in regular physical activity, and eating a low-fat diet with limited meat products.

After age twenty, the lungs begin to lose some of their efficiency, and tiny alveoli sacs that filter air are no longer renewed. Lung function begins to deteriorate and the rate of airflow through the airways slowly declines after age thirty. The biggest change occurs because airways in older people close more readily. They collapse when an older person breathes shallowly or when they are prone for an extended period, increasing the risk for pneumonia and other lung problems. Maintaining lung function can be helped by keeping older people in an upright position as much as possible, especially when ill or after surgery. Other common lung problems include an increase in lung infections because of a diminished immune system, chronically low oxygen levels, and abnormal breathing patterns. Exercise and training can improve lung capacity, even in the very elderly.

Changes in Bone Density

During the aging process, mineral loss in bones, particularly calcium, causes bones to become weaker and more porous, resulting in **osteoporosis**. Although women have higher rates of osteoporosis, it occurs in both genders. Modifiable risk factors include low calcium intake, tobacco use, sedentary lifestyle, and excessive alcohol consumption. Non-modifiable risk factors are aging, being white or of Asian descent, being very thin or having a small body size, and a family history of the disease. Osteoporosis can be treated with medications.

Key Term

Osteoporosis: A progressive disease resulting in fragile and easily broken bones.

Challenge Question: What can you do to reduce your risk of osteoporosis?

Critical Thinking Question: What suggestions could you make to an older family member to help improve lung function?

Urinary Tract Changes

Bladder capacity diminishes with age, resulting in the need to urinate more frequently. Kidney function is reduced and waste is filtered from the blood at one half the rate it was at age thirty.

Urinary incontinence ranges from passing a few drops of urine while laughing, sneezing, or coughing to losing control over urination altogether.[13] Incontinence is more prevalent in women than men, and at least 50 percent of nursing home residents are affected. The U.S. prevalence in men age 60 and older is 17–21 percent, and about 23 percent of women age 60–79 are affected, with nearly half of this population experiencing daily incontinence.[14] Incontinence is most likely caused by multiple factors in the older population, including functional and cognitive impairments and medications.[15] Treatment depends on the severity of the problem and ranges from behavioral techniques and physical therapy to surgery.

Sexual Functioning Changes

Menopause marks the end of fertility for women. It occurs usually between ages 45–55, when estrogen production diminishes, then ceases. The decline in estrogen results in decreased vaginal blood flow, decreased vaginal lubrication, vaginal elasticity, and may cause pain during intercourse.[16] However, onset of menopause does not change sexual drive; it remains at the pre-menopause level.[17] Availability and health of partners may limit sexual activity for the post-menopausal woman and the aging man.

For men, fertility continues throughout life, but because testosterone levels drop as men age, the ability to obtain and maintain an erection is diminished. Orgasms are of shorter duration, and older men need an increase in the length of the refractory period between erections. The National Council on Aging found that almost one half of Americans over age 60 engage in sexual activity at least once a month, and 40 percent would like to have sex more frequently.[18] It is unknown whether the availability of drugs like Viagra (sildenafil) will make sexual activity more prevalent in this age group. There are arguments that erectile dysfunction (ED) is not a disease and should not be treated as such, and in fact, the concept of ED only became a medical issue with the introduction of Viagra.[19]

Key Term

Urinary incontinence: The involuntary excretion of urine.

Mental Changes

Intellectual changes in healthy older people are slight, and the most common psychological illness is depression.[20] Although people age 65 and older make up only 12 percent of the population, in 2004, they accounted for 16 percent of the suicides.[21] Correctly diagnosing and treating the mental challenges faced by the elderly may reduce this suicide rate.

Depression

Depression, one of the conditions most commonly associated with suicide, is often not recognized or treated in older adults.[22] It is not a normal part of aging, and health care professionals may miss depressive symptoms in older patients. The risk for depression increases when ability to function becomes limited; therefore, hospitalized elderly and those requiring home care are more likely to be depressed.[23] Symptoms of depression in this population, are similar to the symptoms experienced in other age groups. Depression can be effectively treated with antidepressant medications and psychotherapy.

Symptoms of Depression

Feeling nervous, empty, worthless

Not enjoying things that were previously enjoyed

Being restless and irritable

Feeling unloved, that life is not worth living

Changes in sleeping habits

Changes in eating habits

FIGURE 16-4. Depression is widely under-recognized in the elderly.

Dementia and Alzheimer's Diseases

Dementia is characterized by a loss of or decline in memory and other cognitive abilities. It is not part of the aging process, but caused by various diseases and conditions that result in damaged brain cells. Diagnosis for dementia requires that the patient meet the following criteria:

- A decline in memory and at least one of the following cognitive abilities:

    - Difficulty speaking or understanding spoken or written language.

    - Difficulty recognizing once familiar objects

    - Difficulty walking.

    - Difficulty thinking, making decisions, and completing tasks.

Alzheimer's disease is the most common form of dementia in the elderly, affecting 5.3 million people, and it is the sixth leading cause of death in the U.S. The cause of Alzheimer's remains unknown, but it likely develops as a result of multiple factors, rather than from a single cause. Although it is not a normal part of aging, the greatest risk for Alzheimer's is advancing age, and one in eight of the baby boom population will develop Alzheimer's disease.[24] There are no treatments to slow or stop the deterioration of brain cells that occurs with Alzheimer's disease. Although the FDA has approved five drugs that temporarily slow Alzheimer's symptoms, these drugs only work for between 6–12 months, and only in about one half of the people that take them.[25] Some data suggest that the health of the brain is linked to the overall health of the heart and blood vessels. Careful management of risk factors for cardiovascular disease, type II diabetes, high blood pressure, being physically active, and not smoking may help or delay cognitive decline.[26]

Memory

Many studies have shown that memory decreases as age advances. This memory loss is seen in short-term rather than long-term memory. An individual may vividly recall events from long ago, but may not remember that he told you about those events just thirty minutes ago.

Diseases Affecting the Elderly

As the number of elderly continues to increase, so does the prevalence of stroke, diabetes, arthritis, and heart disease. Sexually transmitted infection (STI) is significant among the elderly for both newly acquired infections and for residual complications from preceding infections.[27] Twenty-five percent of HIV infections are in people over age fifty, and there may be more elderly people who are infected. Doctors do not always test older people for HIV/AIDS in routine check-ups, and older people are less likely to talk about sex and also less likely to use a condom during sexual activity.[28] Dr. Bodley-Tickell and colleagues found the rate of STIs, other than HIV, more than doubled in older people in 2003, compared with 1996.[29] The results of this study indicate that sexual risk-taking behavior is not limited to young people. Reducing the incidence of STIs in the older population requires more interventions aimed specifically at this age group, and promotion of safer sex practices within it.

One of the challenges the elderly face is managing chronic disease. It may be difficult to track prescription medication use, and because there is no one system that records all prescriptions provided to an individual, negative drug interactions may occur. The risk for adverse drug interactions is higher in people with impaired circulation and declining liver and kidney function. It is rare for older people to abuse illicit drugs, but it is not unusual for some to develop a prescription drug dependency.

Alcohol abuse is a hidden epidemic, with surveys showing as many as 17 percent of those over the age of 65 with an alcohol abuse problem. These drinkers can be classified into two types: hardy survivors who have been abusing alcohol for many years, and those who begin abusing alcohol later in life. Alcohol use is complicated by prescription drug use. The elderly spend over $500 million each year on medications, and combining alcohol with medications frequently produces adverse reactions.[30]

Independence versus Dependence

Sixty-four percent of adults between the ages of 65–74 are married and live with a spouse. For those over 85, 24 percent are married and live with a spouse. Among women over 65, 48 percent are widowers.

Elderly people who engage in 20–30 minutes of moderate to vigorous physical activity have better physical function than those who are active throughout the day or those who are inactive.[31] Maintaining higher levels of physical function increases the likelihood of remaining independent. Figure 16-6 shows the activity limitations caused by chronic conditions among older people.

Challenge Question: What percentage of older people abuse alcohol?

Remaining independent is important among the elderly, and research shows that life expectancy is increased for those who are not in a care facility. About 5 percent of people age 65 and older live in nursing homes, with an average life expectancy of approximately six months upon entrance into the home. Although 14 percent of people over age 65 have 2–3 chronic conditions that erode their ability to live independently, the majority of these individuals live with family members.

Image of Health in Depth

Necessary Elements of Successful Aging

- A place to live

- Health and access to health care

- Friends, a spouse, or family members who care about you

- Financial security

- Interests and hobbies that are enjoyed

FIGURE 16-5. Living independently or with a spouse or family member may extend life.

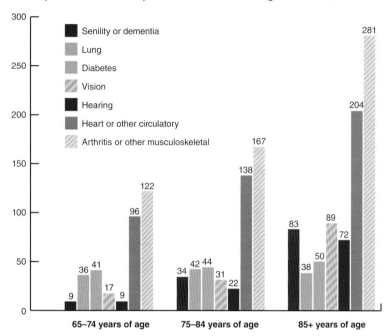

FIGURE 16-6. Activity limitation among adults 2006–2007.
(Source: CDC/NCHS Health, United States, 2009. Numbers in millions.)

Coming to Terms with the Beginning of the End

For the majority of people, extending healthy life is a daily goal, but at some point, we each must face our mortality. With every birthday, the elderly recognize that life is limited. But if life has been lived to the fullest, accepting the inevitable may be easier. Many factors influence coming to terms with death, including age, health status, personal experience with death, religious beliefs, and the circumstances in which death occurs.

The Stages of Dying

Although death is inevitable, most Americans are uncomfortable with the thought, and continue to strive to postpone it. In her landmark work, Elisabeth Kubler-Ross identified five common stages in the dying process. Recognizing and understanding these stages may help with accepting death.

Denial

The first stage begins after receiving a diagnosis that death is inevitable, such as with terminal cancer. During this stage, the patient and perhaps the patient's family members enter the denial phase, refusing to accept that this could possibly happen. More medical tests and treatments may be called for, and some may reach out for spiritual support to help deny death. Individuals may be able to accept intellectually that death is inevitable, but have not come to terms with it emotionally.

Anger

In the second stage, anger may occur when the person wonders why he or she must be the one to die. Life is viewed as unfair, and death is viewed as an unwarranted punishment for unknown deeds. Patients may become hostile as they try to work through this stage.

Bargaining

During the bargaining phase, family members and patients try to create contracts to extend life. The patient may resolve to be a better parent, spouse, member of their faith, or a better individual, or perhaps they may bargain for just a specific amount of time. "If I could only live to see my child marry, I could die comfortably," but with the bargaining phase there may be no end to the attempts at negotiation.

Depression

When the reality of impending death is accepted, depression may occur. This usually occurs as symptoms of death become more evident and options for recovery are depleted. The dying person may feel guilt over the pain being caused to surviving loved ones, and may experience feelings of tremendous loss.

Leslie's Story

Leslie moved from the east coast to the west coast for college. She loved her new life and also loved going home for vacations. One Saturday morning, her father called and asked her to come home to see him. Leslie told him she would be home in just another six weeks, but her father insisted she come right away. When pushed, he told Leslie he just might not be around in six more weeks.

Distraught and overwhelmed, Leslie flew home the next day. On the plane, she relived her mother's death some 8 years ago. Family members had sat with her mother as she died, but Leslie had not been able to handle that. She still felt some guilt about not being there.

At home, her father was in good spirits and seemed to have accepted his pending death. They talked about final details and were even able to joke with one another. Leslie had to fly back to school a few days later, and at the airport, her father took her aside. He told her what a great kid she was, how proud he was of her, and to keep up the good work. He asked her not to grieve too long so that he could get on with his next stage. Leslie held her father, thanked him for his courage, and laughed and said she would grieve as long as she wanted just to irritate him. They joked about that, and then with one last hug, Leslie got on the plane.

When the phone call came a couple of weeks later, Leslie was able to accept what had happened. Although it was still overwhelmingly sad, she was glad that she and her father had talked about death and that she had been able to let him talk. She knew that having the conversation had helped her father, and realized it had been helpful to her, too. ∎

Acceptance

The final stage is acceptance. The fight is over and emotions become more stable. Patients sleep more, and when awake seem ready to move on with the next journey. In this stage, they are not depressed or unhappy, but perhaps void of feelings. They may no longer welcome visitors outside of family, and want to spend the remaining time very quietly with those closest to them. Death usually comes about peacefully, and quietly.

Kubler-Ross' research was done with people who were terminally ill with cancer. She documented stages as the disease progressed from terminal diagnosis to death. Not all people experience the same process in dying—for some, death occurs without warning so they do not experience these stages, while others may move back and forth between stages.

Hospice Care

Dame Cicely Saunders opened the first hospice center in London in 1967. In her work as a physician, she stated that dying "is physically very hard work," and began a movement to offer support and **palliative care** for the terminally ill. Hospice care is usually provided to patients with a life expectancy of less than six months. The first American hospice was opened in Connecticut in 1974.

Today, hospice and palliative care centers offer a full program of support for the terminally ill and for people living with a terminally ill person. The support program includes medical care, as well as spiritual and emotional care for both the patient and family members. Team members include a nurse, social worker, spiritual counselor, home health aide, a volunteer, and a supervising hospice physician. Palliative care is the prevention and relief of pain and suffering, focusing on managing symptoms, and improving quality of life.

Although many cities now have hospice care centers, most hospice care takes place in the patient's own home. Many health insurance providers, including Medicare, now cover some or all of hospice costs. After the patient has died, hospice care continues for surviving family members, offering ongoing grief counseling for up to a year.

Key Term

Palliative care: Care provided to reduce symptoms and manage pain.

Motivation Maximizer

Is It All Worth It?

How can there be a motivation maximizer in a chapter on aging and death? It is here because life is so incredibly worthwhile, even if none of us gets out alive. Each and every day provides a new opportunity to change your life, to make it better, to make it more enjoyable, to give more, to love more, and to smile more. With every choice you make, you have the ability to affect your life's outcome. As you read through this, consider the joys you have already experienced in life. Of course, they have not all come without a cost, and some have already experienced great sorrow and/or hardship. But tomorrow starts it all again, and tomorrow you can begin to enact plans that will lead to a happy, successful, and healthy life for yourself. You have control over your destiny. Knowing this and accepting this is the first step in making positive changes. Go for it.

The Final Act

Acknowledging that death is a reality enables people to plan for it. An individual can make many of the decisions about the dying process and even the after-death process in advance. Making these decisions may help those who survive you, easing their burden.

Defining Death

The need to have an explicit definition for death occurred in 1981, as a result of legal and ethical issues. The Uniform Determination of Death Act was accepted by the American Medical Association, the American Bar Association, and the National Conference on Uniform State Laws. Although it has not been accepted in all states, the act provides a clear description of death:

1. An individual must have sustained either irreversible cessation of all circulatory and respiratory functions, or

2. Irreversible cessation of all functions of the entire brain, including the brain stem.

3. A determination of death must be made in accordance with accepted medical standards.[32]

Certifying brain death requires another set of conditions. Since the brain stem is the relay site for all sensory and motor pathways and is necessary for sustaining critical body functions such as respiration, brain death may be the most credible way to define death. The Harvard Medical School defines brain death as:

1. Unreceptivity and unresponsiveness to any stimuli.

2. No movement for a continuous hour after observation by a physician, and no breathing after three minutes off a respirator.

3. No reflexes, including brainstem reflexes; fixed and dilated pupils.

4. A "flat" **electroencephalogram (EEG)** for at least ten minutes.

5. All of these tests repeated at least 24 hours later with no change.

6. Certainty that **hypothermia** and depression of the central nervous system, which can be caused by certain drugs, such as barbiturates, are not responsible for these conditions.[33]

Key Terms

Electroencephalogram (EEG): An assessment of electrical activity in the brain.

Hypothermia: Extreme loss of body heat.

Final Choices

Making decisions about the end of your life may seem exceptionally hard, but it is a gift you can leave for your loved ones. You may want to make choices about whether mechanical respiration, mechanical resuscitation, or intravenous nutrition are used if you are unable to breathe or to hydrate or feed yourself. As long as a person is conscious, he or she has the right to refuse medical treatment, even if this means death will occur sooner. But if a person is unable to make a decision due to coma or the inability to speak, medical personnel will make the decision, unless an advance directive or living will is in place.

Advance Directive and Living Wills

Advance directive and **living wills** are legal documents that allow an individual to make decisions about end-of-life matters. These documents communicate the patient's choices to both medical professionals and family members, possibly directing or restricting the use of life-extending technology, resuscitation if breathing or heartbeat stop, and organ or tissue donation. A **durable power of attorney** for health care is a document that names an individual of your choosing to make decisions for you if you are unable to do so.

Advance directive, living wills, and durable powers of attorney for health care do not need to be complicated legal documents. Each document can be short and simple, specifying your wishes, but they must comply with state laws, and copies of the directives should be given to personal physicians and family members. These documents can be changed or cancelled at any time, providing the author is considered of sound mind. The U.S. Living Will Registry provides advance directive forms for each of the fifty states (http://uslwr.com/formslist.shtm).

Key Terms

Advance directive: An advance directive is a legal document that may include a living will, a medical power of attorney, and a do not resuscitate order. It allows an individual to convey decisions about end-of-life care ahead of time and provides a way to communicate wishes to family, friends, and health care providers.

Living wills: Living wills are one part of an advance directive that indicates your treatment preferences in end-of-life situations, including whether you want specific kinds of treatment and life sustaining measures such as mechanical breathing and tube feeding.

Durable power of attorney: A durable power of attorney is a general, special, or health care power of attorney that contains special durability provisions. The person named in your durable power of attorney can only make decisions for you if the conditions you specified are met. This might include becoming mentally incompetent, being in a coma, or other medical conditions that prevent or inhibit you from making decisions independently.

Organ Donation

Organs that can be donated at the time of death include kidneys, heart, lungs, liver, pancreas, and the intestines. These must be transplanted within hours of removing them from the donor's body. Certain tissues can also be donated, such as corneas, the middle ear, skin, heart valves, bone, veins, cartilage, tendons, and ligaments. These tissues can be stored in tissue banks and used to restore sight, cover burns, repair hearts, replace veins, and mend damaged connective tissue and cartilage in recipients.

Transplanting organs began in 1954, when the first successful living-related kidney transplant occurred. This was followed in 1962, using a cadaveric (deceased) kidney transplant. Required request laws were passed in 1982, mandating that hospitals develop policies to identify patients as potential donors and approach families about organ donation. Organs cannot be bought or sold in the United States.

At the end of 2005, there were 163,631 persons living with a functioning organ transplant. Survival rates for recipients vary from 75 percent to almost 95 percent at the end of the first year. In the U.S. today, more than 108,000 people need life-saving organ transplants. In 2009, there were just 8,021 deceased organ donors, and each day, an average of 18 people die because of the shortage. Every eleven minutes a new name is added to the transplant waiting list.[34] If you choose to donate your organs, you can access your state's donor registry via the Internet. Your wishes can also be designated on your driving license, by carrying a donor card, and can be included in your living will or advance directive. If you elect not to donate, these same documents can include that information.

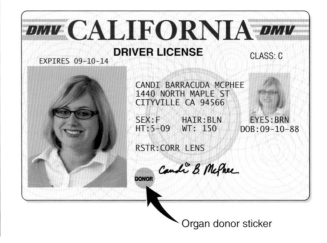

Organ donor sticker

FIGURE 16-7. Your organ donation might save another life.

The Right to Die

Whether a person has the right to choose to die is complicated by as many issues as the right to an abortion. In 1997, Oregon passed the Death with Dignity Act, allowing terminally ill patients the right to end their lives through the voluntary self-administration of lethal medications, expressly prescribed by a physician for that purpose. The Act states that ending one's life in accordance with the law does not constitute suicide.[35] During 2008, 88 lethal medications prescriptions were issued, and of these, 54 patients took the medication. Another 22 died of their underlying causes, and the remaining 12 were alive at the end of 2008. Since the law passed, 401 patients have died under the terms of the law.[36]

Although Oregon now counts the number of people who choose death rather than enduring constant pain and slow decay, experts estimate that thousands of terminally ill people decide to kill themselves each year. This might be done with **passive euthanasia**, in which there is intentional withholding of treatment that would prolong life, or with **active euthanasia**, in which life is terminated with lethal drugs. An example of active euthanasia is in veterinary medicine, when animals have no hope of recovery and are suffering so greatly that death is a more compassionate choice.

Image of Health in Depth

The Right to Die

Under Oregon's right to die law, a person must:

- Be at least 18 years old.

- Have a terminal illness with less than six months to live.

- Make three requests for a prescription (one written and two verbal) with at least 15 days separating each request.

- The prescribing physician and a consulting physician must confirm that the patient is capable and acting voluntarily.

The patient must be referred for counseling if either physician believes the patient's judgment is impaired. The doctor must also advise the patient of alternatives, such as hospice care.

Key Terms

Passive euthanasia: The intentional withholding of life-supporting equipment and services to bring about death in a terminally ill patient.

Active euthanasia: The administration of lethal drugs designed to bring about death in a terminally ill patient.

The Final Preparations

Following a death, survivors must make decisions about the disposition of the body. In the U.S., the choice is either a burial or a cremation. Funerals rank among one of the most expensive purchases for consumers: a traditional funeral, including a casket, costs about $6,000. Though it is now becoming more common for individuals and families to request that no service be conducted, a service can provide important benefits for survivors. Aside from allowing them to honor the deceased, it provides an opportunity for the outward expression of grief, and is often seen as the last act in the dying process. Individuals can make their own arrangements prior to death, or these final tasks may be left to survivors.

Surviving Loss

Coping with the loss of someone you love is a highly individual process. Survivors may go through many emotions during the first days, including overwhelming shock, disbelief, anger, guilt, and grief. William Worden, in his pioneering work, "Grief Counseling and Grief Therapy," identified four "tasks" that need to be accomplished before mourning is complete. The first task is to accept the reality of the loss and accept that the person is gone forever. For most people, this is followed by the second task, having to work through pain and grief. These are uncomfortable feelings that may be accompanied by feelings of unfinished business, worry, and questions that cannot be answered. Ignoring these emotions does not make them disappear, so at some point, they must be addressed. The third task is to adjust to an environment in which the deceased is missing. The rearranging, restructuring, and redefining that take place during this stage helps fill the roles previously held by the deceased. If the person was a major force in your life, this stage can take a significant amount of time, and it may be quite difficult to move to the final task—to emotionally relocate the deceased and move on with life. In this stage, survivors move forward from the feelings of loss and longing and are able to go on with their lives. There may be difficult days still ahead, but the emotional energy that was spent during the first days after the loss is now redirected.

Responsibility and Accountability

Reaching this chapter means you are approaching the end of this course. Have you been responsible during this term? Do you like the consequences of the choices you have made?

Taking Responsibility for Your Life

When a person enters college, he or she is typically considered to be an adult, able to successfully take on adult responsibilities and make appropriate choices and decisions. This does not mean losing the right to have fun, to be spontaneous, or to even be silly once in a while. But it does mean that it is now up to you to take care of yourself, and to behave responsibly. So, do you? Life is expensive. The only way you get your money's worth out of it, to make the cost worthwhile, is by applying yourself each and every day. To get value from your life, it is up to you to ensure you lead the healthiest life you can possibly lead.

Focusing on Accountability

Soon, you will learn how your responsibility in this course has paid off; your accountability will be seen in the grade you earn. As you approach the end of your life, how do you want your accountability to show itself? If you are currently a smoker, fail to quit smoking, and at some point are diagnosed with cancer, will you be able to think that the pleasure you experienced from smoking was worth this cost? If you do not exercise, do not eat well, and do manage your weight, are you going to say, "I have no regrets," if the cost is an earlier death? Most of today's leading causes of death can be postponed or prevented by making better choices. Is it worth it to you to make better choices, beginning right now?

Summary

The Stages of Life

- Gerontology is the study of the aging process and how people cope with aging.

- Biological age refers to the age or condition of the person's biological systems.

- Social age refers to how well you match society's expectations for your age.

- Legal age is the age that must be obtained to achieve certain rights.

- Psychological age refers to how you adapt during the aging process.

- Functional age refers to how well you and your body function compared to others of similar age.

- Medicare is a government sponsored health care system for those over 65.

- Today, minorities are underrepresented in the aged population but this is expected to increase dramatically by 2050.

Health Issues and Aging

- Positive emotions have an independent relationship with coronary heart disease. Being happy improves health outcome.

- Physical changes in the aging process include eyesight, hearing, cardiovascular changes, and sexual functioning changes.

- Mental challenges include memory loss, depression, dementia, and Alzheimer's disease.

- Diseases faced by the elderly are no different than diseases faced by the rest of the population.

- Prescription abuse and prescription drug interactions are a concern in the elderly population.

- Alcohol abuse is a hidden epidemic, with some who have been alcoholic for many years and others who are new alcoholics.

- Most of the elderly live with either a spouse, with family or independently.

- Only about 5 percent of the elderly population live in nursing homes or care facilities. Life expectancy is less for those who do not live independently.

Coming to Terms with the Beginning of the End

- Elisabeth Kubler-Ross identified five stages to the dying process: denial, anger, bargaining, depression and acceptance. Not all people experience all stages, and some move back and forth between stages.

- Defining death has been a difficult process; the Uniform Determination of Death Act and the Harvard Medical School have offered two widely accepted definitions.

- Hospice centers offer palliative care to those facing a terminal illness.

- Advance directives, living wills, and durable power of attorney for health care are all documents that can facilitate an individual's wishes are carried out if they become unable to speak for themselves.

- Organ and tissue donations are less than the numbers of organs and tissues that are needed.

- In 1997, Oregon passed the Death with Dignity Act allowing terminally ill patients to end their lives through voluntary self-administration of a lethal medication. Since the law was passed 401 individuals have elected to use it.

- Passive euthanasia refers to withholding of treatment that would prolong life.

- Active euthanasia refers to terminating life with lethal drugs.

- William Worden identified four tasks that need to be accomplished in the grieving process: accept the reality of the loss, work through the pain, adjust to the environment in which the deceased is missing and emotionally relocate the deceased and move on with life.

Reassessing Your Knowledge

1. Describe the various ways age can be assessed. What can you do to ensure you are maintaining a "younger" status in your aging?

2. Why are minorities underrepresented in the aging population, and what can be done to change this?

3. Describe changing health conditions that affect the elderly.

4. What could be done to reduce the risk of adverse drug interactions within the elderly population, and even other populations?

5. Using the Kubler-Ross stages of dying, how might you be able to help someone who is dying or someone is going through a very difficult time?

To answer these questions, you might choose to work in groups with your colleagues. Check your answers against the written material in the text, and reread those sections in which you made errors.

Health Assessment Toolbox

Are you biologically younger or older than your real age? This site provides a free real-age test and tips to help stay younger. **http://realage.com**

Health assessments for older adults focusing on function, cognitive ability, and psychological functions. **http://www.healthinaging.org**

UC Davis Alzheimer's Disease Research Center explains testing available for neuropsychological assessment. **http://alzheimer.ucdavis.edu/faq/tests/index.php**

Vocabulary Challenge

Match the term in the left-hand column with its correct definition in the right-hand column.

TERM		DEFINITION
Gerontology		A. Clouding of the lens of the eye, causing blurred vision and eventually blindness
Functional Age		B. How well you match society's expectations for your age
Social Age		C. Age-related hearing loss
Biological Age		D. The study of the aging process
Psychological Age		E. A sound in one or both ears that occurs without external stimulus
Palliative Care		F. Age that compares how well you and your body function compared to others of similar age
Cataract		G. Care designed to reduce symptoms and relieve pain
Hypothermia		H. Age that refers to the condition of your biological systems
Presbycusis		I. How you adapt to the aging process
Tinnitus		J. Extreme loss of body heat

D; F; B; H; I; G; A; J; C; E

Answers

Exploring the Internet

American Association of Retired People (AARP)
This organization provides information on aging, including promoting the health of the aged, health care and retirement planning.
http://www.aarp.org

Association for Death Education and Counseling (ADEC)
Resources for education bereavement, and care for the dying.
http://www.adec.org

National Institute on Aging
Fact sheets and related brochures on age related topics.
http://www.nih.gov/nia

U.S. Department of Health and Human Services
Donate Life. Information for organ donation including appropriate forms.
http://www.organdonor.gov

Oregon Department of Health and Human Services
Information on the Death with Dignity Act.
http://egov.Oregon.gov/DHS/ph/pas

Alzheimer's Association
Help for caregivers and patients on the causes and treatment of Alzheimer's disease.
http://www.alz.org

U.S. Administration on Aging
Statistical information and links to resources on aging.
http://www.aoa.gov

Public Agenda Issue Guide
The Right to Die. Provides information on the right to die.
http://www.publicagenda.org/citizen/issueguides/right-to-die

Tragedy Assistance Program for Survivors
TAPS offers compassion and understanding through a peer network for those on a journey through grief.
http://www.taps.org/survivors.aspx

Selected References

1. National Institute on Aging. Life Extension: Science Facts or Science Fiction? Age Page, September, 2002. www.niapublications.org/engagepages/lifeest.asp

2. Age Identity, Gender, and Perceptions of Decline: Does Feeling Older Lead to Pessimistic Dispositions About Cognitive Aging? *The Journals of Gerontology, Series B: Psychological Sciences, Social Sciences,* 65B(1): 91–96. 2010

3. U.S. Census Bureau. National Population Projections, Released 2008, based on Census 2000. Downloaded February 14, 2001, from http://www.census.gov/poulation/www/projections/index.html

4. National Research Council. Preparing for an Aging World: The Case for Cross-National Research. Panel on a Research Agenda and New Data for an Aging World, Committee on Population and Committee on National Statistics, Division of Behavioral and Social Sciences and Education. Washington: National Academy Press. 2001.

5. Cliquet, R., and Nizamuddin, M., eds. Population Aging: Challenges for Policies and Programmes in Developed and Developing Countries. New York: United Nations Population Fund; and Brussels: Centrum voor Bevolkings-en Gezinsstudiën (CBGS). 1999.

6. Davidson, K.W. *European Heart Journal*, published online February18, 2010.

7. Spirduso, W., Francis, K.L., and MacRae, P.G. *Physical Dimensions of Aging*. Published by Human Kinetics. 2005.

8. Friedman D. S., O'Colmain B. J., et al: Prevalence of Open-Angle Glaucoma in the United States. *Archives of Ophthalmology* 122(4): 532–538, 2004.

9. Russell, P., Tamm, E.R., et al. The Presence and Properties of Myocilin in the Aqueous Humor. *Investigative Ophthalmology and Visual Science,* 42(5): 983–986. 2001.

10. Heijl, A., Leske, M.C., et al: Reduction of Intraocular Pressure and Glaucoma Progression: Results from the Early Manifest Glaucoma Trial. *Archives of Ophthalmology,* 120(10): 1268–1279. 2002.

11. National Eye Institute, National Institutes of Health. Cataract: What You Should Know. August, 2004.

12. Parmet, S. Age-Related Macular Degeneration. *JAMA*, 288(18): 2358. 2001.

13. Abrams, P., Cardozo, L., Fall, M., et al. The Standardisation of Terminology of Lower Urinary Tract Function: Report from the Standardisation Subcommittee of the International Continence Society. *Neurourol Urodyn*, 21: 167. 2002.

14. Stothers, L., Thom, D., and Calhoun, E. Urologic Diseases in America Project: Urinary Incontinence in males—Demographics and Economic Burden. *Journal of Urology*, 173: 1302. 2005.

15. DuBeau, C.E., Kuchel, G.A., Johnson T., et al. Incontinence in the Frail Elderly. *Incontinence*, 4th ed. Abrams P., Cardozo L., Khoury S., Wein A. (eds). Health Publication Ltd., Plymouth, UK: 961–1024. 2009.

16. Nachtigall, L.E. Sexual Function in the Menopause and Postmenopause. In R. A. Lobo (Ed.), *Treatment of the Postmenopausal Woman: Basic and Clinical Aspects* (pp. 301–306). New York: Raven Press Ltd. 1994.

17. Koster, A., and Garde, K. Sexual Desire and Menopausal Development. A Prospective Study of Danish Women Born in 1936. *Maturitas*, 16: 49–60. 1993.

18. National Council on Aging. Half of Older Americans Report They Are Sexually Active. September 28, 1998.

19. Moynihan, R. The Rise of Viagra: How the Little Blue Pill Changed Sex in American. B*MJ*, 330: 424. 2005. doi: 10.1136/bmj.330.7488.424 (Published 17 February 2005).

20. Jones, K. Psychological Problems in the Elderly. *Family Physician*, 30: 591–593. 1984.

21. Centers for Disease Control and Prevention, National Center for Injury Prevention and Control. Web-based Injury Statistics Query and Reporting System (WISQARS). (2005) [accessed January 31 2007].

22. Conwell, Y., and Brent, D. Suicide and Aging. I: Patterns of Psychiatric Diagnosis. *International Psychogeriatrics*, 7(2): 149–164. 1995.

23. Hybels, C.F., and Blazer, D.G. Epidemiology of Late-Life Mental Disorders. *Clinics in Geriatric Medicine*, 19: 663–696. November, 2003.

24. Ross, L., K., Brennan, K., Nazareno, C., et al. Alzheimer's Disease Facts and Figures in California: Current Status and Future Projections. Executive Summary. Institute for Health and Aging, School of Nursing, University of California, San Francisco, CA 94143. February, 2009.

25. 2010 Alzheimer's Disease Facts and Figures. The Alzheimer's Association. Chicago, IL.

26. Hendrie, H.C., Albert, M.S., Butters, M.A., Gao S., Knopman, D.S., Launer, L.J., Jaffe, K., et al. The NIH Cognitive and Emotional Health Project: Report of the Critical Evaluation Study Committee. *Alzheimer's & Dementia*, 2: 12–32. 2006.

27. Talashek, M.L., Tichy, A.M., and Epping, H. Sexually Transmitted Diseases in the Elderly- Issues and Recommendations. *Journal of Gerontological Nursing* 4: 33–40. April, 1990.

28. National Institute on Aging, National Institutes of Health: HIV, AIDS and Older People. March, 2009.

29. Bodley-Tickell, A.T., Olowokure, B., Bhaduri, S., et al. Trends in Sexually Transmitted Infections (other than HIV) in Older People: Analysis of Data from an Enhanced Surveillance System. *Sexually Transmitted Infections*, 84: 312–317. 2008.

30. Hays, L., et al. American Academy of Addiction Psychiatry Symposium: Substance Use Disorders in the Elderly: Prevalence, Special Considerations and Treatment. 2002.

31. Brach, J.S., Simonsick, E.M., Kritchevsky, S., et al. The Association Between Physical Function and Lifestyle Activity and Exercise in the Health, Aging and Body Composition Study. *The Journal of the American Geriatrics Society,* 52(4): 502–509. 2004.

32. President's Commission for the Study of Ethical Problems in Medicine and Biomedical and Behavioral Research, Deciding to Forgo Life-Sustaining Treatment. Concern for the Dying. New York, 1983.

33. Ad Hoc Committee of the Harvard Medical School to Examine the Definition of Brain Death. A Definition of Irreversible Coma. *Journal of the American Medical Association,* 205: 377. 1968.

34. Organ Procurement and Transplantation Network. U.S. Department of Health and Human Services. Downloaded November 6, 2010, from http://optn. transplant.hrsa.gov

35. Oregon Death with Dignity Act, Oregon Revised Statute 127.800–127.897. 1997.

36. 2008 Summary of Oregon's Death with Dignity Act. Downloaded October 12, 2010, from http://oregon. gov/DHS/ph/pas/index.shtml

Glossary

Abortifacient: Any agent or substance that induces an abortion.

Abstinence: The act or practice of refraining from sexual intercourse.

Accountability: The willingness to be answerable for consequences of actions and choices.

Active euthanasia: The administration of lethal drugs designed to bring about death in a terminally ill patient.

Adequate intake (AI): A recommended intake value based on estimates of nutrient intake by a group (or groups) of healthy people that are assumed to be adequate; used when an RDA cannot be determined.

Advance directive: A legal document that may include a living will, a medical power of attorney, and a do not resuscitate order. It allows an individual to convey decisions about end-of-life matters care ahead of time, and provides a way to communicate wishes to family, friends, and health care providers.

Aerobic: Literally meaning "with oxygen." Aerobic exercise is continuous, such as running or fast walking, requiring the exchange of oxygen for muscles to perform.

Affiliative: A more submissive communication style that seeks to minimize conflict.

Agorophobia: A fear of being in places where help may not be available, including fear of being outside, in crowds, or on bridges.

Allopathic medicine: The treatment of disease using conventional evidence-based medical therapies.

Alpha-fetoprotein screen (AFP): A prenatal blood test to determine the level of maternal AFP in a pregnant woman. A high level of AFP is a marker for spina bifida.

Alternative medicine: A non-Western form of medical practice, such as the use of botanicals to treat disease.

Amenorrhea: Cessation of menstruation.

Amino acids: The building blocks of proteins.

Amniocentesis: The extraction of amniotic fluid from the amniotic sac surrounding the fetus to screen for genetic abnormalities.

Amniotic fluid: The fluid that suspends the embryo and fetus within the amniotic sac.

Amniotic sac: A thin membrane that forms a sac around the embryo and fetus.

Anaerobic: Literally meaning "without oxygen." Exercise that is explosive and short term, such as sprinting, throwing events in track and field, and heavy weight training.

Analgesic: An agent used to suppress pain.

Anaphylactic shock: An allergic reaction that causes circulatory collapse and suffocation due to bronchial and tracheal swelling.

Androgynous: A blending of male and female behaviors or interests.

Anemia: A condition of having less than the normal number of red blood cells or less than the normal quantity of hemoglobin in the blood. The oxygen-carrying capacity of the blood is, therefore, reduced.

Aneurysm: A burst artery caused by a weakening of the vessel wall.

Angina: Chest pain or discomfort when the heart does not receive enough oxygenated blood.

Angiography: A technique in which dye is injected to determine the movement of blood through vessels and organs, particularly the heart.

Angioplasty: A technique to widen a narrowed or obstructed artery as a result of atherosclerosis.

Anorexia: An eating disorder characterized by a preoccupation with body weight; fear of gaining weight resulting in self-starvation.

Anti-inflammatory drugs: Drugs that reduce inflammation.

Antibodies: Proteins specific to an antigen, usually bacteria that can destroy or weaken it.

Antiemetic drugs: Drugs that prevent nausea and vomiting.

Antigen: Any substance that causes the immune system to produce antibodies.

Antipyretic drugs: Drugs that prevent or reduce fever by lowering body temperature.

Anxiety disorder: A psychoneurotic disorder, sometimes called free-floating anxiety.

Aorta: The largest artery in the body; delivers oxygenated blood from the heart to the body.

Arrhythmia: An irregular heartbeat, in which the heart skips beats or beats too fast. Some arrhythmias can cause the heart to stop beating, leading to sudden cardiac arrest.

Arteriosclerosis: Degenerative changes in the arteries, characterized by thicker vessel walls, accumulation of calcium, and consequent loss of elasticity and lessened blood flow.

Artificial insemination: A procedure in which sperm are inserted directly into the uterus.

Assisted reproductive technology (ART): Includes all fertility treatments wherein both eggs and sperm are handled. It does not include artificial insemination (sperm only) or medically inducing egg production (egg only) unless the intention includes egg retrieval.

Asymptomatic: Not showing or producing indications of a disease or medical condition.

Atherosclerosis: A common form of arteriosclerosis in which fatty substances form a deposit of plaque on the inner lining of arterial walls, restricting blood flow.

Atria: The two upper chambers of the heart where blood collects before exiting through valves to the ventricles.

Ballistic: A force of tension on a muscle that is being stretched with movement.

Binge eating: An eating disorder characterized by episodes of severe overeating.

Bioavailability: The extent to which a medication or nutrient can be used by the body.

Bioequivalence: The condition in which different formulations of the same drug or chemical are absorbed equally by the body.

Biological markers: Measurable and quantifiable indicators of health, such as blood pressure, cholesterol level, and blood glucose level.

Biopsy: The process of removing tissue for examination.

Bipolar disorder: Formerly called manic depression, characterized by severe mood swings from high (manic) to low (depression), with episodes of normal moods in between.

Bisexual: Sexual attraction to members of both genders.

Body mass index (BMI): A measure of relative body weight, correlating highly with more direct measures of body fat, calculated by dividing total body weight in kilograms, by body height in meters squared.

Bradycardia: A heartbeat of less than 60 beats per minute that is physiologically inadequate for the patient. (In some patients, a heart rate of less than 60 is adequate.)

Brain stem: The part of the brain that controls heart rate, respiration, sleep, and other important functions.

Bronchitis: Inflammation of the bronchial tubes, resulting in coughing from increased mucus production.

Bulimia nervosa: An eating disorder characterized by recurrent episodes of excessive eating, followed by purging foods through vomiting and/or the use of laxatives.

Burnout: Psychological exhaustion and diminished efficiency resulting from overwork or prolonged exposure to stress.

Bursitis: An inflammation of a bursa sac, the small cushions in joints that pad and lubricate the area between tendon and bone.

Caesarean section: Abdominal surgical delivery involving multiple incisions through the abdomen and uterus to remove the baby. This also involves an epidural to allow the mother to be conscious and aware, but pain-free during the procedure.

Calorie: A unit of energy, or 1/1,000 of a kilocalorie.

Carbohydrate: One of the main dietary components that includes starches, sugar, and fiber.

Carcinogen: An agent known to cause cancer.

Carcinogenesis: Production of cancer.

Cardiomyopathy: Degenerative heart disease in which the heart muscle becomes enlarged, thickens, and weakens.

Cardiorespiratory endurance training: Sustained large muscle dynamic exercise designed to improve cardiorespiratory fitness.

Cardiorespiratory fitness: The ability of the heart and lungs to work efficiently to supply oxygen to skeletal muscles during sustained physical activity.

Cardiovascular disease: Diseases that involve the heart or blood vessels.

Carpal tunnel syndrome: Compression of the median nerve in the wrist that can cause tingling, itching, or numbness in the palm of the hand and fingers.

Cataracts: Clouding of the lens of the eye, causing blurred vision and eventually blindness.

Causal: Implying a cause.

Central nervous system (CNS): Made up of the spinal cord and the brain that controls both somatic and autonomic responses, such as respiration, heart rate, and blood pressure.

Cerebral cortex: The part of the brain that controls sight, hearing, taste, tactile sensations, and smell.

Certified nurse-midwife: A state-certified registered nurse who holds a master's degree and advanced training in obstetrics and gynecology.

Cervical cap: A thimble-shaped cup that fits over the cervix, used with a spermicide to prevent conception.

Chancre: A sore or ulcer that is painless but highly infectious, appearing at the location where the syphilis bacteria (spirochete) enters the body.

Chloasma: Brown patches on facial skin.

Cholesterol: A white crystalline substance found in animal tissue and some foods. A high blood cholesterol level can contribute to coronary artery disease.

Chronic diseases: Diseases of long duration, such as heart disease or diabetes.

Chronic obstructive pulmonary disease: A group of health conditions resulting in blocked airways and difficulty breathing.

Chyme: The thick semi-fluid mass of partially digested food that is passed from the stomach to the intestinal tract.

Cilia: Minute, hair-like organelles that beat in waves to move protozoans, liquids, dust, pollens, and mucus out of the cells.

Circumcision: The removal of the foreskin from the head of the penis.

Cleft palate: A congenital separation of the roof of the mouth and sometimes the lip.

Cocaine: An illicit drug made from coca leaves, used for its stimulant and euphorigenic properties.

Cohort: A group of persons sharing a particular statistical or demographic characteristic.

Coitus: Sexual intercourse.

Coitus interruptus: The act of withdrawing the penis prior to ejaculation during sexual intercourse.

Commitment: The realization that one feels love in the short term, and the commitment to maintain that love in the long term.

Communication: The exchange of thoughts, opinions, or information in speech, writing, or signs.

Complementary medicine: A type of medical practice that may be performed along with traditional Western medicine practices, such as music therapy while undergoing surgery.

Compulsion: An irresistible urge to behave in a certain way, especially against one's conscious wishes.

Computer tomography scan (CT scan): Also called CAT scan, this radiologic scan produces cross-sectional images of a part of the body onto a computer screen.

Comstock Act: The Comstock Act (1873) is a United States federal law that made it illegal to send any "obscene, lewd, and/or lascivious" materials through the mail, including contraceptive devices and information.

Conception: The fertilization of an egg by sperm, marking the onset of a pregnancy.

Congenital: Existing at birth.

Congenital heart defects: Structural problems with the heart present at birth.

Contraceptive: Any agent that prevents conception.

Contraceptive sponge: A contraceptive method that combines a barrier and spermicide to prevent conception.

Coronary artery disease (CAD): A narrowing of the small blood vessels that supply oxygen and blood to the heart. CAD is also called coronary heart disease (CHD).

Coronary bypass graft surgery: A surgical procedure in which arteries or veins from other parts of the body are grafted onto coronary arteries to bypass blockages and improve blood flow.

Coronary heart disease: Heart disease characterized by atherosclerotic build-up that blocks blood flow to the heart muscle, resulting in a myocardial infarction.

Cowper's glands: Two pea-shaped nodules located just below the prostate gland, that secrete a fluid which lubricates the urethra and neutralizes acid left by urine in the urethra.

Cunnilingus: Oral stimulation of the labia, clitoris, and vaginal entrance.

Cystic fibrosis: A hereditary disease that causes difficulty with digestion and breathing, due to excessive mucus accumulation in airways.

Daily reference intakes (DRI): The recommended daily intake of nutrient requirements.

Deoxyribonucleic acid (DNA): A material present in nearly all living organisms that carries all genetic information.

Depressive disorder: A group of symptoms that reflects a sad or irritable mood beyond normal sadness or grief, characterized by increasingly severe symptoms of longer duration.

Diabetes: A metabolic disorder in which the body ceases to either use or make insulin efficiently.

Diaphragm: A barrier method made of latex or silicone and used with spermicide, designed to cover the cervix and prevent conception.

Diastole: The period of time when the heart fills with blood after systole (contraction).

Distress: From the Latin dis =bad, as in dissonance, disagreement.

Diverticular disease: Bulging pouches in the colon or large intestine that become inflamed.

Dopamine: A neurotransmitter that plays a major role in drug addiction, as it increases pleasure.

Down syndrome: A congenital condition that causes development delays, and physical differences, and may lead to mental retardation.

Drug: Any substance other than food that alters the body and its functions.

Drug expectancy: The expectation a drug user has in regard to feeling certain effects when using a particular drug.

Durable power of attorney: A general, special, or health care power of attorney that contains special durability provisions. The person named your durable power of attorney can only make decisions for you if the conditions you specified are met. This might include becoming mentally incompetent, being in a coma, or other medical conditions that prevent or inhibit you from making decisions independently.

Dysfunctional family: A family in which conflict, misbehavior, and abuse occur continually and regularly, creating a climate that diminishes the emotional and physical health and well-being of family members.

Dyspareunia: Painful intercourse.

Dysplasia: An abnormal change in cellular structure.

Dyspnea: Shortness of breath caused by mild activity.

Echocardiography: A procedure that sends ultrasound waves into the chest to create moving pictures of the heart.

Ectopic pregnancy: Growth of a fertilized embryo outside of the uterus, usually in the fallopian tube.

Efficacy: The therapeutic effect of a given intervention.

Ejaculation: The discharge of semen during orgasm.

Ejection fraction: A test to measure the volume of blood pumped out by the left ventricle.

Electrocardiogram: A quick, painless test that records the activity of the heart.

Electroencephalogram: An assessment of electrical activity in the brain.

Electrolytes: Body salts and minerals that help regulate hydration in the body and are important for nerve and muscle function.

Electronic aggression: Using electronic media to embarrass, harass, or threaten another person.

Elephantiasis: A parasitic worm infection that blocks the lymphatic system, causing limbs to swell so much they resemble parts of an elephant. The prognosis is good for mild, early infections, but it is fatal for heavy parasitic infections.

Emboli: A mass that travels through the bloodstream, lodges in a blood vessel, and stops blood flow. Examples of emboli are a detached blood clot, a clump of bacteria, and foreign material such as air.

Emergency contraceptive pills: Treatment initiated within 72 hours after unprotected intercourse, reducing the risk of pregnancy by at least 75 percent.

Emphysema: Destruction of the lungs over time, as bronchial tubes collapse.

Encephalitis: An inflammation of the brain caused by infection, usually a virus. Symptoms include headache, fever, and vomiting, and can become progressively severe to include loss of consciousness, seizures, and death.

Endocrinology: The branch of medicine dealing with the endocrine glands and their secretions.

Endometrial cancer: A cancer that occurs in the endometrial lining of the uterus.

Endometrium: The mucous membrane lining the uterus that is composed of three layers.

Epidemic: An infection that spreads rapidly throughout a region such as a state.

Epididymis: A system of ducts on the posterior of the testes that stores sperm prior to ejaculation.

Epidural: A local anesthetic injected into the space between the outer membrane covering the spinal cord and the bones of the spine. It is used during childbirth to help alleviate the pain of a vaginal delivery.

Episiotomy: A surgical incision used to enlarge the perineum during childbirth to facilitate delivery.

Erogenous zones: Areas of the body that become hypersensitive to touch during sexual arousal.

Estimated average requirement (EAR): A daily nutrient intake value estimated to meet the requirement of half of the healthy individuals in a life stage and gender group; used to assess dietary adequacy and as the basis for the RDA.

Eustress: From the Greek eu = good, as in euphoria.

External locus of control: Perception that events in your life occur by chance or because of actions outside your control.

Fallopian tubes: A pair of thin ducts also called oviducts, connecting the ovaries to the uterus. Fertilization usually occurs in one of the fallopian tubes.

Fast twitch muscle fibers: Capable of producing short bursts of strength and speed, but fatigue quickly. Ideal for sprinting.

Fee-for-service insurance: A health insurance plan in which the consumer pays a monthly premium. After spending a predetermined amount on medical care each year, the consumer then pays a percentage of expenses incurred, while the plan pays the remainder.

Fellatio: Oral stimulation of the penis.

Female condom: A polyurethane pouch inserted into the vagina prior to sexual intercourse, helping to prevent pregnancy and transmission of STIs.

Fertility: The ability to reproduce.

Fertility awareness method: A set of practices in which a woman uses one or more of her primary fertility signs to determine the fertile and infertile phases of her menstrual cycle.

Fertility drugs: Drugs that treat infertility by causing women to ovulate.

Fetal alcohol spectrum disorders: A range of neurological and physical impairments that can affect a child exposed to alcohol in the womb.

Fiber: The non-digestible component of plant foods.

Fight-or-flight response: The body's response to extreme stress, during which the endocrine system releases stress hormones such as cortisol and adrenaline, and the autonomic nervous system elevates heart rate, blood pressure, and respiration.

Flexibility: The ability to move a joint through its full range of motion.

Follicle stimulating hormone (FSH): A hormone released from the pituitary gland that causes the egg to be released from the ovary.

Food and Drug Administration (FDA): An agency under the federal Department of Health and Human Services that regulates the approval of all prescription and over-the-counter drugs manufactured and sold in the United States.

Frostbite: Tissue damage caused by exposure to temperatures below freezing.

Gamma hydroxybutyric acid: An illegal substance that causes drowsiness, dizziness, nausea, and visual disturbances at lower doses, and

unconsciousness, seizures, severe respiratory depression, and death at higher concentrations.

Gastrointestinal tract: The gastrointestinal tract is the system of organs that takes in food, digests it to extract energy and nutrients, and expels the remaining waste.

Gender: Roles, behaviors, and characteristics that society associates with males and females.

Gender identity: The gender to which you most closely identify.

Gene: The basic physical and functional units of heredity that carry information for developing the proteins that determine the characteristics of specific organisms. When genes are altered so that the proteins cannot carry out their normal functions, genetic disorders can result.

Generic: A non-branded product.

Genome: The complete set of genetic material of an organism.

Gerontology: The study of the collective and individual processes of aging.

Gestational diabetes: High blood sugar levels that occur during pregnancy. About 40 percent of women who develop gestational diabetes will later develop type II diabetes.

Gingivitis: Inflammation of the gums.

Glaucoma: Elevated pressure within the eyeball, causing impaired vision and possible blindness.

Glycogen: A polysaccharide energy source that is stored in liver and muscle tissue.

Hallucinogens: Drugs that cause distortions in time, space and perceptions.

Health: Soundness of body or mind; freedom from disease or ailment; to have one's health; to lose one's health.

Health maintenance organizations: Health insurance plans in which, in exchange for a monthly premium, consumers can select medical treatment from a list of physicians and pay only a co-payment at each visit.

Heart failure: A condition in which the heart cannot pump enough blood to the body. It is caused either by inadequate amounts of blood reaching the heart, or inadequate force to pump the blood.

Heimlich maneuver: Emergency procedure to expel an obstruction in the airway of a choking victim.

Hemoglobin: Red blood cells that transport oxygen.

Hemorrhagic stroke: A stroke caused by the rupture of a blood vessel in the brain, often due to an aneurysm.

Heterosexual: Sexual attraction to someone of the opposite gender.

High blood pressure: A serious condition in which either systolic or diastolic blood pressure remains above normal, possibly leading to coronary heart disease, heart failure, stroke, or kidney disease.

High-density lipoproteins: A blood constituent involved in the transport of cholesterol and associated with a decreased risk of atherosclerosis and heart attack.

Histamine: A chemical released in the blood that causes heat and swelling at the site of an infection. It also can produce an inflammatory reaction in response to excessive antibodies, created as a result of an allergic reaction to a substance.

HIV: Human immunodeficiency virus, the virus that causes AIDS (Acquired Immunodeficiency Syndrome).

Holistic: Emphasizing the importance of the whole and the interdependence of its parts.

Homeopathy: The method of treating symptoms using drugs, given in minute doses that in a healthy person would produce symptoms similar to those of the disease.

Homeostasis: Maintaining equilibrium between interdependent elements, especially those maintained by physiological processes.

Homosexual: Sexual attraction to someone of the same gender.

Human chorionic gonadotropin (hCG): A hormone produced during a pregnancy, first by the embryo and later by the placenta. Its purpose is to maintain production of progesterone.

Human papilloma virus: One of the most commonly spread sexually transmitted infections, sometimes leading to genital warts.

Hydrate: To drink water. Proper hydration is necessary during exercise to prevent dehydration, muscle cramping, and heat stroke.

Hymen: A fold of mucous membrane that surrounds and partially covers the external vaginal opening.

Hyperglycemia: High blood sugar.

Hyperplasia: An abnormal multiplication of cells.

Hyperthermia (heat stroke): Elevated core body temperature when the body produces more heat than can be dissipated. A core body temperature of 104 degrees or more is considered hyperthermic.

Hypoglycemia: Blood glucose values that fall below 70 mg/dl. Symptoms include sweating, rapid change in mood, and inability to follow or engage in conversation. Left untreated, hypoglycemia may lead to seizures.

Hypothermia: Core body temperature drops to 95 degrees or less as a result of exposure to cold temperatures. Extreme loss of body heat.

Illicit: Unlawful, not allowed by law.

Immunotherapy: Treatment of disease by inducing, enhancing, or suppressing immune response.

Impaired fasting blood glucose: In impaired fast blood glucose, the blood glucose is between 100–125 mg/dl. Normal fasting blood glucose levels are below 100 mg/dl and values over 125 mg/dl indicate diabetes.

Infatuation: A strong physical and emotional attraction to another person.

Infectious diseases: Infectious or communicable diseases, caused by a biological agent (e.g., virus, bacterium, or parasite) that can be spread directly or indirectly from one living thing to another.

Infirmity: Physical or mental weakness.

Inhalants: Common home and automotive products—e.g., gasoline—that produce toxic vapors that some drugs users inhale to get high.

Intentional injury: An injury that occurs when harm is intended.

Internal locus of control: Perception that you control and are responsible for events in your life.

Intimacy: Feeling close, connected, and bonded in loving relationships.

Intrauterine device: A plastic device inserted into the uterus as a contraceptive.

Ischemic stroke: A stroke caused by an inadequate supply of oxygen-rich blood reaching part of the brain, resulting in death of brain cells.

Isokinetic: Exercise that maintains constant tension through movement as muscles shorten or lengthen, in exercises such as running, walking, cycling, or swimming.

Isometric: Strength training that involves holding a position or pressing against an immovable object such as the floor or wall.

Isotonic: Contracting and shortening a muscle through a range of motion under constant tension, such as in weight training.

Ketoacidosis: Occurs when the body depends on fat for energy, and is unable to utilize the ketones being produced. Excess ketones in the blood spill over into the urine, pulling body fluid with them. Untreated, this condition can lead to coma and even death.

Ketones: Substances made when the body breaks down fat for energy.

Kilocalorie: 1,000 calories, or the energy needed to raise the temperature of 1 kilogram of water one degree Celsius.

Lactational amenorrhea method: Breastfeeding a newborn that results in amenorrhea, a highly effective, temporary method of contraception.

Laparoscope: A long, thin, telescope-like surgical instrument used to view the interior parts of the body.

Legal: Allowed by law.

Legumes: Peas and bean products that are high in fiber and an excellent source of protein.

Leukoplakia: A disorder of mucous membranes characterized by white patches on the tongue and inner cheeks that can become cancerous.

Limbic system: The reward center of the brain, initiating feelings of pleasure that cause us to want to repeat the behavior, such as eating and sex.

Lipid: Organic compound comprised of fat and found in the blood.

Living wills: Living wills are one part of an advance directive that indicate your treatment preferences in end-of-life situations, including whether you want specific kinds of treatment and life sustaining measures such as mechanical breathing and feeding tubes.

Low-density lipoprotein: A plasma protein that is the major carrier of cholesterol in the blood. High levels are associated with atherosclerosis.

Lumpectomy: Surgical removal of a tumor.

Lupus: An autoimmune disorder that can impair the function of the joints, kidneys, heart, brain, skin, or blood.

Luteinizing hormone (LH): A hormone released from the pituitary gland that initiates the release of estrogen and progesterone into the blood prior to ovulation.

Lymphatic system: Part of the immune system, the lymphatic system is interconnected spaces and vessels between body tissues and organs, by which lymph circulates throughout the body.

Lymphocytes: Special white blood cells that can specifically target a pathogen for destruction, and remember it in case it enters the body in the future.

Macrophages: Special white blood cells that form at the site of an infection to destroy pathogens.

Macular degeneration: Deterioration of the central portion of the retina, resulting in diminished visual difficulties and eventually blindness.

Magnetic resonance imaging (MRI): An imaging technique that uses electromagnetic radiation to obtain images of soft tissue in the body.

Mainstream smoke: Mainstream smoke is a combination of smoke inhaled and exhaled by the smoker.

Major depression: Severe, disabling depression that keeps a person from functioning.

Male condom: A sheath usually made of either latex or polyurethane that covers the penis during sexual intercourse, used as a contraceptive method and/or STI preventative.

Malpractice: Failure of a professional to render proper services through reprehensible ignorance or negligence or through criminal intent, especially when injury or loss results.

Mastectomy: Surgical removal of the breast.

Masturbation: Self-stimulation of the genitals, causing increasing levels of sexual arousal, including orgasm.

Median nerve: A nerve that extends along the forearm and passes through the wrist, affecting movement and sensation in the hand.

Medicaid: Government-sponsored health care system for the indigent and disabled.

Medicare: Government-sponsored health care system for those age 65 or older.

Meditation: Thought practice that results in relaxation and stress reduction.

Menarche: The first menstruation in women.

Metabolic syndrome: A cluster of problems including high cholesterol with high LDL and low HDL levels, high triglycerides, and high blood pressure.

Metabolism: The chemical processes occurring within a living cell or organism that are necessary for the maintenance of life. In metabolism, some substances are broken down to yield energy for vital processes, while other substances necessary for life are synthesized.

Metastasize: The movement of cancerous cells in the body from the original location to a new location.

Methamphetamine: A man-made substance used in medical treatments for hypotension and narcolepsy, and also used illicitly as a stimulant.

Mindfulness: The ability to concentrate on breath and movement while excluding extraneous thoughts.

Minor depression (dysthymia): Minor depression that does not seriously disable the person, but keeps him from functioning at an optimal level.

Monounsaturated fats: A fat that has only one double-bonded carbon atom. Some plant-based fats, including canola, olive, and peanut oils, are monounsaturated.

Morbid obesity: Defined as having a BMI over 40.

Morbidity: State of ill health or disease.

Mortality: Risk of death.

Muscular endurance: The ability of a muscle to engage in sustained effort while resisting fatigue.

Muscular strength: The ability of a muscle to exert force against a physical object.

Myocardial infarction: An interruption in blood flow to the heart, causing part of the heart muscle to die. Commonly called a heart attack.

Naturopathy: A system or method of treating disease that employs no surgery or synthetic drugs, instead using diets, herbs, vitamins, and massage to assist the natural healing processes.

Neuropathy: Damage to the nerves of the peripheral nervous system.

Neurotransmitters: Brain chemicals that allow the transmission of signals from one neuron to the next across nerve synapses.

Nicotine poisoning: Symptoms of dizziness, light-headedness, rapid, erratic pulse, clammy skin, nausea, vomiting, and diarrhea often experienced by beginning smokers.

Nitrosamines: Any of a class of organic compounds present in various foods and other products, and found to be carcinogenic in laboratory animals.

Non-parous women: Women who have never given birth.

Nurse practitioner/physician's assistant (PA): A registered nurse who has received special training and can perform many of the duties of a physician.

Nutrient dense: Food that contains a large number of nutrients relative to the amount and size of the food.

Nutrients: Any element or compound necessary for or contributing to an organism's metabolism, growth, or other function.

Obese: Being at least 20 percent over ideal weight for height, with a BMI greater than 25 percent for men and 33 percent for women.

Obsession: An idea or feeling that completely occupies the mind.

Oncology: The branch of medicine dealing with tumors, including cancerous tumors.

Ophthalmologists: Licensed physicians specializing in the medical care and surgery of the eyes.

Optician: A technician who makes and fits eyeglasses based on prescriptions.

Optometrist: A trained and licensed individual who can prescribe and fit eyeglasses.

Oral contraception (OCs): A variety of hormonal compounds in pill form that prevent ovulation, thereby preventing pregnancy.

Orthotics: Inserts for shoes to provide arch support and stability.

Osteoporosis: A progressive disease resulting in fragile and easily broken bones.

Other-directed: Depend on others to make decisions for you, lacking autonomy.

Ovarian cancer: A malignant tumor located on the ovary.

Ovaries: The female gonads, which contain eggs and produce hormones.

Overweight: Having more body weight, relative to height, than is recommended for the general healthy population.

Oxidized LDL particles: A low-density lipoprotein containing free radicals that can react with tissues, causing damage.

Palliative care: Care provided to reduce symptoms and manage pain.

Pandemic: An infection that spreads continentally, or even globally.

Panic disorder: An anxiety disorder characterized by severe recurring episodes of fear and terror.

Pap test: Test to detect cancerous or precancerous cells of the cervix, allowing for early diagnosis of cancer.

Parous women: Women who have given birth.

Passion: Physical and emotional drives that lead to romance, physical attraction, and sexual consummation in loving relationships.

Passive euthanasia: The intentional withholding of life-supporting equipment and services to bring about death in a terminally ill patient.

Pathogen: A disease-causing organism.

Pedophiles: Adults who are sexually attracted to children.

Peer group: Individuals who are equal in age, education, and social status.

Pelvic inflammatory disease: An inflammation of the female pelvic organs, most commonly the fallopian tubes, usually as a result of a bacterial infection.

Penis: Dual-purpose male organ that delivers sperm to the vagina and discharges urine from the bladder.

Peripheral artery disease: A disease in which arteries become narrowed or blocked, causing a reduced supply of oxygenated blood to parts of the body.

Index